The Expositor's Bible
Jeremiah Volumes I & II
With a Sketch of His Life and Times.
By the Rev. C. J. Ball, M.A.,
and
W. H. Bennett, M.A.
Edited by Anthony Uyl

Woodstock, Ontario, 2017

The Expositor's Bible: Jeremiah Volumes I & II

The Expositor's Bible: The Prophecies of Jeremiah (Volume I)
With a Sketch of His Life and Times.
By the Rev. C. J. Ball, M.A.,
Chaplain of Lincoln's Inn;

and

The Expositor's Bible: The Book of Jeremiah Chapters XXI-LII (Volume II)
By W. H. Bennett, M.A.
Professor of Old Testament Languages and Literature Hackney and new colleges
Originally edited by the Rev. W. Robertson Nicoll, M.A., LL.D.
Edited by Anthony Uyl

Volume I Originally Published by:
New York: A. C. Armstrong & Son, 714 Broadway. 1890.

Volume II Originally Published by:
London; Hodder and Stoughton; 27, Paternoster Row; MDCCCXCV

The text of The Expositor's Bible: Jeremiah Volumes I & II is all in the Public Domain. This edition is published by Devoted Publishing a division of 2165467 Ontario Inc.

What kind of philosophies do you have?
Let us know!

Contact us at: devotedpub@hotmail.com
Visit us on Facebook: Devoted Publishing
Get more products via our website: www.devotedpublishing.com
Published in Woodstock, Ontario, Canada 2017.

For bulk educational rates, please contact us at the above email address.

ISBN: 978-1-988297-95-8

Rev. C. J. Ball, M.A., & W. H. Bennett, M.A.

Table of Contents

VOLUME I 6
PRELIMINARY SKETCH OF THE LIFE AND TIMES OF JEREMIAH 6
    Footnotes: 22
I. THE CALL AND CONSECRATION 24
    Footnotes: 28
II. THE TRUST IN THE SHADOW OF EGYPT 29
    Footnotes: 40
III. ISRAEL AND JUDAH: A CONTRAST 41
    Footnotes: 46
IV. THE SCYTHIANS AS THE SCOURGE OF GOD 47
    Footnotes: 51
V. POPULAR AND TRUE RELIGION 52
    Footnotes: 71
VI. THE IDOLS OF THE HEATHEN AND THE GOD OF ISRAEL 72
    Footnotes: 81
VII. THE BROKEN COVENANT 82
    Footnotes: 90
VIII. THE FALL OF PRIDE 92
    Footnotes: 97
IX. THE DROUGHT AND ITS MORAL IMPLICATIONS 98
    Footnotes: 119
X. THE SABBATH - A WARNING 121
    Footnotes: 124
XI. THE DIVINE POTTER 125
    Footnotes: 131
XII. THE BROKEN VESSEL - A SYMBOL OF JUDGMENT 132
    Footnotes: 135
XIII. JEREMIAH UNDER PERSECUTION 136
    Footnotes: 140
VOLUME II 141
PREFACE 141
CHRONOLOGICAL TABLE 142
    Footnotes: 143
BOOK I 144
    CHAPTER I 144
    Footnotes: 146
    CHAPTER II 147
    Footnotes: 152
    CHAPTER III 153

- Footnotes: 157
- CHAPTER IV: 158
- Footnotes: 160
- CHAPTER V: 162
- Footnotes: 164
- CHAPTER VII: 171
- Footnotes: 176
- CHAPTER VIII: 177
- CHAPTER IX: 184
- Footnotes: 189
- CHAPTER X: 190
- Footnotes: 193
- CHAPTER XI: 194
- Footnotes: 198
- CHAPTER XII: 199
- Footnotes: 204
- CHAPTER XIII: 205
- Footnotes: 209
- CHAPTER XIV: 210
- Footnotes: 213
- CHAPTER XV: 214
- Footnotes: 218

BOOK II: 219
- CHAPTER XVI: 219
- Footnotes: 222
- CHAPTER XVII: 223
- Footnotes: 227
- CHAPTER XVIII: 228
- Footnotes: 229
- CHAPTER XIX: 230
- Footnotes: 233
- CHAPTER XX: 234
- Footnotes: 234
- CHAPTER XXI: 235
- Footnotes: 236
- CHAPTER XXII: 238
- Footnotes: 239
- CHAPTER XXIII: 240
- Footnotes: 241
- CHAPTER XXIV: 242
- Footnotes: 243

Rev. C. J. Ball, M.A., & W. H. Bennett, M.A.

- CHAPTER XXV ... 244
  - Footnotes: ... 246
- BOOK III ... 247
  - CHAPTER XXVI ... 247
    - Footnotes: ... 248
  - CHAPTER XXVII ... 249
    - Footnotes: ... 252
  - CHAPTER XXVIII ... 254
    - Footnotes: ... 257
  - CHAPTER XXIX ... 258
    - Footnotes: ... 261
  - CHAPTER XXX ... 263
    - Footnotes: ... 266
  - CHAPTER XXXI ... 267
    - Footnotes: ... 269
  - CHAPTER XXXII ... 271
    - Footnotes: ... 276
  - CHAPTER XXXIII ... 278
    - Footnotes: ... 280
  - CHAPTER XXXIV ... 282
    - Footnotes: ... 284
- EPILOGUE ... 285
  - CHAPTER XXXV ... 285
    - Footnotes: ... 287

VOLUME I

PRELIMINARY SKETCH OF THE LIFE AND TIMES OF JEREMIAH

A priest by birth, Jeremiah became a prophet by the special call of God. His priestly origin implies a good literary training, in times when literature was largely in the hands of the priests. The priesthood, indeed, constituted a principal section of the Israelitish nobility, as appears both from the history of those times, and from the references in our prophet's writings, where kings and princes and priests are often named together as the aristocracy of the land (i. 18, ii. 26, iv. 9); and this fact would ensure for the young prophet a share in all the best learning of his age. The name of Jeremiah, like other prophetic proper names, seems to have special significance in connexion with the most illustrious of the persons recorded to have borne it. It means Iahvah foundeth, and, as a proper name, The Man that Iahvah foundeth; a designation which finds vivid illustration in the words of Jeremiah's call: "Before I moulded thee in the belly, I knew thee; and before thou camest forth from the womb, I consecrated thee: a spokesman to the nations did I make thee" (i. 5). The not uncommon name of Jeremiah--six other persons of the name are numbered in the Old Testament--must have appeared to the prophet as invested with new force and meaning, in the light of this revelation. Even before his birth he had been "founded" [1] and predestined by God for the work of his life.

The Hilkiah named as his father was not the high priest of that name, [2] so famous in connexion with the reformation of king Josiah. Interesting as such a relationship would be if established, the following facts seem decisive against it. The prophet himself has omitted to mention it, and no hint of it is to be found elsewhere. The priestly family to which Jeremiah belonged was settled at Anathoth (i. 1, xi. 21, xxix. 27). But Anathoth in Benjamin (xxxvii. 12), the present `Anâtâ, between two and three miles NNE. of Jerusalem, belonged to the deposed line of Ithamar (1 Chron. xxiv. 3; comp. with 1 Kings ii. 26, 35). After this it is needless to insist that the prophet, and presumably his father, resided at Anathoth, whereas Jerusalem was the usual residence of the high priest. Nor is the identification of Jeremiah's family with that of the ruling high priest helped by the observation that the father of the high priest was named Shallum (1 Chron. v. 39), and that the prophet had an uncle of this name (Jer. xxxii. 7). The names Hilkiah [3] and Shallum are too common to justify any conclusions from such data. If the prophet's father was head of one of the twenty-four classes or guilds of the priests, that might explain the influence which Jeremiah could exercise with some of the grandees of the court. But we are not told more than that Jeremiah ben Hilkiah was a member of the priestly community settled at Anathoth. It is, however, a gratuitous disparagement of one of the greatest names in Israel's history, to suggest that, had Jeremiah belonged to the highest ranks of his caste, he would not have been equal to the self-renunciation involved in the assumption of the unhonoured and thankless office of a prophet. [4] Such a suggestion is certainly not warranted by the portraiture of the man as delineated by himself, with all the distinctive marks of truth and nature. From the moment that he became decisively convinced of his mission, Jeremiah's career is marked by struggles and vicissitudes of the most painful and perilous kind; his perseverance in his allotted path was met by an ever increasing hardness on the part of the people; opposition and ridicule became persecution, and the messenger of Divine truth persisted in proclaiming his message at the risk of his own life. That life may, in fact, be called a prolonged martyrdom; and, if we may judge of the unknown by the known, the tradition that the prophet was stoned to death by the Jewish refugees in Egypt is only too probable an account of its final scene. If "the natural shrinking of a somewhat feminine character" is traceable in his own report of his conduct at particular junctures, does not the fact shed an intenser glory upon the man, who overcame this instinctive timidity, and persisted, in face of the most appalling dangers, in the path of duty? Is not the victory of a constitutionally timid and shrinking character a nobler moral triumph than that of the man who never knew fear--who marches to the conflict with others, with a light heart, simply because it is his nature to do so--because he has had no experience of the agony of a previous conflict with self? It is easy to sit in one's library and criticize the heroes of old; but the modern censures of Jeremiah betray at once a want of historic imagination, and a defect of sympathy with the sublime fortitude of one who struggled on in a battle which he knew to be lost. In a protracted contest such as that which Jeremiah was called upon to maintain, what wonder if courage sometimes flags, and hopelessness utters its forsaken cry? The moods of the saints are not always the same; they vary, like those of common men, with the stress of the hour. Even our Saviour could cry from the cross, "My God, My God, why hast Thou forsaken Me?" It is not by passing expressions, wrung from their torn hearts by the agony of the hour, that men are to be judged. It is the issue of the crisis that is all-important; not the cries of pain, which indicate its overwhelming pressure.

"It is sad," says a well known writer, with reference to the noble passage, xxxi. 31-34, which he justly characterizes as "one of those which best deserve to be called the Gospel before Christ," "It is sad that Jeremiah could not always keep his spirit under the calming influence of these high thoughts. No book of the Old Testament, except the book of Job and the Psalms, contains so much which is difficult to reconcile with the character of a self-denying servant of Jehovah. Such expressions as those in xi. 20, xv. 15, and especially xviii. 21-23, contrast powerfully with Luke xxiii. 34, and show that the typical character of Jeremiah is not absolutely complete." Probably not. The writer in question is honourably distinguished from a crowd of French and German critics, whose attainments are not superior to his own, by his deep sense of the inestimable value to mankind of those beliefs which animated the prophet, and by the sincerity of his manifest endeavours to judge fairly between Jeremiah and his detractors. He has already remarked truly enough that "the baptism of complicated suffering," which the prophet was called upon to pass through in the reign of Jehoiakim, "has made him, in a very high and true sense, a type of One greater than he." It is impossible to avoid such an impression, if we study the records of his life with any insight or sympathy. And the impression thus created is deepened, when we turn to that prophetic page which may be called the most appealing in the entire range of the Old Testament. In the 53rd of Isaiah the martyrdom of Jeremiah becomes the living image of that other martyrdom, which in the fulness of time was to redeem the world. After this, to say that "the typical character of Jeremiah is not absolutely complete," is no more than the assertion of a truism; for what Old Testament character, what character in the annals of collective humanity, can be brought forward as a perfect type of the Christ, the Man whom, in His sinlessness and His power, unbiassed human reason and conscience instinctively suspect to have been also God? To deplore the fact that this illustrious prophet "could not always keep his spirit under the calming influence of his highest thoughts," is simply to deplore the infirmity that besets all human nature, to regret that natural imperfection which clings to a finite and fallen creature, even when endowed with the most splendid gifts of the spirit. For the rest, a certain degree of exaggeration is noticeable in founding upon three brief passages of so large a work as the collected prophecies of Jeremiah the serious charge that "no book of the Old Testament, except the book of Job and the Psalms, contains so much which is difficult to reconcile with the character of a self-denying servant of Jehovah." The charge appears to me both ill-grounded and misleading. But I reserve the further consideration of these obnoxious passages for the time when I come to discuss their context, as I wish now to complete my sketch of the prophet's life. He has himself recorded the date of his call to the prophetic office. It was in the thirteenth year of the good king Josiah, that the young [5] priest was summoned to a higher vocation by an inward Voice whose urgency he could not resist. [6] The year has been variously identified with 629, 627, and 626 b.c. The place has been supposed to have been Jerusalem, the capital, which was so near the prophet's home, and which, as Hitzig observes, offered the amplest scope and numberless occasions for the exercise of prophetic activity. But there appears no good reason why Jeremiah should not have become known locally as one whom God had specially chosen, before he abandoned his native place for the wider sphere of the capital. This, in truth, seems to be the likelier supposition, considering that his reluctance to take the first decisive step in his career excused itself on the ground of youthful inexperience: "Alas, my Lord Iahvah! behold, I know not (how) to speak; for I am but a youth." [7] The Hebrew term may imply that he was about eighteen or twenty: an age when it is hardly probable that he would permanently leave his father's house. Moreover, he has mentioned a conspiracy of his fellow-townsmen against himself, in terms which have been taken to imply that he had exercised his ministry among them, before his removal to Jerusalem. In chap. xi. 21, we read: "Therefore thus said Iahvah Sabaoth upon the men of `Anathoth that were seeking thy life, saying, Prophesy not in the name of Iahvah, that thou die not by our hand! Therefore thus said Iahvah Sabaoth: Behold I am about to visit it upon them: the young men shall die by the sword; their sons and their daughters shall die by the famine. And a remnant they shall have none; for I will bring evil unto the men of `Anathoth, (in) the year of their visitation." It is natural to see in this wicked plot against his life the reason for the prophet's departure from his native place (but cf. p. 265). We are reminded of the violence done to our Lord by the men of "His own country" (he patris autou), and of His final and, as it would seem, compulsory departure from Nazareth to Capernaum (St. Luke iv. 16-29; St. Matt. iv. 13). In this, as in other respects, Jeremiah was a true type of the Messias.

The prophetic discourses, with which the book of Jeremiah opens (ii. 1-iv. 2), have a general application to all Israel, as is evident not only from the ideas expressed in them, but also from the explicit address, ii. 4: "Hear ye the word of Iahvah, O house of Jacob, and all the clans of the house of Israel!" It is clear enough, that although Jeremiah belongs to the southern kingdom, his reflexions here concern the northern tribes as well, who must be included in the comprehensive phrases "house of Jacob," and "all the clans of the house of Israel." The fact is accounted for by the circumstance that these two discourses are summaries of the prophet's teaching on many distinct occasions, and as such might have been composed anywhere. There can be no doubt, however, that the principal contents of his book have their scene in Jerusalem. In chap. ii. 1, 2, indeed, we have what looks like the prophet's introduction to the scene of his future activity. "And there fell a word of Iahvah unto me, saying, Go and cry in the ears of Jerusalem." But the words are not found in the LXX., which begins chap. ii. thus: "And he said, These things saith the Lord, I remembered the lovingkindness (eleos) of thy youth, and the love of thine espousals (teleiosis)." But whether these words of the received Hebrew text be genuine or not, it is plain that if, as the terms of the prophet's commission affirm, he was to be "an embattled city, and a pillar of iron, and walls of bronze ... to the kings of Judah, to her princes, to her priests," as well as "to the country folk" (i. 18), Jerusalem, the residence of kings and princes and chief priests, and the centre of the land, would be the natural sphere of his operations. The same thing is implied in the Divine statement: "A nabî' to the nations have I made thee" (i. 5). The prophet of Judea could only reach the gôyîm--the surrounding foreign peoples--through the government of his own country, and through his influence upon Judean policy. The leaving of his native place, sooner or later, seems to be involved in the words (i. 7, 8): "And Iahvah said unto me, Say not, I am a youth: for upon whatsoever (journey) I send thee, thou shalt go (Gen. xxiv. 42); and with whomsoever I charge thee, thou shalt speak (Gen. xxiii. 8). Be not afraid of them!" The Hebrew is to some extent ambiguous. We might also render: "Unto whomsoever I send thee, thou shalt go; and whatsoever I charge thee, thou shalt speak." But the difference will not affect my point, which is that the words seem to imply the contingency of Jeremiah's leaving Anathoth. And this implication is certainly strengthened by the twice-given warning: "Be not afraid of them!" (i. 8), "Be not dismayed at them, lest I dismay thee (indeed) before them!" (17). The young prophet might dread the effect of an unpopular message upon his brethren and his father's house. But his fear would reach a far higher pitch of intensity, if he were called upon to confront with the same message of unwelcome truth the king in his palace, or the high priest in the courts of the sanctuary, or the fanatical and easily excited populace of the capital. Accordingly, when after his general prologue or exordium, the prophet plunges at once "into the agitated life of the present,"[8] it is to "the men of Judah and Jerusalem" (iv. 3), to "the great men" (v. 5), and to the throng of worshippers in the temple (vii. 2), that he addresses his burning words. When, however (v. 4), he exclaims: "And for me, I said, They are but poor folk; they do foolishly (Num. xii. 11), for they know not the way of Iahvah, the rule (i.e., religion) of their God (Isa. xlii. 1): I will get me unto the great men, and will speak with them; for they know the way of Iahvah, the rule of their God:" he again seems to suggest a prior ministry, of however brief duration, upon the smaller stage of Anathoth. At all events, there is nothing against the conjecture that the prophet may have passed to and fro between his birthplace and Jerusalem, making occasional sojourn in the capital, until at last the machinations of his neighbours (xi. 19 sqq.), and as appears from xii. 6, his own kinsmen, drove him to quit Anathoth for ever. If Hitzig be right in referring Psalms xxiii., xxvi.-xxviii. to the prophet's pen, we may find in them evidence of the fact that the temple became his favourite haunt, and indeed his usual abode. As a priest by birth, he would have a claim to live in some one of the cells that surrounded the temple on three sides of it. The 23rd Psalm, though written at a later period in the prophet's career--I shall refer to it again by-and-by--closes with the words, "And I will return unto (Ps. vii. 17; Hos. xii. 7) the house of Iahvah as long as I live," or perhaps, "And I will return (and dwell) in" etc., as though the temple were at once his sanctuary and his home. In like manner, Ps. xxvi. speaks of one who "washed his hands, in innocency" (i.e. in a state of innocency; the symbolical action corresponding to the real state of his heart and conscience), and so "compassed the altar of Iahvah"; "to proclaim with the sound of a psalm of thanksgiving, and to rehearse all His wondrous works." The language here seems even to imply (Ex. xxx. 19-21), that the prophet took part, as a priest, in the ritual of the altar. He continues: "Iahvah, I love the abode of thine house, And the place of the dwelling of Thy glory!" and concludes, "My foot, it standeth on a plain; In the congregations I bless Iahvah," speaking as one continually present at the temple services. His prayers "Judge me," i.e., Do me justice, "Iahvah!" and "Take not away my soul among sinners, Nor my life among men of bloodshed!" may point either to the conspiracies of the Anathothites, or to subsequent persecutions at Jerusalem. The former seem to be intended both here, and in Ps. xxvii., which is certainly most appropriate as an Ode of Thanksgiving for the prophet's escape from the murderous attempts of the men of Anathoth. Nothing could be more apposite than the allusions to "evil-doers drawing near against him to eat up his flesh" (i.e., according to the common Aramaic metaphor, to slander him, and destroy him with false accusations); to the "lying witnesses, and the man (or men) breathing out (or panting after) violence" (ver. 12); and to having been forsaken even by his father and mother (ver. 10). With the former, we may compare the prophet's words, chap. ix. 2 sqq., "O that I were in the wilderness, in a lodge of wayfaring men; that I might forsake my people, and depart from among them! For all of them are adulterous, an assembly of traitors. And they have bent their tongue, (as it were) their bow for lying; and it is not by sincerity that they have grown strong in the land. Beware ye, every one of his friend, and have no confidence in any brother: for every brother will assuredly supplant" (qvv yqv a reference to Jacob and Esau), "and every friend will gad about for slander. And each will deceive his friend, and the truth they will not speak: they have taught their tongue to speak lies; with perverseness they have wearied themselves. Thy dwelling is in the midst of deceit.... A murderous arrow is their tongue; deceit hath it spoken; with his mouth one speaketh peace with his neighbour, and inwardly he layeth an ambush for him." Such language, whether in the psalm or in the prophetic oration, could only be the fruit of bitter personal experience. (Cf. also xi. 19 sqq., xx. 2 sqq., xxvi. 8, xxxvi. 26, xxxvii. 15, xxxviii. 6). The allusion of the psalmist to being forsaken by father and mother (Ps. xxvii. 10) may be illustrated by the prophet's words, chap. xii. 6.

Jeremiah came prominently forward at a serious crisis in the history of his people. The Scythian invasion of Asia, described by Herodotus (i. 103-106), but not mentioned in the biblical histories of the time, was threatening Palestine and Judea. According to the old Greek writer, Cyaxares the Mede, while engaged in besieging Nineveh, was attacked by a great horde of Scythians, under their king Madyes, who had entered Asia in pushing their pursuit of the Cimmerians, whom they had expelled from Europe.[9] The Medes lost the battle, and the barbarous victors found themselves masters of Asia. Thereupon they marched for Egypt, and had made their way past Ascalon, when they were met by the envoys of Psammitichus I. the king of Egypt, whose "gifts and prayers," induced them to return. On the way back, some few of them lagged behind the main body, and plundered the famous temple of Atergatis-Derceto, or as Herodotus calls the great Syrian goddess, Ourania Afrodite, at Ascalon (the goddess avenged herself by smiting them and their descendants with impotence--theleian nouson, cf. 1 Sam. v. 6 sqq.). For eight and twenty years the Scythians remained the tyrants of Asia, and by their exactions and plundering raids brought ruin everywhere, until at last Cyaxares and his Medes, by help of treachery, recovered their former sway. After this, the Medes took Nineveh, and reduced the Assyrians to complete subjection; but Babylonia remained independent. Such is the story as related by Herodotus, our sole authority in the matter. It has been supposed [10] that the 59th Psalm was written by king Josiah, while the Scythians were threatening Jerusalem. Their wild hordes, ravenous for plunder, like the Gauls who at a later time struck Rome with panic, are at any rate well described in the verse

> "They return at eventide,
> They howl like the dogs,
> the famished pariah dogs of an eastern town--
> And surround the city."

But the Old Testament furnishes other indications of the terror which preceded the Scythian invasion, and of the merciless havoc which accompanied it. The short prophecy of Zephaniah, who prophesied "in the days of Josiah ben Amon king of Judah," and was therefore a contemporary of Jeremiah, is best explained by reference to this crisis in the affairs of Western Asia. Zephaniah's very first word is a startling menace. "I will utterly away with everything from off the face of the ground, saith Iahvah." "I will away with man and beast, I will away with the birds of the air, and the fishes of the sea, and the stumblingblocks along with the wicked (i.e. the idols with their worshippers); and I will exterminate man from off the face of the ground, saith Iahvah." The imminence of a sweeping destruction is announced. Ruin is to overtake every existing thing; not only the besotted people and their dumb idols, but beasts and birds and even the fish of the sea are to perish in the universal catastrophe. It is exactly what might be expected from the sudden appearance of a horde of barbarians of unknown numbers, sweeping over a civilised country from north to south, like some devastating flood; slaying whatever crossed their path, burning towns and temples, and devouring the flocks and herds. The reference to the fishes of the sea is explained by the fact that the Scythians marched southward by the road which ran along the coast through Philistia. "Gaza," cries the prophet, "shall be forsaken,"--there is an inimitable paronomasia in his words [11] --"And Ascalon a desolation: as for Ashdod, at noonday they shall drive her into exile; and Ekron shall be rooted up. Alas for the dwellers by the shore line, the race of the Cherethites! The word of Iahvah is against you, O Canaan, land of the Philistines! And I will destroy thee, that there shall be no inhabitant." It is true that Herodotus relates that the Scythians, in their retreat, for the most part marched past Ascalon without doing any harm, and that the plunder of the temple was the work of a few stragglers. But neither is this very probable in itself, nor does it harmonize with what he tells us afterwards about the plunder and rapine that marked the period of Scythian domination. We need not suppose that the information of the old historian as to the doings of these barbarians was as exact as that of a modern state paper. Nor, on the other hand, would it be very judicious to press every detail in a highly wrought prophetic discourse, which vividly sets forth the fears of the time, and gives imaginative form to the feelings and anticipations of the hour; as if it were intended by the writer, not for the moral and spiritual good of his contemporaries, but to furnish posterity with a minutely accurate record of the actual course of events in the distant past.

The public danger, which stimulated the reflexion and lent force to the invective of the lesser prophet, intensified the impression produced by the earlier preaching of Jeremiah. The tide of invasion, indeed, rolled past Judea, without working much permanent harm to the little kingdom, with whose destinies were involved the highest interests of mankind at large. But this respite from destruction would be understood by the prophet's hearers as proof of the relentings of Iahvah towards His penitent people; and may, for the time at least, have confirmed the impression wrought upon the popular mind by Jeremiah's passionate censures and entreaties. The time was otherwise favourable; for the year of his call was the year immediately subsequent to that in which the young king Josiah "began to purify Judah and Jerusalem from the high places and the Asherim, and the carven images and the molten images," which he did in the twelfth year of his reign, i.e. in the twentieth year of his age, according to the testimony of the Chronicler (2 Chron. xxxiv. 3), which there is no good reason for disallowing. Jeremiah was probably about the same age as the king, as he calls himself a mere youth (na`ar). After the Scythians had retired--if we are right in fixing their invasion so early in the reign--the official reformation of public worship was taken up again, and completed by the eighteenth year of Josiah, when the prophet might be about twenty-five. The finding of what is called "the book of the Law," and "the book of the Covenant," [12] by Hilkiah the high priest, while the temple was being restored by the king's order, is represented by the histories as having determined the further course of the royal reforms. What this book of the Law was, it is not necessary now to discuss. It is clear from the language of the book of Kings, and from the references of Jeremiah, that the substance of it, at any rate, closely corresponded with portions of Deuteronomy. It appears from his own words (chap. xi. 1-8) that at first, at all events, Jeremiah was an earnest preacher of the positive precepts of this book of the Covenant. It is true that his name does not occur in the narrative of Josiah's reformation, as related in Kings. There the king and his counsellors inquire of Iahvah through the prophetess Huldah (2 Kings xxii. 14). Supposing the account to be both complete and correct, this only shows that five years after his call, Jeremiah was still unknown or little considered at court. But he was doubtless included among the "prophets," who, with "the king and all the men of Judah and all the inhabitants of Jerusalem," "and the priests ... and all the people, both small and great," after the words of the newfound book of the Covenant had been read in their ears, bound themselves by a solemn league and covenant, "to walk after Iahweh, and to keep His commandments, and His laws, and His statutes, with all the heart, and with all the soul" (2 Kings xxiii. 3). It is evident that at first the young prophet hoped great things of this national league and the associated reforms in the public worship. In his eleventh chapter, he writes thus: "The word that fell to Jeremiah from Iahvah, saying: Hear ye the words of this covenant"--presumably the words of the newfound book of the Torah--"And speak ye to the men of Judah, and to the inhabitants of Jerusalem. And thou shalt say unto them"--the change from the second plural "hear ye," "speak ye," is noticeable. In the first instance, no doubt, the message contemplates the leaders of the reforming movement generally; the prophet is specially addressed in the words, "And thou shalt say unto them, Thus said Iahvah, the God of Israel, Cursed is the man that will not hear the words of this covenant, which I commanded your fathers, in the day when I brought them forth from the land of Egypt, from the iron furnace, saying, Hearken to My voice, and do them, according to all that I command you; and ye shall become to Me a people, and I--I will become to you Elohim: in order to make good the oath that I sware to your fathers, to give them a land flowing with milk and honey, as at this day.

"And I answered and said, So be it, Iahvah!

"And Iahvah said unto me, Proclaim all these words in the cities of Judah and in the streets of Jerusalem, saying, Hear ye the words of this covenant, and do them. For I solemnly adjured your fathers, at the time when I brought them up out of the land of Egypt, (and) unto this day, with all earnestness [earnestly and incessantly], saying, Hearken ye to My voice. And they hearkened not, nor inclined their ear, and they walked individually in the stubbornness of their evil heart. So I brought upon them all the words of this covenant"--i.e., the curses, which constituted the sanction of it: see Deut. iv. 25 sqq., xxviii. 15 sqq.--"(this covenant) which I commanded them to do, and they did it not." [Or perhaps, "Because I bade them do, and they did not;" implying a general prescription of conduct, which was not observed. Or, "I who had bidden them do, and they did not"--justifying, as it were, God's assumption of the function of punishment. His law had been set at nought; the national reverses, therefore, were His infliction, and not another's.] This, then, was the first preaching of Jeremiah. "Hear ye the words of this covenant!"--the covenant drawn out with such precision and legal formality in the newfound book of the Torah. Up and down the country, "in the cities of Judah" and "in the streets of Jerusalem," everywhere within the bounds of the little kingdom that acknowledged the house of David, he published this panacea for the actual and imminent evils of the time, insisting, we may be sure, with all the eloquence of a youthful patriot, upon the impressive warnings embodied in the past history of Israel, as set forth in the book of the Law. But his best efforts were fruitless. Eloquence and patriotism and enlightened spiritual beliefs and lofty purity of purpose were wasted upon a generation blinded by its own vices and reserved for a swiftly approaching retribution. Perhaps the plots which drove the prophet finally from his native place were due to the hostility evoked against him by his preaching of the Law. At all events, the account of them immediately follows, in this eleventh chapter (vers. 18 sqq.). But it must be borne in mind that the Law-book was not found until five years after his call to the office of prophet. In any case, it is not difficult to understand the popular irritation at what must have seemed the unreasonable attitude of a prophet, who, in spite of the wholesale destruction of the outward symbols of idolatry effected by the king's orders, still declared that the claims of Iahweh were unsatisfied, and that something more was needed than the purging of Judah and Jerusalem from the high places and the Asherim, if the Divine favour were to be conciliated, and the country restored to permanent prosperity. The people probably supposed that they had sufficiently fulfilled the law of their God, when they had not only demolished all sanctuaries but His, but had done away with all those local holy places where Iahvah was indeed worshipped, but with a deplorable admixture of heathenish rites. The law of the one legal sanctuary, so much insisted upon in Deuteronomy, was formally established by Josiah, and the national worship was henceforth centralized in Jerusalem, which from this time onward remained in the eyes of all faithful Israelites "the place where men ought to worship." It is entirely in accordance with what we know of human nature in general, and not merely of Jewish nature, that the popular mind failed to rise to the level of the prophetic teaching, and that the reforming zeal of the time should have exhausted itself in efforts which effected no more than these external changes. The truth is that the reforming movement began from above, not from below; and however earnest the young king may have been, it is probable that the mass of his subjects viewed the abolition of the high-places, and the other sweeping measures, initiated in obedience to the precepts of the book of the Covenant, either with apathy and indifference, or with feelings of sullen hostility. The priesthood of Jerusalem were, of course, benefited by the abolition of all sanctuaries, except the one wherein they ministered and received their dues. The writings of our prophet amply demonstrate that, whatever zeal for Iahvah, and whatever degree of compunction for the past may have animated the prime movers in the reformation of the eighteenth of Josiah, no radical improvement was effected in the ordinary life of the nation. For some twelve years, indeed, the well-meaning king continued to occupy the throne; years, it may be presumed, of comparative peace and prosperity for Judah, although neither the narrative of Kings and Chronicles nor that of Jeremiah gives us any information about them. Doubtless it was generally supposed that the nation was reaping the reward of its obedience to the law of Iahvah. But at the end of that period, circ. b.c. 608, an event occurred which must have shaken this faith to its foundations. In the thirty-first year of his reign, Josiah fell in the battle of Megiddo, while vainly opposing the small forces at his command to the hosts of Egypt. Great indeed must have been the "searchings of heart" occasioned by this unlooked-for and overwhelming stroke. Strange that it should have fallen at a time when, as the people deemed, the God of Israel was receiving His due at their hands; when the injunctions of the book of the Covenant had been minutely carried out, the false and irregular worships abolished, and Jerusalem made the centre of the cultus; a time when it seemed as if the Lord had become reconciled to His people Israel, when years of peace and plenty seemed to give demonstration of the fact; and when, as may perhaps be inferred from Josiah's expedition against Necho, the extension of the border, contemplated in the book of the Law, was considered as likely to be realised in the near future. The height to which the national aspirations had soared only made the fall more disastrous, complete, ruinous.

The hopes of Judah rested upon a worldly foundation; and it was necessary that a people whose blindness was only intensified by prosperity, should be undeceived by the discipline of overthrow. No hint is given in the meagre narrative of the reign as to whether the prophets had lent their countenance or not to the fatal expedition. Probably they did; probably they too had to learn by bitter experience, that no man, not even a zealous and godfearing monarch, is necessary to the fulfilment of the Divine counsels. And the agony of this irretrievable disaster, this sudden and complete extinction of his country's fairest hopes, may have been the means by which the Holy Spirit led Jeremiah to an intenser conviction that illicit modes of worship and coarse idolatries were not the only things in Judah offensive to Iahvah; that something more was needed to win back His favour than formal obedience, however rigid and exacting, to the letter of a written code of sacred law; that the covenant of Iahvah with His people had an inward and eternal, not an outward and transitory significance; and that not the letter but the spirit of the law was the thing of essential moment. Thoughts like these must have been present to the prophet's mind when he wrote (xxxi. 31 sqq.): "Behold, a time is coming, saith Iahvah, when I will conclude with the house of Israel and with the house of Judah a fresh treaty, unlike the treaty that I concluded with their forefathers, at the time when I took hold of their hand, to bring them out of the land of Egypt; when they, on their part, disannulled my treaty, and I--I disdained [13] them, saith Iahvah. For this is the treaty that I will conclude with the house of Israel after those days [i.e. in due time], saith Iahvah: I will put my Torah within them and upon their heart will I grave it; and I will become to them a God, and they--they shall become to me a people."

It is but a dull eye which cannot see beyond the metaphor of the covenant or treaty between Iahvah and Israel; and it is a strangely dark understanding that fails to perceive here and elsewhere a translucent figure of the eternal relations subsisting between God and man. The error is precisely that against which the prophets, at the high watermark of their inspiration, are always protesting--the universal and inveterate error of narrowing down the requirements of the Infinitely Holy, Just and Good, to the scrupulous observance of some accepted body of canons, enshrined in a book and duly interpreted by the laborious application of recognised legal authorities. It is so comfortable to be sure of possessing an infallible guide in so small a compass; to be spared all further consideration, so long as we have paid the priestly dues, and kept the annual feasts, and carefully observed the laws of ceremonial purity! From the first, the attention of priests and people, including the official prophets, would be attracted by the ritual and ceremonial precepts, rather than by the earnest moral teaching of Deuteronomy. As soon as first impressions had had time to subside, the moral and spiritual element in that noble book would begin to be ignored, or confounded with the purely external and mundane prescriptions affecting public worship and social propriety; and the interests of true religion would hardly be subserved by the formal acceptance of this code as the law of the state. The unregenerate heart of man would fancy that it had at last gotten that for which it is always craving--something final--something to which it could triumphantly point, when urged by the religious enthusiast, as tangible evidence that it was fulfilling the Divine law, that it was at one with Iahvah, and therefore had a right to expect the continuance of His favour and blessing. Spiritual development would be arrested; men would become satisfied with having effected certain definite changes bringing them into external conformity with the written law, and would incline to rest in things as they were. Meanwhile, the truth held good that to make a fetish of a code, a system, a holy book, is not necessarily identical with the service of God. It is, in fact, the surest way to forget God; for it is to invest something that is not He, but, at best, a far-off echo of His voice, with His sole attributes of finality and sufficiency.

The effect of the downfall of the good king was electrical. The nation discovered that the displeasure of Iahvah had not passed away like a morning cloud. Out of the shock and the dismay of that terrible disillusion sprang the conviction that the past was not atoned for, that the evil of it was irreparable. The idea is reflected in the words of Jeremiah (xv. 1): "And Iahvah said unto me, If Moses were to stand before Me (as an intercessor), and Samuel, I should not incline towards this people: dismiss them from My presence, and let them go forth! And when they say unto thee, Whither are we to go forth? thou shalt say unto them, Thus said Iahvah, They that are Death's to death; and they that are the Sword's to the sword; and they that are Famine's to famine; and they that are Captivity's to captivity. And I will set over them four families, saith Iahvah; the sword to slay, and the dogs to draw (2 Sam. xvii. 13), and the birds of the air, and the beasts of the earth, to devour and to destroy. And I will give them for worry (Deut. xxviii. 25) to all the realms of earth; because of (Deut. xv. 10, xviii. 12; vnll) Manasseh ben Hezekiah king of Judah; for what he did in Jerusalem." In the next verses we have what seems to be a reference to the death of Josiah (ver. 7). "I fanned them with a fan"--the fan by which the husbandman separates wheat from chaff in the threshing floor--"I fanned them with a fan, in the gates of the land"--at Megiddo, the point where an enemy marching along the maritime route might enter the land of Israel; "I bereaved, I ruined my people (ver. 9). She that had borne seven, pined away; she breathed out her soul; her sun went down while it was yet day." The national mourning over this dire event became proverbial, as we see from Zech. xii. 11: "In that day, great shall be the mourning in Jerusalem; like the mourning of Hadadrimmon in the valley of Megiddo."

The political relations of the period are certainly obscure, if we confine our attention to the biblical data. Happily, we are now able to supplement these, by comparison with the newly recovered monuments of Assyria. Under Manasseh, the kingdom of Judah became tributary to Esarhaddon; and this relation of dependence, we may be sure, was not interrupted during the vigorous reign of the mighty Ashurbanipal, b.c. 668-626. But the first symptoms of declining power on the side of their oppressors would undoubtedly be the signal for conspiracy and rebellion in the distant parts of the loosely amalgamated empire. Until the death of Ashurbanipal, the last great sovereign who reigned at Nineveh, it may be assumed that Josiah stood true to his fealty. It appears from certain notices in Kings and Chronicles (2 Kings xxiii. 19; 2 Chron. xxxiv. 6) that he was able to exercise authority even in the territories of the ruined kingdom of Israel. This may have been due to the fact that he was allowed to do pretty much as he liked, so long as he proved an obedient vassal; or, as is more likely, the attention of the Assyrians was diverted from the West by troubles nearer home in connection with the Scythians or the Medes and Babylonians. At all events, it is not to be supposed that when Josiah went out to oppose the Pharaoh at Megiddo, he was facing the forces of Egypt alone. The thing is intrinsically improbable. The king of Judah must have headed a coalition of the petty Syrian states against the common enemy. It is not necessary to suppose that the Palestinian principalities resisted Necho's advance, in the interests of their nominal suzerain Assyria. From all we can gather, that empire was now tottering to its irretrievable fall, under the feeble successors of Ashurbanipal. The ambition of Egypt was doubtless a terror to the combined peoples. The further results of Necho's campaign are unknown. For the moment, Judah experienced a change of masters; but the Egyptian tyranny was not destined to last. Some four years after the battle of Megiddo, Pharaoh Necho made a second expedition to the North, this time against the Babylonians, who had succeeded to the empire of Assyria. The Egyptians were utterly defeated in the battle of Carchemish, circ. b.c. 606-5, which left Nebuchadrezzar in virtual possession of the countries west of the Euphrates (Jer. xlvi. 2). It was the fourth year of Jehoiakim, son of Josiah, king of Judah, when this crisis arose in the affairs of the Eastern world. The prophet Jeremiah did not miss the meaning of events. From the first he recognised in Nebuchadrezzar, or Nabucodrossor, an instrument in the Divine hand for the chastisement of the peoples; from the first, he predicted a judgment of God, not only upon the Jews, but upon all nations, far and near. The substance of his oracles is preserved to us in chapters xxv. and xlvi.-xlix. of his book. In the former passage, which is expressly dated from the fourth year of Jehoiakim, and the first of Nebuchadrezzar, the prophet gives a kind of retrospect of his ministry of three-and-twenty years, affirms that it has failed of its end, and that Divine retribution is therefore certain. The "tribes of the north" will come and desolate the whole country (ver. 9), and "these nations"--the peoples of Palestine--"shall serve the king of Babel seventy years" (ver. 11). The judgment on the nations is depicted by an impressive symbolism (ver. 15). "Thus said Iahvah, the God of Israel, unto me, Take this cup of wine, the (Divine) wrath, from My hand, and cause all the nations, unto whom I send thee, to drink it. And let them drink, and reel, and show themselves frenzied, because of the sword that I am sending amongst them!" The strange metaphor recalls our own proverb: Quem Deus vult perdere, prius dementat. "So I took the cup from the hand of Iahvah, and made all the nations drink, unto whom Iahvah had sent me." Then, as in some list of the proscribed, the prophet writes down, one after another, the names of the doomed cities and peoples. The judgment was set for that age, and the eternal books were opened, and the names found in them were these (ver. 18): "Jerusalem, and the cities of Judah, and her kings, and her princes. Pharaoh king of Egypt, and his servants, and his princes, and all his people. And all the hired soldiery, and all the kings of the land of Uz, and all the kings of the land of the Philistines, and Ashkelon, and Gaza, and Ekron, and the remnant of Ashdod. Edom, and Moab, and the benê Ammon. And all the kings of Tyre, and all the kings of Sidon, and the kings of the island (i.e. Cyprus) that is beyond the sea. Dedan and Tema and Buz and all the tonsured folk. And all the kings of Arabia, and all the kings of the hired soldiery, that dwell in the wilderness. And all the kings of Zimri, and all the kings of Elam, and all the kings of Media. And all the kings of the north, the near and the far, one with another; and all the kingdoms of the earth that are upon the surface of the ground."

***

When the mourning for Josiah was ended (2 Chron. xxxv. 24 sqq.), the people put Jehoahaz on his father's throne. But this arrangement was not suffered to continue, for Necho, having defeated and slain Josiah, naturally asserted his right to dispose of the crown of Judah as he thought fit. Accordingly, he put Jehoahaz in bonds at Riblah in the land of Hamath, whither he had probably summoned him to swear allegiance to Egypt, or whither, perhaps, Jehoahaz had dared to go with an armed force to resist the Egyptian pretensions, which, however, is an unlikely supposition, as the battle in which Josiah had fallen must have been a severe blow to the military resources of Judah. Necho carried the unfortunate but also unworthy king (2 Kings xxiii. 32) a prisoner to Egypt, where he died (ibid. 34). These events are thus alluded to by Jeremiah (xxii. 10-12): "Weep ye not for one dead (i.e. Josiah), nor make your moan for him: weep ever for him that is going away; for he will not come back again, and see his native land! For thus hath Iahvah said of Shallum (i.e. Jehoahaz, 1 Chron. iii. 15) ben Josiah, king of Judah, that reigned in the place of Josiah his father, who is gone forth out of this place (i.e. Jerusalem, or the palace, ver. 1), He will not come back thither again. For in the place whither they have led him into exile, there he will die; and this land he will not see again." The pathos of this lament for one whose dream of greatness was broken for ever within three short months, does not conceal the prophet's condemnation of Necho's prisoner. Jeremiah does not condole with the captive king as the victim of mere misfortune. In this, as in all the gathering calamities of his country, he sees a retributive meaning. The nine preceding verses of the chapter demonstrate the fact.

In the place of Jehoahaz, Necho had set up his elder brother Eliakim, with the title of Jehoiakim (2 Kings xxiii. 34). This prince also is condemned in the narrative of Kings (ver. 37), as having done "the evil thing in the eyes of Iahvah, according to all that his forefathers had done;" an estimate which is thoroughly confirmed by what Jeremiah has added to his lament for the deposed king his brother. The pride, the grasping covetousness, the high-handed violence and cruelty of Jehoiakim, and the doom that will overtake him, in the righteousness of God, are thus declared: "Woe to him that buildeth his house by injustice, and his chambers by iniquity! that layeth on his neighbour work without wages, and giveth him not his hire! That saith, I will build me a lofty house, with airy chambers; and he cutteth him out the windows thereof, panelling it with cedar, and painting it with vermilion. Shalt thou reign, that thou art hotly intent upon cedar?" (Or, according to the LXX. Vat., thou viest with Ahaz--LXX. Alex., with Ahab; perhaps a reference to "the ivory house" mentioned in 1 Kings xxii. 39). "Thy father, did he not eat and drink and do judgment and justice? Then it was well with him. He judged the cause of the oppressed and the needy: then it was well. Was not this to know Me? saith Iahvah. For thine eyes and thine heart are set upon nought but thine own lucre [thy plunder], and upon the blood of the innocent, to shed it, and upon extortion and oppression to do it. Therefore, thus hath Iahvah said of Jehoiakim ben Josiah, king of Judah: They shall not lament for him with Ah, my brother! or Ah, sister! They shall not lament for him with Ah, lord! or Ah, his majesty! With the burial of an ass shall he be buried; with dragging and casting forth beyond the gates of Jerusalem!"

In the beginning of the reign of this worthless tyrant, the prophet was impelled to address a very definite warning to the throng of worshippers in the court of the temple (xxvi. 4 sqq.). It was to the effect that if they did not amend their ways, their temple should become like Shiloh, and their city a curse to all the nations of the earth. There could be no doubt of the meaning of this reference to the ruined sanctuary, long since forsaken of God (Ps. lxxviii. 60). It so wrought upon that fanatical audience, that priests and prophets and people rose as one man against the daring speaker; and Jeremiah was barely rescued from immediate death by the timely intervention of the princes. The account closes with the relation of the cruel murder of another prophet of the school of Jeremiah, by command of Jehoiakim the king; and it is very evident from these narratives that, screened as he was by powerful friends, Jeremiah narrowly escaped a similar fate.

We have reached the point in our prophet's career when, taking a broad survey of the entire world of his time, he forecasts the character of the future that awaits its various political divisions. He has left the substance of his reflexions in the 25th chapter, and in those prophecies concerning the foreign peoples, which the Hebrew text of his works relegates to the very end of the book, as chapters xlvi.-li., but which the Greek recension of the Septuagint inserts immediately after chap. xxv. 13. In the decisive battle at Carchemish, which crippled the power of Egypt, the only other existing state which could make any pretensions to the supremacy of Western Asia, and contend with the trans-Euphratean empires for the possession of Syria-Palestine, Jeremiah had recognised a signal indication of the Divine Will, which he was not slow to proclaim to all within reach of his inspired eloquence. In common with all the great prophets who had preceded him, he entertained a profound conviction that the race was not necessarily to the swift, nor the battle to the strong; that the fortune of war was not determined simply and solely by chariots and horsemen and big battalions; that behind all material forces lay the spiritual, from whose absolute will they derived their being and potency, and upon whose sovereign pleasure depended the issues of victory and defeat, of life and death. As his successor, the second Isaiah, saw in the polytheist Cyrus, king of Anzan, a chosen servant of Iahvah, whose whole triumphant career was foreordained in the counsels of heaven; so Jeremiah saw in the rise of the Babylonian domination, and the rapid development of the new empire upon the ruins of the old, a manifest token of the Divine purpose, a revelation of a Divine secret. His point of view is strikingly illustrated by the warning which he was directed to send a few years later to the kings who were seeking to draw Judah into the common alliance against Babylon (chap. xxvii. 1 sqq.). "In the beginning of the reign of Zedekiah [14] ben Josiah, king of Judah, fell this word to Jeremiah from Iahvah. Thus said Iahvah unto me, Make thee thongs and poles, and put them upon thy neck; and send them to the king of Edom, and to the king of Moab, and to the king of the benê Ammon, and to the king of Tyre, and to the king of Zidon, by the hand of the messengers that are come to Jerusalem, unto Zedekiah the king of Judah. And give them a charge unto their masters, saying, Thus said Iahvah Sabaoth, the God of Israel, Thus shall ye say to your masters: I it was that made the earth, mankind, and the cattle that are on the face of the earth, by My great strength, and by Mine outstretched arm; and I give it to whom it seemeth good in My sight. And now, I will verily give all these countries into the hand of Nebuchadrezzar king of Babel, My servant; and even the wild creatures of the field will I give unto him to serve him."

Nebuchadrezzar was invincible, and the Jewish prophet clearly perceived the fact. But it must not be imagined that the Jewish people generally, or the neighbouring peoples, enjoyed a similar degree of insight. Had that been so, the battle of Jeremiah's life would never have been fought out under such cruel, such hopeless conditions. The prophet saw the truth, and proclaimed it without ceasing in reluctant ears, and was met with derision, and incredulity, and intrigue, and slander, and pitiless persecution. By-and-by, when his word had come to pass, and all the principalities of Canaan were crouching abjectly at the feet of the conqueror, and Jerusalem was a heap of ruins, the scattered communities of banished Israelites could remember that Jeremiah had foreseen and foretold it all. In the light of accomplished facts, the significance of his prevision began to be realised; and when the first dreary hours of dumb and desperate suffering were over, the exiles gradually learned to find consolation in the few but precious promises that had accompanied the menaces which were now so visibly fulfilled. While they were yet in their own land, two things had been predicted by this prophet in the name of their God. The first was now accomplished; no cavil could throw doubt upon actual experience. Was there not here some warrant, at least for reasonable men, some sufficient ground for trusting the prophet at last, for believing in his Divine mission, for striving to follow his counsels, and for looking forward with steadfast hope out of present affliction, to the gladness of the future which the same seer had foretold, even with the unwonted precision of naming a limit of time? So the exiles were persuaded, and their belief was fully justified by the event. Never had they realised the absolute sovereignty of their God, the universality of Iahvah Sabaoth, the shadowy nature, the blank nothingness of all supposed rivals of His dominion, as now they did, when at length years of painful experience had brought home to their minds the truth that Nebuchadrezzar had demolished the temple and laid Jerusalem in the dust, not, as he himself believed, by the favour of Bel-Merodach and Nebo, but by the sentence of the God of Israel; and that the catastrophe, which had swept them out of political existence, occurred not because Iahvah was weaker than the gods of Babylon, but because He was irresistibly strong; stronger than all powers of all worlds; stronger therefore than Israel, stronger than Babylon; stronger than the pride and ambition of the earthly conqueror, stronger than the self-will, and the stubbornness, and the wayward rebellion, and the fanatical blindness, and the frivolous unbelief, of his own people. The conception is an easy one for us, who have inherited the treasures both of Jewish and of Gentile thought; but the long struggle of the prophets, and the fierce antagonism of their fellow-countrymen, and the political extinction of the Davidic monarchy, and the agonies of the Babylonian exile, were necessary to the genesis and germination of this master-conception in the heart of Israel, and so of humanity.

To return from this hasty glance at the remoter consequences of the prophet's ministry, it was in the fourth year of Jehoiakim, and the first of Nebuchadrezzar (xxv. 1) that, in obedience to a Divine intimation, he collected the various discourses which he had so far delivered in the name of God. Some doubt has been raised as to the precise meaning of the record of this matter (xxxvi.). On the one hand, it is urged that "An historically accurate reproduction of the prophecies would not have suited Jeremiah's object, which was not historical but practical: he desired to give a salutary shock to the people, by bringing before them the fatal consequences of their evil deeds:" and that "the purport of the roll (ver. 29) which the king burned was [only] that the king of Babylon should 'come and destroy this land,' whereas it is clear that Jeremiah had uttered many other important declarations in the course of his already long ministry." And on the other hand, it is suggested that the roll, of which the prophet speaks in chap. xxxvi., contained no more than the prophecy concerning the Babylonian invasion and its consequences, which is preserved in chap. xxv., and dated from the fourth year of Jehoiakim.

Considering the unsatisfactory state of the text of Jeremiah, it is perhaps admissible to suppose, for the sake of this hypothesis, that the second verse of chap. xxv., which expressly declares that this prophecy was spoken by its author "to all the people of Judah, and to all the inhabitants of Jerusalem," is "a loose inaccurate statement due to a later editor;" although this inconvenient statement is found in the Greek of the LXX. as well as in the Massoretic Hebrew text. But let us examine the alleged objections in the light of the positive statements of chap. xxxvi. It is there written thus: "In the fourth year of Jehoiakim ben Josiah king of Judah, this word fell to Jeremiah from Iahvah. Take thee a book-roll, and write on it all the words that I have spoken unto thee, concerning Israel and Judah and all the nations, from the day when I (first) spake unto thee,--from the days of Josiah,--unto this day." This certainly seems plain enough. The only possible question is whether the command was to collect within the compass of a single volume, a sort of author's edition, an indefinite number of discourses preserved hitherto in separate MSS. and perhaps to a great extent in the prophet's memory, or whether we are to understand by "all the words" the substance of the various prophecies to which reference is made. If the object was merely to impress the people on a particular occasion by placing before them a sort of historical review of the prophet's warnings in the past, it is evident that a formal edition of his utterances, so far as he was able to prepare such a work, would not be the most natural or ready method of attaining that purpose. Such a review for practical purposes might well be comprised within the limits of a single continuous composition, such as we find in chap. xxv., which opens with a brief retrospect of the prophet's ministry during twenty-three years (vers. 3-7), and then denounces the neglect with which his warnings have been received, and declares the approaching subjugation of all the states of Phenicia-Palestine by the king of Babylon. But the narrative itself gives not a single hint that such was the sole object in view. Much rather does it appear from the entire context that, the crisis having at length arrived, which Jeremiah had so long foreseen, he was now impelled to gather together, with a view to their preservation, all those discourses by which he had laboured in vain to overcome the indifference, the callousness, and the bitter antagonism of his people. These utterances of the past, collected and revised in the light of successive events, and illustrated by their substantial agreement with what had actually taken place, and especially by the new danger which seemed to threaten the whole West, the rising power of Babylon, might certainly be expected to produce a powerful impression by their coincidence with the national apprehensions; and the prophet might even hope that warnings, hitherto disregarded, but now visibly justified by events in course of development, would at last bring "the house of Judah" to consider seriously the evil that, in God's Providence, was evidently impending, and "return every man from his evil way," that even so late the consequences of their guilt might be turned aside. This doubtless was the immediate aim, but it does not exclude others, such as the vindication of the prophet's own claims, in startling contrast with those of the false prophets, who had opposed him at every step, and misled his countrymen so grievously and fatally. Against these and their delusive promises, the volume of Jeremiah's past discourses would constitute an effective protest, and a complete justification of his own endeavours. We must also remember that, if the repentance and salvation of his own contemporaries was naturally the first object of the prophet in all his undertakings, in the Divine counsels prophecy has more than a temporary value, and that the writings of this very prophet were destined to become instrumental in the conversion of a succeeding generation.

Those twenty-three years of patient thought and earnest labour, of high converse with God, and of agonised pleading with a reprobate people, were not to be without their fruit, though the prophet himself was not to see it. It is matter of history that the words of Jeremiah wrought with such power upon the hearts of the exiles in Babylonia, as to become, in the hands of God, a principal means in the regeneration of Israel, and of that restoration which was its promised and its actual consequence; and from that day to this, not one of all the goodly fellowship of the prophets has enjoyed such credit in the Jewish Church as he who in his lifetime had to encounter neglect and ridicule, hatred and persecution, beyond what is recorded of any other.

"So Jeremiah called Baruch ben Neriah; and Baruch wrote, from the mouth of Jeremiah, all the words of Iahvah, that He had spoken unto him, upon a book-roll" (ver. 4). Nothing is said about time; and there is nothing to indicate that what the scribe wrote at the prophet's dictation was a single brief discourse. The work probably occupied a not inconsiderable time, as may be inferred from the datum of the ninth verse (vid. infr.). Jeremiah would know that haste was incompatible with literary finish; he would probably feel that it was equally incompatible with the proper execution of what he had recognised as a Divine command. The prophet hardly had all his past utterances lying before him in the form of finished compositions. "And Jeremiah commanded Baruch, saying: I am detained (or confined); I cannot enter the house of Iahvah; so enter thou, and read in the roll, that thou wrotest from my mouth, the words of Iahvah, in the ears of the people, in the house of Iahvah, upon a day of fasting: and also in the ears of all Judah (the Jews), that come in (to the temple) from their (several) cities, thou shalt read them. Perchance their supplication will fall before Iahvah, and they will return, every one from his evil way; for great is the anger and the hot displeasure that Iahvah hath spoken (threatened) unto this people. And Baruch ben Neriah did according to all that Jeremiah the prophet commanded him, reading in the book the words of Iahvah in Iahvah's house." This last sentence might be regarded as a general statement, anticipative of the detailed account that follows, as is often the case in Old Testament narratives. But I doubt the application of this well-known exegetical device in the present instance. The verse is more likely an interpolation; unless we suppose that it refers to divers readings of which no particulars are given, but which preceded the memorable one described in the following verses. The injunction, "And also in the ears of all Judah that come out of their cities thou shalt read them!" might imply successive readings, as the people flocked into Jerusalem from time to time. But the grand occasion, if not the only one, was without doubt that which stands recorded in the text. "And it came to pass in the fifth year of Jehoiakim ben Josiah king of Judah, in the ninth month, they proclaimed a fast before Iahvah,--all the people in Jerusalem and all the people that were come out of the cities of Judah into Jerusalem. And Baruch read in the book the words of Jeremiah, in the house of Iahvah, in the cell of Gemariah ben Shaphan the scribe, in the upper (inner) court, at the entry of the new gate of Iahvah's house, in the ears of all the people." The dates have an important bearing upon the points we are considering. It was in the fourth year of Jehoiakim that the prophet was bidden to commit his oracles to writing. If, then, the task was not accomplished before the ninth month of the fifth year, it is plain that it involved a good deal more than penning such a discourse as the twenty-fifth chapter. This datum, in fact, strongly favours the supposition that it was a record of his principal utterances hitherto, that Jeremiah thus undertook and accomplished. It is not at all necessary to assume that on this or any other occasion Baruch read the entire contents of the roll to his audience in the temple. We are told that he "read in the book the words of Jeremiah," that is, no doubt, some portion of the whole. And so, in the famous scene before the king, it is not said that the entire work was read, but the contrary is expressly related (ver. 23): "And when Jehudi had read three columns or four, he (the king) began to cut it with the scribe's knife, and to cast it into the fire." Three or four columns of an ordinary roll might have contained the whole of the twenty-fifth chapter; and it must have been an unusually diminutive document, if the first three or four columns of it contained no more than the seven verses of chap. xxv. (3-6), which declare the sin of Judah, and announce the coming of the king of Babylon. And, apart from these objections, there is no ground for the presumption that "the purport of the roll which the king burnt was [only] that the king of Babylon should 'come and destroy this land.'" As the learned critic, from whom I have quoted these words, further remarks, with perfect truth, "Jeremiah had uttered many other important declarations in the course of his already long ministry."

That, I grant, is true; but then there is absolutely nothing to prove that this roll did not contain them all. Chap. xxxvi. 29, cited by the objector, is certainly not such proof. That verse simply gives the angry exclamation with which the king interrupted the reading of the roll, "Why hast thou written upon it, The king of Babylon shall surely come and destroy this land, and cause to cease from it man and beast?"

This may have been no more than Jehoiakim's very natural inference from some one of the many

Rev. C. J. Ball, M.A., & W. H. Bennett, M.A.

allusions to the enemy "from the north," which occur in the earlier part of the book of Jeremiah. At all events, it is evident that, whether the king of Babylon was directly mentioned or not in the portion of the roll read in his presence, the verse in question assigns, not the sole import of the entire work, but only the particular point in it, which, at the existing crisis, especially roused the indignation of Jehoiakim. The 25th chapter may of course have been contained in the roll read before the king.

And this may suffice to show how precarious are the assertions of the learned critic in the Encyclop. Brit. upon the subject of Jeremiah's roll. The plain truth seems to be that, perceiving the imminence of the peril that threatened his country, the prophet was impressed with the conviction that now was the time to commit his past utterances to writing; and that towards the end of the year, after he had formed and carried out this project, he found occasion to have his discourses read in the temple, to the crowds of rural folk who sought refuge in Jerusalem, before the advance of Nebuchadrezzar. So Josephus understood the matter (Ant., x. 6, 2).

On the approach of the Babylonians, Jehoiakim made his submission; but only to rebel again, after three years of tribute and vassalage (2 Kings xxiv. 1). Drought and failure of the crops aggravated the political troubles of the country; evils in which Jeremiah was not slow to discern the hand of an offended and alienated God. "How long," he asks (xii. 4), "shall the country mourn, and the herbage of the whole field wither? From the wickedness of them that dwell therein the beasts and the birds perish." And in chap. xiv. we have a highly poetical description of the sufferings of the time.

> *"Judah mourneth, and her gates languish;*
> *They sit in black on the ground;*
> *And the outcry of Jerusalem hath gone up.*
> *And their nobles, they sent their menial folk for water;*
> *They came to the pits, they found no water;*
> *They returned with their vessels empty;*
> *They were ashamed and confounded and covered their head.*
> *On account of ye ground that is chapt,*
> *For rain hath not fallen in the land,*
> *The plowmen are ashamed--they cover their head.*
> *For even the hind in the field--*
> *She calveth and forsaketh her young;*
> *For there is no grass.*
> *And the wild asses, they stand on the scaurs;*
> *They snuff the wind* [15] *like jackals;*
> *Their eyes fail, for there is no herbage."*

And then, after this graphic and almost dramatic portrayal of the sufferings of man and beast, in the blinding glare of the towns, and in the hot waterless plains, and on the bare hills, under that burning sky, whose cloudless splendours seemed to mock their misery, the prophet prays to the God of Israel.

> *"If our misdeeds answer against us,*
> *O Iahvah, work for Thy name sake!*
> *Verily, our fallings away are many;*
> *Towards thee we are in fault.*
> *Hope of Israel, that savest him in time of trouble!*
> *Why shouldst thou be as a sojourner in the land,*
> *And as a traveller, that turneth aside to pass the night?*
> *Why shouldst thou be as a man stricken dumb,*
> *As a champion that cannot save?*
> *Yet Thou art in our midst, O Iahvah,*
> *And Thy name is called over us:*
> *Leave us not!"*
> And again, at the end of the chapter,
> *"Hast Thou wholly rejected Judah?*
> *Hath Thy soul loathed Zion?*
> *Why hast Thou smitten us,*
> *That there is no healing for us?*
> *We looked for welfare, but bootlessly,*
> *For a time of healing, and behold terror!*
> *We know, Iahvah, our wickedness, the guilt of our fathers:*
> *Verily, we are in fault toward Thee!*
> *Be not scornful, for Thy name's sake!*

> Dishonour not Thy glorious throne! [i.e. Jerusalem.]
> Remember, break not Thy covenant with us!
> Among the Vanities of the nations are there indeed raingivers?
> Or the heavens, can they yield showers?
> Art not Thou He (that doeth this), Iahvah our God?
> And we wait for Thee,
> For 'tis Thou that madest all this world."

In these and the like pathetic outpourings, which meet us in the later portions of the Old Testament, we may observe the gradual development of the dialect of stated prayer; the beginnings and the growth of that beautiful and appropriate liturgical language in which both the synagogue and the church afterwards found so perfect an instrument for the expression of all the harmonies of worship. Prayer, both public and private, was destined to assume an increasing importance, and, after the destruction of temple and altar, and the forcible removal of the people to a heathen land, to become the principal means of communion with God.

The evils of drought and dearth appear to have been accompanied by inroads of foreign enemies, who took advantage of the existing distress to rob and plunder at will. This serious aggravation of the national troubles is recorded in chap. xii. 7-17. There it is said, in the name of God, "I have left My house, I have cast off My heritage; I have given the Darling of My soul into the hands of her enemies." The reason is Judah's fierce hostility to her Divine Master: "Like a lion in the forest she hath uttered a cry against Me." The result of this unnatural rebellion is seen in the ravages of lawless invaders, probably nomads of the desert, always watching their opportunity, and greedy of the wealth, while disdainful of the pursuits of their civilised neighbours. It is as if all the wild beasts, that roam at large in the open country, had concerted a united attack upon the devoted land; as if many shepherds with their innumerable flocks had eaten bare and trodden down the vineyard of the Lord. "Over all the bald crags in the wilderness freebooters (Obad. 5) are come; for a sword of Iahweh's is devouring: from land's end to land's end no flesh hath security" (ver. 12). The rapacious and heathenish hordes of the desert, mere human wolves intent on ravage and slaughter, are a sword of the Lord's, for the chastisement of His people; just as the king of Babylon is His "servant" for the same purpose.

Only ten verses of the book of Kings are occupied with the reign of Jehoiakim (2 Kings xxiii. 34-xxiv. 6); and when we compare that flying sketch with the allusions in Jeremiah, we cannot but keenly regret the loss of that "Book of the chronicles of the kings of Judah," to which the compiler of Kings refers as his authority. Had that work survived, many things in the prophets, which are now obscure and baffling, would have been clear and obvious. As it is, we are often obliged to be contented with surmises and probabilities, where certainty would be right welcome. In the present instance, the facts alluded to by the prophet appear to be included in the statement that the Lord sent against Jehoiakim bands of Chaldeans, and bands of Arameans, and bands of Moabites, and bands of benê Ammon. The Hebrew term implies marauding or predatory bands, rather than regular armies, and it need not be supposed that they all fell upon the country at the same time or in accordance with any preconcerted scheme. In the midst of these troubles, Jehoiakim died in the flower of his age, having reigned no more than eleven years, and being only thirty-six years old (2 Kings xxiii. 36). The prophet thus alludes to his untimely end. "Like the partridge that sitteth on eggs that she hath not laid, so is he that maketh riches, and not by right: in the midst of his days they leave him; and in his last end he proveth a fool" (xvii. 11). We have already considered the detailed condemnation of this evil king in the 22nd chapter. The prophet Habakkuk, a contemporary of Jeremiah, seems to have had Jehoiakim in his mind's eye, when denouncing (ii. 9) woe to one that "getteth an evil gain for his house, that he may set his nest on high, that he may escape from the hand of evil!" The allusion is to the forced labour on his new palace, and on the defences of Jerusalem, as well as to the fines and presents of money, which this oppressive ruler shamelessly extorted from his unhappy subjects. "The stone out of the wall," says the prophet, "crieth out; and the beam out of the woodwork answereth it."

The premature death of the tyrant removed a serious obstacle from the path of Jeremiah. No longer forced to exercise a wary vigilance in avoiding the vengeance of a king whose passions determined his conduct, the prophet could now devote himself heart and soul to the work of his office. The public danger, imminent from the north, and the way to avert it, is the subject of the discourses of this period of his ministry. His unquenchable faith appears in the beautiful prayer appended to his reflexions upon the death of Jehoiakim (xvii. 12 sqq.). We cannot mistake the tone of quiet exultation, with which he expresses his sense of the absolute righteousness of the catastrophe. "A throne of glory, a height higher than the first (?), (or, higher than any before) is the place of our sanctuary." Never before in the prophet's experience has the God of Israel so clearly vindicated that justice which is the inalienable attribute of His dread tribunal.

For himself, the immediate result of this renewal of an activity that had been more or less suspended, was persecution and even violence. The earnestness with which he besought the people to honestly keep the law of the Sabbath, an obligation which was recognised in theory though disregarded in practice; and his striking illustration of the true relations between Iahvah and Israel as parallel to those that hold between the potter and the clay (chap. xvii. 19 sqq.), only brought down upon him the fierce hostility and organised opposition of the false prophets, and the priests, and the credulous and self-willed populace, as we read in chap. xviii. 18 sqq. "And they said, Come, and let us contrive plots against Jeremiah.... Come, and let us smite him with the tongue, and let us not listen to any of his words. Should evil be repaid for good, that they have digged a pit for my life?" And after his solemn testimony before the elders in the valley of Ben-Hinnom, and before the people generally, in the court of the Lord's house (chap. xix.), the prophet was seized by order of Pashchûr, the commandant of the temple, who was himself a leading false prophet, and cruelly beaten, and set in the stocks for a day and a night. That the spirit of the prophet was not broken by this shameful treatment, is evident from the courage with which he confronted his oppressor on the morrow, and foretold his certain punishment. But the apparent failure of his mission, the hopelessness of his life's labour, indicated by the deepening hostility of the people, and the readiness to proceed to extremities against him thus evinced by their leaders, wrung from Jeremiah that bitter cry of despair, which has proved such a stumbling-block to some of his modern apologists.

Soon the prophet's fears were realised, and the Divine counsel, of which he alone had been cognisant, was fulfilled. Within three short months of his accession to the throne, the boy-king Jeconiah (or Jehoiachin or Coniah), with the queen-mother, the grandees of the court, and the pick of the population of the capital, was carried captive to Babylon by Nebuchadrezzar (2 Kings xxiv. 8 sqq.; Jer. xxiv. 1).

Jeremiah has appended his forecast of the fate of Jeconiah, and a brief notice of its fulfilment, to his denunciations of that king's predecessors (xxii. 24 sqq.). "As I live, saith Iahvah, verily, though Coniah ben Jehoiakim king of Judah be a signet ring upon My own right hand, verily thence will I pluck thee away! And I will give thee into the hand of them that seek thy life, and into the hand of those of whom thou art afraid; and into the hand of Nebuchadrezzar king of Babel, and into the hand of the Chaldeans. And I will cast thee forth, and thy mother that bare thee, into the foreign land, wherein ye were not born; and there ye shall die. But unto the land whither they long to return, thither shall they not return. Is this man Coniah a despised broken vase, or a vessel devoid of charm? Why were he and his offspring cast forth, and hurled into the land that they knew not? O land, land, land, hear thou the word of Iahvah. Thus hath Iahvah said, Write ye down this man childless, a person that shall not prosper in his days: for none of his offspring shall prosper, sitting on the throne of David, and ruling again in Judah."

No better success attended the prophet's ministry under the new king Zedekiah, whom Nebuchadrezzar had placed on the throne as his vassal and tributary. So far as we can judge from the accounts left us, Zedekiah was a wellmeaning but unstable character, whose weakness and irresolution were too often played upon by unscrupulous and scheming courtiers, to the fatal miscarriage of right and justice. Soon the old intrigues began again, and in the fourth year of the new reign (xxviii. 1) envoys from the neighbour-states arrived at the Jewish court, with the object of drawing Judah into a coalition against the common suzerain, the king of Babylon. This suicidal policy of combination with heathenish and treacherous allies, most of whom were the heirs of immemorial feuds with Judah, against a sovereign who was at once the most powerful and the most enlightened of his time, called forth the prophet's immediate and strenuous opposition. Boldly affirming that Iahvah had conferred universal dominion upon Nebuchadrezzar, and that consequently all resistance was futile, he warned Zedekiah himself to bow his neck to the yoke, and dismiss all thought of rebellion. It would seem that about this time (circ. 596 b.c.) the empire of Babylon was passing through a serious crisis, which the subject peoples of the West hoped and expected would result in its speedy dissolution. Nebuchadrezzar was, in fact, engaged in a life-and-death struggle with the Medes; and the knowledge that the Great King was thus fully occupied elsewhere, encouraged the petty princes of Phenicia-Palestine in their projects of revolt. If chaps. l., li., are genuine, it was at this juncture that Jeremiah foretold the fall of Babylon; for, at the close of the prophecy in question (li. 59), it is said that he gave a copy of it to one of the princes who accompanied Zedekiah to Babylon in the fourth year of his reign, i.e. in 596 b.c. But the style and thought of these two chapters, and the general posture of things which they presuppose, are decisive against the view that they belong to Jeremiah. At all events the prophet gave the clearest evidence that he did not himself share in the general delusion that the fall of Babylon was near at hand. He declared that all the nations must be content to serve Nebuchadrezzar, and his son, and his son's son (xxvii. 7); and as chap. xxix. shows, he did his best to counteract the evil influence of those fanatical visionaries, who were ever promising a speedy restoration to the exiles who had been deported to Babylon with Jeconiah. At last, however, in spite of all Jeremiah's warnings and entreaties, the vacillating king Zedekiah, was persuaded to rebel; and the natural consequence followed--the Chaldeans appeared before Jerusalem. King and people had refused salvation, and were now no more to be saved.

During the siege, the prophet was more than once anxiously consulted by the king as to the issue of the crisis. Although kept in ward by Zedekiah's orders, lest he should weaken the defence by his discouraging addresses, Jeremiah showed that he was far above the feeling of private ill-will, by the answers he returned to his sovereign's inquiries. It is true that he did not at all modify the burden of his message; to the king as to the people he steadily counselled surrender. But strongly as he denounced further resistance, he did not predict the king's death; and the tone of his prophecy concerning Zedekiah is in striking contrast with that concerning his predecessor Jehoiakim. It was in the tenth year of Zedekiah and the eighteenth of Nebuchadrezzar, that is to say, circ. 589 b.c., when Jeremiah was imprisoned in the court of the royal guard, within the precincts of the palace (xxxii. 1 sqq.); when the siege of Jerusalem was being pressed on with vigour, and when of all the strong cities of Judah, only two, Lachish and Azekah, were still holding out against the Chaldean blockade; that the prophet thus addressed the king (xxxiv. 2 sqq.): "Thus hath Iahvah said, Behold, I am about to give this city into the hand of the king of Babel, and he shall burn it with fire. And thou wilt not escape out of his hand; for thou wilt certainly be taken, and into his hand thou wilt be given. And thine eyes shall see the king of Babel's eyes, and his mouth shall speak with thy mouth, and to Babel wilt thou come. But hear thou Iahvah's word, O Zedekiah king of Judah! Thus hath Iahvah said upon thee, Thou wilt not die by the sword. In peace wilt thou die; and with the burnings of thy fathers, the former kings that were before thee, so will men burn (spicery) for thee, and with Ah, Lord! will they wail for thee; for a promise have I given, saith Iahvah." Zedekiah was to be exempted from the violent death, which then seemed so probable; and was to enjoy the funeral honours of a king, unlike his less worthy brother Jehoiakim, whose body was cast out to decay unburied like that of a beast. The failure of Jeremiah's earnest and consistent endeavours to bring about the submission of his people to what he foresaw to be their inevitable destiny, is explained by the popular confidence in the defences of Jerusalem, which were enormously strong for the time, and were considered impregnable (xxi. 13); and by the hopes entertained that Egypt, with whom negotiations had long been in progress, would raise the siege ere it was too late. The low state of public morals is vividly illustrated by an incident which the prophet has recorded (chap. xxxiv. 7 sqq.). In the terror inspired by the approach of the Chaldeans, the panic-stricken populace of the capital bethought them of that law of their God, which they had so long set at nought; and the king and his princes and the entire people bound themselves by a solemn covenant in the temple, to release all slaves of Israelitish birth, who had served six years and upwards, according to the law. The enfranchisement was accomplished with all the sanctions of law and of religion; but no sooner had the Chaldeans retired from before Jerusalem in order to meet the advancing army of Egypt, than the solemn covenant was cynically and shamelessly violated, and the unhappy freedmen were recalled to their bondage. After this, further warning was evidently out of place; and nothing was left for Jeremiah but to denounce the outrage upon the majesty of heaven, and to declare the speedy return of the besiegers, and the desolation of Jerusalem. His own liberty had not yet been restricted (xxxvii. 4) when these events happened; but a pretext was soon found for venting upon him the malice of his enemies. After assuring the king that the respite was not to be permanent, but that Pharaoh's army would return to Egypt without accomplishing any deliverance, and that the Chaldeans would "come again, and fight against the city, and take it, and burn it with fire" (xxxvii. 8), Jeremiah availed himself of the temporary absence of the besieging forces, to attempt to leave his City of Destruction; but he was arrested in the gate by which he was going out, and brought before the princes on a charge of attempted desertion to the enemy. Ridiculous as was this accusation, when thus levelled against one whose whole life was conspicuous for sufferings entailed by a lofty and unflinching patriotism and a devotion, at the time almost unique, to the sacred cause of religion and morality; it was at once received and acted upon. Jeremiah was beaten and thrown into a dungeon, where he languished for a long time in subterranean darkness and misery, until the king desired to consult him again. This was the saving of the prophet's life; for after once more declaring his unalterable message, byr mlr bvl tntn, "Into the king of Babel's hand thou wilt be given!" he made indignant protest against his cruel wrongs, and obtained from Zedekiah some mitigation of his sentence. He was not sent back to the loathsome den under the house of Jonathan the scribe, in whose dark recesses he had well nigh perished (xxxvii. 20), but was detained in the court of the guard, receiving a daily dole of bread for his maintenance. Here he appears to have still used such opportunity as he had, in dissuading the people from continuing the defence. At all events, four of the princes induced the king to deliver him into their power, on the ground that he "weakened the hands of the men of war," and sought not the welfare but the hurt of the nation (xxxviii. 4). Unwilling for some reason or other, probably a superstitious one, to imbrue their hands in the prophet's blood, they let him down with cords into a miry cistern (bvr) in the court of the guard, and left him there to die of cold and hunger. Timely help sanctioned by the king rescued Jeremiah from this horrible fate; but not before he had undergone sufferings of the severest character, as may easily be understood from his own simple narrative, and from the indelible impression wrought upon others by the record of his sufferings, which led the poet of the Lamentations to refer to this time of deadly peril, and torture both mental and physical, in the following terms:

"They chased me sore like a bird,
They that were my foes without a cause.
They silenced my life in the pit,
And they cast a stone upon me.
Waters overflowed mine head;
Methought, I am cut off.
I called Thy name, Iahvah,
Out of the deepest pit.
My voice Thou heardest (saying),
'Hide not Thine ear at my breathing, at my cry.'
Thou drewest near when I called Thee;
Thou saidst, 'Fear not'!
Thou pleadedst, O Lord, my souls pleadings;
Thou ransomedst my life."

After this signal escape, Jeremiah's counsel was once more sought by the king, in a secret interview, which was jealously concealed from the princes. But neither entreaties, nor assurances of safety, could persuade Zedekiah to surrender the city. Nothing was now left for the prophet, but to await, in his milder captivity, the long foreseen catastrophe. The form now taken by his solitary musings was not anxious speculation upon the question whether any possible resources were as yet unexhausted, whether by any yet untried means king and people might be convinced, and the end averted. Taking that end for granted, he looks forth beyond his own captivity, beyond the scenes of famine and pestilence and bloodshed that surround him, beyond the strife of factions within the city, and the lines of the besiegers without it, to a fair prospect of happy restoration and smiling peace, reserved for his ruined country in the far-off yet ever-approaching future (xxxii., xxxiii.).

Strong in this inspired confidence, like the Roman who purchased at its full market value the ground on which the army of Hannibal lay encamped, he did not hesitate to buy, with all due formalities of transfer, a field in his native place, at this supreme moment, when the whole country was wasted with fire and sword, and the artillery of the foe was thundering at the walls of Jerusalem. And the event proved that he was right. He believed in the depth of his heart that God had not finally cast off His people. He believed that nothing, not even human error and revolt, could thwart and turn aside the Eternal purposes. He was sure--it was demonstrated to him by the experience of an eventful life--that, amid all the vicissitudes of men and things, one thing stands immutable, and that is the will of God. He was sure that Abraham's family had not become a nation, merely in order to be blotted out of existence by a conqueror who knew not Iahvah; that the torch of a true religion, a spiritual faith, had not been handed on from prophet to prophet, burning in its onward course with an ever clearer and intenser flame, merely to be swallowed up before its final glory was attained, in utter and eternal darkness. The covenant with Israel would no more be broken than the covenant of day and night (xxxiii. 20). The laws of the natural world are not more stable and secure than those of the spiritual realm; for both have their reason and their ground of prevalence in the Will of the One Unchangeable Lord of all. And as the prophet had been right in his forecast of the destruction of his country, so did he prove to have been right in his joyful anticipation of the future renascence of all the best elements in Israel's life. The coming time fulfilled his word; a fact which must always remain unaccountable to all but those who believe as Jeremiah believed.

After the fall of the city, special care was taken to ensure the safety of Jeremiah, in accordance with the express orders of Nebuchadrezzar, who had become cognisant of the prophet's consistent advocacy of surrender, probably from the exiles previously deported to Babylonia, with whom Jeremiah had maintained communications, advising them to settle down peaceably, accepting Babylon as their country for the time being, and praying for its welfare and that of its rulers. Nebuzaradan, the commander-in-chief, further allowed the prophet his choice between following him to Babylon, or remaining with the wreck of the population in the ruined country. Patriotism, which in his case was identified with a burning zeal for the moral and spiritual welfare of his fellow-countrymen, prevailed over regard for his own worldly interests; and Jeremiah chose to remain with the survivors--disastrously for himself, as the event proved (xxxix. 2, xl. 1).

An old man, worn out with strife and struggle, and weighed down by disappointment and the sense of failure, he might well have decided to avail himself of the favour extended to him by the conqueror, and to secure a peaceful end for a life of storm and conflict. But the calamities of his country had not quenched his prophetic ardour; the sacred fire still burnt within his aged spirit; and once more he sacrificed himself to the work he felt called upon to do, only to experience again the futility of offering wise counsel to headstrong, proud, and fanatical natures. Against his earnest protestations, he was forced to accompany the remnant of his people in their hasty flight into Egypt (xlii.); and, in the last glimpse afforded us, we see him there among his fellow-exiles making a final, and alas! ineffectual protest against their stubborn idolatry (xliv.). A tradition mentioned by Tertullian and St. Jerome which may be of earlier and Jewish origin, states that these apostates in their wicked rage against the prophet stoned him to death (cf. Heb. xi. 37).

The last chapter of his book brings the course of events down to about 561 b.c. The fact has naturally suggested a conjecture that the same year witnessed the close of the prophet's life. In that case, Jeremiah must have attained to an age of somewhere about ninety years; which, taking all the circumstances into consideration, is hardly credible. A celibate life is said to be unfavourable to longevity; but however that may be, the other conditions in this instance make it extremely unlikely. Jeremiah's career was a vexed and stormy one; it was his fate to be divided from his kindred and his fellow-countrymen by the widest and deepest differences of belief; like St. Athanasius, he was called upon to maintain the cause of truth against an opposing world. "Woe's me, my mother!" he cries, in one of his characteristic fits of despondency, which were the natural fruit of a passionate and almost feminine nature, after a period of noble effort ending in the shame of utter defeat; "Woe's me, that thou gavest me birth, a man of strife, and a man of contention to all the land! Neither lender nor borrower have I been; yet all are cursing me" (xv. 10). The persecutions he endured, the cruelties of his long imprisonment, the horrors of the protracted siege, upon which he has not dwelt at length, but which have stamped themselves indelibly upon his language (xviii. 21, 22, xx. 16), would certainly not tend to prolong his life. In the 71st Psalm, which seems to be from his pen, and which wants the usual heading "A Psalm of David," he speaks of himself as conscious of failing powers, and as having already reached the extreme limit of age. Writing after his narrow escape from death in the miry cistern of his prison, he prays

> "Cast me not off in the time of old age;
> Forsake me not, when my strength faileth."
> And again,
> "Yea, even when I am old and grey-headed,
> O God forsake me not!"
> And, referring to his signal deliverance,
> "Thou that shewedst me many and sore troubles,
> Thou makest me live again;
> And out of the deeps of the earth again Thou bringest me up."

The allusion in the 90th Psalm, as well as the case of Barzillai, who is described as extremely old and decrepit at fourscore (2 Sam. xix. 33), proves that life in ancient Palestine did not ordinarily transcend the limits of seventy to eighty years. Still, after all that may be urged to the contrary, Jeremiah may have been an exception to his contemporaries in this, as in most other respects. Indeed, his protracted labours and sufferings seem almost to imply that he was endowed with constitutional vigour and powers of endurance above the average of men; and if, as some suppose, he wrote the book of Job in Egypt, to embody the fruits of his life's experience and reflexion, as well as arranged and edited his other writings, it is evident that he must have sojourned among the exiles in that country for a considerable time.

The tale is told. In meagre and broken outline I have laid before you the known facts of a life which must always possess permanent interest, not only for the student of religious development, but for all men who are stirred by human passion, and stimulated by human thought. And fully conscious as I am of failure in the attempt to reanimate the dry bones of history, to give form and colour and movement to the shadows of the past; I shall not have spent my pains for nought, if I have awakened in a single heart some spark of living interest in the heroes of old; some enthusiasm for the martyrs of faith; some secret yearning to cast in their own lot with those who have fought the battle of truth and righteousness and to share with the saints departed in the victory that overcometh the world. And even if in this also I have fallen short of the mark, these desultory and imperfect sketches of a good man's life and work will not have been wholly barren of result, if they lead any one of my readers to renewed study of that truly sacred text which preserves to all time the living utterances of this last of the greater prophets.

Footnotes:

1. The same root is used in the Targ. on i. 15 for setting or fixing thrones, cf. Dan. vii. 9: (rmyv)

2. Clem. Alex., Strom., I., § 120.
3. At least seven times.
4. Hitzig.
5. i. 6.
6. i. 2, xxv. 3.
7. nr puer; (1) Ex. ii. 6, of a three months' babe; (2) of a young man up to about the twentieth year, Gen. xxxiv. 19, of Shechem ben Hamor; 1 Kings iii. 7, of Solomon, as here.
8. Hitzig, Vorbemerkungen.
9. The Cimmerians are the Gomer of Scripture, the Gimirrâ'a of the cuneiform inscriptions.
10. Ewald, Die Psalmen, 165.
11. Zeph. ii. 4 sqq., qrvn tqr ... zh zvvh thyh
12. sphr htvrh, 2 Kings xxii. 8; sphr hvryt, 2 Kings xxiii. 2.
13. Comparing the Hebrew verb with the Arabic Arabic script timuit, fastidivit. LXX., kago emelesa auton, Cf. Jer. iii. 14. Gesenius rendered fastidivit, rejecit.
14. So rightly the Syriac, for Jehoiakim.
15. i.e. To scent food afar off, like beasts of prey. There was no occasion to alter A.V.

I. THE CALL AND CONSECRATION

In the foregoing pages we have considered the principal events in the life of the prophet Jeremiah, by way of introduction to the more detailed study of his writings. Preparation of this kind seemed to be necessary, if we were to enter upon that study with something more than the vaguest perception of the real personality of the prophet. On the other hand, I hope we shall not fail to find our mental image of the man, and our conception of the times in which he lived, and of the conditions under which he laboured as a servant of God, corrected and perfected by that closer examination of his works to which I now invite you. And so we shall be better equipped for the attainment of that which must be the ultimate object of all such studies; the deepening and strengthening of the life of faith in ourselves, by which alone we can hope to follow in the steps of the saints of old, and like them to realise the great end of our being, the service of the All-Perfect.

I shall consider the various discourses in what appears to be their natural order, so far as possible, taking those chapters together which appear to be connected in occasion and subject. Chap. i. evidently stands apart, as a self-complete and independent whole. It consists of a chronological superscription (vv. 1-3), assigning the temporal limits of the prophet's activity; and secondly, of an inaugural discourse, which sets before us his first call, and the general scope of the mission which he was chosen to fulfil. This discourse, again, in like manner falls into two sections, of which the former (vv. 4-10) relates how the prophet was appointed and qualified by Iahvah to be a spokesman for Him; while the latter (vv. 11-19), under the form of two visions, expresses the assurance that Iahvah will accomplish His word, and pictures the mode of fulfilment, closing with a renewed summons to enter upon the work, and with a promise of effectual support against all opposition.

It is plain that we have before us the author's introduction to the whole book; and if we would gain an adequate conception of the meaning of the prophet's activity both for his own time and for ours, we must weigh well the force of these prefatory words. The career of a true prophet, or spokesman for God, undoubtedly implies a special call or vocation to the office. In this preface to the summarized account of his life's work, Jeremiah represents that call as a single and definite event in his life's history. Must we take this in its literal sense? We are not astonished by such a statement as "the word of the Lord came unto me;" it may be understood in more senses than one, and perhaps we are unconsciously prone to understand it in what is called a natural sense. Perhaps we think of a result of pious reflexion pondering the moral state of the nation and the needs of the time: perhaps of that inward voice which is nothing strange to any soul that has attained to the rudiments of spiritual development. But when we read such an assertion as that of ver. 9, "Then the Lord put forth His hand, and touched my mouth," we cannot but pause and ask what it was that the writer meant to convey by words so strange and startling. Thoughtful readers cannot avoid the question whether such statements are consonant with what we otherwise know of the dealings of God with man; whether an outward and visible act of the kind spoken of conforms with that whole conception of the Divine Being, which is, so far as it reflects reality, the outcome of His own contact with our human spirits. The obvious answer is that such corporeal actions are incompatible with all our experience and all our reasoned conceptions of the Divine Essence, which fills all things and controls all things, precisely because it is not limited by a bodily organism, because its actions are not dependent upon such imperfect and restricted media as hands and feet. If, then, we are bound to a literal sense, we can only understand that the prophet saw a vision, in which a Divine hand seemed to touch his lips, and a Divine voice to sound in his ears. But are we bound to a literal sense? It is noteworthy that Jeremiah does not say that Iahvah Himself appeared to him. In this respect, he stands in conspicuous contrast with his predecessor Isaiah, who writes (vi. 1), "In the year that king Uzziah died, I saw the Lord sitting upon a throne, high and lifted up;" and with his successor Ezekiel, who affirms in his opening verse (i. 1) that on a certain definite occasion "the heavens opened," and he saw "visions of God." Nor does Jeremiah use that striking phrase of the younger prophet's, "The hand of Iahvah was upon me," or "was strong upon me." But when he says, "Iahvah put forth His hand and touched my mouth," he is evidently thinking of the seraph that touched Isaiah's mouth with the live coal from the heavenly altar (vi. 7). The words are identical (I phy vyg), and might be regarded as a quotation. It is true that, supposing Jeremiah to be relating the experience of a trance-like condition or ecstasy, we need not assume any conscious imitation of his predecessor. The sights and sounds which affect a man in such a condition may be partly repetitions of former experience, whether one's own or that of others;

Rev. C. J. Ball, M.A., & W. H. Bennett, M.A.

and in part wholly new and strange. In a dream one might imagine things happening to oneself, which one had heard or read of in connexion with others. And Jeremiah's writings generally prove his intimate acquaintance with those of Isaiah and the older prophets. But as a trance or ecstasy is itself an involuntary state, so the thoughts and feelings of the subject of it must be independent of the individual will, and as it were imposed from without. Is then the prophet describing the experience of such an abnormal state--a state like that of St. Peter in his momentous vision on the housetop at Joppa, or like that of St. Paul when he was "caught up to the third heaven," and saw many wonderful things which he durst not reveal? The question has been answered in the negative on two principal grounds. It is said that the vision of vv. 11, 12, derives its significance not from the visible thing itself, but from the name of it, which is, of course, not an object of sight at all; and consequently, the so-called vision is really "a well-devised and ingenious product of cool reflexion." But is this so? We may translate the original passage thus: And there fell a word of Iahvah unto me, saying, What seest thou, Jeremiah? And I said, A rod of a wake-tree (i.e. an almond) is what I see. And Iahvah said unto me, Thou hast well seen; for wakeful am I over My word, to do it. Doubtless there is here one of those plays on words which are so well known a feature of the prophetic style; but to admit this is by no means tantamount to an admission that the vision derives its force and meaning from the "invisible name" rather than from the visible thing. Surely it is plain that the significance of the vision depends on the fact which the name implies; a fact which would be at once suggested by the sight of the tree. It is the well known characteristic of the almond tree that it wakes, as it were, from the long sleep of winter before all other trees, and displays its beautiful garland of blossom, while its companions remain leafless and apparently lifeless. This quality of early wakefulness is expressed by the Hebrew name of the almond tree; for shaq?d means waking or wakeful. If this tree, in virtue of its remarkable peculiarity, was a proverb of watching and waking, the sight of it, or of a branch of it, in a prophetic vision would be sufficient to suggest that idea, independently of the name. The allusion to the name, therefore, is only a literary device for expressing with inimitable force and neatness the significance of the visible symbol of the "rod of the almond tree," as it was intuitively apprehended by the prophet in his vision.

Another and more radical ground is discovered in the substance of the Divine communication. It is said that the anticipatory statement of the contents and purpose of the subsequent prophesyings of the seer (ver. 10), the announcement beforehand of his fortunes (vv. 8, 18, 19), and the warning addressed to the prophet personally (ver. 17), are only conceivable as results of a process of abstraction from real experience, as prophecies conformed to the event (ex eventu). "The call of the prophet," says the writer whose arguments we are examining, "was the moment when, battling down the doubts and scruples of the natural man (vv. 7, 8), and full of holy courage, he took the resolution (ver. 17) to proclaim God's word. Certainly he was animated by the hope of Divine assistance (ver. 18), the promise of which he heard inwardly in the heart. More than this cannot be affirmed. But in this chapter (vv. 17, 18), the measure and direction of the Divine help are already clear to the writer; he is aware that opposition awaits him (ver. 19); he knows the content of his prophecies (ver. 10). Such knowledge was only possible for him in the middle or at the end of his career; and therefore the composition of this opening chapter must be referred to such a later period. As, however, the final catastrophe, after which his language would have taken a wholly different complexion, is still hidden from him here; and as the only edition of his prophecies prepared by himself, that we know of, belongs to the fourth year of Jehoiakim (xxxvi. 45); the section is best referred to that very time, when the posture of affairs promised well for the fulfilment of the threatenings of many years (cf. xxv. 9 with vv. 15, 10; xxv. 13 with vv. 12-17; xxv. 6 with ver. 16. And ver. 18 is virtually repeated, chap. xv. 20, which belongs to the same period)."

The first part of this is an obvious inference from the narrative itself. The prophet's own statement makes it abundantly clear that his conviction of a call was accompanied by doubts and fears, which were only silenced by that faith which moves mountains. That lofty confidence in the purpose and strength of the Unseen, which has enabled weak and trembling humanity to endure martyrdom, might well be sufficient to nerve a young man to undertake the task of preaching unpopular truths, even at the risk of frequent persecution and occasional peril. But surely we need not suppose that, when Jeremiah started on his prophetic career, he was as one who takes a leap in the dark. Surely it is not necessary to suppose him profoundly ignorant of the subject-matter of prophecy in general, of the kind of success he might look for, of his own shrinking timidity and desponding temperament, of "the measure and direction of the Divine help." Had the son of Hilkiah been the first of the prophets of Israel instead of one of the latest; had there been no prophets before him; we might recognise some force in this criticism. As the facts lie, however, we can hardly avoid an obvious answer. With the experience of many notable predecessors before his eyes; with the message of a Hosea, an Amos, a Micah, an Isaiah, graven upon his heart; with his minute knowledge of their history, their struggles and successes, the fierce antagonisms they roused, the cruel persecutions they were called upon to face in the discharge of their Divine commission; with his profound sense that nothing but the good help of their God had enabled them to endure the strain of a lifelong battle; it is not in the least wonderful that Jeremiah should have foreseen the like experience for himself. The wonder would have been, if, with such speaking examples before him, he had not anticipated "the measure and direction of the Divine help"; if he had been ignorant "that opposition awaited him"; if he had not already possessed a general knowledge of the "contents" of his own as of all prophecies. For there is a substantial unity underlying all the manifold outpourings of the prophetic spirit. Indeed, it would seem that it is to the diversity of personal gifts, to differences of training and temperament, to the rich variety of character and circumstance, rather than to any essential contrasts in the substance and purport of prophecy itself, that the absence of monotony, the impress of individuality and originality is due, which characterises the utterances of the principal prophets.

Apart from the unsatisfactory nature of the reasons alleged, it is very probable that this opening chapter was penned by Jeremiah as an introduction to the first collection of his prophecies, which dates from the fourth year of Jehoiakim, that is, circ. b.c. 606. In that case, it must not be forgotten that the prophet is relating events which, as he tells us himself (chap. xxv. 3), had taken place three and twenty years ago; and as his description is probably drawn from memory, something may be allowed for unconscious transformation of facts in the light of after experience. Still, the peculiar events that attended so marked a crisis in his life as his first consciousness of a Divine call must, in any case, have constituted, cannot but have left a deep and abiding impress upon the prophet's memory; and there really seems to be no good reason for refusing to believe that that initial experience took the form of a twofold vision seen under conditions of trance or ecstasy. At the same time, bearing in mind the Oriental passion for metaphor and imagery, we are not perhaps debarred from seeing in the whole chapter a figurative description, or rather an attempt to describe through the medium of figurative language, that which must always ultimately transcend description--the communion of the Divine with the human spirit. Real, most real of real facts, as that communion was and is, it can never be directly communicated in words; it can only be hinted and suggested through the medium of symbolic and metaphorical phraseology. Language itself, being more than half material, breaks down in the attempt to express things wholly spiritual.

I shall not stop to discuss the importance of the general superscription or heading of the book, which is given in the first three verses. But before passing on, I will ask you to notice that, whereas the Hebrew text opens with the phrase Dibrê Yirmeyáhu (dvry yrmyhv), "The words of Jeremiah," the oldest translation we have, viz. the Septuagint, reads: "The word of God which came to Jeremiah" (to rema tou Theou ho egeneto epi Hieremian). It is possible, therefore, that the old Greek translator had a Hebrew text different from that which has come down to us, and opening with the same formula which we find at the beginning of the older prophets Hosea, Joel, and Micah. In fact, Amos is the only prophet, besides Jeremiah, whose book begins with the phrase in question (dvry mvs--Logoi Amos); and although it is more appropriate there than here, owing to the continuation "And he said," it looks suspicious even there, when we compare Isaiah i. 1, and observe how much more suitable the term "vision" (chzvn) would be. It is likely that the LXX. has preserved the original reading of Jeremiah, and that some editor of the Hebrew text altered it because of the apparent tautology with the opening of ver. 2: "To whom the word of the Lord (LXX. tou Theou) came in the days of Josiah."

Such changes were freely made by the scribes in the days before the settlement of the O. T. canon; changes which may occasion much perplexity to those, if any there be, who hold by the unintelligent and obsolete theory of verbal and even literal inspiration, but none at all to such as recognise a Divine hand in the facts of history, [16] and are content to believe that in holy books, as in holy men, there is a Divine treasure in earthen vessels. The textual difference in question may serve to call our attention to the peculiar way in which the prophets identified their work with the Divine will, and their words with the Divine thoughts; so that the words of an Amos or a Jeremiah were in all good faith held and believed to be self-attesting utterances of the Unseen God. The conviction which wrought in them was, in fact, identical with that which in after times moved St. Paul to affirm the high calling and inalienable dignity of the Christian ministry in those impressive words, "Let a man so account of us as of the ministers of Christ, and stewards of the mysteries of God."

Vv. 5-10, which relate how the prophet became aware that he was in future to receive revelations from above, constitute in themselves an important revelation. Under Divine influence he becomes aware of a special mission. Ere I began to form (mould, fashion, ytsr, as the potter moulds the clay) thee in the belly, I knew thee; and ere thou begannest to come forth from the womb, [17] I had dedicated thee, not "regarded thee as holy," Isa. viii. 13; nor perhaps "declared thee holy," as Ges.; but "hallowed thee," i.e. dedicated thee to God, Judg. xvii. 3; 1 Kings ix. 3; especially Lev. xxvii. 14; of money and houses. The pi. of consecrating priests, Ex. xxviii. 41; altar, Ex. xxix. 36, temple, mountain, etc.; perhaps also, "consecrated thee" for the discharge of a sacred office. Even soldiers are called consecrated (mqdsym Isa. xiii. 3), as ministers of the Lord of Hosts, and probably as having been formally devoted to His service at the outset of a campaign by special solemnities of lustration and sacrifice; while guests bidden to a sacrificial feast had to undergo a preliminary form of consecration (1 Sam. xvi. 5; Zeph. i. 7), to fit them for communion with Deity.

With the certainty of his own Divine calling, it became clear to the prophet that the choice was not an arbitrary caprice; it was the execution of a Divine purpose, conceived long, long before its realisation in time and space. The God whose foreknowledge and will directs the whole course of human history--whose control of events and direction of human energies is most signally evident in precisely those instances where men and nations are most regardless of Him, and imagine the vain thought that they are independent of Him (Isa. xxii. 11, xxxvii. 26)--this sovereign Being, in the development of whose eternal purposes he himself, and every son of man was necessarily a factor, had from the first "known him,"--known the individual character and capacities which would constitute his fitness for the special work of his life;--and "sanctified" him; devoted and consecrated him to the doing of it when the time of his earthly manifestation should arrive. Like others who have played a notable part in the affairs of men, Jeremiah saw with clearest vision that he was himself the embodiment in flesh and blood of a Divine idea; he knew himself to be a deliberately planned and chosen instrument of the Divine activity. It was this seeing himself as God saw him, which constituted his difference from his fellows, who only knew their individual appetites, pleasures and interests, and were blinded, by their absorption in these, to the perception of any higher reality. It was the coming to this knowledge of himself, of the meaning and purpose of HIS individual unity of powers and aspirations in the great universe of being, of his true relation to God and to man, which constituted the first revelation to Jeremiah, and which was the secret of his personal greatness.

This knowledge, however, might have come to him in vain. Moments of illumination are not always accompanied by noble resolves and corresponding actions. It does not follow that, because a man sees his calling, he will at once renounce all, and pursue it. Jeremiah would not have been human, had he not hesitated a while, when, after the inward light, came the voice, A spokesman, or Divine interpreter (nvy'), to the nations appoint I thee. To have passing flashes of spiritual insight and heavenly inspiration is one thing; to undertake now, in the actual present, the course of conduct which they unquestionably indicate and involve, is quite another. And so, when the hour of spiritual illumination has passed, the darkness may and often does become deeper than before.

And I said, Alas! O Lord Iahvah, behold I know not how to speak; for I am but a youth. The words express that reluctance to begin which a sense of unpreparedness, and misgivings about the unknown future, naturally inspire. To take the first step demands decision and confidence; but confidence and decision do not come of contemplating oneself and one's own unfitness or unpreparedness, but of steadfastly fixing our regards upon God, who will qualify us for all that He requires us to do. Jeremiah does not refuse to obey His call; the very words "My Lord Iahvah"--'Adonai, Master, or my Master--imply a recognition of the Divine right to his service; he merely alleges a natural objection. The cry, "Who is sufficient for these things?" rises to his lips, when the light and the glory are obscured for a moment, and the reaction and despondency natural to human weakness ensue. And Iahvah said unto me, Say not, I am but a youth; for unto all that I send thee unto, thou shalt go, and all that I command thee thou shalt speak. Be not afraid of them; for with thee am I to rescue thee, is the utterance of Iahvah. "Unto all that I send thee unto"; for he was to be no local prophet; his messages were to be addressed to the surrounding peoples as well as to Judah; his outlook as a seer was to comprise the entire political horizon (ver. 10, xxv. 9, 15, xlvi. sqq.). Like Moses (Ex. iv. 10), Jeremiah objects that he is no practised speaker; and this on account of youthful inexperience. The answer is that his speaking will depend not so much upon himself as upon God: "All that I command thee, thou shalt speak." The allegation of his youth also covers a feeling of timidity, which would naturally be excited at the thought of encountering kings and princes and priests, as well as the common people, in the discharge of such a commission. This implication is met by the Divine assurance: "Unto all"--of whatever rank--"that I send thee unto, thou shalt go"; and by the encouraging promise of Divine protection against all opposing powers: "Be not afraid of them; for with thee am I to rescue thee." [18]

And Iahvah put forth His hand and touched my mouth: and Iahvah said unto me, Behold I have put My words in thy mouth! This word of the Lord, says Hitzig, is represented as a corporeal substance; in accordance with the Oriental mode of thought and speech, which invests everything with bodily form. He refers to a passage in Samuel (2 Sam. xvii. 5) where Absalom says, "Call now Hushai the Archite, and let us hear that which is in his mouth also;" as if what the old counsellor had to say were something solid in more senses than one. But we need not press the literal force of the language. A prophet who could write (v. 14): "Behold I am about to make my words in thy mouth fire and this people logs of wood; and it shall devour them;" or again (xv. 16), "Thy words were found, and I did eat them; and Thy word became unto me a joy and my heart's delight," may also have written, "Behold I have put My words in thy mouth!" without thereby becoming amenable to a charge of confusing fact with figure, metaphor with reality. Nor can I think the prophet means to say that, although, as a matter of fact, the Divine word already dwelt in him, it was now "put in his mouth," in the sense that he was henceforth to utter it. Stripped of the symbolism of vision, the verse simply asserts that the spiritual change which came over Jeremiah at the turning point in his career was due to the immediate operation of God; and that the chief external consequence of this inward change was that powerful preaching of Divine truth, by which he was henceforth known. The great Prophet of the Exile twice uses the phrase,

"I have set My words in thy mouth" (Isa. li. 16, lix. 21) with much the same meaning as that intended by Jeremiah, but without the preceding metaphor about the Divine hand.

See I have this day set thee over the nations and over the kingdoms, to root out and to pull down, and to destroy and to overturn; to rebuild and to replant. Such, following the Hebrew punctuation, are the terms of the prophet's commission; and they are well worth consideration, as they set forth with all the force of prophetic idiom his own conception of the nature of that commission. First, there is the implied assertion of his own official dignity: the prophet is made a paqîd (Gen. xli. 34, "officers" set by Pharaoh over Egypt; 2 Kings xxv. 19 a military prefect) a prefect or superintendent of the nations of the world. It is the Hebrew term corresponding to the episkopos of the New Testament and the Christian Church (Judg. ix. 28; Neh. xi. 9). And secondly, his powers are of the widest scope; he is invested with authority over the destinies of all peoples. If it be asked in what sense it could be truly said that the ruin and renascence of nations was subject to the supervision of the prophets, the answer is obvious. The word they were authorised to declare was the word of God. But God's word is not something whose efficacy is exhausted in the human utterance of it. God's word is an irreversible command, fulfilling itself with all the necessity of a law of nature. The thought is well expressed by a later prophet: "For as the rain cometh down, and the snow from heaven, and returneth not thither, but watereth the earth, and maketh it bring forth and spring; and yieldeth seed to the sower and bread to the eater: so shall My word become, that goeth forth out of My mouth; it shall not return to Me empty (ryqm), but shall surely do that which I have willed, and shall carry through that for which I sent it" (or "shall prosper him whom I have sent," Isa. lv. 10, 11). All that happens is merely the selfaccomplishment of this Divine word, which is only the human aspect of the Divine will. If, therefore, the absolute dependence of the prophets upon God for their knowledge of this word be left out of account, they appear as causes, when they are in truth but instruments, as agents when they are only mouthpieces. And so Ezekiel writes, "when I came to destroy the city" (Ezek. xliii. 3), meaning when I announced the Divine decree of its destruction. The truth upon which this peculiar mode of statement rests--the truth that the will of God must be and always is done in the world that God has made and is making--is a rock upon which the faith of His messengers may always repose. What strength, what staying power may the Christian preacher find in dwelling upon this almost visible fact of the self-fulfilling will and word of God, though all around him he hear that will questioned, and that word disowned and denied! He knows--it is his supreme comfort to know--that, while his own efforts may be thwarted, that will is invincible; that though he may fail in the conflict, that word will go on conquering and to conquer, until it shall have subdued all things unto itself.

Footnotes:

16. Even in the history of the transmission of ancient writings.
17. Isa. xliv. 24, yvtsrk mbtn, xlix. 5, ytsry mbtn lvd lv.
18. For the words of this promise, cf. ver. 19 infr., xv. 20, xlii. 11.

Rev. C. J. Ball, M.A., & W. H. Bennett, M.A.

II. THE TRUST IN THE SHADOW OF EGYPT

Jeremiah ii. 1-iii. 5.

The first of the prophet's public addresses is, in fact, a sermon which proceeds from an exposure of national sin to the menace of coming judgment. It falls naturally into three sections, of which the first (ii. 1-13) sets forth Iahvah's tender love to His young bride Israel in the old times of nomadic life, when faithfulness to Him was rewarded by protection from all external foes; and then passes on to denounce the unprecedented apostasy of a people from their God. The second (14-28) declares that if Israel has fallen a prey to her enemies, it is the result of her own infidelity to her Divine Spouse; of her early notorious and inveterate falling away to the false gods, who are now her only resource, and that a worthless one. The third section (ii. 29-iii. 5) points to the failure of Iahvah's chastisements to reclaim a people hardened in guilt, and in a self-righteousness which refused warning and despised reproof; affirms the futility of all human aid amid the national reverses; and cries woe on a too late repentance. It is not difficult to fix the time of this noble and pathetic address. That which follows it, and is intimately connected with it in substance, was composed "in the days of Josiah the king" (iii. 6), so that the present one must be placed a little earlier in the same reign; and, considering its position in the book, may very probably be assigned to the thirteenth year of Josiah, i.e. b.c. 629, in which the prophet received his Divine call. This is the ordinary opinion; but one critic (Knobel) refers the discourse to the beginning of the reign of Jehoiakim, on account of the connexion with Egypt which is mentioned in vv. 18, 36, and the humiliation suffered at the hands of the Egyptians which is mentioned in ver. 16; while another (Graf) maintains that chaps. ii.-vi. were composed in the fourth year of Jehoiakim, as if the prophet had committed nothing to writing before that date--an assumption which seems to run counter to the implication conveyed by his own statement, chap. xxxvi. 2. This latter critic has failed to notice the allusions in chaps. iv. 14, vi. 8, to an approaching calamity which may be averted by national reformation, to which the people are invited;--an invitation wholly incompatible with the prophet's attitude at that hopeless period. The series of prophecies beginning at chap. iv. 3 is certainly later in time than the discourse we are now considering; but as certainly belongs to the immediate subsequent years.

It does not appear that the first two of Jeremiah's addresses were called forth by any striking event of public importance, such as the Scythian invasion. His new-born consciousness of the Divine call would urge the young prophet to action; and in the present discourse we have the firstfruits of the heavenly impulse. It is a retrospect of Israel's entire past and an examination of the state of things growing out of it. The prophet's attention is not yet confined to Judah; he deplores the rupture of the ideal relations between Iahvah and His people as a whole (ii. 4; cf. iii. 6). As Hitzig has remarked, this opening address, in its finished elaboration, leaves the impression of a first outpouring of the heart, which sets forth at once without reserve the long score of the Divine grievances against Israel. At the same time, in its closing judgment (iii. 5), in its irony (ii. 28), in its appeals (ii. 21, 31), and its exclamations (ii. 12), it breathes an indignation stern and deep to a degree hardly characteristic of the prophet in his other discourses, but which was natural enough, as Hitzig observes, in a first essay at moral criticism, a first outburst of inspired zeal.

In the Hebrew text the chapter begins with the same formula as chap. i. (ver. 4): "And there fell a word of Iahvah unto me, saying." But the LXX. reads: "And he said, Thus saith the Lord," (kai eipe, tade legei kurios); a difference which is not immaterial, as it may be a trace of an older Hebrew recension of the prophet's work, in which this second chapter immediately followed the original superscription of the book, as given in chap. i. 1, 2, from which it was afterwards separated by the insertion of the narrative of Jeremiah's call and visions (vy'mr: cf. Amos i. 2). Perhaps we may see another trace of the same thing in the fact that whereas chap. i. sends the prophet to the rulers and people of Judah, this chapter is in part addressed to collective Israel (ver. 4); which constitutes a formal disagreement. If the reference to Israel is not merely retrospective and rhetorical,--if it implies, as seems to be assumed, that the prophet really meant his words to affect the remnant of the northern kingdom as well as Judah,--we have here a valuable contemporary corroboration of the much disputed assertion of the author of Chronicles, that king Josiah abolished idolatry "in the cities of Manasseh and Ephraim and Simeon even unto Naphtali, to wit, in their ruins round about" (2 Chron. xxxiv. 6), as well as in Judah and Jerusalem; and that Manasseh and Ephraim and "the remnant of Israel" (2 Chron. xxxiv. 9, cf. 21) contributed to his restoration of the temple. These statements of the Chronicler imply that Josiah exercised authority in the ruined northern kingdom, as well as in the more fortunate south; and so far as this first discourse of Jeremiah was actually addressed to Israel as well as to Judah, those disputed statements find in it an undesigned confirmation. However this may be, as a part of the first collection of the author's prophecies, there is little doubt that the chapter was read by Baruch to the people of Jerusalem in the fourth year of Jehoiakim (chap. xxxvi. 6).

Go thou and cry in the ears of Jerusalem: Thus hath Iahvah said (or thought: This is the Divine thought concerning thee!) I have remembered for thee the kindness of thy youth, the love of thine espousals; thy following Me (as a bride follows her husband to his tent) in the wilderness, in a land unsown. A dedicated thing (qrs: like the high priest, on whose mitre was graven qrs lyhvh) was Israel to Iahvah, His firstfruits of increase; all who did eat him were held guilty, ill would come to them, saith Iahvah (vers. 2, 3).--"I have remembered for thee," i.e. in thy favour, to thy benefit--as when Nehemiah prays, "Remember in my favour, O my God, for good, all that I have done upon this people," (Neh. v. 19)--"the kindness"--chsd--the warm affection of thy youth, "the love of thine espousals," or the charm of thy bridal state (Hos. ii. 15, xi. 1); the tender attachment of thine early days, of thy new born national consciousness, when Iahvah had chosen thee as His bride, and called thee to follow Him out of Egypt. It is the figure which we find so elaborately developed in the pages of Hosea. The "bridal state" is the time from the Exodus to the taking of the covenant at Sinai (Ezek. xvi. 8), which was, as it were, the formal instrument of the marriage; and Israel's young love is explained as consisting in turning her back upon "the flesh-pots of Egypt" (Ex. xvi. 3), at the call of Iahvah, and following her Divine Lord into the barren steppes. This forsaking of all worldly comfort for the hard life of the desert was proof of the sincerity of Israel's early love. [The evidently original words "in the wilderness, a land unsown," are omitted by the LXX., which renders: "I remembered the mercy of thy youth, and the love of thy nuptials (teleiosis, consummation), so that thou followedst the Holy One of Israel, saith Iahvah."] Iahvah's "remembrance" of this devotion, that is to say, the return He made for it, is described in the next verse. Israel became not "holiness" but a holy or hallowed thing; a dedicated object, belonging wholly and solely to Iahvah, a thing which it was sacrilege to touch; Iahvah's "firstfruits of increase" (Heb. r'syt tvv'th). This last phrase is to be explained by reference to the well-known law of the firstfruits (Ex. xxiii. 19; Deut. xviii. 4, xxvi. 10), according to which the first specimens of all agricultural produce were given to God. Israel, like the firstlings of cattle and the firstfruits of corn and wine and oil, was qds lyhvh consecrated to Iahweh; and therefore none might eat of him without offending. "To eat" or devour is a term naturally used of vexing and destroying a nation (x. 25, l. 7; Deut. vii. 16, "And thou shalt eat up all the peoples, which Jehovah thy God is about to give thee;" Isa. i. 7; Ps. xiv. 4, "Who eat up My people as they eat bread"). The literal translation is, "All his eaters become guilty (or are treated as guilty, punished); evil cometh to them;" and the verbs, being in the imperfect, denote what happened again and again in Israel's history; Iahvah suffered no man to do His people wrong with impunity. This, then, is the first count in the indictment against Israel, that Iahvah had not been unmindful of her early devotion, but had recognised it by throwing the shield of sanctity around her, and making her inviolable against all external enemies (vv. 1-3). The prophet's complaint, as developed in the following section (vv. 4-8), is that, in spite of the goodness of Iahvah, Israel has forsaken Him for idols. "Hear ye the word of Iahvah, O house of Jacob, and all the clans of the house of Israel!" All Israel is addressed, and not merely the surviving kingdom of Judah, because the apostasy had been universal. A special reference apparently made in ver. 8 to the prophets of Baal, who flourished only in the northern kingdom. We may compare the word of Amos "against the whole clan," which Iahvah "brought up from the land of Egypt" (Amos iii. 1), spoken at a time when Ephraim was yet in the heyday of his power.

Thus hath Iahvah said, What found your fathers in Me, that was unjust, (vl a single act of injustice, Ps. vii. 4; not to be found in Iahvah, Deut. xxxii. 4) that they went far from Me and followed the Folly and were befooled (or the Delusion and were deluded) (ver. 5). The phrase is used 2 Kings xvii. 15 in the same sense; hhvl "the (mere) breath," "the nothingness" or "vanity," being a designation of the idols which Israel went after (cf. also chap. xxiii. 16; Ps. lxii. 11; Job xxvii. 12); much as St. Paul has written that "an idol is nothing in the world" (1 Cor. viii. 4), and that, with all this boasted culture, the nations of classical antiquity "became vain," or were befooled "in their imaginations" (emataiothesan = vyhvlv), "and their foolish heart was darkened" (Rom. i. 21). Both the prophet and the apostle refer to that judicial blindness which is a consequence of persistently closing the eyes to truth, and deliberately putting darkness for light and light for darkness, bitter for sweet, and sweet for bitter, in compliance with the urgency of the flesh. For ancient Israel, the result of yielding to the seductions of foreign worship was, that "They were stultified in their best endeavours. They became false in thinking and believing, in doing and forbearing, because the fundamental error pervaded the whole life of the nation and of the individual. They supposed that they knew and honoured God, but they were entirely mistaken; they supposed they were doing His will, and securing their own welfare, while they were doing and securing the exact contrary" (Hitzig). And similar consequences will always flow from attempts to serve two masters; to gratify the lower nature, while not breaking wholly with the higher. Once the soul has accepted a lower standard than the perfect law of truth, it does not stop there. The subtle corruption goes on extending its ravages farther and farther; while the consciousness that anything is wrong becomes fainter and fainter as the deadly mischief increases, until at last the ruined spirit believes itself in perfect health, when it is, in truth, in the last stage of mortal disease. Perversion of the will and the affections leads to the perversion of the intellect. There is a profound meaning in the old saying that, Men make their gods in their own likeness. As a man is, so will God appear to him to be. "With the loving, Thou wilt shew Thyself loving; With the perfect, Thou wilt shew Thyself perfect; With the pure, Thou wilt shew Thyself pure; And with the perverse, Thou wilt shew Thyself froward" (Ps. xviii. 25 sq.). Only hearts pure of all worldly taint see God in His purity. The rest worship some more or less imperfect semblance of Him, according to the varying degrees of their selfishness and sin.

And they said not, Where is Iahvah, who brought us up out of the land of Egypt, that guided us in the wilderness, in a land of wastes and hollows (or desert and defile), in a land of drought and darkness (dreariness tslmvt), in a land that no man passed through, and where no mortal dwelt (ver. 6). "They said not, Where is Iahvah, who brought us up out of the land of Egypt." It is the old complaint of the prophets against Israel's black ingratitude. So, for instance, Amos (ii. 10) had written: "Whereas I--I brought you up from the land of Egypt, and guided you in the wilderness forty years;" and Micah (vi. 3 sq.): "My people, what have I done unto thee, and how have I wearied thee? Answer against Me. For I brought thee up from the land of Egypt, and from a house of bondmen redeemed I thee." In common gratitude, they were bound to be true to this mighty Saviour; to enquire after Iahvah, to call upon Him only, to do His will, and to seek His grace (cf. xxix. 12 sq.). Yet, with characteristic fickleness, they soon forgot the fatherly guidance, which had never deserted them in the period of their nomadic wanderings in the wilds of Arabia Petræa; a land which the prophet poetically describes as "a land of wastes and hollows"--alluding probably to the rocky defiles through which they had to pass--and "a land of drought and darkness;" [19] the latter an epithet of the Grave or Hades (Job x. 21), fittingly applied to that great lone wilderness of the south, which Isaiah had called "a fearsome land" (xxi. 1), and "a land of trouble and anguish" (xxx. 6), whither, according to the poet of Job, "The caravans go up and are lost" (vi. 18).

And I brought you into the garden land, to eat its fruits and its choicest things (tvvh Isa. i. 19; Gen. xlv. 18, 20, 23); and ye entered and defiled My land, and My domain ye made a loathsome thing! (ver. 7). With the wilderness of the wanderings is contrasted the "land of the carmel," the land of fruitful orchards and gardens, as in chap. iv. 26.; Isa. x. 18, xvi. 10, xxix. 17. This was Canaan, Iahvah's own land, which He had chosen out of all countries to be His special dwelling-place and earthly sanctuary; but which Israel no sooner possessed, than they began to pollute this holy land by their sins, like the guilty peoples whom they had displaced, making it thereby an abomination to Iahvah (Lev. xviii. 24 sq., cf. chap. iii. 2).

The priests they said not, Where is Iahvah? and they that handle the law, they knew (i.e. regarded, heeded) Me not; and as for the shepherds (i.e. the king and princes, ver. 26), they rebelled against Me, and the prophets, they prophesied by (through) the Baal, and them that help not (i.e. the false gods) they followed (ver. 8). In the form of a climax, this verse justifies the accusation contained in the last, by giving particulars. The three ruling classes are successively indicted (cf. ver. 26, ch. xviii. 18). The priests, part of whose duty was to "handle the law," i.e. explain the Torah, to instruct the people in the requirements of Iahvah, by oral tradition and out of the sacred law-books, gave no sign of spiritual aspiration (cf. ver. 6); like the reprobate sons of Eli, "they knew not" (1 Sam. ii. 12) "Iahvah," that is to say, paid no heed to Him and His will as revealed in the book of the law; the secular authorities, the king and his counsellors ("wise men," xviii. 18), not only sinned thus negatively, but positively revolted against the King of kings, and resisted His will; while the prophets went further yet in the path of guilt, apostatizing altogether from the God of Israel, and seeking inspiration from the Phenician Baal, and following worthless idols that could give no help. There seems to be a play on the words Baal and Belial, as if Baal meant the same as Belial, "profitless," "worthless" (cf. 1 Sam. ii. 12: "Now Eli's sons were sons of Belial; they knew not Iahvah." The phrase l'yvlv "they that help not," or "cannot help," suggests the term blyl Belial; which, however, may be derived from bly "not," and l "supreme," "God," and so mean "not-God," "idol," rather than "worthlessness," "unprofitableness," as it is usually explained). The reference may be to the Baal-worship of Samaria, the northern capital, which was organised by Ahab, and his Tyrian queen (chap. xxiii. 13).

Therefore--on account of this amazing ingratitude of your forefathers,--I will again plead (reason, argue forensically) with you (the present generation in whom their guilt repeats itself) saith Iahvah, and with your sons' sons (who will inherit your sins) will I plead. The nation is conceived as a moral unity, the characteristics of which are exemplified in each successive generation. To all Israel, past, present, and future, Iahvah will vindicate his own righteousness. For cross (the sea) to the coasts of the Citieans (the people of Citium in Cyprus) and see; and to Kedar (the rude tribes of the Syrian desert) send ye, and mark well, and see whether there hath arisen a case like this. Hath a nation changed gods--albeit they are no-gods? Yet My people hath changed his (true) glory for that which helpeth not (or is worthless). Upheave, ye heavens (smym smv, a fine paronomasia), at this, and shudder (and) be petrified (chrvv m'd Ges., "be sore amazed" = smm; but Hitzig "be dry" = stiff and motionless, like syn. yvs in 1 Kings xiii. 4), saith Iahvah; for two evil things hath My people done: Me they have forsaken--a Fountain of living water--to hew them out cisterns, broken cisterns, that cannot (imperf. = potential) hold water (Heb. the waters: generic article) (vv. 9-13). In these five verses, the apostasy of Israel from his own God is held up as a fact unique in history--unexampled and inexplicable by comparison with the doings of other nations. Whether you look westward or eastward, across the sea to Cyprus, or beyond Gilead to the barbarous tribes of the Cedrei (Ps. cxx. 5), nowhere will you find a heathen people that has changed its native worship for another; and if you did find such, it would be no precedent or palliation of Israel's behaviour. The heathen in adopting a new worship simply exchanges one superstition for another; the objects of his devotion are "non-gods" (ver. 11). The heinousness and the eccentricity of Israel's conduct lies in the fact that he has bartered truth for falsehood; he has exchanged "his Glory"--whom Amos (viii. 7) calls the Pride (A.V. Excellency) of Jacob--for a useless idol; an object which the prophet elsewhere calls "The Shame" (iii. 24, xi. 13), because it can only bring shame and confusion upon those whose hopes depend upon it. The wonder of the thing might well be supposed to strike the pure heavens, the silent witnesses of it, with blank astonishment (cf. a similar appeal in Deut. iv. 26, xxxi. 28, xxxii. 1, where the earth is added). For the evil is not single but twofold. With the rejection of truth goes the adoption of error; and both are evils. Not only has Israel turned his back upon "a fountain of living waters;" he has also "hewn him out cisterns, broken cisterns, that cannot hold water." The "broken cisterns" are, of course, the idols which Israel made to himself. As a cistern full of cracks and fissures disappoints the wayfarer, who has reckoned on finding water in it; so the idols, having only the semblance and not the reality of life, avail their worshippers nothing (vv. 8, 11). In Hebrew the waters of a spring are called "living" (Gen. xxi. 19), because they are more refreshing and, as it were, life-giving, than the stagnant waters of pools and tanks fed by the rains. Hence by a natural metaphor, the mouth of a righteous man, or the teaching of the wise, and the fear of the Lord, are called a fountain of life (Prov. x. 11, xiii. 14, xiv. 27). "The fountain of life" is with Iahvah (Ps. xxxvi. 10); nay, He is Himself the Fountain of living waters (Jer. xvii. 13); because all life, and all that sustains or quickens life, especially spiritual life, proceeds from Him. Now in Ps. xix. 8 it is said that "The law of the Lord--or, the teaching of Iahvah--is perfect, reviving (or restoring) the soul" (cf. Lam. i. 11; Ruth iv. 15); and a comparison of Micah and Isaiah's statement that "Out of Zion will go forth the law, and the word of the Lord from Jerusalem" (Isa. ii. 3; Mic. iv. 2), with the more figurative language of Joel (iii. 18) and Zechariah (xiv. 8), who speak of "a fountain going forth from the house of the Lord," and "living waters going forth from Jerusalem," suggests the inference that "the living waters," of which Iahvah is the perennial fountain, are identical with His law as revealed through priests and prophets. It is easy to confirm this suggestion by reference to the river "whose streams make glad the city of God" (Ps. xlvi. 4); to Isaiah's poetic description of the Divine teaching, of which he was himself the exponent, as "the waters of Shiloah that flow softly" (viii. 6), Shiloah being a spring that issues from the temple rock; and to our Lord's conversation with the woman of Samaria, in which He characterises His own teaching as "living waters" (St. John iv. 10), and as "a well of waters, springing up unto eternal Life" (ibid. 14).

 Is Israel a bondman, or a homeborn serf? Why hath he become a prey? Over him did young lions roar; they uttered their voice; and they made his land a waste; his cities, they are burnt up (or thrown down), so that they are uninhabited. Yea, the sons of Noph and Tahpan(h)es, they did bruise thee on the crown. Is not this what (the thing that) thy forsaking Iahvah thy God brought about for thee, at the time He was guiding thee in the way? (vv. 14-17). As Iahvah's bride, as a people chosen to be His own, Israel had every reason to expect a bright and glorious career. Why was this expectation falsified by events? But one answer was possible, in view of the immutable righteousness, the eternal faithfulness of God. The ruin of Israel was Israel's own doing. It is a truth which applies to all nations, and to all individuals capable of moral agency, in all periods and places of their existence. Let no man lay his failure in this world or in the world to come at the door of the Almighty. Let none venture to repeat the thoughtless blasphemy which charges the All-Merciful with sending frail human beings to expiate their offences in an everlasting hell! Let none dare to say or think, God might have made it otherwise, but He would not! Oh, no; it is all a monstrous misconception of the true relations of things. You and I are free to make our choice now, whatever may be the case hereafter. We may choose to obey God, or to disobey; we may seek His will, or our own. The one is the way of life; the other, of death, and nothing can alter the facts; they are part of the laws of the universe. Our destiny is in our own hands, to make or to mar. If we qualify ourselves for nothing better than a hell--if our daily progress leads us farther and farther from God and nearer and nearer to the devil--then hell will be our eternal home. For God is love, and purity, and truth, and glad obedience to righteous laws; and these things, realized and rejoiced in, are heaven. And the man that lives without these as the sovereign aims of his existence--the man whose heart's worship is centred upon something else than God--stands already on the verge of hell, which is "the place of him that knows not (and cares not for) God." And unless we are prepared to find fault with that natural arrangement whereby like things are aggregated to like, and all physical elements gravitate towards their own kind; I do not see how we can disparage the same law in the spiritual sphere, in virtue of which all spiritual beings are drawn to their own place, the heavenly-minded rising to the heights above, and the contrary sort sinking to the depths beneath.

The precise bearing of the question (ver. 14), "Is Israel a bondman, or a homeborn slave?" is hardly self-evident. One commentator supposes that the implied answer is an affirmative. Israel is a "servant," the servant, that is, the worshipper of the true God. Nay, he is more than a mere bondservant; he occupies the favoured position of a slave born in his lord's house (cf. Abram's three hundred and eighteen young men, Gen. xiv. 14), and therefore, according to the custom of antiquity, standing on a different footing from a slave acquired by purchase. The "home" or house is taken to mean the land of Canaan, which the prophet Hosea had designated as Iahvah's "house" (Hosea ix. 15, cf. 3); and the "Israel" intended is supposed to be the existing generation born in the holy land. The double question of the prophet then amounts to this: If Israel be, as is generally admitted, the favourite bondservant of Iahvah, how comes it that his lord has not protected him against the spoiler? But, although this interpretation is not without force, it is rendered doubtful by the order of the words in the Hebrew, where the stress lies on the terms for "bondman" and "homeborn slave"; and by its bold divergence from the sense conveyed by the same form of question in other passages of the prophet, e.g. ver. 31 infr., where the answer expected is a negative one (cf. also chap. viii. 4, 5, xiv. 19, xlix. 1. The formula is evidently characteristic). The point of the question seems to lie in the fact of the helplessness of persons of servile condition against occasional acts of fraud and oppression, from which neither the purchased nor the homebred slave could at all times be secure. The rights of such persons, however humane the laws affecting their ordinary status, might at times be cynically disregarded both by their masters and by others (see a notable instance, Jer. xxxiv. 8 sqq.). Moreover, there may be a reference to the fact that slaves were always reckoned in those times as a valuable portion of the booty of conquest; and the meaning may be that Israel's lot as a captive is as bad as if he had never known the blessings of freedom, and had simply exchanged one servitude for another by the fortune of war. The allusion is chiefly to the fallen kingdom of Ephraim. We must remember that Jeremiah is reviewing the whole past, from the outset of Iahvah's special dealings with Israel. The national sins of the northern and more powerful branch had issued in utter ruin. The "young lions," the foreign invaders, had "roared against" Israel properly so called, and made havoc of the whole country (cf. iv. 7). The land was dispeopled, and became an actual haunt of lions (2 Kings xvii. 25), until Esarhaddon colonised it with a motley gathering of foreigners (Ezra iv. 2). Judah too had suffered greatly from the Assyrian invasion in Hezekiah's time, although the last calamity had then been mercifully averted (Sanherib boasts that he stormed and destroyed forty-six strong cities, and carried off 200,000 captives, and an innumerable booty). The implication is that the evil fate of Ephraim threatens to overtake Judah; for the same moral causes are operative, and the same Divine will, which worked in the past, is working in the present, and will continue to work in the future. The lesson of the past was plain for those who had eyes to read and hearts to understand it. Apart from this prophetic doctrine of a Providence which shapes the destinies of nations, in accordance with their moral deserts, history has no value except for the gratification of mere intellectual curiosity.

Aye, and the children of Noph and Tahpanhes they bruise (? used to bruise; are bruising: the Heb. yrv may mean either) thee on the crown (ver. 16). This obviously refers to injuries inflicted by Egypt, the two royal cities of Noph or Memphis, and Tahpanhes or Daphnæ, being mentioned in place of the country itself. Judah must be the sufferer, as no Egyptian attack on Ephraim is anywhere recorded; while we do read of Shishak's invasion of the southern kingdom in the reign of Rehoboam, both in the Bible (1 Kings xiv. 25), and in Shishak's own inscriptions on the walls of the temple of Amen at Karnak. But the form of the Hebrew verb seems to indicate rather some contemporary trouble; perhaps plundering raids by an Egyptian army, which about this time was besieging the Philistine stronghold of Ashdod (Herod., ii. 157). "The Egyptians are bruising (or crushing) thee" seems to be the sense; and so it is given by the Jewish commentator Rashi (yrtstsv diffringunt). Our English marginal rendering ("fed on") follows the traditional pronunciation of the Hebrew term (yrv), which is also the case with the Targum and the Syriac versions; but this can hardly be right, unless we suppose that the Egyptians infesting the frontier are scornfully compared to vermin (read yrv with J. D. Mich.) of a sort which, as Herodotus tells us, the Egyptians particularly disliked (but cf. Mic. v. 5; Ges., depascunt, "eating down.")

The A.V. of ver. 17 presents a curious mistake, which the Revisers have omitted to correct. The words should run, as I have rendered them, "Is not this"--thy present ill fortune--"the thing that thy forsaking of Iahvah thy God did for thee--at the time when He was guiding thee in the way?" The Hebrew verb does not admit of the rendering in the perf. tense, for it is an impf., nor is it a 2nd pers. fem. (tsh not tsy) but a 3rd. The LXX. has it rightly (ouchi tauta epoiese soi to katalipein se eme?), but leaves out the next clause which specifies the time. The words, however, are probably original; for they insist, as vv. 5 and 31 insist, on the groundlessness of Israel's apostasy. Iahvah had given no cause for it; He was fulfilling His part of the covenant by "guiding them in the way." Guidance or leading is ascribed to Iahvah as the true "Shepherd of Israel" (chap. xxxi. 9; Ps. lxxx. 1). It denotes not only the spiritual guidance which was given through the priests and prophets; but also that external prosperity, those epochs of established power and peace and plenty, which were precisely the times chosen by infatuated Israel for defection from the Divine Giver of her good things. As the prophet Hosea expresses it, ii. 8 sq., "She knew not that it was I who gave her the corn and the new wine and the oil; and silver I multiplied unto her, and gold, which they made into the Baal. Therefore will I take back My corn in the time of it, and My new wine in its season, and will snatch away My wool and My flax, which were to cover her nakedness." And (chap. xiii. 6) the same prophet gives this plain account of his people's thankless revolt from their God: "When I fed them, they were sated; sated were they, and their heart was lifted up: therefore they forgot Me." It is the thought so forcibly expressed by the minstrel of the Book of the Law (Deut. xxxii. 15), first published in the early days of Jeremiah: "And Jeshurun waxed fat and kicked; Thou waxedst fat, and gross and fleshy! And he forsook the God that made him, And made light of his protecting Rock." And, lastly, the Chronicler has pointed the same moral of human fickleness and frailty in the case of an individual, Uzziah or Azariah, the powerful king of Judah, whose prosperity seduced him into presumption and profanity (2 Chron. xxvi. 16): "When he grew strong, his heart rose high, until he dealt corruptly, and was unfaithful to Iahvah his God." I need not enlarge on the perils of prosperity; they are known by bitter experience to every Christian man. Not without good reason do we pray to be delivered from evil "In all time of our wealth;" nor was that poet least conversant with human nature who wrote that "Sweet are the uses of adversity."

And now--a common formula in drawing an inference and concluding an argument--what hast thou to do with the way of Egypt, to drink the waters of Shihor (the Black River, the Nile); and what hast thou to do with the way to Assyria, to drink the waters of the River? (par excellence, i.e., the Euphrates). Thy wickedness correcteth thee, and thy revolts it is that chastise thee. Know then, and see that evil and bitter is thy forsaking Iahvah thy God, and thine having no dread of Me, saith the Lord Iahvah Sabaoth (vv. 18, 19). And now--as the cause of all thy misfortunes lies in thyself--what is the use of seeking a cure for them abroad? Egypt will prove as powerless to help thee now, as Assyria proved in the days of Ahaz (ver. 36 sq.). The Jewish people, anticipating the views of certain modern historians, made a wrong diagnosis of their own evil case. They traced all that they had suffered, and were yet to suffer, to the ill will of the two great Powers of their time; and supposed that their only salvation lay in conciliating the one or the other. And as Isaiah found it necessary to cry woe on the rebellious children, "that walk to go down into Egypt, and have not asked at My mouth; to strengthen themselves in the strength of Pharaoh, and to trust in the shadow of Egypt!" (Isa. xxx. 1 sq.), so now, after so much experience of the futility and positive harmfulness of these unequal alliances, Jeremiah has to lift his voice against the same national folly.

The "young lions" of ver. 15 must denote the Assyrians, as Egypt is expressly named in ver. 16. The figure is very appropriate, for not only was the lion a favourite subject of Assyrian sculpture; not only do the Assyrian kings boast of their prowess as lion-hunters, while they even tamed these fierce creatures, and trained them to the chase; but the great strength and predatory habits of the king of beasts made him a fitting symbol of that great empire whose irresistible power was founded upon and sustained by wrong and robbery. This reference makes it clear that the prophet is contemplating the past; for Assyria was at this time already tottering to its fall, and the Israel of his day, i.e. the surviving kingdom of Judah, had no longer any temptation to court the countenance of that decaying if not already ruined empire. The sin of Israel is an old one; both it and its consequences belong to the past (ver. 20 compared with ver. 14); and the national attempts to find a remedy must be referred to the same period. Ver. 36 makes it evident that the prophet's contemporaries concerned themselves only about an Egyptian alliance.

It is an interesting detail that for "the waters of Shihor," the LXX. gives "waters of Gihon" (Geon), which it will be remembered is the name of one of the four rivers of Paradise, and which appears to have been the old Hebrew name of the Nile (Ecclus. xxiv. 27; Jos., Ant., i. 1, 3). Shihor may be an explanatory substitute. For the rest, it is plain that the two rivers symbolize the two empires (cf. Isa. viii. 7; chap. xlvi. 7); and the expression "to drink the waters" of them must imply the receiving and, as it were, absorption of whatever advantage might be supposed to accrue from friendly relations with their respective countries. At the same time, a contrast seems to be intended between these earthly waters, which could only disappoint those who sought refreshment in them, and that "fountain of living waters" (ver. 13) which Israel had forsaken. The nation sought in Egypt its deliverance from self-caused evil, much as Saul had sought guidance from witches when he knew himself deserted by the God whom by disobedience he had driven away. In seeking thus to escape the consequences of sin by cementing alliances with heathen powers, Israel added sin to sin. Hence (in ver. 19) the prophet reiterates with increased emphasis what he has already suggested by a question (ver. 17): "Thy wickedness correcteth thee, and thy revolts it is that chastise thee. Know then, and see that evil and bitter is thy forsaking of Iahweh thy God, and thine having no dread of Me!" Learn from these its bitter fruits that the thing itself is bad (Read phhdty 'ly as a 2nd pers. instead of phchdty. Job xxi. 33, quoted by Hitzig, is not a real parallel; nor can the sentence, as it stands, be rendered, "Und dass die Scheu vor mir nicht an dich kam"); and renounce that which its consequences declare to be an evil course, instead of aggravating the evil of it by a new act of unfaithfulness.

For long ago didst thou break thy yoke, didst thou burst thy bonds, and saidst, I will not serve: for upon every high hill, and under each evergreen tree thou wert crouching in fornication (vv. 20-24). Such seems to be the best way of taking a verse which is far from clear as it stands in the Masoretic text. The prophet labours to bring home to his hearers a sense of the reality of the national sin; and he affirms once more (vv. 5, 7) that Israel's apostasy originated long ago, in the early period of its history, and implies that the taint thus contracted is a fact which can neither be denied nor obliterated. (The punctuators of the Hebrew text, having pointed the first two verbs as in the 1st pers. instead of the 2nd feminine, were obliged, further, to suggest the reading l' 'vvr, "I will not transgress," for the original phrase l' 'vvr "I will not serve;" a variant which is found in the Targum, and many MSS. and editions. "Serving" and "bearing the yoke" are equivalent expressions (xxvii. 11, 12); so that, if the first two verbs were really in the 1st pers., the sentence ought to be continued with, "And I said, Thou shalt not serve." But the purport of this verse is to justify the assertion of the last, as is evident from the introductory particle "for," ky. The Syriac supports 'vvr; and the LXX. and Vulg. have the two leading verbs in the 2nd pers., iv. 19.) The meaning is that Israel, like a stubborn ox, has broken the yoke imposed on him by Iahvah; a statement which is repeated in v. 5: "But these have altogether broken the yoke, they have burst the bonds" (cf. ver. 31, infr.; Hos. iv. 16; Acts xxvi. 14).

Yet I--I planted thee with (or, as) noble vines, all of them genuine shoots; and how hast thou turned Me thyself into the wild offshoots of a foreign vine? (ver. 21). The thought seems to be borrowed from Isaiah's Song of the Beloved's Vineyard (Isa. v. 1 sqq.). The nation is addressed as a person, endowed with a continuity of moral existence from the earliest period. "The days of the life of a man may be numbered; but the days of Israel are innumerable" (Ecclus. xxxvii. 25). It was with the true seed of Abraham, the real Israel, that Iahvah had entered into covenant (Ex. xviii. 19; Rom. ix. 7); and this genuine offspring of the patriarch had its representatives in every succeeding generation, even in the worst of times (1 Kings xix. 18). But the prophet's argument seems to imply that the good plants had reverted to a wild state, and that the entire nation had become hopelessly degenerate; which was not far from the actual condition of things at the close of his career. The culmination of Israel's degeneracy, however, was seen in the rejection of Him to whom "gave all the prophets witness." The Passion of Christ sounded a deeper depth of sacred sorrow than the passion of any of His forerunners. "O Jerusalem, Jerusalem! Thou that killest the prophets, and stonest them that are sent unto thee!"

> "Then on My head a crown of thorns I wear;
> For these are all the grapes Sion doth bear,
> Though I My vine planted and watered there:
> Was ever grief like Mine?"

For if thou wash with nation, and take thee much soap, spotted (crimsoned; Targ. Isa. i. 18: or written, recorded) is thy guilt before Me, saith My Lord Iahvah. Comparison with Isa. i. 18, "Though thy sins be as scarlet ... though they be red like crimson," suggests that the former rendering of the doubtful word (nktm) is correct; and this idea is plainly better suited to the context than a reference to the Books of Heaven, and the Recording Angel; for the object of washing is to get rid of spots and stains.

How canst thou say, I have not defiled myself; after the Baals I have not gone: See thy way in the valley, know what thou hast done, O swift she-camel, running hither and thither (literally intertwining or crossing her ways) (ver. 23). The prophet anticipates a possible attempt at self-justification; just as in ver. 35 he complains of Israel's self-righteousness. Both here and there he is dealing with his own contemporaries in Judah; whereas the idolatry described in ver. 20 sqq. is chiefly that of the ruined kingdom of Ephraim (ch. iii. 24; 2 Kings xvii. 10). It appears that the worship of Baal proper only existed in Judah for a brief period in the reign of Ahaziah's usurping queen Athaliah, side by side with the worship of Iahvah (2 Chron. xxiii. 17); while on the high-places and at the local sanctuaries the God of Israel was honoured (2 Kings xviii. 22). So far as the prophet's complaints refer to old times, Judah could certainly boast of a relatively higher purity than the northern kingdom; and the manifold heathenism of Manasseh's reign had been abolished a whole year before this address was delivered (2 Chron. xxxiv. 3 sqq.). "The valley" spoken of as the scene of Judah's misdoings is that of Ben-Hinnom, south of Jerusalem, where, as the prophet elsewhere relates (vii. 31, xxxii. 35; 2 Kings xxiii. 10), the people sacrificed children by fire to the god Molech, whom he expressly designates as a Baal (xix. 5, xxxii. 35), using the term in its wider significance, which includes all the aspects of the Canaanite sun-god. And because Judah betook herself now to Iahvah, and now to Molech, varying, as it were, her capricious course from right to left and from left to right, and halting evermore between two opinions (1 Kings xviii. 21), the prophet calls her "a swift young she-camel,"--swift, that is, for evil--"intertwining, or crossing her ways." The hot zeal with which the people wantonly plunged into a sensual idolatry is aptly set forth in the figure of the next verse. A wild ass, used to the wilderness (Job xxiv. 5), in the craving of her soul she snuffeth up (xiv. 6) the wind (not "lässt sie kaum Athem genug finden, indem sie denselben vorweg vergeudet," as Hitzig; but, as a wild beast scenting prey, cf. xiv. 6, or food afar off, she scents companions at a distance); her greedy lust, who can turn it back? None that seek her need weary themselves; in her month they find her. While passion rages, animal instinct is too strong to be diverted from its purpose; it is idle to argue with blind appetite; it goes straight to its mark, like an arrow from a bow. Only when it has had its way, and the reaction of nature follows, does the influence of reason become possible. Such was Israel's passion for the false gods. They had no need to seek her (Hos. ii. 7; Ezek. xvi. 34); in the hour of her infatuation, she fell an easy victim to their passive allurements. (The "month" is the season when the sexual instinct is strong.) Warnings fell on deaf ears. Keep back thy foot from bareness, and thy throat from thirst! This cry of the prophets availed nothing: Thou saidst, It is vain! (sc. that thou urgest me.) No, for I love the strangers and after them will I go! The meaning of the admonition is not very clear. Some (e.g. Rosenmüller) have understood a reference to the shameless doings, and the insatiable cravings of lust. Others (as Gesenius) explain the words thus: "Do not pursue thy lovers in such hot haste, as to wear thy feet bare in the wild race!" Others, again, take the prohibition literally, and connect the barefootedness and the thirst with the orgies of Baal-worship (Hitz.), in which the priests leaped or rather limped with bare feet (what proof?) on the blazing âltar, as an act of religious mortification, shrieking the while till their throats were parched and dry (Ps. lxix. 4, nchr grvny), in frenzied appeal to their lifeless god (cf. Ex. iii. 5; 2 Sam. xv. 30; 1 Kings xviii. 26). In this case, the command is, Cease this self-torturing and bootless worship! But the former sense seems to agree better with the context.

Like the shame of a thief, when he is detected, so are the house of Israel ashamed--they, their kings, their princes, and their priests, and their prophets; in that they say (are ever saying) to the wood (iii. 9 in Heb. masc.), Thou art my father! (iii. 4) and to the stone (in Heb. fem.), Thou didst bring me forth! For they (xxxii. 33) have turned towards Me the back and not the face; but in the time of their trouble they say (begin to say), O rise and save us! But where are thy gods that thou madest for thyself? Let them arise, if they can save thee in the time of thy trouble; for numerous as thy cities are thy gods become, O Judah! (vv. 26-28). "The Shame" (hvst) is the well-known title of opprobrium which the prophets apply to Baal. Even in the histories, which largely depend on prophetic sources, we find such substitutions as Ishbosheth for Eshbaal, the "Man of Shame" for "Baal's Man." Accordingly, the point of ver. 26 sqq. is, that Israel has served the Shame, the idol-gods, instead of Iahvah, shame has been and will be her reward: in the hour of bitter need, when she implores help from the One true God, she is put to shame by being referred back to her senseless idols. The "Israel" intended is the entire nation, as in ver. 3, and not merely the fallen kingdom of Ephraim. In ver. 28 the prophet specially addresses Judah, the surviving representative of the whole people. In the book of Judges (x. 10-14) the same idea of the attitude of Iahvah towards His faithless people finds historical illustration. Oppressed by the Ammonites they "cried unto the Lord, saying, We have sinned against Thee, in that we have both forsaken our own God, and have served the Baals;" but Iahvah, after reminding them of past deliverances followed by fresh apostasies, replies: "Go, and cry unto the gods which ye have chosen; let them save you in the time of your distress!" Here also we hear the echoes of a prophetic voice. The object of such ironical utterances was by no means to deride the self-caused miseries in which Israel was involved; but, as is evident from the sequel of the narrative in Judges, to deepen penitence and contrition, by making the people realize the full flagrancy of their sin, and the suicidal folly of their desertions of the God whom, in times of national distress, they recognised as the only possible Saviour. In the same way and with the same end in view, the prophetic psalmist of Deut. xxxii. represents the God of Israel as asking (ver. 37) "Where are their gods; the Rock in which they sought refuge? That used to eat the flesh of their sacrifices, that drank the wine of their libation? Let them arise and help you; let them be over you a shelter!" The purpose is to bring home to them a conviction of the utter vanity of idol-worship; for the poet continues: "See now that I even I am He"--the one God--"and there is no God beside Me" (with Me, sharing My sole attributes); "'Tis I that kill and save alive; I have crushed, and I heal." The folly of Israel is made conspicuous, first by the expression "Saying to the wood, Thou art my father, and to the stone, Thou didst bring me forth;" and secondly, by the statement, "Numerous as thy cities are thy gods become, O Judah!" In the former, we have a most interesting glimpse of the point of view of the heathen worshipper of the seventh century b.c., from which it appears that by a god he meant the original, i.e., the real author of his own existence. Much has been written in recent years to prove that man's elementary notions of deity are of an altogether lower kind than those which find expression in the worship of a Father in heaven; but when we see that such an idea could subsist even in connexion with the most impure nature-worships, as in Canaan, and when we observe that it was a familiar conception in the religion of Egypt several thousand years previously, we may well doubt whether this idea of an Unseen Father of our race is not as old as humanity itself.

The sarcastic reference to the number of Judah's idols may remind us of what is recorded of classic Athens, in whose streets it was said to be easier to find a god than a man. The irony of the prophet's remark depends on the consideration that there is, or ought to be, safety in numbers. The impotence of the false gods could hardly be put in a stronger light in words as few as the prophet has used. In chap. xi. 13 he repeats the statement in an amplified form: "For numerous as thy cities have thy gods become, O Judah; and numerous as the streets of Jerusalem have ye made altars for The Shame, altars for sacrificing to the Baal." From this passage, apparently, the LXX. derived the words which it adds here: "And according to the number of the streets of Jerusalem did they sacrifice to the (image of) Baal" (ethuon te Baal).

Why contend ye with Me? All of you have rebelled against Me, saith Iahvah. (LXX. esebesate, kai pantes humeis enomesate eis eme. "Ebenfalls authentisch" says Hitzig). In vain have I smitten your sons; correction they (i.e., the people; but LXX. edexasthe may be correct), received not! your own sword hath eaten up your prophets, like a destroying lion. Generation that ye are! See the word of Iahvah! Is it a wilderness that I have been to Israel, or a land of deepest gloom? Why have My people said, We are free; we will come no more unto Thee? Doth a virgin forget her ornaments, a bride her bands (or garlands, Rashi)? yet My people hath forgotten Me days without number (vv. 29-32). The question, "Why contend, or dispute ye (tryvv), or, as the LXX. has it, talk ye (tdvrv) towards or about Me ('ly)?" implies that the people murmured at the reproaches and menaces of the prophet (ver. 26 sqq.). He answers them by denying their right to complain. Their rebellion has been universal; no chastisement has reformed them; Iahvah has done nothing which can be alleged in excuse of their unfaithfulness; their sin is, therefore, a portentous anomaly, for which it is impossible to find a parallel in ordinary human conduct. In vain have had "their sons," the young men of military age, fallen in battle (Amos iv. 10); the nation had stubbornly refused to see in such disasters a sign of Iahvah's displeasure, a token of Divine chastisement; or rather, while recognising the wrath of heaven, they had obstinately persisted in believing in false explanations of its motive, and refused to admit that the purpose of it was their religious and moral amendment. And not only had the nation refused warning, and despised instruction, and defeated the purposes of the Divine discipline. They had slain their spiritual monitors, the prophets, with the sword; the prophets who had founded upon the national disasters their rebukes of national sin, and their earnest calls to penitence and reform (1 Kings xix. 10; Neh. ix. 26; St. Matt. xxiii. 37). And so when at last the long deferred judgment arrived, it found a political system ready to go to pieces through the feebleness and corruption of the ruling classes; a religious system, of which the spirit had long since evaporated, and which simply survived in the interests of a venal priesthood, and its intimate allies, who made a trade of prophecy; and a kingdom and people ripe for destruction.

At the thought of this crowning outrage, the prophet cannot restrain his indignation. "Generation that ye are!" he exclaims, "behold the word of the Lord. Is it a wilderness that I have been to Israel, or a land of deepest gloom?" Have I been a thankless, barren soil, returning nothing for your culture? The question is more pointed in Hebrew than in English; for the same term (vd `abad) means both to till the ground, and to serve and worship God. We have thus an emphatic repetition of the remonstrance with which the address opens: Iahweh has not been unmindful of Israel's service; Israel has been persistently ungrateful for Iahvah's gracious love. The cry "We are free!" (rdnv) implies that they had broken away from a painful yoke and a burdensome service (cf. ver. 20); the yoke being that of the Moral Law, and the service that perfect freedom which consists in subjection to Divine Reason. Thus sin always triumphs in casting away man's noblest prerogative; in trampling under foot that loyalty to the higher ideal which is the bridal adornment and the peculiar glory of the soul.

Why hurriest thou to seek thy love? (Lit. why dost thou make good thy way? somewhat as we say, "to make good way with a thing") (ver. 33). The key to the meaning here is supplied by ver. 36: Why art thou in such haste to change thy way? In (Of) Egypt also thou shalt be disappointed, as thou wert in Assyria. The "way" is that which leads to Egypt; and the "love" is that apostasy from Iahvah which invariably accompanies an alliance with foreign peoples (ver. 18). If you go to Assyria, you "drink the waters of the Euphrates," i.e., you are exposed to all the malign influences of the heathen land. Elsewhere, also (iv. 30), Jeremiah speaks of the foreign peoples, whose connexion Israel so anxiously courted, as her "lovers"; and the metaphor is a common one in the prophets.

The words which follow are obscure. Therefore the evil things also hast thou taught thy ways. What "evil things"? Elsewhere the term denotes misfortunes, calamities (Lam. iii. 38); and so probably here (cf. iii. 5). The sense seems to be: Thou hast done evil, and in so doing hast taught Evil to dog thy steps! The term evil obviously suggests the two meanings of sin and the punishment of sin; as we say, "Be sure your sin will find you out!" Ver. 34 explains what was the special sin that followed and clung to Israel: Also, in thy skirts--the borders of thy garments--are they (the evil things) found, viz., the life-blood of innocent helpless ones; not that thou didst find them house-breaking, and so hadst excuse for slaying them (Exod. xxii. 2); but for all these warnings or, because of all these apostasies and dallyings with the heathen, which they denounced (cf. iii. 7), thou slewest them. The murder of the prophets (ver. 30) was the unatoned guilt which clung to the skirts of Israel.

And thou saidst, Certainly I am absolved! Surely His wrath is turned away from me! Behold I wilt reason with thee, because thou sayest, I sinned not! (ver. 35). This is what the people said when they murdered the prophets. They, and doubtless their false guides, regarded the national disasters as so much atonement for their sins. They believed that Iahvah's wrath had exhausted itself in the infliction of what they had already endured, and that they were now absolved from their offences. The prophets looked at the matter differently. To them, national disasters were warnings of worse to follow, unless the people would take them in that sense, and turn from their evil ways. The people preferred to think that their account with Iahvah had been balanced and settled by their misfortunes in war (ver. 30). Hence they slew those who never wearied of affirming the contrary, and threatening further woe, as false prophets (Deut. xviii. 20). The saying, "I sinned not!" refers to these cruel acts; they declared themselves guiltless in the matter of slaying the prophets, as if their blood was on their own heads. The only practical issue of the national troubles was that instead of reforming, they sought to enter into fresh alliances with the heathen, thus, from the point of view of the prophets, adding sin to sin. Why art thou in such haste to change thy way? (i.e. thy course of action, thy foreign policy). Through Egypt also shalt thou be shamed, as thou hast been shamed through Assyria. Out of this affair also (or, from him, as the country is perhaps personified as a lover of Judah;) shalt thou go forth with thine hands upon thine head (in token of distress, 2 Sam. xiii. 19: Tamar); for Iahvah hath rejected the objects of thy trust, so that thou canst not be successful regarding them (vv. 36, 37). The Egyptian alliance, like the former one with Assyria, was destined to bring nothing but shame and confusion to the Jewish people. The prophet urges past experience of similar undertakings, in the hope of deterring the politicians of the day from their foolish enterprise. But all that they had learnt from the failure and loss entailed by their intrigues with one foreign power was, that it was expedient to try another. So they made haste to "change their way," to alter the direction of their policy from Assyria to Egypt. King Hezekiah had renounced his vassalage to Assyria, in reliance, as it would seem, on the support of Taharka, king of Egypt and Ethiopia (2 Kings xviii. 7; cf. Isa. xxx. 1-5); and now again the nation was coquetting with the same power. As has been stated, an Egyptian force lay at this time on the confines of Judah, and the prophet may be referring to friendly advances of the Jewish princes towards its leaders.

In the Hebrew, ch. iii. opens with the word "saying" (l'mr). No real parallel to this can be found elsewhere, and the Sept. and Syriac omit the term. Whether we follow these ancient authorities, and do the same, or whether we prefer to suppose that the prophet originally wrote, as usually, "And the Word of Iahvah came unto me, saying," will not make much difference. One thing is clear; the division of the chapters is in this instance erroneous, for the short section, iii. 1-5, obviously belongs to and completes the argument of ch. ii. The statement of ver. 37, that Israel will not prosper in the negotiations with Egypt, is justified in iii. 1 by the consideration that prosperity is an outcome of the Divine favour, which Israel has forfeited. The rejection of Israel's "confidences" implies the rejection of the people themselves (vii. 29). If a man divorce his wife and she go away from him (m'tv de chez lul), and become another man's, doth he (her former husband) return unto her again? Would not that land be utterly polluted? It is the case contemplated in the Book of the Law (Deut. xxiv. 1-4), the supposition being that the second husband may divorce the woman, or that the bond between them may be dissolved by his death. In either contingency, the law forbade reunion with the former husband, as "abomination before Iahvah;" and David's treatment of his ten wives, who had been publicly wedded by his rebel son Absalom, proves the antiquity of the usage in this respect (2 Sam. xx. 3). The relation of Israel to Iahvah is the relation to her former husband of the divorced wife who has married another. If anything it is worse. And thou, thou hast played the harlot with many paramours; and shalt thou return unto Me? saith Iahvah. The very idea of it is rejected with indignation. The Author of the law will not so flagrantly break the law. (With the Heb. form of the question, cf. the Latin use of the infin. "Mene incepto desistere victam?") The details of the unfaithfulness of Israel--the proofs that she belongs to others and not to Iahvah--are glaringly obvious; contradiction is impossible. Lift up thine eyes upon the bare fells, and see! cries the prophet; where hast thou not been forced? By the roadsides thou satest for them like a Bedawi in the wilderness, and thou pollutedst the land with thy whoredom and with thine evil (Hos. vi. 13). On every hill-top the evidence of Judah's sinful dalliance with idols was visible; in her eagerness to consort with the false gods, the objects of her infatuation, she was like a courtesan looking out for paramours by the wayside (Gen. xxxviii. 14), or an Arab lying in wait for the unwary traveller in the desert. (There may be a reference to the artificial bamoth or "high places" erected at the top of the streets, on which the wretched women, consecrated to the shameful rites of the Canaanite goddess Ashtoreth, were wont to sit plying their trade of temptation: 2 Kings xxiii. 8; Ezek. xvi. 25). We must never forget that, repulsive and farfetched as these comparisons of an apostate people to a sinful woman may seem to us, the ideas and customs of the time made them perfectly apposite. The worship of the gods of Canaan involved the practice of the foulest impurities; and by her revolt from Iahvah, her lord and husband, according to the common Semitic conception of the relation between a people and their god, Israel became a harlot in fact as well as in figure. The land was polluted with her "whoredoms," i.e., her worship of the false gods, and her practice of their vile rites; and with her "evil," as instanced above (ii. 30, 35) in the murder of those who protested against these things (Num. xxxv. 33; Ps. cvi. 38). As a punishment for these grave offences, the showers were withholden, and the spring rains fell not; but the merciful purpose of this Divine chastisement was not fulfilled; the people were not stirred to penitence, but rather hardened in their sins: but thou hadst a harlot's forehead; thou refusedst to be made ashamed! And now the day of grace is past, and repentance comes too late. Hast thou not but now called unto Me, My Father! Friend of my youth wert Thou? Will He retain His wrath for ever? or keep it without end? (vv. 3, 5). The reference appears to be to the external reforms accomplished by the young king Josiah in his twelfth year--the year previous to the utterance of this prophecy; when, as we read in 2 Chron. xxxiv. 3, "He began to purge Judah and Jerusalem from the high places, and the Asherim, and the carven images, and the molten images." To all appearance, it was a return of the nation to its old allegiance; the return of the rebellious child to its father, of the erring wife to the husband of her youth. By those two sacred names which in her inexcusable fickleness and ingratitude she had lavished upon stocks and stones, Israel now seemed to be invoking the relenting compassion of her alienated God (ii. 27, ii. 2). But apart from the doubt attaching to the reality of reformations to order, carried out in obedience to a royal decree; apart from the question whether outward changes so easily and rapidly accomplished, in accordance with the will of an absolute monarch, were accompanied by any tokens of a genuine national repentance; the sin of Israel had gone too far, and been persisted in too long, for its terrible consequences to be averted. Behold--it is the closing sentence of the address; a sentence fraught with despair, and the certainty of coming ruin;--Behold, thou hast planned and accomplished the evil (ii. 33); and thou hast prevailed! The approaches of the people are met by the assurance that their own plans and doings, rather than Iahvah's wrath, are the direct cause of past and prospective adversity; ill doing is the mother of ill fortune. Israel inferred from her troubles that God was angry with her; and she is informed by His prophet that, had she been bent on bringing those troubles about, she could not have chosen any other line of conduct than that which she had actually pursued. The term "evils" again suggests both the false and impure worships, and their calamitous moral consequences. Against the will of Iahvah, His people had wrought for its own ruin, and had prevailed.

And now let us take a farewell look at the discourse in its entirety. Beginning at the beginning, the dawn of his people's life as a nation, the young prophet declares that in her early days, in the old times of simple piety and the uncorrupted life of the desert, Israel had been true to her God; and her devotion to her Divine spouse had been rewarded by guidance and protection. "Israel was a thing consecrated to Iahvah; whoever eat of it was held guilty, and evil came upon them" (ii. 1-3). This happy state of mutual love and trust between the Lord and His people began to change with the great change in outward circumstances involved in their conquest of Canaan and settlement among the aboriginal inhabitants as the ruling race. With the lands and cities of the conquered, the conquerors soon learned to adopt also their customs of worship, and the licentious merriment of their sacrifices and festivals. Gradually they lost all sense of any radical distinction between the God of Israel and the local deities at whose ancient sanctuaries they now worshipped Him. Soon they forgot their debt to Iahvah; His gracious and long-continued guidance in the Arabian steppes, and the loving care which had established them in the goodly land of orchards and vineyards and cornfields. The priests ceased to care about ascertaining and declaring His will; the princes openly broke His laws; and the popular prophets spoke in the name of the popular Baals (vv. 4-8). There was something peculiarly strange and startling in this general desertion of the national God and Deliverer; it was unparalleled among the surrounding heathen races. They were faithful to gods that were no gods; Israel actually exchanged her Glory, the living source of all her strength and well-being, for a useless, helpless idol. Her behaviour was as crazy as if she had preferred a cistern, all cracks and fissures, that could not possibly hold water, to a never-failing fountain of sweet spring water (vv. 9-13). The consequences were only too plain to such as had eyes to see. Israel, the favoured slave of Iahvah, was robbed and spoiled. The "lions," the fierce and rapacious warriors of Assyria had ravaged his land, and ruined his cities; while Egypt was proving but a treacherous friend, pilfering and plundering on the borders of Judah. It was all Israel's own doing; forsaking his God, he had forfeited the Divine protection. It was his own apostasy, his own frequent and flagrant revolts which were punishing him thus. Vain, therefore, utterly vain were his endeavours to find deliverance from trouble in an alliance with the great heathen powers of South or North (vv. 14-19). Rebellion was no new feature in the national history. No; for of old the people had broken the yoke of Iahvah, and burst the bonds of His ordinances, and said, I will not serve! and on every high hill, and under every evergreen tree, Israel had bowed down to the Baalim of Canaan, in spiritual adultery from her Divine Lord and Husband. The change was a portent; the noble vine-shoot had degenerated into a worthless wilding (vv. 20-21). The sin of Israel was inveterate and ingrained; nothing could wash out the stain of it. Denial of her guilt was futile; the dreadful rites in the valley of Hinnom witnessed against her. Her passion for the foreign worships was as insatiable and headstrong as the fierce lust of the camel or the wild ass. To protests and warnings her sole reply was: "It is in vain! I love the strangers, and them will I follow!" The outcome of all this wilful apostasy was the shame of defeat and disaster, the humiliation of disappointment, when the helplessness of the stocks and stones, which had supplanted her Heavenly Father, was demonstrated by the course of events. Then she bethought her of the God she had so lightly forsaken, only to hear in His silence a bitterly ironical reference to the multitude of her helpers, the gods of her own creation. The national reverses failed of the effect intended in the counsels of Providence. Her sons had fallen in battle; but instead of repenting of her evil ways, she slew the faithful prophets who warned her of the consequences of her misdeeds (vv. 20-30). It was the crowning sin; the cup of her iniquity was full to overflowing. Indignant at the memory of it, the prophet once more insists that the national crimes are what has put misfortune on the track of the nation; and chiefly, this heinous one of killing the messengers of God like housebreakers caught in the act; and then aggravating their guilt by self-justification, and by resorting to Egypt for that help, which they despaired of obtaining from an outraged God. All such negotiations, past or present, were doomed to failure beforehand; the Divine sentence had gone forth, and it was idle to contend against it (vv. 31-37). Idle also it was to indulge in hopes of the restoration of Divine favour. Just as it was not open to a discarded wife to return to her husband after living with another; so might not Israel be received back into her former position of the Bride of Heaven, after she had "played the harlot with many lovers." Doubtless of late she had given tokens of remembering her forgotten Lord, calling upon the Father who had been the guide of her youth, and deprecating the continuance of His wrath. But the time was long since past, when it was possible to avert the evil consequences of her misdoings. She had, as it were, steadily purposed and wrought out her own evils; both her sins and her sufferings past and to come: the iron sequence could not be broken; the ruin she had courted lay before her in the near future: she had "prevailed." All efforts such as she was now making to stave it off were like a deathbed repentance; in the nature of things, they could not annihilate the past, nor undo what had been done, nor substitute the fruit of holiness for the fruit of sin, the reward of faithfulness and purity for the wages of worldliness, sensuality, and forgetfulness of God.

Thus the discourse starts with impeachment, and ends with irreversible doom. Its tone is comminatory throughout; nowhere do we hear, as in other prophecies, the promise of pardon in return for penitence. Such preaching was necessary, if the nation was to be brought to a due sense of its evil; and the reformation of the eighteenth of Josiah, which was undoubtedly accompanied by a considerable amount of genuine repentance among the governing classes, was in all likelihood furthered by this and similar prophetic orations. [20]

Footnotes:

19. tslmvt, so far as the punctuation suggests that the term is a compound, meaning "shadow of death," is one of the fictions of the Masorets, like lg'yvnym and chlk'ym and chlkh in the Psalms.

20. Perhaps, too, the immediate object of the prophet was attained, which was, as Ewald thinks, to dissuade the people from alliance with Psammitichus, the vigorous monarch who was then reviving the power and ambition of Egypt. Jeremiah dreaded the effects of Egyptian influence upon the religion and morals of Judah. Ewald notes the significant absence of all reference to the enemy from the north, who appears in all the later pieces.

III. ISRAEL AND JUDAH: A CONTRAST

Jeremiah iii. 6-iv. 2.

The first address of our prophet was throughout of a sombre cast, and the darkness of its close was not relieved by a single ray of hope. It was essentially a comminatory discourse, the purpose of it being to rouse a sinful nation to the sense of its peril, by a faithful picture of its actual condition, which was so different from what it was popularly supposed to be. The veil is torn aside; the real relations between Israel and his God are exposed to view; and it is seen that the inevitable goal of persistence in the course which has brought partial disasters in the past, is certain destruction in the imminent future. It is implied, but not said, that the only thing that can save the nation is a complete reversal of policies hitherto pursued, in Church and State and private life; and it is apparently taken for granted that the thing implied is no longer possible. The last word of the discourse was: "Thou hast purposed and performed the evils, and thou hast conquered" (iii. 5). The address before us forms a striking contrast to this dark picture. It opens a door of hope for the penitent. The heart of the prophet cannot rest in the thought of the utter rejection of his people; the harsh and dreary announcement that his people's woes are self-caused cannot be his last word. "His anger was only love provoked to distraction; here it has come to itself again," and holds out an offer of grace first to that part of the whole nation which needs it most, the fallen kingdom of Ephraim, and then to the entire people. The all Israel of the former discourse is here divided into its two sections, which are contrasted with each other, and then again considered as a united nation. This feature distinguishes the piece from that which begins chap. iv. 3, and which is addressed to "Judah and Jerusalem" rather than to Israel and Judah, like the one before us. An outline of the discourse may be given thus. It is shown that Judah has not taken warning by Iahvah's rejection of the sister kingdom (6-10); and that Ephraim may be pronounced less guilty than Judah, seeing that she had witnessed no such signal example of the Divine vengeance on hardened apostasy. She is, therefore, invited to repent and return to her alienated God, which will involve a return from exile to her own land; and the promise is given of the reunion of the two peoples in a restored Theocracy, having its centre in Mount Zion (11-19). All Israel has rebelled against God; but the prophet hears the cry of universal penitence and supplication ascending to heaven; and Iahvah's gracious answer of acceptance (iii. 20-iv. 2).

The opening section depicts the sin which had brought ruin on Israel, and Judah's readiness in following her example, and refusal to take warning by her fate. This twofold sin is aggravated by an insincere repentance. And Iahvah said unto me, in the days of Josiah the king, Sawest thou what the Turncoat or Recreant Israel did? she would go up every high hill, and under every evergreen tree, and play the harlot there. And methought that after doing all this she would return to Me; but she returned not; and the Traitress, her sister Judah saw it. And I [21] saw that when for the very reason that she, the Turncoat Israel, had committed adultery, I had put her away, and given her her bill of divorce, the Traitress Judah, her sister, was not afraid, but she too went off and played the harlot. And so, through the cry (cf. Gen. iv. 10, xviii. 20 sq.) of her harlotry (or read rv for ql, script. defect. through her manifold or abounding harlotry) she polluted the land (vtchnph ver. 2), in that she committed adultery with the Stone and with the Stock. And yet though she was involved in all this guilt (lit. and even in all this. Perhaps the sin and the penalties of it are identified; and the meaning is: And yet for all this liability: cf. Isa. v. 25), the Traitress Judah returned not unto Me with all her heart (with a whole or undivided heart, with entire sincerity [22]) but in falsehood saith Iahvah. The example of the northern kingdom is represented as a powerful influence for evil upon Judah. This was only natural; for although from the point of view of religious development Judah is incomparably the more important of the sister kingdoms; the exact contrary is the case as regards political power and predominance. Under strong kings like Omri and Ahab, or again, Jeroboam II., Ephraim was able to assert itself as a first-rate power among the surrounding principalities; and in the case of Athaliah, we have a conspicuous instance of the manner in which Canaanite idolatry might be propagated from Israel to Judah. The prophet declares that the sin of Judah was aggravated by the fact that she had witnessed the ruin of Israel, and yet persisted in the same evil courses of which that ruin was the result. She sinned against light. The fall of Ephraim had verified the predictions of her prophets; yet "she was not afraid," but went on adding to the score of her own offences, and polluting the land with her unfaithfulness to her Divine Spouse. The idea that the very soil of her country was defiled by Judah's idolatry may be illustrated by reference to the well-known words of Ps. cvi. 38: "They shed innocent blood, even the blood of their sons and their daughters whom they sacrificed unto the idols of Canaan; and the land was defiled with the bloodshed." We may also remember Elohim's word to Cain: "The voice of thy brother's blood is crying unto Me from the ground!" (Gen. iv. 10). As Iahvah's special dwelling-place, moreover, the land of Israel was holy; and foreign rites desecrated and profaned it, and made it offensive in His sight. The pollution of it cried to heaven for vengeance on those who had caused it. To such a state had Judah brought her own land, and the very city of the sanctuary; "and yet in all this"--amid this accumulation of sins and liabilities--she turned not to her Lord with her whole heart. The reforms set on foot in the twelfth year of Josiah were but superficial and half-hearted; the people merely acquiesced in them, at the dictation of the court, and gave no sign of any inward change or deep-wrought repentance. The semblance without the reality of sorrow for sin is but a mockery of heaven, and a heinous aggravation of guilt. Hence the sin of Judah was of a deeper dye than that which had destroyed Israel. And Iahvah said unto me, The Turncoat or Recreant Israel hath proven herself more righteous than the Traitress Judah. Who could doubt it, considering that almost all the prophets had borne their witness in Judah; and that, in imitating her sister's idolatry, she had resolutely closed her eyes to the light of truth and reason? On this ground, that Israel has sinned less, and suffered more, the prophet is bidden to hold out to her the hope of Divine mercy. The greatness of her ruin, as well as the lapse of years since the fatal catastrophe, might tend to diminish in the prophet's mind the impression of her guilt; and his patriotic yearning for the restoration of the banished Ten Tribes, who, after all, were the near kindred of Judah, as well as the thought that they had borne their punishment, and thus atoned for their sin (Isa. xl. 2), might cooperate with the desire of kindling in his own countrymen a noble rivalry of repentance, in moving the prophet to obey the impulse which urged him to address himself to Israel. Go thou, and cry these words northward (toward the desolate land of Ephraim), and say: Return, Turncoat or Recreant Israel, saith Iahvah; I will not let My countenance fall at the sight of you (lit. against you, cf. Gen. iv. 5); for I am loving, saith Iahvah, I keep not anger for ever. Only recognise thy guilt, that thou hast rebelled against Iahvah thy God, and hast scattered (or lavished: Ps. cxii. 9) thy ways to the strangers (hast gone now in this direction, now in that, worshipping first one idol and then another; cf. ii. 23; and so, as it were, dividing up and dispersing thy devotion) under every evergreen tree; but My voice ye have not obeyed, saith Iahvah. The invitation, "Return Apostate Israel!"-- [23] svvh msvh ys--contains a play on words, which seems to suggest that the exile of the Ten Tribes was voluntary, or self-imposed; as if, when they turned their backs upon their true God, they had deliberately made choice of the inevitable consequence of that rebellion, and made up their minds to abandon their native land. So close is the connexion, in the prophet's view, between the misfortunes of his people and their sins.

Return, ye apostate children (again there is a play on words--svvv vnym svvvym--Turn back, ye back-turning sons, or ye sons that turn the back to Me) saith Iahvah; for it was I that wedded you (ver. 14), and am, therefore, your proper lord. The expression is not stranger than that which the great prophet of the Return addresses to Zion: "Thy sons shall marry thee." But perhaps we should rather compare another passage of the book of Isaiah, where it is said: "Iahvah, our God! other lords beside Thee have had dominion over us" (blvnv Isa. xxvi. 13), and render: For it is I that will be your lord; or perhaps, For it is I that have mastered you, and put down your rebellion by chastisements; and I will take you, one of a city and two of a clan, and will bring you to Zion. As a "city" is elsewhere spoken of as a "thousand" (Mic. v. 1), and a "thousand" ('lph) is synonymous with a "clan" (msphchh), as providing a thousand warriors in the national militia; it is clear that the promise is that one or two representatives of each township in Israel shall be restored from exile to the land of their fathers. In other words, we have here Isaiah's doctrine of the remnant, which he calls a "tenth" (Isa. vi. 13), and of which he declared that "the survivors of the house of Judah that remain, shall again take root downwards, and bear fruit upwards" (Isa. xxxvii. 31). And as Zion is the goal of the returning exiles, we may see, as doubtless the prophets saw, a kind of anticipation and foreshadowing of the future in the few scattered members of the northern tribes of Asher, Manasseh and Zebulun, who "humbled themselves," and accepted Hezekiah's invitation to the passover (2 Chron. xxx. 11, 18); and, again, in the authority which Josiah is said to have exercised in the land of the Ten Tribes (2 Chron. xxxiv. 6; cf. 9). We must bear in mind that the prophets do not contemplate the restoration of every individual of the entire nation; but rather the return of a chosen few, a kind of "firstfruits" of Israel, who are to be a "holy seed" (Isa. vi. 13), from which the power of the Supreme will again build up the entire people according to its ancient divisions. So the holy Apostle in the Revelation hears that twelve thousand of each tribe are sealed as servants of God (Rev. vii.).

The happy time of restoration will also be a time of reunion. The estranged tribes will return to their old allegiance. This is implied by the promise, "I will bring you to Zion," and by that of the next verse: And I will give you shepherds after My own heart; and they shall shepherd you with knowledge and wisdom. Obviously, kings of the house of David are meant; the good shepherds of the future are contrasted with the "rebellious" ones of the past (ii. 8). It is the promise of Isaiah (i. 26): "And I will restore thy judges as at the first, and thy counsellors as at the beginning." In this connexion, we may recall the fact that the original schism in Israel was brought about by the folly of evil shepherds. The coming King will resemble not Rehoboam but David. Nor is this all; for It shall come to pass, when ye multiply and become fruitful in the land, in those days, saith Iahvah, men shall not say any more, The ark of the covenant of Iahvah, (or, as LXX., of the Holy One of Israel); nor shall it (the ark) come to mind; nor shall men remember it, nor miss it; nor shall it be made any more (pointing ysh although the verb may be impersonal. I do not understand why Hitzig asserts "Man wird keine andere machen (Movers) oder; sie wird nicht wieder gemacht (Ew., Graf) als wäre nicht von der geschichtlichen Lade die Rede, sondern von ihr begrifflich, können die Worte nicht bedeuten." But cf. Exod. xxv. 10; Gen. vi. 14; where the same verb sh is used. Perhaps, however, the rendering of C. B. Michaelis, which he prefers, is more in accordance with what precedes: nor shall all that be done any more, Gen. xxix. 26, xli. 34. But phqd does not mean nachforschen: cf. 1 Sam. xx. 6, xxv. 15). In that time men will call Jerusalem the throne of Iahvah; and all the nations will gather into it (Gen. i. 9), for the name of Iahvah [at Jerusalem: LXX. om.]; and they (the heathen) will no longer follow the stubbornness of their evil heart (vii. 24; Deut. xxix. 19).

In the new Theocracy, the true kingdom of God, the ancient symbol of the Divine presence will be forgotten in the realization of that presence. The institution of the New Covenant will be characterized by an immediate and personal knowledge of Iahvah in the hearts of all His people (xxxi. 31 sq.). The small object in which past generations had loved to recognise the earthly throne of the God of Israel, will be replaced by Jerusalem itself, the Holy City, not merely of Judah, nor of Judah and Israel, but of the world. Thither will all the nations resort "to the name of Iahvah;" ceasing henceforth "to follow the hardness (or callousness) of their own evil heart." That the more degraded kinds of heathenism have a hardening effect upon the heart; and that the cruel and impure worships of Canaan especially tended to blunt the finer sensibilities, to enfeeble the natural instincts of humanity and justice, and to confuse the sense of right and wrong, is beyond question. Only a heart rendered callous by custom, and stubbornly deaf to the pleadings of natural pity, could find genuine pleasure in the merciless rites of the Molech-worship; and they who ceased to follow these inhuman superstitions, and sought light and guidance from the God of Israel, might well be said to have ceased "to walk after the hardness of their own evil heart." [24] The more repulsive features of heathenism chime in too well with the worst and most savage impulses of our nature; they exhibit too close a conformity with the suggestions and demands of selfish appetite; they humour and encourage the darkest passions far too directly and decidedly, to allow us to regard as plausible any theory of their origin and permanence which does not recognise in them at once a cause and an effect of human depravity (cf. Rom. i.).

The repulsiveness of much that was associated with the heathenism with which they were best acquainted, did not hinder the prophets of Israel from taking a deep spiritual interest in those who practised and were enslaved by it. Indeed, what has been called the universalism of the Hebrew seers--their emancipation in this respect from all local and national limits and prejudices--is one of the clearest proofs of their divine mission. Jeremiah only reiterates what Micah and Isaiah had preached before him; that "in the latter days the mountain of Iahvah's House shall be established as the chief of mountains, and shall be exalted above the hills; and all the nations will flow unto it" (Isa. ii. 2). In ch. xvi. 19 sq. our prophet thus expresses himself upon the same topic. "Iahvah, my strength and my stronghold, and my refuge in the day of distress! unto Thee shall nations come from the ends of the earth, and shall say: Our forefathers inherited nought but a lie, vanity, and things among which is no helper. Shall a man make him gods, when they are no gods?" How largely this particular aspiration of the prophets of the seventh and eighth centuries b.c. has since been fulfilled in the course of the ages is a matter of history. The religion which was theirs has, in the new shape given it by our Lord and His Apostles, become the religion of one heathen people after another, until at this day it is the faith professed, not only in the land of its origin, but by the leading nations of the world. So mighty a fulfilment of hopes, which at the time of their first conception and utterance could only be regarded as the dreams of enthusiastic visionaries, justifies those who behold and realize it in the joyful belief that the progress of true religion has not been maintained for six and twenty centuries to be arrested now; and that these old-world aspirations are destined to receive a fulness of illustration in the triumphs of the future, in the light of which the brightest glories of the past will pale and fade away.

The prophet does not say, with a prophet of the New Covenant, that all Israel shall be saved (Rom. xi. 26). We may, however, fairly interpret the latter of the true Israel, the remnant according to the election of grace, rather than of Israel according to the flesh, and so both will be at one, and both at variance with the unspiritual doctrine of the Talmud, that All Israel, irrespective of moral qualifications, will have a portion in the world to come, on account of the surpassing merits of Abraham, Isaac and Jacob, and even of Abraham alone (cf. St. Matt. iii. 9; St. John viii. 33).

The reference to the ark of the covenant in the sixteenth verse is remarkable upon several grounds. This sacred symbol is not mentioned among the spoils which Nebuzaradan (Nabû-zir-iddin) took from the temple (lii. 17 sqq.); nor is it specified among the treasures appropriated by Nebuchadrezzar at the surrender of Jehoiachin. The words of Jeremiah prove that it cannot be included among "the vessels of gold" which the Babylonian conqueror "cut in pieces" (2 Kings xxiv. 13). We learn two facts about the ark from the present passage: (1) that it no longer existed in the days of the prophet; (2) that people remembered it with regret, though they did not venture to replace the lost original by a new substitute. It may well have been destroyed by Manasseh, the king who did his utmost to abolish the religion of Iahvah. However that may be, the point of the prophet's allusion consists in the thought that in the glorious times of Messianic rule the idea of holiness will cease to be attached to things, for it will be realized in persons; the symbol will become obsolete, and its name and memory will disappear from the minds and affections of men, because the fact symbolized will be universally felt and perceived to be a present and self-evident truth. In that great epoch of Israel's reconciliation, all nations will recognise in Jerusalem the throne of Iahvah, the centre of light and source of spiritual truth; the Holy City of the world. Is it the earthly or the heavenly Jerusalem that is meant? It would seem, the former only was present to the consciousness of the prophet, for he concludes his beautiful interlude of promise with the words: In those days will the house of Judah walk beside the house of Israel; and they will come together from the land of the North [and from all the lands: LXX add. cf. xvi. 15] unto the land that I caused your fathers to possess. Like Isaiah (xi. 12 sqq.) and other prophets his predecessors, Jeremiah forecasts for the whole repentant and united nation a reinstatement in their ancient temporal rights, in the pleasant land from which they had been so cruelly banished for so many weary years.

"The letter killeth, but the spirit giveth life." If, when we look at the whole course of subsequent events, when we review the history of the Return and of the narrow religious commonwealth which was at last, after many bitter struggles, established on mount Sion; when we consider the form which the religion of Iahvah assumed in the hands of the priestly caste, and the half-religious, half-political sects, whose intrigues and conflicts for power constitute almost all we know of their period; when we reflect upon the character of the entire post-exilic age down to the time of the birth of Christ, with its worldly ideals, its fierce fanaticisms, its superstitious trust in rites and ceremonies; if, when we look at all this, we hesitate to claim that the prophetic visions of a great restoration found fulfilment in the erection of this petty state, this paltry edifice, upon the ruins of David's capital; shall we lay ourselves open to the accusation that we recognise no element of truth in the glorious aspirations of the prophets? I think not.

After all, it is clear from the entire context that these hopes of a golden time to come are not independent of the attitude of the people towards Iahvah. They will only be realized, if the nation shall truly repent of the past, and turn to Him with the whole heart. The expressions "at that time," "in those days" (vv. 17, 18), are only conditionally determinate; they mean the happy time of Israel's repentance, if such a time should ever come. From this glimpse of glorious possibilities, the prophet turns abruptly to the dark page of Israel's actual history. He has, so to speak, portrayed in characters of light the development as it might have been; he now depicts the course it actually followed. He restates Iahvah's original claim upon Israel's grateful devotion (ii. 2), putting these words into the mouth of the Divine Speaker: And I indeed thought, How will I set thee among the sons (of the Divine household), and give thee a lovely land, a heritage the fairest among the nations! And methought, thou wouldst call Me 'My Father,' and wouldst not turn back from following Me. Iahvah had at the outset adopted Israel, and called him from the status of a groaning bondsman to the dignity of a son and heir. When Israel was a child, He had loved him, and called His son out of Egypt (Hos. xi. 1), to give him a place and a heritage among nations. It was Iahvah, indeed, who originally assigned their holdings to all the nations, and separated the various tribes of mankind, fixing the territories of peoples, according to the number of the sons of God (Deut. xxxii. 8 Sept.). If He had brought up Israel from Egypt, He had also brought up the Philistines from Caphtor, and the Arameans from Kir (Amos ix. 7). But He had adopted Israel in a more special sense, which may be expressed in St. Paul's words, who makes it the chief advantage of Israel above the nations that unto them were committed the oracles of God. (Rom. iii. 2). What nobler distinction could have been conferred upon any race of men than that they should have been thus chosen, as Israel actually was chosen, not merely in the aspirations of prophets, but as a matter of fact in the divinely-directed evolution of human history, to become the heralds of a higher truth, the hierophants of spiritual knowledge, the universally recognised interpreters of God? Such a calling might have been expected to elicit a response of the warmest gratitude, the most enthusiastic loyalty and unswerving devotion. But Israel as a nation did not rise to the level of these lofty prophetic views of its vocation; it knew itself to be the people of Iahvah, but it failed to realize the moral significance of that privilege, and the moral and spiritual responsibilities which it involved. It failed to adore Iahvah as the Father, in the only proper and acceptable sense of that honourable name, the sense which restricts its application to one sole Being. Heathenism is blind and irrational as well as profane and sinful; and so it does not scruple to confer such absolutely individual titles as "God" and "Father" upon a multitude of imaginary powers.

Methought thou wouldst call Me 'My Father,' and wouldst not turn back from following Me. But (Zeph. iii. 7) a woman is false to her fere; so were ye false to Me, O house of Israel, saith Iahvah. The Divine intention toward Israel, God's gracious design for her everlasting good, God's expectation of a return for His favour, and how that design was thwarted so far as man could thwart it, and that expectation disappointed hitherto; such is the import of the last two verses (19, 20). Speaking in the name of God, Jeremiah represents Israel's past as it appears to God. He now proceeds to shew dramatically, or as in a picture, how the expectation may yet be fulfilled, and the design realized. Having exposed the national guilt, he supposes his remonstrance to have done its work, and he overhears the penitent people pouring out its heart before God. Then a kind of dialogue ensues between the Deity and His suppliants. Hark! upon the bare hills is heard the weeping of the supplications of the sons of Israel, that they perverted their way, forgot Iahvah their God. The treeless hill-tops had been the scene of heathen orgies miscalled worship. There the rites of Canaan performed by Israelites had insulted the God of heaven (vv. 2 and 6). Now the very places which witnessed the sin, witness the national remorse and confession. The 'high-places' are not condemned even by Jeremiah as places of worship, but only as places of heathen and illicit worships. The solitude and quiet and purer air of the hill-tops, their unobstructed view of heaven and suggestive nearness thereto, have always made them natural sanctuaries both for public rites and private prayer and meditation: cf. 2 Sam. xv. 32; and especially St. Luke vi. 12.

In this closing section of the piece (iii. 19-iv. 2) 'Israel' means not the entire people, but the northern kingdom only, which is spoken of separately also in iii. 6-18, with the object of throwing into higher relief the heinousness of Judah's guilt. Israel--the northern kingdom--was less guilty than Judah, for she had no warning example, no beacon-light upon her path, such as her own fall afforded to the southern kingdom; and therefore the Divine compassion is more likely to be extended to her, even after a century of ruin and banishment, than to her callous, impenitent sister. Whether at the time Jeremiah was in communication with survivors of the northern Exile, who were faithful to the God of their fathers, and looked wistfully toward Jerusalem as the centre of the best traditions and the sole hope of Israelite nationality, cannot now be determined. The thing is not unlikely, considering the interest which the prophet afterwards took in the Judean exiles who were taken to Babylon with Jehoiachin (chap. xxix.) and his active correspondence with their leaders. We may also remember that "divers of Asher and Manasseh and Zebulun humbled themselves" and came to keep passover with king Hezekiah at Jerusalem. It cannot, certainly, be supposed, with any show of reason, that the Assyrians either carried away the entire population of the northern kingdom, or exterminated all whom they did not carry away. The words of the Chronicler who speaks of "a remnant ... escaped out of the hand of the kings of Assyria," are themselves perfectly agreeable to reason and the nature of the case, apart from the consideration that he had special historical sources at his command (2 Chron. xxx. 6, 11). We know that in the Maccabean and Roman wars the rocky fastnesses of the country were a refuge to numbers of the people, and the history of David shews that this had been the case from time immemorial (cf. Judg. vi. 2). Doubtless in this way not a few survived the Assyrian invasions and the destruction of Samaria (b.c. 721). But to return to the text. After the confession of the nation that they have perverted their way (that is, their mode of worship, by adoring visible symbols of Iahvah, and associating with Him as His compeers a multitude of imaginary gods, especially the local Baalim, ii. 23, and Ashtaroth), the prophet hears another voice, a voice of Divine invitation and gracious promise, responsive to penitence and prayer: Return, ye apostate sons, let Me heal your apostasies! or If ye return, ye apostate sons, I will heal your apostasies! It is an echo of the tenderness of an older prophet (Hos. xiv. 1, 4). And the answer of the penitents quickly follows: Behold us, we are come unto Thee, for Thou art Iahvah our God. The voice that now calls us, we know by its tender tones of entreaty, compassion and love to be the voice of Iahvah our own God; not the voice of sensual Chemosh, tempting to guilty pleasures and foul impurities, not the harsh cry of a cruel Molech, calling for savage rites of pitiless bloodshed. Thou, Iahvah--not these nor their fellows--art our true and only God.

Surely, in vain (for nought, bootlessly, 1 Sam. xxv. 21; chap. v. 2, xvi. 19) on the hills did we raise a din (lit. 'hath one raised'; reading bgvvt and hrym); surely, in Iahvah our God is the safety of Israel! The Hebrew cannot be original as it now stands in the Masoretic text, for it is ungrammatical. The changes I have made will be seen to be very slight, and the sense obtained is much the same as Ewald's Surely in vain from the hills is the noise, from the mountains (where every reader must feel that from the mountains is a forcible-feeble addition which adds nothing to the sense). We might also perhaps detach the mem from the term for 'hills,' and connect it with the preceding word, thus getting the meaning: Surely, for Lies are the hills, the uproar of the mountains! (lsqrym ... hmvn hrym); that is to say, the high-places are devoted to delusive nonentities, who can do nothing in return for the wild orgiastic worship bestowed on them; a thought which contrasts very well with the second half of the verse: Surely, in Iahvah our God is the safety of Israel!

The confession continues: And as for the Shame--the shameful idol, the Baal whose worship involved shameful rites (chap. xi. 13; Hos. ix. 10), and who put his worshippers to shame, by disappointing them of help in the hour of their need (ii. 8, 26, 27)--as for the Shame--in contrast with Iahvah, the Safety of Israel, who gives all, and requires little or nothing of this kind in return--it devoured the labour of our fathers from our youth, their flocks and their herds, their sons and their daughters. The allusion is to the insatiable greed of the idol-priests, and the lavish expense of perpetually recurring feasts and sacrifices, which constituted a serious drain upon the resources of a pastoral and agricultural community; and to the bloody rites which, not content with animal offerings, demanded human victims for the altars of an appalling superstition. Let us lie down in our shame, and let our infamy cover us! for toward Iahvah our God we trespassed, we and our fathers, from our youth even unto this day, and obeyed not the voice of Iahvah our God. A more complete acknowledgment of sin could hardly be conceived; no palliating circumstances are alleged, no excuses devised, of the kind with which men usually seek to soothe a disturbed conscience. The strong seductions of Canaanite worship, the temptation to join in the joyful merriment of idol-festivals, the invitation of friends and neighbours, the contagion of example,--all these extenuating facts must have been at least as well known to the prophet as to modern critics, but he is expressively silent on the point of mitigating circumstances in the case of a nation to whom such light and guidance had come, as came to Israel. No, he could discern no ground of hope for his people except in a full and unreserved admission of guilt, an agony of shame and contrition before God, a heartfelt recognition of the truth that from the outset of their national existence to the passing day they had continually sinned against Iahvah their God and resisted His holy Will.

Finally, to this cry of penitents humbled in the dust, and owning that they have no refuge from the consequences of their sin but in the Divine Mercy, comes the firm yet loving answer: If thou wilt return, O Israel, saith Iahvah, unto Me wilt return, and if thou wilt put away thine Abominations [out of thy mouth and, LXX.] out of My Presence, and sway not to and fro (1 Kings xiv. 15), but wilt swear 'By the Life of Iahvah!' in good faith, justice, and righteousness; then shall the nations bless themselves by Him, and in Him shall they glory (iv. 1, 2). Such is the close of this ideal dialogue between God and man. It is promised that if the nation's repentance be sincere--not half-hearted like that of Judah (iii. 10; 2 Chron. xxxiv. 33)--and if the fact be demonstrated by a resolute and unwavering rejection of idol-worship, evinced by the disuse of their names in oaths, and the expulsion of their symbols from the Presence, that is, out of the sanctuaries and domain of Iahvah, and by adhering to the Name of the God of Israel in oaths and compacts of all kinds, and by a scrupulous loyalty to such engagements (Ps. xv. 4; Deut. x. 20; Isa. xlviii. 1); then the ancient oracle of blessing will be fulfilled, and Israel will become a proverb of felicity, the pride and boast of mankind, the glorious ideal of perfect virtue and perfect happiness (Gen. xii. 3; Isa. lxv. 16). Then, all the nations will gather together unto Jerusalem for the Name of Iahvah (iii. 17); they will recognise in the religion of Iahvah the answer to their highest longings and spiritual necessities, and will take Israel for what Iahvah intended him to be, their example and priest and prophet.

Jeremiah could hardly have chosen a more extreme instance for pointing the lesson he had to teach than the long-since ruined and depopulated kingdom of the Ten Tribes. Hopeless as their actual condition must have seemed at the time, he assures his own countrymen in Judah and Jerusalem that even yet, if only the moral requirements of the case were fulfilled, and the heart of the poor remnant and of the survivors in banishment aroused to a genuine and permanent repentance, the Divine promises would be accomplished in a people whose sun had apparently set in darkness for ever. And so he passes on to address his own people directly in tones of warning, reproof, and menace of approaching wrath (iv. 3-vi. 30).

Footnotes:

21. She saw: Pesh. This may be right. And the Traitress, her sister Judah, saw it: yea, saw that even because the Turncoat Israel had committed adultery, I put her away.... And yet the Traitress Judah, her sister, was not afraid, etc.

22. 1 Kings ii. 4, b'mt = bkllvvm

23. As if "Turn back, back-turning Israel!" i.e. Thou that turnedst thy back upon Iahvah, and, therefore, upon His pleasant land.

24. Cf. also the Arabic Arabic script pravus, Arabic script pravitas, with the Hebrew term.

IV. THE SCYTHIANS AS THE SCOURGE OF GOD

Jeremiah iv. 3-vi. 30.

If we would understand what is written here and elsewhere in the pages of prophecy, two things would seem to be requisite. We must prepare ourselves with some knowledge of the circumstances of the time, and we must form some general conception of the ideas and aims of the inspired writer, both in themselves, and in their relation to passing events. Of the former, a partial and fragmentary knowledge may suffice, provided it be true so far as it goes; minuteness of detail is not necessary to general accuracy. Of the latter, a very full and complete conception may be gathered from a careful study of the prophetic discourses.

The chapters before us were obviously composed in the presence of a grave national danger; and what that danger was is not left uncertain, as the discourse proceeds. An invasion of the country appeared to be imminent; the rumour of approaching war had already made itself heard in the capital; and all classes were terror-stricken at the tidings.

As usual in such times of peril, the country people were already abandoning the uncalled towns and villages, to seek refuge in the strong places of the land, and, above all, in Jerusalem, which was at once the capital and the principal fortress of the kingdom. The evil news had spread far and near; the trumpet-signal of alarm was heard everywhere; the cry was, Assemble yourselves, and let us go into the fenced cities! (iv. 5).

The ground of this universal terror is thus declared: The lion is gone up from his thicket, and the destroyer of nations is on his way, is gone forth from his place; to make thy land a desolation, that thy cities be laid waste, without inhabitant (ver. 7). A hot blast over the bare hills in the wilderness, on the road to the daughter of my people, not for winnowing, nor for cleansing; a full blast from those hills cometh at My beck (ver. 11). Lo, like clouds he cometh up, and, like the whirlwind, his chariots; swifter than vultures are his horses. Woe unto us! We are verily destroyed (ver. 13). Besiegers (lit. watchmen, Isa. i. 8) are coming from the remotest land, and they utter their cry against the cities of Judah. Like keepers of a field become they against her on every side (vv. 16-17). At the same time, the invasion is still only a matter of report; the blow has not yet fallen upon the trembling people. Behold, I am about to bring upon you a nation from afar, O house of Israel, saith Iahvah; an inexhaustible nation it is, a nation of old time it is, a nation whose tongue thou knowest not, nor understandest (lit. hearest) what it speaketh. Its quiver is like an opened grave; they all are heroes. And it will eat up thine harvest and thy bread, which thy sons and thy daughters should eat; it will eat up thy flock and thine herd; it will eat up thy vine and thy figtree; it will shatter thine embattled cities, wherein thou art trusting, with the sword (v. 15-17). Thus hath Iahvah said: Lo, a people cometh from a northern land, and a great nation is awaking from the uttermost parts of earth. Bow and lance they hold; savage it is, and pitiless; the sound of them is like the sea, when it roareth; and on horses they ride; he is arrayed as a man for battle, against thee, O daughter of Zion. We have heard the report of him; our hands droop; anguish hath taken hold of us, throes, like hers that travaileth (vi. 22 sq.). With the graphic force of a keen observer, who is also a poet, the priest of Anathoth has thus depicted for all time the collapse of terror which befel his contemporaries, on the rumoured approach of the Scythians in the reign of Josiah. And his lyric fervour carries him beyond this; it enables him to see with the utmost distinctness the havoc wrought by these hordes of savages; the surprise of cities, the looting of houses, the flight of citizens to the woods and the hills at the approach of the enemy; the desertion of the country towns, the devastation of fields and vineyards, confusion and desolation everywhere, as though primeval chaos had returned; and he tells it all with the passion and intensity of one who is relating an actual personal experience. In my vitals, my vitals, I quake, in the walls of my heart! My heart is murmuring to me; I cannot hold my peace; for my soul is listening to the trumpet-blast, the alarm of war! Ruin on ruin is cried, for all the land is ravaged; suddenly are my tents ravaged, my pavilions in a moment! How long must I see the standards, must I listen to the trumpet-blast? (iv. 19-21). I look at the earth, and lo, 'tis chaos: at the heavens, and their light is no more. I look at the mountains, and lo, they rock, and all the hills sway to and fro. I look, and lo, man is no more, and the birds of the air are gone, I look, and lo, the fruitful soil is wilderness, and all the cities of it are overthrown (iv. 23-26). At the noise of horseman and archer all the city is in flight! They are gone into the thickets, and up the rocks they have clomb: all the city is deserted (ver. 29). His eye follows the course of devastation until it reaches Jerusalem: Jerusalem, the proud, luxurious capital, now isolated on her hills, bereft of all her daughter cities, abandoned, even betrayed, by her foreign allies. And thou, that art doomed to destruction, what canst thou do? Though thou clothe thee in scarlet, though thou deck thee with decking of gold, though thou broaden thine eyes with henna, in vain dost thou make thyself fair; the lovers have scorned thee, thy life are they seeking. [25] The "lovers"--the false foreigners--have turned against her in the time of her need; and the strange gods, with whom she dallied in the days of prosperity, can bring her no help. And now, while she witnesses, but cannot avert, the slaughter of her children, her shrieks ring in the prophet's ear: A cry, as of one in travail, do I hear; pangs as of her that beareth her firstborn; the cry of the daughter of Zion, that panteth, that spreadeth out her hands: Woe's me! my soul swooneth for the slayers! (vv. 30, 31).

Even the strong walls of Jerusalem are no sure defence; there is no safety but in flight. Remove your goods, ye sons of Benjamin, from within Jerusalem! And in Tekoah (as if Blaston or Blowick or Trumpington) blow a trumpet-blast, and upon Beth-hakkérem raise a signal (or beacon)! for evil hath looked forth from the north, and mighty ruin (vi. 1, 2). The two towns mark the route of the fugitives, making for the wilderness of the south; and the trumpet-call, and the beacon-light, muster the scattered companies at these rallying points or haltingplaces. The beautiful and the pampered one will I destroy-- the daughter of Sion. (Perhaps: The beautiful and the pampered woman art thou like, O daughter of Sion! 3rd fem. sing. in -i.) To her come the shepherds and their flocks; they pitch the tents upon her round about; they graze each at his own side (i.e. on the ground nearest him). The figure changes, with lyric abruptness, from the fair woman, enervated by luxury (ver. 2) to the fair pasture-land, on which the nomad shepherds encamp, whose flocks soon eat the herbage down, and leave the soil stripped bare (ver. 3); and then, again, to an army beleaguering the fated city, whose cries of mutual cheer, and of impatience at all delay, the poet-prophet hears and rehearses. Hallow ye war against her! Arise ye, let us go up (to the assault) at noontide! Unhappy we! the day hath turned; the shadows of eventide begin to lengthen! Arise ye, and let us go up in the night, to destroy her palaces! (vv. 4, 5).

As a fine example of poetical expression, the discourse obviously has its own intrinsic value. The author's power to sketch with a few bold strokes the magical effect of a disquieting rumour; the vivid force with which he realizes the possibilities of ravage and ruin which are wrapped up in those vague, uncertain tidings; the pathos and passion of his lament over his stricken country, stricken as yet to his perception only; the tenderness of feeling; the subtle sweetness of language; the variety of metaphor; the light of imagination illuminating the whole with its indefinable charm; all these characteristics indicate the presence and power of a master-singer. But with Jeremiah, as with his predecessors, the poetic expression of feeling is far from being an end in itself. He writes with a purpose to which all the endowments of his gifted nature are freely and resolutely subordinated. He values his powers as a poet and orator solely as instruments which conduce to an efficient utterance of the will of Iahvah. He is hardly conscious of these gifts as such. He exists to "declare in the house of Jacob and to publish in Judah" the word of the Lord.

It is in this capacity that he now comes forward, and addresses his terrified countrymen, in terms not calculated to allay their fears with soothing suggestions of comfort and reassurance, but rather deliberately chosen with a view to heightening those fears, and deepening them to a sense of approaching judgment. For, after all, it is not the rumoured coming of the Scythian hordes that impels him to break silence. It is his consuming sense of the moral degeneracy, the spiritual degradation of his countrymen, which flames forth into burning utterance. Whom shall I address and adjure, that they may hear? Lo, their ear is uncircumcised, and they cannot hearken; lo, the word of Iahvah hath become to them a reproach; they delight not therein. And of the fury of Iahvah I am full; I am weary of holding it in. Then the other voice in his heart answers: Pour thou it forth upon the child in the street, and upon the company of young men together! (vi. 10, 11). It is the righteous indignation of an offended God that wells up from his heart, and overflows at his lips, and cries woe, irremediable woe, upon the land he loves better than his own life.

He begins with encouragement and persuasion, but his tone soon changes to denunciation and despair (iv. 3 sq.). Thus hath Iahvah said to the men of Judah and to Jerusalem, Break you up the fallows, and sow not into thorns! Circumcise yourselves to Iahvah, and remove the foreskins of your heart, ye men of Judah, and ye inhabitants of Jerusalem! lest My fury come forth like fire, and burn with none to quench it, because of the evil of your doings. Clothed with the Spirit, as Semitic speech might express it, his whole soul enveloped in a garment of heavenly light--a magical garment whose virtues impart new force as well as new light--the prophet sees straight to the heart of things, and estimates with God-given certainty the real state of his people, and the moral worth of their seeming repentance. The first measures of Josiah's reforming zeal have been inaugurated; at least within the limits of the capital, idolatry in its coarser and more repellent forms has been suppressed; there is a shew of return to the God of Israel. But the popular heart is still wedded to the old sanctuaries, and the old sensuous rites of Canaan; and, worse than this, the priests and prophets, whose centre of influence was the one great sanctuary of the Book of the Law, the temple at Jerusalem, have simply taken advantage of the religious reformation for their own purposes of selfish aggrandisement. From the youngest to the oldest of them,

they all ply the trade of greed; and from prophet to priest, they all practice lying. And they have repaired
the ruin of [the daughter] of my people in light fashion, saying, It is well, it is well! though it be not well
(vi. 13, 14). The doctrine of the one legitimate sanctuary, taught with disinterested earnestness by the
disciples of Isaiah, and enforced by that logic of events which had demonstrated the feebleness of the
local holy places before the Assyrian destroyers, had now come to be recognised as a convenient
buttress of the private gains of the Jerusalem priesthood and the venal prophets who supported their
authority. The strong current of national reform had been utilized for the driving of their private
machinery; and the sole outcome of the self-denying efforts and sufferings of the past appeared to be the
enrichment of these grasping and unscrupulous worldlings who sat, like an incubus, upon the heart of
the national church. So long as money flowed steadily into their coffers, they were eager enough to
reassure the doubting, and to dispel all misgivings by their deceitful oracle that all was well. So long as
the sacrifices, the principal source of the priestly revenue, abounded, and the festivals ran their yearly
round, they affirmed that Iahweh was satisfied, and that no harm could befal the people of His care. This
trading in things Divine, to the utter neglect of the higher obligations of the moral law, was simply
appalling to the sensitive conscience of the true prophet of that degenerate age. A strange and a startling
thing it is, that is come to pass in the land. The prophets, they have prophesied in the Lie, and the
priests, they tyrannise under their direction; and My people, they love it thus; and what will ye do for
the issue thereof? (v. 30, 31.) For such facts must have an issue; and the present moral and spiritual ruin
of the nation points with certainty to impending ruin in the material and political sphere. The two things
go together; you cannot have a decline of faith, a decay of true religion, and permanent outward
prosperity; that issue is incompatible with the eternal laws which regulate the life and progress of
humanity. One sits in the heavens, over all things from the beginning, to whom all stated worship is a
hideous offence when accompanied by hypocrisy and impurity and fraud and violence in the ordinary
relations of life. What good to me is incense that cometh from Sheba, and the choice calamus from a far
country? your burnt offerings (holocausts) are not acceptable, and your sacrifices are not sweet unto Me.
Instead of purchasing safety, they will ensure perdition: Therefore thus hath Iahvah said: Lo, I am about
to lay for this people stumblingblocks, and they shall stumble upon them, fathers and sons together, a
neighbour and his friend; and they shall perish (vi. 20 sq.).

In the early days of reform, indeed, Jeremiah himself appears to have shared in the sanguine views
associated with a revival of suspended orthodoxy. The tidings of imminent danger were a surprise to
him, as to the zealous worshippers who thronged the courts of the temple. So then, after all, "the burning
anger of Iahvah was not turned away" by the outward tokens of penitence, by the lavish gifts of
devotion; this unexpected and terrifying rumour was a call for the resumption of the garb of mourning
and for the renewal of those public fasts which had marked the initial stages of reformation (iv. 8). The
astonishment and the disappointment of the man assert themselves against the inspiration of the prophet,
when, contemplating the helpless bewilderment of kings and princes, and the stupefaction of priests and
prophets in face of the national calamities, he breaks out into remonstrance with God. And I said, Alas,
O Lord Iahvah! of a truth, Thou hast utterly beguiled this people and Jerusalem, saying, It shall be well
with you; whereas the sword will reach to the life. The allusion is to the promises contained in the Book
of the Law, the reading of which had so powerfully conduced to the movement for reform. That book
had been the text of the prophet-preachers, who were most active in that work; and the influence of its
ideas and language upon Jeremiah himself is apparent in all his early discourses.

The prophet's faith, however, was too deeply rooted to be more than momentarily shaken; and it
soon told him that the evil tidings were evidence not of unfaithfulness or caprice in Iahvah, but of the
hypocrisy and corruption of Israel. With this conviction upon him, he implores the populace of the
capital to substitute an inward and real for an outward and delusive purification. Break up the fallows!
Do not dream that any adequate reformation can be superinduced upon the mere surface of life: Sow not
among thorns! Do not for one moment believe that the word of God can take root and bear fruit in the
hard soil of a heart that desires only to be secured in the possession of present enjoyments, in immunity
for self-indulgence, covetousness, and oppression of the poor. Wash thine heart from wickedness, O
Jerusalem! that thou mayst be saved. How long shall the schemings of thy folly lodge within thee? For
hark! one declareth from Dan, and proclaimeth folly from the hills of Ephraim (iv. 14 sq.). The "folly"
('awen) is the foolish hankering after the gods which are nothing in the world but a reflexion of the
diseased fancy of their worshippers; for it is always true that man makes his god in his own image,
when he does make him, and does not receive the knowledge of him by revelation. It was a folly
inveterate and, as it would seem, hereditary in Israel, going back to the times of the Judges, and
recalling the story of Micah the Ephraimite and the Danites who stole his images. That ancient sin still
cried to heaven for vengeance; for the apostatizing tendency, which it exemplified, was still active in the
heart of Israel. [26] The nation had "rebelled against" the Lord, for it was foolish and had never really
known Him; the people were silly children, and lacked insight; skilled only in doing wrong, and
ignorant of the way to do right (iv. 22). Like the things they worshipped, they had eyes, but saw not;
they had ears, but heard not. Enslaved to the empty terrors of their own imaginations, they, who

cowered before dumb idols, stood untrembling in the awful presence of Him whose laws restrained the ocean within due limits, and upon whose sovereign will the fall of the rain and increase of the field depended (v. 21-24). The popular blindness to the claims of the true religion, to the inalienable rights of the God of Israel, involved a corresponding and ever-increasing blindness to the claims of universal morality, to the rights of man. Competent observers have often called attention to the remarkable influence exercised by the lower forms of heathenism in blunting the moral sense; and this influence was fully illustrated in the case of Jeremiah's contemporaries. So complete, so universal was the national decline that it seemed impossible to find one good man within the bounds of the capital. Every aim in life found illustration in those gay, crowded streets, in the bazaars, in the palaces, in the places by the gate where law was administered, except the aim of just and righteous and merciful dealing with one's neighbour. God was ignored or misconceived of, and therefore man was wronged and oppressed. Perjury, even in the Name of the God of Israel, whose eyes regard faithfulness and sincerity, and whose favour is not to be won by professions and presents; a self-hardening against both Divine chastisement and prophetic admonition; a fatal inclination to the seductions of Canaanite worship and the violations of the moral law, which that worship permitted and even encouraged as pleasing to the gods; these vices characterized the entire population of Jerusalem in that dark period. Run ye to and fro in the streets of Jerusalem, and see now, and know, and seek ye in the broad places thereof, if ye can find a man, if indeed there be one that doeth justice, that seeketh sincerity; that I may pardon her. And if they say, By the life of Iahvah! even so they swear falsely. Iahvah, are not thine eyes toward sincerity? Thou smotest them, and they trembled not; Thou consumedst them, they refused to receive instruction; they made their faces harder than a rock, they refused to repent. And for me, I said (methought), These are but poor folk; they behave foolishly, because they know not the way of Iahvah, the justice (ver. 1) of their God: let me betake myself to the great, and speak with them; for they at least know the way of Iahvah, the justice of their God: but these with one consent had broken the yoke, had burst the bonds in sunder (v. 1-5).

Then, as now, the debasement of the standard of life among the ruling classes was a far more threatening symptom of danger to the commonwealth than laxity of principle among the masses, who had never enjoyed the higher knowledge and more thorough training which wealth and rank, as a matter of course, confer. If the crew turn drunken and mutinous, the ship is in unquestionable peril; but if they who have the guidance of the vessel in their hands, follow the vices of those whom they should command and control, wreck and ruin are assured.

The profligacy allowed by heathenism, against which the prophets cried in vain, is forcibly depicted in the words: Why should I pardon thee? Thy sons have forsaken Me, and have sworn by them that are no gods: though I had bound them (to Me) by oath, [27] they committed (spiritual) adultery, and into the house of the Fornicatress (the idol's temple, where the harlot priestess sat for hire) they would flock. Stallions roaming at large were they; neighing each to his neighbour's wife. Shall I not punish such offences, saith Iahvah; and shall not My soul avenge herself on such a nation as this? The cynical contempt of justice, the fraud and violence of those who were in haste to become rich, are set forth in the following: Among My people are found godless men; one watcheth, as birdcatchers lurk; they have set the trap, they catch men. Like a cage filled with birds, so are their houses filled with fraud: therefore they are become great, and have amassed wealth. They are become fat, they are sleek; also they pass over (Isa. xl. 27) cases (Ex. xxii. 9, xxiv. 14; cf. also 1 Sam. x. 2) of wickedness--neglect to judge heinous crimes; the cause they judge not, the cause of the fatherless, to make it succeed; and the right of the needy they vindicate not (v. 26-28).

She is the city doomed to be punished! she is all oppression within. As a spring poureth forth its waters, so she poureth forth her wickedness; violence and oppression resound in her; before Me continually is sickness and wounds (vi. 6, 7). There would seem to be no hope for such a people and such a city. The prophet, indeed, cannot forget the claims of kindred, the thousand ties of blood and feeling that bind him to this perverse and sinful nation. Thrice, even in this dark forecast of destruction, he mitigates severity with the promise, yet will I not make a full end. The door is still left open, on the chance that some at least may be won to penitence. But the chance was small. The difficulty was, and the prophet's yearning tenderness towards his people could not blind him to the fact, that all the lessons of God's providence were lost upon this reprobate race: They have belied the Lord, and said, it is not He; neither shall evil come upon us; neither shall we see sword and famine. The prophets, they insisted, were wrong both in the significance which they attributed to occasional calamities, and in the disasters, which they announced as imminent: The prophets will become wind, and the Word of God is not in them; so will it turn out with them. It was, therefore, wholly futile to appeal to their better judgment against themselves: Thus said Iahvah, Stop on the ways, and consider, and ask after the eternal paths, where is the good way, and walk therein, and find rest for your soul: and they said, We will not walk therein. And I will set over you watchmen (the prophets); hearken ye to the call of the trumpet! (the warning note of prophecy) and they said We will not hearken. From such wilful hardness and impenitence, disdaining correction and despising reproof, God appeals to the heathen themselves, and to the dumb earth, to attest the justice of His sentence of destruction against this people: Therefore, hear, O ye nations, and know, and testify what is among them! Hear, O earth! Lo, I am about to bring evil upon this people, the fruit of their own devisings; for unto My words they have not hearkened, and as for Mine instruction, they have rejected it. Their doom was inevitable, for it was the natural and necessary consequence of their own doings: Thine own way and thine Own deeds have brought about these evils for thee; this is thine own evil; verily, it is bitter, verily, it reacheth unto thine heart. The discourse ends with a despairing glance at the moral reprobation of Israel. An assayer did I make thee among My people, a refiner (reading mec?aref, Mal. iii. 2, 3), that thou mightest know and assay their kind (lit. way). Jeremiah's call had been to "sit as a refiner and purifier of silver" in the name of his God: in other words, to separate the good elements from the bad in Israel, and to gather around himself the nucleus of a people "prepared for Iahvah." But his work had been vain. In vain had the prophetic fire burnt within him; in vain had the vehemency of the spirit fanned the flame; the Divine word--that solvent of hearts-- had been expended in vain; no good metal could come of an ore so utterly base. They are all the worst (1 Ki. xx. 43) of rebels (or, deserters to the rebels), going about with slander; they are brass and iron; they all deal corruptly. [28] The bellows blow; the lead (used for fining the ore) is consumed by the fire; in vain do they go on refining (or, does the refiner refine [29]); and the wicked are not separated. Refuse silver are they called, for Iahvah hath refused them.

Footnotes:

25. The modern singer has well caught the echo of this ancient strain.

"Wilt thou cover thine hair with gold, and with silver thy feet?
Hast thou taken the purple to fold thee, and made thy mouth sweet?
Behold, when thy face is made bare, he that loved thee shall hate:
Thy face shall be no more fair at the fall of thy fate."
      Atalanta in Calydon.

26. The second 'awen, however, probably means "trouble," "calamity," as in Hab. iii. 7. The Sept. renders ponos, and this agrees with the mention of Dan in viii. 16. As Ewald puts it, "from the north of Palestine the misery that is coming from the further north is already being proclaimed to all the nations in the south (vi. 18)."

27. With a different point: "When I had fed them to the full" (cf. Hos. xiii. 6).

28. This term--mashchîthîm--is certainly not the plur. of the mashchîth, "pitfall" or "trap," of v. 26. The meaning is the same as in Isa. i. 4. The original force of the root shachath is seen in the Assyrian shachâtu, "to fall down."

29. The form--c?arOf--is like bachOn, "assayer," in ver. 27.

V. POPULAR AND TRUE RELIGION

Jeremiah vii.-x., xxvi.

In the four chapters which we are now to consider we have what is plainly a finished whole. The only possible exception (x. 1-16) shall be considered in its place. The historical occasion of the introductory prophecy (vii. 1-15), and the immediate effect of its delivery, are recorded at length in the twenty-sixth chapter of the book, so that in this instance we are happily not left to the uncertainties of conjecture. We are there told that it was in the beginning of the reign of Jehoiakim son of Josiah, king of Judah, that Jeremiah received the command to stand in the fore-court of Iahvah's house, and to declare to all the cities of Judah that were come to worship there, that unless they repented and gave ear to Iahvah's servants the prophets, He would make the temple like Shiloh, and Jerusalem itself a curse to all the nations of the earth. The substance of the oracle is there given in briefer form than here, as was natural, where the writer's object was principally to relate the issue of it as it affected himself. In neither case is it probable that we have a verbatim report of what was actually said, though the leading thoughts of his address are, no doubt, faithfully recorded by the prophet in the more elaborate composition (chap. vii.). Trifling variations between the two accounts must not, therefore, be pressed.

Internal evidence suggests that this oracle was delivered at a time of grave public anxiety, such as marked the troubled period after the death of Josiah, and the early years of Jehoiakim. All Judah, or all the cities of Judah (xxvi. 2), that is to say, the people of the country towns as well as the citizens of Jerusalem, were crowding into the temple to supplicate their God (vii. 2). This indicates an extraordinary occasion, a national emergency affecting all alike. Probably a public fast and humiliation had been ordered by the authorities, on the reception of some threatening news of invasion. "The opening paragraphs of the address are marked by a tone of controlled earnestness, by an unadorned plainness of statement, without passion, without exclamation, apostrophe, or rhetorical device of any kind; which betokens the presence of a danger which spoke too audibly to the general ear to require artificial heightening in the statement of it. The position of affairs spoke for itself" (Hitzig). The very words with which the prophet opens his message, Thus said Iahvah Sabaoth, the God of Israel, Make good your ways and your doings, that I may cause you to dwell (permanently) in this place! (ver. 3, cf. ver. 7) prove that the anxiety which agitated the popular heart and drove it to seek consolation in religious observances, was an anxiety about their political stability, about the permanence of their possession of the fair land of promise. The use of the expression Iahvah Sabaoth "Iahvah (the God) of Hosts" is also significant, as indicating that war was what the nation feared; while the prophet reminds them thus that all earthly powers, even the armies of heathen invaders, are controlled and directed by the God of Israel for His own sovereign purposes. A particular crisis is further suggested by the warning: Trust ye not to the lying words, 'The Temple of Iahvah, the Temple of Iahvah, the Temple of Iahvah, is this!' The fanatical confidence in the inviolability of the temple, which Jeremiah thus deprecates, implies a time of public danger. A hundred years before this time the temple and the city had really come through a period of the gravest peril, justifying in the most palpable and unexpected manner the assurances of the prophet Isaiah. This was remembered now, when another crisis seemed imminent, another trial of strength between the God of Israel and the gods of the heathen. Only part of the prophetic teachings of Isaiah had rooted itself in the popular mind--the part most agreeable to it. The sacrosanct inviolability of the temple, and of Jerusalem for its sake, was an idea readily appropriated and eagerly cherished. It was forgotten that all depended on the will and purposes of Iahvah himself; that the heathen might be the instruments with which He executed his designs, and that an invasion of Judah might mean, not an approaching trial of strength between His omnipotence and the impotency of the false gods, but the judicial outpouring of His righteous wrath upon His own rebellious people.

Jeremiah, therefore, affirms that the popular confidence is ill-founded; that his countrymen are lulled in a false security; and he enforces his point, by a plain exposure of the flagrant offences, which render their worship a mockery of God.

Again, it may be supposed that the startling word, Add your burnt-offerings to your (ordinary) offerings, and eat the flesh (of them) (vii. 21), implies a time of unusual activity in the matter of honouring the God of Israel with the more costly offerings of which the worshippers did not partake, but which were wholly consumed on the altar; which fact also might point to a season of special danger.

And, lastly, the references to taking refuge behind the walls of 'defenced cities' (viii. 14; x. 17), as we know that the Rechabites and doubtless most of the rural populace took refuge in Jerusalem on the approach of the third and last Chaldean expedition, seem to prove that the occasion of the prophecy was the first Chaldean invasion, which ended in the submission of Jehoiakim to the yoke of Babylon (2 Kings xxiv. 1). Already the northern frontier had experienced the destructive onslaught of the invaders, and rumour announced that they might soon be expected to arrive before the walls of Jerusalem (viii. 16, 17).

The only other historical occasion which can be suggested with any plausibility is the Scythian invasion of Syria-Palestine, to which the previous discourse was assigned. This would fix the date of the prophecy at some point between the thirteenth and the eighteenth years of Josiah (b.c. 629-624). But the arguments for this view do not seem to be very strong in themselves, and they certainly do not explain the essential identity of the oracle summarized in chap. xxvi. 1-6, with that of vii. 1-15. The "undisguised references to the prevalence of idolatry in Jerusalem itself (vii. 17; cf. 30, 31), and the unwillingness of the people to listen to the prophet's teaching, (vii. 27)," are quite as well accounted for by supposing a religious or rather an irreligious reaction under Jehoiakim--which is every way probable considering the bad character of that king (2 Kings xxiii. 37; Jer. xxii. 13 sqq.), and the serious blow inflicted upon the reforming party by the death of Josiah; as by assuming that the prophecy belongs to the years before the extirpation of idolatry in the eighteenth year of the latter sovereign.

And now let us take a rapid glance at the salient points of this remarkable utterance. The people are standing in the outer court, with their faces turned toward the court of the priests, in which stood the holy house itself (Ps. v. 7). The prophetic speaker stands facing them, "in the gate of the Lord's house," the entry of the upper or inner court, the place whence Baruch was afterwards to read another of his oracles to the people (xxxvi. 10). Standing here, as it were between his audience and the throne of Iahvah, Jeremiah acts as visible mediator between them and their God. His message to the worshippers who throng the courts of Iahvah's sanctuary is not one of approval. He does not congratulate them upon their manifest devotion, upon the munificence of their offerings, upon their ungrudging and unstinted readiness to meet an unceasing drain upon their means. His message is a surprise, a shock to their self-satisfaction, an alarm to their slumbering consciences, a menace of wrath and destruction upon them and their holy place. His very first word is calculated to startle their self-righteousness, their misplaced faith in the merit of their worship and service. Amend your ways and your doings! Where was the need of amendment? they might ask. Were they not at that moment engaged in a function most grateful to Iahvah? Were they not keeping the law of the sacrifices, and were not the Levitical priesthood ministering in their order, and receiving their due share of the offerings which poured into the temple day by day? Was not all this honour enough to satisfy the most exacting of deities? Perhaps it was, had the deity in question been merely as one of the gods of Canaan. So much lip-service, so many sacrifices and festivals, so much joyous revelling in the sanctuary, might be supposed to have sufficiently appeased one of the common Baals, those half-womanish phantoms of deity whose delight was imagined to be in feasting and debauchery. Nay, so much zeal might have propitiated the savage heart of a Molech. But the God of Israel was not as these, nor one of these; though His ancient people were too apt to conceive thus of Him, and certain modern critics have unconsciously followed in their wake.

Let us see what it was that called so loudly for amendment, and then we may become more fully aware of the gulf that divided the God of Israel from the idols of Canaan, and His service from all other service. It is important to keep this radical difference steadily before our minds, and to deepen the impression of it, in days when the effort is made by every means to confuse Iahvah with the gods of heathendom, and to rank the religion of Israel with the lower surrounding systems.

Jeremiah accuses his countrymen of flagrant transgression of the universal laws of morality. Theft, murder, adultery, perjury, fraud and covetousness, slander and lying and treachery (vii. 9, ix. 3-8), are charged upon these zealous worshippers by a man who lived amongst them, and knew them well, and could be contradicted at once if his charges were false.

He tells them plainly that, in virtue of their frequenting it, the temple is become a den of robbers.

And this trampling upon the common rights of man has its counterpart and its climax in treason against God, in burning incense to the Baal, and walking after other gods whom they know not (vii. 9); in an open and shameless attempt to combine the worship of the God who had from the outset revealed Himself to their prophets as a "jealous," i.e., an exclusive God, with the worship of shadows who had not revealed themselves at all, and could not be "known," because devoid of all character and real existence. They thus ignored the ancient covenant which had constituted them a nation (vii. 23).

In the cities of Judah, in the streets of the very capital, the cultus of AshtOreth, the Queen of Heaven, the voluptuous Canaanite goddess of love and dalliance, was busily practised by whole families together, in deadly provocation of the God of Israel. The first and great commandment said, Thou shalt love Iahvah thy God, and Him only shalt thou serve. And they loved and served and followed and sought after and worshipped the sun and the moon and the host of heaven, the objects adored by the nation that was so soon to enslave them (viii. 2). Not only did a worldly, covetous and sensual priesthood connive in the restoration of the old superstitions which associated other gods with Iahvah, and set up idol symbols and altars within the precincts of His temple, as Manasseh had done (2 Kings xxi. 4-5); they went further than this in their "syncretism," or rather in their perversity, their spiritual blindness, their wilful misconception of the God revealed to their fathers. They actually confounded Him--the Lord who exercised loving kindness, justice, and righteousness, and delighted in the exhibition of these qualities by His worshippers (ix. 24)--with the dark and cruel sun-god of the Ammonites. They rebuilt the high-places of the Tophet, in the valley of ben Hinnom, on the north side of Jerusalem, to burn their sons and their daughters in the fire; if by means so revolting to natural affection they might win back the favour of heaven--means which Iahvah commanded not, neither came they into His mind (vii. 31). Such fearful and desperate expedients were doubtless first suggested by the false prophets and priests in the times of national adversity under king Manasseh. They harmonized only too well with the despair of a people, who saw in a long succession of political disasters the token of Iahvah's unforgiving wrath. That these dreadful rites were not a "survival" in Israel, seems to follow from the horror which they excited in the allied armies of the two kingdoms, when the king of Moab, in the extremity of the siege, offered his eldest son as a burnt-offering on the wall of his capital before the eyes of the besiegers. So appalled were the Israelite forces by this spectacle of a father's despair, that they at once raised the blockade, and retreated homeward (2 Kings iii. 27). It is probable, then, that the darker and bloodier aspects of heathen worship were of only recent appearance among the Hebrews, and that the rites of Molech had not been at all frequent or familiar, until the long and harassing conflict with Assyria broke the national spirit and inclined the people, in their trouble, to welcome the suggestion that costlier sacrifices were demanded, if Iahvah was to be propitiated and His wrath appeased. Such things were not done, apparently, in Jeremiah's time; he mentions them as the crown of the nation's past offences; as sins that still cried to heaven for vengeance, and would surely entail it, because the same spirit of idolatry which had culminated in these excesses, still lived and was active in the popular heart. It is the persistence in sins of the same character which involves our drinking to the dregs the cup of punishment for the guilty past. The dark catalogue of forgotten offences witnesses against us before the Unseen Judge, and is only obliterated by the tears of a true repentance, and by the new evidence of a change of heart and life. Then, as in some palimpsest, the new record covers and conceals the old; and it is only if we fatally relapse, that the erased writing of our misdeeds becomes visible again before the eye of Heaven. Perhaps also the prophet mentions these abominations because at the time he saw around him unequivocal tendencies to the renewal of them. Under the patronage or with the connivance of the wicked king Jehoiakim, the reactionary party may have begun to set up again the altars thrown down by Josiah, while their religious leaders advocated both by speech and writing a return to the abolished cultus. At all events, this supposition gives special point to the emphatic assertion of Jeremiah, that Iahvah had not commanded nor even thought of such hideous rites. The reference to the false labours of the scribes (chap. viii. 8) lends colour to this view. It may be that some of the interpreters of the sacred law actually anticipated certain writers of our own day, in putting this terrible gloss upon the precept, The firstborn of thy sons shalt thou give unto Me (Ex. xxii. 29).

The people of Judah were misled, but they were willingly misled. When Jeremiah declares to them, Lo, ye are trusting, for your part, upon the words of delusion, so that ye gain no good! (vii. 8) it is perhaps not so much the smooth prophecies of the false prophets as the fatal attitude of the popular mind, out of which those misleading oracles grew, and which in turn they aggravated, that the speaker deprecates. He warns them that an absolute trust in the præsentia Numinis is delusive; a trust, cherished like theirs independently of the condition of its justification, viz., a walk pleasing to God. What! will ye break all My laws, and then come and stand with polluted hands before Me in this house (Isa. i. 15), which is named after Me 'Iahvah's House', (Isa. iv. 1), and reassure yourselves with the thought, We are absolved from the consequences of all these abominations? (vv. 9-10. Lit. We are saved, rescued, secured, with regard to having done all these abominations: cf. ii. 35. But perhaps, with Ewald, we should point the Hebrew term differently, and read, "Save us!" to do all these abominations, as if that were the express object of their petition, which would really ensue, if their prayer were granted: a fine irony. For the form of the verb, cf. Ezek. xiv. 14.) They thought their formal devotions were more than enough to counterbalance any breaches of the decalogue; they laid that flattering unction to their souls. They could make it up with God for setting His moral law at nought. It was merely a question of compensation. They did not see that the moral law is as immutable as laws physical; and that the consequences of violating or keeping it are as inseparable from it as pain from a blow, or death from poison. They did not see that the moral law is simply the law of man's health and wealth, and that the transgression of it is sorrow and suffering and death.

"If men like you," argues the prophet, "dare to tread these courts, it must be because you believe it a proper thing to do. But that belief implies that you hold the temple to be something other than what it really is; that you see no incongruity in making the House of Iahvah a meeting-place of murderers (spelunca latronum: Matt. xxi. 13). That you have yourselves made it, in the full view of Iahvah, whose seeing does not rest there, but involves results, such as the present crisis of public affairs; the national danger is proof that He has seen your heinous misdoings." For Iahvah's seeing brings a vindication of right, and vengeance upon evil (2 Chron. xxiv. 22; Ex. iii. 7). He is the watchman that never slumbers nor sleeps; the eternal Judge, Who ever upholds the law of righteousness in the affairs of man, nor suffers the slightest infringement of that law to go unpunished. And this unceasing watchfulness, this perpetual dispensation of justice, is really a manifestation of Divine mercy; for the purpose of it is to save the human race from self-destruction, and to raise it ever higher in the scale of true well-being, which essentially consists in the knowledge of God and obedience to His laws.

Jeremiah gives his audience further ground for conviction. He points to a striking instance in which conduct like theirs had involved results such as his warning holds before them. He establishes the probability of chastisement by an historical parallel. He offers them, so to speak, ocular demonstration of his doctrine. I also, lo, I have seen, saith Iahvah! Your eyes are fixed on the temple; so are Mine, but in a different way. You see a national palladium; I see a desecrated sanctuary, a shrine polluted and profaned. This distinction between God's view and yours is certain: for, go ye now to My place which was at Shiloh, where I caused My Name to abide at the outset (of your settlement in Canaan); and see the thing that I have done to it, because of the wickedness of My people Israel (the northern kingdom). There is the proof that Iahvah seeth not as man seeth; there, in that dismantled ruin, in that historic sanctuary of the more powerful kingdom of Ephraim, once visited by thousands of worshippers like Jerusalem to-day, now deserted and desolate, a monument of Divine wrath.

The reference is not to the tabernacle, the sacred Tent of the Wanderings, which was first set up at Nob (1 Sam. xxi. 22) and then removed to Gibeon (2 Chron. i. 3), but obviously to a building more or less like the temple, though less magnificent. The place and its sanctuary had doubtless been ruined in the great catastrophe, when the kingdom of Samaria fell before the power of Assyria (721 b.c.).

In the following words (vv. 13-15) the example is applied. And now--stating the conclusion--because of your having done all these deeds (saith Iahvah, LXX. omits), and because I spoke unto you (early and late, LXX. omits), and ye hearkened not, and I called you and ye answered not (Prov. i. 24): I will do unto the house upon which My Name is called, wherein ye are trusting, and unto the place which I gave to you and to your fathers--as I did unto Shiloh.

Some might think that if the city fell, the holy house would escape, as was thought by many likeminded fanatics when Jerusalem was beleaguered by the Roman armies seven centuries later: but Jeremiah declares that the blow will fall upon both alike; and to give greater force to his words, he makes the judgment begin at the house of God. (The Hebrew reader will note the dramatic effect of the disposition of the accents. The principal pause is placed upon the word "fathers," and the reader is to halt in momentary suspense upon that word, before he utters the awful three which close the verse: as I--did to--Shiloh. The Massorets were masters of this kind of emphasis.)

And I will cast you away from My Presence, as I cast (all: LXX. omits [30]) your kinsfolk, all the posterity of Ephraim (2 Kings xvii. 20). Away from My Presence: far beyond the bounds of that holy land where I have revealed Myself to priests and prophets, and where My sanctuary stands; into a land where heathenism reigns, and the knowledge of God is not; into the dark places of the earth, that lie under the blighting shadow of superstition, and are enveloped in the moral midnight of idolatry. Projiciam vos a facie mea. The knowledge and love of God--heart and mind ruled by the sense of purity and tenderness and truth and right united in an Ineffable Person, and enthroned upon the summit of the universe--these are light and life for man; where these are, there is His Presence. They who are so endowed behold the face of God, in Whom is no darkness at all. Where these spiritual endowments are non-existent; where mere power, or superhuman force, is the highest thought of God to which man has attained; where there is no clear sense of the essential holiness and love of the Divine Nature; there the world of man lies in darkness that may be felt; there bloody rites prevail; there harsh oppression and shameless vices reign: for the dark places of the earth are full of the habitations of cruelty.

And thou, pray thou not for this people (xviii. 20), and lift not up for them outcry nor prayer, and urge not Me, for I hear thee not. Seest thou not what they do in the cities of Judah and in the streets of Jerusalem? The children gather sticks, and the fathers light the fire, and the women knead dough, to make sacred buns (xliv. 19) for the Queen of Heaven, and to pour libations to other gods, in order to grieve Me (Deut. xxxii. 16, 21). Is it Me that they grieve? saith Iahvah; is it not themselves (rather), in regard to the shame of their own faces (16-19).

From one point of view, all human conduct may be said to be indifferent to God; He is autarkes, self-sufficing, and needs not our praises, our love, our obedience, any more than He needed the temple ritual and the sacrifices of bulls and goats. Man can neither benefit nor injure God; he can only affect his own fortunes in this world and the next, by rebellion against the laws upon which his welfare depends, or by a careful observance of them. In this sense, it is true that wilful idolatry, that treason against God, does not "provoke" or "grieve" the Immutable One. Men do such things to their own sole hurt, to the shame of their own faces: that is, the punishment will be the painful realization of the utter groundlessness of their confidence, of the folly of their false trust; the mortification of disillusion, when it is too late. That Jeremiah should have expressed himself thus is sufficient answer to those who pretend that the habitual anthropomorphism of the prophetic discourses is anything more than a mere accident of language and an accommodation to ordinary style.

In another sense, of course, it is profoundly true to say that human sin provokes and grieves the Lord. God is Love; and love may be pained to its depths by the fault of the beloved, and stirred to holy indignation at the disclosure of utter unworthiness and ingratitude. Something corresponding to these emotions of man may be ascribed, with all reverence, to the Inscrutable Being who creates man "in His own image," that is, endowed with faculties capable of aspiring towards Him, and receiving the knowledge of His being and character.

Pray not thou for this people ... for I hear thee not! Jeremiah was wont to intercede for his people (xi. 14, xviii. 20, xv. 1; cf. 1 Sam. xii. 23). The deep pathos which marks his style, the minor key in which almost all his public utterances are pitched, proves that the fate which he saw impending over his country, grieved him to the heart. "Our sweetest songs are those which tell of saddest thought;" and this is eminently true of Jeremiah. A profound melancholy had fallen like a cloud upon his soul; he had seen the future, fraught as it was with suffering and sorrow, despair and overthrow, slaughter and bitter servitude; a picture in which images of terror crowded one upon another, under a darkened sky, from which no ray of blessed hope shot forth, but only the lightnings of wrath and extermination. Doubtless his prayers were frequent, alive with feeling, urgent, imploring, full of the convulsive energy of expiring hope. But in the midst of his strong crying and tears, there arose from the depths of his consciousness the conviction that all was in vain. Pray not thou for this people, for I will not hear thee. The thought stood before him, sharp and clear as a command; the unuttered sound of it rang in his ears, like the voice of a destroying angel, a messenger of doom, calm as despair, sure as fate. He knew it was the voice of God.

In the history of nations as in the lives of individuals there are times when repentance, even if possible, would be too late to avert the evils which long periods of misdoing have called from the abyss to do their penal and retributive work. Once the dike is undermined, no power on earth can hold back the flood of waters from the defenceless lands beneath. And when a nation's sins have penetrated and poisoned all social and political relations, and corrupted the very fountains of life, you cannot avert the flood of ruin that must come, to sweep away the tainted mass of spoiled humanity; you cannot avert the storm that must break to purify the air, and make it fit for men to breathe again.

Therefore--because of the national unfaithfulness--thus said the Lord Iahvah, Lo, Mine anger and My fury are being poured out toward this place--upon the men, and upon the cattle, and upon the trees of the field, and upon the fruit of the ground; and it will burn, and not be quenched! (vii. 20). The havoc wrought by war, the harrying and slaying of man and beast, the felling of fruit trees and firing of the vineyards, are intended; but not so as to exclude the ravages of pestilence and droughts (chap. xiv.) and famine. All these evils are manifestations of the wrath of Iahvah. Cattle and trees and "the fruit of the ground," i.e. of the cornlands and vineyards, are to share in the general destruction (cf. Hos. iv. 3), not, of course, as partakers of man's guilt, but only by way of aggravating his punishment. The final phrase is worthy of consideration, because of its bearing upon other passages. It will burn and not be quenched, or it will burn unquenchably. The meaning is not that the Divine wrath once kindled will go on burning for ever; but that once kindled, no human or other power will be able to extinguish it, until it has accomplished its appointed work of destruction.

Thus said Iahvah Sabaoth, the God of Israel: Your holocausts add ye to your common sacrifices, and eat ye flesh! that is, Eat flesh in abundance, eat your fill of it! Stint not yourselves by devoting any portion of your offerings wholly to Me. I am as indifferent to your "burnt-offerings," your more costly and splendid gifts, as to the ordinary sacrifices, over which you feast and make merry with your friends (1 Sam. i. 4, 13). The holocausts which you are now burning on the altar before Me will not avail to alter My settled purpose. For I spake not with your fathers, nor commanded them, in the day that I brought them forth out of the land of Egypt, concerning matters of holocaust and sacrifice, but this matter commanded I them, "Hearken ye unto My voice, so become I God to you, and you--ye shall become to Me a people; and walk ye in all the way that I shall command you, that it may go well with you!" (22-23) cf. Deut. vi. 3. Those who believe that the entire priestly legislation as we now have it in the Pentateuch is the work of Moses, may be content to find in this passage of Jeremiah no more than an extreme antithetical expression of the truth that to obey is better than sacrifice. There can be no question that from the outset of its history, Israel, in common with all the Semitic nations, gave outward expression to its religious ideas in the form of animal sacrifice. Moses cannot have originated the institution, he found it already in vogue, though he may have regulated the details of it. Even in the Pentateuch, the term "sacrifice" is nowhere explained; the general understanding of the meaning of it is taken for granted (see Ex. xii. 27, xxiii. 18). Religious customs are of immemorial use, and it is impossible in most cases to specify the period of their origin. But while it is certain that the institution of sacrifice was of extreme antiquity in Israel as in other ancient peoples, it is equally certain, from the plain evidence of their extant writings, that the prophets before the Exile attached no independent value either to it or to any other part of the ritual of the temple. We have already seen how Jeremiah could speak of the most venerable of all the symbols of the popular faith (iii. 16). Now he affirms that the traditional rules for the burnt-offerings and other sacrifices were not matters of special Divine institution, as was popularly supposed at the time. The reference to the Exodus may imply that already in his day there were written narratives which asserted the contrary; that the first care of the Divine Saviour after He had led His people through the sea was to provide them with an elaborate system of ritual and sacrifice, identical with that which prevailed in Jeremiah's day. The important verse already quoted (viii. 8) seems to glance at such pious fictions of the popular religious teachers: How say ye, We are wise, and the instruction (A. V. "law") of Iahvah is with us? But behold for lies hath it wrought--the lying pen of the scribes!

It is, indeed, difficult to see how Jeremiah or any of his predecessors could have done otherwise than take for granted the established modes of public worship, and the traditional holy places. The prophets do not seek to alter or abolish the externals of religion as such; they are not so unreasonable as to demand that stated rites and traditional sanctuaries should be disregarded, and that men should worship in the spirit only, without the aid of outward symbolism of any sort, however innocent and appropriate to its object it might seem. They knew very well that rites and ceremonies were necessary to public worship; what they protested against was the fatal tendency of their time to make these the whole of religion, to suppose that Iahvah's claims could be satisfied by a due performance of these, without regard to those higher moral requirements of His law which the ritual worship might fitly have symbolized but could not rightly supersede. It was not a question with Hosea, Amos, Micah, Isaiah, Jeremiah, whether or not Iahvah could be better honoured with or without temples and priests and sacrifices. The question was whether these traditional institutions actually served as an outward expression of that devotion to Him and His holy law, of that righteousness and holiness of life, which is the only true worship, or whether they were looked upon as in themselves comprising the whole of necessary religion. Since the people took this latter view, Jeremiah declares that their system of public worship is futile.

Hearken unto My voice: not as giving regulations about the ritual, but as inculcating moral duty by the prophets, as is explained immediately (ver. 25), and as is clear also from the statement that they walked in the schemes of their own evil heart [omit: in the stubbornness, with LXX., and read mô' açôth stat. constr.], and fell to the rear and not the front. As they did not advance in the knowledge and love of the spiritual God, who was seeking to lead them by His prophets, from Moses downwards (Deut. xviii. 15), they steadily retrograded and declined in moral worth, until they had become hopelessly corrupt and past correction. (Lit. and they became back and not face, which may mean, they turned their backs upon Iahvah and His instruction.) This steady progress in evil is indicated by the words, and they hardened their neck, they did worse than their fathers (ver. 26). It is implied that this was the case with each successive generation, and the view of Israel's history thus expressed is in perfect harmony with common experience. Progress, one way or the other, is the law of character; if we do not advance in goodness, we go back, or, what is the same thing, we advance in evil.

Finally, the prophet is warned that his mission also must fail, like that of his predecessors, unless indeed the second clause of ver. 27, which is omitted by the Septuagint, be really an interpolation. At all events, the failure is implied if not expressed, for he is to pronounce a sentence of reprobation upon his people. And thou shalt speak all these words unto them [and they will not hearken unto thee, and thou shalt call unto them, and they will not answer thee: LXX. omits]. And thou shalt say unto them, This is the nation that hearkened not unto the voice of Iahvah its God, and received not correction: Good faith is perished and cut off from their mouth (cf. ix. 3 sq.). The charge is remarkable. It is one which Jeremiah reiterates: see ver. 9, vi. 13, viii. 5, ix. 3 sqq., xii. 1. His fellow-countrymen are at once deceivers and deceived. They have no regard for truth and honour in their mutual dealings; grasping greed and lies and trickery stamp their everyday intercourse with each other; and covetousness and fraud equally characterise the behaviour of their religious leaders. Where truth is not prized for its own sake, there debased ideas of God and lax conceptions of morality creep in and spread. Only he who loves truth comes to the light; and only he who does God's will sees that truth is divine. False belief and false living in turn beget each other; and as a matter of experience it is often impossible to say which was antecedent to the other.

In the closing section of this first part of his long address (vv. 29-viii. 3), Jeremiah apostrophizes the country, bidding her bewail her imminent ruin. Shear thy tresses (coronal of long hair) and cast them away, and lift upon the bare hills a lamentation!--sing a dirge over thy departed glory and thy slain children, upon those unhallowed mountain-tops which were the scene of thine apostasies (iii. 21); for Iahvah hath rejected and forsaken the generation of His wrath. The hopeless tone of this exclamation (cf. also vv. 15, 16, 20) seems to agree better with the times of Jehoiakim, when it had become evident to the prophet that amendment was beyond hope, than with the years prior to Josiah's reformation. His own contemporaries are 'the generation of Iahvah's wrath,' i.e. upon which His wrath is destined to be poured out, for the day of grace is past and gone; and this, because of the desecration of the temple itself by such kings as Ahaz and Manasseh, but especially because of the horrors of the child-sacrifices in the valley of ben Hinnom (2 Kings xvi. 3, xxi. 3-6), which those kings had been the first to introduce in

Judah. Therefore behold days are coming, saith Iahvah, and it shall no more be called the Tophet (an obscure term, probably meaning something like Pyre or Burningplace: cf. the Persian tab-idan "to burn," and the Greek thapto, taph-ein "to bury," strictly "to burn" a corpse; also tupho, "to smoke," Sanskrit dhûp: to suppose a reproachful name like "Spitting" = "Object of loathing," is clearly against the context: the honourable name is to be exchanged for one of dishonour), and the Valley of ben Hinnom, but the Valley of Slaughter, and people shall bury in [the] Tophet for want of room (elsewhere)! A great battle is contemplated, as is evident also from Deut. xxviii. 25, 26, the latter verse being immediately quoted by the prophet (ver. 33). The Tophet will be defiled for ever by being made a burial place; but many of the fallen will be left unburied, a prey to the vulture and the jackal. In that fearful time, all sounds of joyous life will cease in the cities of Judah and in the capital itself, for the land will become a desolation. And the scornful enemy will not be satisfied with wreaking his vengeance upon the living; he will insult the dead, by breaking into the sepulchres of the kings and grandees, the priests and prophets and people, and haling their corpses forth to lie rotting in face of the sun, moon and stars, which they had so sedulously worshipped in their lifetime, but which will be powerless to protect their dead bodies from this shameful indignity. And as for the survivors, death will be preferred to life in the case of all the remnant that remain of this evil tribe, in all the places whither I shall have driven them, saith Iahvah Sabaoth (omit the second that remain, with LXX. as an accidental repetition from the preceding line, and as breaking the construction). The prophet has reached the conviction that Judah will be driven into banishment; but the details of the destruction which he contemplates are obviously of an imaginative and rhetorical character. It is, therefore, superfluous to ask whether a great battle was actually fought afterwards in the valley of ben Hinnom, and whether the slain apostates of Judah were buried there in heaps, and whether the conquerors violated the tombs. Had the Chaldeans or any of their allies done this last, in search of treasure for instance, we should expect to find some notice of it in the historical chapters of Jeremiah. But it was probably known well enough to the surrounding peoples that the Jews were not in the habit of burying treasure in their tombs. The prophet's threat however, curiously corresponds to what Josiah is related to have done at Bethel and elsewhere, by way of irreparably polluting the high places (2 Kings xxiii. 16 sqq.); and it is probable that his recollection of that event, which he may himself have witnessed, determined the form of Jeremiah's language here. [31]

In the second part of this great discourse (viii. 4-23) we have a fine development of thoughts which have already been advanced in the opening piece, after the usual manner of Jeremiah. The first half (or strophe) is mainly concerned with the sins of the nation (vv. 4-13), the second with a despairing lament over the punishment (14-23 = ix. 1). And thou shalt say unto them: Thus said Iahvah, Do men fall and not rise again? Doth a man turn back, and not return? Why doth Jerusalem make this people to turn back with an eternal (or perfect, utter, absolute) turning back? Why clutch they deceit, refuse to return? (The LXX. omits "Jerusalem," which is perhaps only a marginal gloss. We should then have to read svvv shobab for svvvh shobebah, as "this people" is masc. The He has been written twice by inadvertence. The verb, however, is transitive in l. 19; Isa. xlvii. 10, etc.; and I find no certain instance of the intrans. form besides Ezek. xxxviii. 8, participle.) I listened and heard; they speak not aright (Ex. x. 29; Isa. xvi. 6); not a man repenteth over his evil, saying (or thinking), "What have I done?" They all (lit. all of him, i.e. the people) turn back into their courses (plur. Heb. text; sing. Heb. marg.), like the rushing horse into the battle.

There is something unnatural in this obstinate persistence in evil. If a man happens to fall he does not remain on the ground, but quickly rises to his feet again; and if he turn back on his way for some reason or other, he will usually return to that way again. There is a play on the word 'turn back' or 'return,' like that in iii. 12, 14. The term is first used in the sense of turning back or away from Iahvah, and then in that of returning to Him, according to its metaphorical meaning "to repent." Thus the import of the question is: Is it natural to apostatize and never to repent of it? (Perhaps we should rather read, after the analogy of iii. 1, "Doth a man go away (hylk) on a journey, and not return?")

Others interpret: Doth a man return, and not return? That is, if he return, he does it, and does not stop midway; whereas Judah only pretends to repent, and does not really do so. This, however, does not agree with the parallel member, nor with the following similar questions.

It is very noticeable how thoroughly the prophets, who, after all, were the greatest of practical moralists, identify religion with right aims and right conduct. The beginning of evil courses is turning away from Iahvah; the beginning of reform is turning back to Iahvah. For Iahvah's character as revealed to the prophets is the ideal and standard of ethical perfection; He does and delights in love, justice and equity (ix. 23). If a man look away from that ideal, if he be content with a lower standard than the Will and Law of the All-Perfect, then and thereby he inevitably sinks in the scale of morality. The prophets are not troubled by the idle question of medieval schoolmen and sceptical moderns. It never occurred to them to ask the question whether God is good because God wills it, or whether God wills good because it is good. The dilemma is, in truth, no better than a verbal puzzle, if we allow the existence of a personal Deity. For the idea of God is the idea of a Being who is absolutely good, the only Being who is such; perfect goodness is understood to be realized nowhere else but in God. It is part of His essence and conception; it is the aspect under which the human mind apprehends Him. To suppose goodness existing apart from Him, as an independent object which He may choose or refuse, is to deal in empty abstractions. We might as well ask whether convex can exist apart from concave in nature, or motion apart from a certain rate of speed. The human spirit can apprehend God in His moral perfections, because it is, at however vast a distance, akin to Him--a divinæ particula auræ; and it can strive towards those perfections by help of the same grace which reveals them. The prophets know of no other origin or measure of moral endeavour than that which Iahvah makes known to them. In the present instance, the charge which Jeremiah makes against his contemporaries is a radical falsehood, insincerity, faithlessness: they clutch or cling to deceit, they speak what is not right or honest, straightforward (Gen. xlii. 11, 19). Their treason to God and their treachery to their fellows are opposite sides of the same fact. Had they been true to Iahvah, that is, to His teachings through the higher prophets and their own consciences, they would have been true to one another. The forbearing love of God, His tender solicitude to hear and save, are illustrated by the words: I listened and heard ... not a man repented over his evil, saying, What have I done? (The feeling of the stricken conscience could hardly be more aptly expressed than by this brief question.) But in vain does the Heavenly Father wait for the accents of penitence and contrition: they all return--go back again and again (Ps. xxiii. 6)--into their own race or courses, like a horse rushing (lit. pouring forth: of rushing waters, Ps. lxxviii. 20) into the battle. The eagerness with which they follow their own wicked desires, the recklessness with which they "give their sensual race the rein," in set defiance of God, and wilful oblivion of consequences, is finely expressed by the simile of the warhorse rushing in headlong eagerness into the fray (Job xxxix. 25). Also (or even) the stork in the heavens knoweth her appointed times, and turtledove, swift and crane observe the season of their coming; but My people know not the ordinance of Iahvah--what He has willed and declared to be right for man (His Law; jus divinum, relligio divina). The dullest of wits can hardly fail to appreciate the force of this beautiful contrast between the regularity of instinct and the aberrations of reason. All living creatures are subject to laws upon obedience to which their well-being depends. The life of man is no exception; it too is subject to a law--a law which is as much higher than that which regulates mere animal existence, as reason and conscience and spiritual aspiration are higher than instinct and sexual impulse. But whereas the lower forms of life are obedient to the laws of their being, man rebels against them, and dares to disobey what he knows to be for his good; nay, he suffers himself to be so blinded by lust and passion and pride and self-will that at last he does not even recognise the Law--the ordinance of the Eternal--for what it really is, the organic law of his true being, the condition at once of his excellence and his happiness.

The prophet next meets an objection. He has just alleged a profound moral ignorance--a culpable ignorance--against the people. He supposes them to deny the accusation, as doubtless they often did in answer to his remonstrances (cf. xvii. 15, xx. 7 sq.) How can ye say, "We are wise"--morally wise--"and the teaching of Iahvah is with us!" [but behold: LXX. omits: either term would be sufficient by itself] for the Lie hath the lying pen of the scribes made it! The reference clearly is to what Jeremiah's opponents call "the teaching (or law: torah) of Iahvah"; and it is also clear that the prophet charges the "scribes" of the opposite party with falsifying or tampering with the teaching of Iahvah in some way or other. Is it meant that they misrepresented the terms of a written document, such as the Book of the Covenant, or Deuteronomy? But they could hardly do this without detection, in the case of a work which was not in their exclusive possession. Or does Jeremiah accuse them of misinterpreting the sacred law, by putting false glosses upon its precepts, as might be done in a legal document wherever there seemed room for a difference of opinion, or wherever conflicting traditional interpretations existed side by side? (Cf. my remarks on vii. 31.) The Hebrew may indicate this, for we may translate: But lo, into the lie the lying pen of the scribes hath made it! which recalls St. Paul's description of the heathen as changing the truth of God into a lie (Rom. i. 26). The construction is the same as in Gen. xii. 2; Isa. xliv. 17. Or, finally, does he boldly charge these abettors of the false prophets with forging supposititious law-books, in the interest of their own faction, and in support of the claims and doctrines of the worldly priests and prophets? This last view is quite admissible, so far as the Hebrew goes, which, however, is not free from ambiguity. It might be rendered, But behold, in vain, or bootlessly (iii. 23) hath the lying pen of the scribes laboured; taking the verb in an absolute sense, which is not a common use (Ruth ii. 19). Or we might transpose the terms for "pen" and "lying," and render, But behold, in vain hath the pen of the scribes fabricated falsehood. In any case, the general sense is the same: Jeremiah charges not only the speakers, but the writers, of the popular party with uttering their own inventions in the name of Iahvah. These scribes were the spiritual ancestors of those of our Saviour's time, who "made the word of God of none effect for the sake of their traditions" (Matt. xv. 6). For the Lie means, to maintain the popular misbelief. (It might also be rendered, for falsehood, falsely, as in the phrase to swear falsely, i.e., for deceit; Lev. v. 24.) It thus appears that conflicting and competing versions of the law were current in that age. Has the Pentateuch preserved elements of both kinds, or is it homogeneous throughout? Of the scribes of the period we, alas! know little beyond what this passage tells us. But Ezra must have had predecessors, and we may remember that Baruch, the friend and amanuensis of

Jeremiah, was also a scribe (xxxvi. 26).

The "wise" will blush, they will be dismayed and caught! Lo, the word of Iahvah they rejected, and wisdom of what sort have they? (vi. 10). The whole body of Jeremiah's opponents, the populace as well as the priests and prophets, are intended by the wise, that is, the wise in their own conceits (ver. 8); there is an ironical reference to their own assumption of the title. These self-styled wise ones, who preferred their own wisdom to the guidance of the prophet, will be punished by the mortification of discovering their folly when it is too late. Their folly will be the instrument of their ruin, for "He taketh the wise in their own craftiness" as in a snare (Prov. v. 22).

They who reject Iahvah's word, in whatever form it comes to them, have no other light to walk by; they must needs walk in darkness, and stumble at noonday. For Iahvah's word is the only true wisdom, the only true guide of man's footsteps. And this is the kind of wisdom which the Holy Scriptures offer us; not a merely speculative wisdom, not what is commonly understood by the terms science and art, but the priceless knowledge of God and of His will concerning us; a kind of knowledge which is beyond all comparison the most important for our well-being here and hereafter. If this Divine wisdom, which relates to the proper conduct of life and the right education of the highest faculties of our being, seem a small matter to any man, the fact argues spiritual blindness on his part; it cannot diminish the glory of heavenly wisdom.

Some well-meaning but mistaken people are fond of maintaining what they call "the scientific accuracy of the Bible," meaning thereby an essential harmony with the latest discoveries, or even the newest hypotheses, of physical science. But even to raise such a preposterous question, whether as advocate or as assailant, is to be guilty of a crude anachronism, and to betray an incredible ignorance of the real value of the Scriptures. That value I believe to be inestimable. But to discuss "the scientific accuracy of the Bible" appears to me to be as irrelevant to any profitable issue, as it would be to discuss the meteorological precision of the Mahabharata, or the marvellous chemistry of the Zendavesta, or the physiological revelations of the Koran, or the enlightened anthropology of the Nibelungenlied.

A man may reject the word of Iahvah, he may reject Christ's word, because he supposes that it is not sufficiently attested. He may urge that the proof that it is of GOD breaks down, and he may flatter himself that he is a person of superior discernment, because he perceives a fact to which the multitude of believers are apparently blind. But what kind of proof would he have? Does he demand more than the case admits of? Some portent in earth or sky or sea, which in reality would be quite foreign to the matter in hand, and could have none but an accidental connexion with it, and would, in fact, be no proof at all, but itself a mystery requiring to be explained by the ordinary laws of physical causation? To demand a kind of proof which is irrelevant to the subject is a mark not of superior caution and judgment, but of ignorance and confusion of thought. The plain truth is, and the fact is abundantly illustrated by the teachings of the prophets and, above all, of our Divine Lord, that moral and spiritual truths are self-attesting to minds able to realize them; and they no more need supplementary corroboration than does the ultimate testimony of the senses of a sane person.

Now the Bible as a whole is an unique repertory of such truths; this is the secret of its age-long influence in the world. If a man does not care for the Bible, if he has not learned to appreciate this aspect of it, if he does not love it precisely on this account, I, in turn, care very little for his opinion about the Bible. There may be much in the Bible which is otherwise valuable, which is precious as history, as tradition, as bearing upon questions of interest to the ethnologist, the antiquarian, the man of letters. But these things are the shell, that is the kernel; these are the accidents, that is the substance; these are the bodily vesture, that is the immortal spirit. A man who has not felt this, has yet to learn what the Bible is.

In his text as we now have it, Jeremiah proceeds to denounce punishment on the priests and prophets, whose fraudulent oracles and false interpretations of the Law ministered to their own greedy covetousness, and who smoothed over the alarming state of things by false assurances that all was well (vv. 10-12). The Septuagint, however, omits the whole passage after the words, Therefore I will give their wives to others, their fields to conquerors! and as these words are obviously an abridgment of the threat, vi. 12 (cf. Deut. xxviii. 30), while the rest of the passage agrees verbatim with vi. 13-15, it may be supposed that a later editor inserted it in the margin here, as generally apposite (cf. vi. 10 with ver. 9), whence it has crept into the text. It is true that Jeremiah himself is fond of repetition, but not so as to interrupt the context, as the "therefore" of ver. 10 seems to do. Besides, the "wise" of ver. 8 are the self-confident people; but if this passage be in place here, "the wise" of ver. 9 will have to be understood of their false guides, the prophets and priests. Whereas, if the passage be omitted, there is manifest continuity between the ninth verse and the thirteenth: "I will sweep, sweep them away," saith Iahvah; no grapes on the vine, and no figs on the fig tree, and the foliage is withered, and I have given them destruction (or blasting).

The opening threat is apparently quoted from the contemporary prophet Zephaniah (i. 2, 3). The point of the rest of the verse is not quite clear, owing to the fact that the last clause of the Hebrew text is undoubtedly corrupt. We might suppose that the term "laws" (chqym) had fallen out, and render, and I gave them laws which they transgress (cf. v. 22, xxxi. 35). The Vulgate has an almost literal translation, which gives the same sense: "et dedi eis quæ praetergressa sunt." [32] The Septuagint omits the clause, probably on the ground of its difficulty. It may be that bad crops and scarcity are threatened (cf. chap. xiv., v. 24, 25). In that case, we may correct the text in the manner suggested above svrym or brvsn xvii. 18, for yvrvm; or sdphvn Amos iv. 9, for the yvdvm of other MSS.. Others understand the verse in a metaphorical sense. The language seems to be coloured by a reminiscence of Micah vii. 1, 2; and the "grapes" and "figs" and "foliage" may be the fruits of righteousness, and the nation is like Isaiah's unfruitful vineyard (Isa. v.) or our Lord's barren fig tree (Matt. xxi. 19), fit only for destruction (cf. also vi. 9 and ver. 20). Another passage which resembles the present is Hab. iii. 17: "For the fig tree will not blossom, and there will be no yield on the vines; the produce of the olive will disappoint, and the fields will produce no food." It was natural that tillage should be neglected upon the rumour of invasion. The country-folk would crowd into the strong places, and leave their vineyards, orchards and cornfields to their fate (ver. 14). This would, of course, lead to scarcity and want, and aggravate the horrors of war with those of dearth and famine. I think the passage of Habakkuk is a precise parallel to the one before us. Both contemplate a Chaldean invasion, and both anticipate its disastrous effects upon husbandry.

It is possible that the original text ran: And I have given (will give) unto them their own work (i.e., the fruit of it, vdtm: used of field-work, Ex. i. 14; of the earnings of labour, Isa. xxxii. 17). This, which is a frequent thought in Jeremiah, forms a very suitable close to the verse. The objection is that the prophet does not use this particular term for "work" elsewhere. But the fact of its only once occurring might have caused its corruption. (Another term, which would closely resemble the actual reading, and give much the same sense as this last, is vvrm "their produce." This, too, as a very rare expression, only known from Josh. v. 11, 12, might have been misunderstood and altered by an editor or copyist. It is akin to the Aramaic bvr, and there are other Aramaisms in our prophet.) One thing is certain; Jeremiah cannot have written what now appears in the Masoretic text.

It is now made clear what the threatened evil is, in a fine closing strophe, several expressions of which recall the prophet's magnificent alarm upon the coming of the Scythians (cf. iv. 5 with viii. 14; iv. 15 with viii. 16; iv. 19 with viii. 18). Here, however, the colouring is darker, and the prevailing gloom of the picture unrelieved by any ray of hope. The former piece belongs to the reign of Josiah, this to that of the worthless Jehoiakim. In the interval between the two, moral decline and social and political disintegration had advanced with fearfully accelerated speed, and Jeremiah knew that the end could not be far off.

The fatal news of invasion has come, and he sounds the alarm to his countrymen. Why are we sitting still (in silent stupefaction)? assemble yourselves, that we may go into the defenced cities, and be silent (or amazed, stupefied, with terror) there! for Iahvah our God hath silenced us (with speechless terror) and given us water of gall to drink; for we trespassed toward Iahvah. We looked for peace (or, weal, prosperity), and there is no good; for a time of healing, and behold panic fear! So the prophet represents the effect of the evil tidings upon the rural population. At first they are taken by surprise; then they rouse themselves from their stupor to take refuge in the walled cities. They recognise in the trouble a sign of Iahvah's anger. Their fond hopes of returning prosperity are nipped in the bud; the wounds of the past are not to be healed; the country has hardly recovered from one shock, before another and more deadly blow falls upon it. The next verse describes more particularly the nature of the bad news; the enemy, it would seem, had actually entered the land, and given no uncertain indication of what the Judeans might expect, by his ravages on the northern frontier. From Dan was heard the snorting of his horses; at the sound of the neighings of his chargers all the land did quake: and they came in (into the country) and eat up the land and the fulness thereof, a city and them that dwelt therein. This was what the invaders did to city after city, once they had crossed the border; ravaging its domain, and sacking the place itself. Perhaps, however, it is better to take the perfects as prophetic, and to render: "From Dan shall be heard ... shall quake: and they shall come and eat up the land," etc. This makes the connexion easier with the next verse, which certainly has a future reference: For behold I am about to send (or simply, I send) against you serpents, basilisks (Isa. xi. 8, the çif·oni was a small but very poisonous snake; Aquila basiliskos, Vulg. regulus), for whom there is no charm, and they will bite you! saith Iahvah. If the tenses be supposed to describe what has already happened, then the connexion of thought may be expressed thus: all this evil that you have heard of has happened, not by mere ill fortune, but by the Divine will: Iahvah Himself has done it, and the evil will not stop there, for He purposes to send these destroying serpents into your very midst (cf. Num. xxi. 6).

The eighteenth verse begins in the Hebrew with a highly anomalous word, which is generally supposed to mean "my source of comfort" (mvlygyty). But both the strangeness of the form itself, which can hardly be paralleled in the language, and the indifferent sense which it yields, and the uncertainty of the Hebrew MSS., and the variations of the old versions, indicate that we have here another corruption of the text. Some Hebrew copies divide the word, and this is supported by the Septuagint and the Syro-Hexaplar version, which treat the verse as the conclusion of ver. 17, and render "and they shall bite you incurably, with pain of your perplexed heart" (Syro-Hex. "without cure"). But if the first part of the word is "without" (mbly "for lack of" ...), what is the second? No such root as the existing letters imply is found in Hebrew or the cognate languages. The Targum does not help us: Because they were scoffing (mlygyn) against the prophets who prophesied unto them, sorrow and sighing will I bring ('yty) upon them on account of their sins: upon them, saith the prophet, my heart is faint. It is evident that this is no better than a kind of punning upon the words of the Masoretic text. [33] I incline to read "How shall I cheer myself? Upon me is sorrow; upon me my heart is sick." (The prophet would write l not ly for "against," without a suffix. Read mh 'vlygh ly ygvn Job ix. 27, x. 20; Ps. xxxix. 14.) The passage is much like iv. 19.

Another possible emendation is: "Iahvah causeth sorrow to flash forth upon me" (mvlyg yhvh; after the archetype of Amos v. 9); but I prefer the former.

Jeremiah closes the section with an outpouring of his own overwhelming sorrow at the heart-rending spectacle of the national calamities. No reader endued with any degree of feeling can doubt the sincerity of the prophet's patriotism, or the willingness with which he would have given his own life for the salvation of his country. This one passage alone says enough to exonerate its author from the charge of indifference, much more of treachery to his fatherland. He imagines himself to hear the cry of the captive people, who have been carried away by the victorious invader into a distant land: Hark! the sound of the imploring cry of the daughter of my people from a land far away! "Is Iahvah not in Sion? or is not her King in her?" (cf. Mic. iv. 9). Such will be the despairing utterance of the exiles of Judah and Jerusalem; and the prophet hastens to answer it with another question, which accounts for their ruin by their disloyalty to that heavenly King; O why did they vex Me with their graven images, with alien vanities? Compare a similar question and answer in an earlier discourse (v. 19). It may be doubted whether the pathetic words which follow--The harvest is past, the fruit-gathering is finished, but as for us, we are not delivered!--are to be taken as a further complaint of the captives, or as a reference by the prophet himself to hopes of deliverance which had been cherished in vain, month after month, until the season of campaigns was over. In Palestine, the grain crops are harvested in April and May, the ingathering of the fruit falls in August. During all the summer months, Jehoiakim, as a vassal of Egypt, may have been eagerly hoping for some decisive interference from that quarter. That he was on friendly terms with that power at the time appears from the fact that he was allowed to fetch back refugees from its territory (xxvi. 22 sq.). A provision for the extradition of offenders is found in the far more ancient treaty between Ramses II. and the king of the Syrian Chetta (fourteenth cent. b.c.). But perhaps the prophet is alluding to one of those frequent failures of the crops, which inflicted so much misery upon his people (cf. vers. 13, iii. 3, v. 24, 25), and which were a natural incident of times of political unsettlement and danger. In that case, he says, the harvest has come and gone, and left us unhelped and disappointed. I prefer the political reference, though our knowledge of the history of the period is so scanty, that the particulars cannot be determined.

It is clear enough from the lyrical utterance which follows (vv. 21-23), that heavy disasters had already befallen Judah: For the shattering of the daughter of my people am I shattered; I am a mourner; astonishment hath seized me! This can hardly be pure anticipation. The next two verses may be a fragment of one of the prophet's elegies (qinoth). At all events, they recall the metre of Lam. iv. and v.:

Doth balm in Gilead fail?
Fails the healer there?
Why is not bound up
My people's deadly wound?
O that my head were springs,
Mine eye a fount of tears!
To weep both day and night
Over my people's slain.

It is not impossible that these two quatrains are cited from the prophet's elegy upon the last battle of Megiddo and the death of Josiah. Similar fragments seem to occur below (ix. 17, 18, 20) in the instructions to the mourning-women, the professional singers of dirges over the dead.

The beauty of the entire strophe, as an outpouring of inexpressible grief, is too obvious to require much comment. The striking question "Is there no balm in Gilead, is there no physician there?" has passed into the common dialect of religious aphorism; and the same may be said of the despairing cry, "The harvest is past, the summer is ended, and we are not saved!"

The wounds of the state are past healing; but how, it is asked, can this be? Does nature yield a balm which is sovereign for bodily hurts, and is there nowhere a remedy for those of the social organism? Surely that were something anomalous, strange and unnatural (cf. viii. 7). Is there no balm in Gilead? Yes, it is found nowhere else (cf. Plin., Hist. Nat., xii. 25 ad init. "Sed omnibus odoribus præfertur balsamum, uni terrarum Judææ concessum"). Then has Iahvah mocked us, by providing a remedy for the lesser evil, and leaving us a hopeless prey to the greater? The question goes deep down

Rev. C. J. Ball, M.A., & W. H. Bennett, M.A.

to the roots of faith. Not only is there an analogy between the two realms of nature and spirit; in a sense, the whole physical world is an adumbration of things unseen, a manifestation of the spiritual. Is it conceivable that order should reign everywhere in the lower sphere, and chaos be the normal state of the higher? If our baser wants are met by provisions adapted in the most wonderful way to their satisfaction, can we suppose that the nobler--those cravings by which we are distinguished from irrational creatures--have not also their satisfactions included in the scheme of the world? To suppose it is evidence either of capricious unreason, or of a criminal want of confidence in the Author of our being.

Is there no balm in Gilead? Is there no healer there? There is a panacea for Israel's woes--the "law" or teaching of Iahvah; there is a Healer in Israel, Iahvah Himself (iii. 22, xvii. 14), who has declared of Himself, I wound and I heal (Deut. xxxii. 39; chap. xxx. 17, xxxiii. 6). Why then is no bandage applied to the daughter of my people? This is like the cry of the captives, Is Iahvah not in Sion, is not her King in her? (ver. 19). The answer there is, Yes! it is not that Iahvah is wanting; it is that the national guilt is working out its own retribution. He leaves this to be understood here; having framed his question so as to compel people, if it might be, to the right inference and answer.

The precious balsam is the distinctive glory of the mountain land of Gilead, and the knowledge of Iahvah is the distinctive glory of His people Israel. Will no one, then, apply the true remedy to the hurt of the state? No, for priests and prophets and people know not--they have refused to know Iahvah (ver. 5). The nation will not look to the Healer and live. It is their misfortunes that they hate, not their sins. There is nothing left for Jeremiah but to sing the funeral song of his fatherland.

While weeping over their inevitable doom, the prophet abhors with his whole soul his people's wickedness, and longs to fly from the dreary scene of treachery and deceit. O that I had in the wilderness a lodging-place of wayfaring men--some lonely khan on a caravan track, whose bare, unfurnished walls, and blank almost oppressive stillness, would be a grateful exchange for the luxury and the noisy riot of Judah's capital--that I might leave my people and go away from among them! The same feeling finds expression in the sigh of the psalmist, who is perhaps Jeremiah himself: O for the wings of a dove! (Ps. lv. 6 sqq.) The same feeling has often issued in actual withdrawal from the world. And under certain circumstances, in certain states of religion and society, the solitary life has its peculiar advantages. The life of towns is doubtless busy, practical, intensely real; but its business is not always of the ennobling sort, its practice in the strain and struggle of selfish competition is often distinctly hostile to the growth and play of the best instincts of human nature; its intensity is often the mere result of confining the manifold energies of the mind to one narrow channel, of concentrating the whole complex of human powers and forces upon the single aim of self-advancement and self-glorification; and its reality is consequently an illusion, phenomenal and transitory as the unsubstantial prizes which absorb all its interest, engross its entire devotion, and exhaust its whole activity. It is not upon the broad sea, nor in the lone wilderness, that men learn to question the goodness, the justice, the very being of their Maker. Atheism is born in the populous wastes of cities, where human beings crowd together, not to bless but to prey upon each other; where rich and poor dwell side by side, but are separated by the gulf of cynical indifference and social disdain; where selfishness in its ugliest forms is rampant, and is the rule of life with multitudes:--the selfishness which grasps at personal advantage and is deaf to the cries of human pain; the selfishness which calls all manner of fraud and trickery lawful means for the achievement of its sordid ends; and the selfishness of flagrant vice, whose activity is not only earthly and sensual but also devilish, as directly involving the degradation and ruin of human souls. No wonder that they whose eyes have been blinded by the god of this world, fail to see evidence of any other God; no wonder that they in whose hearts a coarse or a subtle self-worship has dried the springs of pity and love can scoff at the very idea of a compassionate God; no wonder that a soul, shaken to its depths by the contemplation of this bewildering medley of heartlessness and misery, should be tempted to doubt whether there is indeed a Judge of all the earth, who doeth right.

***

There is no truth, no honour in their dealings with one another; falsehood is the dominant note of their social existence: They are all adulterers, a throng of traitors! The charge of adultery is no metaphor (chap. v. 7, 8). Where the sense of religious sanctions is weakened or wanting, the marriage tie is no longer respected; and that which perhaps lust began, is ended by lust, and man and woman are faithless to each other, because they are faithless to God.

And they bend their tongue, their bow, falsely. [34] The tongue is as a bow of which words are the arrows. Evildoers "stretch their arrow, the bitter word, to shoot in ambush at the blameless man" (Ps. lxiv. 4; cf. Ps. xi. 2). The metaphor is common in the language of poetry; we have an instance in Longfellow's "I shot an arrow into the air," and Homer's familiar epea pteroenta, "winged words," is a kindred expression. (Others render, and they bend their tongue as their bow of falsehood, as though the term sheqer, mendacium, were an epithet qualifying the term for "bow." I have taken it adverbially, a use justified by Pss. xxxviii. 20, lxix. 5, cxix. 78, 86.) In colloquial English a man who exaggerates a story is said to "draw the long bow."

Their tongue is a bow with which they shoot lies at their neighbours, and it is not by truth--faithfulness, honour, integrity--that they wax mighty in the land; their riches and power are the fruit of craft and fraud and overreaching. As was said in a former discourse, "their houses are full of deceit, therefore they become great, and amass wealth" (v. 27). By truth, or more literally unto truth, according to the rule or standard of truth (cf. Isa. xxxii. 1, "according to right;" Gen. i. 11, "according to its kind"). With the idea of the verb, we may compare Ps. cxii. 2: "Mighty in the land shall his seed become" (cf. also Gen. vii. 18, 19). The passage chap. v. 2, 3, is essentially similar to the present, and is the only one besides where we find the term "by truth" (l'mvnh le'emunah). The idiom seems certain, and the parallel passages, especially v. 27, appear to establish the translation above given; otherwise one might be tempted to render: they stretch their tongue, their bow, for lying (lsqr, v. 2), and it is not for truth that they are strong in the land. "Noblesse oblige" is no maxim of theirs; they use their rank and riches for unworthy ends.

For out of evil unto evil they go forth--they go from one wickedness to another, adding sin to sin. Apparently, a military metaphor. What they have and are is evil, and they go forth to secure fresh conquests of the same kind. Neither good nor evil is stationary; progress is the law of each--and Me they know not, saith Iahvah--they know not that I am truth itself, and therefore irreconcilably opposed to all this fraud and falsehood.

Beware ye, every one of his companion, and in no brother confide ye; for every brother will surely play the Jacob,--and every companion will go about slandering. And they deceive each his neighbour, and truth they speak not: they have trained their tongue to speak falsehood, to pervert (their way, iii. 21) they toil (chap. xx. 9; cf. Gen. xix. 11). Thine inhabiting is in the midst of deceit; through deceit they refuse to know Me, saith Iahvah (3-5). [35] As Micah had complained before him (Mic. vii. 5), and as bitter experience had taught our prophet (xi. 18 sqq., xii. 6), neither friend nor brother was to be trusted; and that this was not merely the melancholy characteristic of a degenerate age, is suggested by the reference to the unbrotherly intrigues of the far-off ancestor of the Jewish people, in the traditional portrait of whom the best and the worst features of the national character are reflected with wonderful truth and liveliness. [36] Every brother will not fail to play the Jacob (Gen. xxv. 29 sqq., xxvii. 36; Hos. xii. 4), to outwit, defraud, supplant; cunning and trickery will subserve acquisitiveness. But though an inordinate love of acquisition may still seem to be specially characteristic of the Jewish race, as in ancient times it distinguished the Canaanite and Semitic nations in general, the tendency to cozen and overreach one's neighbour is so far from being confined to it, that some modern ethical speculators have not hesitated to assume this tendency to be an original and natural instinct of humanity. The fact, however, for which those who would account for human nature upon purely "natural" grounds are bound to supply some rational explanation, is not so much that aspect of it which has been well-known to resemble the instincts of the lower animals ever since observation began, but the aspect of revolt and protest against those lower impulses which we find reflected so powerfully in the documents of the higher religion, and which makes thousands of lives a perpetual warfare.

Jeremiah presents his picture of the universal deceit and dissimulation of his own time as something peculiarly shocking and startling to the common sense of right, and unspeakably revolting in the sight of God, the Judge of all. And yet the difficulty to the modern reader is to detect any essential difference between human nature then and human nature now--between those times and these. It is still true that avarice and lust destroy natural affection; that the ties of blood and friendship are no protection against a godless love of self. The work of slander and misrepresentation is not left to avowed enemies; your own acquaintance will gratify their envy, spite, or mere ill-will in this unworthy way. A simple child may tell the truth; but tongues have to be trained to expertness in lying, whether in commerce or in diplomacy, in politics or in the newspaper press, in the art of the salesman or in that of the agitator and the demagogue. Men still make a toil of perverting their way, and spend as much pains in becoming accomplished villains as honest folk take to excel in virtue. Deceit is still the social atmosphere and environment, and through deceit men refuse to know Iahvah. The knowledge, the recognition, the steady recollection of what Iahvah is, and what His law requires, does not suit the man of lies; his objects oblige him to shut his eyes to the truth. Men do not will and will not, to know the moral impediments that lie in the way of self-seeking and self-pleasing. Sinning is always a matter of choice, not of nature, nor of circumstances alone. To desire to be delivered from moral evil is, so far, a desire to know God.

Thine inhabiting is in the midst of deceit: who that ever lifts an eye above the things of time, has not at times felt thus? "This is a Christian country." Why? Because the majority are as bent on self-pleasing, as careless of God, as heartlessly and systematically forgetful of the rights and claims of others, as they would have been had Christ never been heard of? A Christian country? Why? Is it because we can boast of some two hundred forms or fashions of supposed Christian belief, differentiated from each other by heaven knows what obscure shibboleths, which in the lapse of time have become meaningless and obsolete; while the old ill-will survives, and the old dividing lines remain, and Christians stand apart from Christians in a state of dissension and disunion that does despite and dishonour to Christ, and must be very dear to the devil? Some people are bold enough to defend this horrible condition of things by raising a cry of Free Trade in Religion. But religion is not a trade, not a thing to make a profit of, except with Simon Magus and his numerous followers both inside and outside of the Church.

A Christian country! But the rage of avarice, the worship of Mammon, is not less rampant in London than in old Jerusalem. If the more violent forms of oppression and extortion are restrained among us by the more complete organization of public justice, the fact has only developed new and more insidious modes of attack upon the weak and the unwary. Deceit and fraud have been put upon their mettle by the challenge of the law, and thousands of people are robbed and plundered by devices which the law can hardly reach or restrain. Look where the human spider sits, weaving his web of guile, that he may catch and devour men! Look at the wonderful baits which the company-monger throws out day by day to human weakness and cupidity! Do you call him shrewd and clever and enterprising? It is a sorry part to play in life, that of Satan's decoy, tempting one's fellow-creatures to their ruin. Look at the lying advertisements, which meet your eyes wherever you turn, and make the streets of this great city almost as hideous from the point of view of taste as from that of morality! What a degrading resource! To get on by the industrious dissemination of lies, by false pretences, which one knows to be false! And to trade upon human misery--to raise hopes that can never be fulfilled--to add to the pangs of disease the smart of disappointment and the woe of a deeper despair, as countless quacks in this Christian country do!

A Christian country: where God is denied on the platform and through the press; where a novel is certain of widespread popularity, if its aim be to undermine the foundations of the Christian faith; where atheism is mistaken for intelligence, and an inconsistent Agnosticism for the loftiest outcome of logic and reason; where flagrant lust walks the streets unrebuked, unabashed; where every other person you meet is a gambler in one form or another, and shopmen and labourers and loafers and errand boys are all eager about the result of races, and all agog to know the forecasts of some wily tipster, some wiseacre of the halfpenny press!

A Christian country: where the rich and noble have no better use for profuse wealth than horse-training, and no more elevating mode of recreation than hunting and shooting down innumerable birds and beasts; where some must rot in fever-dens, clothed in rags, pining for food, stifling for lack of air and room; while others spend thousands of pounds upon a whim, a banquet, a party, a toy for a fair woman. I am not a Socialist; I do not deny a man's right to do what he will with his own, and I believe that state interference would be in the last degree disastrous to the country. But I affirm the responsibility before God of the rich and great; and I deny that they who live and spend for themselves alone are worthy of the name of Christian.

A Christian country: where human beings die, year after year, in the unspeakable, unimaginable agonies of canine madness, and dogs are kept by the thousand in crowded cities, that the sacrifice to the fiend of selfishness and the mocking devil of vanity may never lack its victims! There is a more than Egyptian worship of Anubis, in the silly infatuation which lavishes tenderness upon an unclean brute, and credulously invests instinct with the highest attributes of reason; and there is a worse than heathenish besottedness in the heart that can pamper a dog, and be utterly indifferent to the helplessness and the sufferings of the children of the poor. And people will go to church, and hear what the preacher has to say, and "think he said what he ought to have said," or not, as the case may be, and return to their own settled habits of worldly living, as a matter of course. Oh yes! it is a Christian country--the name of Christ has been named in it for fifteen centuries past; and for that reason Christ will judge it.

**

Therefore, thus said Iahvah Sabaoth: Lo, I am about to melt them and put them to proof (Job xii. 11; Judg. xvii. 4; ch. vi. 25.); for how am I to deal in face of [the wickedness of, LXX: the term has fallen out of the Heb. text: cf. iv. 4, vii. 12] the daughter of My people? This is the meaning of the disasters that have fallen and are even now falling upon the country. Iahvah will melt and assay this rough, intractable human ore, in the fiery furnace of affliction; the strain of insincerity that runs through it, the base earthy nature, can only thus be separated and purged away (Isa. xlviii. 10). A deadly arrow [LXX. a wounding one, i.e., one which does not miss, but hits and kills] is their tongue; deceit it spake: with his mouth peace with his companion he speaketh, and inwardly he layeth his ambush (Ps. lv. 22). The verse again specifies the wickedness complained of, and justifies our restoration of that word in the previous verse.

Perhaps, with the Peshito Syriac and the Targum, we ought rather to render: a sharp arrow is their tongue. There is an Arabic saying quoted by Lane, "Thou didst sharpen thy tongue against us," which seems to present a kindred root [37] (cf. Ps. lii. 3, lvii. 4; Prov. xxv. 18). The Septuagint may be right, with its probable reading: deceit are the words of his mouth. This certainly improves the symmetry of the verse.

For such things (emphatic) shall I not--or should I not, with an implied ought--shall I not punish them, saith Iahvah, or on such a nation shall not My soul avenge herself? (v. 9, 29, after which the LXX. omits them here.) These questions, like the previous one, How am I to deal--or, how could I act--in face of the wickedness of the daughter of My people? imply the moral necessity of the threatened evils. If Iahweh be what He has taught man's conscience that He is, national sin must involve national suffering, and national persistence in sin must involve national ruin. Therefore He will melt and try this people, both for their punishment and their reformation, if it may be so. For punishment is properly retributive, whatever may be alleged to the contrary. Conscience tells us that we deserve to suffer for ill-doing, and conscience is a better guide than ethical or sociological speculators who have lost faith in God. But God's chastisements as known to our experience, that is to say, in the present life, are reformatory as well as retributive; they compel us to recollect, they bring us, like the Prodigal, back to ourselves, out of the distractions of a sinful career, they humble us with the discovery that we have a Master, that there is a Power above ourselves and our apparently unlimited capacity to choose evil and to do it: and so by Divine grace we may become contrite and be healed and restored.

The prophet thus, perhaps, discerns a faint glimmer of hope, but his sky darkens again immediately. The land is already to a great extent desolate, through the ravages of the invaders, or through severe droughts (cf. iv. 25, viii. 20(?), xii. 4). Upon the mountains will I lift up weeping and wailing, and upon the pastures of the prairie a lamentation, for they have been burnt up (ii. 15; 2 Kings xxii. 13), so that no man passeth over them, and they have not heard the cry of the cattle: from the birds of the air to the beasts, they are fled, are gone (iv. 25). The perfects may be prophetic and announce what is certain to happen hereafter. The next verse, at all events, is unambiguous in this respect: And I will make Jerusalem into heaps, a haunt of jackals; and the cities of Judah will I make a desolation without inhabitant. Not only the country districts, but the fortified towns, and Jerusalem itself, the heart and centre of the nation, will be desolated. Sennacherib boasts that he took forty-six strong cities, and "little towns without number," and carried off 200,150 male and female captives, and an immense booty in cattle, before proceeding to invest Jerusalem itself; a state which shews how severe the sufferings of Judah might be, before the enemy struck at its vitals.

In the words I will make Jerusalem heaps, there is not necessarily a change of subject. Jeremiah was authorized to "root up and pull down and destroy" in the name of Iahvah.

He now challenges the popular wise men (viii. 8, 9) to account for what, on their principles, must appear an inexplicable phenomenon. Who is the (true) wise man, so that he understands this (Hos. xiv. 9), and who is he to whom the mouth of Iahvah hath spoken, so that he can explain it [unto you? LXX.]. Why is the land undone, burnt up like the prairie, without a passer by? Both to Jeremiah and to his adversaries the land was Iahvah's land; what befel it must have happened by His will, or at least with His consent. Why had He suffered the repeated ravages of foreign invaders to desolate His own portion, where, if anywhere on earth, He must display His power and the proof of His deity? Not for lack of sacrifices, for these were not neglected. Only one answer was possible, to those who recognised the validity of the Book of the Law, and the binding character of the covenant which it embodied. The people and their wise men cannot account for the national calamities; Jeremiah himself can only do so, because he is inwardly taught by Iahvah himself (ver. 12): And Iahvah said. It may be supposed that ver. 11 states the popular dilemma, the anxious question which they put to the official prophets, whose guidance they accepted. The prophets could give no reasonable or satisfying answer, because their teaching hitherto had been that Iahvah could be appeased "with thousands of rams, and ten thousand torrents of oil" (Mic. vi. 7). On such conditions they had promised peace, and their teaching had been falsified by events. Therefore Jeremiah gives the true answer for Iahvah. But why did not the people cease to believe those whose word was thus falsified? Perhaps the false prophets would reply to objectors, as the refugees in Egypt answered Jeremiah's reproof of their renewed worship of the Queen of Heaven: "It was in the years that followed the abolition of this worship that our national disasters began" (xliv. 18). It is never difficult to delude those whose evil and corrupt hearts make them desire nothing so much as to be deluded.

And Iahvah said: Because they forsook (lit. upon = on account of their forsaking) "My Law which I set before them" (Deut. iv. 18), and they hearkened not unto My voice (Deut. xxviii. 15), and walked not therein (in My Law; LXX. omits the clause); and walked after the obstinacy of their own (evil: LXX.) heart, and after the Baals (Deut. iv. 3) which their fathers taught them--instead of teaching them the laws of Iahvah (Deut. xi. 19). Such were, and had always been, the terms of the answer of Iahvah's true prophets. Do you ask upon what ground ('al mah) misfortune has overtaken you? Upon the ground of your having forsaken Iahvah's "law" or instruction, His doctrine concerning Himself and your consequent obligations towards Him. They had this teaching in the Book of the Law, and had solemnly undertaken to observe it, in that great national assembly of the eighteenth year of Josiah. And they had had it from the first in the living utterances of the prophets.

This, then, is the reason why the land is waste and deserted. And therefore--because past and present experience is an index of the future, for Iahvah's character and purpose are constant--therefore the desolation of the cities of Judah and of Jerusalem itself, will ere long be accomplished. Therefore thus said Iahvah Sabaoth, the God of Armies and the God of Israel; Lo, I am about to feed them--or, I continue to feed them--to wit, this people (an epexegetical gloss omitted by the LXX.) with wormwood, and I will give them to drink waters of gall (Deut. xxix. 17. An Israelite inclining to foreign gods is "a root bearing wormwood and gall"--bearing a bitter harvest of defeat, a cup of deadly disaster for his people; cf. Am. vi. 12), and I will "scatter them among the nations," "whom they and their fathers knew not" (Deut. xxviii. 36, 64). The last phrase is remarkable as evidence of the isolation of Israel, whose country lay off the beaten track between the Trans-Euphratean empires and Egypt, which ran along the sea-coast. They knew not Assyria, until Tiglath Pileser's intervention (circ. 734), nor Babylon till the times of the New Empire. In Hezekiah's day, Babylon is still "a far country" (2 Kings xx. 14). Israel was in fact an agricultural people, trading directly with Phenicia and Egypt, but not with the lands beyond the Great River. The prophets heighten the horror of exile by the strangeness of the land whither Israel is to be banished.

And I will send after them the sword, until I have consumed them. The survivors are to be cut off (cf. viii. 3); there is no reserve, as in iv. 27, v. 10, 18; a "full end" is announced; which, again, corresponds to the aggravation of social and private evils in the time of Jehoiakim, and the prophet's despair of reform.

The judgment of Judah is the ruin of her cities, the dispersion of her people in foreign lands, and extermination by the sword. Nothing is left for this doomed nation but to sing its funeral song; to send for the professional wailing women, that they may come and chant their dirges, not over the dead but over the living who are condemned to die: Thus said Iahvah Sabaoth (here as in ver. 6, LXX. omits the expressive Sabaoth), Mark ye well the present crisis, and what it implies (cf. ii. 10; LXX. wrongly omits this emphatic term), and summon the women that sing dirges, that they come, and unto the skilful women send ye, that they come [LXX. omits], and hasten [LXX. and speak and] to lift up the death-wail over us, that our eyes may run down with tears, and our eyelids pour down waters. The "singing women" of 2 Chron. xxxv. 25, or the "minstrels" of St. Matt. ix. 23, are intended. The reason assigned for thus inviting them assumes that the prophet's forecast is already fulfilled. Already, as in viii. 19, Jeremiah hears the loud wailing of the captives as they are driven away from their ruined homes: For the sound of the death-wail is heard from Sion, "How are we undone! We are sore ashamed"--of our false confidence and foolish security and deceitful hopes--"for, after all, we have left the land, for our dwellings have cast (us) out!" The last two lines appear to be parallels, which is against the rendering, For men have cast down our dwellings. Cf. Lev. xviii. 25; chap. xxii. 28. From the wailing women, the address now seems to turn to the Judean women generally; but perhaps the former are still intended, as their peculiar calling was probably hereditary and passed on from mother to daughter: For hear, ye women, the word of Iahvah, and let your ear take in the word of His mouth! and teach ye your daughters the death-wail, and each her companion the lamentation; for

> "Death scales our lattices,
> Enters our palaces,
> To cut off boy without,
> The young men from the streets."

And the corpses of men will fall--the tense certifies the future reference of the others--like dung (viii. 2) on the face of the field (2 Kings ix. 37, of Jezebel's corpse)--left without burial rites to rot and fatten the soil--and like the corn-swath behind the reaper, and none shall gather (them). The quatrain (ver. 20) is possibly quoted from some familiar elegy; and the allusion seems to be to a mysterious visitation like the plague, which used to be known in Europe as "the Black Death" (cf. xv. 2, xviii. 21, xliii. 11). In this time of closed gates and barred doors, death is represented as entering the house, not by the door, but "climbing up some other way" like a thief (Joel ii. 9; St. John x. 1). Bars and bolts will be futile against such an invader. The figure is not continued in the second half of the stanza. [38] The point of the closing comparison seems to be that whereas the corn-swaths are gathered up in sheaves and taken home, the bodies will lie where the reaper Death cuts them down.

Thus said Iahvah: Let not a wise man glory in his wisdom, and let not the mighty man glory in his might! Let not a rich man glory in his riches, but in this let him glory that glorieth, in being prudent and knowing Me (LXX. omits pronoun, cf. Gen. i. 4), that I, Iahvah, do lovingkindness (and: LXX. and Orientals), justice and righteousness upon the earth; for in these I delight, saith Iahvah.

It is not easy, at first sight, to see the connexion of this, one of the finest and deepest of Jeremiah's oracles, with the sentence of destruction which precedes it. It is not satisfactory to regard it as stating "the only means of escape and the reason why it is not used" (the latter being set forth in vv. 24, 25); for the leading idea of the whole composition, from vii. 13 to ix. 22, is that retribution is coming, and no escape, not even that of a remnant, is contemplated. The passage looks like an appendix to the previous pieces, such as the prophet might have added at a later period when the crisis was over, and the country had begun to breathe again, after the shock of invasion had rolled away. And this impression is confirmed by its contents. We have no details about the first interference of the new Chaldean power in Judah; we only read that in Jehoiakim's days Nebuchadrezzar the king of Babylon came up, and Jehoiakim became his servant three years: then he turned and rebelled against him (2 Kings xxiv. 1). But before this, for some two or three years, Jehoiakim was the vassal of the king of Egypt to whom he owed his crown, and Nebuchadrezzar had to reduce Necho before he could attend to Jehoiakim. It may be, therefore, that the worst apprehensions of the time not having been realized, in the year or two of lull which followed, the politicians of Judah began to boast of their foresight and the caution and sagacity of their measures for the public safety, instead of ascribing the respite to God; the warrior class might vaunt the bravery which it had exhibited or intended to exhibit in the service of the country; and the rich nobles might exult in the apparent security of their treasures and the new lease of enjoyment accorded to themselves. To these various classes, who would not be slow to ridicule his dark forebodings as those of a moody and unpatriotic pessimist (xx. 7, xxvi. 11, xxix. 26, xxxvii. 13), Jeremiah now speaks, to remind them that if the danger is over for the present, it is the lovingkindness and the righteous government of Iahvah which has removed it, and to declare that it is only suspended and postponed, not abolished for ever: Behold, days are coming, saith Iahvah, when I will visit (his guilt) upon every one that is circumcised in foreskin (only, and not in heart also): upon Egypt and upon Judah, and upon Edom and upon the benê Ammon and upon Moab, and upon all the tonsured folk that dwell in the wilderness: For all the nations are uncircumcised, and all the house of Israel are uncircumcised in heart. Egypt is mentioned first, as the leading nation, to which at the time the petty states of the west looked for help in their struggle against Babylon (cf. xxvii. 3). The prophet numbers Judah with the rest, not only as a member of the same political group, but as standing upon the same level of unspiritual life. Like Israel, Egypt also practised circumcision, and both the context here requires and their kinship with the Hebrews makes it probable that the other peoples mentioned observed the same custom (Herod., ii. 36, 104), which is actually portrayed in a wall-painting at Karnak. The "tonsured folk" or "cropt-heads" of the wilderness are north Arabian nomads like the Kedarenes (xlix. 28, 32), and the tribes of Dedan, Tema and Buz (xxv. 23), whose ancestor was the circumcised Ishmael (Gen. xxv. 13 sqq., xvii. 23). Herodotus records their custom of shaving the temples all round, and leaving a tuft of hair on the top of the head (Herod., iii. 8), which practice, like circumcision, had a religious significance, and was forbidden to the Israelites (Lev. xix. 27, xxi. 5).

Now why does Jeremiah mention circumcision at all? The case is, I think, parallel to his mention of another external distinction of the popular religion, the Ark of the Covenant (iii. 15). Just as in that place God promises shepherds according to Mine heart which shall shepherd the restored Israel with knowledge and prudence, and then directly adds that, in the light and truth of those days, the ark will be forgotten (iii. 15, 16); so here, he bids the ruling classes, the actual shepherds of the nation, not to trust in their own wisdom or valour or wealth (cf. xvii. 5 sqq.), but in being prudent and knowing Iahvah, and then adds that the outward sign of circumcision, upon which the people prided themselves as the mark of their dedication to Iahvah, was in itself of no value, apart from a "circumcised heart," i.e., a heart purified of selfish aims and devoted to the will and glory of God (iv. 4). So far as Iahvah is concerned, all Judah's heathen neighbours are uncircumcised, in spite of their observance of the outward rite. The Jews themselves would hardly admit the validity of heathen circumcision, because the manner of it was different, just as at this day the Muhammadan method differs from the Jewish. But Jeremiah puts "all the house of Israel," who were circumcised in the orthodox manner, on a level with the imperfectly circumcised heathen peoples around them. All alike are uncircumcised before God; those who have the orthodox rite, and those who have but an inferior semblance of it; and all alike will in the day of judgment be visited for their sins (cf. Amos i.).

With the increasing carelessness of moral obligations, an increasing importance would be attached to the observance of such a rite as circumcision, which was popularly supposed to devote a man to Iahvah in such sense that the tie was indissoluble. Jeremiah says plainly that this is a mistaken view. The outward sign must have an inward and spiritual grace corresponding thereto; else the Judeans are no better than those whose circumcision they despise as defective. His meaning is that of the Apostle, "Circumcision verily profiteth, if thou keep the law; but if thou be a breaker of law, thy circumcision hath become uncircumcision" (Rom. ii. 25). "Circumcision is nothing, and uncircumcision is nothing, but the keeping of the commandments of God," scil. is everything (1 Cor. vii. 19). It is "faith working by love," it is the "new creature" that is essential in spiritual religion (Gal. v. 6, vi. 15).

Hæc dicit Dominus: Non glorietur sapiens in sapientia sua. Glancing back over the whole passage, we discern an inward relation between these verses and the preceding discourse. It is not the outward props of state-craft, and strong battalions, and inexhaustible wealth, that really and permanently uphold a nation; not these, but the knowledge of Iahvah, a just insight into the true nature of God, and a national life regulated in all its departments by that insight. At the outset of this third section of his discourse (ix. 3-6), Jeremiah declared that corrupt Israel knew not and refused to know its God. At the beginning of the entire piece (vii. 3 sq.), he urged his countrymen to amend their ways and their doings, and not go on trusting in lying words and doing the opposite of lovingkindness and justice and righteousness, which alone are pleasing to Iahvah (Mic. vi. 8), Who delighteth in lovingkindness and not sacrifice, and in the knowledge of God more than in burnt-offerings (Hos. vi. 6). And just as in the opening section the sacrificial worship was disparaged, taken as an "opus operatum," so here at the close circumcision is declared to have no independent value as a means of securing Divine favour (ix. 25). Thus the entire discourse is rounded off by the return of the end to the beginning; and the main thought of the whole, which Jeremiah has developed and enforced with so much variety of feeling and oratorical and poetical ornament, is the eternally true thought that a service of God which is purely external is no service at all, and that rites without a loving obedience are an insult to the Majesty of Heaven.

 x. 17-25. The latter part of chap. x. resumes the subject suspended at ix. 22. It evidently contemplates the speedy departure of the people into banishment. Away out of the land with thy pack (or thy goods; LXX. hupostasis, "property," Targ. "merchandise," the Heb. term, which is related to "Canaan," occurs here only), O thou that sittest in distress! (or abidest in the siege: lii. 5; 2 Kings xxiv. 10). Sion is addressed, and bidden to prepare her scanty bundle of bare necessaries for the march into exile. So Egypt is bidden to "make for herself vessels of exile," xlvi. 19. Some think that Sion is warned to withdraw her goods from the open country to the protection of her strong walls, before the siege begins, as in viii. 14; but we have passed that stage in the development of the piece, and the next verse seems to shew the meaning: For thus hath Iahvah said, Lo, I am about to sling forth the inhabitants of the land this time--as opposed to former occasions, when the enemy retired unsuccessful (2 Kings xvi. 5, xix. 36), or went off satisfied with plunder or an indemnity, like the Scythians (see also 2 Kings xiv. 14)--and I will distress them that they may find out the truth, which now they refuse to see. The aposiopesis that they may find out! is very striking. The Vulgate renders the verb in the passive: "Tribulabo eos ita ut inveniantur." This, however, does not give so good a sense as the Masoretic pointing, and Ewald's reference of the term to the goods of the panic-stricken fugitives seems flat and tasteless ("the inhabitants of the land will this time ... not be able to hide their goods from the enemy!"). The best comment on the phrase is supplied by a later oracle: Lo, I am about to make them know this time--I will make them know My hand and My might; that they may know that My name is Iahvah (xvi. 21). Cf. also xvii. 9; Eccles. viii. 17.

 The last verse (17) resembles a poetical quotation; and this one looks like the explication of it. There the population is personified as a woman; here we have instead the plain prose expression, "inhabitants of the land." The figurative, "I will sling them forth" or "cast them out," explains the bidding of Sion to pack up her bundle or belongings--there seems to be a touch of contempt in this isolated word, as much as to signify that the people must go forth into exile with no more of their possessions than they can carry like a beggar in a bundle. The expression, "I will distress them," seems to shew that "thou that sittest in the distress" is proleptic, or to be rendered "thou that art to sit in distress," which comes to the same thing.

***

 And now the prophet imagines the distress and the remorse of this forlorn mother, as it will manifest itself when her house is ruined and her children are gone and she realizes the folly of the past (cf. iv. 31):--

> *"Woe's me for my wound!*
> *Fatal is my stroke!"*

(perhaps quoted from a familiar elegy). And yet I--I thought (chap. xxii. 21; Ps. xxx. 7), Only this--no more than this--is my sickness: I can bear it! (chlyy 's'n 'k vh; LXX. sou, Vulg. mea). The people had never fully realized the threatenings of the prophets, until they began to be accomplished. When they heard them, they had said, half-incredulously, half-mockingly, Is that all? Their false guides, too, had treated apparent danger as a thing of little moment, assuring them that their half reforms, and zealous outward worship, were sufficient to turn away the Divine displeasure (vi. 14). And so they said to themselves, as sinners are still in the habit of saying, "If the worst come to the worst, I can bear it. Besides, God is merciful, and things may turn out better for frail humanity than your preachers of wrath and woe predict. Meanwhile--I shall do as I please, and take my chance of the issue."

 The lament of the mourning mother continues: My tent is laid waste and all my cords are broken; My sons went forth of me (to battle) and are not; There is none to spread my tent any more, And to set up my curtains (cf. Amos ix. 11). Overhearing, as it were, this sorrowful lamentation (qinah), the prophet interposes with the reason of the calamity: For the shepherds became brutish or behaved foolishly, stulte egerunt (Vulg.)--the leaders of the nation shewed themselves as insensate and silly as cattle--and Iahvah they sought not (ii. 8); Therefore--as they had no regard for Divine counsel--they dealt not wisely (iii. 15, ix. 23, xx. 11), and all their flock was scattered abroad.

Once more, and for the last time, the prophet sounds the alarm: Hark! a rumour! lo, it cometh! and a great uproar from the land of the north; to make the cities of Judah a desolation, a haunt of jackals! It is not likely that the verse is to be regarded as spoken by the mourning country; she contemplates the evil as already done, whereas here it is only imminent (cf. iv. 6, vi. 22, i. 15). The piece concludes with a prayer (vv. 23-25), which may be considered either as an intercession by the prophet on behalf of the nation (cf. xviii. 20), or as a form of supplication which he suggests as suitable to the existing crisis. I know, Iahvah, that man's way is not his own; That it pertaineth not to a man to walk and direct his own steps: Correct me, Iahvah, but with justice; Not in Thine anger, lest Thou make me small! (Partly quoted, Ps. vi. 1, xxxviii. 1.) Pour out Thy fury upon the nations that know Thee not, And upon tribes that have not called upon Thy name; For they have devoured Jacob [and will devour him], [and consumed him], and his pasture they have desolated! (Ps. lxxix. 6, 7, quoted from this place. In Jer. the LXX. omits "and will devour him;" while the psalm omits both of the bracketed expressions.)

The Vulgate renders ver. 23: "Scio, Domine, quia non est hominis via ejus; nec viri est ut ambulet, et dirigat gressus suos." I think this indicates the correct reading of the Hebrew text (hlk vhkyn; cf. ix. 23, where two infinitives absolute are used in a similar way). The Septuagint also must have had the same text, for it translates, "nor will (= can) a man walk and direct his own walking." The Masoretic punctuation is certainly incorrect; and the best that can be made of it is Hitzig's version, which, however, disregards the accents, although their authority is the same as that of the vowel points: I know Iahvah that not to man belongeth his way, not to a perishing (lit. "going," "departing") man--and to direct his steps. Any reader of Hebrew may see at once that this is a very unusual form of expression. (For the thought, cf. Prov. xvi. 9, xix. 21; Ps. xxxvii. 23.)

The words express humble submission to the impending chastisement. The penitent people does not deprecate the penalty of its sins, but only prays that the measure of it may be determined by right rather than by wrath (cf. xlvi. 27, 28). The very idea of right and justice implies a limit, whereas wrath, like all passions, is without limit, blind and insatiable. "In the Old Testament, justice is opposed, not to mercy, but to high-handed violence and oppression, which recognise no law but subjective appetite and desire. The just man owns the claims of an objective law of right."

Non est hominis via ejus. Neither individuals nor nations are masters of their own fortunes in this world. Man has not his fate in his own hands; it is controlled and directed by a higher Power. By sincere submission, by a glad, unswerving loyalty, which honours himself as well as its Object, man may co-operate with that Power, to the furtherance of ends which are of all possible ends the wisest, the loftiest, the most beneficial to his kind. Self-will may oppose those ends, it cannot thwart them; at the most it can but momentarily retard their accomplishment, and exclude itself from a share in the universal blessing.

Israel now confesses, by the mouth of his best and truest representative, that he has hitherto loved to choose his own path, and to walk in his own strength, without reference to the will and way of God. Now, the overwhelming shock of irresistible calamity has brought him to his senses, has revealed to him his powerlessness in the hands of the Unseen Arbiter of events, has made him see, as he never saw, that mortal man can determine neither the vicissitudes nor the goal of his journey. Now he sees the folly of the mighty man glorying in his might, and the rich man glorying in his riches; now he sees that the how and the whither of his earthly course are not matters within his own control; that all human resources are nothing against God, and are only helpful when used for and with God. Now he sees that the path of life is not one which we enter upon and traverse of our own motion, but a path along which we are led; and so, resigning his former pride of independent choice, he humbly prays, "Lead Thou me on!" Lead me whither Thou wilt, in the way of trouble and disaster and chastisement for my sins; but remember my human frailty and weakness, and let not Thy wrath destroy me! Finally, the suppliant ventures to remind God that others are guilty as well as he, and that the ruthless destroyers of Israel are themselves fitted to be objects as well as instruments of Divine justice. They are such (i) because they have not "known" nor "called upon" Iahvah; and (ii) because they have "devoured Jacob" who was a thing consecrated to Iahvah (ii. 3), and therefore are guilty of sacrilege (cf. l. 28, 29).

It has never been our lot to see our own land overrun by a barbarous invader, our villages burnt, our peasantry slaughtered, our towns taken and sacked with all the horrors permitted or enjoined by a non-Christian religion. We read of but hardly realize the atrocities of ancient warfare. If we did realize them, we might even think a saint justified in praying for vengeance upon the merciless destroyers of his country. But apart from this, I see a deeper meaning in this prayer. The justice of this terrible visitation upon Judah is admitted by the prophet. Yet in Judah many righteous were involved in the general calamity. On the other hand, Jeremiah knew something of the vices of the Babylonians, against which his contemporary Habakkuk inveighs so bitterly. They "knew not" nor "called upon" Iahvah; but a base polytheism reflected and sanctioned the corruption of their lives. A kind of moral dilemma, therefore, is proposed here. If the purpose of this outpouring of Divine wrath be to bring Israel to "find out" (ver. 18) and to acknowledge the truth of God and his own guiltiness, can wrath persist, when that result is attained? Does not justice demand that the torrent of destruction be diverted upon the proud oppressor? So prayer, the forlorn hope of poor humanity, strives to overcome and compel and prevail with God, and to wrest a blessing even from the hand of Eternal Justice.

Footnotes:

30. The omissions of the Septuagint are not always intelligent. The repetition of the "all" here intensifies the idea of the totality of the ruin of the northern kingdom. The two clauses balance each other: all your brethren--all the seed of Ephraim. The objection that Edom was also a "brother" of Israel (Deut. xxiii. 8; Amos i. 11) shews a want of rhetorical sense. In vii. 4 the Septuagint tastelessly omits the third "The Temple of Iahvah!" upon which the rhetorical effect largely depends: cf. chap. xxii. 29; Isa. vi. 3.

31. Note on vii. 25.--The word answering to "daily" in the Heb. simply means "day," and ought to be omitted, as an accidental repetition either from the previous line, or of the last two letters of the preceding word "prophets." Cf. ver. 13, where a similar phrase, "rising early and speaking," occurs in a similar context, but without "daily."

32. Wa'etten lahem can only mean "and I gave (in prophetic idiom 'and I will give') unto them," and this, of course, requires an object. "I will give them to those who shall pass over them" is the rendering proposed by several scholars. But lahem does not mean "to those," and the thought does not harmonize with what precedes, and this use of vr is doubtful, and the verb "to give" absolutely requires an object. The Vulgate rendering is really more in accordance with Hebrew syntax, as the masc. suffix of the verb might be used in less accurate writing. Targum: "because I gave them My law from Sinai, and they transgressed against it;" Peshito: "and I gave unto them, and they transgressed them." So also the Syro-Hexaplar of Milan (participle: "were transgressing") between asterisks.

33. It seems to take the ly each time as lyhvnly and to read mlygym 'yty for mvlygyty: thus getting "Scoffers! I will bring upon them sorrow; upon them my heart is faint."

34. The irregular Hiphil form of the verb--cf. 1 Sam. xiv. 22; Job xix. 4--may be justified by Job xxviii. 8; we are not, therefore, bound to render the Masoretic text: and they make their tongue bend their lying bow. Probably, however, Qal is right, the Hiphil being due to a misunderstanding, like that of the Targum, "And they taught their tongue words of lying."

35. Ewald prefers the reading of the LXX., which divides the words differently. If we suppose their version correct, they must have read: "They have trained their tongue to speak falsehood, to distort. They are weary of returning. Oppression in oppression, deceit in deceit! They refuse to know Me, saith Iahvah." But I do not think this an improvement on the present Masoretic text.

36. If Jeremiah wrote Ps. lv., as Hitzig supposes, he may be alluding to the treachery of a particular friend; cf. Ps. lv. 13, 14.

37. Shahadhta lisânaka `alaina. In this case, we should follow the Heb. margin or Q'rê.

38. Speak thou, Thus saith Iahweh, is undoubtedly a spurious addition, and does not appear in the LXX. Jeremiah never says Koh ne'um Iahvah, and never uses the imperative dabber!

VI. THE IDOLS OF THE HEATHEN AND THE GOD OF ISRAEL

Jeremiah x. 1-16.

This fine piece is altogether isolated from the surrounding context, which it interrupts in a very surprising manner. Neither the style nor the subject, neither the idioms nor the thoughts expressed in them, agree with what we easily recognise as Jeremiah's work. A stronger contrast can hardly be imagined than that which exists between the leading motive of this oracle as it stands, and that of the long discourse in which it is embedded with as little regard for continuity as an aerolite exhibits when it buries itself in a plain. In what precedes, the prophet's fellow-countrymen have been accused of flagrant and defiant idolatry (vii. 17 sqq., 30 sqq.); the opening words of this piece imply a totally different situation. To the way of the nations become not accustomed, and of the signs of heaven be not afraid; for the nations are afraid of them. [39] Jeremiah would not be likely to warn inveterate apostates not to "accustom themselves" to idolatry. The words presuppose, not a nation whose idolatry was notorious, and had just been the subject of unsparing rebuke and threats of imminent destruction; they presuppose a nation free from idolatry, but exposed to temptation from surrounding heathenism. The entire piece contains no syllable of reference to past or present unfaithfulness on the part of Israel. Here at the outset, and throughout, Israel is implicitly contrasted with "the nations" (ta ethne) as the servant of Iahvah with the foolish worshippers of lifeless gods. There is a tone of contempt in the use of the term goyim--"To the way of the goyim accustom not yourselves ... for the goyim are afraid of them" (of the signs of heaven); or as the Septuagint puts it yet more strongly, "for they (the besotted goyim) are afraid (i.e., worship) before them;" as though that alone--the sense of Israel's superiority--should be sufficient to deter Israelites from any bowings in the house of Rimmon. [40] Neither this contemptuous use of the term goyim, "Gentiles," nor the scathing ridicule of the false gods and their devotees, is in the manner of Jeremiah. Both are characteristic of a later period. The biting scorn of image-worship, the intensely vivid perception of the utter incommensurableness of Iahvah, the Creator of all things, with the handiwork of the carpenter and the silversmith, are well-known and distinctive features of the great prophets of the Exile (see especially Isa. xl.-lxvi.). There are plenty of allusions to idolatry in Jeremiah; but they are expressed in a tone of fervid indignation, not of ridicule. It was the initial offence, which issued in a hopeless degradation of public and private morality, and would have for its certain consequence the rejection and ruin of the nation (ii. 5-13, 20-28, iii. 1-9, 23 sqq.). All the disasters, past and present, which had befallen the country, were due to it (vii. 9, 17 sqq., 30 sqq., viii. 2 etc.). The people are urged to repent and return to Iahvah with their whole heart (iii. 12 sqq., iv. 3 sqq., v. 21 sqq., vi. 8), as the only means of escape from deadly peril. The Baals are things that cannot help or save (ii. 8, 11); but the prophet does not say, as here (x. 5), "Fear them not; they cannot harm you!" The piece before us breathes not one word about Israel's apostasy, the urgent need of repentance, the impending ruin. Taken as a whole, it neither harmonizes with Jeremiah's usual method of argument, nor does it suit the juncture of affairs implied by the language which precedes and follows (vii. 1-ix. 26, x. 17-25). For let us suppose that this oracle occupies its proper place here, and was actually written by Jeremiah at the crisis which called forth the preceding and following utterances. Then the warning cry, "Be not afraid of the signs of heaven!" can only mean "Be not afraid of the Powers under whose auspices the Chaldeans are invading your country; Iahvah, the true and living God, will protect you!" But consolation of this kind would be diametrically opposed to the doctrine which Jeremiah shares with all his predecessors; the doctrine that Iahvah Himself is the prime cause of the coming trouble, and that the heathen invaders are His instruments of wrath (v. 9 sq., vi. 6); it would imply assent to that fallacious confidence in Iahvah, which the prophet has already done his utmost to dissipate (vi. 14, vii. 4 sq.).

The details of the idolatry satirized in the piece before us point to Chaldea rather than to Canaan. We have here a zealous worship of wooden images overlaid and otherwise adorned with silver and gold, and robed in rich garments of violet and purple (cf. Josh. vii. 21). This does not agree with what we know of Judean practice in Jeremiah's time, when, besides the worship of the Queen of Heaven, the people adored "stocks and stones;" probably the wooden symbols of the goddess Asherah and rude sun-pillars, but hardly works of the costly kind described in the text, which indicate a wealthy people whose religion reflected an advanced condition of the arts and commerce. The designation of the objects of heathen worship as "the signs of heaven," and the gibe at the custom of carrying the idol-statues in procession (Isa. xlvi. 1, 7), also point us to Babylon, "the land of graven images" (l. 38), and the home of star-worship and astrological superstition (Isa. xlvii. 13).

From all these considerations, it would appear that not Israel in Canaan but Israel in Chaldea is addressed in this piece by some unknown prophet, whose leaflet has been inserted among the works of Jeremiah. In that case, the much disputed eleventh verse, written in Aramaic, and as such unique in the volume of the prophets proper, may really have belonged to the original piece. Aramaic was the common language of intercourse between East and West both before and during the captivity (cf. 2 Kings xviii. 26); and the suggestion that the tempted exiles should answer in this dialect the heathen who pressed them to join in their worship, seems suitable enough. The verse becomes very suspicious, if we suppose that the whole piece is really part and parcel of Jeremiah's discourse, and as such addressed to the Judeans in the reign of Jehoiakim. Ewald, who maintains this view upon grounds that cannot be called convincing, thinks the Aramaic verse was originally a marginal annotation on verse 15, and suggests that it is a quotation from some early book similar to the book of Daniel. At all events, it is improbable that the verse proceeded from the pen of Jeremiah, who writes Aramaic nowhere else, not even in the letter to the exiles of the first Judean captivity (chap. xxix.).

But might not the piece be an address which Jeremiah sent to the exiles of the Ten Tribes, who were settled in Assyria, and with whom it is otherwise probable that he cultivated some intercourse? The expression "House of Israel" (ver. 1) has been supposed to indicate this. That expression, however, occurs in the immediately preceding context (ix. 26), as does also that of "the nations"; facts which may partially explain why the passage we are discussing occupies its present position. The unknown author of the Apocryphal Letter of Jeremiah and the Chaldee Targumist appear to have held the opinion that Jeremiah wrote the piece for the benefit of the exiles carried away with Jehoiachin in the first Judean captivity. The Targum introduces the eleventh verse thus: "This is a copy of the letter which Jeremiah the prophet sent to the remnant of the elders of the captivity which was in Babylon. And if the peoples among whom ye are shall say unto you, Fear the Errors, O house of Israel! thus shall ye answer and thus shall ye say unto them: The Errors whom ye fear are (but) errors, in which there is no profit: they from the heavens are not able to bring down rain, and from the earth they cannot make fruits to spring: they and those who fear them will perish from the earth, and will be brought to an end from under these heavens. And thus shall ye say unto them: We fear Him that maketh the earth by His power," etc. (ver. 12). The phrase "the remnant of the elders of the captivity which was (or who were) in Babylon" is derived from Jer. xxix. 1. But how utterly different are the tone and substance of that message from those of the one before us! Far from warning his captive countrymen against the state-worship of Babylon, far from satirizing its absurdity, Jeremiah bids the exiles be contented in their new home, and to pray for the peace of the city. The false prophets who appear at Babylon prophesy in Iahvah's name (vv. 15, 21), and in denouncing them Jeremiah says not a word about idolatry. It is evident from the whole context that he did not fear it in the case of the exiles of Jehoiachin's captivity. (See also the simile of the Good and Bad Figs, chap. xxiv., which further illustrates the prophet's estimation of the earlier body of exiles.)

The Greek Epistle of Jeremiah, which in MSS. is sometimes appended to Baruch, and which Fritzsche refers to the Maccabean times, appear to be partially based upon the passage we are considering. Its heading is: "Copy of a letter which Jeremiah sent unto those who were about to be carried away captives to Babylon, by the king of the Babylonians; to announce to them as was enjoined him by God." It then begins thus: "On account of your sins which ye have sinned before God ye will be carried away to Babylon as captives by Nabuchodonosor king of the Babylonians. Having come, then, into Babylon, ye will be there many years, and a long time, until seven generations; but after this I will bring you forth from thence in peace. But now ye will see in Babylon gods, silvern and golden and wooden, borne upon shoulders, shewing fear (an object of fear) to the nations. Beware then, lest ye also become like unto the nations, and fear take you at them, when ye see a multitude before and behind them worshipping them. But say ye in the mind: Thee it behoveth us to worship, O Lord! For Mine angel is with you, and He is requiring your lives." The whole epistle is well worth reading as a kind of paraphrase of our passage. "For their tongue is carven (or polished) by a carpenter, and themselves are overlaid with gold and silver, but lies they are and they cannot speak." "They being cast about with purple apparel have their face wiped on account of the dust from the house, which is plentiful upon them" (13). "But he holds a dagger with right hand and an axe, but himself from war and robbers he will not (= cannot) deliver" (15), cf. Jer. x. 15. "He is like one of the house-beams" (20, cf. Jer. x. 8, and perhaps 5). "Upon their body and upon their head alight bats, swallows, and the birds, likewise also the cats; whence ye will know that they are not gods; therefore fear them not" (cf. Jer. x. 5). "At all cost are they purchased, in which there is no spirit" (25; cf. Jer. x. 9, 14). "Footless, upon shoulders they are carried, displaying their own dishonour to men" (26). "Neither if they suffer evil from any one, nor if good, will they be able to recompense" (34; cf. ver. 5). "But they that serve them will be ashamed" (39; cf. ver. 14). "By carpenters and goldsmiths are they prepared; they become nothing but what the craftsmen wish them to become. And the very men that prepare them cannot last long; how then are the things prepared by them likely to do so? for they left lies and a reproach to them that come after. For whenever war and evils come upon them, the priests consult together where to hide with them. How then is it possible not to perceive that they are not gods, who neither save themselves from war nor from evils? For being of wood and overlaid with gold and silver they will be known hereafter, that they are lies. To all the nations and to the kings it will be manifest that they are not gods but works of men's hands, and no work of God is in them" (45-51; cf. Jer. x. 14-15). "A wooden pillar in a palace is more useful than the false gods" (59). "Signs among nations they will not shew in heaven, nor yet will they shine like the sun, nor give light as the moon" (67). "For as a scarecrow in a cucumber-bed guarding nothing, so their gods are wooden and overlaid with gold and with silver" (70; cf. Jer. x. 5). The mention of the sun, moon and stars, the lightning, the wind, the clouds, and fire "sent forth from above," as totally unlike the idols in "forms and powers," seems to shew that the author had verses 12, 13 before him.

When we turn to the Septuagint, we are immediately struck by its remarkable omissions. The four verses 6-8 and 10 do not appear at all in this oldest of the versions; while the ninth is inserted between the first clause and the remainder of the fifth verse. Now, on the one hand, it is just the verses which the LXX. translates, which both in style and matter contrast so strongly with Jeremiah's authentic work, and are plainly incongruous with the context and occasion; while, on the other hand, the omitted verses contain nothing which points positively to another author than Jeremiah, and, taken by themselves, harmonise very well with what may be supposed to have been the prophet's feeling at the actual juncture of affairs.

> "There is none at all like Thee, O Iahvah!
> Great art Thou, and great is Thy Name in might!
> Who should not fear Thee, O King of the nations? for 'tis Thy due
> For among all the wise of the nations and in all their kingdom there is none at all like Thee.
> And in one thing they are brute-like and dull;
> In the doctrine of Vanities, which are wood!
> But Iahvah Elohim is truth;
> He is a living God, and an eternal King:
> At His wrath the earth quaketh,
> And nations abide not His indignation."

As Hitzig has observed, it is natural that now, as the terrible decision approaches, the prophet should seek and find comfort in the thought of the all-overshadowing greatness of the God of Israel. If, however, we suppose these verses to be Jeremiah's, we can hardly extend the same assumption to verses 12-16, in spite of one or two expressions of his which occur in them; and, upon the whole, the linguistic argument seems to weigh decisively against Jeremiah's authorship of this piece (see Naegelsbach).

It may be true enough that "the basis and possibility of the true prosperity and the hope of the genuine community are unfolded in these strophes" (Ewald); but that does not prove that they belong to Jeremiah. Nor can I see much force in the remark that "didactic language is of another kind than that of pure prophecy." But when the same critic affirms that "the description of the folly of idolatry ... is also quite new, and clearly serves as a model for the much more elaborate ones, Isa. xl. 19-24 (20), xli. 7, xliv. 8-20, xlvi. 5-7;" he is really giving up the point in dispute. Verses 12-16 are repeated in the prophecy against Babylon (li. 15-19); but this hardly proves that "the later prophet, chap. l.-li., found all these words in our piece;" it is only evidence, so far as it goes, for those verses themselves.

The internal connexion which Ewald assumes, is not self-evident. There is no proof that "the thought that the gods of the heathen might again rule" occurred for one moment to Jeremiah on this occasion; nor the thought that "the maintenance of the ancient true religion in conflict with the heathen must produce the regeneration of Israel." There is no reference throughout the disputed passage to the spiritual condition of the people, which is, in fact, presupposed to be good; and the return in verses 17-25 "to the main subject of the discourse" is inexplicable on Ewald's theory that the whole chapter, omitting verse 11, is one homogeneous structure.

Hear ye the word that Iahvah spake upon you, O house of Israel! Thus said Iahvah. The terms imply a particular crisis in the history of Israel, when a Divine pronouncement was necessary to the guidance of the people. Iahvah speaks indeed in all existence and in all events, but His voice becomes audible, is recognised as His, only when human need asserts itself in some particular juncture of affairs. Then, in view of the actual emergency, the mind of Iahweh declares itself by the mouth of His proper spokesmen; and the prophetic Thus said Iahvah contrasts the higher point of view with the lower, the heavenly and spiritual with the earthly and the carnal; it sets forth the aspect of things as they appear to God, in the sharpest antithesis to the aspect of things as they appear to the natural unilluminated man. Thus said Iahvah: This is the thought of the Eternal, this is His judgment upon present conditions and passing events, whatever your thought and your judgment may happen or incline to be! Such, I think, is the essential import of this vox solennis, this customary formula of the dialect of prophecy.

On the present occasion, the crisis in view of which a prophet declares the mind of Iahvah is not a political emergency but a religious temptation. The day for the former has long since passed away, and the depressed and scattered communities of exiled Israelites are exposed among other trials to the constant temptation to sacrifice to present expediency the only treasure which they have saved from the wreck of their country, the faith of their fathers, the religion of the prophets. The uncompromising tone of this isolated oracle, the abruptness with which the writer at once enters in medias res, the solemn emphasis of his opening imperatives, proves that this danger pressed at the time with peculiar intensity. Thus said Iahvah: Unto the way of the nations use not yourselves, And of the signs of heaven stand not in awe, for that the nations stand in awe of them! (cf. Lev. xviii. 3; Ezek. xx. 18). The "way" of the nations is their religion, the mode and manner of their worship (v. 4, 5); and the exiles are warned not to suffer themselves to be led astray by example, as they had been in the land of Canaan; they are not to adore the signs of heaven, simply because they see their conquerors adoring them. The "signs of heaven" would seem to be the sun, moon and stars, which were the objects of Babylonian worship; although the passage is unhappily not free from ambiguity. Some expositors have preferred to think of celestial phenomena such as eclipses and particular conjunctions of the heavenly bodies, which in those days were looked upon as portents, foreshadowing the course of national and individual fortunes. That there is really a reference to the astrological observation of the stars, is a view which finds considerable support in the words addressed to Babylon on the eve of her fall, by a prophet, who, if not identical was at least contemporary with him whose message we are discussing. In the forty-seventh chapter of the book of Isaiah, it is said to Babylon: "Let now them that parcel out the heavens, that gaze at the stars, arise and save thee, prognosticating month by month the things that will come upon thee" (Isa. xlvii. 13). The signs of heaven are, in this case, the supposed indications of coming events furnished by the varying appearances of the heavenly bodies; and one might even suppose that the immediate occasion of our prophecy was some eclipse of the sun or moon, or some remarkable conjunction of the planets which at the time was exciting general anxiety among the motley populations of Babylonia. The prophecy then becomes a remarkable instance of the manner in which an elevated spiritual faith, free from all the contaminating and blinding influences of selfish motives and desires, may rise superior to universal superstition, and boldly contradict the suggestions of what is accounted the highest wisdom of the time, anticipating the results though not the methods nor the evidence of science, at an epoch when science is as yet in the mythological stage. And the prophet might well exclaim in a tone of triumph, Among all the wise of the nations none at all is like unto thee, O Lord, as a source of true wisdom and understanding for the guidance of life (ver. 7).

The inclusion of eclipses and comets among the signs of heaven here spoken of has been thought to be barred by the considerations that these are sometimes alleged by the prophets themselves as signs of coming judgment exhibited by the God of Israel; that, as a matter of fact, they were as mysterious and awful to the Jews as to their heathen neighbours; and that what is here contemplated is not the terror inspired by rare occasional phenomena of this kind, but an habitual superstition in relation to some ever-present causes. It is certain that in another prophecy against Babylon, preserved in the book of Isaiah, it is declared that, as a token of the impending destruction, "the stars of heaven and the Orions thereof shall not give their light: the sun shall be darkened in his going forth, and the moon shall not cause his light to shine" (Isa. xiii. 10); and the similar language of the prophet Joel is well known (Joel ii. 2, 10, 30, 31, iii. 15). But these objections are not conclusive, for what our author is denouncing is the heathen association of "the signs of the heavens," whatever may be intended by that expression, with a false system of religious belief. It is a special kind of idolatry that he contemplates, as is clear from the immediate context. Not only does the parallel clause "Unto the way of the nations use not yourselves" imply a gradual conformity to a heathen religion; not only is it the fact that the Hebrew phrase rendered in our versions "Be not dismayed!" may imply religious awe or worship (Mal. ii. 5), as indeed terms denoting fear or dread are used by the Semitic languages in general; but the prophet at once proceeds to an exposure of the absurdity of image-worship: For the ordinances (established modes of worship; 2 Kings xvii. 8; here, established objects of worship) of the peoples are a mere breath (i.e., nought)! for it (the idol) is a tree, which out of the forest one felled (so the accents); the handiwork of the carpenter with the bill. With silver and with gold one adorneth it (or, maketh it bright); with nails and with hammers they make them fast, that one sway not (or, that there be no shaking). Like the scarecrow of a garden of gourds are they, and they cannot speak; they are carried and carried, for they cannot take a step (or, march): be not afraid of them, for they cannot hurt, neither is it in their power to benefit! "Be not afraid of them!" returns to the opening charge: "Of the signs of heaven stand not in awe!" (cf. Gen. xxxi. 42, 53; Isa. viii. 12, 13). Clearly, then, the signa coeli are the idols against whose worship the prophet warns his people; and they denote "the sun, the moon, the constellations (of the Zodiac), and all the host of heaven" (2 Kings xxiii. 5). We know that the kings of Judah, from Ahaz onwards, derived this worship from Assyria, and that its original home was Babylon, where in every temple the exiles would see images of the deities presiding over the heavenly bodies, such as Samas (the sun) and his consort Aa (the moon) at Sippara, Merodach (Jupiter) and his son Nebo (Mercurius) at Babylon and Borsippa, Nergal (Mars) at Cutha, daily served with a splendid and attractive ritual, and honoured with festivals and processions on the most costly and magnificent scale. The prophet looks through all this outward display to the void within, he draws no subtle distinction between the symbol and the thing symbolized; he accepts the popular confusion of the god with his image, and identifies all the deities of the heathen with the materials out of which their statues are made by the hands of men. And he is justified in doing this, because there can be but one god in his sense of the word; a multitude of gods is a contradiction in terms. From this point of view, he exposes the absurdity of the splendid idolatry which his captive countrymen see all around them. Behold that thing, he cries, which they call a god, and before which they tremble with religious fear! It is nothing but a tree trunk hewn in the forest, and trimmed into shape by the carpenter, and plated with silver and gold, and fixed on its pedestal with hammer and nails, for fear it should fall! Its terrors are empty terrors, like those of the palm-trunk, rough-hewn into human shape, and set up among the melons to frighten the birds away.

> *"Olim truncus eram ficulnus, inutile lignum,*
> *Cum faber, incertus scamnum faceretne Priapum,*
> *Maluit esse deum. Deus inde ego, furum ariumque*
> *Maxima formido."* (Hor., Sat. i. 8, 1, sqq.)

Though the idol has the outward semblance of a man, it lacks his distinguishing faculty of speech; it is as dumb as the scarecrow, and as powerless to move from its place; so it has to be borne about on men's shoulders (a mocking allusion to the grand processions of the gods, which distinguished the Babylonian festivals). Will you then be afraid of things that can do neither good nor harm? asks the prophet; in terms that recall the challenge of another, or perchance of himself, to the idols of Babylon: Do good or do evil, that we may look at each other and see it together (Isa. xli. 23).

In utter contrast with the impotence, the nothingness of all the gods of the nations, whether Israel's neighbours or his invaders, stands for ever the God of Israel. There is none at all like Thee, O Iahweh! great art Thou, and great is Thy Name in might! With different vowel points, we might render, Whence (cometh) Thy like, O Iahvah? This has been supported by reference to chap. xxx. 7: Alas! for great is that day. Whence (is one) like it? (me`ayin?); but there too, as here, we may equally well translate, there is none like it. The interrogative, in fact, presupposes a negative answer; and the Hebrew particle usually rendered there is not, are not (`ayin, `ên) has been explained as originally identical with the interrogative where? (`ayin, implied in me`ayin, "from where?" "whence?" cf. Job. xiv. 10: where is he? = he is not). The idiom of the text expresses a more emphatic negation than the ordinary form would do; and though rare, is by no means altogether unparalleled (see Isa. xl. 17, xli. 24; and other references in Gesenius). Great art Thou and great is Thy Name in might; that is to say, Thou art great in Thyself, and great in repute or manifestation among men, in respect of might, virile strength or prowess (Ps. xxi. 14). Unlike the do-nothing idols, Iahvah reveals His strength in deeds of strength (cf. Exod. xv. 3 sqq.). Who should not fear Thee, Thou King of the nations? (cf. v. 22) for Thee it beseemeth (= it is Thy due, and Thine only): for among all the wise of the nations and in all their realm, there is none at all (as in ver. 6) like Thee. Religious fear is instinctive in man; but, whereas the various nations lavish reverence upon innumerable objects utterly unworthy of the name of deity, rational religion sees clearly that there can be but One God, working His supreme will in heaven and earth; and that this Almighty being is the true "King of the nations," and disposes their destinies as well as that of His people Israel, although they know Him not, but call other imaginary beings their kings (a common Semitic designation of a national god: Ps. xx. 9; Isa. vi. 5, viii. 21). He, then, is the proper object of the instinct of religious awe; all the peoples of the earth owe Him adoration, even though they be ignorant of their obligation; worship is His unshared prerogative.

Among all the wise of the nations and in all their realm, not one is like Thee! Who are the wise thus contrasted with the Supreme God? Are the false gods the reputed wise ones, giving pretended counsel to their deluded worshippers through the priestly oracle? The term "kingdom" seems to indicate this view, if we take "their kingdom" to mean the kingdom of the wise ones of the nations, that is, the countries whose "kings" they are, where they are worshipped as such. The heathen in general, and the Babylonians in particular, ascribed wisdom to their gods. But there is no impropriety from an Old Testament point of view in comparing Iahvah's wisdom with the wisdom of man. The meaning of the prophet may be simply this, that no earthly wisdom, craft or political sagacity, not even in the most powerful empires such as Babylon, can be a match for Iahvah the All-wise, or avail to thwart His purposes (Isa. xxxi. 1, 2). "Wise" and "sagacious" are titles which the kings of Babylon continually assert for themselves in their extant inscriptions; and the wisdom and learning of the Chaldeans was famous in the ancient world. Either view will agree with what follows: But in one thing they--the nations, or their wise men--will turn out brutish and besotted: (in) the teaching of Vanities which are wood. The verse is difficult; but the expression "the teaching (or doctrine) of Vanities" may perhaps be regarded as equivalent to the idols taught of; and then the second half of the verse is constructed like the first member of ver. 3: The ordinances of the peoples are Vanity, and may be rendered, the idols taught of are mere wood (cf. ver. 3 b, ii. 27, iii. 9). It is possible also that the right reading is "foundation" (mûsad) not "doctrine" (mûsar): the foundation (basis, substratum, substance) of idols is wood. (The term "Vanities"--habalim--is used for "idols," viii. 19, xiv. 22; Ps. xxxi. 7). And, lastly, I think, the clause might be rendered: a doctrine of Vanities, of mere wood, it--their religion--is! [41] This supreme folly is the "one thing" that discredits all the boasted wisdom of the Chaldeans; and their folly will hereafter be demonstrated by events (ver. 14).

The body of the idol is wood, and outwardly it is decorated with silver and gold and costly apparel; but the whole and every part of it is the work of man. Silver plate (lit. beaten out) from Tarshish--from far away Tartessus in Spain--is brought, and gold from Uphaz (Dan. x. 5), the work of the smith, and of the hands of the founder--who have beaten out the silver and smelted the gold: blue and purple is their clothing (Ex. xxvi. 31, xxviii. 8): the work of the wise--of skilled artists (Isa. xl. 20)-- is every part of them. Possibly the verse might better be translated: Silver to be beaten out--argentum malleo diducendum--which is brought from Tarshish, and gold which is brought from Uphaz, are the work of the smith and of the hands of the smelter; the blue and purple which are their clothing, are the work of the wise all of them. At all events, the point of the verse seems to be that, whether you look at the inside or the outside of the idol, his heart of wood or his casing of gold and silver and his gorgeous robes, the whole and every bit of him as he stands before you is a manufactured article, the work of men's hands. The supernatural comes in nowhere. In sharpest contrast with this lifeless fetish, Iahvah is a God that is truth, i.e., a true God (cf. Prov. xxii. 21), or Iahvah is God in truth--is really God--He is a living God, and an eternal King; the sovereign whose rule is independent of the vicissitudes of time, and the caprices of temporal creatures: at His wrath the earth quaketh, and nations cannot abide His indignation: the world of nature and the world of man are alike dependent upon His Will, and He exhibits His power and his righteous anger in the disturbances of the one and the disasters of the other.

According to the Hebrew punctuation, we should rather translate: But Iahvah Elohim (the designation of God in the second account of creation, Gen. ii. 4-iii. 24) is truth, i.e., reality; as opposed to the falsity and nothingness of the idols; or permanence, lastingness (Ps. xix. 10), as opposed to their transitoriness (vv. 11-15).

The statement of the tenth verse respecting the eternal power and godhead of Iahvah is confirmed in the twelfth and thirteenth by instances of His creative energy and continual activity as exhibited in the world of nature. The Maker of the earth by His power, Establishing the habitable world by His wisdom, And by His insight He did stretch out the heavens: At the sound of His giving voice (Ps. lxxvii. 18; i.e., thundering) there is an uproar of waters in the heavens, And He causeth the vapours to rise from the end of the earth; Lightnings for the rain He maketh, And causeth the wind to go forth out of His treasuries. There is no break in the sense between these sentences and the tenth verse. The construction resembles that of Amos v. 8, ix. 5, 6, and is interrupted by the eleventh verse, which in all probability was, to begin with, a marginal annotation.

The solid earth is itself a natural symbol of strength and stability. The original creation of this mighty and enduring structure argues the omnipotence of the Creator; while the "establishing" or "founding" of it upon the waters of the great deep is a proof of supreme wisdom (Ps. xxiv. 2; cxxxvi. 6), and the "spreading out" of the visible heavens or atmosphere like a vast canopy or tent over the earth (Ps. civ. 2; Isa. xl. 22), is evidence of a perfect insight into the conditions essential to the existence and wellbeing of man.

It is, of course, clear enough that physical facts and phenomena are here described in popular language as they appear to the eye, and by no means with the severe precision of a scientific treatise. It is not to be supposed that this prophet knew more about the actual constitution of the physical universe than the wise men of his time could impart. But such knowledge was not necessary to the enforcement of the spiritual truths which it was his mission to proclaim; and the fact that his brief oracle presents those truths in a garb which we can only regard as poetical, and which it would argue a want of judgment to treat as scientific prose, does not affect their eternal validity, nor at all impair their universal importance. The passage refers us to God as the ultimate source of the world of nature. It teaches us that the stability of things is a reflexion of His eternal being; that the persistence of matter is an embodiment of His strength; that the indestructibility which science ascribes to the materials of the physical universe is the seal which authenticates their Divine original. Persistence, permanence, indestructibleness, are properly sole attributes of the eternal Creator, which He communicates to His creation. Things are indestructible as regards man, not as regards the Author of their being.

Thus the wisdom enshrined in the laws of the visible world, all its strength and all its stability, is a manifestation of the Unseen God. Invisible in themselves, the eternal power and godhead of Iahvah become visible in His creation. And, as the Hebrew mode of expression indicates, His activity is never suspended, nor His presence withdrawn. The conflict of the elements, the roar of the thunder, the flash of the lightning, the downpour of waters, the rush of the stormwind, are His work; and not less His work, because we have found out the "natural" causes, that is, the established conditions of their occurrence; not less His work, because we have, in the exercise of faculties really though remotely akin to the Divine Nature, discovered how to imitate, or rather mimic, even the more awful of these marvellous phenomena. Mimicry it cannot but appear, when we compare the overwhelming forces that rage in a tropical storm with our electric toys. The lightnings in their glory and terror are still God's arrows, and man cannot rob His quiver.

Nowadays more is known about the machinery of the world, but hardly more of the Intelligence that contrived it, and keeps it continually in working order, nay, lends it its very existence. More is known about means and methods, but hardly more about aims and purposes. The reflexion, how few are the master-conceptions which modern speculation has added to the treasury of thought, should suggest humility to the vainest and most self-confident of physical inquirers. In the very dawn of philosophy the human mind appears to have anticipated as it were by sudden flashes of insight some of the boldest hypotheses of modern science, including that of Evolution itself.

The unchangeable or invariable laws of nature, that is to say, the uniformity of sequence which we observe in physical phenomena, is not to be regarded as a thing that explains itself. It is only intelligible as the expression of the unchanging will of God. The prophet's word is still true. It is God who "causes the vapours to rise from the end of the earth," drawing them up into the air from oceans and lakes by the simple yet beautiful and efficient action of the solar heat; it is God who "makes lightnings for the rain," charging the clouds with the electric fluid, to burst forth in blinding flashes when the opposing currents meet. It is God who "brings the wind out of His treasuries." In the prophet's time the winds were as great a mystery as the thunder and lightning; it was not known whence they came nor whither they went. But the knowledge that they are but currents of air due to variations of temperature does not really deprive them of their wonder. Not only is it impossible, in the last resort, to comprehend what heat is, what motion is, what the thing moved is. A far greater marvel remains, which cries aloud of God's wisdom and presence and sovereignty over all; and that is the wonderful consilience of all the various powers and forces of the natural world in making a home for man, and enabling so apparently feeble a creature as he to live and thrive amidst the perpetual interaction and collision of the manifold and mighty elements of the universe.

The true author of all this magnificent system of objects and forces, to the wonder and the glory of which only custom can blind us, is the God of the prophet. This sublime, this just conception of God was possible, for it was actually realized, altogether apart from the influence of Hellenic philosophy and modern European science. But it was by no means as common to the Semitic peoples. In Babylon, which was at the time the focus of all earthly wisdom and power, in Babylon the ancient mother of sciences and arts, a crude polytheism stultified all the wisdom of the wise, and lent its sanction to a profound moral corruption. Rapid and universal conquests, enormous wealth accruing from the spoils and tributes of all nations, only subserved the luxury and riotous living which issued in a general effeminacy and social enervation; until the great fabric of empire, which Nabopalassar and Nebuchadrezzar had reared by their military and political genius, sank under the weight of its own vices.

Looking round upon this spectacle of superstitious folly, the prophet declares that all men are become too brute-like for knowledge; too degraded to appreciate the truth, the simplicity of a higher faith; too besotted with the worship of a hundred vain idols, which were the outward reflexion of their own diseased imaginations, to receive the wisdom of the true religion, and to perceive especially the truth just enunciated, that it is Iahvah who gives the rain and upon whom all atmospheric changes depend (cf. xiv. 22): and thus, in the hour of need, every founder blushes for the image, because his molten figure is a lie, and there is no breath in them; because the lifeless idol, the work of his hands, can lend no help. Perhaps both clauses of the verse rather express a prophecy: All men will be proven brutish, destitute of knowledge; every founder will blush for the graven image. Wise and strong as the Babylonians supposed themselves to be, the logic of events would undeceive them. They were doomed to a rude awakening; to discover in the hour of defeat and surrender that the molten idol was a delusion, that the work of their hands was an embodied lie, void of life, powerless to save. Vanity--a mere breath, nought--are they, a work of knaveries (a term recurring only in li. 18; the root seems to mean "to stammer," "to imitate"); in the time of their visitation they will perish! or simply they perish!--in the burning temples, in the crash of falling shrines.

It has happened so. At this day the temples of cedar and marble, with their woodwork overlaid with bronze and silver and gold, of whose glories the Babylonian sovereigns so proudly boast in their still existing records, as "shining like the sun, and like the stars of heaven," are shapeless heaps or rather mountains of rubbish, where Arabs dig for building materials and treasure trove, and European explorers for the relics of a civilisation and a superstition which have passed away for ever. "Vana sunt, et opus risu dignum." In the revolutions of time, which are the outward measures of the eternally self-unfolding purposes of God, the word of the Judean prophets has been amply fulfilled. Babylon and her idols are no more.

All other idols, too, must perish in like manner. Thus shall ye say of them: The gods who the heavens and earth did not make, perish from the earth and from under the heavens shall these! The assertion that the idols of Babylon were doomed to destruction, was not the whole of the prophetic message. It is connected with and founded upon the antithetic assertion of the eternity of Iahvah. They will perish, but He endures. The one eternal is El Elyon, the Most High God, the Maker of heaven and earth. But heaven and earth and whatever partakes only of their material nature are also doomed to pass away. And in that day of the Lord, when the elements melt with fervent heat, and the earth and the works that are therein shall be burnt up (2 Pet. iii. 10), not only will the idols of the heathen world, and the tawdry dolls which a degenerate church suffers to be adored as a kind of magical embodiment of the Mother of God, but all other idols which the sensebound heart of man makes to itself, vanish into nothingness before that overwhelming revelation of the supremacy of God.

There is something amazing in the folly of worshipping man, whether in the abstract form of the cultus of "Humanity," or in any of the various forms of what is called "Hero-worship," or in the vulgar form of self-worship, which is the religion of the selfish and the worldly. To ascribe infallibility to any mortal, whether Pope or politician, is to sin in the spirit of idolatry. The Maker of heaven and earth, and He alone, is worthy of worship. "Where wast thou when I laid the foundations of the earth? declare, if thou hast understanding" (Job xxxviii. 4). No human wisdom nor power presided there; and to produce the smallest of asteroids is still a task which lies infinitely beyond the combined resources of modern science. Man and all that man has created is nought in the scale of God's creation. He and all the mighty works with which he amazes, overshadows, enslaves his little world, will perish and pass away; only that will survive which he builds of materials which are imperishable, fabrics of spiritual worth and excellence and glory (1 Cor. iii. 13). A Nineveh, a Babylon, a London, a Paris, may disappear; but he that doeth the will of God abideth for ever (1 John ii. 17). Not like these (cf. verse 11 ad fin.) is Jacob's Portion, but the Maker and Moulder of the All--He is his heritage; Iahvah Sabaoth is His name! (Both here and at li. 19 = xxviii. 19 the LXX. omits: and Israel is the tribe, which seems to have been derived from Deut. xxxii. 9. Israel is elsewhere called Iahvah's heritage, Ps. xxxiii. 12, and portion, Deut. xxxii. 9; but that thought hardly suits the connexion here.)

Not like these: for He is the Divine Potter who moulded all things, including the signs of heaven, and the idols of wood and metal, and their foolish worshippers. And he is Jacob's portion; for the knowledge and worship of Him was, in the Divine counsels, originally assigned to Israel (cf. Deut. iv. 19; and xxxii. 8, according to the true reading, preserved in the LXX.); and therefore Israel alone knows Him and His glorious attributes. Iahvah Sabaoth is His name: the Eternal, the Maker and Master of the hosts of heaven and earth, is the aspect under which He has revealed Himself to the true representatives of Israel, His servants the prophets.

The portion of Israel is his God--his abiding portion; of which neither the changes of time nor the misconceptions of man can avail to rob him. When all that is accidental and transitory is taken away, this distinction remains: Israel's portion is his God. Iahvah was indeed the national God of the Jews, argue some of our modern wise ones; and therefore He cannot be identified with the universal Deity. He has been developed, expanded, into this vast conception; but originally He was but the private god of a petty tribe, the Lar of a wandering household. Now herein is a marvellous thing. How was it that this particular household god thus grew to infinite proportions, like the genius emerging from the unsealed jar of Arab fable, until, from His prime foothold on the tent-floor of a nomad family, He towered above the stars and His form overshadowed the universe? How did it come to pass that His prophet could ask in a tone of indisputable truth, recognised alike by friend and foe, "Do not I fill heaven and earth, saith Iahvah"? (Jer. xxiii. 24). How, that this immense, this immeasurable expansion took place in this instance, and not in that of any one of the thousand rival deities of surrounding and more powerful tribes and nations? How comes it that we to-day are met to adore Iahvah, and not rather one of the forgotten gods of Canaan or Egypt or Babylon? Merodach and Nebo have vanished, but Iahvah is the Father of our Lord Jesus Christ. It certainly looks very much as if the Hebrew prophets were right; as if Iahvah were really the God of the creation as well as the Portion of Jacob.

The portion of Jacob. Is His relation to that one people a stumbling-block? Can we see no eternal truth in the statement of the Psalmist that the Lord's portion is His people? Who can find fault with the enthusiastic faith of holy men thus exulting in the knowledge and love of God? It is a characteristic of all genuine religion, this sweet, this elevating consciousness that God is our God; this profound sense that He has revealed Himself to us in a special and peculiar and individual manner. But the actual historical results, as well as the sacred books, prove that the sense of possessing God and being possessed by Him was purer, stronger, deeper, more effectual, more abiding, in Israel than in any other race of the ancient world.

One must tread warily upon slippery ground; but I cannot help thinking that many of the arguments alleged against the probability of God revealing Himself to man at all or to a single nation in particular, are sufficiently met by the simple consideration that He has actually done so. Any event whatever may be very improbable until it has happened; and assuming that God has not revealed Himself, it may perhaps be shewn to be highly improbable that He would reveal Himself. But, meanwhile, all religions and all faith and the phenomena of conscience and the highest intuitions of reason presuppose this improbable event as the fact apart from which they are insoluble riddles. This is not to say that the precise manner of revelation--the contact of the Infinite with the Finite Spirit--is definable. There are many less lofty experiences of man which also are indefinable and mysterious, but none the less actual and certain. Facts are not explained by denial, which is about the most barren and feeble attitude a man can take up in the presence of a baffling mystery. Nor is it for man to prescribe conditions to God. He who made us and knows us far better than we know ourselves, knows also how best to reveal Himself to His creatures.

The special illumination of Israel, however, does not imply that no light was vouchsafed elsewhere. The religious systems of other nations furnish abundant evidence to the contrary. God "left not Himself without witness," the silent witness of that beneficent order of the natural world, which makes it possible for man to live, and to live happily. St. Paul did not scruple to compliment even the degenerate Athenians of his own day on the ground of their attention to religious matters, and he could cite a Greek poet in support of his doctrine that man is the offspring of the one God and Father of all.

We may see in the fact a sufficient indication of what St. Paul would have said, had the nobler non-Christian systems fallen under his cognisance; had heathenism become known to him not in the heterogeneous polytheism of Hellas, which in his time had long since lost what little moral influence it had ever possessed, nor in the wild orgiastic nature worships of the Lesser Asia, which in their thoroughly sensuous basis did dishonour alike to God and to man; but in the sublime tenets of Zarathustra, with their noble morality and deep reverence for the One God, the Spirit of all goodness and truth, or in the reformed Brahmanism of Gautama the Buddha, with its grand principle of self-renunciation and universal charity.

The peculiar glories of Bible religion are not dimmed in presence of these other lights. Allowing for whatever is valuable in these systems of belief, we may still allege that Bible religion comprises all that is good in them, and has, besides, many precious features peculiar to itself; we may still maintain that their excellences are rather testimonies to the truth of the biblical teachings about God, than difficulties in the way of a rational faith; that it would be far more difficult to a thoughtful mind to accept the revelation of God conveyed in the Bible, if it were the fact that no rays of Divine light had cheered the darkness of the millions of struggling mortals beyond the pale of Judaism, than it is under the actual circumstances of the case: in short, that the truths implicated in imperfect religions, isolated from all contact with Hebrew or Christian belief, are a witness to and a foreshadowing of the truths of the gospel.

Our prophet declares that Jacob's portion--the God of Israel--is not like the gods of contemporary peoples. How, then, does he conceive of Him? Not as a metaphysical entity--a naked, perhaps empty abstraction of the understanding. Not as the Absolute and Infinite Being, who is out of all relation to space and time. His language--the language of the Old Testament--possesses no adjectives like "Infinite," "Absolute," "Eternal," "Omniscient," "Omnipresent," nor even "Almighty," although that word so often appears in our venerable Authorized Version. It is difficult for us, who are the heirs of ages of thought and intellectual toil, and whose thinking is almost wholly carried on by means of abstract ideas, to realize a state of mind and a habit of thought so largely different from our own as that of the Hebrew people and even of the Hebrew prophets. Yet unless we make an effort to realize it, however inadequately, unless we exert ourselves, and strive manfully to enter through the gate of an instructed imagination into that far-off stage of life and thought which presents so many problems to the historical student, and hides in its obscurity so many precious truths; we must inevitably fail to appreciate the full significance, and consequently fail of appropriating the full blessing of those wonderful prophecies of ancient Israel, which are not for an age but for all time.

Let us, then, try to apprehend the actual point of view from which the inspired Israelite regarded his God. In the first place, that point of view was eminently practical. As a recent writer has forcibly remarked, "The primitive mind does not occupy itself with things of no practical importance, and it is only in the later stages of society that we meet with traditional beliefs nominally accepted by every one but practically regarded by none; or with theological speculations which have an interest for the curious, but are not felt to have a direct bearing on the concerns of life."

The pious Israelite could not indulge a morbidly acute and restlessly speculative intellect with philosophical or scientific theories about the Deity, His nature in Himself, His essential and accidental attributes, His relation to the visible world. Neither did such theories then exist ready made to his hand, nor did his inward impulses and the natural course of thought urge him to pry into such abstruse matters, and with cold irreverence to subject his idea of God to critical analysis. Could he have been made to understand the attitude and the demands of some modern disputants, he would have been apt to exclaim, "Canst thou by searching find out God? Canst thou find out Shaddai unto perfection? It is as high as heaven, what canst thou do? deeper than hell, what canst thou know?" To find out and to know

God as the understanding finds out and knows, how can that ever become possible to man? Such knowledge depends entirely upon processes of comparison; upon the perception of similarity between the object investigated and other known objects; upon accurate naming and classification. But who can dream of successfully referring the Deity to a class? "To what will ye liken God, or what likeness will ye compare unto Him?" In the brief prophecy before us, as in the fortieth chapter of Isaiah, with which it presents so many points of contact, we have a splendid protest against all attempts at bringing the Most High within the limitations of human cognition, and reducing God to the category of things known and understood. Directed in the first instance against idolatry--against vain efforts to find an adequate likeness of the Supreme in some one of the numberless creations of His hand, and so to compare and gauge and comprehend Himself,--that protest is still applicable, and with even greater force, against the idolatrous tendencies of the present age: when one school of devotees loudly declares,

> "Thou, Nature, art our goddess; to thy law
> Our services are bound: wherefore should we
> Stand in the plague of custom?"

and another is equally loud in asserting that it has found the true god in man himself; and another proclaims the divinity of brute force, and feels no shame in advocating the sovereignty of those gross instincts and passions which man shares with the beasts that perish. It is an unworthy and an inadequate conception of God, which identifies Him with Nature; it is a deplorably impoverished idea, the mere outcome of philosophic despair, which identifies him with Humanity; but what language can describe the grovelling baseness of that habit of thought which knows of nothing higher than the sensual appetite, and seeks nothing better than its continual indulgence; which sees the native impress of sovereignty on the brow of passing pleasure, and recognises the image and likeness of God in a temporary association of depraved instincts?

It is to this last form of idolatry, this utter heathenism in the moral life, that all other forms really converge, as St. Paul has shewn in the introduction of his Epistle to the Romans, where, in view of the unutterable iniquities which were familiar occurrences in the world of his contemporaries, he affirms that moral decadence of the most appalling character is ultimately traceable to a voluntary indulgence of those idolatrous tendencies which ignore God's revelation of Himself to the heart and reason, and prefer to find their deity in something less awful in purity and holiness, less averse to the defilements of sin, less conversant with the secrets of the soul; and so, not liking to retain the true and only God in knowledge, change His truth into a lie, and worship and serve the creature more than the Creator: changing the glory of the incorruptible God into an image made like unto corruptible man, or even to birds and fourfooted beasts and creeping things.

Footnotes:

39. LXX. "for they are afraid before them," ky ychtv hmh lphnyhm.

40. This is the most natural interpretation of the passage according to the Hebrew punctuation. Another is given below.

41. It is against usage to divide the clause as Naegelsbach does, "Vain instruction! It is wood!" or to render with Ewald "Simply vain doctrine is the wood!" which would require the article (ha'eç).

VII. THE BROKEN COVENANT

Jeremiah xi., xii.

There is no visible break between these two chapters. They seem to summarize the history of a particular episode in the prophet's career. At the same time, the style is so peculiar, that it is not so easy, as it might appear at a first glance, to determine exactly what it is that the section has to tell us. When we come to take a closer look at it, we find a thoroughly characteristic mixture of direct narrative and soliloquy, of statement of facts and reflexion upon those facts, of aspiration and prayer and prophecy, of self-communing and communing with God. Careful analysis may perhaps furnish us with a clue to the disentanglement of the general sense and drift of this characteristic medley. We may thus hope to get a clearer insight into the bearing of this old-world oracle upon our own needs and perplexities, our sins and the fruit of our sins, what we have done and what we may expect as the consequence of our doings. For the Word of God is "quick and powerful." Its outward form and vesture may change with the passing of time; but its substance never changes. The old interpreters die, but the Word lives, and its life is a life of power. By that Word men live in their successive generations; it is at once creative and regulative; it is the seed of life in man, and it is the law of that life. Apart from the Divine Word, man would be no more than a brute gifted with understanding, but denied all answer to the higher cravings of soul and spirit; a being whose conscious life was a mere mockery; a self-tormentor, tantalized with vain surmises, tortured with ever-recurring problems; longing for light, and beset with never-lifting clouds of impenetrable darkness; the one sole instance, among the myriads of sentient beings, of a creature whose wants Nature refuses to satisfy, and whose lot it is to consume for ever in the fires of hopeless desire.

The sovran Lord, who is the Eternal Wisdom, has not made such a mistake. He provides satisfaction for all His creatures, according to the varying degrees of their capacity, according to their rank in the scale of being, so that all may rejoice in the fulness and the freedom of a happy life for their allotted time. Man is no exception to the universal rule. His whole constitution as God has fashioned it is such that he can find his perfect satisfaction in the Word of the Lord. And the depth of his dissatisfaction, the poignancy and the bitterness of his disappointment and disgust at himself and at the world in which he finds himself, are the strongest evidence that he has sought satisfaction in things that cannot satisfy; that he has foolishly endeavoured to feed his soul upon ashes, to still the cravings of his spirit with something other than that Word of God which is the Bread of Life.

You will observe that the discourse we are to consider, is headed: "The word that fell to Jeremiah from Iahvah (lit. from with, that is, from the presence of the Eternal), saying." I think that expression "saying" covers all that follows, to the end of the discourse. The prophet's preaching the Law, and the consequences of that preaching as regarded himself; his experience of the stubbornness and treachery of the people; the varying moods of his own mind under that bitter experience; his reflexions upon the condition of Judah, and the condition of Judah's ill-minded neighbours; his forecasts of the after-course of events as determined by the unchanging will of a righteous God; all these things seem to be included in the scope of that "Word from the presence of Iahvah," which the prophet is about to put on record. You will see that it is not a single utterance of a precise and definite message, which he might have delivered in a few moments of time before a single audience of his countrymen. The Word of the Lord is progressively revealed; it begins with a thought in the prophet's mind, but its entire content is unfolded gradually, as he proceeds to act upon that thought or Divine impulse; it is, as it were, evolved as the result of collision between the prophet and his hearers; it emerges into clear light out of the darkness of storm and conflict; a conflict both internal and external; a conflict within, between his own contending emotions and impulses and sympathies; and a conflict without, between an unpopular teacher, and a wayward and corrupt and incorrigible people. From with Iahvah. There may be strife and tumult and the darkness of ignorance and passion upon earth; but the star of truth shines in the firmament of heaven, and the eye of the inspired man sees it. This is his difference from his fellows.

Hear ye the words of this covenant, and speak ye unto the men of Judah, and upon the dwellers in Jerusalem! And say thou unto them, Thus saith Iahvah, the God of Israel, Accursed are the men that hear not the words of this covenant, which I lay on your fathers, in the day that I brought them forth from the land of Egypt, from the furnace of iron, saying, Hearken unto My voice, and do these things, according to all that I shall charge you: that ye may become for Me a people, and that I Myself may become for you a God. That I may make good (lhqym vid. infr.) the oath which I sware to your forefathers, that I would give them a land flowing with milk and honey, as it now is (or simply, to-day). And I answered and said, Amen, Iahvah! (xi. 1-5). "Hear ye ... speak ye unto the men of Judah!" The occasion referred to is that memorable crisis in the eighteenth year of king Josiah, when Hilkiah the high priest had "found the book of the law in the house of the Lord" (2 Kings xxii. 8 sqq.), and the pious king had read in the hearing of the assembled people those fervid exhortations to obedience, those promises fraught with all manner of blessing, those terrible denunciations of wrath and ruin reserved for rebellion and apostasy, which we may still read in the closing chapters of the book of Deuteronomy (Deut. xxvii. sq.). Jeremiah is recalling the events of his own ministry, and passes in rapid review from the time of his preaching upon the Book of the Law, to the Chaldean invasion in the reign of Jehoiachin (xiii. 18 sqq.). He recalls the solemn occasion when king and people bound themselves by oath to observe the law of their God; when "the king stood upon the platform, and made the covenant before Iahvah, that he would follow Iahvah, and keep his commandments, and his laws and his statutes, with whole heart and with whole soul; to make good (lhqym) the words of this covenant, that were written upon this roll; and all the people stood to the covenant" (2 Kings xxiii. 3). At or soon after this great meeting, the prophet gives, in the name of Iahvah, an emphatic approval to the public undertaking; and bids the leaders in the movement not to rest contented with this good beginning, but to impress the obligation more deeply upon the community at large, by sending a mission of properly qualified persons, including himself, which should at once enforce the reforms necessitated by the covenant of strict obedience to the Law, and reconcile the people both of the capital and of the rural towns and hamlets to the sudden and sweeping changes demanded of them, by shewing their entire consonance with the Divine precepts. "Hear ye"--princes and priests--"the words of this covenant; and speak ye unto the men of Judah!" Then follows, in brief, the prophet's own commission, which is to reiterate, with all the force of his impassioned rhetoric, the awful menaces of the Sacred Book: Cursed be the men that hear not the words of this covenant! Now again, in these last years of their national existence, the chosen people are to hear an authoritative proclamation of that Divine Law upon which all their weal depends; the Law given them at the outset of their history, when the memory of the great deliverance was yet fresh in their minds; the Law which was the condition of their peculiar relation to the Universal God. At Sinai they had solemnly undertaken to observe that Law; and Iahweh had fulfilled His promise to their "fathers"--to Abraham, Isaac, and Jacob--and had given them a goodly land, in which they had now been established for at least six hundred years. The Divine truth and righteousness were manifest upon a retrospect of this long period of eventful history; and Jeremiah could not withhold his inward assent, in the formula prescribed by the Book of the Law (Deut. xxvii. 15 sqq.), to the perfect justice of the sentence: "Cursed be the men that hear not the words of this covenant." And I answered and said, Amen, Iahvah! [42] So to this true Israelite, thus deeply communing with his own spirit, two things had become clear as day. The one was the absolute righteousness of God's entire dealing with Israel, from first to last; the righteousness of disaster and overthrow as well as of victory and prosperity: the other was his own present duty to bring this truth home to the hearts and consciences of his fellow-countrymen. This is how he states the fact: And Iahvah said unto me, Proclaim thou all these words in the cities of Judah and in the streets of Jerusalem, saying, Hear ye the words of this covenant and do them. For I earnestly adjured your fathers, when I brought them up from the land of Egypt (and I have done so continually) even unto this very day, saying, Obey ye My voice! And they obeyed not, nor inclined their ear; and they walked, each and all, in the hardness of their wicked heart. So I brought upon them all the threats (lit. words) of this covenant, which I had charged them to keep, and they kept it not. (xi. 6-8). God is always self-consistent; man is often inconsistent with himself; God is eternally true, man is ever giving fresh proofs of his natural faithlessness. God is not only just in keeping His promises; He is also merciful, in labouring ever to induce man to be self-consistent, and true to moral obligations. And Divine mercy is revealed alike in the pleadings of the Holy Spirit by the mouth of prophets, by the voice of conscience, and in the retribution that overtakes persistence in evil. The Divine Law is life and health to them that keep it; it is death to them that break it. "Thou, Lord, art merciful; for thou rewardest every man according to his works."

The relation of the One God to this one people was neither accidental nor arbitrary. It is sometimes spoken of as a thing glaringly unjust to the other nations of the ancient world, that the Father of all should have chosen Israel only to be the recipient of His special favours. Sometimes it is demanded, as an unanswerable dilemma, How could the Universal God be the God of the Jews, in the restricted sense implied by the Old Testament histories? But difficulties of this kind rest upon misunderstanding, due to a slavishly literal interpretation of certain passages, and inability to take a comprehensive view of the general drift and tenor of the Old Testament writings as they bear upon this subject. God's choice of Israel was proof of His love for mankind. He did not select one people, because He was indifferent or hostile to all other peoples; but because He wished to bring all the nations of the earth to the knowledge of Himself, and the observance of His law. The words of our prophet shew that he was profoundly convinced that the favour of Iahvah had from the outset depended upon the obedience of Israel: Hearken unto My voice, and do these things ... that ye may become for Me a people, and that I Myself may become for you a God. How strangely must such words have sounded in the ears of people who believed, as the masses both in town and country appear for the most part to have done, that Iahvah as the ancestral god was bound by an indissoluble tie to Israel, and that He could not suffer the nation to perish without incurring irreparable loss, if not extinction, for Himself! It is as if the prophet had said: You call yourselves the people of God; but it is not so much that you are His people, as that you may become such by doing His will. You suppose that Iahvah, the Eternal, the Creator, is to you what Chemosh is to Moab, or Molech to Ammon, or Baal to Tyre; but that is just what He is not. If you entertain such ideas of Iahvah, you are worshipping a figment of your own carnal imaginations; your god is not the Universal God but a gross unspiritual idol. It is only upon your fulfilment of His conditions, only upon your yielding an inward assent to His law, a hearty acceptance to His rule of life, that He Himself--the One only God--can truly become your God. In accepting His law, you accept Him, and in rejecting His law, you reject Him; for His law is a reflexion of Himself; a revelation, so far as such can be made to a creature like man, of His essential being and character. Therefore think not that you can worship Him by mere external rites; for the true worship is "righteousness, and holiness of life."

The progress of the reforming movement, which was doubtless powerfully stimulated by the preaching of Jeremiah, is briefly sketched in the chapter of the book of Kings, to which I have already referred (2 Kings xxiii.). That summary of the good deeds of king Josiah records apparently a very complete extirpation of the various forms of idolatry, and even a slaughter of the idol-priests upon their own altars. Heathenism, it would seem, could hardly have been practised again, at least openly, during the twelve remaining years of Josiah. But although a zealous king might enforce outward conformity to the Law, and although the earnest preaching of prophets like Zephaniah and Jeremiah might have considerable effect with the better part of the people, the fact remained that those whose hearts were really open to the word of the Lord were still, as always, a small minority; and the tendency to apostasy, though checked, was far from being rooted up. Here and there the forbidden rites were secretly observed; and the harsh measures which had accompanied their public suppression may very probably have intensified the attachment of many to the local forms of worship. Sincere conversions are not effected by violence; and the martyrdom of devotees may give new life even to degraded and utterly immoral superstitions. The transient nature of Josiah's reformation, radical as it may have appeared at the time to the principal agents engaged in it, is evident from the testimony of Jeremiah himself. And Iahvah said unto me, There exists a conspiracy among the men of Judah, and among the inhabitants of Jerusalem. They have returned to the old sins of their fathers, who refused to hear My words; and they too have gone away after other gods, to serve them: the house of Israel and the house of Judah have broken My covenant, which I made with their forefathers. Therefore thus saith Iahvah, Behold I am about to bring unto them an evil from which they cannot get forth; and they will cry unto Me, and I will not listen unto them. And the cities of Judah and the inhabitants of Jerusalem will go and cry unto the gods to whom they burn incense (i.e., now; ptcp.); and they will yield them no help at all in the time of their evil. For many as thy cities are thy gods become, O Judah! and many as the streets of Jerusalem have ye appointed altars to the Shame, altars for burning incense to the Baal. And as for thee, intercede thou not for this people, nor lift up for them outcry (i.e., mourning) and intercession; for I intend not to hearken, in the time when they call unto Me, in the time of their evil (so read: cf. vers. 12, vt instead of vd) (vv. 9-14). All this appears to indicate the course of the prophet's reflexion, after it had become clear to him that the reformation was illusory, and that his own labours had failed of their purpose. He calls the relapse of the people a plot or conspiracy; thereby suggesting, perhaps, the secrecy with which the prohibited worships were at first revived, and the intrigues of the unfaithful nobles and priests and prophets, in order to bring about a reversal of the policy of reform, and a return to the old system; and certainly suggesting that the heart of the nation, as a whole, was disloyal to its Heavenly King, and that its renewed apostasy was a wicked disavowal of lawful allegiance, and an act of unpardonable treason against God.

But the word further signifies that a bond has been entered into, a bond which is the exact antithesis of the covenant with Iahvah; and it implies that this bond has about it a fatal strength and permanence, involving as its necessary consequence the ruin of the nation. Breaking covenant with Iahvah meant making a covenant with other gods; it was impossible to do the one thing without the other. And that is as true now, under totally different conditions, as it was in the land of Judah, twenty-four centuries ago. If you have broken faith with God in Christ, it is because you have entered into an agreement with another; it is because you have foolishly taken the tempter at his word, and accepted his conditions, and surrendered to his proposals, and preferred his promises to the promises of God. It is because, against all reason, against conscience, against the Holy Spirit, against the witness of God's Word, against the witness of His Saints and Confessors in all ages, you have believed that a Being less than the Eternal God could ensure your weal and make you happy. And now your heart is no longer at unity in itself, and your allegiance is no longer single and undivided. Many as thy cities are thy gods become, O Judah! The soul that is not unified and harmonized by the fear of the One God, is torn and distracted by a thousand contending passions: and vainly seeks peace and deliverance by worship at a thousand unholy shrines. But Mammon and Belial and Ashtaroth and the whole rout of unclean spirits, whose seductions have lured you astray, will fail you at last; and in the hour of bitter need, you will learn too late that there is no god but God, and no peace nor safety nor joy but in Him.

It is futile to pray for those who have deliberately cast off the covenant of Iahvah, and made a covenant with His adversary. Intercede not for this people, nor lift up outcry and intercession for them! Prayer cannot save, nothing can save, the impenitent; and there is a state of mind, in which one's own prayer is turned into sin; the state of mind in which a man prays, merely to appease God, and escape the fire, but without a thought of forsaking sin, without the faintest aspiration after holiness. There is a degree of guilt upon which sentence is already passed, which is "unto death," and for which intercession is interdicted alike by the Apostle of the New as to the prophet of the Old Covenant.

What availeth it My beloved, that she fulfilleth her intent in Mine house? Can vows and hallowed flesh make thine evil to pass from thee? Then mightest thou indeed rejoice [43] (ver. 15). Such appears to be the true sense of this verse, the only difficult one in the chapter. The prophet had evidently the same thought in his mind as in ver. 11: I will bring unto them an evil, from which they cannot get forth; and they will cry unto Me, and I will not hearken unto them. The words also recall those of Isaiah (Isa. i. 11 sqq.): "For what to Me are your many sacrifices, saith Iahvah? When ye enter in to see My face, who hath sought this at your hand, to trample My courts? Bring no more a vain oblation; loathly incense it is to Me!" The term which I have rendered "intent," usually denotes an evil intention; so that, like Isaiah, our prophet implies that the popular worship is not only futile but sinful. So true it is that "He that turneth away his ear from hearing the law, even his prayer is an abomination" (Prov. xxviii. 9); or, as the Psalmist puts the same truth, "If I incline unto wickedness with my heart, the Lord will not hear me."

"A flourishing olive, fair with shapely fruit, did Iahvah call thy name. To the sound of a great uproar will He set her on fire; and his hanging boughs will crackle (in the flames). And Iahvah Sabaoth, that planted thee, Himself hath pronounced evil upon thee; because of the evil of the house of Israel and the house of Judah, which they have done to themselves (iv. 18, vii. 19) in provoking Me, in burning incense to the Baal" (vers. 16-17). The figure of the olive seems a very natural one (cf. Rom. xi. 17), when we remember the beauty and the utility for which that tree is famous in Eastern lands. Iahvah called thy name; that is, called thee into determinate being; endowed thee at thine origin with certain characteristic qualities. Thine original constitution, as thou didst leave thy Maker's hand, was fair and good. Israel among the nations was as beautiful to the eye as the olive among trees; and his "fruit," his doings, were a glory to God and a blessing to men, like that precious oil, for "which God and man honour" the olive (Judg. ix. 9). (Zech. iv. 3; Hos. xiv. 7; Ps. lii. 10.) But now the noble stock had degenerated; the "green olive tree," planted in the very court of Iahvah's house, had become no better than a barren wilding, fit only for the fire. The thought is essentially similar to that of an earlier discourse: "I planted thee a noble vine, wholly a right seed; how then hast thou turned into the degenerate plant of a strange vine unto Me?" (ii. 21). Here, there is an abrupt transition, which forcibly expresses the suddenness of the destruction that must devour this degenerate people: To the sound of a great uproar--the din of invading armies--he will set her (the beloved, symbolized by the tree) on fire; and his (the olive's) hanging boughs will crackle in the flames. And this fierce work of a barbarous soldiery is no chance calamity; it is the execution of a Divine judgment: Iahvah Sabaoth ... Himself hath pronounced evil upon thee. And yet further, it is the nation's own doing; the two houses of Israel have persistently laboured for their own ruin; they have brought it upon themselves. Man is himself the author of his own weal and woe; and they who are not "working out their own salvation," are working out their own destruction.

And it was Iahvah that gave Me knowledge, so that I well knew; at that time, Thou didst shew me their doings. But, for myself, like a favourite (lit. tame, friendly, gentle: iii. 4) lamb that is led to the slaughter, I wist not that against me they had laid a plot. 'Let us fell the tree in its prime, [44] and let us cut him off out of the land of the living, that his name be remembered no more.' 'Yea, but Iahvah [45] Sabaoth judgeth righteously, trieth reins and heart. I shall see Thy vengeance on them; for unto Thee have I laid bare my cause.' Therefore thus said Iahvah; Upon the men of Anathoth that were seeking thy life, saying, Thou shalt not prophesy in the name of Iahvah, that thou die not by our hand:--therefore thus said Iahvah Sabaoth, Behold I am about to visit it upon them: the young men will die by the sword; their sons and their daughters will die by the famine. And a remnant they shall not have: for I will bring an evil unto the men of Anathoth, the year of their visitation (vv. 18-23).

The prophet, it would seem, had made the round of the country places, and come to Anathoth, on his return journey to Jerusalem. Here, in his native town, he proclaimed to his own people that same solemn message which he had delivered to the country at large. It is very probable that the preceding verses (9-17) contain the substance of his address to his kinsfolk and acquaintance; an address which stirred them, not to repentance towards God but to murderous wrath against His prophet. A plot was laid for Jeremiah's life by his own neighbours and even his own family (xii. 6); and he owed his escape to some providential circumstance, some "lucky accident," as men might say, which revealed to him their unsuspected perfidy. What the event was which thus suddenly disclosed the hidden danger, is not recorded; and the whole episode is rather alluded to than described. But it is clear that the prophet knew nothing about the plot, until it was ripe for execution. He was as wholly unconscious of the death prepared for him, as a petted lamb on the way to the altar. "Then"--when his fate seemed sure--then it was that something happened by which "Iahvah gave him knowledge," and "shewed him their doings." The thought or saying attributed to his enemies, "Let us fell the tree(s) in the prime thereof!" may contain a sarcastic allusion really made to the prophet's own warning (ver. 16): "A flourishing olive, fair with shapely fruit, did Iahvah call thy name: to the noise of a great uproar will He set it on fire, and the branches thereof shall crackle in the flames." The words that follow (ver. 20), "yea, but (or, and yet) Iahvah Sabaoth judgeth righteously; trieth reins and heart" (cf. xx. 12), is the prophet's reply, in the form of an unexpressed thought, or a hurried ejaculation upon discovering their deadly malice. The timely warning which he had received, was fresh proof to him of the truth that human designs are, after all that their authors can do, dependent on the will of an Unseen Arbiter of events; and the Divine justice, thus manifested towards himself, inspired a conviction that those hardened and bloodthirsty sinners would, sooner or later, experience in their own destruction that display of the same Divine attribute which was necessary to its complete manifestation. It was this conviction, rather than personal resentment, however excusable under the circumstances that feeling would have been, which led Jeremiah to exclaim: "I shall see Thy vengeance on them, for unto Thee have I laid bare my cause."

He had appealed to the Judge of all the earth, that doeth right; and he knew the innocency of his own heart in the quarrel. He was certain, therefore, that his cause would one day be vindicated, when that ruin overtook his enemies, of which he had warned them in vain. Looked at in this light, his words are a confident assertion of the Divine justice, not a cry for vengeance. They reveal what we may perhaps call the human basis of the formal prophecy which follows; they shew by what steps the prophet's mind was led on to the utterance of a sentence of destruction upon the men of Anathoth. That Jeremiah's invectives and threatenings of wrath and ruin should provoke hatred and opposition was perhaps not wonderful. Men in general are slow to recognise their own moral shortcomings, to believe evil of themselves; and they are apt to prefer advisers, whose optimism, though ill-founded and misleading, is pleasant and reassuring and confirmatory of their own prejudices. But it does seem strange that it should have been reserved for the men of his own birthplace, his own "brethren and his father's house," to carry opposition to the point of meditated murder. Once more Jeremiah stands before us, a visible type of Him whose Divine wisdom declared that a prophet finds no honour in his own country, and whose life was attempted on that Sabbath day at Nazareth (St. Luke iv. 24 sqq.).

The sentence was pronounced, but the cloud of dejection was not at once lifted from the soul of the seer. He knew that justice must in the end overtake the guilty; but, in the meantime, "his enemies lived and were mighty," and their criminal designs against himself remained unnoticed and unpunished. The more he brooded over it, the more difficult it seemed to reconcile their prosperous immunity with the justice of God. He has given us the course of his reflections upon this painful question, ever suggested anew by the facts of life, never sufficiently answered by toiling reason. Too righteous art Thou, Iahvah, for me to contend with Thee: I will but lay arguments before Thee (i.e., argue the case forensically). Wherefore doth the way of the wicked prosper? Wherefore are they undisturbed, all that deal very treacherously? Thou plantest them, yea, they take root; they grow ever, yea, they bear fruit: Thou art nigh in their mouth, and far from their reins. And Thou, Iahvah, knowest me; Thou seest me, and triest mine heart in Thy mind. Separate them like sheep for the slaughter, and consecrate them for the day of killing! How long shall the land mourn, and the herbage of all the country wither? From the evil of the dwellers therein, beasts and birds perish: for they have said (or, thought), He cannot see our end (xii. 1-4). It is not merely that his would-be murderers thrive; it is that they take the holy Name upon their unclean lips; it is that they are hypocrites combining a pretended respect for God, with an inward and thorough indifference to God. He is nigh in their mouth and far from their reins. They "honour Him with their lips, but have removed their heart far from Him; and their worship of Him is a mere human commandment, learned by rote" (Isa. xxix. 13). They swear by His Name, when they are bent on deception (ch. v. 2). It is all this which especially rouses the prophet's indignation; and contrasting therewith his own conscious integrity and faithfulness to the Divine law, he calls upon Divine Justice to judge between himself and them: Pull them out like sheep for slaughter, and consecrate them (set them apart--from the rest of the flock) for the day of killing! It has been said that Jeremiah throughout this whole paragraph speaks not as a prophet but as a private individual; and that in this verse especially he "gives way to the natural man, and asks the life of his enemies" (1 Kings iii. 11; Job xxxi. 30). This is perhaps a tenable opinion. We have to bear in mind the difference of standpoint between the writers of the Old Covenant and those of the New. Not much is said by the former about the forgiveness of injuries, about withholding the hand from vengeance. The most ancient law, indeed, contained a noble precept, which pointed in this direction: "If thou meet thine enemy's ox or his ass going astray, thou shalt surely bring it back to him again. If thou see the ass of him that hateth thee lying under his burden, and wouldest forbear to help him, thou shalt surely help with him" (Ex. xxiii. 4, 5).

And in the book of Proverbs we read: "Rejoice not when thine enemy falleth, And let not thine heart be glad when he is overthrown." But the impression of magnanimity thus produced is somewhat diminished by the reason which is added immediately: "Lest the Lord see it and it displease Him, And He turn away His wrath from him:" a motive of which the best that can be said is that it is characteristic of the imperfect morality of the time (Prov. xxiv. 17 sq.). The same objection may be taken to that other famous passage of the same book: "If thine enemy be hungry, give him bread to eat; And if he be thirsty, give him water to drink: For thou shalt heap coals of fire upon his head, And the Lord shall reward thee" (Prov. xxv. 21 sq.). The reflexion that the relief of his necessities will mortify and humiliate an enemy to the utmost, which is what seems to have been originally meant by "heaping coals of fire upon his head," however practically useful in checking the wild impulses of a hot-blooded and vindictive race, such as the Hebrews were, and such as their kindred the Bedawi Arabs have remained to this day under a system of faith which has not said, "Love your enemies"; and however capable of a new application in the more enlightened spirit of Christianity (Rom. xii. 19 sqq.); is undoubtedly a motive marked by the limitations of Old Testament ethical thought. And edifying as they may prove to be, when understood in that purely spiritual and universal sense, to which the Church has lent her authority, how many of the psalms were, in their primary intention, agonizing cries for vengeance; prayers that the human victim of oppression and wrong might "see his desire upon his enemies"? All this must be borne in mind; but there are other considerations also which must not be omitted, if we would get at the exact sense of our prophet in the passage before us.

We must remember that he is laying a case before God. He has admitted at the outset that God is absolutely just, in spite of and in view of the fact that his murderous enemies are prosperous and unpunished. When he pleads his own sincerity and purity of heart, in contrast with the lip-service of his adversaries, it is perhaps that God may grant, not so much their perdition, as the salvation of the country from the evils they have brought and are bringing upon it. Ascribing the troubles already present and those which are yet to come, the desolations which he sees and those which he foresees, to their steady persistence in wickedness, he asks, How long must this continue? Would it not be better, would it not be more consonant with Divine wisdom and righteousness to purify the land of its fatal taint by the sudden destruction of those heinous and hardened offenders, who scoff at the very idea of a true forecast of their "end" (ver. 4)? But this is not all. There would be more apparent force in the allegation we are discussing if it were. The cry to heaven for an immediate act of retributive justice is not the last thing recorded of the prophet's experience on this occasion. He goes on to relate, for our satisfaction, the Divine answer to his questionings, which seems to have satisfied his own troubled mind. If thou hast run but with footracers, and they have wearied thee, how then wilt thou compete with the coursers? And if thy confidence be in a land of peace (or, a quiet land), how then wilt thou do in the thickets (jungles) of Jordan?[46] For even thine own brethren and thy father's house, even they will deal treacherously with thee; even they will cry aloud after thee: trust thou not in them, though they speak thee fair! (xii. 5, 6). The metaphors convey a rebuke of impatience and premature discouragement. Hitzig aptly quotes Demosthenes: "If they cannot face the candle, what will they do when they see the sun?" (Plut. de vitioso pudore, c. 5.) It is "the voice of the prophet's better feeling, and of victorious self-possession," adds the critic; and we, who earnestly believe that, of the two voices which plead against each other in the heart of man, the voice that whispers good is the voice of God, find it not hard to accept his statement in that sense. The prophet is giving us the upshot of his reflexion upon the terrible danger from which he had been mercifully preserved; and we see that his thoughts were guided to the conclusion that, having once accepted the Divine Call, it would be unworthy to abdicate his mission on the first signal of danger. Great as that danger had been, he now, in his calmer hour, perceives that, if he is to fulfil his high vocation, he must be prepared to face even worse things. With serious irony he asks himself, if a runner who is overcome in a footrace can hope to outstrip horses? or how a man, who is only bold where no danger is, will face the perils that lurk in the jungles of the Jordan? He remembers that he has to fight a more arduous battle and on a greater scene. Jerusalem is more than Anathoth; and "the kings of Judah and the princes thereof" are mightier adversaries than the conspirators of a country town. And his present escape is an earnest of deliverance on the wider field: They shall fight against thee, but they shall not prevail against thee: for I am with thee, said Iahvah, to deliver thee (see i. 17-19). But to a deeply affectionate and sensitive nature like Jeremiah's, the thought of being forsaken by his own kindred might well appear as a trial worse than death. This is the "contending with horses," the struggle that is almost beyond the powers of man to endure; this is the deadly peril, like that of venturing into the lion-haunted thickets of Jordan, which he clearly foresees as awaiting him: For even thine own brethren and thy father's house, even they will deal treacherously with thee.[47] It would seem that the prophet, with whose "timidity" some critics have not hesitated to find fault, had to renounce all that man holds dear, as a condition of faithfulness to his call. Again we are reminded of One, of whom it is recorded that "Neither did His brethren believe in Him" (St. John vii. 5), and that "His friends went out to lay hold on Him, for they said, He is beside Himself" (St. Mark iii. 21). The closeness of the parallel between type and antitype, between the sorrowful prophet and the Man of Sorrows, is seen yet further in the words, "Even they will cry aloud after thee" (lit. with full cry). The meaning may be: They will join in the hue and cry of thy pursuers, the mad shouts of "Stop him!" or "Strike him down!" such as may perhaps have rung in the prophet's ears as he fled from Anathoth. But we may also understand a metaphorical description of the efforts of his family to recall him from the unpopular path on which he had entered; and this perhaps agrees better with the warning: "Trust them not, though they speak thee fair." And understood in this sense, the words coincide with what is told us in the Gospel of the attempt of our Lord's nearest kin to arrest the progress of His Divine mission, when His mother and His brethren "standing without, sent unto Him, calling Him" (St. Mark iii. 31).

The lesson for ourselves is plain. The man who listens to the Divine call, and makes God his portion, must be prepared to surrender everything else. He must be prepared, not only to renounce much which the world accounts good; he must be prepared for all kinds of opposition, passive and active, tacit and avowed; he may even find, like Jeremiah, that his foes are the members of his own household (St. Matt. x. 36). And, like the prophet, his acceptance of the Divine call binds him to close his ears against entreaties and flatteries, against mockery and menace; and to act upon his Master's word: "If any man would come after Me, let him deny himself, and take up his cross, and follow Me. For whosoever would save his life shall lose it; and whosoever shall lose his life for My sake and the gospel's shall save it" (St. Mark viii. 34 sq.). "If any man come unto Me, and hate not his father and mother and wife and children and brethren and sisters, yea and his own life also, he cannot be My disciple" (St. Luke xiv. 26). A great prize is worth a great risk; and eternal life is a prize infinitely great. It is therefore worth the hazard and the sacrifice of all (St. Luke xviii. 29 sq.).

The section which follows (vv. 7-17) has been supposed to belong to the time of Jehoiakim, and consequently to be out of place here, having been transposed from its original context, because the peculiar Hebrew term which is rendered "dearly beloved" (ver. 7), is akin to the term rendered "My beloved," chap. xi. 15. But this supposition depends on the assumption that the "historical basis of the section" is to be found in the passage 2 Kings xxiv. 2, which relates briefly that in Jehoiakim's time plundering bands of Chaldeans, Syrians, Moabites and Ammonites overran the country. The prophecy concerning Iahvah's "evil neighbours" is understood to refer to these marauding inroads, and is accordingly supposed to have been uttered between the eighth and the eleventh years of Jehoiakim (Hitzig). It has, however, been pointed out (Naegelsbach) that the prophet does not once name the Chaldeans in the present discourse; which "he invariably does in all discourses subsequent to the decisive battle of Carchemish in the fourth year of Jehoiakim," which gave the Chaldeans the sovereignty of Western Asia. This discourse must, therefore, be of earlier date, and belong either to the first years of Jehoiakim, or to the time immediately subsequent to the eighteenth of Josiah. The history as preserved in Kings and Chronicles is so incomplete, that we are not bound to connect the reference to "evil neighbours" with what is so summarily told in 2 Kings xxiv. 2. There may have been other occasions when Judah's jealous and watchful enemies profited by her internal weakness and dissensions to invade and ravage the land; and throughout the whole period the country was exposed to the danger of plundering raids by the wild nomads of the eastern and southern borders. It is possible, however, that vv. 14-17 are a later postscript, added by the prophet when he wrote his book in the fifth or sixth year of Jehoiakim (xxxvi. 9, 32).

There is, in reality, a close connexion of thought between ver. 7 sqq. and what precedes. The relations of the prophet to his own family are made to symbolise the relations of Iahvah to His rebellious people; just as a former prophet finds in his own merciful treatment of a faithless wife a parable of Iahvah's dealings with faithless Israel. I have forsaken My house, I have cast away My domain; I have given My soul's love into the grasp of her foes. My domain hath become to Me like the lion in the wood; she hath given utterance with her voice against Me; therefore I hate her. It is Iahvah who still speaks, as in ver. 6; the "house" is His holy house, [48] the temple; the domain is His domain, the land of Judah; His "soul's love," is the Jewish people. Yet the expressions, "my house," "my domain," "my soul's love," equally suit the prophet's own family and their estate; the mention of the "lion in the wood" and its threatening roar, and the enmity provoked thereby, recalls what was said about the "wilds of the Jordan" in ver. 5, and the full outcry of his kindred after the prophet in ver. 6; and the solemn words "I have forsaken Mine house, I have cast away My domain" ... "I hate her," clearly correspond with the sentence of destruction upon Anathoth, ch. xi. 21 sqq. The double reference of the language becomes intelligible when we remember that in rejecting His messengers, Israel, nay mankind, rejects God; and that words and deeds done and uttered by Divine authority may be ascribed directly to God Himself. And regarded in the light of the prophet's commission "to pluck up and to break down, and to destroy and to overthrow, to build and to plant" nations and kingdoms (i. 10), all that is here said may be taken to be the prophet's own deliverance concerning his country. This, at all events, is the case with verses 12, 13.

What! do I see my domain (all) vultures (and) hyenas? [49] Are vultures all around her? Go ye, assemble all the beasts of the field! Bring them to devour (ver. 9). The questions express astonishment at an unlooked-for and unwelcome spectacle. The loss of Divine favour has exposed Judah to the active hostility of man; and her neighbours eagerly fall upon her, like birds and beasts of prey, swarming over a helpless quarry. It is--so the prophet puts it--it is as if a proclamation had gone forth to the wolves and jackals of the desert, bidding them come and devour the fallen carcase. [50] In another oracle he speaks of the heathen as "devouring Jacob" (x. 25). The people of Iahvah are their natural prey (Ps. xiv. 4: "who eat up My people as they eat bread"); but they are not suffered to devour them, until they have forfeited His protection.

The image is now exchanged for another, which approximates more nearly to the fact pourtrayed. Many shepherds have marred My vineyard; they have trodden down My portion; they have turned My pleasant portion into a desolate wilderness. He (the foe, the instrument of this ruin) hath made it a desolation; it mourneth against Me, being desolate; desolated is all the land, for there is no man that giveth heed (vv. 10, 11). As in an earlier discourse, ch. vi. 3, the invaders are now compared to hordes of nomad shepherds, who enter the land with their flocks and herds, and make havoc of the crops and pastures. From time immemorial the wandering Bedawis have been a terror to the settled peasantry of the East, whose way of life they despise as ignoble and unworthy of free men. Of this traditional enmity we perhaps hear a far-off echo in the story of Cain the tiller of the ground and Abel the keeper of sheep; and certainly in the statement that "every shepherd was an abomination unto the Egyptians" (Gen. xlvi. 34). The picture of utter desolateness, which the prophet suggests by a fourfold repetition, is probably sketched from a scene which he had himself witnessed; if it be not rather a representation of the actual condition of the country at the time of his writing. That the latter is the case might naturally be inferred from a consideration of the whole passage; and the twelfth verse seems to lend much support to this view: Over all bare hills in the wilderness have come ravagers; for Iahvah hath a devouring sword: from land's end to land's end no flesh hath peace. [51] The language indeed recalls that of ch. iv. 10, 11; and the entire description might be taken as an ideal picture of the ruin that must ensue upon Iahvah's rejection of the land and people, especially if the closing verses (14-17) be considered as a later addition to the prophecy, made in the light of accomplished facts. But, upon the whole, it would seem to be more probable that the prophet is here reading the moral of present or recent experience. He affirms (ver. 11) that the affliction of the country is really a punishment for the religious blindness of the nation: there is no man that layeth to heart the Divine teaching of events as interpreted by himself (cf. ver. 4). The fact that we are unable, in the scantiness of the records of the time, to specify the particular troubles to which allusion is made, is no great objection to this view, which is at least effectively illustrated by the brief statement of 2 Kings xxiv. 2. The reflexion appended in ver. 13 points in the same direction: They have sown wheat, and have reaped thorns; they have put themselves to pain (or, exhausted themselves) without profit, (or, made themselves sick with unprofitable toil); and they are ashamed of their [52] produce (ingatherings), through the heat of the wrath of Iahvah. When the enemy had ravaged the crops, thorns would naturally spring up on the wasted lands; and "the heat of the wrath of Iahvah" appears to have been further manifested in a parching drought, which ruined what the enemy had left untouched (ver. 4, ch. xiv.).

Thus, then, Jeremiah receives the answer to his doubts in a painfully visible demonstration of what the wrath of Iahvah means. It means drought and famine; it means the exposure of the country, naked and defenceless, to the will of rapacious and vindictive enemies. For Iahvah's wrongs are far deeper and more bitter than the prophet's. The misdeeds of individuals are lighter in the balance than the sins of a nation; the treachery of a few persons on a particular occasion is as nothing beside the faithlessness of many generations. The partial evils, therefore, under which the country groans, can only be taken as indications of a far more complete and terrible destruction reserved for final impenitence. The perception of this truth, we may suppose, sufficed for the time to silence the prophet's complaints; and in the revulsion of feeling inspired by the awful vision of the unimpeded outbreak of Divine wrath, he utters an oracle concerning his country's destroyers, in which retributive justice is tempered by compassion and mercy. Thus hath Jehovah said, Upon all Mine evil neighbours, who touch the heritage which I caused My people Israel to inherit: Lo I am about to uproot (i. 10) them from off their own land, and the house of Judah will I uproot from their midst. And after I have uprooted them, I will have compassion on them again, and will restore them each to their own heritage and their own land. And if they truly learn the ways of My people, to swear by My name, 'as Iahvah liveth!' even as they taught My people to swear by the Baal; they shall be rebuilt in the midst of My people. And if they will not hear, I will uproot that nation, utterly and fatally; it is an oracle of Iahvah (14-17). The preceding section (vv. 7-14), as we have seen, rapidly yet vividly sketches the calamities which have ensued and must further ensue upon the Divine desertion of the country. Iahvah has forsaken the land, left her naked to her enemies, for her causeless, capricious, thankless revolt against her Divine Lord. In this forlorn, defenceless condition, all manner of evils befall her; the vineyards and cornfields are ravaged, the goodly land is desolated, by hordes of savage freebooters pouring in from the eastern deserts. These invaders are called Iahvah's "evil neighbours;" an expression which implies, not individuals banded together for purposes of brigandage, but hostile nations. [53] Upon these nations also will the justice of God be vindicated; for that justice is universal in its operation, and cannot therefore be restricted to

Israel. Judgment must "begin at the house of God;" but it will not end there. The "evil neighbours," the surrounding heathen kingdoms, have been Iahvah's instruments for the chastisement of His rebellious people; but they are not on that account exempted from recompense. They too must reap what they have sown. They have insulted Iahvah, by violating His territory; they have indulged their malice and treachery and rapacity, in utter disregard of the rights of neighbours, and the moral claims of kindred peoples. As they have done, so shall it be done unto them: Drasanti pathein. They have laid hands on the possessions of their neighbour, and their own shall be taken from them; I am about to uproot them from off their own land (cf. Amos i. 3-ii. 3). And not only so, but the house of Judah will I pluck up from their midst. The Lord's people shall be no more exposed to their unneighbourly ill-will; the butt of their ridicule, the victim of their malice, will be removed to a foreign soil as well as they; but oppressed and oppressors will no longer be together; their new settlements will lie far apart; under the altered state of things, under the shadow of the great conqueror of the future, there will be no opportunity for the old injurious dealings. All alike, Judah and the enemies of Judah, will be subject to the will of the foreign lord. But that is not the end. The Judge of all the earth is merciful as well as just. He is loth to blot whole peoples out of existence, even though they have merited destruction by grievous and prolonged transgression of His laws. Therefore banishment will be followed by restoration, not in the case of Judah only, but of all the expatriated peoples. After enduring the Divine probation of adversity, they will be brought again, by the Divine compassion, "each to their own heritage and their own land." And then, if they will profit by the teaching of Iahvah's prophets, and "learn the ways," that is, the religion of His people, making their supreme appeal to Iahvah, as the fountain of all truth and the sovran vindicator of right and justice, as hitherto they have appealed to the Baal, and misled Israel into the same profane and futile course; then "they shall be built up," or rebuilt, or brought to great and ever-growing prosperity, "in the midst of My people." Such is to be the blessing of the Gentiles; they shall share in the glorious future that awaits repentant Israel. The present condition of things is to be completely reversed: now Judah sojourns in their midst; then they will be surrounded on every side by the emancipated and triumphant people of God: now they beset Judah with jealousies, suspicions, enmities; then Judah will embrace them all with the arms of an unselfish and protecting love. A last word of warning is added. The doom of the nation that will not accept the Divine teaching will be utter and absolute extermination.

The forecast is plainly of a Messianic nature; it recognises in Iahvah the Saviour, not of a nation, but of the world. It perceives that the disunion and mutual hatred of peoples, as of individuals, is a breach of Divine law; and it proclaims a general return to God, and submission to His guidance in all political as well as private affairs, as the sole cure for the numberless evils that flow from that hatred and disunion. It is only when men have learnt that God is their common Father and Lord, that they come to see with the clearness and force of practical conviction that they themselves are all members of one family, bound as such to mutual offices of kindness and charity; it is only when there is a conscious identity of interest with all our fellows, based upon the recognition that all alike are children of God and heirs of eternal life, that true freedom and universal brotherhood become possible for man.

Footnotes:

42. But perhaps it is rather the prophet's love for his people, which fervently prays that the oath of blessing may be observed, and Judah maintained in the goodly land.

43. Hitzig supposed that the "vows" and "hallowed flesh" were thank-offerings for the departure of the Scythians. "It is plain that the people are really present in the temple; they bring, presumably after the retreat of the Scythians, the offerings vowed at that time." But, considering the context, the reference appears to be more general. I have partly followed the LXX. in emending an obviously corrupt verse; the only one in the chap. which presents any textual difficulty. Read: mlyky rtky 'z tl zy mh lydydy vvyty svth hmzmth hndrym vvsr qds yvrv. The article with a noun with suffix, and the peculiar form of the 2 pers. pron. f., are found elsewhere in Jer. But I incline to correct further thus: "What avail to My beloved is her dealing (or sacrificing: sh 2 Kings xvii. 32) in My house?" hmzbchvt hrbym vvsr qds vgv. "Can the many altars (ver. 13) and hallowed flesh cause thine evil to pass away from thee (or pass thee by)?" This seems very apposite to what precedes. The Hebrew, as it stands, cannot possibly mean what we read both in the A. V. and R. V., nor indeed anything else.

44. Reading blchv, with Hitzig, instead of blchmv, which is meaningless. Deut. xxxiv. 7; Ezek. xxi. 3. Perhaps it would be better to keep all the letters, and point blchmv, understanding ts as collective, "the trees."

45. Not a vocative: xx. 12, xvii. 10.

46. That "the swelling" or "the pride of Jordan" should rather be read "the wilds" or "jungles of Jordan," is clear from xlix. 19; Zech. xi. 3; quoted by Hitzig. g'vn means "growth," "overgrowth," among other things; and the Heb. phrase coincides with the Iarden drumos of Josephus (Bell. Jud., vii. 6, 5).

47. The form of the Heb. verbs implies the certainty of the event. Hitzig supposes that ver. 6

simply explains the expression "land of peace" in ver. 5. At Anathoth the prophet was at home; if he "ran away" (reading vvrch "fleest" for vvtch "art confident") there, what would he do, when he had gone forth as a "sheep among wolves" (St. Luke x. 3)? But I think it is much better to regard ver. 6 as explaining the whole of ver. 5 in the manner suggested above.

48. Or perhaps rather the holy land itself, as Hitzig suggested: Hos. ix. 15.

49. Lit. "Is my domain vultures, hyenas, to me?" The dative expresses the interest of the speaker in the fact (dat. ethic.). The Heb. term tsvv only occurs here. It is the Arabic dhabu`, "hyena" (so Sept.). St. Jerome renders avis discolor. So the Targum: "a strewn" "sprinkled," or "spotted fowl."

50. The references to "birds of prey," "beasts of the field," and "spoilers" (ver. 12), are interpreted by the phrase "mine evil neighbours" (ver. 14); and this constitutes a link between vv. 7-14 and 14-17.

51. Such seems to be the best punctuation of the sentence. It involves the transfer of Athnach to 'klh.

52. So the LXX. This agrees better with the context than "So be ye ashamed of your fruits."

53. As Hitzig has observed, only a people, or a king, or a national god, could be spoken of as a "neighbour" to the God of Israel.

VIII. THE FALL OF PRIDE

Jeremiah xiii.

This discourse is a sort of appendix to the preceding; as is indicated by its abrupt and brief beginning with the words "Thus said Iahvah unto me," without the addition of any mark of time, or other determining circumstance. It predicts captivity, in retribution for the pride and ingratitude of the people; and thus suitably follows the closing section of the last address, which announces the coming deportation of Judah and her evil neighbours. The recurrence here (ver. 9) of the peculiar term rendered "swelling" or "pride" in our English versions (ch. xii. 5), points to the same conclusion. We may subdivide it thus: It presents us with (i) a symbolical action, or acted parable, with its moral and application (vv. 1-11); (ii) a parabolic saying and its interpretation, which leads up to a pathetic appeal for penitence (vv. 12-17); (iii) a message to the sovereigns (vv. 18, 19); and (iv) a closing apostrophe to Jerusalem--the gay and guilty capital, so soon to be made desolate for her abounding sins (vv. 20-27).

In the first of these four sections, we are told how the prophet was bidden of God to buy a linen girdle, and after wearing it for a time, to bury it in a cleft of the rock at a place whose very name might be taken to symbolize the doom awaiting his people. A long while afterwards he was ordered to go and dig it up again, and found it altogether spoiled and useless. The significance of these proceedings is clearly enough explained. The relation between Israel and the God of Israel had been of the closest kind. Iahvah had chosen this people, and bound it to Himself by a covenant, as a man might bind a girdle about his body; and as the girdle is an ornament of dress, so had the Lord intended Israel to display His glory among men (ver. 11). But now the girdle is rotten; and like that rotten girdle will He cause the pride of Judah to rot and perish (vv. 9, 10).

It is natural to ask, whether Jeremiah really did as he relates; or whether the narrative about the girdle be simply a literary device intended to carry a lesson home to the dullest apprehension. If the prophet's activity had been confined to the pen; if he had not been wont to labour by word and deed for the attainment of his purposes; the latter alternative might be accepted. For mere readers, a parabolic narrative might suffice to enforce his meaning. But Jeremiah, who was all his life a man of action, probably did the thing he professes to have done, not in thought nor in word only, but in deed and to the knowledge of certain competent witnesses. There was nothing novel in this method of attracting attention, and giving greater force and impressiveness to his prediction. The older prophets had often done the same kind of things, on the principle that deeds may be more effective than words. What could have conveyed a more vivid sense of the Divine intention, than the simple act of Ahijah the Shilonite, when he suddenly caught away the new mantle of Solomon's officer, and rent it into twelve pieces, and said to the astonished courtier, "Take thee ten pieces! for thus said Iahvah, the God of Israel, Behold I am about to rend the kingdom out of the hand of Solomon, and will give the ten tribes to thee"? (1 Kings xi. 29 sqq.) In like manner, when Ahab and Jehoshaphat, dressed in their robes of state, sat enthroned in the gateway of Samaria, and "all the prophets were prophesying before them" about the issue of their joint expedition to Ramoth-gilead, Zedekiah, the son of a Canaanitess--as the writer is careful to add of this false prophet--"made him horns of iron and said, Thus said Iahvah, With these shalt thou butt the Arameans, until thou make an end of them" (1 Kings xxii. 11). Isaiah, Hosea, and Ezekiel, record similar actions of symbolical import. Isaiah for a time walked half-clad and barefoot, as a sign that the Egyptians and Ethiopians, upon whom Judah was inclined to lean, would be led away captive, in this comfortless guise, by the king of Assyria (Isa. xx.). Such actions may be regarded as a further development of those significant gestures, with which men in what is called a state of nature are wont to give emphasis and precision to their spoken ideas. They may also be compared with the symbolism of ancient law. "An ancient conveyance," we are told, "was not written but acted. Gestures and words took the place of written technical phraseology, and any formula mispronounced, or symbolical act omitted, would have vitiated the proceeding as fatally as a material mistake in stating the uses or setting out the remainders would, two hundred years ago, have vitiated an English deed." (Maine, Ancient Law, p. 276.) Actions of a purely symbolical nature surprise us, when we first encounter them in Religion or Law, but that is only because they are survivals. In the ages when they originated, they were familiar occurrences in all transactions between man and man. And this general consideration tends to prove that those expositors are wrong who maintain that the prophets did not really perform the symbolical actions of which they speak. Just as it is argued that the visions which they describe, are merely a literary device; so the reality of these symbolical actions has needlessly enough been called in question. The learned Jews Abenezra and Maimonides in the twelfth century, and David Kimchi in the thirteenth, were the first to affirm this opinion. Maimonides held that all such actions passed in vision before the prophets; a view which has found a modern advocate in Hengstenberg: and Stäudlin, in the last century, affirmed that they had neither an objective nor a subjective reality, but were simply a "literary device." This, however, is only true, if true at all, of the declining period of prophecy, as in the case of the visions. In the earlier period, while the prophets were still accustomed to an oral delivery of their discourses, we may be quite sure that they suited the action to the word in the way that they have themselves recorded; in order to stir the popular imagination, and to create a more vivid and lasting impression. The narratives of the historical books leave no doubt about the matter. But in later times, when spoken addresses had for the most part become a thing of the past, and when prophets published their convictions in manuscript, it is possible that they were content with the description of symbolical doings, as a sort of parable, without any actual performance of them. Jeremiah's hiding his girdle in a cleft of the rock at "Euphrates" has been regarded by some writers as an instance of such purely ideal symbolism. And certainly it is difficult to suppose that the prophet made the long and arduous journey from Jerusalem to the Great River for such a purpose. It is, however, a highly probable conjecture that the place whither he was directed to repair was much nearer home: the addition of a single letter to the name rendered "Euphrates" gives the far preferable reading "Ephrath," that is to say, Bethlehem in Judah (Gen. xlviii. 7). Jeremiah may very well have buried his girdle at Bethlehem, a place only five miles or so to the south of Jerusalem; a place, moreover, where he would have no trouble in finding a "cleft of the rock," which would hardly be the case upon the alluvial banks of the Euphrates. If not accidental, the difference may be due to the intentional employment of an unusual form of the name, by way of hinting at the source whence the ruin of Judah was to flow. The enemy "from the north" (ver. 20) is of course the Chaldeans.

The mention of the queen-mother (ver. 18) along with the king appears to point unmistakably to the reign of Jehoiachin or Jechoniah. The allusion is compared with the threat of ch. xxii. 26: "I will cast thee out, and thy mother that bare thee into another country." Like Josiah, this king was but eight years old when he began to reign (2 Chron. xxxvi. 9, after which 2 Kings xxiv. 8 must be corrected); and he had enjoyed the name of king only for the brief period of three months, when the thunderbolt fell, and Nebuchadrezzar began his first siege of Jerusalem. The boy-king can hardly have had much to do with the issue of affairs, when "he and his mother and his servants and his princes and his eunuchs" surrendered the city, and were deported to Babylon, with ten thousand of the principal inhabitants (2 Kings xxiv. 12 sqq.). The date of our discourse will thus be the beginning of the year b.c. 599, which was the eighth year of Nebuchadrezzar (2 Kings xxiv. 12).

It is asserted, indeed, that the difficult verse 21 refers to the revolt from Babylon as an accomplished fact; but this is by no means clear from the verse itself. What wilt thou say, demands the prophet, when He shall appoint over thee--albeit, thou thyself hast instructed them against thyself;-- lovers to be thy head? The term "lovers" or "lemans" applies best to the foreign idols, who will one day repay the foolish attachment of Iahvah's people by enslaving it (cf. ch. iii. 4, where Iahvah himself is called the "lover" of Judah's youthful days); and this question might as well have been asked in the days of Josiah, as at any later period. At various times in the past Israel and Judah had courted the favour of foreign deities. Ahaz had introduced Aramean and Assyrian novelties; Manasseh and Amon had revived and aggravated his apostasy. Even Hezekiah had had friendly dealings with Babylon, and we must remember that in those times friendly intercourse with a foreign people implied some recognition of their gods, which is probably the true account of Solomon's chapels for Tyrian and other deities.

The queen of ver. 18 might conceivably be Jedidah, the mother of Josiah, for that king was only eight at his accession, and only thirty-nine at his death (2 Kings xxii. 1). And the message to the sovereigns (ver. 18) is not couched in terms of disrespect nor of reproach: it simply declares the imminence of overwhelming disaster, and bids them lay aside their royal pomp, and behave as mourners for the coming woe. Such words might perhaps have been addressed to Josiah and his mother, by way of deepening the impression produced by the Book of the Law, and the rumoured invasion of the Scythians. But the threat against "the kings that sit on David's throne" (ver. 13) is hardly suitable on this supposition; and the ruthless tone of this part of the address--I will dash them in pieces, one against another, both the fathers and the sons together: I will not pity, nor spare, nor relent from destroying them--considered along with the emphatic prediction of an utter and entire captivity (ver. 19), seems to indicate a later period of the prophet's ministry, when the obduracy of the people had revealed more fully the hopelessness of his enterprise for their salvation. The mention of the enemy "from the north" will then be a reference to present circumstances of peril, as triumphantly vindicating the prophet's former menaces of destruction from that quarter. The carnage of conquest and the certainty of exile are here threatened in the plainest and most direct style; but nothing is said by way of heightening the popular terror of the coming destroyer. The prophet seems to take it for granted that the nature of the evil which hangs over their heads, is well known to the people, and does not need to be dwelt upon or amplified with the lyric fervour of former utterances (see ch. iv., v. 15 sqq., vi. 22 sqq.). This appears quite natural, if we suppose that the first invasion of the Chaldeans was now a thing of the past; and that the nation was awaiting in trembling uncertainty the consequences of Jehoiakim's breach of faith with his Babylonian suzerain (2 Kings xxiv. i. 10). The prophecy may therefore be assigned with some confidence to the short reign of Jehoiachin, to which perhaps the short section, ch. x. 17-25, also belongs; a date which harmonizes better than any other with the play on the name Euphrates in the opening of the chapter. It agrees, too, with the emphatic Iahvah hath spoken! (ver. 15), which seems to be more than a mere assertion of the speaker's veracity, and to point rather to the fact that the course of events had reached a crisis; that something had occurred in the political world, which suggested imminent danger; that a black cloud was looming up on the national horizon, and signalling unmistakably to the prophet's eye the intention of Iahvah. What other view so well explains the solemn tone of warning, the vivid apprehension of danger, the beseeching tenderness, that give so peculiar a stamp to the three verses in which the address passes from narrative and parable, to direct appeal? Hear ye and give ear: be not proud: for Iahvah hath spoken! Give glory to Iahvah your God--the glory of confession, of avowing your own guilt and His perfect righteousness (Josh. vii. 19; St. John ix. 24); of recognising the due reward of your deeds in the destruction that threatens you; the glory involved in the cry, "God be merciful to me a sinner!"--Give glory to Iahvah your God, before the darkness fall, and before your feet stumble upon the twilight mountains; and ye wait for dawn, and He make it deepest gloom, He turn it to utter darkness. The day was declining; the evening shadows were descending and deepening; soon the hapless people would be wandering bewildered in the twilight, and lost in the darkness, unless, ere it had become too late, they would yield their pride, and throw themselves upon the pity of Him who "maketh the seven stars and Orion, and turneth the deepest gloom into the morning" (Amos v. 8).

The verbal allusiveness of the opening section does not, according to Oriental taste, diminish the solemnity of the speaker; on the contrary, it tends to deepen the impression produced by his words. And perhaps there is a psychological reason for the fact, beyond the peculiar partiality of Oriental peoples for such displays of ingenuity. It is, at all events, remarkable that the greatest of all masters of human feeling has not hesitated to make a dying prince express his bitter and desponding thoughts in what may seem an artificial toying and trifling with the suggestiveness of his own familiar name; and when the king asks: "Can sick men play so nicely with their names?" the answer is: "No, misery makes sport to mock itself." (Rich. II., Act 2, Sc. i., 72 sqq.) The Greek tragedian, too, in the earnestness of bitter sport, can find a prophecy in a name. "Who was for naming her thus, with truth so entire? (Was it One whom we see not, wielding tongue happily with full foresight of what was to be?) the Bride of Battles, fiercely contested Helen: seeing that, in full accord with her name, haler of ships, haler of men, haler of cities, forth of the soft and precious tapestries away she sailed, under the gale of the giant West" (Æsch., Ag., 681 sqq.). And so, to Jeremiah's ear, Ephrath is prophetic of Euphrates, upon whose distant banks the glory of his people is to languish and decay. "I to Ephrath, and you to Phrath!" is his melancholy cry. Their doom is as certain as if it were the mere fulfilment of an old-world prophecy, crystallized long ages ago in a familiar name; a word of destiny fixed in this strange form, and bearing its solemn witness from the outset of their history until now concerning the inevitable goal.

There is nothing so very surprising, as Ewald seems to have thought, in the suggestion that the Perath of the Hebrew text may be the same as Ephrath. But perhaps the valley and spring now called Furah (or Furat) which lies at about the same distance N.E. of Jerusalem, is the place intended by the prophet. The name, which means fresh or sweet water is identical with the Arabic name of the Euphrates (Furat, Arabic script), which again is philologically identical with the Hebrew Perath. It is obvious that this place would suit the requirements of the text quite as well as the other, while the coincidence of name enables us to dispense with the supposition of an unusual form or even a corruption of the original; but Furat or Forah is not mentioned elsewhere in the Old Testament. The old versions send the prophet to the river Euphrates, which Jeremiah calls simply "The River" in one place (ii. 18), and "The river of Perath" in three others (xlvi. 2, 6, 10); while the rare "Perath," without any addition, is only found in the second account of the Creation (Gen. ii. 14), in 2 Chron. xxxv. 20, and in a passage of this book which does not belong, nor profess to belong, to Jeremiah (li. 63). We may, therefore, conclude that "Perath" in the present passage means not the great river of that name, but a place near Jerusalem, although that place was probably chosen with the intention, as above explained, of alluding to the Euphrates.

I cannot assent to the opinion which regards this narrative of the spoiled girdle as founded upon some accidental experience of the prophet's life, in which he afterwards recognised a Divine lesson. The precision of statement, and the nice adaptation of the details of the story to the moral which the prophet wished to convey, rather indicate a symbolical course of action, or what may be called an acted parable. The whole proceeding appears to have been carefully thought out beforehand. The intimate connexion between Iahvah and Israel is well symbolized by a girdle--that part of an Eastern dress which "cleaves to the loins of a man," that is, fits closest to the body, and is most securely attached thereto. And if the nations be represented by the rest of the apparel, as the girdle secures and keeps that in its place, we may see an implication that Israel was intended to be the chain that bound mankind to God. The girdle was of linen, the material of the priestly dress, not only because Jeremiah was a priest, but because Israel was called to be "a kingdom of priests," or the Priest among nations (Ex. xix. 6). The significance of the command to wear the girdle, but not to put it into water, seems to be clear enough. The unwashed garment which the prophet continues to wear for a time represents the foulness of Israel; just as the order to bury it at Perath indicates what Iahvah is about to do with His polluted people.

The exposition begins with the words, Thus will I mar the great pride of Judah and of Jerusalem! The spiritual uncleanness of the nation consisted in the proud self-will which turned a deaf ear to the warnings of Iahvah's prophets, and obstinately persisted in idolatry (ver. 10). It continues: For as the girdle cleaveth to the loins of a man, so made I the whole house of Israel and the whole house of Judah to cleave unto Me, saith Iahvah; that they might become to Me for a people, and for a name, and for a praise, and for an ornament (Ex. xxviii. 2). Then their becoming morally unclean, through the defilements of sin, is briefly implied in the words, And they obeyed not (ver. 11).

It is not the pride of the tyrant king Jehoiakim that is here threatened with destruction. It is the national pride which had all along evinced itself in rebellion against its heavenly King--the great pride of Judah and Jerusalem; and this pride, inasmuch as it "trusted in man and made flesh its arm" (xvii. 5), and boasted in a carnal wisdom, and material strength and riches (ix. 23, xxi. 13), was to be brought low by the complete extinction of the national autonomy, and the reduction of a high-spirited and haughty race to the status of humble dependents upon a heathen power.

2. A parabolic saying follows, with its interpretation. And say thou unto them this word: Thus said Iahvah, the God of Israel: Every jar is wont to be filled (or shall be filled) with wine. And if they say unto thee, Are we really not aware that every jar is wont to be filled with wine? say thou unto them, Thus said Iahvah, Lo, I am about to fill all the inhabitants of this land, and the kings that sit for David upon his throne, and the priests and the prophets, and all the inhabitants of Jerusalem, with drunkenness; and I will dash them in pieces against one another, and the fathers and the sons together, saith Iahvah: I will not forbear nor spare nor pity, so as not to mar them (cf. vv. 7, 9).

The individual members of the nation, of all ranks and classes, are compared to earthenware jars, not "skins," as the LXX. gives it, for they are to be dashed in pieces, "like a potter's vessel" (Ps. ii. 9; cf. ver. 14). [54] Regarding them all as ripe for destruction, Jeremiah exclaims, "Every jar is filled with wine," in the ordinary course of things; that is its destiny. His hearers answer with the mocking question, "Do you suppose that we don't know that?" They would, of course, be aware that a prophet's figure, however homely, covered an inner meaning of serious import; but derision was their favourite retort against unpopular truths (xvii. 15, xx. 7, 8). They would take it for granted that the thing suggested was unfavourable, from their past experience of Jeremiah. Their ill-timed banter is met by the instant application of the figure. They, and the kings then sitting on David's throne, i.e., the young Jehoiachin and the queen-mother Nehushta (who probably had all the authority if not the title of a regent), and the priests and prophets who fatally misled them by false teachings and false counsels, are the wine-jars intended, and the wine that is to fill them is the wine of the wrath of God (Ps. lxxv. 8; Jer. xxv. 15; cf. li. 7; Rev. xvi. 19; Isa. xix. 14, 15). The effect is intoxication--a fatal bewilderment, a helpless lack of decision, an utter confusion and stupefaction of the faculties of wisdom and foresight, in the very moment of supreme peril (cf. Isa. xxviii. 7; Ps. lx. 5). Like drunkards, they will reel against and overthrow each other. The strong term I will dash them in pieces is used, to indicate the deadly nature of their fall, and because the prophet has still in his mind the figure of the wine-jars, which were probably amphoræ, pointed at the end, like those depicted in Egyptian mural paintings, so that they could not stand upright without support. By their fall they are to be utterly "marred" (the term used of the girdle, ver. 9).

But even yet one way of escape lies open. It is to sacrifice their pride, and yield to the will of Iahvah. Hear ye, and give ear, be not haughty! for Iahvah hath spoken: give ye to Iahvah your God the glory, before it grow dark (or He cause darkness), and before your feet stumble upon mountains of twilight; and ye wait for the dawn, and He make it gloom, turning it to cloudiness! (Isa. v. 30, viii. 20, 22; Amos viii. 9). It is very remarkable, that even now, when the Chaldeans are actually in the country, and blockading the strong places of southern Judah (ver. 19), which was the usual preliminary to an advance upon Jerusalem itself (2 Chron. xii. 4, xxxii. 9; Isa. xxxvi. 1, 2), Jeremiah should still speak thus; assuring his fellow-citizens that confession and self-humiliation before their offended God might yet deliver them from the bitterest consequences of past misdoing. Iahvah had indeed spoken audibly enough, as it seemed to the prophet, in the calamities that had already befallen the country; these were an indication of more and worse to follow, unless they should prove efficacious in leading the people to repentance. If they failed, nothing would be left for the prophet but to mourn in solitude over his country's ruin (ver. 17). But Jeremiah was fully persuaded that the Hand that had stricken could heal; the Power that had brought the invaders into Judah, could cause them to "return by the way that they had come" (Isa. xxxvii. 34). Of course such a view is unintelligible from the standpoint of unbelief; but then the standpoint of the prophets is faith.

3. After this general appeal for penitence, the discourse turns to the two exalted persons whose position and interest in the country were the highest of all, the youthful king, and the empress or queen-mother. They are addressed in a tone which, though not disrespectful, is certainly despairing. They are called upon, not so much to set the example of penitence (cf. Jonah iii. 6), as to take up the attitude of mourners (Job ii. 13; Isa. iii. 26; Lam. ii. 10; Ezek. xxvi. 16) in presence of the public disasters. Say thou to the king and to the empress, Sit ye low on the ground! (lit. make low your seat! cf. Isa. vii. for the construction) for it is fallen from your heads [55] --your beautiful crown! (Lam. v. 16). The cities of the south are shut fast, and there is none that openeth (Josh. vi. 1): Judah is carried away captive all of her, she is wholly carried away. There is no hope; it is vain to expect help; nothing is left but to bemoan the irreparable. The siege of the great fortresses of the south country and the sweeping away of the rural population were sure signs of what was coming upon Jerusalem. The embattled cities themselves may be suggested by the fallen crown of beauty; Isaiah calls Samaria "the proud crown of the drunkards of Ephraim" (Isa. xxviii. 1), and cities are commonly represented in ancient art by female figures wearing mural crowns. In that case, both verses are addressed to the sovereigns, and the second is exegetical of the first.

As already observed, there is here no censure, but only sorrowful despair over the dark outlook. In the same way, Jeremiah's utterance (xxii. 20 sqq.) about the fate of Jehoiachin is less a malediction than a lament. And when we further consider his favourable judgment of the first body of exiles, who were carried away with this monarch soon after the time of the present oracle (chap. xxiv.), we may perhaps see reason to conclude that the surrender of Jerusalem to the Chaldeans on this occasion was partly due to his advice. The narrative of Kings, however, is too brief to enable us to come to any certain decision about the circumstances of Jehoiachin's submission (2 Kings xxiv. 10-12).

4. From the sovereigns, the prophet turns to Jerusalem. Lift up thine eyes (O Jerusalem [56]), and behold them that came from the north! Where is the flock that was given to thee, thy beautiful sheep? What wilt thou say when He shall appoint over thee--nay, thou thyself hast spurred them against thyself!--lovers (iii. 4, xi. 19) for head? Will not pangs take thee, as a woman in travail? Jerusalem sits upon her hills, as a beautiful shepherdess. The country towns and unwalled villages lay about her, like a fair flock of sheep and goats entrusted to her care and keeping. But now these have been destroyed and their pastures are made a silent solitude, and the destroyer is advancing against herself. What pangs of shame and terror will be hers, when she recognises in the enemy triumphing over her grievous downfall the heathen "friends" whose love she had courted so long! Her sin is to be her scourge. She shall be made the thrall of her foreign lovers. Iahvah will "appoint them over her" (xv. 3, li. 27); they will become the "head," and she the "tail" (Lam. i. 5; Deut. xxviii. 44). Yet this will, in truth, be her own doing, not Iahvah's; she has herself "accustomed them to herself" (x. 2), or "instructed" or "spurred them on" against herself (ii. 33, iv. 18). The revolt of Jehoiakim, his wicked breach of faith with Nebuchadrezzar, had turned friends to enemies (iv. 30). But the chief reference seems to be more general--the continual craving of Judah for foreign alliances and foreign worships. And if thou say in thine heart, "Wherefore did these things befall me?" through the greatness of thy guilt were thy skirts uncovered, thine heels violated (Nah. iii. 5) or exposed. Will a Cushite change his skin, or a leopard his spots? ye, too, are ye able to do good, O ye that are wont to do evil? If amid the sharp throes of suffering Jerusalem should still fail to recognise the moral cause of them (v. 19), she may be assured beforehand that her unspeakable dishonour is the reward of her sins; that is why "the virgin daughter of Sion" is surprised and ravished by the foe (a common figure: Isa. xlvii. 1-3). Sin has become so ingrained in her, that it can no more be eradicated than the blackness of an African skin, or the spots of a leopard's hide. The habit of sinning has become "a second nature," and, like nature, is not to be expelled (cf. viii. 4-7).

The effect of use and wont in the moral sphere could hardly be expressed more forcibly, and Jeremiah's comparison has become a proverb. Custom binds us all in every department of life; it is only by enlisting this strange influence upon the side of virtue, that we become virtuous. Neither virtue nor vice can be pronounced perfect, until the habit of either has become fixed and invariable. It is the tendency of habitual action of any kind to become automatic; and it is certain that sin may attain such a mastery over the active powers of a man that its indulgence may become almost an unconscious exercise of his will, and quite a matter of course. But this fearful result of evil habits does not excuse them at the bar of common sense, much less at the tribunal of God. The inveterate sinner, the man totally devoid of scruple, whose conscience is, as it were, "seared with a hot iron," is not on that account excused by the common judgment of his kind; the feeling he excites is not forbearance, but abhorrence; he is regarded not as a poor victim of circumstances over which he has no control, but as a monster of iniquity. And justly so; for if he has lost control of his passions, if he is no longer master of himself, but the slave of vice, he is responsible for the long course of self-indulgence which has made him what he is. The prophet's comparison cannot be applied in support of a doctrine of immoral fatalism. The very fact that he makes use of it, implies that he did not intend it to be understood in such a sense. "Will a

Cushite change his skin, or a leopard his spots? Ye also--supposing such a change as that--will be able to do good, O ye that are taught--trained, accustomed--to do evil!" (perhaps the preferable rendering).

Not only must we abstain from treating a rhetorical figure as a colourless and rigorous proposition of mathematical science; not only must we allow for the irony and the exaggeration of the preacher: we must also remember his object, which is, if possible, to shock his hearers into a sense of their condition, and to awaken remorse and repentance even at the eleventh hour. His last words (ver. 27) prove that he did not believe this result, improbable as it was, to be altogether impossible. Unless some sense of sin had survived in their hearts, unless the terms, "good" and "evil," had still retained a meaning for his countrymen, Jeremiah would hardly have laboured still so strenuously to convince them of their sin.

For the present, when retribution is already at the doors, when already the Divine wrath has visibly broken forth, his prevailing purpose is not so much to suggest a way of escape, as to bring home to the heart and conscience of the nation the true meaning of the public calamities. They are the consequence of habitual rebellion against God. And I will scatter them like stubble passing away to (= before: cf. xix. 10) the wind of the wilderness. This is thy lot (fem. thine, O Jerusalem), the portion of thy measures (others: lap) from Me, saith Iahvah; because thou forgattest Me, and didst trust in the Lie. And I also--I will surely strip thy skirts to thy face, and thy shame shall be seen! (Nah. iii. 5). Thine adulteries and thy neighings, the foulness of thy fornications upon the hills in the field (iii. 2-6)--I have seen thine abominations! (For the construction, compare Isa. i. 13.) Woe unto thee, O Jerusalem! After how long yet wilt thou not become clean? (2 Kings v. 12, 13). That which lies before the citizens in the near future is not deliverance, but dispersion in foreign lands. The onset of the foe will sweep them away, as the blast from the desert drives before it the dry stubble of the corn-fields (cf. iv. 11, 12). This is no chance calamity, but a recompense allotted and meted out by Iahvah to the city that forgot Him and "trusted in the Lie" of Baal-worship and the associated superstitions. The city that dealt shamefully in departing from her God, and dallying with foul idols, shall be put to shame by Him before all the world (ver. 26 recurring to the thought of ver. 22, but ascribing the exposure directly to Iahvah). Woe--certain woe--awaits Jerusalem; and it is but a faint and far-off glimmer of hope that is reflected in the final question, which is like a weary sigh: After how long yet wilt thou not become clean? How long must the fiery process of cleansing go on, ere thou be purged of thine inveterate sins? It is a recognition that the punishment will not be exterminative; that God's chastisements of His people can no more fail at last than His promises; that the triumph of a heathen power and the disappearance of Iahvah's Israel from under His heaven cannot be the final phase of that long eventful history which began with the call of Abraham.

Footnotes:

54. Also xlviii. 12; Lam. iv. 2; Isa. xxx. 14.

55. LXX. apo kephales humon.. Read mr'stykm = mr'sykm; and cf. Assyrian re?u, plur. re?êtu (= r'svt).

56. For ynykm we might read, with LXX., Vat., ynyk (yrvsl)m. The Arabic has Israel. But Vulg. and Targ. agree with the Q'rê, and take the verbs as plur.: "Lift ye up your eyes and see who are coming from the north." The sing. fem. is to be preferred as the more difficult reading, and on account of ver. 21, where it recurs. Jerusalem is addressed (ver. 27), and "your eyes," plur. masc. pron., may be justified as indicating the collective sense of the fem. sing. The population of the capital is meant. Cf. Mic. i. 11; Jer. xxi. 13, 14. In ver. 23, the masc. plur. appears again, the figure for a moment being dropped.

IX. THE DROUGHT AND ITS MORAL IMPLICATIONS

Jeremiah xiv., xv. (xvii.?).

Various opinions have been expressed about the division of these chapters. They have been cut up into short sections, supposed to be more or less independent of each other;[57] and they have been regarded as constituting a well-organized whole, at least so far as the eighteenth verse of chap. xvii. The truth may lie between these extremes. Chapters xiv., xv. certainly hang together; for in them the prophet represents himself as twice interceding with Iahvah on behalf of the people, and twice receiving a refusal of his petition (xiv. 1-xv. 4), the latter reply being sterner and more decisive than the first. The occasion was a long period of drought, involving much privation for man and beast. The connexion between the parts of this first portion of the discourse is clear enough. The prophet prays for his people, and God answers that He has rejected them, and that intercession is futile. Thereupon, Jeremiah throws the blame of the national sins upon the false prophets; and the answer is that both the people and their false guides will perish. The prophet then soliloquises upon his own hard fate as a herald of evil tidings, and receives directions for his own personal guidance in this crisis of affairs (xv. 10-xvi. 9). There is a pause but no real break at the end of chap. xv. The next chapter resumes the subject of directions personally affecting the prophet himself; and the discourse is then continuous so far as xvii. 18, although, naturally enough, it is broken here and there by pauses of considerable duration, marking transitions of thought, and progress in the argument.

The heading of the entire piece is marked in the original by a peculiar inversion of terms, which meets us again, chap. xlvi. 1, xlvii. 1, xlix. 34, but which, in spite of this recurrence, wears a rather suspicious look. We might render it thus: "What fell as a word of Iahvah to Jeremiah, on account of the droughts" (the plural is intensive, or it signifies the long continuance of the trouble--as if one rainless period followed upon another). Whether or not the singular order of the words be authentic, the recurrence at chap. xvii. 8 of the remarkable term for "drought" (Heb. bacc?óreth of which bac?c?aróth here is plur.) favours the view that that chapter is an integral portion of the present discourse. The exordium (xiv. 1-9) is a poetical sketch of the miseries of man and beast, closing with a beautiful prayer. It has been said that this is not "a word of Iahvah to Jeremiah," but rather the reverse. If we stick to the letter, this no doubt is the case; but, as we have seen in former discourses, the phrase "Iahvah's word" meant in prophetic use very much more than a direct message from God, or a prediction uttered at the Divine instigation. Here, as elsewhere, the prophet evidently regards the course of his own religious reflexion as guided by Him who "fashioneth the hearts of men," and "knoweth their thoughts long before;" and if the question had suggested itself, he would certainly have referred his own poetic powers--the tenderness of his pity, the vividness of his apprehension, the force of his passion,--to the inspiration of the Lord who had called and consecrated him from the birth, to speak in His Name.

There lies at the heart of many of us a feeling, which has lurked there, more or less without our cognisance, ever since the childish days when the Old Testament was read at the mother's knee, and explained and understood in a manner proportioned to the faculties of childhood. When we hear the phrase "The Lord spake," we instinctively think, if we think at all, of an actual voice knocking sensibly at the door of the outward ear. It was not so; nor did the sacred writer mean it so. A knowledge of Hebrew idiom--the modes of expression usual and possible in that ancient speech--assures us that this statement, so startlingly direct in its unadorned simplicity, was the accepted mode of conveying a meaning which we, in our more complex and artificial idioms, would convey by the use of a multitude of words, in terms far more abstract, in language destitute of all that colour of life and reality which stamps the idiom of the Bible. It is as though the Divine lay farther off from us moderns; as though the marvellous progress of all that new knowledge of the measureless magnitude of the world, of the power and complexity of its machinery, of the surpassing subtlety and the matchless perfection of its laws and processes, had become an impassable barrier, at least an impenetrable veil, between our minds and God. We have lost the sense of His nearness, of His immediacy, so to speak; because we have gained, and are ever intensifying, a sense of the nearness of the world with which He environs us. Hence, when we speak of Him, we naturally cast about either for poetical phrases and figures, which must always be more or less vague and undefined, or for highly abstract expressions, which may suggest scientific exactness, but are, in truth, scholastic formulæ, dry as the dust of the desert, untouched by the breath of life; and even if they affirm a Person, destitute of all those living characters by which we instinctively and without effort recognise Personality. We make only a conventional use of the language of the sacred writers, of the prophets and prophetic historians, of the psalmists, and the legalists of the Old Testament; the language which is the native expression of a peculiar intensity of religious faith, realizing the Unseen as the Actual and, in truth, the only Real.

> "Judah mourneth and the gates thereof languish,
> They are clad in black down to the ground;
> And the cry of Jerusalem hath gone up.
> And their nobles have sent their lesser folk for water;
> They have been to the pits, and found no water:
> Their vessels have come back empty;
> Ashamed and confounded, they have covered their heads.
> "Because the ground is chapt, for there hath not been rain in the land,
> The plowmen are ashamed, they have covered their heads.
> "For even the hind in the field hath yeaned and forsaken her fawn,
> For there is no grass.
> And the wild asses stand on the bare fells;
> They snuff the wind like jackals;
> Their eyes fail, for there is no pasturage.
> "If our sins have answered against us,
> Iahweh, act for Thine own Name sake;
> For our relapses are many;
> Against Thee have we trespassed.
> "Hope of Israel, that savest him in time of trouble,
> Wherefore wilt Thou be as a stranger in the land,
> And as a traveller that leaveth the road but for the night?
> Wherefore wilt Thou be as a man o'erpowered with sleep,
> As a warrior that cannot rescue?
> "Sith Thou art in our midst, O Iahvah,
> And Thy Name upon us hath been called;
> Cast us not down!"

How beautiful both plaint and prayer! The simple description of the effects of the drought is as lifelike and impressive as a good picture. The whole country is stricken; the city-gates, the place of common resort, where the citizens meet for business and for conversation, are gloomy with knots of mourners robed in black from head to foot, or, as the Hebrew may also imply, sitting on the ground, in the garb and posture of desolation (Lam. ii. 10, iii. 28). The magnates of Jerusalem send out their retainers to find water; and we see them returning with empty vessels, their heads muffled in their cloaks, in sign of grief at the failure of their errand (cf. 1 Kings xviii. 5, 6). The parched ground everywhere gapes with fissures; [58] the yeomen go about with covered heads in deepest dejection. The distress is universal, and affects not man only, but the brute creation. Even the gentle hind, that proverb of maternal tenderness, is driven by sorest need to forsake the fruit of her hard travail; her starved dugs are dry, and she flies from her helpless offspring. The wild asses of the desert, fleet, beautiful and keen-eyed creatures, scan the withered landscape from the naked cliffs, and snuff the wind, like jackals scenting prey; but neither sight nor smell suggests relief. There is no moisture in the air, no glimpse of pasture in the wide sultry land.

The prayer is a humble confession of sin, an unreserved admission that the woes of man evince the righteousness of God. Unlike certain modern poets, who bewail the sorrows of the world as the mere infliction of a harsh and arbitrary and inevitable Destiny, Jeremiah makes no doubt that human sufferings are due to the working of Divine justice. "Our sins have answered against our pleas at Thy judgment seat; our relapses are many; against Thee have we trespassed," against Thee, the sovereign Disposer of events, the Source of all that happens and all that is. If this be so, what plea is left? None, but that appeal to the Name of Iahvah, with which the prayer begins and ends. "Act for Thine own Name sake."... "Thy Name upon us hath been called." Act for Thine own honour, that is, for the honour of Mercy, Compassion, Truth, Goodness; which Thou hast revealed Thyself to be, and which are parts of Thy glorious Name (Ex. xxxiv. 6). Pity the wretched, and pardon the guilty; for so will Thy glory increase amongst men; so will man learn that the relentings of love are diviner affections than the ruthlessness of wrath and the cravings of vengeance.

There is also a touching appeal to the past. The very name by which Israel was sometimes designated as "the people of Iahvah," just as Moab was known by the name of its god as "the people of

Chemosh" (Num. xxi. 29), is alleged as proof that the nation has an interest in the compassion of Him whose name it bears; and it is implied that, since the world knows Israel as Iahvah's people, it will not be for Iahvah's honour that this people should be suffered to perish in their sins. Israel had thus, from the outset of its history, been associated and identified with Iahvah; however ill the true nature of the tie has been understood, however unworthily the relation has been conceived by the popular mind, however little the obligations involved in the call of their fathers have been recognised and appreciated. God must be true, though man be false. There is no weakness, no caprice, no vacillation in God. In bygone "times of trouble" the "Hope of Israel" had saved Israel over and over again; it was a truth admitted by all--even by the prophet's enemies. Surely then He will save His people once again, and vindicate His Name of Saviour. Surely He who has dwelt in their midst so many changeful centuries, will not now behold their trouble with the lukewarm feeling of an alien dwelling amongst them for a time, but unconnected with them by ties of blood and kin and common country; or with the indifference of the traveller who is but coldly affected by the calamities of a place where he has only lodged one night. Surely the entire past shews that it would be utterly inconsistent for Iahvah to appear now as a man so buried in sleep that He cannot be roused to save His friends from imminent destruction (cf. 1 Kings xviii. 27) (St. Mark iv. 38). He who had borne Israel and carried him as a tender nurseling all the days of old (Isa. lxiii. 9) could hardly without changing His own unchangeable Name, His character and purposes, cast down His people and forsake them at last.

Such is the drift of the prophet's first prayer. To this apparently unanswerable argument his religious meditation upon the present distress has brought him. But presently the thought returns with added force, with a sense of utmost certitude, with a conviction that it is Iahvah's Word, that the people have wrought out their own affliction, that misery is the hire of sin.

> *"Thus hath Iahvah said of this people:*
> *Even so have they loved to wander,*
> *Their feet they have not refrained;*
> *And as for Iahvah, He accepteth them not;*
> *"He now remembereth their guilt,*
> *And visiteth their trespasses.*
> *And Iahvah said unto me,*
> *Intercede thou not for this people for good!*
> *If they fast, I will not hearken unto their cry;*
> *And if they offer whole-offering and oblation,*
> *I will not accept their persons;*
> *But by the sword, the famine, and the plague, will I consume them.*
> *"And I said, Ah, Lord Iahvah!*
> *Behold the prophets say to them, Ye shall not see sword,*
> *And famine shall not befall you;*
> *For peace and permanence will I give you in this place.*
> *"And Iahvah said unto me:*
> *Falsehood it is that the prophets prophesy in My Name.*
> *I sent them not, and I charged them not, and I spake not unto them.*
> *A vision of falsehood and jugglery and nothingness, and the guile of their own heart,*
> *They, for their part, prophesy you.*
> *"Therefore thus said Iahvah:*
> *Concerning the prophets who prophesy in My Name, albeit I sent them not,*
> *And of themselves say, Sword and famine there shall not be in this land;*
> *By the sword and by the famine shall those prophets be fordone.*
> *And the people to whom they prophesy shall lie thrown out in the streets of Jerusalem,*
> *Because of the famine and the sword,*
> *With none to bury them,--*
> *Themselves, their wives, and their sons and their daughters:*
> *And I will pour upon them their own evil.*
> *And thou shalt say unto them this word:*
> *Let mine eyes run down with tears, night and day,*
> *And let them not tire;*
> *For with mighty breach is broken*
> *The virgin daughter of my people--*
> *With a very grievous blow.*
> *If I go forth into the field,*
> *Then behold! the slain of the sword;*
> *And if I enter the city,*

Then behold! the pinings of famine:
For both prophet and priest go trafficking about the land,
And understand not." [59]

It has been supposed that this whole section is misplaced, and that it would properly follow the close of chap. xiii. The supposition is due to a misapprehension of the force of the pregnant particle which introduces the reply of Iahvah to the prophet's intercession. "Even so have they loved to wander;" even so, as is naturally implied by the severity of the punishment of which thou complainest. The dearth is prolonged; the distress is widespread and grievous. So prolonged, so grievous, so universal, has been their rebellion against Me. The penalty corresponds to the offence. It is really "their own evil" that is being poured out upon their guilty heads (ver. 16; cf. iv. 18). Iahvah cannot accept them in their sin; the long drought is a token that their guilt is before His mind, unrepented, unatoned. Neither the supplications of another, nor their own fasts and sacrifices, avail to avert the visitation. So long as the disposition of the heart remains unaltered; so long as man hates, not his darling sins, but the penalties they entail, it is idle to seek to propitiate Heaven by such means as these. And not only so. The droughts are but a foretaste of worse evils to come; by the sword, the famine, and the plague will I consume them. The condition is understood, If they repent and amend not. This is implied by the prophet's seeking to palliate the national guilt, as he proceeds to do, by the suggestion that the people are more sinned against than sinning, deluded as they are by false prophets; as also by the renewal of his intercession (ver. 19). Had he been aware in his inmost heart that an irreversible sentence had gone forth against his people, would he have been likely to think either excuses or intercessions availing? Indeed, however absolute the threats of the prophetic preachers may sound, they must, as a rule, be qualified by this limitation, which, whether expressed or not, is inseparable from the object of their discourses, which was the moral amendment of those who heard them.

Of the "false," that is, the common run of prophets, who were in league with the venal priesthood of the time, and no less worldly and self-seeking than their allies, we note that, as usual, they foretell what the people wishes to hear; "Peace (Prosperity), and Permanence," is the burden of their oracles. They knew that invectives against prevailing vices, and denunciations of national follies, and forecasts of approaching ruin, were unlikely means of winning popularity and a substantial harvest of offerings. At the same time, like other false teachers, they knew how to veil their errors under the mask of truth; or rather, they were themselves deluded by their own greed, and blinded by their covetousness to the plain teaching of events. They might base their doctrine of "Peace and Permanence in this place!" upon those utterances of the great Isaiah, which had been so signally verified in the lifetime of the seer himself; but their keen pursuit of selfish ends, their moral degradation, caused them to shut their eyes to everything else in his teachings, and, like his contemporaries, they "regarded not the work of Iahvah, nor the operation of His hand." Jeremiah accuses them of "lying visions;" visions, as he explains, which were the outcome of magical ceremonies, by aid of which, perhaps, they partially deluded themselves, before deluding others, but which were, none the less, "things of nought," devoid of all substance, and mere fictions of a deceitful and self-deceiving mind (ver. 14). He expressly declares that they have no mission; in other words, their action is not due to the overpowering sense of a higher call, but is inspired by purely ulterior considerations of worldly gain and policy. They prophesy to order; to the order of man, not of God. If they visit the country districts, it is with no spiritual end in view; priest and prophet alike make a trade of their sacred profession, and, immersed in their sordid pursuits, have no eye for truth, and no perception of the dangers hovering over their country. Their misconduct and misdirection of affairs are certain to bring destruction upon themselves and upon those whom they mislead. War and its attendant famine will devour them all.

But the day of grace being past, nothing is left for the prophet himself but to bewail the ruin of his people (ver. 17). He will betake himself to weeping, since praying and preaching are vain. The words which announce this resolve may portray a sorrowful experience, or they may depict the future as though it were already present (vv. 17, 18). The latter interpretation would suit ver. 17, but hardly the following verse, with its references to "going forth into the field," and "entering into the city." The way in which these specific actions are mentioned seems to imply some present or recent calamity; and there is apparently no reason why we may not suppose that the passage was written at the disastrous close of the reign of Josiah, in the troublous interval of three months, when Jehoahaz was nominal king in Jerusalem, but the Egyptian arms were probably ravaging the country, and striking terror into the hearts of the people. In such a time of confusion and bloodshed, tillage would be neglected, and famine would naturally follow; and these evils would be greatly aggravated by drought. The only other period which suits is the beginning of the reign of Jehoiakim; [60] but the former seems rather to be indicated by chap. xv. 6-9.

Heartbroken at the sight of the miseries of his country, the prophet once more approaches the eternal throne. His despairing mood is not so deep and dark as to drown his faith in God. He refuses to believe the utter rejection of Judah, the revocation of the covenant. (The measure is Pentameter).

The Expositor's Bible: Jeremiah Volumes I & II

> "Hast Thou indeed cast off Judah?
> Hath Thy soul revolted from Sion?
> Why hast Thou smitten us, past healing?
> Waiting for peace, and no good came,
> For a time of healing, and behold terror!
> "We know, Iahvah, our wickedness, our fathers' guilt;
> For we have trespassed toward Thee.
> Scorn Thou not, for Thy Name sake,
> Disgrace not Thy glorious throne!
> Remember, break not, Thy covenant with us!
> "Are there, in sooth, among the Nothings of the nations senders of rain?
> And is it the heavens that bestow the showers?
> Is it not Thou, Iahvah our God?
> And we wait for Thee,
> For Thou it was that madest the world." [61]

To all this the Divine answer is stern and decisive. And Iahvah said unto me: If Moses and Samuel were to stand (pleading) before Me, My mind would not be towards this people: send them away from before Me (dismiss them from My Presence), that they may go forth! After ages remembered Jeremiah as a mighty intercessor, and the brave Maccabeus could see him in his dream as a grey-haired man "exceeding glorious" and "of a wonderful and excellent majesty," who "prayed much for the people and for the holy city" (2 Macc. xv. 14). And the beauty of the prayers which lie like scattered pearls of faith and love among the prophet's soliloquies is evident at a glance. But here Jeremiah himself is conscious that his prayers are unavailing; and that the office to which God has called him is rather that of pronouncing judgment than of interceding for mercy. Even a Moses or a Samuel, the mighty intercessors of the old heroic times, whose pleadings had been irresistible with God, would now plead in vain (Ex. xvii. 11 sqq., xxxii. 11 sqq.; Num. xiv. 13 sqq. for Moses; 1 Sam. vii. 9 sqq., xii. 16 sqq.; Ps. xcix. 6; Ecclus. xlvi. 16 sqq. for Samuel). The day of grace has gone, and the day of doom is come. His sad function is to "send them away" or "let them go" from Iahvah's Presence; to pronounce the decree of their banishment from the holy land where His temple is, and where they have been wont to "see His face." The main part of his commission was "to root out, and to pull down, and to destroy, and to overthrow" (i. 10). And if they say unto thee, Whither are we to go forth? Thou shalt say unto them, thus hath Iahvah said: They that belong to the Death (i.e. the Plague; as the Black Death was spoken of in medieval Europe) to death; and they that belong to the Sword, to the sword; and they that belong to the Famine, to famine; and they that belong to Captivity, to captivity! The people were to "go forth" out of their own land, which was, as it were, the Presence-chamber of Iahvah, just as they had at the outset of their history gone forth out of Egypt, to take possession of it. The words convey a sentence of exile, though they do not indicate the place of banishment. The menace of woe is as general in its terms as that lurid passage of the Book of the Law upon which it appears to be founded (Deut. xxviii. 21-26). The time for the accomplishment of those terrible threatenings "is nigh, even at the doors." On the other hand, Ezekiel's "four sore judgments" (Ezek. xiv. 21) were suggested by this passage of Jeremiah.

The prophet avoids naming the actual destination of the captive people, because captivity is only one element in their punishment. The horrors of war--sieges and slaughters and pestilence and famine--must come first. In what follows, the intensity of these horrors is realized in a single touch. The slain are left unburied, a prey to the birds and beasts. The elaborate care of the ancients in the provision of honourable resting places for the dead is a measure of the extremity thus indicated. In accordance with the feeling of his age, the prophet ranks the dogs and vultures and hyenas that drag and disfigure and devour the corpses of the slain, as three "kinds" of evil equally appalling with the sword that slays. The same feeling led our Spenser to write:

> "To spoil the dead of weed
> Is sacrilege, and doth all sins exceed."

And the destruction of Moab is decreed by the earlier prophet Amos, "because he burned the bones of the king of Edom into lime," thus violating a law universally recognised as binding upon the conscience of nations (Amos ii. 1). Cf. also Gen. xxiii.

Thus death itself was not to be a sufficient expiation for the inveterate guilt of the nation. Judgment was to pursue them even after death. But the prophet's vision does not penetrate beyond this present scene. With the visible world, so far as he is aware, the punishment terminates. He gives no hint here, nor elsewhere, of any further penalties awaiting individual sinners in the unseen world. The scope of his prophecy indeed is almost purely national, and limited to the present life. It is one of the recognised conditions of Old Testament religious thought.

And the ruin of the people is the retribution reserved for what Manasseh did in Jerusalem. To the prophet, as to the author of the book of Kings, who wrote doubtless under the influence of his words, the guilt contracted by Judah under that wicked king was unpardonable. But it would convey a false impression if we left the matter here; for the whole course of his after-preaching--his exhortations and promises, as well as his threats--prove that Jeremiah did not suppose that the nation could not be saved by genuine repentance and permanent amendment. What he intends rather to affirm is that the sins of the fathers will be visited upon children, who are partakers of their sins. It is the doctrine of St. Matt. xxiii. 29 sqq.; a doctrine which is not merely a theological opinion, but a matter of historical observation.

And I will set over them four kinds--It is an oracle of Iahvah--the sword to slay, and the dogs to hale, and the fowls of the air, and the beasts of the earth, to devour and to destroy. And I will make them a sport for all the realms of earth; on account of Manasseh ben Hezekiah king of Judah, for what he did in Jerusalem.

Jerusalem!--the mention of that magical name touches another chord in the prophet's soul; and the fierce tones of his oracle of doom change into a dirge-like strain of pity without hope.

> "For who will have compassion on Thee, O Jerusalem?
> And who will yield thee comfort?
> And who will turn aside to ask of thy welfare?
> 'Twas thou that rejectedst Me (it is Iahvah's word);
> Backward wouldst thou wend:
> So I stretched forth My hand against thee and destroyed thee;
> I wearied of relenting.
> And I winnowed them with a fan in the gates of the land;
> I bereaved, I undid My people:
> Yet they returned not from their own ways.
> His widows outnumbered before Me the sand of seas:
> I brought them against the Mother of Warriors a harrier at high noon;
> I threw upon her suddenly anguish and horrors.
> She that had borne seven sons did pine away;
> She breathèd out her soul.
> Her sun did set, while it yet was day;
> He blushed and paled.
> But their remnant will I give to the sword
> Before their foes: (It is Iahvah's word)."

The fate of Jerusalem would strike the nations dumb with horror; it would not inspire pity, for man would recognise that it was absolutely just. Or perhaps the thought rather is, in proving false to Me, thou wert false to thine only friend: Me thou hast estranged by thy faithlessness; and from the envious rivals, who beset thee on every side, thou canst expect nothing but rejoicing at thy downfall (Ps. cxxxvi.; Lam. ii. 15-17; Obad. 10 sqq.). The peculiar solitariness of Israel among the nations (Num. xxiii. 9) aggravated the anguish of her overthrow.

In what follows, the dreadful past appears as a prophecy of the yet more terrible future. The poet-seer's pathetic monody moralizes the lost battle of Megiddo--that fatal day when the sun of Judah set in what seemed the high day of her prosperity, and all the glory and the promise of good king Josiah vanished like a dream in sudden darkness. Men might think--doubtless Jeremiah thought, in the first moments of despair, when the news of that overwhelming disaster was brought to Jerusalem, with the corpse of the good king, the dead hope of the nation--that this crushing blow was proof that Iahvah had rejected His people, in the exercise of a sovereign caprice, and without reference to their own attitude towards Him. But, says or chants the prophet, in solemn rhythmic utterance,

> "'Twas thou that rejectedst Me;
> Backward wouldst thou wend:
> So I stretched forth My hand against thee, and wrought thee hurt;
> I wearied of relenting."

The cup of national iniquity was full, and its baleful contents overflowed in a devastating flood. "In the gates of the land"--the point on the north-west frontier where the armies met--Iahvah "winnowed His people with a fan," separating those who were doomed to fall from those who were to survive, as the winnowing fan separates the chaff from the wheat in the threshing-floor. There He "bereaved" the nation of their dearest hope, "the breath of their nostrils, the Lord's Anointed" (Lam. iv. 20); there He multiplied their widows. And after the lost battle He brought the victor in hot haste against the "Mother" of the fallen warriors, the ill-fated city, Jerusalem, to wreak vengeance upon her for her ill-timed opposition. But, for all this bitter fruit of their evil doings, the people "turned not back from their own ways"; and therefore the strophe of lamentation closes with a threat of utter extermination: "Their remnant"--the poor survival of these fierce storms--"Their remnant will I give to the sword before their foes." [62]

If the thirteenth and fourteenth verses be not a mere interpolation in this chapter (see xvii. 3, 4), their proper place would seem to be here, as continuing and amplifying the sentence upon the residue of the people. The text is unquestionably corrupt, and must be amended by help of the other passage, where it is partially repeated. The twelfth verse may be read thus:

"Thy wealth and thy treasures will I make a prey,
For the sin of thine high places in all thy borders." [63]

Then the fourteenth verse follows, naturally enough, with an announcement of the Exile:

"And I will enthral thee to thy foes
In a land thou knowest not:
'For a fire is kindled in Mine anger,'
That shall burn for evermore!" [64]

The prophet has now fulfilled his function of judge by pronouncing upon his people the extreme penalty of the law. His strong perception of the national guilt and of the righteousness of God has left him no choice in the matter. But how little this duty of condemnation accorded with his own individual feeling as a man and a citizen is clear from the passionate outbreak of the succeeding strophe.

"Woe's me, my mother," he exclaims, "that thou barest me,
A man of strife and a man of contention to all the country!
Neither lender nor borrower have I been;
Yet all of them do curse me."

A desperately bitter tone, evincing the anguish of a man wounded to the heart by the sense of fruitless endeavour and unjust hatred. He had done his utmost to save his country, and his reward was universal detestation. His innocence and integrity were requited with the odium of the pitiless creditor who enslaves his helpless victim, and appropriates his all; or the fraudulent borrower who repays a too ready confidence with ruin. [65]

The next two verses answer this burst of grief and despair:
"Said Iahvah, Thine oppression shall be for good;
I will make the foe thy suppliant in time of evil and in time of distress.
Can one break iron,
Iron from the north, and brass?"

In other words, faith counsels patience, and assures the prophet that all things work together for good to them that love God. The wrongs and bitter treatment which he now endures will only enchance his triumph, when the truth of his testimony is at last confirmed by events, and they who now scoff at his message, come humbly to beseech his prayers. The closing lines refer, with grave irony, to that unflinching firmness, that inflexible resolution, which, as a messenger of God, he was called upon to maintain. He is reminded of what he had undertaken at the outset of his career, and of the Divine Word which made him "a pillar of iron and walls of brass against all the land" (i. 18). Is it possible that the pillar of iron can be broken, and the walls of brass beaten down by the present assault?

There is a pause, and then the prophet vehemently pleads his own cause with Iahvah. Smarting with the sense of personal wrong, he urges that his suffering is for the Lord's own sake; that consciousness of the Divine calling has dominated his entire life, ever since his dedication to the prophetic office; and that the honour of Iahvah requires his vindication upon his heartless and hardened adversaries.

"Thou knowest, Iahvah!
Remember me, and visit me, and avenge me on my persecutors.
Take me not away in thy longsuffering;
Regard my bearing of reproach for Thee.
"Thy words were found, and I did eat them,
And it became to me a joy and mine heart's gladness;

For I was called by Thy Name, O Iahvah, God of Sabaoth!
"I sate not in the gathering of the mirthful, nor rejoiced;
Because of Thine hand I sate solitary,
For with indignation Thou didst fill me.
"Why hath my pain become perpetual,
And my stroke malignant, incurable?
Wilt Thou indeed become to me like a delusive stream,
Like waters which are not lasting?"

The pregnant expression, "Thou knowest, Iahvah!" does not refer specially to anything that has been already said; but rather lays the whole case before God in a single word. The Thou is emphatic; Thou, Who knowest all things, knowest my heinous wrongs: Thou knowest and seest it all, though the whole world beside be blind with passion and self-regard and sin (Ps. x. 11-14). Thou knowest how pressing is my need; therefore Take me not away in Thy longsuffering: sacrifice not the life of Thy servant to the claims of forbearance with his enemies and Thine. The petition shews how great was the peril in which the prophet perceived himself to stand: he believes that if God delay to strike down his adversaries, that longsuffering will be fatal to his own life.

The strength of his case is that he is persecuted, because he is faithful; he bears reproach for God. He has not abused his high calling for the sake of worldly advantage; he has not prostituted the name of prophet to the vile ends of pleasing the people, and satisfying personal covetousness. He has not feigned smooth prophecies, misleading his hearers with flattering falsehood; but he has considered the privilege of being called a prophet of Iahvah as in itself an all-sufficient reward; and when the Divine Word came to him, he has eagerly received, and fed his inmost soul upon that spiritual aliment, which was at once his sustenance and his deepest joy. Other joys, for the Lord's sake, he has abjured. He has withdrawn himself even from harmless mirth, that in silence and solitude he might listen intently to the inward Voice, and reflect with indignant sorrow upon the revelation of his people's corruption. Because of Thine Hand--under Thy influence; conscious of the impulse and operation of Thy informing Spirit;--I sate solitary; for with indignation Thou didst fill me. The man whose eye has caught a glimpse of eternal Truth, is apt to be dissatisfied with the shows of things; and the lighthearted merriment of the world rings hollow upon the ear that listens for the Voice of God. And the revelation of sin--the discovery of all that ghastly evil which lurks beneath the surface of smooth society--the appalling vision of the grim skeleton hiding its noisome decay behind the mask of smiles and gaiety; the perception of the hideous incongruity of revelling over a grave; has driven others, besides Jeremiah, to retire into themselves, and to avoid a world from whose evil they revolted, and whose foreseen destruction they deplored.

The whole passage is an assertion of the prophet's integrity and consistency, with which, it is suggested, that the failure which has attended his efforts, and the serious peril in which he stands, are morally inconsistent, and paradoxical in view of the Divine disposal of events. Here, in fact, as elsewhere, Jeremiah has freely opened his heart, and allowed us to see the whole process of his spiritual conflict in the agony of his moments of doubt and despair. It is an argument of his own perfect sincerity; and, at the same time, it enables us to assimilate the lesson of his experience, and to profit by the heavenly guidance he received, far more effectually, than if he had left us ignorant of the painful struggles at the cost of which that guidance was won.

The seeming injustice or indifference of Providence is a problem which recurs to thoughtful minds in all generations of men.

"O, goddes cruel, that govérne
This world with byndyng of youre word eterne ...
What governance is in youre prescience
That gilteles tormenteth innocence?...
Alas! I see a serpent or a theif,
That many a trewé man hath doon mescheit,
Gon at his large, and wher him luste may turne;
But I moste be in prisoun."

That such apparent anomalies are but a passing trial, from which persistent faith will emerge victorious in the present life, is the general answer of the Old Testament to the doubts which they suggest. The only sufficient explanation was reserved, to be revealed by Him, who, in the fulness of time, "brought life and immortality to light."

The thought which restored the failing confidence and courage of Jeremiah was the reflexion that such complaints were unworthy of one called to be a spokesman for the Highest; that the supposition of the possibility of the Fountain of Living Waters failing like a winter torrent, that runs dry in the summer heats, was an act of unfaithfulness that merited reproof; and that the true God could not fail to protect His messenger, and to secure the triumph of truth in the end.

> "To this Iahvah said thus:
> If thou come again,
> I will make thee again to stand before Me;
> And if thou utter that is precious rather than that is vile,
> As My mouth shalt thou become:
> They shall return unto thee,
> But Thou shalt not return unto them.
> "And I will make thee to this people an embattled wall of brass;
> And they shall fight against thee, but not overcome thee,
> For I will be with thee to help thee and to save thee;
> It is Iahvah's word.
> And I will save thee out of the grasp of the wicked,
> And will ransom thee out of the hand of the terrible."

In the former strophe, the inspired poet set forth the claims of the psychic man, and poured out his heart before God. Now he recognises a Word of God in the protest of his better feeling. He sees that where he remains true to himself, he will also stand near to his God. Hence springs the hope, which he cannot renounce, that God will protect His accepted servant in the execution of the Divine commands. Thus the discords are resolved; and the prophet's spirit attains to peace, after struggling through the storm.

It was an outcome of earnest prayer, of an unreserved exposure of his inmost heart before God. What a marvel it is--that instinct of prayer! To think that a being whose visible life has its beginning and its end, a being who manifestly shares possession of this earth with the brute creation, and breathes the same air, and partakes of the same elements with them for the sustenance of his body; who is organized upon the same general plan as they, has the same principal members discharging the same essential functions in the economy of his bodily system; a being who is born and eats and drinks and sleeps and dies like all other animals;--that this being and this being only of all the multitudinous kinds of animated creatures, should have and exercise a faculty of looking off and above the visible which appears to be the sole realm of actual existence, and of holding communion with the Unseen! That, following what seems to be an original impulse of his nature, he should stand in greater awe of this Invisible than of any power that is palpable to sense; should seek to win its favour, crave its help in times of pain and conflict and peril; should professedly live, not according to the bent of common nature and the appetites inseparable from his bodily structure, but according to the will and guidance of that Unseen Power! Surely there is here a consummate marvel. And the wonder of it does not diminish, when it is remembered that this instinct of turning to an unseen Guide and Arbiter of events, is not peculiar to any particular section of the human race. Wide and manifold as are the differences which characterize and divide the families of man, all races possess in common the apprehension of the Unseen and the instinct of prayer. The oldest records of humanity bear witness to its primitive activity, and whatever is known of human history combines with what is known of the character and workings of the human mind to teach us that as prayer has never been unknown, so it is never likely to become obsolete.

May we not recognise in this great fact of human nature a sure index of a great corresponding truth? Can we avoid taking it as a clear token of the reality of revelation; as a kind of immediate and spontaneous evidence on the part of nature that there is and always has been in this lower world some positive knowledge of that which far transcends it, some real apprehension of the mystery that enfolds the universe? a knowledge and an apprehension which, however imperfect and fragmentary, however fitful and fluctuating, however blurred in outline and lost in infinite shadow, is yet incomparably more and better than none at all. Are we not, in short, morally driven upon the conviction that this powerful instinct of our nature is neither blind nor aimless; that its Object is a true, substantive Being; and that this Being has discovered, and yet discovers, some precious glimpses of Himself and His essential character to the spirit of mortal man? It must be so, unless we admit that the soul's dearest desires are a mocking illusion, that her aspirations towards a truth and a goodness of superhuman perfection are moonshine and madness. It cannot be nothingness that avails to evoke the deepest and purest emotions of our nature; not mere vacuity and chaos, wearing the semblance of an azure heaven. It is not into a measureless waste of outer darkness that we reach forth trembling hands.

Surely the spirit of denial is the spirit that fell from heaven, and the best and highest of man's thoughts aim at and affirm something positive, something that is, and the soul thirsts after God, the Living God.

We hear much in these days of our physical nature. The microscopic investigations of science leave nothing unexamined, nothing unexplored, so far as the visible organism is concerned. Rays from many distinct sources converge to throw an ever-increasing light upon the mysteries of our bodily constitution. In all this, science presents to the devout mind a valuable subsidiary revelation of the power and goodness of the Creator. But science cannot advance alone one step beyond the things of time and sense; her facts belong exclusively to the material order of existence; her cognition is limited to the various modes and conditions of force that constitute the realm of sight and touch; she cannot climb above these to a higher plane of being. And small blame it is to science, that she thus lacks the power of overstepping her natural boundaries. The evil begins when the men of science venture, in her much-abused name, to ignore and deny realities not amenable to scientific tests, and immeasurably transcending all merely physical standards and methods.

Neither the natural history nor the physiology of man, nor both together, are competent to give a complete account of his marvellous and many-sided being. Yet some thinkers appear to imagine that when a place has been assigned him in the animal kingdom, and his close relationship to forms below him in the scale of life has been demonstrated; when every tissue and structure has been analysed, and every organ described and its function ascertained; then the last word has been spoken, and the subject exhausted. Those unique and distinguishing faculties by which all this amazing work of observation, comparison, reasoning, has been accomplished, appear either to be left out of the account altogether, or to be handled with a meagre inadequacy of treatment that contrasts in the strongest manner with the fulness and the elaboration which mark the other discussion. And the more this physical aspect of our composite nature is emphasized; the more urgently it is insisted that, somehow or other, all that is in man and all that comes of man may be explained on the assumption that he is the natural climax of the animal creation, a kind of educated and glorified brute--that and nothing more;--the harder it becomes to give any rational account of those facts of his nature which are commonly recognised as spiritual, and among them of this instinct of prayer and its Object.

Under these discouraging circumstances, men are fatally prone to seek escape from their self-involved dilemma, by a hardy denial of what their methods have failed to discover and their favourite theories to explain. The soul and God are treated as mere metaphysical expressions, or as popular designations of the unknown causes of phenomena; and prayer is declared to be an act of foolish superstition which persons of culture have long since outgrown. Sad and strange this result is; but it is also the natural outcome of an initial error, which is none the less real because unperceived. Men "seek the living among the dead"; they expect to find the soul by post mortem examination, or to see God by help of an improved telescope. They fail and are disappointed, though they have little right to be so, for "spiritual things are discerned spiritually," and not otherwise.

In speculating on the reasons of this lamentable issue, we must not forget that there is such a thing as an unpurified intellect as well as a corrupt and unregenerate heart. Sin is not restricted to the affections of the lower nature; it has also invaded the realm of thought and reason. The very pursuit of knowledge, noble and elevating as it is commonly esteemed, is not without its dangers of self-delusion and sin. Wherever the love of self is paramount, wherever the object really sought is the delight, the satisfaction, the indulgence of self, no matter in which of the many departments of human life and action, there is sin. It is certain that the intellectual consciousness has its own peculiar pleasures, and those of the keenest and most transporting character; certain that the incessant pursuit of such pleasures may come to absorb the entire energies of a man, so that no room is left for the culture of humility or love or worship. Everything is sacrificed to what is called the pursuit of truth, but is in sober fact a passionate prosecution of private pleasure. It is not truth that is so highly valued; it is the keen excitement of the race, and not seldom the plaudits of the spectators when the goal is won. Such a career may be as thoroughly selfish and sinful and alienated from God as a career of common wickedness. And thus employed or enthralled, no intellectual gifts, however splendid, can bring a man to the discernment of spiritual truth. Not self-pleasing and foolish vanity and arrogant self-assertion, but a self-renouncing humility, an inward purity from idols of every kind, a reverence of truth as divine, are indispensable conditions of the perception of things spiritual.

The representation which is often given is a mere travesty. Believers in God do not want to alter His laws by their prayers--neither His laws physical, nor His laws moral and spiritual. It is their chief desire to be brought into submission or perfect obedience to the sum of His laws. They ask their Father in heaven to lead and teach them, to supply their wants in His own way, because He is their Father; because "It is He that made us, and His we are." Surely, a reasonable request, and grounded in reason.

To a plain man, seeking for arguments to justify prayer may well seem like seeking a justification of breathing, or eating and drinking and sleeping, or any other natural function. Our Lord never does anything of the kind, because His teaching takes for granted the ultimate prevalence of common sense, in spite of all the subtleties and airspun perplexities, in which a speculative mind delights to lose itself. So long as man has other wants than those which he can himself supply, prayer will be their natural expression.

If there be a spiritual as distinct from a material world, the difficulty to the ordinary mind is not to conceive of their contact but of their absolute isolation from each other. This is surely the inevitable result of our own individual experience, of the intimate though not indissoluble union of body and spirit in every living person.

How, it may be asked, can we really think of his Maker being cut off from man, or man from his Maker? God were not God, if He left man to himself. But not only are His wisdom, justice and love manifested forth in the beneficent arrangements of the world in which we find ourselves; not only is He "kind to the unjust and the unthankful." In pain and loss He quickens our sense of Himself (cf. xiv. 19-22). Even in the first moments of angry surprise and revolt, that sense is quickened; we rebel, not against an inanimate world or an impersonal law, but against a Living and Personal Being, whom we acknowledge as the Arbiter of our destinies, and whose wisdom and love and power we affect for the time to question, but cannot really gainsay. The whole of our experience tends to this end--to the continual rousing of our spiritual consciousness. There is no interference, no isolated and capricious interposition or interruption of order within or without us. Within and without us, His Will is always energizing, always manifesting forth His Being, encouraging our confidence, demanding our obedience and homage.

Thus prayer has its Divine as well as its human side; it is the Holy Spirit drawing the soul, as well as the soul drawing nigh unto God. The case is like the action and reaction of the magnet and the steel. And so prayer is not a foolish act of unauthorised presumption, not a rash effort to approach unapproachable and absolutely isolated Majesty. Whenever man truly prays, his Divine King has already extended the sceptre of His mercy, and bidden him speak.

xvi.-xvii. After the renewal of the promise there is a natural pause, marked by the formula with which the present section opens. When the prophet had recovered his firmness, through the inspired and inspiring reflexions which took possession of his soul after he had laid bare his inmost heart before God (xv. 20, 21), he was in a position to receive further guidance from above. What now lies before us is the direction, which came to him as certainly Divine, for the regulation of his own future behaviour as the chosen minister of Iahvah at this crisis in the history of his people. "And there fell a word of Iahvah unto me, saying: Thou shalt not take thee a wife; that thou get not sons and daughters in this place." Such a prohibition reveals, with the utmost possible clearness and emphasis, the gravity of the existing situation. It implies that the "peace and permanence," so glibly predicted by Jeremiah's opponents, will never more be known by that sinful generation. "This place," the holy place which Iahvah had "chosen, to establish His name there," as the Book of the Law so often describes it; "this place," which had been inviolable to the fierce hosts of the Assyrian in the time of Isaiah (Isa. xxxvii. 33), was now no more a sure refuge, but doomed to utter and speedy destruction. To beget sons and daughters there was to prepare more victims for the tooth of famine, and the pangs of pestilence, and the devouring sword of a merciless conqueror. It was to fatten the soil with unburied carcases, and to spread a hideous banquet for birds and beasts of prey. Children and parents were doomed to perish together; and Iahvah's witness was to keep himself unencumbered by the sweet cares of husband and father, that he might be wholly free for his solemn duties of menace and warning, and be ready for every emergency.

> "For thus hath Iahvah said:
> Concerning the sons and concerning the daughters that are born in this place,
> And concerning their mothers that bear them,
> And concerning their fathers that beget them, in this land:
> By deaths of agony shall they die;
> They shall not be mourned nor buried;
> For dung on the face of the ground shall they serve;
> And by the sword and by the famine shall they be fordone:
> And their carcase shall serve for food
> To the fowls of the air and to the beasts of the earth" (xvi. 3-4).

The "deaths of agony" seem to indicate the pestilence, which always ensued upon the scarcity and vile quality of food, and the confinement of multitudes within the narrow bounds of a besieged city (see Josephus' well-known account of the last siege of Jerusalem).

The attitude of solitary watchfulness and strict separation, which the prophet thus perceived to be required by circumstances, was calculated to be a warning of the utmost significance, among a people who attached the highest importance to marriage, and the permanence of the family.

It proclaimed more loudly than words could do, the prophet's absolute conviction that offspring was no pledge of permanence; that universal death was hanging over a condemned nation. But not only this. It marks a point of progress in the prophet's spiritual life. The crisis, through which we have seen him pass, has purged his mental vision. He no longer repines at his dark lot; no longer half envies the false prophets, who may win the popular love by pleasing oracles of peace and well-being; no longer complains of the Divine Will, which has laid such a burden upon him. He sees now that his part is to refuse even natural and innocent pleasures for the Lord's sake; to foresee calamity and ruin; to denounce unceasingly the sin he sees around him; to sacrifice a tender and affectionate heart to a life of rigid asceticism; and he manfully accepts his part. He knows that he stands alone--the last fortress of truth in a world of falsehood; and that for truth it becomes a man to surrender his all.

That which follows tends to complete the prophet's social isolation. He is to give no sign of sympathy in the common joys and sorrows of his kind.

> "For thus hath Iahvah said:
> Enter thou not into the house of mourning,
> Nor go to lament, nor comfort thou them:
> For I have taken away My friendship from this people ('Tis Iahvah's utterance!)
> The lovingkindness and the compassion;
> And old and young shall die in this land,
> They shall not be buried, and men shall not wail for them;
> Nor shall a man cut himself, nor make himself bald, for them:
> Neither shall men deal out bread to them in mourning,
> To comfort a man over the dead;
> Nor shall they give them to drink the cup of consolation,
> Over a man's father and over his mother.
> "And the house of feasting thou shalt not enter,
> To sit with them to eat and to drink.
> For thus hath Iahvah Sabaoth, the God of Israel, said:
> Lo, I am about to make to cease from this place,
> Before your own eyes and in your own days,
> Voice of mirth and voice of gladness,
> The voice of the bridegroom and the voice of the bride."

Acting as prophet, that is, as one whose public actions were symbolical of a Divine intent, Jeremiah is henceforth to stand aloof, on occasions when natural feeling would suggest participation in the outward life of his friends and acquaintance. He is to quell the inward stirrings of affection and sympathy, and to abstain from playing his part in those demonstrative lamentations over the dead, which the immemorial custom and sentiment of his country regarded as obligatory; and this, in order to signify unmistakably that what thus appeared to be the state of his own feelings, was really the aspect under which God would shortly appear to a nation perishing in its guilt. "Enter not into the house of mourning ... for I have taken away My friendship from this people, the lovingkindness and the compassion." An estranged and alienated God would view the coming catastrophe with the cold indifference of exact justice. And the consequence of the Divine aversion would be a calamity so overwhelming, that the dead would be left without those rites of burial, which the feeling and conscience of all races of mankind have always been careful to perform. There should be no burial, much less ceremonial lamentation, and those more serious modes of evincing grief by disfigurement of the person, [66] which, like tearing the hair and rending the garments, are natural tokens of the first distraction of bereavement. Not for wife or child (mt: see Gen. xxiii. 3), nor for father or mother should the funeral feast be held; for men's hearts would grow hard at the daily spectacle of death, and at last there would be no survivors.

In like manner, the prophet is forbidden to enter as guest "the house of feasting." He is not to be seen at the marriage-feast,--that occasion of highest rejoicing, the very type and example of innocent and holy mirth; to testify by his abstention that the day of judgment was swiftly approaching, which would desolate all homes, and silence for evermore all sounds of joy and gladness in the ruined city. And it is expressly added that the blow will fall "before your own eyes and in your own days;" shewing that the hour of doom was very near, and would no more be delayed.

In all this, it is noticeable that the Divine answer appears to bear special reference to the peculiar terms of the prophet's complaint. In despairing tones he had cried (xv. 10), "Woe's me, my mother, that thou didst bear me!" and now he is himself warned not to take a wife, and seek the blessing of children. The outward connexion here may be: "Let it not be that thy children speak of thee, as thou hast spoken of thy mother!" [67] But the inner link of thought may rather be this, that the prophet's temporary unfaithfulness evinced in his outcry against God and his lament that ever he was born is punished by the denial to him of the joys of fatherhood--a penalty which would be severe to a loving, yearning nature like his, but which was doubtless necessary to the purification of his spirit from all worldly taint, and to the discipline of his natural impatience and tendency to repine under the hand of God. His punishment, like that of Moses, may appear disproportionate to his offence; but God's dealings with man are not regulated by any mechanical calculation of less and more, but by His perfect knowledge of the needs of the case; and it is often in truest mercy that His hand strikes hard. "As gold in the furnace doth He try them"; and the purest metal comes out of the hottest fire.

Further, it is not the least prominent but the leading part of a man's nature that most requires this heavenly discipline, if the best is to be made of it that can be made. The strongest element, that which is most characteristic of the person, that which constitutes his individuality, is the chosen field of Divine influence and operation; for here lies the greatest need. In Jeremiah this master element was an almost feminine tenderness; a warmly affectionate disposition, craving the love and sympathy of his fellows, and recoiling almost in agony from the spectacle of pain and suffering. And therefore it was that the Divine discipline was specially applied to this element in the prophet's personality. In him, as in all other men, the good was mingled with evil, which, if not purged away, might spread until it spoiled his whole nature. It is not virtue to indulge our own bent, merely because it pleases us to do so; nor is the exercise of affection any great matter to an affectionate nature. The involved strain of selfishness must be separated, if any naturally good gift is to be elevated to moral worth, to become acceptable in the sight of God. And so it was precisely here, in his most susceptible point, that the sword of trial pierced the prophet through. He was saved from all hazard of becoming satisfied with the love of wife and children, and forgetting in that earthly satisfaction the love of his God. He was saved from absorption in the pleasures of friendly intercourse with neighbours, from passing his days in an agreeable round of social amenities; at a time when ruin was impending over his country, and well nigh ready to fall. And the means which God chose for the accomplishment of this result were precisely those of which the prophet had complained (xv. 17); his social isolation, which though in part a matter of choice, was partly forced upon him by the irritation and ill-will of his acquaintance. It is now declared that this trial is to continue. The Lord does not necessarily remove a trouble, when entreated to do it. He manifests His love by giving strength to bear it, until the work of chastening be perfected.

An interruption is now supposed, such as may often have occurred in the course of Jeremiah's public utterances. The audience demands to know why all this evil is ordained to fall upon them. What is our guilt and what our trespass, that we have trespassed against Iahvah our God? The answer is a twofold accusation. Their fathers were faithless to Iahvah, and they have outdone their fathers' sin; and the penalty will be expulsion and a foreign servitude.

> *"Because your fathers forsook Me (It is Iahvah's word!)*
> *And went after other gods, and served them, and bowed down to them,*
> *And Me they forsook, and My teaching they observed not:*
> *And ye yourselves (or, as for you) have done worse than your fathers;*
> *And lo, ye walk each after the stubbornness of his evil heart,*
> *So as not to hearken unto Me.*
> *Therefore will I hurl you from off this land,*
> *On to the land that ye and your fathers knew not;*
> *And ye may serve there other gods, day and night,*
> *Since I will not grant you grace."*

The damning sin laid to Israel's charge is idolatry, with all the moral consequences involved in that prime transgression. That is to say, the offence consisted not barely in recognising and honouring the gods of the nations along with their own God, though that were fault enough, as an act of treason against the sole majesty of Heaven; but it was aggravated enormously by the moral declension and depravity, which accompanied this apostasy. They and their fathers forsook Iahvah "and kept not His teaching;" a reference to the Book of the Law, considered not only as a collection of ritual and ceremonial precepts for the regulation of external religion, but as a guide of life and conduct. And there had been a progress in evil; the nation had gone from bad to worse with fearful rapidity: so that now it could be said of the existing generation that it paid no heed at all to the monitions which Iahvah uttered by the mouth of His prophet, but walked simply in stubborn self-will and the indulgence of every corrupt inclination. And here too, as in so many other cases, the sin is to be its own punishment. The Book of the Law had declared that revolt from Iahvah should be punished by enforced service of strange gods in a strange land (Deut. iv. 28, xxviii. 36, 64); and Jeremiah repeats this threat, with the addition of a tone of ironical concession: there, in your bitter banishment, you may have your wish to the full; you may serve the foreign gods, and that without intermission (implying that the service would be a slavery).

The whole theory of Divine punishment is implicit in these few words of the prophet. They who sin persistently against light and knowledge are at last given over to their own hearts' lust, to do as they please, without the gracious check of God's inward voice. And then there comes a strong delusion, so that they believe a lie, and take evil for good and good for evil, and hold themselves innocent before God, when their guilt has reached its climax; so that, like Jeremiah's hearers, if their evil be denounced, they can ask in astonishment: "What is our iniquity? or what is our trespass?"

They are so ripe in sin that they retain no knowledge of it as sin, but hold it virtue.

> "And they, so perfect is their misery,
> Not once perceive their foul disfigurement,
> But boast themselves more comely than before."

And not only do we find in this passage a striking instance of judicial blindness as the penalty of sin. We may see also in the penalty predicted for the Jews a plain analogy to the doctrine that the permanence of the sinful state in a life to come is the penalty of sin in the present life. "He that is unjust, let him be unjust still; and he that is filthy, let him be filthy still!" and know himself to be what he is.

The prophet's dark horizon is here apparently lit up for a moment by a gleam of hope. The fourteenth and fifteenth verses, however, with their beautiful promise of restoration, really belong to another oracle, whose prevailing tones are quite different from the present gloomy forecast of retribution (xxiii. 7 sqq.). Here they interrupt the sense, and make a cleavage in the connexion of thought, which can only be bridged over artificially, by the suggestion that the import of the two verses is primarily not consolatory but minatory; that is to say, that they threaten Exile rather than promise Return; a mode of understanding the two verses which does manifest violence to the whole form of expression, and, above all, to their obvious force in the original passage from which they have been transferred hither. Probably some transcriber of the text wrote them in the margin of his copy, by way of palliating the otherwise unbroken gloom of this oracle of coming woe. Then, at some later time, another copyist, supposing the marginal note indicated an omission, incorporated the two verses in his transcription of the text, where they have remained ever since. (See on xxiii. 7, 8.)

After plainly announcing in the language of Deuteronomy the expulsion of Judah from the land which they had desecrated by idolatry, the prophet develops the idea in his own poetic fashion; representing the punishment as universal, and insisting that it is a punishment, and not an unmerited misfortune.

> "Lo, I am about to send many fishers (It is Iahvah's word!)
> And they shall fish them;
> And afterwards will I send many hunters,
> And they shall hunt them,
> From off every mountain,
> And from off every hill,
> And out of the clefts of the rocks."

Like silly fish, crowding helplessly one over another into the net, [68] when the fated moment arrives, Judah will fall an easy prey to the destroyer. And "afterwards," to ensure completeness, those who have survived this first disaster will be hunted like wild beasts, out of all the dens and caves in the mountains, the Adullams and Engedis, where they have found a refuge from the invader.

There is clearly reference to two distinct visitations of wrath, the latter more deadly than the former; else why the use of the emphatic note of time "afterwards"? If we understand by the "fishing" of the country the so-called first captivity, the carrying away of the boy-king Jehoiachin and his mother and his nobles and ten thousand principal citizens, by Nebuchadrezzar to Babylon (2 Kings xxiv. 10 sqq.); and by the "hunting" the final catastrophe in the time of Zedekiah; we get, as we shall see, a probable explanation of a difficult expression in the eighteenth verse, which cannot otherwise be satisfactorily accounted for. The next words (ver. 17) refute an assumption, implied in the popular demand to know wherein the guilt of the nation consists, that Iahvah is not really cognisant of their acts of apostasy.

> "For Mine eyes are upon all their ways,
> They are not hidden away from before My face;
> Nor is their guilt kept secret from before Mine eyes."

The verse is thus an indirect reply to the questions of verse 10; questions which in some mouths might indicate that unconsciousness of guilt, which is the token of sin finished and perfected; in others, the presence of that unbelief which doubts whether God can, or at least whether He does regard human conduct. But "He that planted the ear, can He not hear? He that formed the eye, can He not see?" (Ps. xciv. 9). It is really an utterly irrational thought, that sight, and hearing, and the higher faculties of reflexion and consciousness, had their origin in a blind and deaf, a senseless and unconscious source such as inorganic matter, whether we consider it in the atom or in the enormous mass of an embryo system of stars.

The measure of the penalty is now assigned.

> "And I will repay first the double of their guilt and their trespass
> For that they profaned My land with the carcases of their loathly offerings,
> And their abominations filled Mine heritage." [69]

"I will repay first." The term "first," which has occasioned much perplexity to expositors, means "the first time" (Gen. xxxviii. 28; Dan. xi. 29), and refers, if I am not mistaken, to the first great blow, the captivity of Jehoiachin, of which I spoke just now; an occasion which is designated again (ver. 21), by the expression "this once" or rather "at this time." And when it is said "I will repay the double of their guilt and of their trespass," we are to understand that the Divine justice is not satisfied with half measures; the punishment of sin is proportioned to the offence, and the cup of self-entailed misery has to be drained to the dregs. Even penitence does not abolish the physical and temporal consequences of sin; in ourselves and in others whom we have influenced they continue--a terrible and ineffaceable record of the past. The ancient law required that the man who had wronged his neighbour by theft or fraud should restore double (Ex. xxii. 4, 7, 9); and thus this expression would appear to denote that the impending chastisement would be in strict accordance with the recognised rule of law and justice, and that Judah must repay to the Lord in suffering the legal equivalent for her offence. In a like strain, towards the end of the Exile, the great prophet of the captivity comforts Jerusalem with the announcement that "her hard service is accomplished, her punishment is held sufficient; for she hath received of Iahvah's hand twofold for all her trespasses" (Isa. xl. 2). The Divine severity is, in fact, truest mercy. Only thus does mankind learn to realize "the exceeding sinfulness of sin," only as Judah learned the heinousness of desecrating the Holy Land with "loathly offerings" to the vile Nature-gods, and with the symbols in wood and stone of the cruel and obscene deities of Canaan; viz. by the fearful issue of transgression, the lesson of a calamitous experience, confirming the forecasts of its inspired prophets.

> "Iahvah my strength and my stronghold and my refuge in the day of distress!
> Unto Thee the very heathen will come from the ends of the earth, and will say:
> 'Mere fraud did our fathers receive as their own,
> Mere breath, and beings among whom is no helper.
> Should man make him gods,
> When such things are not gods?'
> "Therefore, behold I am about to let them know--
> At this time will I let them know My hand and My might,
> And they shall know that My name is Iahvah!"

In the opening words Jeremiah passionately recoils from the very mention of the hateful idols, the loathly creations, the lifeless "carcases," which his people have put in the place of the Living God. An overmastering access of faith lifts him off the low ground where these dead things lie in their helplessness, and bears him in spirit to Iahvah, the really and eternally existing, Who is his "strength and stronghold and refuge in the day of distress." From this height he takes an eagle glance into the dim future, and discerns--O marvel of victorious faith!--that the very heathen, who have never so much as known the Name of Iahvah, must one day be brought to acknowledge the impotence of their hereditary gods, and the sole deity of the Mighty One of Jacob. He enjoys a glimpse of Isaiah's and Micah's glorious vision of the latter days, when "the mountain of the Lord's House shall be exalted as chief of mountains, and all nations shall flow unto it."

In the light of this revelation, the sin and folly of Israel in dishonouring the One only God, by associating Him with idols and their symbols, becomes glaringly visible. The very heathen (the term is emphatic by position), will at last grope their way out of the night of traditional ignorance, and will own the absurdity of manufactured gods. Israel, on the other hand, has for centuries sinned against knowledge and reason. They had "Moses and the prophets"; yet they hated warning and despised reproof. They resisted the Divine teachings, because they loved to walk in their own ways, after the imaginings of their own evil hearts. And so they soon fell into that strange blindness, which suffered them to see no sin in giving companions to Iahvah, and neglecting His severer worship for the sensuous rites of Canaan.

A rude awakening awaits them. Once more will Iahvah interpose to save them from their infatuation. "This time" they shall be taught to know the nothingness of idols, not by the voice of prophetic pleadings, not by the fervid teachings of the Book of the Law, but by the sword of the enemy, by the rapine and ruin, in which the resistless might of Iahvah will be manifested against His rebellious people. Then, when the warnings which they have ridiculed find fearful accomplishment, then will they know that the name of the One God is Iahvah--He Who alone was and is and shall be for evermore. In the shock of overthrow, in the sorrows of captivity, they will realize the enormity of assimilating the Supreme Source of events, the Fountain of all being and power, to the miserable phantoms of a darkened and perverted imagination.

xvii. 1-18. Jeremiah, speaking for God, returns to the affirmation of Judah's guiltiness. He has answered the popular question (xvi. 10), so far as it implied that it was no mortal sin to associate the worship of alien gods with the worship of Iahvah. He now proceeds to answer it with an indignant contradiction, so far as it suggested that Judah was no longer guilty of the grossest forms of idolatry.

1?"The trespass of Judah," he affirms, "is written with pen of iron, with point of adamant;

> Graven upon the tablet of their heart,
> And upon the horns of their altars:
> Even as their sons remember their altars,
> And their sacred poles by the evergreen trees,
> Upon the high hills.
> 2?"O My mountain in the field!
> Thy wealth and all thy treasures will I give for a spoil,
> For the trespass of thine high-places in all thy borders.
> And thou shalt drop thine hand [70] from thy demesne which I gave thee;
> And I will enslave thee to thine enemies,
> In the land that thou knowest not;
> "For a fire have ye kindled in Mine anger;
> It shall burn for evermore."

It is clear from the first strophe that the outward forms of idolatry were no longer openly practised in the country. Where otherwise would be the point of affirming that the national sin was "written with pen of iron, and point of adamant"--that it was "graven upon the tablet of the people's heart?" Where would be the point of alluding to the children's memory of the altars and sacred poles, which were the visible adjuncts of idolatry? Plainly it is implied that the hideous rites, which sometimes involved the sacrifice of children, are a thing of the past; yet not of the distant past, for the young of the present generation remember them; those terrible scenes are burnt in upon their memories, as a haunting recollection which can no more be effaced, than the guilt contracted by their parents as agents in those abhorrent rites can be done away. The indelible characters of sin are graven deeply upon their hearts; no need for a prophet to remind them of facts to which their own consciences, their own inward sense of outraged affections, and of nature sacrificed to a dark and bloody superstition, bears irrefragable witness. Rivers of water cannot cleanse the stain of innocent blood from their polluted altars. The crimes of the past are unatoned for, and beyond reach of atonement; they cry to heaven for vengeance, and the vengeance will surely fall (xv. 4).

Hitzig rather prosaically remarks that Josiah had destroyed the altars. But the stains of which the poet-seer speaks are not palpable to sense; he contemplates unseen realities.

> "Will all great Neptune's ocean wash this blood
> Clean from my hand? No, this my hand will rather
> The multitudinous seas incarnadine,
> Making the green one red."

The second strophe declares the nature of the punishment. The tender, yearning, hopeless love of the cry with which Iahvah resigns His earthly seat to profanation and plunder and red-handed ruin, enhances the awful impression wrought by the slow, deliberate enunciation of the details of the sentence--the utter spoliation of temple and palaces; the accumulated hoards of generations--all that represented the wealth and culture and glory of the time--carried away for ever; the enforced surrender of home and country; the harsh servitude to strangers in a far-off land.

It is difficult to fix the date of this short lyrical outpouring, if it be assumed, with Hitzig, that it is an independent whole. He refers it to the year b.c. 602, after Jehoiakim had revolted from Babylon--"a proceeding which made a future captivity well-nigh certain, and made it plain that the sin of Judah remained still to be punished." Moreover, the preceding year (b.c. 603) was what was known to the Law as a Year of Release or Remission (shenath shemittah); and the phrase "thou shalt drop thine hand," i.e. "loose thine hold of" the land (xvii. 4), appears to allude to the peculiar usages of that year, in which the debtor was released from his obligations, and the corn-lands and vineyards were allowed to lie fallow. The Year of Release was also called the Year of Rest (shenath shabbathon, Lev. xxv. 5); and both in the present passage of Jeremiah, and in the book of Leviticus, the time to be spent by the Jews in exile is regarded as a period of rest for the desolate land, which would then "make good her sabbaths" (Lev. xxvi. 34, 35, 43). The Chronicler indeed seems to refer to this very phrase of Jeremiah; at all events, nothing else is to be found in the extant works of the prophet with which his language corresponds (2 Chron. xxxvi. 21).

If the rendering of the second verse, which we find in both our English versions, and which I have adopted above, be correct, there arises an obvious objection to the date assigned by Hitzig; and the same objection lies against the view of Naegelsbach, who translates:

"As their children remember their altars,
And their images of Baal by (i.e. at the sight of) the green trees, by the high hills."

For in what sense could this have been written "not long before the fourth year of Jehoiakim," which is the date suggested by this commentator for the whole group of chapters, xiv.-xvii. 18? The entire reign of Josiah had intervened between the atrocities of Manasseh and this period; and it is not easy to suppose that any sacrifice of children had occurred in the three months' reign of Jehoahaz, or in the early years of Jehoiakim. Had it been so, Jeremiah, who denounces the latter king severely enough, would certainly have placed the horrible fact in the forefront of his invective; and instead of specifying Manasseh as the king whose offences Iahvah would not pardon, would have thus branded Jehoiakim, his own contemporary. This difficulty appears to be avoided by Hitzig, who explains the passage thus: "When they (the Jews) think of their children, they remember, and cannot but remember, the altars to whose horns the blood of their immolated children cleaves. In the same way, by a green tree on the hills, i.e., when they come upon any such, their Asherim are brought to mind, which were trees of that sort." And since it is perhaps possible to translate the Hebrew as this suggests, "When they remember their sons, their altars, and their sacred poles, by (i.e. by means of) the evergreen trees (collective term) upon the high hills," and this translation agrees well with the statement that the sin of Judah is "graven upon the tablet of their heart," his view deserves further consideration. The same objection, however, presses again, though with somewhat diminished force. For if the date of the section be 602, the eighth year of Jehoiakim, more than forty years must have elapsed between the time of Manasseh's bloody rites and the utterance of this oracle. Would many who were parents then, and surrendered their children for sacrifice, be still living at the supposed date? And if not, where is the appropriateness of the words "When they remember their sons, their altars, and their Asherim?"

There seems no way out of the difficulty, but either to date the piece much earlier, assigning it, e.g., to the time of the prophet's earnest preaching in connexion with the reforming movement of Josiah, when the living generation would certainly remember the human sacrifices under Manasseh; or else to construe the passage in a very different sense, as follows. The first verse declares that the sin of Judah is graven upon the tablet of their heart, and upon the horns of their altars. The pronouns evidently shew that it is the guilt of the nation, not of a particular generation, that is asserted. The subsequent words agree with this view. The expression, "Their sons" is to be understood in the same way as the expressions "their heart," "their altars." It is equivalent to the "sons of Judah" (benê Jehudah), and means simply the people of Judah, as now existing, the present generation. Now it does not appear that image-worship and the cultus of the high-places revived after their abolition by Josiah. Accordingly, the symbols of impure worship mentioned in this passage are not high-places and images but altars and Asherim, i.e., the wooden poles which were the emblems of the reproductive principle of Nature. What the passage therefore intends to say would seem to be this: "The guilt of the nation remains, so long as its children are mindful of their altars and Asherim erected beside [71] the evergreen trees on the high hills"; i.e., so long as they remain attached to the modified idolatry of the day.

The general force of the words remains the same, whether they accuse the existing generation of serving sun-pillars (maççeboth) and sacred poles (asherim), or merely of hankering after the old forbidden rites. For so long as the popular heart was wedded to the former superstitions, it could not be said that any external abolition of idolatry was a sufficient proof of national repentance. The longing to indulge in sin is sin; and sinful it is not to hate sin. The guilt of the nation remained, therefore, and would remain, until blotted out by the tears of a genuine repentance towards Iahvah.

But understood thus, the passage suits the time of Jehoiachin, as well as any other period.

"Why," asks Naegelsbach, "should not Moloch have been the terror of the Israelitish children, when there was such real and sad ground for it, as in wanting in other bugbears which terrify the children of the present day?" To this we may reply, (1) Moloch is not mentioned at all, but simply altars and asherim; (2) would the word "remember" be appropriate in this case?

The beautiful strophes which follow (5-13) are not obviously connected with the preceding text. They wear a look of self-completeness, which suggests that here and in many other places Jeremiah has left us, not whole discourses, written down substantially in the form in which they were delivered, but rather his more finished fragments; pieces which being more rhythmical in form, and more striking in thought, had imprinted themselves more deeply upon his memory.

Rev. C. J. Ball, M.A., & W. H. Bennett, M.A.

> "Thus hath Iahvah said:
> Cursed is the man that trusteth in human kind,
> And maketh flesh his arm,
> And whose heart swerveth from Iahvah!
> And he shall become like a leafless tree in the desert,
> And shalt not see when good cometh;
> And shall dwell in parched places in the steppe,
> A salt land and uninhabited.
> "Blessed is the man that trusteth in Iahvah,
> And whose trust Iahvah becometh!
> And he shall become like a tree planted by water,
> That spreadeth its roots by a stream,
> And is not afraid when heat cometh,
> And its leaf is evergreen;
> And in the year of drought it feareth not,
> Nor leaveth off from making fruit."

The form of the thought expressed in these two octostichs, the curse and the blessing, may have been suggested by the curses and blessings of that Book of the Law of which Jeremiah had been so faithful an interpreter (Deut. xxvii. 15-xxviii. 20); while both the thought and the form of the second stanza are imitated by the anonymous poet of the first psalm. The mention of "the year of drought" in the penultimate line may be taken, perhaps, as a link of connexion between this brief section and the whole of what precedes it so far as chap. xiv., which is headed "Concerning the droughts." If, however, the group of chapters thus marked out really constitute a single discourse, as Naegelsbach assumes, one can only say that the style is episodical rather than continuous; that the prophet has often recorded detached thoughts, worked up to a certain degree of literary form, but hanging together as loosely as pearls on a string. Indeed, unless we suppose that he had kept full notes of his discourses and soliloquies, or that, like certain professional lecturers of our own day, he had been in the habit of indefinitely repeating to different audiences the same carefully elaborated compositions, it is difficult to understand how he would be able without the aid of a special miracle, to write down in the fourth year of Jehoiakim the numerous utterances of the previous three and twenty years. Neither of these suppositions appears probable. But if the prophet wrote from memory, so long after the original delivery of many of his utterances, the looseness of internal connexion, which marks so much of his book, is readily understood.

The internal evidence of the fragment before us, so far as any such is traceable, appears to point to the same period as what precedes, the time immediately subsequent to the death of Jehoiakim. The curse pronounced upon trusting in man may be an allusion to that king's confidence in the Egyptian alliance, which probably induced him to revolt from Nebuchadrezzar, and so precipitate the final catastrophe of his country. He owed his throne to the Pharaoh's appointment (2 Kings xxiii. 34), and may perhaps have regarded this as an additional reason for defection from Babylon. But the chastisement of Egypt preceded that of Judah; and when the day came for the latter, the king of Egypt durst no longer go to the help of his too trustful allies (2 Kings xxiv. 7). Jehoiakim had died, but his son and successor was carried captive to Babylon. In the brief interval between those two events, the prophet may have penned these two stanzas, contrasting the issues of confidence in man and confidence in God. On the other hand, they may also be referred to some time not long before the fourth year of Jehoiakim, when that king, egged on by Egypt, was meditating rebellion against his suzerain; an act of which the fatal consequences might easily be foreseen by any thoughtful observer, who was not blinded by fanatical passion and prejudice, and which might itself be regarded as an index of the kindling of Divine wrath against the country.

> "Deep is the heart above all things else;
> And sore-diseased it is: who can know it?
> I, Iahvah, search the heart, I try the reins,
> And that, to give to a man according to his own ways,
> According to the fruit of his own doings.
> "A partridge that gathereth young which are not hers,
> Is he that maketh wealth not by right.
> In the middle of his days it will leave him,
> And in his end he shall prove a fool.
> "A throne of glory, a high seat from of old,
> Is the place of our sanctuary.
> Hope of Israel, Iahvah!

> All that leave Thee shall be ashamed;
> Mine apostates shall be written in earth;
> For they left the Well of Living Waters, even Iahvah.
> "Heal Thou me, Iahvah, and I shall be healed,
> Save Thou me, and I shall be saved,
> For Thou art my praise.
> "Lo, they say unto me,
> Where is the Word of Iahvah? Prithee, let it come!
> Yet I, I hasted not from being a shepherd after Thee,
> And woeful day I desired not--Thou knowest;
> The issue of my lips, before Thy face it fell.
> "Become not a terror to me!
> Thou art my refuge in the day of evil.
> Let my pursuers be ashamed, and let not me be ashamed!
> Let them be dismayed, and let not me be dismayed;
> Let Thou come upon them a day of evil,
> And doubly with breaking break Thou them!"

In the first of these stanzas, the word "heart" is the connecting link with the previous reflexions. The curse and the blessing had there been pronounced not upon any outward and visible distinctions, but upon a certain inward bent and spirit. He is called accursed, whose confidence is placed in changeable, perishable man, and "whose heart swerveth from Iahvah." And he is blessed, who pins his faith to nothing visible; who looks for help and stay not to the seen, which is temporal, but to the Unseen, which is eternal.

The thought now occurs that this matter of inward trust, being a matter of the heart, and not merely of the outward bearing, is a hidden matter, a secret which baffles all ordinary judgment. Who shall take upon him to say whether this or that man, this or that prince confided or not confided in Iahvah? The human heart is a sea, whose depths are beyond human search; or it is a shifty Proteus, transforming itself from moment to moment under the pressure of changing circumstances, at the magic touch of impulse, under the spell of new perceptions and new phases of its world. And besides, its very life is tainted with a subtle disease, whose hereditary influence is ever interfering with the will and affections, ever tampering with the conscience and the judgment, and making difficult a clear perception, much more a wise decision. Nay, where so many motives press, so many plausible suggestions of good, so many palliations of evil, present themselves upon the eve of action; when the colours of good and evil mingle and gleam together in such rich profusion before the dazzled sight, that the mind is bewildered by the confused medley of appearances, and wholly at a loss to discern and disentangle them one from another; is it wonderful, if in such a case the heart should take refuge in the comfortable illusion of self-deceit, and seek, with too great success, to persuade itself into contentment with something which it calls not positive evil but merely a less sublime good?

It is not for man, who cannot see the heart, to pronounce upon the degree of his fellow's guilt. All sins, all crimes, are in this respect relative to the intensity of passion, the force of circumstances, the nature of surroundings, the comparative stress of temptation. Murder and adultery are absolute crimes in the eye of human law, and subject as such to fixed penalties; but the Unseen Judge takes cognizance of a thousand considerations, which though they abolish not the exceeding sinfulness of these hideous results of a depraved nature, yet modify to a vast extent the degree of guilt evinced in particular cases by the same outward acts. In the sight of God, a life socially correct may be stained with a deeper dye than that of profligacy or bloodshed; and nothing so glaringly shows the folly of inquiring what is the unpardonable sin, as the reflexion that any sin whatever may become such in an individual case.

Before God, human justice is often the liveliest injustice. And how many flagrant wrongs, how many monstrous acts of cruelty and oppression, how many wicked frauds and perjuries, how many of those vile deeds of seduction and corruption, which are, in truth, the murder of immortal souls; how many of those fearful sins, which make a sorrow-laden hell beneath the smiling surface of this pleasure-wooing world, are left unheeded, unavenged by any earthly tribunal! But all these things are noted in the eternal record of Him who searches the heart, and penetrates man's inmost being, not from a motive of mere curiosity, but with fixed intent to award a righteous recompense for all choice and all conduct.

The calamities which marked the last years of Jehoiakim, and his ignominious end, were a signal instance of Divine retribution. Here that king's lawless avarice is branded as not only wicked but foolish. He is compared to the partridge, which gathers and hatches the eggs of other birds, only to be deserted at once by her stolen brood. [72] "In the middle of his days, it shall leave him" (or "it may leave him," for in Hebrew one form has to do duty for both shades of meaning). The uncertainty of possession, the certainty of absolute surrender within a few short years, this is the point which demonstrates the unreason of making riches the chief end of one's earthly activity. "Truly man walketh in a vain shadow, and disquieteth himself in vain: he heapeth up riches, and cannot tell who shall gather them." It is the point which is put with such terrible force in the parable of the Rich Fool. "Soul, thou hast much goods laid up for thyself for many years; take thine ease, eat, drink, and be merry." "And the Lord said unto him, Thou fool! this night shall thy soul be required of thee."

The covetousness, oppression, and bloodthirstiness of Jehoiakim are condemned in a striking prophecy (xxii. 13-19), which we shall have to consider hereafter. A vivid light is thrown upon the words, "In the middle of his days it shall leave him," by the fact recorded in Kings (2 Kings xxiii. 36), that he died in the thirty-sixth year of his age; when, that is, he had fulfilled but half of the threescore years and ten allotted to the ordinary life of man. We are reminded of that other psalm which declares that "bloody and deceitful men shall not live out half their days" (lv. 23).

Apart indeed from all consideration of the future, and apart from all reference to that loyalty to the Unseen Ruler which is man's inevitable duty, a life devoted to Mammon is essentially irrational. The man is most truly a "fool"--that is, one who fails to understand his own nature, one who has not attained to even a tolerable working hypothesis as to the needs of life, and the way to win a due share of happiness;--who has not discovered that

"riches have their proper stint
In the contented mind, not mint;"
and that
"those who have the itch
Of craving more, are never rich;"
and who has missed all apprehension of the grand secret that
"Wealth cannot make a life, but love."

From the vanity of earthly thrones, whether of Egypt or of Judah, thrones whose glory is transitory, and whose power to help and succour is so ill-assured, the prophet lifts his eyes to the one throne whose glory is everlasting, and whose power and permanence are an eternal refuge.

"Thou Throne of Glory, High Seat from of old,
Place of our Sanctuary, Hope of Israel, Iahvah!
All who leave Thee blush for shame;
Mine apostates are written in earth;
For they have forsaken the Well of Living Water, even Iahvah!"

It is his concluding reflexion upon the unblest, unhonoured end of the apostate Jehoiakim. If Isaiah could speak of Shebna as a "throne of glory," [73] i.e., the honoured support and mainstay of his family, there seems no reason why Iahvah might not be so addressed, as the supporting power and sovereign of the world.

The terms "Throne of Glory" ... "Place of our Sanctuary" seem to be used much as we use the expressions, "the Crown," "the Court," "the Throne," when we mean the actual ruler with whom these things are associated. And when the prophet declares "Mine [74] apostates are written in earth," he asserts that oblivion is the portion of those of his people, high or low, who forsake Iahvah for another god. Their names are not written in the Book of Life (Ex. xxxii. 32; Ps. lxix. 28), but in the sand whence they are soon effaced. The prophets do not attempt to expose

"The sweet strange mystery
Of what beyond these things may lie."

They do not in express terms promise eternal life to the individual believer.

But how often do their words imply that comfortable doctrine! They who forsake Iahvah must perish, for there is neither permanence nor stay apart from Iahvah, whose very Name denotes He who Is, the sole Principle of Being and Fountain of Life. If they--nations and persons--who revolt from Him must die, the implication, the truth necessary to complete this affirmation, is that they who trust in Him, and make Him their arm, will live; for union with Him is eternal life.

In this Fountain of Living Water Jeremiah now seeks healing for himself. The malady that afflicts him is the apparent failure of his oracles. He suffers as a prophet whose word seems idle to the multitude. He is hurt with their scorn, and wounded to the heart with their scoffing. On all sides men press the mocking question, "Where is the word of Iahvah? Prithee, let it come to pass!" His threats of national overthrow had not been speedily realized; and men made a mock of the delays of Divine mercy. Conscious of his own integrity, and keenly sensitive to the ridicule of his triumphant adversaries, and scarcely able to endure longer his intolerable position, he pours out a prayer for healing and help. Heal me, he cries, and I shall be healed, Save me and I shall be saved--really and truly saved, as the form of the Hebrew term implies; for Thou art my praise, my boast and my glory, as the Book of the Law affirms (Deut. x. 21). I have not trusted in man, but in God; and if this my sole glory be taken away, if events prove me a false prophet, as my friends allege, applying the very test of the sacred Law (Deut. xviii. 21 sq.), then shall I be of all men most forsaken and forlorn. The bitterness of his woe is intensified by the consciousness that he has not thrust himself without call into the prophetic office, like the false prophets whose aim was to traffic in sacred things (xiv. 14, 15); for then the consciousness of guilt might have made the punishment more tolerable, and the facts would have justified the jeers of his persecutors. But the case was far otherwise. He had been most unwilling to assume the function of prophet; and it was only in obedience to the stress of repeated calls that he had yielded. "But as for me," he protests, "I hasted not from being a shepherd to follow Thee." It would seem, if this be the correct, as it certainly is the simplest rendering of his words, that, at the time when he first became aware of his true vocation, the young prophet was engaged in tending the flocks that grazed in the priestly pasture-grounds of Anathoth. In that case, we are reminded of David, who was summoned from the sheepfold to camp and court, and of Amos the prophet-herdsman of Tekoa. But the Hebrew term translated "from being a shepherd" is probably a disguise of some other original expression; and it would involve no very violent change to read "I made no haste to follow after Thee fully" or "entirely" [75] (Deut. i. 36); a reading which is partially supported by the oldest version. Or it may be even better, as involving a mere change in the punctuation, [76] to amend the text thus: "But as for me, I made no haste, in following thee," more literally, "in accompanying thee" (Judg. xiv. 20). This, however, is a point of textual criticism, which leaves the general sense the same in any case.

When the prophet adds: "and the ill day I desired not," some think that he means the day when he surrendered to the Divine calling, and accepted his mission. But it seems to suit the context better, if we understand by the "ill day" the day of wrath whose coming was the burden of his preaching; the day referred to in the taunts of his enemies, when they asked "Where is the word of Iahvah?" adding with biting sarcasm: "Prithee, let it come to pass." They sneered at Jeremiah as one who seized every occasion to predict evil, as one who longed to witness the ruin of his country. The utter injustice of the charge, in view of the frequent cries of anguish which interrupt his melancholy forecasts, is no proof that it was not made. In all ages, God's representatives have been called upon to endure false accusations. Hence the prophet appeals from man's unrighteous judgment to God the Searcher of hearts. "Thou knowest; the utterance of my lips (Deut. xxiii. 24) before Thy face it fell": as if to say, No word of mine, spoken in Thy name, was a figment of my own fancy, uttered for my own purposes, without regard of Thee. I have always spoken as in Thy presence, or rather, in Thy presence. Thou, who hearest all, didst hear each utterance of mine; and therefore knowest that all I said was truthful and honest and in perfect accord with my commission.

If only we who, like Jeremiah, are called upon to speak for God, could always remember that every word we say is uttered in that Presence, what a sense of responsibility would lie upon us; with what labour and prayers should we not make our preparation! Too often alas! it is to be feared that our perception of the presence of man banishes all sense of any higher presence; and the anticipation of a fallible and frivolous criticism makes us forget for the time the judgment of God. And yet "by our words we shall be justified, and by our words we shall be condemned."

In continuing his prayer, Jeremiah adds the remarkable petition, "Become not Thou to me a cause of dismay!" He prays to be delivered from that overwhelming perplexity, which threatens to swallow him up, unless God should verify by events that which His own Spirit has prompted him to utter. He prays that Iahvah, his only "refuge in the day of evil," will not bemock him with vain expectations; will not falsify His own guidance; will not suffer His messenger to be "ashamed," disappointed and put to the blush by the failure of his predictions. And then once again, in the spirit of his time, he implores vengeance upon his unbelieving and cruel persecutors: "Let them be ashamed," disappointed in their expectation of immunity, "let them be dismayed," crushed in spirit and utterly overcome by the fulfilment of his dark presages of evil. "Let Thou come upon them a day of evil, And doubly with breaking break Thou them!" This indeed asks no more than that what has been spoken before in the way of prophecy--"I will repay the double of their guilt and their trespass" (xvi. 18)--may be forthwith accomplished. And the provocation was, beyond all question, immense. The hatred that burned in the taunt "Where is the word of Iahvah? Prithee, let it come to pass!" was doubtless of like kind with that which at a later stage of Jewish history expressed itself in the words "He trusted in God, let Him deliver Him!" "If He be the Son of God, let Him now come down from the cross, and we will believe on Him!"

And how much fierce hostility that one term "my pursuers" may cover, it is easy to infer from the narratives of the prophet's evil experience in chaps. xx., xxvi. and xxxviii. But allowing for all this, we can at best only affirm that the prophet's imprecations on his foes are natural and human; we cannot pretend that they are evangelical and Christ-like. [77] [78] Besides, the latter would be a gratuitous anachronism, which no intelligent interpreter of Scripture is called upon to perpetrate. It is neither necessary to the proper vindication of the prophet's writings as truly inspired of God, nor helpful to a right conception of the method of revelation.

Rev. C. J. Ball, M.A., & W. H. Bennett, M.A.

Footnotes:

57. Hitzig: (1) xiv. 1-9, 19-22: "Lament and Prayer on occasion of a Drought." (2) xiv. 10-18. "Oracle against the false Prophets and the misguided People" (Hitzig mistakes the import of the phrase kn 'hvv lnv, "Thus have they loved to wander," ver. 10; supposing that the "thus" refers to xiii. 27, and that xiv. 1-9 is misplaced). (3) xv. 1-9. "The incorrigible People will be punished mercilessly." Hitzig thinks C. B. Michaelis wrong in asserting close connexion with the end of the preceding chapter, because the intercession, vv. 2-9, does not agree with the prohibition, xiv. 11; and because xiv. 19-22, merely prays for cessation of the Drought; while the rejection of "the hypothetical intercession," xv. 1, delivers the people over to all the horrors which follow in the train of war. xv. 1-9 may originally have followed xiv. 18. But this is far from cogent reasoning. There is nothing surprising in the renewal of the prophet's intercession, except on a theory of strictly verbal inspiration; and xv. 1 sqq. in refusing deliverance from the Drought, or rather in answer to the prayer imploring it, announces further and worse evils to follow. (4) "Complaint of the Seer against Iahvah, and Soothing of his Dejection," xv. 10-21. Hitzig thinks internal evidence here points to the fourth year of Jehoiakim; and that xvii. 1-4 originally preceded this section, especially as ch. xvi. connects closely with xv. 9. (5) xvi. 1-20. "Prediction of an imminent general Judgment by Plague and Captivity." Written immediately after xv. 1-9, and falls with that in the short reign of Jehoiachin. (6) xvii. 1-4. "Judah's unforgotten Guilt will be punished by Captivity." Wanting in LXX. (as early as Jerome), but contains original of xv. 13, 14, and must therefore be genuine. Belongs 602 b.c., year of Jehoiakim's revolt. (7) xvii. 5-18. "The Vindication of Trust in God on Despisers and Believers. Prayer for its Vindication." Date immediately after death of Jehoiakim. (8) 19-27. "Warning to keep the Sabbath." Time of Jehoiachin.

58. The Heb. verb chth "is broken" may probably have this meaning. "Dismayed" is not nearly so suitable, though it is the usual meaning of the term. Cf. Isa. vii. 8.

59. Cf. viii. 9. "And no wisdom is in them."

60. So Dathe, Naegelsbach.

61. Lit. "all these things," i.e., this visible world. There is no Heb. special term for the "universe" or "world." "The all" or "heaven and earth," or the phrase in the text, are used in this sense.

62. The reference to an eclipse of the sun in the words
"Her sun went down, while it yet was day;
He blushed and paled." appears fairly certain. Such an event is said to have occurred in that part of the world, Sept. 30, b.c. 610.

63. 13. Read vmtyk "Thine high places" for l' vmchyr "without price"; and transpose vcht't (xvii. 3).

64. 14. Read vhvrtyk "and I will make thee serve" (xvii. 4) for vhvrty "and I will make to pass through...." The third member is a quotation from Deut. xxxii. 22. In the fourth, read lvlm "for ever" (xvii. 4) instead of lykm "upon you."

65. The tone of all this indicates that the prophet was no novice in his office. It does not suit the time of Josiah; but agrees very well with the time of confusion and popular dismay which followed his death. That event must have brought great discredit upon Jeremiah and upon all who had been instrumental in the religious changes of his reign.

66. Practices forbidden, Lev. xxi. 5; Deut. xiv. 1. Jeremiah mentions them as ordinary signs of mourning, and doubtless they were general in his time. An ancient usage, having its root in natural feeling, is not easily extirpated.

67. Naegelsbach.

68. The figure recalls the Persian custom of sweeping off the whole population of an island, by forming a line and marching over it, a process of extermination called by the Greek writers sageneuein, "fishing with a seine or drag-net" (Herod. iii. 149, iv. 9, vi. 31).

69. For the construction, cf. Gen. i. 22; Jer. li. 11. Or "With their abominations they filled, etc.," a double accusative.

70. i.e., Loose thine hold of ... let go ... release. Read ydk for vvk. The uses of smt "to throw down," "let fall," resemble those of the Greek hiemi and its compounds. I corrected the passage thus, to find afterwards that I had been anticipated by J. D. Michaelis, Graf, and others.

71. There is something strange about the phrase "by (upon, `al) the evergreen tree." Twenty-five Heb. MSS., the Targ., and the Syriac, read "every" (kol) for "upon" (`al). We still feel the want of a preposition, and may confidently restore "under" (ta?ath), from the nine other passages in which "evergreen tree" (`ec? ra`anan) occurs in connexion with idolatrous worship. In all these instances the expression is "under every evergreen tree" (ta?ath kol `ec? ra`anan); from the Book of the Law (Deut. xii. 2), whence Jeremiah probably drew the phrase, to 2 Chron. xxviii. 4. Jeremiah has already used the phrase thrice (ii. 20, iii. 6, 13), in exactly the same form. The other passages are Ezek. vi. 13; Isa. lvii. 5; 2 Kings xvi. 4, xvii. 10. The corruption of kol into `al is found elsewhere. Probably ta?ath had dropt out of the text, before the change took place here.

72. A popular opinion of the time.
73. Isa. xxii. 23.
74. The Heb. term is probably written with omission of the final mem, a common abbreviation; and the right reading may be vsvrym "and apostates."
75. ml' for mrh.
76. mrh for mrh.
77. I have left this paragraph as I wrote it, although I feel great doubts upon the subject. What I have remarked elsewhere on similar passages, should be considered along with the present suggestions. We have especially to remember, (i) the peculiar status of the speaker as a true prophet; and (ii) the terrible invectives of Christ Himself on certain occasions (St. Matt. xxiii. 33-35; St. Luke x. 15; St. John viii. 44).
78. The context is against supposing, with Graf, that the prophet's call "hear ye!" extends also to princes yet unborn (cf. xiii. 13; xxv. 18 is different). If, however, it be thought that Jeremiah addressed not the sovereigns personally, but only the people passing in and out of the gates; then the expression becomes intelligible as a generalised plural, like the parallels in 2 Chron. xxviii. 3 ("his children"), ibid. 16 ("the kings of Assyria" = Tiglath-pileser II.). The prophet might naturally avoid the singular as too personal, in affirming an obligation which lay upon the Judean kings in general.

X. THE SABBATH – A WARNING

Jeremiah xvii. 19-27.

"Thus said Iahvah unto me: Go and stand in the gate of Benjamin, whereby the kings of Judah come in, and whereby they go out; and in all the gates of Jerusalem. And say unto them, Hear ye the word of Iahvah, O kings of Judah, and all Judah, and all inhabitants of Jerusalem, who come in by these gates!

"Thus said Iahvah: Beware, on your lives, and bear ye not a burden on the Day of Rest, nor bring it in by the gates of Jerusalem! Nor shall ye bring a burden forth out of your houses on the Day of Rest, nor shall ye do any work; but ye shall hallow the Day of Rest, as I commanded your fathers. (Albeit, they hearkened not, nor inclined their ear, but stiffened their neck against hearkening, and against receiving instruction.)

"And it shall come to pass, if ye will indeed hearken unto Me, saith Iahvah, not to bring a burden in by the gates of this city on the Day of Rest, but to hallow the Day of Rest, not to do therein any work; then there shall come in by the gates of this city kings [and princes] sitting upon the throne of David, riding on the chariots and on the horses, they and their princes, O men of Judah and inhabitants of Jerusalem! and this city shall be inhabited for ever. And people shall come in from the cities of Judah and from the places round Jerusalem, and from the land of Benjamin, and from the lowlands, and from the hill-country, and from the south, bringing in burnt-offering and thank-offering, and oblation and incense; and bringing a thanksgiving into the house of Iahvah.

"And if ye hearken not unto Me to hallow the Day of Rest, and not to bear a burden and come in by the gates of Jerusalem on the Day of Rest: I will kindle a fire in her gates, and it shall devour the palaces of Jerusalem, and shall not be quenched."

The matter and manner of this brief oracle mark it off from those which precede it as an independent utterance, and a whole complete in itself. Its position may be accounted for by its probable date, which may be fixed a little after the previous chapters, in the three months' reign of the ill-starred Jehoiachin; and by the writer's or his editor's desire to break the monotony of commination by an occasional gleam of hope and promise. At the same time, the introductory formula with which it opens is so similar to that of the two following oracles (chaps. xviii., xix.), as to suggest the idea of a connexion in time between the members of the group. Further, there is an obvious connexion of thought between chaps. xviii., xix. In the former, the house of Israel is represented as clay in the hand of the Divine Potter; in the latter, Judah is a potter's vessel destined to be broken in pieces. And if we assume the priority of the piece before us, a logical progress is observable, from the alternative here presented for the people's choice, to their decision for the worse part (xviii. 12 sqq.), and then to the corresponding decision on the part of Iahvah (xix.). Or, as Hitzig puts it otherwise, in the piece before us the scales are still in equipoise; in chap. xviii. one goes down; Iahvah intends mischief (ver. 11), and the people are invited to appease His anger. But the warning is fruitless; and therefore the prophet announces their destruction, depicting it in the darkest colours (chap. xix.). The immediate consequence to Jeremiah himself is related in chap. xx. 1-6; and it is highly probable that the section, chap. xxi. 11-xxii. 9, is the continuation of the oracle addressed to Pashchur: so that we have before us a whole group of prophecies belonging to the same eventful period of the prophet's activity (xvii. 20 agrees closely with xxii. 2, and xvii. 25 with xxii. 4).

The circumstances of the present oracle are these. Jeremiah is inwardly bidden to station himself first in "the gate of the sons of the people"--a gate of Jerusalem which we cannot further determine, as it is not mentioned elsewhere under this designation, but which appears to have been a special resort of the masses of the population, because it was the one by which the kings were wont to enter and leave the city, and where they doubtless were accustomed to hear petitions and to administer justice; and afterwards, he is to take his stand in all the gates in turn, so as not to miss the chance of delivering his message to any of his countrymen. He is there to address the "kings of Judah" (ver. 20); an expression which may denote the young king Jehoiachin and his mother (xiii. 18), or the king and the princes of the blood, the "House of David" of chap. xxi. 12. The promise "kings shall come in by the gates of this city ... and this city shall be inhabited for ever," and the threat "I will kindle a fire in her gates, and it shall devour the palaces of Jerusalem," may be taken to imply a time when the public danger was generally recognised. The first part of the promise may be intended to meet an apprehension, such as might naturally be felt after the death of Jehoiakim, that the incensed Chaldeans would come and take away the Jewish place and nation. In raising the boy Jehoiachin to the throne of his fathers, men may have sorrowfully foreboded that, as the event proved, he would never keep his crown till manhood, nor beget a race of future kings.

The matter of the charge to rulers and people is the due observance of the fourth commandment: "ye shall hallow the Day of Rest, as I commanded your fathers" (see Ex. xx. 8, "Remember the Day of Rest, to hallow it"--which is probably the original form of the precept. Jeremiah, however, probably had in mind the form of the precept as it appears in Deuteronomy: "Observe the Day of Rest to hallow it, as Iahvah thy God commanded thee:" Deut. v. 12). The Hebrew term for "hallow" means to separate a thing from common things, and devote it to God.

To hallow the Day of Rest, therefore, is to make a marked distinction between it and ordinary days, and to connect it in some way with religion. What is here commanded is to abstain from "bearing burdens," and doing any kind of work (melakah, Gen. ii. 2, 3; Ex. xx. 9, 10, xxxi. 14, 15; Gen. xxxix. 11, "appointed task," "duty," "business"). The bearing of burdens into the gates and out of the houses clearly describes the ordinary commerce between town and country. The country folk are forbidden to bring their farm produce to the market in the city gates, and the townspeople to convey thither from their houses and shops the manufactured goods which they were accustomed to barter for these. Nehemiah's memoirs furnish a good illustration of the general sense of the passage (Neh. xiii. 15), relating how he suppressed this Sabbath traffic between town and country. Dr. Kuenen has observed that "Jeremiah is the first of the prophets who stands up for a stricter sanctification of the seventh day, treating it, however, merely as a day of rest.... What was traditional appears to have been only abstinence from field-work, and perhaps also from professional pursuits." In like manner, he had before stated that "tendencies to such an exaggeration of the Sabbath rest as would make it absolute, are found from the Chaldean period. Isaiah (i. 13) regards the Sabbath purely as a sacrificial day." The last statement here is hardly a fair inference. In the passage referred to Isaiah is inveighing against the futile worship of his contemporaries; and he only mentions the Sabbath in this connexion. And that "tradition" required more than "abstinence from field-work" is evident from words of the prophet Amos, written at least a century and a half before the present oracle, and implying that very abstinence from trading which Jeremiah prescribes. Amos makes the grasping dealers of his time cry impatiently, "When will the new moon be gone, that we may sell corn? and the sabbath, that we may set out wheat for sale?" (Amos viii. 5); a clear proof that buying and selling were suspended on the sabbath festival in the eighth century b.c.

It is hardly likely that, when law or custom compelled covetous dealers to cease operations on the Sabbath, and buying and selling, the principal business of the time, was suspended, the artisans of town or country would be allowed by public opinion to ply their everyday tasks. Accordingly, when Jeremiah adds to his prohibition of Sabbath trading, a veto upon any kind of "work"--a term which includes this trafficking, but also covers the labour of handicraftsmen (cf. 1 Kings v. 30; 2 Kings xii. 12; Ex. xxxv. 35)--he is not really increasing the stringency of the traditional rule about Sabbath observance.

Further, it is difficult to understand how Dr. Kuenen could gather from this passage that Jeremiah treats the Sabbath "merely as a day of rest." This negative character of mere cessation from work, of enforced idleness, is far from being the sole feature of the Sabbath, either in Jeremiah's view of it, or as other more ancient authorities represent it. The testimony of the passage before us proves, if proof were needed, that the Sabbath was a day of worship. This is implied both by the phrase "ye shall hallow the Day of Rest," that is, consecrate it to Iahvah; and by the promise that if the precept be observed faithfully, abundant offerings shall flow into the temple from all parts of the country, that is, as the context seems to require, for the due celebration of the Sabbath festival. There is an intentional contrast between the bringing of innumerable victims, and "bearing burdens" of flour and oil and incense on the Sabbath, for the joyful service of the temple, including the festal meal of the worshippers, and that other carriage of goods for merely secular objects. And as the wealth of the Jerusalem priesthood chiefly depended upon the abundance of the sacrifices, it may be supposed that Jeremiah thus gives them a hint that it is really their interest to encourage the observance of the law of the Sabbath. For if men were busy with their buying and selling, their making and mending, upon the seventh as on other days, they would have no more time or inclination for religious duties, than the Sunday traders of our large towns have under the vastly changed conditions of the present day. Moreover, the teaching of our prophet in this matter takes for granted that of his predecessors, with whose writings he was thoroughly acquainted. If in this passage he does not expressly designate the Sabbath as a religious festival, it is because it seemed needless to state a thing so obvious, so generally recognised in theory, however loosely observed in practice. The elder prophets Hosea, Amos, Isaiah, associate Sabbath and new moon together as days of festal rejoicing, when men appeared before Iahvah, that is, repaired to the sanctuary for worship and sacrifice (Hos. ii. 11; Isa. i. 11-14), and when all ordinary business was consequently suspended (Amos viii. 5).

It is clear, then, from this important passage of Jeremiah that in his time and by himself the

Sabbath was still regarded under the double aspect of a religious feast and a day of cessation from labour, the latter being, as in the ancient world generally, a natural consequence of the former characteristic. Whether the abolition of the local sanctuaries in the eighteenth year of Josiah resulted in any practical modification of the conception of the Sabbath, so that, in the words of Professor Robertson Smith, "it became for most Israelites an institution of humanity divorced from ritual," is rendered doubtful by the following considerations. The period between the reform of Josiah and the fall of Jerusalem was very brief, including not more than about thirty-five years (621-586, according to Wellhausen). But that a reaction followed the disastrous end of the royal Reformer, is both likely under the circumstances, and implied by the express assertions of the author of Kings, who declares of the succeeding monarchs that they "did evil in the sight of the Lord according to all that their fathers had done." As Wellhausen writes: "the battle of Megiddo had shown that in spite of the covenant with Jehovah the possibilities of non-success in war remained the same as before": so at least it would appear to the unspiritual mind of a populace, still hankering after the old forms of local worship, with their careless connivance at riot and disorder. It is not probable that a rapacious and bloody tyrant, like Jehoiakim, would evince more tenderness for the ritual laws than for the moral precepts of Deuteronomy. It is likely, then, that the worship at the local high places revived during this and the following reigns, just as it had revived after its temporary abolition by Hezekiah (2 Kings xviii. 22). Moreover, it is with Judah, not ruined and depopulated Israel, that we have to deal; and even in Judah the people must by this time have been greatly reduced by war and its attendant evils, so that Jerusalem itself and its immediate neighbourhood probably comprised the main part of the population to which Jeremiah addressed his discourses during this period. The bulk of the little nation would, in fact, naturally concentrate upon Jerusalem, in the troublous times that followed the death of Josiah. If so, it is superfluous to assume that "most men could only visit the central altar at rare intervals" during these last decades of the national existence. [79] The change of view belongs rather to the sixth than the seventh century, to Babylonia rather than to Judea.

The Sabbath observance prescribed by the old Law, and recommended by Jeremiah, was indeed a very different thing from the pedantic and burdensome obligation which it afterwards became in the hands of scribes and Pharisees. These, with their long catalogue of prohibited works, and their grotesque methods of evading the rigour of their own rules, had succeeded in making what was originally a joyous festival and day of rest for the weary, into an intolerable interlude of joyless restraint; when our Lord reminded them that the Sabbath was made for man, and not man for the Sabbath (St. Mark ii. 27). Treating the strict observance of the day as an end in itself, they forgot or ignored the fact that the oldest forms of the sacred Law agreed in justifying the institution by religious and humanitarian considerations (Ex. xx. 8, 10; Deut. v. 12). The difference in the grounds assigned by the different legislations-- Deuteronomy alleging neither the Divine Rest of Exodus xx., nor the sign of Exodus xxxi. 13, but the enlightened and enduring motive "that thy bondman and thine handmaid may rest as well as thou," coupled with the feeling injunction, "Remember that thou wast a bondman in the land of Egypt" (Deut. v. 14, 15)--need not here be discussed; for in any case, the different motives thus suggested were enough to make it clear to those who had eyes to see, that the Sabbath was not anciently conceived as an arbitrary institution established purely for its own sake, and without reference to ulterior considerations of public benefit. The Book of the Covenant affirmed the principle of Sabbath rest in these unmistakable terms: "Six days thou mayst do thy works, and on the seventh day thou shalt leave off, that thine ox and thine ass may rest, and the son of thine handmaid"--the home-born slave--"and the alien may be refreshed" (Ex. xxiii. 12), lit. recover breath, have respite. The humane care of the lawgiver for the dumb toilers and slaves requires no comment; and we have already noticed the same spirit of humanity in the later precept of the Book of the Law (Deut. v. 14, 15). These older rules, it will be observed, are perfectly general in their scope, and forbid not particular actions (Ex. xvi. 23, xxxv. 3; Num. xv. 32), but the continuance of ordinary labour; prescribing a merciful intermission alike for the cattle employed in husbandry and as beasts of burden, and for all classes of dependents.

The origin of the Sabbath festival is lost in obscurity. When the unknown writer of Gen. i. so beautifully connects it with the creation of the world, he betrays not only the belief of his contemporaries in its immemorial antiquity, but also a true perception of the utility of the institution, its perfect adaptation to the wants of humanity. He expresses his sense of the fact in the most emphatic way possible, by affirming the Divine origin of an institution whose value to man is divinely great; and by carrying back that origin to the very beginning, he implies that the Sabbath was made for mankind and not merely for Israel. To whom indeed could an ancient Jewish writer refer as the original source of this unique blessing of a Day of Rest and drawing near to God, if not to Iahvah, the fountain of all things good?

That Moses, the founder of the nation, gave Israel the Sabbath, is as likely as anything can be. Whether, in doing so, he simply sanctioned an ancient and salutary custom (investing it perhaps with new and better associations), dating from the tribal existence of the fathers in Chaldea, or ordered the matter so in purposeful contrast to the Egyptian week of ten days, cannot at present be determined. The

Sabbath of Israel, both that of the prophets and that of the scribes, was an institution which distinguished the nation from all others in the period open to historical scrutiny; and with this knowledge we may rest content. That which made Israel what it was, and what it became to the world; the total of the good which this people realized, and left as a priceless heritage to mankind for ever, was the outcome, not of what it had in common with heathen antiquity, but of what was peculiar to itself in ideas and institutions. We cannot be too strongly on our guard against assuming external, superficial, and often accidental resemblances, to be an index of inward and essential likeness and unity. Whatever approximations may be established by modern archæology between Israel and kindred peoples, it will still be true that those points of contact do not explain, though to the apprehension of individuals they may obscure what is truly characteristic of Israel, and what alone gives that nation its imperishable significance in the history of the world. After all deductions made upon such grounds, nothing can abolish the force of the fact that Moses and the prophets do not belong to Moab, Ammon, or Edom; that the Old Testament, though written in the language of Canaan, is not a monument of Canaanite but of Israelite faith; that the Christ did not spring out of Babylon or Egypt, and that Christianity is not explicable as the last development of Accadian magic or Egyptian animal worship.

To those who believe that the prophets enjoyed a higher and less fallible guidance than human fancy, reflexion, experience; who recognise in the general aim and effect of their teaching, as contrasted with that of other teachers, the best proof that their minds were subject to an influence and a spirit transcending the common limits of humanity; the prominence given by Jeremiah to the law of the Sabbath will be sufficient evidence of the importance of that law to the welfare of his contemporaries, if not of all subsequent generations. If we have rightly assigned the piece to the reign of Jehoiachin, we may suppose that among the contrary currents which agitated the national life at that crisis, there were indications of repentance and remorse at the misdoings of the late reign. The present utterance of the prophet might then be regarded as a test of the degree and worth of the revulsion of popular feeling towards the God of the Fathers. The nation was trembling for its existence; and Jeremiah met its fears, by pointing out the path of safety. Here was one special precept hitherto but little observed. Would they keep it now and henceforth, in token of a genuine obedience? Repentance in general terms is never difficult. The rub is conduct. Recognition of the Divine Law is easy, so long as life is not submitted to its control. The prophet thus proposes, in a single familiar instance, a plain test of sincerity, which is perhaps not less applicable in our own day than it was then.

***

The wording of the final threat suggests a thought of solemn consequence for ourselves. "I will kindle a fire in her gates, and it shall devour the castles of Jerusalem--and shall not be quenched!" The gates were the scene of Judah's sinful breach of the Sabbath law, and in them her punishment is to begin. So in the after life of the lost those parts of the physical and mental organism which have been the principal seats of sin, the means and instruments of man's misdoing, will also be the seat of keenest suffering, the source and abode of the most poignant misery. "The fire that never shall be quenched"-- Jesus has spoken of that awful mystery, as well as Jeremiah. It is the ever-kindling, never-dying fire of hopeless and insatiable desire; it is the withering flame of hatred of self, when the castaway sees with open eyes what that self has become; it is the burning pain of a sleepless memory of the unalterable past; it is the piercing sense of a life flung recklessly to ruin; it is the scorching shame, the scathing self-contempt, the quenchless, raging thirst for deliverance from ourselves; it is the fearful consciousness of self-destruction, branded upon the soul for ever and ever!

Footnotes:

79. Encycl. Britann., s.v. Sabbath, p. 125.

Rev. C. J. Ball, M.A., & W. H. Bennett, M.A.

XI. THE DIVINE POTTER

Jeremiah xviii.

Jeremiah goes down into the Lower Town, or the valley between the upper and lower city; and there his attention is arrested by a potter sitting at work before his wheel. As the prophet watches, a vessel is spoiled in the making under the craftsman's hand; so the process begins afresh, and out of the same lump of clay another vessel is moulded, according to the potter's fancy.

Reflecting upon what he had seen, Jeremiah recognised a Divine Word alike in the impulse which led him thither, and in the familiar actions of the potter. Perhaps as he sat meditating at home, or praying in the court of the temple, the thought had crossed his mind that Iahvah was the Potter, and mankind the clay in His hands; a thought which recurs so often in the eloquent pages of the second Isaiah, who was doubtless indebted to the present oracle for the suggestion of it. Musing upon this thought, Jeremiah wandered half-unconsciously down to the workshop of the potter; and there, under the influence of the Divine Spirit, his thought developed itself into a lesson for his people and for us.

Cannot I do unto you like this potter, O house of Israel? saith Iahvah; Behold, as the clay in the potter's hand, so are ye in My hand, O house of Israel. Iahvah has an absolute control over His people and over all peoples, to shape their condition and to alter their destiny; a control as absolute as that of the potter over the clay between his hands, which he moulds and remoulds at will. Men are wholly malleable in the hands of their Maker; incapable, by the nature of things, of any real resistance to His purpose. If the first intention of the potter fail in the execution, he does not fail to realize his plan on a second trial. And if man's nature and circumstances appear for a time to thwart the Maker's design; if the unyielding pride and intractable temper of a nation mar its beauty and worth in the eyes of its Creator, and render it unfit for its destined uses and functions; He can take away the form He has given, and reduce His work to shapelessness, and remodel the ruined mass into accordance with His sovereign design. Iahvah, the supreme Author of all existence, can do this. It is evident that the Creator can do as He will with His creature. But all His dealings with man are conditioned by moral considerations. He meddles with no nation capriciously, and irrespective of its attitude towards His laws. At one moment I threaten a nation and a kingdom that I will uproot and pull down and destroy. And that nation which I threatened returneth from its evil, and I repent of the evil that I purposed to do it. And at another moment, I promise a nation and a kingdom that I will build and plant. And it doeth the Evil in Mine eyes, in not hearkening unto My voice; and I repent of the good that I said I would do it (vv. 7-10).

This is a bold affirmation, impressive in its naked simplicity and directness of statement, of a truth which in all ages has taken possession of minds at all capable of a comprehensive survey of national experience; the truth that there is a power revealing itself in the changes and chances of human history, shaping its course, and giving it a certain definite direction, not without regard to the eternal principles of morality. When in some unexpected calamity which strikes down an individual sinner, men recognise a "judgment" or an instance of "the visitation of God," they infringe the rule of Christian charity, which forbids us to judge our brethren. Yet such judgment, liable as it is to be too readily suggested by private ill-will, envy and other evil passions, which warp the even justice that should guide our decisions, and blind the mind to its own lack of impartiality, is in general the perversion of a true instinct which persists in spite of all scientific sophistries and philosophic fallacies. For it is an irrepressible instinct rather than a reasoned opinion which makes us all believe, however inconsistently and vaguely, that God rules; that Providence asserts itself in the stream of circumstance, in the current of human affairs. The native strength of this instinctive belief is shewn by its survival in minds that have long since cast off allegiance to religious creeds. It only needs a sudden sense of personal danger, the sharp shock of a serious accident, the foreboding of bitter loss, the unexpected but utter overthrow of some well-laid scheme that seemed assured of success, to stir the faith that is latent in the depths of the most callous and worldly heart, and to force the acknowledgment of a righteous Judge enthroned above.

Compared with the mysterious Power which evinces itself continuously in the apparent chaos of conflicting events, man's free will is like the eddy whirling round upon the bosom of a majestic river as it floats irresistibly onward to its goal, bearing the tiny vortex along with it. Man's power of self-determination no more interferes with the counsels of Providence than the diurnal revolution of the earth on its axis interferes with its annual revolution round the sun. The greater comprises the less; and God includes the world.

The Creator has implanted in the creature a power of choice between good and evil, which is a pale reflexion of His own tremendous Being. But how can we even imagine the dependent, the limited, the finite, acting independently of the will of the Absolute and Infinite? The fish may swim against the ocean current; but can it swim at all out of the ocean? Its entire activity depends upon the medium in which it lives and moves and has its being.

But Jeremiah exposes the secret of Providence to the eyes of his fellow-countrymen for a particular purpose. His aim is to eradicate certain prevalent misconceptions, so as to enable them to rightly apprehend the meaning of God's present dealings with themselves. The popular belief was that Zion was an inviolable sanctuary; that whatever disasters might have befallen the nation in the past, or might be imminent in the future, Iahvah could not, for His own sake, permit the extinction of Judah as a nation. For then His worship, the worship of the temple, the sacrifices of the one altar, would be abolished; and His honour and His Name would be forgotten among men. These were the thoughts which comforted them in the trying time when a thousand rumours of the coming of the Chaldeans to punish their revolt were flying about the land; and from day to day men lived in trembling expectation of impending siege and slaughter. These were the beliefs which the popular prophets, themselves probably in most cases fanatical believers in their own doctrine, vehemently maintained in opposition to Jeremiah. Above all, there was the covenant between Iahvah and His people, admitted as a fact both by Jeremiah and his opponents. Was it conceivable that the God of the Fathers, who had chosen them and their posterity to be His people for ever, would turn from His purpose, and reject His chosen utterly?

Jeremiah meets these popular illusions by applying his analogy of the potter. The potter fashions a mass of clay into a vessel; and Iahvah had fashioned Israel into a nation. But as though the mass of inert matter had proven unwieldy or stubborn to the touches of his plastic hands; as the wheel revolved, a misshapen product resulted, which the artist broke up again, and moulded afresh on his wheel, till it emerged a fair copy of his ideal. And so, in the revolutions of time, Israel had failed of realizing the design of his Maker, and had become a vessel of wrath fitted to destruction. But as the rebellious lump was fashioned again by the deft hand of the master, so might this refractory people be broken and built up anew by the Divine master hand.

In the light of this analogy, the prophet interprets the existing complications of the political world. The serious dangers impending over the nation are a sure symptom that the Divine Potter is at work, "moulding" an evil fate for Judah and Jerusalem. "And now prithee say unto the men of Judah and the inhabitants of Jerusalem:

"Thus hath Iahvah said,
Behold I am moulding evil against you,
And devising a device against you!"

But Iahvah's menaces are not the mere vent of a tyrant's caprice or causeless anger: they are a deliberate effort to break the hard heart, to reduce it to contrition, to prepare it for a new creation in a more glorious likeness. Therefore the threat closes with an entreaty:

"Return ye, I pray you, each from his evil way,
And make good your ways and your doings!"

If the prophetic warning fulfil its purpose, and the nation repent, then as in the case of Nineveh, which repented at the preaching of Jonah, the sentence of destruction is revoked, and the doomed nation is granted a new lease of life. The same truth holds good reversely. God's promises are as conditional as His threats. If a nation lapse from original righteousness, the sure consequence is the withdrawal of Divine favour, and all of blessing and permanence that it confers. It is evident that the prophet directly contradicts the popular persuasion, which was also the current teaching of his professional opponents, that Iahvah's promises to Israel are absolute, that is, irrespective of moral considerations. Jeremiah is revealing, in terms suited to the intelligence of his time, the true law of the Divine dealings with Israel and with man. And what he has here written, it is important to bear in mind, when we are studying other passages of his writings and those of his predecessors, which foreshow judgments and mercies to individual peoples. However absolute the language of prediction, the qualification here supplied must usually be understood; so that it is not too much to say that this remarkable utterance is one of the keys to the comprehension of Hebrew prophecy.

But now, allowing for antique phraseology, and for the immense difference between ancient and modern modes of thought and expression; allowing also for the new light shed upon the problems of life and history by the teaching of Him who has supplemented all that was incomplete in the doctrine of the prophets and the revelation granted to the men of the elder dispensation; must we pronounce this oracle of Jeremiah's substantially true or the contrary? Is the view thus formulated an obsolete opinion, excusable in days when scientific thinking was unknown; useful indeed for the furtherance of the immediate aims of its authors, but now to be rejected wholly as a profound mistake, which modern enlightenment has at once exposed and rendered superfluous to an intelligent faith in the God of the prophets?

Here and everywhere else, Jeremiah's language is in form highly anthropomorphic. If it was to arrest the attention of the multitude, it could not well have been otherwise. He seems to say that God changes His intentions, according as a nation changes its behaviour. Something must be allowed for style, in a writer whose very prose is more than half poetry, and whose utterances are so often lyrical in form as well as matter. The Israelite thinkers, however, were also well aware that the Eternal is superior to change; as is clear from that striking word of Samuel: "The Glory of Israel lieth not nor repenteth; for He is not man, that He should repent" (1 Sam. xv. 29). And prophetic passages like that in Kings, which so nobly declares that the heaven and the heaven of heavens cannot contain God (cf. Jer. xxiii. 24), or that of the second Isaiah which affirms that the Divine ways and purposes are as much higher than those of His people, as the heavens are higher than the earth (Isa. lv. 9), prove that the vivid anthropomorphic expressions of the popular teaching of the prophets ought in mere justice to be limited by these wider conceptions of the Divine Nature and attributes. These passages are quite enough to clear the prophets of the accusation of entertaining such gross and crude ideas of Deity as those which Xenophanes ridiculed, and which find their embodiment in most mythologies.

There is indeed a sense in which all thinking, not only thought about God, but about the natural world, must be anthropomorphic. Man is unquestionably "the measure of all things," and he measures by a human standard. He interprets the world without in terms of his own consciousness; he imposes the forms and moulds of his own mind upon the universal mass of things. Time, space, matter, motion, number, weight, organ, function,--what are all these but inward conceptions by which the mind reduces a chaos of conflicting impressions to order and harmony? What the external world may be, apart from our ideas of it, no philosopher pretends to be able to say; and an equal difficulty embarrasses those who would define what the Deity is, apart from His relations to man. But then it is only those relations that really concern us; everything else is idle speculation, little becoming to creatures so frail and ephemeral as we.

From this point of view, we may fairly ask, what difference it makes whether the prophet affirm that Iahvah repents of retributive designs, when a nation repents of its sins, or that a nation's repentance will be followed by the restoration of temporal prosperity. It is a mere matter of statement; and the former way of putting the truth was the more intelligible way to his contemporaries, and has, besides, the advantage of implying the further truth that the fortunes of nations do not depend upon a blind and inexorable fate, but upon the Will and Law of a holy God. It affirms a Lawmaker as well as a Law, a Providence as well as an uniform sequence of events.

The prophet asserts, then, that nations reap what they have sown; that their history is, in general, a record of God's judgments upon their ways and doings. This is, of course, a matter of faith, as are all beliefs about the Unseen; but it is a faith which has its root in an apparently ineradicable instinct of humanity. Drasanti pathein, "The doer must suffer," is not a conviction of Hebrew religion only; it belongs to the universal religious consciousness. Some critics are fond of pronouncing the "policy" of the prophets a mistaken one. They commend the high tone of their moral teachings, but consider their forecasts of the future and interpretations of passing events, as erroneous deductions from their general views of the Divine nature. We are not well acquainted with the times and circumstances under which the prophets wrote and spoke. This is true even in the case of Jeremiah; the history of the time exists only in the barest outline. But the writings of an Isaiah or an Amos make it difficult to suppose that their authors would not have occupied a leading position in any age and nation; their thought is the highest product of the Hebrew mind; and the policy of Isaiah at least, during the Assyrian crisis, was gloriously justified by the event.

We need not, however, stop here in attempting to vindicate the attitude and aims of the prophets. Without claiming infallibility for every individual utterance of theirs--without displaying the bad taste and entire lack of literary tact which would be implied by insisting upon the minute accuracy and close correspondence to fact, of all that the prophets foreboded, all that they suggested as possible or probable, and by turning all their poetical figures and similes into bald assertions of literal fact; we may, I think, steadfastly affirm that the great principles of revealed religion, which it was their mission to enunciate and impress by all the resources of a fervid oratory and a high-wrought poetical imagination, are absolutely and eternally true. Man does reap as he sows; all history records it. The present welfare and future permanence of a nation do depend, and have always depended, upon the strength of its adhesion to religious and moral convictions. What was it that enabled Israel to gain a footing in Canaan, and to reduce, one after another, nations and communities far more advanced in the arts of civilization than they? What but the physical and moral force generated by the hardy and simple life of the desert, and disciplined by wise obedience to the laws of their Invisible King? What but a burning faith in the Lord of Hosts, Iahvah Sabaoth, the true Leader of the armies of Israel? Had they only remained uncontaminated by the luxuries and vices of the conquered races; had they not yielded to the soft seduction of sensuous forms of worship; had they continued faithful to the God who had brought them out of Egypt, and lived, on the whole, by the teaching of the true prophets; who can say that they might not have successfully withstood the brunt of Assyrian or Chaldean invasion?

The disruption of the kingdom, the internecine conflicts, the dynastic revolutions, the entanglements with foreign powers which mark the progressive decline of the empire of David and Solomon, would hardly have found place in a nation that steadily lived by the rule of the prophets, clinging to Iahvah and Iahvah only, and "doing justice and loving mercy" in all the relations of life. The gradual differentiation of the idea of Iahvah into a multitude of Baals at the local sanctuaries must have powerfully tended to disintegrate the national unity. Solomon's temple and the recognition of the one God of all the tribes of Israel as supreme, which that religious centre implied, was, on the other hand, a real bond of union for the nation. We cannot forget that, at the outset of the whole history, Moses created or resuscitated the sense of national unity in the hearts of the Egyptian serfs, by proclaiming to them Iahvah, the God of their fathers. It is a one-sided representation which treats the policy of the prophets as purely negative; as confined to the prohibition of leagues with the foreigner, and the condemnation of walls and battlements, chariots and horses, and all the elements of social strength and display. The prophets condemn these things, regarded as substitutes for trust in the One God, and faithful obedience to His laws. They condemn the man who puts his confidence in man, and makes flesh his arm, and forgets the only true source of strength and protection. To those who allege that the policy of the prophets was a failure, we may reply that it never had a full and fair trial.

> *And they will say, Hopeless! for we will follow after our own*
> *devices, and will each practise the stubbornness of his own evil*
> *heart. Therefore thus hath Iahvah said:*
> *1.?"Ask ye now among the heathen,*
> *Who hath heard the like?*
> *The virgin (daughter) of Israel*
> *Hath done a very horrible thing.*
> *2.?"Doth the snow of Lebanon cease*
> *From overflowing the field?*
> *Do the running waters dry up,*
> *The icy streams?* [80]
> *3.?"For My people have forgotten me,*
> *To vain things they burn incense;*
> *And they have made them stumble in their ways, the ancient paths,*
> *To walk in bypaths, a way not cast up:*
> *4.?"To make their land a desolation,*
> *Perpetual hissings;*
> *Every one that passeth her by shall be amazed,*
> *And shall shake his head.*
> *5.?"Like an east wind will I scatter them*
> *In the face of the foe;*
> *The back and not the face will I shew them,*
> *In the day of their overthrow."*

God foresees that His gracious warning will be rejected as heretofore; the prophet's hearers will cry "It is hopeless!" thy appeal is in vain, thine enterprise desperate; "for after our own devices" or thoughts "will we walk," not after thine, though thou urge them as Iahvah's; "and we will each practise the stubbornness of his own evil heart"--this last in a tone of irony, as if to say, Very well; we accept thy description of us; our ways are stubborn, and our hearts evil: we will abide by our character, and stand true to your unflattering portrait. Otherwise, the words may be regarded as giving the substance of the popular reply, in terms which at the same time convey the Divine condemnation of it; but the former view seems preferable.

God foresees the obstinacy of the people, and yet the prophet does not cease his preaching. A cynical assent to his invective only provokes him to more strenuous endeavours to convince them that they are in the wrong; that their behaviour is against reason and nature. Once more (ii. 10 sqq.) he strives to shame them into remorse by contrasting their conduct with that of other nations. These were faithful to their own gods; among them such a crime as national apostasy was unheard of and unknown. It was reserved for Israel to give the first example of this abnormal offence; a fact as strange and fearful in the moral world, as some unnatural revolution in the physical sphere. That Israel should forget his duty to Iahvah was as great and inexplicable a portent, as if the perennial snows of the Lebanon should cease to supply the rivers of the land; or as if the ice-cold streams of its glens and gorges should suddenly cease to flow. And certainly, when we look at the matter with the eye of calm reason, the prophet cannot be said to have here exaggerated the mystery of sin. For, however strong the temptation that lures man from the path of duty, however occasion may suggest, and passion urge, and desire yearn, these influences cannot of themselves silence conscience, and obliterate experience, and overpower judgment, and defeat reason. As surely as it is possible to know anything, man knows that his vital interests coincide with duty; and that it is not only weak but absolutely irrational to sacrifice duty to the importunities of appetite.

When man forsakes the true God, it is to "burn incense to vain gods" or things of nought. He who worships what is less than God, worships nothing. No being below God can yield any true satisfaction to that human nature which was made for God. The man who fixes his hope upon things that perish in the using, the man who seeks happiness in things material, the man whose affections have sole regard to the joys of sense, and whose devotion is given wholly to worldly objects, is the man who will at the last cry out, in hopeless disappointment and bitterness of spirit, Vanity of vanities! all is vanity! "For what shall it profit a man, if he shall gain the whole world, and lose his own soul? Or what shall a man give in exchange for his soul?" The soul's salvation consists in devotion to its Lord and Maker; its eternal loss and ruin, in alienation from Him who is its true and only life. The false gods are nought as regards help and profit; they are powerless to bless, but they are potent to hurt and betray. They "make men stumble out of their ways, out of the ancient paths, to walk in bypaths, in a way not cast up." So it was of old; so it is now. When the heart is estranged from God, and devoted to some meaner pursuit than the advancement of His glory, it soon deserts the straight road of virtue, the highway of honour, and falls into the crooked and uneven paths of fraud and hypocrisy, of oppression and vice. The end appears to sanctify the means, or at least to make them tolerable; and, once the ancient path of the Law is forsaken, men will follow the most tortuous, and often thorny and painful courses, to the goal of their choice. The path which leads away from God, leads both individuals and nations to final ruin. Degraded ideas of the Deity, false ideas of happiness, a criminal indifference to the welfare of others, a base devotion to private and wholly selfish ends, must in the long run sap the vigour of a nation, and render it incapable of any effectual resistance to its enemies. Moral declension is a sure symptom of approaching political dissolution; so sure, that if a nation chooses and persists in evil, in the face of all dissuasion, it may be assumed to be bent on suicide. Like Israel, it may be said to do thus, "in order to make its land an astonishment, perpetual hissings." Men will be surprised at the greatness of its fall, and at the same time will acknowledge by voice and gesture that its doom is absolutely just.

So far as his immediate hearers were concerned, the effect of the prophet's words was exactly what had been anticipated (ver. 18; cf. ver. 12). Jeremiah's preaching was a ministry of hardening, in a far more complete sense than Isaiah's had been. On the present occasion, the popular obduracy and unbelief evinced itself in a conspiracy to destroy the prophet by false accusation. They would doubtless find it not difficult to construe his words as blasphemy against Iahvah, and treason against the state. And they said: Come and let us devise devices--lay a plot--against Jeremiah. Dispassionate wisdom, mere worldly prudence, would have said, Let us weigh well the probability or even possibility of the truth of his message. Moral earnestness, a sincere love of God and goodness, would have recognised in the prophet's fearful earnest a proof of good faith, a claim to consideration. Unbiassed common sense would have asked, What has Jeremiah to gain by persistence in unpopular teaching? What will be his reward, supposing his words come true? Is it to be supposed that a man whose woeful tidings are uttered in a voice broken with sobs, and interrupted by bursts of wild lamentation, will look with glad eyes upon destruction when it comes, if it come after all? But habitual sin blinds as well as pollutes the soul. And when admonition is unacceptable, it breeds hatred. The heart that is not touched by appeal becomes harder than it was before. The ice of indifference becomes the adamant of malignant opposition. The populace of Jerusalem, like that of more modern capitals, was enervated by ease and luxury, altogether given over to the pursuit of wealth and pleasure as the end of life. They hated the man who rebuked in the gate, and abhorred him that spoke uprightly (Amos v. 10). They could not abide one whose life and labours were a continual protest against their own. And now he had done his best to rob them of their pleasant confidence, to destroy the delusion of their fool's paradise. He had burst into the heathenish sanctuary where they offered a worship congenial to their hearts, and done his best to wreck their idols, and dash their altars to the ground. He had affirmed that the accredited oracles were all a lie, that the guides whom they blindly followed were leading them to ruin. So the passive dislike of good blazes out into murderous fury against the good man who dares to be good alone in the face of a sinful multitude. That they are made thoroughly uneasy by his message of judgment, that they are more than half convinced that he is right, is plain from the frantic passion with which they repeat and deny his words. Law shall not perish from the priest, nor counsel from the wise, nor the word from the prophet: these things cannot, shall not be. When people have pinned their faith to a false system--a system which accords with their worldly prejudices, and flatters their ungodly pride, and winks at or even sanctions their vices; when they have anchored their entire confidence upon certain men and certain teachings which are in perfect harmony with their own aims in life and their own selfish predilections, they are not only disturbed and distressed but often enraged by a demonstration that they are lulled in a false security. And anger of this kind is apt to be so irrational, that they may think to escape from the threatened evil by silencing its prophet. Come and let us smite him with the tongue, and let us not hearken to any of his words! They will first get rid of him, and then forget his words of warning. Their policy is no better than that of the bird which buries its head in the sand, when its pursuers have run it down; an infatuated Out of sight, out of mind. And Jeremiah's recompense for his disinterested zeal is another conspiracy against his life.

Once more he lays his cause before the one impartial Judge; the one Being who is exalted above all passion, and therefore sees the truth as it is.

> *"Hearken Thou, O Iahvah, unto me,*
> *And hear Thou the voice of mine adversaries.*
> *Should evil be recompensed for good?*
> *For they have digged a pit for my life.*
> *Remember my standing before Thee to speak good about them,*
> *To turn back Thy wrath from them."*

Hearken Thou, since they refuse to hearken; hear both sides, and pronounce for the right. Behold the glaring contrast between my innocence of all hurtful intent, and their clamorous injustice, between my truth and their falsehood, my prayers for their salvation and their outcry for my blood.

As we read this prayer of Jeremiah's, we are reminded of the very similar language of the thirty-fifth and hundred and ninth psalms, of which he was himself perhaps the author (see especially Ps. xxxv. 1, 4, 5, 7, 11, 12; cix. 2, 5). We have already partially considered the moral aspect of such petitions. It is necessary to bear in mind that the prophet is speaking of persons who have persistently rejected warning, and ridiculed reproof; and now, in return for his intercessions on their behalf, are attempting his life, not in a sudden outbreak of uncontrollable fury, but with craft and deliberate malice, after seeking, apparently, like their spiritual successors in a later age, to entrap him into admissions that might be construed as treason or blasphemy (Ps. xxxv. 19-21).

> *"Therefore give their sons to the famine,*
> *And pour them into the hands of the sword;*
> *And let their wives be bereaved and widows,*
> *And let their husbands be slain of Death;*
> *Let their young men be stricken down of the sword in the battle!*
> *"Let a cry be heard from their houses,*
> *When Thou bringest a troop upon them suddenly!*
> *For they digged a pit to catch me,*
> *And snares they hid for my feet.*
> *"But of Thyself, Iahvah, Thou knowest all their plan against me for death;*
> *Pardon Thou not their iniquity,*
> *And blot not out their trespass from before Thee;*
> *But let them be made to stumble before Thee,*
> *In the time of Thine anger deal Thou with them!"*

The passage is lyrical in form and expression, and something must be allowed for the fact in estimating its precise significance. Jeremiah had entreated God and man that all these things might not come to pass. Now, when the attitude of the people towards his message and himself at last leaves no doubt that their obduracy is invincible, in his despair and distraction he cries, Be it so, then! They are bent on destruction; let them have their will! Let the doom overtake them, that I have laboured in vain to avert! With a weary sigh, and a profound sense of the ripeness of his country for ruin, he gives up the struggle to save it. The passage thus becomes a rhetorical or poetical expression of the prophet's despairing recognition of the inevitable.

How vivid are the touches with which he brings out upon his canvas the horrors of war! In language lurid with all the colours of destruction, he sets before us the city taken by storm, he makes us hear the cry of the victims, as house after house is visited by pillage and slaughter. But stripped of its poetical form, all this is no more than a concentrated repetition of the sentence which he has over and over again pronounced against Jerusalem in the name of Iahvah. The imprecatory manner of it may be considered to be simply a solemn signification of the speaker's own assent and approval. He recalls the sentence, and he affirms its perfect consonance with his own sense of justice. Moreover all these terrible things actually happened in the sequel. The prophet's imprecations received the Divine seal of accomplishment. This fact alone seems to me to distinguish his prayer from a merely human cry for vengeance. So far as his feelings as a man and a patriot were concerned, we cannot doubt that he would have averted the catastrophe, had that been possible, by the sacrifice of his own life. That indeed was the object of his entire ministry. We may call the passage an emotional prediction; and it was probably the predictive character of it which led the prophet to put it on record.

While we admit that no Christian may ordinarily pray for the annihilation of any but spiritual enemies, we must remember that no Christian can possibly occupy the same peculiar position as a prophet of the Old Covenant; and we may fairly ask whether any who may incline to judge harshly of Jeremiah on the ground of passages like this, have fully realized the appalling circumstances which wrung these prayers from his cruelly tortured heart? We find it hard to forgive small personal slights, often less real than imaginary; how should we comport ourselves to persons whose shameless ingratitude rewarded evil for good to the extent of seeking our lives? Few would be content, as Jeremiah was, with putting the cause in the hand of God, and abstaining from all attempts at personal vindication of wrongs. It surely betrays a failure of imaginative power to realize the terrible difficulties which beset the path of one who, in a far truer sense than Elijah, was left alone to uphold the cause of true religion in Israel, and not less, a very inadequate knowledge of our own spiritual weakness, when we are bold to censure or even to apologise for the utterances of Jeremiah.

The whole question assumes a different aspect, when it is noticed that the brief "Thus said Iahvah!" of the next chapter (xix.) virtually introduces the Divine reply to the prophet's prayer. He is now bidden to foreshow the utter destruction of the Jewish polity by a symbolic act which is even more unambiguous than the language of the prayer. He is to take a common earthenware bottle (baqbûq, as if "pour-pour"; from baqaq, "to pour out"), and, accompanied by some of the leading personages of the capital, heads of families and priests, to go out of the city to the valley of ben Hinnom, and there, after a solemn rehearsal of the crimes perpetrated on that very spot in the name of religion, and after predicting the consequent retribution which will shortly overtake the nation, he is to dash the vessel in pieces before his companions' eyes, in token of the utter and irreparable ruin which awaits their city and people.

Having enacted his part in this striking scene, Jeremiah returns to the court of the temple, and there repeats the same terrible message in briefer terms before all the people; adding expressly that it is the reward of their stubborn obstinacy and deafness to the Divine voice.

The prophet's imprecations of evil thus appear to have been ratified at the time of their conception by the Divine voice, which spoke in the stillness of his after reflexion.

Footnotes:

80. Instead of mtsvr sdy "from the rock of the field," I have ventured to read mtsvph sdy (Lam. iii. 54; Deut. xi. 4; 2 Kings vi. 6). For yntsv "plucked up" "uprooted," which is inappropriate in connexion with water, Schnurrer's yntsv "dried up" (Isa. xix. 5; Jer. li. 30), is probably right. In the second couplet, I read zvym for zrym, which is meaningless, and transpose qrym with nvzlym.

XII. THE BROKEN VESSEL – A SYMBOL OF JUDGMENT

Jeremiah xix.

The result of his former address, founded upon the procedure of the potter, had only been to bring out into clearer distinctness the appalling extent of the national corruption. It was evident that Judah was incorrigible, and the Potter's vessel must be broken in pieces by its Maker.

Thus said Iahvah: Go and buy a bottle (baqbûq, as if "a pour-pour"; the meaning is alluded to in the first word of ver. 7: ubaqqothi, "and I will pour out") of a moulder of pottery (so the accents; but perhaps the Vulgate is right: "lagunculam figuli testeam," "a potter's earthen vessel," A.V.; lit. a potter's bottle, viz., earthenware), and (take: LXX. rightly adds) some of the elders of the people and of the elders of the priests, and go out into the valley of ben Hinnom at the entry of the Pottery Gate (a postern, where broken earthenware and rubbish were shot forth into the valley: the term is connected with that for "pottery," ver. 1, which is the same as that in Job ii. 8), and cry there the words that I shall speak unto thee,--Jeremiah does not pause here, to relate how he followed the Divine impulse, but goes on at once to communicate the tenor of the Divine "words"; a circumstance which points to the fact that this narrative was only written some time after the symbolical action which it records;--and say thou, Hear ye Iahvah's word, O kings of Judah and inhabitants of Jerusalem! Thus said Iahvah Sabaoth, the God of Israel: Lo, I am about to bring an evil upon this place, such that, whoever heareth it, his ears shall tingle! If we suppose, as seems likely, that this series of oracles (xviii.-xx.) belongs to the reign of Jehoiachin, the expression "kings of Judah" may denote that king and the queen-mother. Another view is that the kings of Judah in general are addressed "as an indefinite class of persons," here and elsewhere (xvii. 20, xxii. 4), because the prophet did not write the main portion of his book until after the siege of Jerusalem (Ewald). The announcement of this verse is quoted by the compiler of Kings in relation to the crimes of king Manasseh (2 Kings xxi. 12).

Because that they forsook Me, and made this place strange--alienated it from Iahvah by consecrating it to "strange gods"; or as the Targum and Syriac, "polluted" it--and burnt incense therein to other gods, whom neither they nor their fathers knew (xvi. 13); and the kings of Judah did fill this place with blood of innocents (so the LXX. "Nor the kings of Judah" gives a poor sense; they are included in the preceding phrase), and built the bamoth Baal (High-places of Baal; a proper name, Josh. xiii. 17), to burn their sons in the fire, [as burnt-offerings to the Baal: LXX. omits, and it is wanting, vii. 31, xxxii. 35. It may be a gloss, but is probably genuine, as there are slight variations in each passage], which I commanded not, [nor spake: LXX. omits], neither came it into My mind: therefore, behold days are coming, saith Iahvah, when this place will no more be called the Tophet and valley of ben Hinnom but the Valley of Slaughter! [and in Tophet shall they bury, so that there be--remain--no room to bury! This clause, preserved at the end of ver. 11, but omitted there by the LXX., probably belongs here: see vii. 42]. And I will pour out (ver. 1; Isa. xix. 3) the counsel of Judah and Jerusalem in this place--that is, I will empty the land of all wisdom and resourcefulness, as one empties a bottle of its water, so that the heads of the state shall be powerless to devise any effectual scheme of defence in the face of calamity (cf. xiii. 13)--and I will cause them to fall by the sword "before their enemies" (Deut. xxviii. 25), and by the hand of them that seek their life; and I will make "their carcases food unto the birds of the air and the beasts of the earth" (Deut. xxviii. 26; chap. vii. 33, xvi. 4). And I will set this city "for an astonishment" (Deut. xxviii. 37) and a hissing (xviii. 16); every one that passeth by her shall be astonished and hiss at all her "strokes" (xlix. 17, l. 13) or "plagues" (Deut. xxviii. 59). And I will cause them to "eat the flesh of their sons and the flesh of their daughters," and each the flesh of his fellow shall they eat--"in the stress and the straitness wherewith their enemies" and they that seek their life "shall straiten them." It will be seen from the references that the Deuteronomic colouring of these closing threats (vv. 7-9) is very strong, the last verse being practically a quotation (Deut. xxviii. 53). The effect of the whole oracle would thus be to suggest that the terrible sanctions of the sacred Law would not remain inoperative; but that the shameless violation of the solemn covenant under Josiah, by which the nation undertook to observe the code of Deuteronomy, would soon be visited with the retributive calamities so vividly foreshadowed in that book.

And break thou the bottle, to the eyes of the men that go with thee, and say unto them: Thus said

Iahvah Sabaoth; So will I break this people and this city, as one breaketh the potter's vessel so that it cannot be mended again! Thus will I do to this place, saith Iahvah, and to the inhabitants thereof and make (infin. constr. as in xvii. 10, continuing the mood and person of the preceding verb; which is properly a function of the infin. absol., as in ver. 13) this city like a Tophet--make it one huge altar of human sacrifice, a burning-place for thousands of human victims. And the houses of Jerusalem, and the houses of the kings of Judah--the palace of David and Solomon, in which king after king had reigned, and "done the evil in Iahvah's eyes,"--shall become like the place of the Tophet, the defiled ones! even all the houses upon the roofs of which they burnt incense unto all the host of heaven, and poured outpourings (libations of wine and honey) unto other gods. (So the Heb. punctuation, which seems to give a very good sense. The principal houses, those of the kings and grandees, are called "the defiled," because their roofs especially have been polluted with idolatrous rites. The last clause of the verse explains the epithet, which might have been referred to "the kings of Judah," had it preceded "like the place of the Tophet." The houses were not to become "defiled"; they were already so, past all cleansing; they were to be destroyed with fire, and in their destruction to become the Tophet or sacrificial pyre of their inhabitants. We need not, therefore, read Tophteh, after Isa. xxx. 33, as I at first thought of doing, to find afterwards that Ewald had already suggested it. The term rendered "even all," is lit. "unto all," that is, "including all"; cf. Ezek. xliv. 9). [81]

The command and break thou the bottle ... and say unto them ... compared with that of ver. 2, and cry there the words that I shall speak unto thee! seems to indicate the proper point of view from which the whole piece is to be regarded. Jeremiah is recalling and describing a particular episode in his past ministry; and he includes the whole of it, with the attendant circumstances and all that he said; first to the elders in the vale of ben Hinnom, and then to the people assembled in the temple, under the comprehensive Thus said Iahvah! with which he begins his narrative. In other words, he affirms that he was throughout the entire occurrence guided by the impulses of the Spirit of God. It is very possible that the longer first address (vv. 2-9) really gives the substance of what he said to the people in the temple on his return from the valley, which is merely summarized in verse 15.

And Jeremiah came in--into the temple--from the Tophet, whither Iahvah had sent him to prophesy, and took his stand in the court of Iahvah's House, and said unto all the people: Thus said Iahvah Sabaoth Israels God; Lo, I am about to bring upon (ver. 3) this city and upon all her cities [and upon her villages: LXX. adds] all the evil that I have spoken concerning her; because they stiffened their neck (vii. 26), not to hear My words! In this apparent epitome of His discourse to the people in the temple, the prophet seems to sum up all his past labours, in view of an impending crisis. "All the evil" spoken hitherto concerning Jerusalem is upon the point of being accomplished (cf. xxv. 3).

In reviewing the entire oracle, we may note as in former instances, the care with which all the circumstances of the symbolical action are chosen, in order to enhance the effect of it upon the minds of the witnesses. The Oriental mind delights in everything that partakes of the nature of an enigma; it loves to be called upon to unravel the meaning of dark sentences, and to disentangle the wisdom wrapped up in riddling words and significant actions. It would have found eloquence in Tarquin's unspoken answer to his son's messenger. "Rex velut deliberabundus in hortum ædium transit, sequente nuncio filii: ibi inambulans tacitus summa papaverum capita dicitur baculo decussisse" (Liv. i. 54). No doubt Jeremiah's companions would watch his every step, and would not miss the fact that he carried his earthenware vessel out of the city by the "Sherd Gate." Here was a vessel yet whole, treated as though it were already a shattered heap of fragments! They would be prepared for the oracle in the valley.

It is worth while, by the way, to notice who those companions were. They were certain of "the elders of the people" and of the "the elders of the priests." Jeremiah, it seems, was no wild revolutionary dreamer and schemer, whose hand and voice were against all established authority in Church and State. This was not the character of the Hebrew prophets in general, though some writers have conceived thus of them. There is no evidence that Jeremiah ever sought to divest himself of the duties and privileges of his hereditary priesthood; or that he looked upon the monarchy and the priestly guilds and the entire social organisation of Israel, as other than institutions divinely originated and divinely preserved through all the ages of the national history. He did not believe that man created these institutions though experience taught him that man might abuse and pervert them from their lawful uses. His aim was always to reform, to restore, to lead the people back to "the old paths" of primitive simplicity and rectitude; not to abolish hereditary institutions, and substitute for the order which had become an integral part of the national life, some brand-new constitution which had never been tried, and would be no more likely to fit the body corporate than the armour of Saul fitted the free limbs of the young shepherd who was to slay Goliath.

The prophets never called for the abolition of those laws and customs, civil and ecclesiastical, which were the very framework of the state, and the pillars of the social edifice. They did not cry, "Down with kings and priests!" but to both kings and priests they cried, "Hear ye Iahvah's word!" And all experience proves that they were right. Paper constitutions have never yet redeemed a nation from its vices, nor delivered a community from the impotence and the decay which are the inevitable fruits of moral corruption. Arbitrary legislative changes will not alter the inward condition of a people; covetousness and hypocrisy, pride and selfishness, intemperance and uncleanness and cruelty, may be as rampant in a commonwealth as in a kingdom.

The contents of the oracle are much what we have had many times already. The chief difference lies in a calm definiteness of assurance, a tone of distinct certitude, as though the end were so near at hand, as to leave no room for doubt or hesitation. And this difference is fittingly and impressively suggested by the particular symbol chosen--the shattering of an earthenware vessel, beyond the possibility of repair. The direct mention of the king of Babylon and the Babylonian captivity, in the sequel (chap. xx.), points to the presence of a Babylonian invasion, probably that which ended with the exile of Jeconiah and the chief citizens of Jerusalem.

The fatal sin, from which the oracle starts and to which it returns, is forsaking Iahvah, and making the city of His choice "strange" to Him, that is, hateful and unclean, by contact with foreign and bloody superstitions, which were even falsely declared by their promoters to be pleasing to Iahvah, the Avenger of innocent blood! (chap. vii. 31). The punishment corresponds to the offence. The sacrifices of blood will be requited with blood, shed in torrents on the very spot which had been so foully polluted; they who had not scrupled to slay their children for the sacrifice, were to slay them again for food under the stress of siege and famine; the city and its houses, defiled with the foreign worships, will become one vast Molech-fire (xxxii. 35), in which all will perish together.

It may strike a modern reader that there is something repulsive and cold-blooded in this detailed enumeration of appalling horrors. But not only is it the case that Jeremiah is quoting from the Book of the Law, at a time when, to an unprejudiced eye, there was every likelihood that the course of events would verify his dark forebodings; in the dreadful experience of those times such incidents as those mentioned (ver. 9) were familiar occurrences in the obstinate defence and protracted sufferings of beleaguered cities. The prophet, therefore, simply affirms that obstinate persistence in following their own counsels and rejecting the higher guidance will bring upon the nation its irretrievable ruin. We know that in the last siege he did his utmost to prevent the occurrence of these unnatural horrors by urging surrender; but then, as always, the people "stiffened their neck, not to hear Iahvah's words."

Jeremiah knew his countrymen well. No phrase could have better described the resolute obstinacy of the national character. How were the headstrong self-will, the inveterate sensuality, the blind tenacity of fanatical and non-moral conceptions which characterized this people, to be purified and made serviceable in the interests of true religion, except by means of the fiery ordeal which all the prophets foresaw and foretold? As we have seen, polytheism exercised upon the popular mind a spell which we can hardly comprehend from our modern point of view; a polytheism foul and murderous, which violated the tenderest affections of our nature by demanding of the father the sacrifice of his child, and violated the very instinct of natural purity by the shameless indulgence of its worship. It was a consecration of lust and cruelty,--that worship of Molech, those rites of the Baals and Asheras. Meagre and monotonous as the sacred records may on these heads appear to be, their witness is supplemented by other sources, by the monuments of Babylon and Phenicia.

It is hard to see how the religious instinct of men in this peculiar stage of belief and practice was to be enlightened and purified in any other way than the actual course of Providence. What arguments can be imagined that would have appealed to minds which found a fatal fascination, nay, we must suppose an intense satisfaction, in rites so hideous that one durst not even describe them; minds to which the lofty monotheism of Amos, the splendid eloquence of an Isaiah, the plaintive lyrical strain of a Jeremiah, appealed in vain? Appeals to the order of the world, to the wonders of organic life, were lost upon minds which made gods of the most obvious subjects of that order, the sun, moon, and stars; which even personified and adored the physical principle whereby the succession of life after life is perpetuated.

Nothing short of the perception that the word of the prophets had come to pass, the recognition, therefore, that the prophetic idea of God was the true idea, could have succeeded in keeping the remnant of Judah safe from the contagion of surrounding heathenism in the land of their exile, and in radically transforming once for all the religious tendencies of the Jewish race.

In Jeremiah's view, the heinousness of Judah's idolatry is heightened by the consideration that the gods of their choice are gods "whom neither they nor their fathers knew" (ver. 4). The kings Ahaz, Manasseh, Amon, had introduced novel rites, and departed from "the old paths" more decidedly than any of their predecessors. In this connexion, we may remember that, while modern Romish controversialists do not scruple to accuse the Church of this country of having unlawfully innovated at the Reformation, the Anglican appeal has always been to Scripture and primitive antiquity. Such, too, was the appeal of the prophets (Hos. vi. 1, 7, xi. 1; Jer. ii. 2, vi. 16, xi. 3). It is the glory of our Church, a glory of which neither the lies of Jesuits nor the envy of the sectaries can rob her, that she returned to "the old paths," boldly overleaping the dark ages of medieval ignorance, imposture, and corruption, and planting her foot firmly upon the rock of apostolic practice and the consent of the undivided Church.

Disunion among Christians is a sore evil, but union in the maintenance and propaganda of falsehood is a worse; and the guilt of disunion lies at the door of that system which abused its authority to crush out legitimate freedom of thought, to retard the advancement of learning, and to establish those monstrous innovations in doctrine and worship, which subtle dialecticians may prove to their own satisfaction to be innocent and non-idolatrous in essence and intention, though all the world can see that in practice they are grossly idolatrous. God preserve England from that toleration of serious error, which is so easy to sceptical indifference! God preserve her from lending an ear to the siren voices that would seduce her to yield her hard-won independence, her noble freedom, her manly rational piety, to the unhistorical and unscriptural claims of the Papacy!

If we reverence those Scriptures of the Old Testament to which our Lord and His Apostles made their constant appeal, we shall keep steadily before our minds the fact that, in the estimation of a prophet like Jeremiah, the sin of sins, the sin that involved the ruin of Israel and Judah, was the sin of associating other objects of worship with the One Only God. The temptation is peculiarly strong to some natures. The continual relapse of ancient Israel is not so great a wonder to those of us who have any knowledge of mankind, and who can observe what is passing around them at the present day. It is the severe demand of God's holy law, which makes men cast about for some plausible compromise--it is that demand which also makes them yearn after some intermediary power, whose compassion will be less subject to considerations of justice, whom prayers and entreaties and presents may overcome, and induce to wink at unrepented sin. In an age of unsettlement, the more daring spirits will be prone to silence their inconvenient scruples by rushing into atheism, while the more timid may take refuge in Popery. "For to disown a Moral Governour, or to admit that any observances of superstition can release men from the duty of obeying Him, equally serves the purpose of those, who resolve to be as wicked as they dare, or as little virtuous as they can" (Bp. Hurd).

Then, too, there is the glory of the saints and angels of God. How can frail man refuse to bow before the vision of their power and splendour, as they stand, the royal children of the King of kings, around the heavenly throne, deathless, radiant with love and joy and purity, exalted far above all human weakness and human sorrows? If the holy angels are "ministering spirits," why not the entire community of the Blessed? And what is to hinder us from casting ourselves at the feet of saint or angel, one's own appointed guardian, or chosen helper? Let good George Herbert answer for us all.

> "Oh glorious spirits, who after all your bands
> See the smooth face of God, without a frown,
> Or strict commands;
> Where every one is king, and hath his crown,
> If not upon his head, yet in his hands:
> "Not out of envy or maliciousness
> Do I forbear to crave your special aid.
> I would address
> My vows to thee most gladly, blessed Maid,
> And Mother of my God, in my distress:

***

> "But now, (alas!) I dare not; for our King,
> Whom we do all jointly adore and praise,
> Bids no such thing:
> And where His pleasure no injunction lays,
> ('Tis your own case) ye never move a wing.
> "All worship is prerogative, and a flower
> Of His rich crown, from whom lies no appeal
> At the last hour:
> Therefore we dare not from His garland steal,
> To make a posy for inferior power."

In this sense also, as in many others, the warning of St. John applies:
LITTLE CHILDREN, KEEP YOURSELVES FROM IDOLS!

Footnotes:

81. LXX. apo ton akatharsion auton makes it possible that they read mtm'ym which would represent mtm'ym "defiled."

XIII. JEREMIAH UNDER PERSECUTION

Jeremiah xx.

The prophet has now to endure something more than a scornful rejection of his message. And Pashchur ben Immer the priest (he was chief officer in the house of Iahvah) heard Jeremiah prophesying these words. And Pashchur smote Jeremiah the prophet and put him in the stocks, which were in the upper gate of Benjamin in the house of Iahvah. Like the priest of Bethel, who abruptly put an end to the preaching of Amos in the royal sanctuary, Pashchur suddenly interferes, apparently before Jeremiah has finished his address to the people; and enraged at the tenour of his words, he causes him--"Jeremiah the prophet," as it is significantly added, to indicate the sacrilege of the act--to be beaten in the cruel Eastern manner on the soles of the feet, inflicting probably the full number of forty blows permitted by the Law (Deut.), and then leaving him, in his agony of mind and body, fast bound in "the stocks." For the remainder of that day and all night long the prophet sat there in the gate, at first exposed to the taunts and jeers of his adversaries and the rabble of their followers, and as the weary hours slowly crept on, becoming painfully cramped in his limbs by the barbarous machine which held his hands and feet near together, and bent his body double. This cruel punishment seems to have been the customary mode of dealing with such as were accounted false prophets by the authorities. It was the treatment which Hanani endured in return for his warning to king Asa (2 Chron. xvi. 10), some three centuries earlier than Jeremiah's time; and a few years later in our prophet's history, an attempt was made to enforce it again in his case (Jer. xxix. 26). Thus, like the holy apostles of our Lord, was Jeremiah "counted worthy to suffer shame" for the Name in which he spoke (Acts v. 40, 41); and like Paul and Silas at Philippi, after enduring "many stripes" his feet were "made fast in the stocks" (Acts xvi. 23, 24). The message of Jeremiah was a message of judgment, that of the apostles was a message of forgiveness; and both met with the same response from a world whose heart was estranged from God. The heart that loves its own way, is only at ease when it can forget God. Any reminder of His Presence, of His perpetual activity in mercy and judgment, is unwelcome, and makes its authors odious. From the outset, transgressors of the Divine law have sought to hide among the trees of the garden--in the engrossing pursuits and pleasures of life--from the Presence of God.

Pashchur's object was not to destroy Jeremiah, but to break his spirit, and discredit him with the multitude, and so silence him for ever. But in this expectation he was as signally disappointed as his successor was in the case of St. Peter (Acts v. 24, 29). Now as then, God's messenger scould not be turned from his conviction that we ought to obey God rather than men. And as he sat alone in his intolerable anguish, brooding over his shameful wrongs, and despairing of redress, a Divine Word came in the stillness of night to this victim of human tyranny. For it came to pass on the morrow that Pashchur brought Jeremiah forth out of the stocks; and Jeremiah said unto him, Not Pashchur [82] --as if "Glad and free"--but Magor-missabib--"Fear on every side"--hath Iahvah called thy name! Sharpened with misery, the seer's eye pierces through the shows of life, and discerns the grim contrast of truth and appearance. Before him stands this great man, clothed with all the dignity of high office, and able to destroy him with a word; but Iahvah's prophet does not quail before abused authority. He sees the sword suspended by a hair over the head of this haughty and supercilious official; and he realizes the solemn irony of circumstance, which has connected a name suggestive of gladness and freedom with a man destined to become the thrall of perpetual terrors. For thus hath Iahvah said: Lo, I am about to make thee a Fear to thyself and to all thy lovers; and they will fall by the sword of their foes, while thine eyes look on! This "glad and free" persecutor, wantoning in the abuse of power, blindly fearless of the future, is not doomed to be slain out of hand; a heavier fate is in store for him, a fate prefigured and foreshadowed by his present sins. His proud confidence is to give place to a haunting sense of danger and insecurity; he is to see his followers perish one after another, and evermore to be expecting the same end for himself: while the freedom which he has enjoyed and abused so long, is to be exchanged for a lifelong captivity in a foreign land. And all Judah will I give into the hand of the king of Babylon, and he will transport them to Babylon, and smite them with the sword. And I will give all the store of this city--the hoarded wealth of all sorts, which constitutes its strength and reserve force--and all the gain thereof--the produce of labour--and all the value thereof--things rare and precious of every kind, works of the carver's and the goldsmith's and the potter's and the weaver's art;--and all the treasures of the kings of Judah will I give into the hand of their foes, that they may spoil them and take them and bring them to

Babylon.

And for thyself, Pashchur, and all that dwell in thine house, ye shall depart among the captives; and to Babylon thou shall come, and there thou shalt die, and there be buried, thyself and all thy lovers, to whom thou hast prophesied with untruth, or rather by the Lie, i.e., by the Baal (ii. 8, xxiii. 13, cf. xii. 16).

The play on the name of Pashchur is like that on Perath (ch. xiii.), and the change to Magor-missabib is like the change of Tophet into "Valley of Slaughter" (ch. xix.). Like Amos (vii. 16), Jeremiah repeats his obnoxious prophecy, with a special application to his cruel persecutor, and with the added detail that all the wealth of Jerusalem will be carried as spoil to Babylon; a detail in which there may lie an oblique reference to the covetous worldliness and the interested opposition of such men as Pashchur. Riches and ease and popularity were the things for which he and those like him had bargained away their integrity, prophesying with conscious falsehood to the deluded people. His "lovers" are his partisans, who eagerly welcomed his presages of peace and prosperity, and doubtless actively opposed Jeremiah with ridicule and threats. The last detail is remarkable, for we do not otherwise know that Pashchur affected to prophesy. If it be not meant simply that Pashchur accepted and lent the weight of his official sanction to the false prophets, and especially those who uttered their divinations in the name of "the Baal," that is to say, either Molech, or the popular and delusive conception of the God of Israel, we see in this man one who combined a steady professional opposition to Jeremiah with power to enforce his hostility by legalized acts of violence. The conduct of Hananiah on a later occasion (xxviii. 10), clearly proves that, where the power was present, the will for such acts was not wanting in Jeremiah's professional adversaries.

It is generally taken for granted that the name of "Pashchur" has been substituted for that of "Malchijah" in the list of the priestly families which returned with Zerubbabel from the Babylonian captivity (Ezra ii. 38; Neh. vii. 41; cf. 1 Chron. xxiv. 9); but it seems quite possible that "the sons of Pashchur" were a subdivision of the family of Immer, which had increased largely during the Exile. In that case, the list affords evidence of the fulfilment of Jeremiah's prediction to Pashchur. The prophet elsewhere mentions another Pashchur, who was also a priest, of the course or guild of Malchijah (xxi. 1, xxxviii. 1), which was the designation of the fifth class of the priests, as "Immer" was that of the sixteenth (1 Chron. xxiv. 9, 14). The prince Gedaliah, who was hostile to Jeremiah, was apparently a son of the present Pashchur (Jer. xxxviii. 1).

It is not easy to determine the relation of the lyrical section which immediately follows the doom of Pashchur, to the preceding account (vv. 7-8). If the seventh verse be in its original place, it would seem that the prophet's word had failed of accomplishment, with the result of intensifying the unbelief and the ridicule which his teachings encountered. There is also something very strange in the sequence of the thirteenth and fourteenth verses, where, as the text now stands, the prophet passes at once, in the most abrupt fashion imaginable, from a fervid ascription of praise, a heartfelt cry of thanksgiving for deliverance either actual or contemplated as such, to utterances of unrelieved despair. I do not think that this is in the manner of Jeremiah; nor do I see how the violent contrast of the two sections (7-13 and 14-18) can fairly be accounted for, except by supposing either that we have here two unconnected fragments, placed in juxtaposition with each other because they belong to the same general period of the prophet's ministry; or that the two passages have by some accident of transcription been transposed, which is by no means an uncommon occurrence in the MSS. of the Biblical writers. Assuming this latter as the more probable alternative, we see in the entire passage a powerful representation of the mental conflict into which Jeremiah was thrown by Pashchur's high-handed violence and the seeming triumph of his enemies. Smarting with the sense of utter injustice, humiliated in his inmost soul by shameful indignities, crushed to the earth with the bitter consciousness of defeat and failure, the prophet like Job opens his mouth and curses his day.

> 1.?"Cursed be the day wherein I was born!
> The day that my mother bare me,
> Let it not be blest!
> 2.?Cursed be the man who told the glad tidings to my father,
> 'There is born to thee a male child;'
> Who made him rejoice greatly.
> 3.?And let that man become like the cities that Iahweh overthrew, without relenting,
> And let him hear a cry in the morning,
> And an alarm at the hour of noon!
> 4.?For that he slew me not in the womb,
> That my mother might have become my grave,
> And her womb have been laden evermore!
> 5.?O why from the womb came I forth
> To see labour and sorrow,

The Expositor's Bible: Jeremiah Volumes I & II
And my days fordone with shame?"

These five triplets afford a glimpse of the lively grief, the passionate despair, which agitated the prophet's heart as the first effect of the shame and the torture to which he had been so wickedly and wantonly subjected. The elegy, of which they constitute the proem, or opening strophe, is not introduced by any formula ascribing it to Divine inspiration; it is simply written down as a faithful record of Jeremiah's own feelings and reflexions and self-communings, at this painful crisis in his career. The poet of the book of Job has apparently taken the hint supplied by these opening verses, and has elaborated the idea of cursing the day of birth through seven highly wrought and imaginative stanzas. The higher finish and somewhat artificial expansion of that passage leave little doubt that it was modelled upon the one before us. But the point to remember here is that both are lyrical effusions, expressed in language conditioned by Oriental rather than European standards of taste and usage. As the prophets were not inspired to express their thoughts and feelings in a modern English dress, it is superfluous to inquire whether Jeremiah was morally justified in using these poetic formulas of imprecation. To insist on applying the doctrine of verbal inspiration to such a passage is to evince an utter want of literary tact and insight, as well as adhesion to an exploded and pernicious relic of sectarian theology. The prophet's curses are simply a highly effective form of poetical rhetoric, and are in perfect harmony with the immemorial modes of Oriental expression; and the underlying thought, so equivocally expressed, according to our ways of looking at things, is simply that his life has been a failure, and therefore it would have been better not to have been born. Who that is at all earnest for God's truth, nay, for far lower objects of human interest and pursuit, has not in moments of despondency and discouragement been overwhelmed for a time by the like feeling? Can we blame Jeremiah for allowing us to see in this faithful transcript of his inner life how intensely human, how entirely natural the spiritual experience of the prophets really was? Besides, the revelation does not end with this initial outburst of instinctive astonishment, indignation and despair. The proem is succeeded by a psalm in seven stanzas of regular poetical form--six quatrains rounded off with a final couplet--in which the prophet's thought rises above the level of nature, and finds in an overruling Providence both the source and the justification of the enigma of his life.

1.?"Thou enticedst me, Iahvah, and I was enticed,
Thou urgedst [83] me, and didst prevail!
I am become a derision all the day long.
Every one mocketh at me.
2.?"For as oft as I speak, I cry alarm,
Violence and havoc do I proclaim;
For Iahvah's word is become to me a reproach,
And a scoff all the day long.
3.?"And if I say, I will not mind it,
Nor speak any more in His Name;
Then it becometh in my heart like a burning fire prisoned in my bones.
And I weary of holding it in [84] and am not able.
4.?"For I have heard the defaming of many, the terror on every side; [85]
All the men of my friendship are watching for my fall;
'Perchance he will be enticed, and we shall prevail over him,
And take our revenge of him.'
5.?"Yet Iahvah is with me as a dread warrior,
Therefore my pursuers shall stumble and not prevail;
They shall be greatly ashamed, for that they have not prospered,
With eternal dishonour that shall not be forgotten.
6.?"And Iahvah Sabaoth trieth the righteous,
Seeth the reins and the heart;
I shall see Thy revenge of them,
For unto Thee have I committed my quarrel.
7.?Sing ye to Iahvah, acclaim ye Iahvah!

For He hath snatched the poor man's life out of the hand of evildoers."
The cause was of God. Thou didst lure me, Iahvah, and I let myself be lured; Thou urgedst me and wert victorious. He had not rashly and presumptuously taken upon himself this office of prophet; he had been called, and had resisted the call, until his scruples and his pleadings were overcome, as was only natural, by a Will more powerful than his own (chap. i. 6). In speaking of the inward persuasions which determined the course of his life, he uses the very terms which are used by the author of Kings in connexion with the spirit that misled the prophets of Arab before the fatal expedition to Ramoth Gilead.

And he said, Thou shalt entice, and also be victorious (1 Kings xxii. 22). Iahvah, therefore, has treated him as an enemy rather than a friend, for He has lured him to his own destruction. Half in irony, half in bitter complaint, the prophet declares that Iahvah has succeeded only too well in His malign purpose: I am become a derision all the day long; Every one mocketh at me.

In the second stanza, the thought appears to be continued thus: Thou overcamest me; for as often as I speak, I am a prophet of evil, I cry alarm ('ez'aq; cf. zE'aqah, vers. 16); I proclaim the imminence of invasion, the violence and havoc of a ruthless conqueror. Thou overcamest me also, in Thy purpose of making me a laughing-stock to my adversaries; for Iahvah's word is become to me a reproach, and a scoff all the day long (the relation between the two halves of the stanza is that of coordination; each gives the reason of the corresponding couplet in the first stanza). His continual threats of a judgment that was still delayed, brought upon him the merciless ridicule of his opponents.

Or the prophet may mean to complain that the monotony of his message, his ever-recurring denunciation of prevalent injustice, is made a reproach against him. For as often as I speak I make an outcry of indignation at foul wrongdoing (Gen. iv. 10, xviii. 21, xix. 13); wrong and robbery do I proclaim (Hab. i. 2, 3)--the oppression of the poor by the covetous and luxurious ruling classes. A third view is that Jeremiah complains of the frequent attacks upon himself: For as often as I speak I have to exclaim; Of assault and violence do I cry; but the first suggestion appears to suit best, as giving a reason for the ridicule which the prophet finds so intolerable (cf. xvii. 15).

The third stanza carries this plea for justice a step further. Not only was the prophet's overwhelming trouble due to his having yielded to the persuasions and promises of Iahvah; not only has he been rewarded with scorn and the scourge and the stocks for his compliance with a Divine call. He has been in a manner forced and driven into his intolerable position by the coercive power of Iahvah, which left him no choice but to utter the word that burnt like a fire within him. Sometimes his fears of perfidy and betrayal suggested the thought of succumbing to the insuperable obstacles which seemed to block his path; of giving up once for all a thankless and fruitless and dangerous enterprise: but then the inward flame burnt so fiercely, that he could find no relief for his anguish but by giving it vent in words (cf. Ps. xxxix. 1-3).

The verse finely illustrates that vivid sense of a Divine constraint which distinguishes the true prophet from pretenders to the office. Jeremiah does not protest the purity of his motives; indirectly and unconsciously he expresses it with a simplicity and a strength which leave no room for suspicion. He has himself no doubt at all that what he speaks is "Iahvah's word." The inward impulse is overpowering; he has striven in vain against its urgency; like Jacob at Peniel, he has wrestled with One stronger than himself. He is no vulgar fanatic or enthusiast, in whom rooted prejudices and irrational frenzies overbalance the judgment, making him incapable of estimating the hazards and the chances of his enterprise; he is as well aware of the perils that beset his path as the coolest and craftiest of his worldly adversaries. Thanks to his natural quickness of perception, his developed faculty of reflexion, he is fully alive to the probable consequences of perpetually thwarting the popular will, of taking up a position of permanent resistance to the policy and the aims and the interests of the ruling classes. But while he has his mortal hopes and fears, his human capacity for anxiety and pain; while his heart bleeds at the sight of suffering, and aches for the woes that thickly crowd the field of his prophetic vision; his speech and his behaviour are dominated, upon the whole, by an altogether higher consciousness. His emotions may have their moments of mastery; at times they may overpower his fortitude, and lay him prostrate in an agony of lamentation and mourning and woe; at times they may even interpose clouds and darkness between the prophet and his vision of the Eternal; but these effects of mortality do not last: they shake but cannot loosen his grasp of spiritual realities; they cannot free him from the constraining influence of the Word of Iahvah. That word possesses, leads him captive, "triumphs over him," over all the natural resistance of flesh and blood; for he is "not as the many"--the false prophets--"who corrupt the Word of God; but as of sincerity, but as of God, in the sight of God, he speaks" (2 Cor. ii. 14, 17).

And still, unless a man be thus impelled by the Spirit; unless he have counted the cost and is prepared to risk all for God; unless he be ready to face unpopularity and social contempt and persecution; unless he knows what it is to suffer for and with Jesus Christ; I doubt if he has any moral right to speak in that most holy Name. For if the all-mastering motive be absent, if the love of Christ constrain him not, how can his desires and his doings be such as the Unseen Judge will either approve or bless?

***

The fourth stanza explains why the prophet laboured, though vainly, to keep silence. It was because of the malicious reports of his utterances, which were carefully circulated by his watchful antagonists. They beset him on every side; like Pashchur, they were to him a "magor-missabib," an environing terror (cf. vi. 25), as they listened to his harangues, and eagerly invited each other to inform against him as a traitor (The words "Inform ye, and let us inform against him!" or "Denounce ye, and let us denounce him!" may be an ancient gloss upon the term dibbah, "ill report," "calumny;" Gen. xxxvii. 2; Num. xiii. 32; Job xvii. 5. For the construction, cf. Job xxxi. 37. They spoil the symmetry of the line. That dibbah really means "defaming," or "slander," appears not only from the passages in which it occurs, but also from the Arabic dabûb; "one who creeps about with slander," from dabba, "to move gently or slowly about." The Heb. ragal, riggel, "to go about slandering," and rakîl, "slander," are analogous).

And not only open enemies thus conspired for the prophet's destruction. Even professed friends (for the phrase, cf. xxxviii. 22; Ps. xli. 10) were treacherously watchful to catch him tripping (cf. ix. 2, xii. 6). Those on whom he had a natural claim for sympathy and protection, bore a secret and determined grudge against him. His unpopularity was complete, and his position full of peril. We have in the thirty-first and several of the following psalms outpourings of feeling under circumstances very similar to those of Jeremiah on the present occasion, even if they were not actually written by him at the same crisis in his career, as certain striking coincidences of expression seem to suggest (ver. 10; cf. Ps. xxxi. 13, xxxv. 15, xxxviii. 17, xli. 9; ver. 13 with Ps. xxxv. 9, 10).

The prophet closes his psalm-like monologue with an act of faith. He remembers that he has a Champion who is mightier than a thousand enemies. Iahvah is with him, not with them (cf. 2 Kings vi. 16); their plots, therefore, are foredoomed to failure, and themselves to the vengeance of a righteous God (xi. 20). The last words are an exultant anticipation of deliverance.

We thus see that the whole piece, like a previous one (xv. 10-21), begins with cursing and ends with an assurance of blessing.

Footnotes:

82. The name is probably a quadriliteral from phsch, Arabic script Ethiopic ???? "to be glad," Assyrian Assyrian script pashâchu "to be at ease," "to rest," (which comes nearest to the Hebrew root). The Arabic verb means "The place was roomy, wide, ample"; whence Arabic script "free from distress or narrowness of mind." Thus Pashchur = "case," "tranquillity," and is formed like Achbor, kaphtor, "a capital," (LXX. Pashchor). But the name might remind a Hebrew of the root phvs "to leap," "prance," Jer. l. 11, and chr "free" (plur. only), as if it were a compound of pash and chOr. "Glad and free:" cf. the LXX. vocalisation Paschor. I think this popular etymology pash + chor is probably what Jeremiah thought of.

83. Ex. xii. 33; Isa. viii. 11; Ezek. iii. 14; Jer. xv. 17.
84. vi. 11 (or, of enduring, Mal. iii. 2).
85. 'Denounce ye, and we will denounce him!'

Rev. C. J. Ball, M.A., & W. H. Bennett, M.A.

VOLUME II

PREFACE

The present work deals primarily with Jeremiah xxi.-lii., thus forming a supplement to the volume of the Expositor's Bible on Jeremiah by the Rev. C. J. Ball, M.A. References to the earlier chapters are only introduced where they are necessary to illustrate and explain the later sections.

I regret that two important works, Prof. Skinner's Ezekiel in this series, and Cornill's Jeremiah in Dr. Haupt's Sacred Books of the Old Testament, were published too late to be used in the preparation of this volume.

I have again to acknowledge my indebtedness to the Rev. T. H. Darlow, M.A., for a careful reading and much valuable criticism of my MS.

CHRONOLOGICAL TABLE

In the present stage of investigation of Old Testament Chronology, absolute accuracy cannot be claimed for such a table as the following. Hardly any, if any, of these dates are supported by a general consensus of opinion. On the other hand, the range of variation is, for the most part, not more than three or four years, and the table will furnish an approximately accurate idea of sequences and synchronisms. In other respects also the data admit of alternative interpretations, and the course of events is partly a matter of theory--hence the occasional insertion of (?).

CLASSICAL SYNCHRONISMS JUDAH AND JEREMIAH ASSYRIA EGYPT Traditional date of the foundation of Rome, 753 MANASSEH (?)

Esarhaddon, 681 Assurbanipal, 668 XXVIth Dynasty Psammetichus I., 666

Jeremiah born, probably between 655 and 645 AMON, 640 JOSIAH, 638

Jeremiah's call in the 13th year of Josiah, 626 Scythian inroad into Western Asia Last kings of Assyria, number and names uncertain, 626-607-6 Psammetichus besieges Ashdod for twenty-nine years

Habakkuk Zephaniah Publication of Deuteronomy, 621 BABYLON. Nabopolassar, 626

Josiah slain at Megiddo, 608 JEHOAHAZ, 608 (xxii. 10-12, Ch. I.) Deposed by Necho, who appoints JEHOIAKIM, 608 (xxii. 13-19, xxxvi. 30, 31, VI.) Jeremiah predicts ruin of Judah and is tried for blasphemy (xxvi., II.) FALL OF NINEVEH, 607-6 Necho, 612

FOURTH YEAR OF JEHOIAKIM, 605-4 BATTLE OF CARCHEMISH (xlvi., XVII.)

Nebuchadnezzar [1] advances into Syria, is suddenly recalled to Babylon--before subduing Judah (?) Nebuchadnezzar, 604

Baruch writes Jeremiah's prophecies in a roll, which is read successively to the people, the nobles, and Jehoiakim, and destroyed by the king (xxxvi., III.; xlv., V.)

Nebuchadnezzar invades Judah (?), the Rechabites take refuge in Jerusalem (?), the Jews rebuked by their example (xxxv., IV.)

Jehoiakim submits to Nebuchadnezzar, revolts after three years, is attacked by various "bands," but dies before Nebuchadnezzar arrives

JEHOIACHIN, 597 (xxii. 20-30, VII.) Continues revolt, but surrenders to Nebuchadnezzar on hisarrival; is deposed and carried to Babylon with many of his subjects. Nebuchadnezzar appoints

ZEDEKIAH, 596Psammetichus II., 596

Jeremiah attempts to keep Zedekiah loyal to Nebuchadnezzar, and contends with priests and prophets who support Egyptian party (xxiii., xxiv., VIII.) Ezekiel

Solon's legislation, 594 Proposed confederation against Nebuchadnezzar denounced by Jeremiah, but supported by Hananiah; proposal abandoned; Hananiah dies (xxvii., xxviii., IX.), 593-2

Controversy by letter with hostile prophets at Babylon (xxix., X.)

Judah revolts, encouraged by Hophra. Jerusalem is beseiged by Chaldeans. There bing no prospect of relief by Egypt, Jeremiah regains his influence and pledges the people by covenant to release their slaves.

On the news of Hophra's advance, the Chaldeans raise the siege; the Egyptian party again become supreme and annul the covenant (xxi. 1-10, xxxiv., xxxvii. 1-10, XI.)

Jeremiah attempts to leave the city, is arrested and imprisoned

Hophra retreats into Egypt and the Chaldeans renew the siege (xxxvii. 11-21, xxxviii., xxxix. 15-18, XII.)

While imprisoned Jeremiah buys his kinsman's inheritance (xxxii., XXX.)

DESTRUCTION OF JERUSALEM, 586 Siege of Tyre

Jeremiah remains for a month a prisoner amongst the other captives. Nebuzaradan arrives; arranges for deportation of bulk of population; appoints Gedaliah governor of residue; releases Jeremiah, who elects to join Gedaliah at Mizpah. Gedaliah murdered. Jeremioah carried off, but rescued by Johanan (xxxix.-xli., lii., XIII.)

Rev. C. J. Ball, M.A., & W. H. Bennett, M.A.

Johanan, in spite of Jeremiah's protest, goes down to Egypt and takes Jeremiah with him (xlii., xliii., XIV.)

Jews in Egypt hold festival in honour of Queen of Heaven. Ineffectual protest of Jeremiah (xliv., XV.)Amasis, 570

  Nebuchadnezzar invades Egypt, (?) 568
  Evil-Merodach, 561
  Pistratus, 560-527 Release of Jehoiachin

CYRUS CONQUERS BABYLON AND GIVES THE JEWS PERMISSION TO RETURN, 538

Footnotes:

1. For spelling see note, page [115]4

BOOK I

PERSONAL UTTERANCES AND NARRATIVES

CHAPTER I

INTRODUCTORY: [2] JEHOAHAZ

xxii. 10-12.

"Weep ye not for the dead, neither bemoan him: but weep sore for him that goeth away: for he shall return no more."--Jer. xxii. 10.

As the prophecies of Jeremiah are not arranged in the order in which they were delivered, there is no absolute chronological division between the first twenty chapters and those which follow. For the most part, however, chapters xxi.-lii. fall in or after the fourth year of Jehoiakim (b.c. 605). We will therefore briefly consider the situation at Jerusalem in this crisis. The period immediately preceding b.c. 605 somewhat resembles the era of the dissolution of the Roman Empire or of the Wars of the French Revolution. An old-established international system was breaking in pieces, and men were quite uncertain what form the new order would take. For centuries the futile assaults of the Pharaohs had only served to illustrate the stability of the Assyrian supremacy in Western Asia. Then in the last two decades of the seventh century b.c. the Assyrian Empire collapsed, like the Roman Empire under Honorius and his successors. It was as if by some swift succession of disasters modern France or Germany were to become suddenly and permanently annihilated as a military power. For the moment, all the traditions and principles of European statesmanship would lose their meaning, and the shrewdest diplomatist would be entirely at fault. Men's reason would totter, their minds would lose their balance at the stupendous spectacle of so unparalleled a catastrophe. The wildest hopes would alternate with the extremity of fear; everything would seem possible to the conqueror.

Such was the situation in b.c. 605, to which our first great group of prophecies belongs. Two oppressors of Israel--Assyria and Egypt--had been struck down in rapid succession. When Nebuchadnezzar [3] was suddenly recalled to Babylon by the death of his father, the Jews would readily imagine that the Divine judgment had fallen upon Chaldea and its king. Sanguine prophets announced that Jehovah was about to deliver His people from all foreign dominion, and establish the supremacy of the Kingdom of God. Court and people would be equally possessed with patriotic hope and enthusiasm. Jehoiakim, it is true, was a nominee of Pharaoh Necho; but his gratitude would be far too slight to override the hopes and aspirations natural to a Prince of the House of David.

In Hezekiah's time, there had been an Egyptian and an Assyrian party at the court of Judah; the recent supremacy of Egypt had probably increased the number of her partisans. Assyria had disappeared, but her former adherents would retain their antipathy to Egypt, and their personal feuds with Jews of the opposite faction; they were as tools lying ready to any hand that cared to use them. When Babylon succeeded Assyria in the overlordship of Asia, she doubtless inherited the allegiance of the anti-Egyptian party in the various Syrian states. Jeremiah, like Isaiah, steadily opposed any dependence upon Egypt; it was probably by his advice that Josiah undertook his ill-fated expedition against Pharaoh Necho. The partisans of Egypt would be the prophet's enemies; and though Jeremiah never became a mere dependent and agent of Nebuchadnezzar, yet the friends of Babylon would be his friends, if only because her enemies were his enemies.

We are told in 2 Kings xxiii. 37 that Jehoiakim did evil in the sight of Jehovah according to all that his father had done. Whatever other sins may be implied by this condemnation, we certainly learn that the king favoured a corrupt form of the religion of Jehovah in opposition to the purer teaching which Jeremiah inherited from Isaiah.

When we turn to Jeremiah himself, the date "the fourth year of Jehoiakim" reminds us that by this time the prophet could look back upon a long and sad experience; he had been called in the thirteenth year of Josiah, some twenty-four years before. With what sometimes seems to our limited intelligence the strange irony of Providence, this lover of peace and quietness was called to deliver a message of ruin and condemnation, a message that could not fail to be extremely offensive to most of his hearers, and to make him the object of bitter hostility.

Much of this Jeremiah must have anticipated, but there were some from whose position and character the prophet expected acceptance, even of the most unpalatable teaching of the Spirit of Jehovah. The personal vindictiveness with which priests and prophets repaid his loyalty to the Divine mission and his zeal for truth came to him with a shock of surprise and bewilderment, which was all the greater because his most determined persecutors were his sacerdotal kinsmen and neighbours at Anathoth. "Let us destroy the tree," they said, "with the fruit thereof, and let us cut him off from the land of the living, that his name may be no more remembered." [4]

He was not only repudiated by his clan, but also forbidden by Jehovah to seek consolation and sympathy in the closer ties of family life: "Thou shalt not take a wife, thou shalt have no sons or daughters." [5] Like Paul, it was good for Jeremiah "by reason of the present distress" to deny himself these blessings. He found some compensation in the fellowship of kindred souls at Jerusalem. We can well believe that, in those early days, he was acquainted with Zephaniah, and that they were associated with Hilkiah and Shaphan and King Josiah in the publication of Deuteronomy and its recognition as the law of Israel. Later on Shaphan's son Ahikam protected Jeremiah when his life was in imminent danger.

The twelve years that intervened between Josiah's Reformation and his defeat at Megiddo were the happiest part of Jeremiah's ministry. It is not certain that any of the extant prophecies belong to this period. With Josiah on the throne and Deuteronomy accepted as the standard of the national life, the prophet felt absolved for a season from his mission to pluck up and break down, and perhaps began to indulge in hopes that the time had come to build and to plant. Yet it is difficult to believe that he had implicit confidence in the permanence of the Reformation or the influence of Deuteronomy. The silence of Isaiah and Jeremiah as to the ecclesiastical reforms of Hezekiah and Josiah stands in glaring contrast to the great importance attached to them by the Books of Kings and Chronicles. But, in any case, Jeremiah must have found life brighter and easier than in the reigns that followed. Probably, in these happier days, he was encouraged by the sympathy and devotion of disciples like Baruch and Ezekiel.

But Josiah's attempt to realise a Kingdom of God was short-lived; and, in a few months, Jeremiah saw the whole fabric swept away. The king was defeated and slain; and his religious policy was at once reversed either by a popular revolution or a court intrigue. The people of the land made Josiah's son Shallum king, under the name of Jehoahaz. This young prince of twenty-three only reigned three months, and was then deposed and carried into captivity by Pharaoh Necho; yet it is recorded of him, that he did evil in the sight of Jehovah, according to all that his fathers had done. [6] He--or, more probably, his ministers, especially the queen-mother [7] --must have been in a hurry to undo Josiah's work. Jeremiah utters no condemnation of Jehoahaz; he merely declares that the young king will never return from his exile, and bids the people lament over his captivity as a more grievous fate than the death of Josiah:--

"Weep not for the dead,
Neither lament over him;
But weep sore for him that goeth into captivity;
For he shall return no more,
Neither shall he behold his native land." [8]

Ezekiel adds admiration to sympathy: Jehoahaz was a young lion skilled to catch the prey, he devoured men, the nations heard of him, he was taken in their pit, and they brought him with hooks into the land of Egypt. [9] Jeremiah and Ezekiel could not but feel some tenderness towards the son of Josiah; and probably they had faith in his personal character, and believed that in time he would shake off the yoke of evil counsellors and follow in his father's footsteps. But any such hopes were promptly disappointed by Pharaoh Necho, and Jeremiah's spirit bowed beneath a new burden as he saw his country completely subservient to the dreaded influence of Egypt.

Thus, at the time when we take up the narrative, the government was in the hands of the party hostile to Jeremiah, and the king, Jehoiakim, seems to have been his personal enemy. Jeremiah himself was somewhere between forty and fifty years old, a solitary man without wife or child. His awful mission as the herald of ruin clouded his spirit with inevitable gloom. Men resented the stern sadness of his words and looks, and turned from him with aversion and dislike. His unpopularity had made him somewhat harsh; for intolerance is twice curst, in that it inoculates its victims with the virus of its own bitterness. His hopes and illusions lay behind him; he could only watch with melancholy pity the eager excitement of these stirring times. If he came across some group busily discussing the rout of the Egyptians at Carchemish, or the report that Nebuchadnezzar was posting in hot haste to Babylon, and wondering as to all that this might mean for Judah, his countrymen would turn to look with contemptuous curiosity at the bitter, disappointed man who had had his chance and failed, and now grudged them their prospect of renewed happiness and prosperity. Nevertheless Jeremiah's greatest work still lay before him. Jerusalem was past saving; but more was at stake than the existence of Judah and its capital. But for Jeremiah the religion of Jehovah might have perished with His Chosen People. It was his mission to save Revelation from the wreck of Israel. Humanly speaking, the religious future of the world depended upon this stern solitary prophet.

Footnotes:

2. Cf. Preface.

3. We know little of Nebuchadnezzar's campaigns. In 2 Kings xxiv. 1 we are told that Nebuchadnezzar "came up" in the days of Jehoiakim, and Jehoiakim became his servant three years. It is not clear whether Nebuchadnezzar "came up" immediately after the battle of Carchemish, or at a later time after his return to Babylon. In either case the impression made by his hasty departure from Syria would be the same. Cf. Cheyne, Jeremiah (Men of the Bible), p. 132. I call the Chaldean king Nebuchadnezzar--not Nebuchadrezzar--because the former has been an English household word for centuries.

4. xi. 19.

5. xvi. 2.

6. 2 Kings xxiii. 30-32.

7. Cf. xxii. 26.

8. xxii. 10-12.

9. Ezek. xix. 3, 4.

Rev. C. J. Ball, M.A., & W. H. Bennett, M.A.

CHAPTER II

A TRIAL FOR HERESY

xxvi.: cf. vii.-x.
"When Jeremiah had made an end of speaking all that Jehovah had commanded him to speak unto all the people, the priests and the prophets and all the people laid hold on him, saying, Thou shalt surely die."--Jer. xxvi. 8.

The date of this incident is given, somewhat vaguely, as the beginning of the reign of Jehoiakim. It was, therefore, earlier than b.c. 605, the point reached in the previous chapter. Jeremiah could offer no political resistance to Jehoiakim and his Egyptian suzerain; yet it was impossible for him to allow Josiah's policy to be reversed without a protest. Moreover, something, perhaps much, might yet be saved for Jehovah. The king, with his court and prophets and priests, was not everything. Jeremiah was only concerned with sanctuaries, ritual, and priesthoods as means to an end. For him the most important result of the work he had shared with Josiah was a pure and holy life for the nation and individuals. Renan--in some passages, for he is not always consistent--is inclined to minimise the significance of the change from Josiah to Jehoiakim; in fact, he writes very much as a cavalier might have done of the change from Cromwell to Charles II. Both the Jewish kings worshipped Jehovah, each in his own fashion: Josiah was inclined to a narrow puritan severity of a life; Jehoiakim was a liberal, practical man of the world. Probably this is a fair modern equivalent of the current estimate of the kings and their policy, especially on the part of Jehoiakim's friends; but then, as unhappily still in some quarters, "narrow puritan severity" was a convenient designation for a decent and honourable life, for a scrupulous and self-denying care for the welfare of others. Jeremiah dreaded a relapse into the old half-heathen ideas that Jehovah would be pleased with homage and service that satisfied Baal, Moloch, and Chemosh. Such a relapse would lower the ethical standard, and corrupt or even destroy any beginnings of spiritual life. Our English Restoration is an object-lesson as to the immoral effects of political and ecclesiastical reaction; if such things were done in sober England, what must have been possible to hot Eastern blood! In protesting against the attitude of Jehoiakim, Jeremiah would also seek to save the people from the evil effects of the king's policy. He knew from his own experience that a subject might trust and serve God with his whole heart, even when the king was false to Jehovah. What was possible for him was possible for others. He understood his countrymen too well to expect that the nation would continue to advance in paths of righteousness which its leaders and teachers had forsaken; but, scattered here and there through the mass of the people, was Isaiah's remnant, the seed of the New Israel, men and women to whom the Revelation of Jehovah had been the beginning of a higher life. He would not leave them without a word of counsel and encouragement.

At the command of Jehovah, Jeremiah appeared before the concourse of Jews, assembled at the Temple for some great fast or festival. No feast is expressly mentioned, but he is charged to address "all the cities of Judah" [10] ; all the outlying population would only meet at the Temple on some specially holy day. Such an occasion would naturally be chosen by Jeremiah for his deliverance, just as Christ availed Himself of the opportunities offered by the Passover and the Feast of Tabernacles, just as modern philanthropists seek to find a place for their favourite topics on the platform of May Meetings.

The prophet was to stand in the court of the Temple and repeat once more to the Jews his message of warning and judgment, "all that I have charged thee to speak unto them, thou shalt not keep back a single word." The substance of this address is found in the various prophecies which expose the sin and predict the ruin of Judah. They have been dealt with in the former volume [11] on Jeremiah in this series, and are also referred to in Book III.

According to the universal principle of Hebrew prophecy, the predictions of ruin were conditional; they were still coupled with the offer of pardon to repentance, and Jehovah did not forbid his prophet to cherish a lingering hope that "perchance they may hearken and turn every one from his evil way, so that I may repent Me of the evil I purpose to inflict upon them because of the evil of their doings." Probably the phrase "every one from his evil way" is primarily collective rather than individual, and is intended to describe a national reformation, which would embrace all the individual citizens; but the actual words suggest another truth, which must also have been in Jeremiah's mind. The nation is, after all, an aggregate of men and women; there can be no national reformation, except through the repentance and amendment of individuals.

Jeremiah's audience, it must be observed, consisted of worshippers on the way to the Temple, and would correspond to an ordinary congregation of church-goers, rather than to the casual crowd gathered round a street preacher, or to the throngs of miners and labourers who listened to Whitfield and Wesley. As an acknowledged prophet, he was well within his rights in expecting a hearing from the attendants at the feast, and men would be curious to see and hear one who had been the dominant influence in Judah during the reign of Josiah. Moreover, in the absence of evening newspapers and shop-windows, a prophet was too exciting a distraction to be lightly neglected. From Jehovah's charge to speak all that He had commanded him to speak and not to keep back a word, we may assume that Jeremiah's discourse was long: it was also avowedly an old sermon [12] ; most of his audience had heard it before, all of them were quite familiar with its main topics. They listened in the various moods of a modern congregation "sitting under" a distinguished preacher. Jeremiah's friends and disciples welcomed the ideas and phrases that had become part of their spiritual life. Many enjoyed the speaker's earnestness and eloquence, without troubling themselves about the ideas at all. There was nothing specially startling about the well-known threats and warnings; they had become

"A tale of little meaning tho' the words were strong."

Men hardened their hearts against inspired prophets as easily as they do against the most pathetic appeals of modern evangelists. Mingled with the crowd were Jeremiah's professional rivals, who detested both him and his teaching--priests who regarded him as a traitor to his own caste, prophets who envied his superior gifts and his force of passionate feeling. To these almost every word he uttered was offensive, but for a while there was nothing that roused them to very vehement anger. He was allowed to finish what he had to say, "to make an end of speaking all that Jehovah had commanded him." But in this peroration he had insisted on a subject that stung the indifferent into resentment and roused the priests and prophets to fury.

"Go ye now unto My place which was in Shiloh, where I caused My name to dwell at the first, and see what I did to it for the wickedness of My people Israel. And now, because ye have done all these works, saith Jehovah, and I spake unto you, rising up early and speaking, but ye heard not; and I called you, but ye answered not: therefore will I do unto the house, that is called by My name, wherein ye trust, and unto the place which I gave to you and to your fathers, as I have done to Shiloh." [13]

The Ephraimite sanctuary of Shiloh, long the home of the Ark and its priesthood, had been overthrown in some national catastrophe. Apparently when it was destroyed it was no mere tent, but a substantial building of stone, and its ruins remained as a permanent monument of the fugitive glory of even the most sacred shrine.

The very presence of his audience in the place where they were met showed their reverence for the Temple: the priests were naturally devotees of their own shrine; of the prophets Jeremiah himself had said, "The prophets prophesy falsely, and the priests rule in accordance with their teaching." [14] Can we wonder that "the priests and the prophets and all the people laid hold on him, saying, Thou shalt surely die"? For the moment there was an appearance of religious unity in Jerusalem; the priests, the prophets, and the pious laity on one side, and only the solitary heretic on the other. It was, though on a small scale, as if the obnoxious teaching of some nineteenth-century prophet of God had given an unexpected stimulus to the movement for Christian reunion; as if cardinals and bishops, chairmen of unions, presidents of conferences, moderators of assemblies, with great preachers and distinguished laymen, united to hold monster meetings and denounce the Divine message as heresy and blasphemy. In like manner Pharisees, Sadducees, and Herodians found a basis of common action in their hatred of Christ, and Pilate and Herod were reconciled by His cross.

Meanwhile the crowd was increasing: new worshippers were arriving, and others as they left the Temple were attracted to the scene of the disturbance. Doubtless too the mob, always at the service of persecutors, hurried up in hope of finding opportunities for mischief and violence. Some six and a half centuries later, history repeated itself on the same spot, when the Asiatic Jews saw Paul in the Temple and "laid hands on him, crying out, Men of Israel, help: This is the man, that teacheth all men everywhere against the people and the law and this place, ... and all the city was moved, and the people ran together and laid hold on Paul." [15]

Our narrative, as it stands, is apparently incomplete: we find Jeremiah before the tribunal of the princes, but we are not told how he came there; whether the civil authorities intervened to protect him, as Claudius Lysias came down with his soldiers and centurions and rescued Paul, or whether Jeremiah's enemies observed legal forms, as Annas and Caiaphas did when they arrested Christ. But, in any case, "the princes of Judah, when they heard these things, came up from the palace into the Temple, and took their seats as judges at the entry of the new gate of the Temple." The "princes of Judah" play a conspicuous part in the last period of the Jewish monarchy: we have little definite information about them, and are left to conjecture that they were an aristocratic oligarchy or an official clique, or both; but it is clear that they were a dominant force in the state, with recognised constitutional status, and that they often controlled the king himself. We are also ignorant as to the "new gate"; it may possibly be the upper gate built by Jotham [16] about a hundred and fifty years earlier.

Before these judges, Jeremiah's ecclesiastical accusers brought a formal charge; they said, almost in the very words which the high priest and the Sanhedrin used of Christ, "This man is worthy of death, for he hath prophesied against this city, as ye have heard with your ears"--i.e. when he said, "This house shall be like Shiloh, and this city shall be desolate without inhabitant." Such accusations have been always on the lips of those who have denounced Christ and His disciples as heretics. One charge against Himself was that He said, "I will destroy this Temple that is made with hands, and in three days I will build another that is made without hands." [17] Stephen was accused of speaking incessantly against the Temple and the Law, and teaching that Jesus of Nazareth would destroy the Temple and change the customs handed down from Moses. When he asserted that "the Most High dwelleth not in temples made with hands," the impatience of his audience compelled him to bring his defence to an abrupt conclusion. [18] Of Paul we have already spoken.

How was it that these priests and prophets thought that their princes might be induced to condemn Jeremiah to death for predicting the destruction of the Temple? A prophet would not run much risk nowadays by announcing that St. Paul's should be made like Stonehenge, or St. Peter's like the Parthenon. Expositors of Daniel and the Apocalypse habitually fix the end of the world a few years in advance of the date at which they write, and yet they do not incur any appreciable unpopularity. It is true that Jeremiah's accusers were a little afraid that his predictions might be fulfilled, and the most bitter persecutors are those who have a lurking dread that their victims are right, while they themselves are wrong. But such fears could not very well be evidence or argument against Jeremiah before any court of law.

In order to realise the situation we must consider the place which the Temple held in the hopes and affections of the Jews. They had always been proud of their royal sanctuary at Jerusalem, but within the last hundred and fifty years it had acquired a unique importance for the religion of Israel. First Hezekiah, and then Josiah, had taken away the other high places and altars at which Jehovah was worshipped, and had said to Judah and Jerusalem, "Ye shall worship before this altar." [19] Doubtless the kings were following the advice of Isaiah and Jeremiah. These prophets were anxious to abolish the abuses of the local sanctuaries, which were a continual incentive to an extravagant and corrupt ritual. Yet they did not intend to assign any supreme importance to a priestly caste or a consecrated building. Certainly for them the hope of Israel and the assurance of its salvation did not consist in cedar and hewn stones, in silver and gold. And yet the unique position given to the Temple inevitably became the starting-point for fresh superstition. Once Jehovah could be worshipped not only at Jerusalem, but at Beersheba and Bethel and many other places where He had chosen to set His name. Even then, it was felt that the Divine Presence must afford some protection for His dwelling-places. But now that Jehovah dwelt nowhere else but at Jerusalem, and only accepted the worship of His people at this single shrine, how could any one doubt that He would protect His Temple and His Holy City against all enemies, even the most formidable? Had He not done so already?

When Hezekiah abolished the high places, did not Jehovah set the seal of approval upon his policy by destroying the army of Sennacherib? Was not this great deliverance wrought to guard the Temple against desecration and destruction, and would not Jehovah work out a like salvation in any future time of danger? The destruction of Sennacherib was essential to the religious future of Israel and of mankind; but it had a very mingled influence upon the generations immediately following. They were like a man who has won a great prize in a lottery, or who has, quite unexpectedly, come into an immense inheritance. They ignored the unwelcome thought that the Divine protection depended on spiritual and moral conditions, and they clung to the superstitious faith that at any moment, even in the last extremity of danger and at the eleventh hour, Jehovah might, nay, even must, intervene. The priests and the inhabitants of Jerusalem could look on with comparative composure while the country was ravaged, and the outlying towns were taken and pillaged; Jerusalem itself might seem on the verge of falling into the hands of the enemy, but they still trusted in their Palladium. Jerusalem could not perish, because it contained the one sanctuary of Jehovah; they sought to silence their own fears and to drown the warning voice of the prophet by vociferating their watchword: "The Temple of Jehovah! the Temple of Jehovah! The Temple of Jehovah is in our midst!" [20]

In prosperous times a nation may forget its Palladium, and may tolerate doubts as to its efficacy; but the strength of the Jews was broken, their resources were exhausted, and they were clinging in an agony of conflicting hopes and fears to their faith in the inviolability of the Temple. To destroy their confidence was like snatching away a plank from a drowning man. When Jeremiah made the attempt, they struck back with the fierce energy of despair. It does not seem that at this time the city was in any immediate danger; the incident rather falls in the period of quiet submission to Pharaoh Necho that preceded the battle of Carchemish. But the disaster of Megiddo was fresh in men's memories, and in the unsettled state of Eastern Asia no one knew how soon some other invader might advance against the city. On the other hand, in the quiet interval, hopes began to revive, and men were incensed when the prophet made haste to nip these hopes in the bud, all the more so because their excited anticipations of future glory had so little solid basis. Jeremiah's appeal to the ill-omened precedent of Shiloh naturally roused the sanguine and despondent alike into frenzy.

Jeremiah's defence was simple and direct: "Jehovah sent me to prophesy all that ye have heard against this house and against this city. Now therefore amend your ways and your doings, and hearken unto the voice of Jehovah your God, that He may repent Him of the evil that He hath spoken against you. As for me, behold, I am in your hands: do unto me as it seems good and right unto you. Only know assuredly that, if ye put me to death, ye will bring the guilt of innocent blood upon yourselves, and upon this city and its inhabitants: for of a truth Jehovah sent me unto you to speak all these words in your ears." There is one curious feature in this defence. Jeremiah contemplates the possibility of two distinct acts of wickedness on the part of his persecutors: they may turn a deaf ear to his appeal that they should repent and reform, and their obstinacy will incur all the chastisements which Jeremiah had threatened; they may also put him to death and incur additional guilt. Scoffers might reply that his previous threats were so awful and comprehensive that they left no room for any addition to the punishment of the impenitent. Sinners sometimes find a grim comfort in the depth of their wickedness; their case is so bad that it cannot be made worse, they may now indulge their evil propensities with a kind of impunity. But Jeremiah's prophetic insight made him anxious to save his countrymen from further sin, even in their impenitence; the Divine discrimination is not taxed beyond its capabilities even by the extremity of human wickedness.

But to return to the main feature in Jeremiah's defence. His accusers' contention was that his teaching was so utterly blasphemous, so entirely opposed to every tradition and principle of true religion--or, as we should say, so much at variance with all orthodoxy--that it could not be a word of Jehovah. Jeremiah does not attempt to discuss the relation of his teaching to the possible limits of Jewish orthodoxy. He bases his defence on the bare assertion of his prophetic mission--Jehovah had sent him. He assumes that there is no room for evidence or discussion; it is a question of the relative authority of Jeremiah and his accusers, whether he or they had the better right to speak for God. The immediate result seemed to justify him in this attitude. He was no obscure novice, seeking for the first time to establish his right to speak in the Divine name. The princes and people had been accustomed for twenty years to listen to him, as to the most fully acknowledged mouthpiece of Heaven; they could not shake off their accustomed feeling of deference, and once more succumbed to the spell of his fervid and commanding personality. "Then said the princes and all the people unto the priests and the prophets, This man is not worthy of death; for he hath spoken to us in the name of Jehovah our God." For the moment the people were won over and the princes convinced; but priests and prophets were not so easily influenced by inspired utterances; some of these probably thought that they had an inspiration of their own, and their professional experience made them callous.

At this point again the sequence of events is not clear; possibly the account was compiled from the imperfect recollections of more than one of the spectators. The pronouncement of the princes and the people seems, at first sight, a formal acquittal that should have ended the trial, and left no room for the subsequent intervention of "certain of the elders," otherwise the trial seems to have come to no definite conclusion, and the incident simply terminated in the personal protection given to Jeremiah by Ahikam ben Shaphan. Possibly, however, the tribunal of the princes was not governed by any strict rules of procedure; and the force of the argument used by the elders does not depend on the exact stage of the trial at which it was introduced.

Either Jeremiah was not entirely successful in his attempt to get the matter disposed of on the sole ground of his own prophetic authority, or else the elders were anxious to secure weight and finality for the acquittal, by bringing forward arguments in its support. The elders were an ancient Israelite institution, and probably still represented the patriarchal side of the national life; nothing is said as to their relation to the princes, and this might not be very clearly defined. The elders appealed, by way of precedent, to an otherwise unrecorded incident of the reign of Hezekiah. Micah the Morasthite had uttered similar threats against Jerusalem and the Temple: "Zion shall be ploughed as a field, and Jerusalem shall become heaps, and the mountain of the house as the high places of the forest." [21] But Hezekiah and his people, instead of slaying Micah, had repented, and the city had been spared. They evidently wished that the precedent could be wholly followed in the present instance; but, at any rate, it was clear that one of the most honoured and successful of the kings of Judah had accepted a threat against the Temple as a message from Jehovah. Therefore the mere fact that Jeremiah had uttered such a threat was certainly not primâ facie evidence that he was a false prophet. We are not told how this argument was received, but the writer of the chapter, possibly Baruch, does not attribute Jeremiah's escape either to his acquittal by the princes or to the reasoning of the elders. The people apparently changed sides once more, like the common people in the New Testament, who heard Christ gladly and with equal enthusiasm clamoured for His crucifixion. At the end of the chapter we find them eager to have the prophet delivered into their hands that they may put him to death. Apparently the prophets and priests, having brought matters into this satisfactory position, had retired from the scene of action; the heretic was to be delivered over to the secular arm. The princes, like Pilate, seemed inclined to yield to popular pressure; but Ahikam, a son of the Shaphan who had to do with the finding of Deuteronomy, stood by Jeremiah, as John of Gaunt stood by Wyclif, and the Protestant Princes by Luther, and the magistrates of Geneva by Calvin; and Jeremiah could say with the Psalmist:--

"I have heard the defaming of many,
Terror on every side:
While they took counsel together against me,
They devised to take away my life.
But I trusted in Thee, O Jehovah:
I said, Thou art my God.
My times are in Thy hand:
Deliver me from the hand of mine enemies, and from them that persecute me.

***

Let the lying lips be dumb,
Which speak against the righteous insolently,
With pride and contempt.
Oh, how great is Thy goodness, which Thou hast laid up for them that fear Thee,
Which Thou hast wrought for them that put their trust in Thee, before the sons of men." [22]

We have here an early and rudimentary example of religious toleration, of the willingness, however reluctant, to hear as a possible Divine message unpalatable teaching, at variance with current theology; we see too the fountain-head of that freedom which since has "broadened down from precedent to precedent."

But unfortunately no precedent can bind succeeding generations, and both Judaism and Christianity have sinned grievously against the lesson of this chapter. Jehoiakim himself soon broke through the feeble restraint of this new-born tolerance. The writer adds an incident that must have happened somewhat later, [23] to show how real was Jeremiah's danger, and how transient was the liberal mood of the authorities. A certain Uriah ben Shemaiah of Kirjath Jearim had the courage to follow in Jeremiah's footsteps and speak against the city "according to all that Jeremiah had said." With the usual meanness of persecutors, Jehoiakim and his captains and princes vented upon this obscure prophet the ill-will which they had not dared to indulge in the case of Jeremiah, with his commanding personality and influential friends. Uriah fled into Egypt, but was brought back and slain, and his body cast out unburied into the common cemetery. We can understand Jeremiah's fierce and bitter indignation against the city where such things were possible.

This chapter is so full of suggestive teaching that we can only touch upon two or three of its more obvious lessons. The dogma which shaped the charge against Jeremiah and caused the martyrdom of Uriah was the inviolability of the Temple and the Holy City. This dogma was a perversion of the teaching of Isaiah, and especially of Jeremiah himself, [24] which assigned a unique position to the Temple in the religion of Israel. The carnal man shows a fatal ingenuity in sucking poison out of the most wholesome truth. He is always eager to discover that something external, material, physical, concrete--some building, organisation, ceremony, or form of words--is a fundamental basis of the faith and essential to salvation. If Jeremiah had died with Josiah, the "priests and prophets" would doubtless have quoted his authority against Uriah. The teaching of Christ and His apostles, of Luther and Calvin and their fellow-reformers, has often been twisted and forged into weapons to be used against their true followers. We are often tempted in the interest of our favourite views to lay undue stress on secondary and accidental statements of great teachers. We fail to keep the due proportion of truth which they themselves observed, and in applying their precepts to new problems we sacrifice the kernel and save the husk. The warning of Jeremiah's persecutors might often "give us pause." We need not be surprised at finding priests and prophets eager and interested champions of a perversion of revealed truth. Ecclesiastical office does not necessarily confer any inspiration from above. The hereditary priest follows the traditions of his caste, and even the prophet may become the mouthpiece of the passions and prejudices of those who accept and applaud him. When men will not endure sound doctrine, they heap to themselves teachers after their own lusts; having itching ears, they turn away their ears from the truth and turn unto fables. [25] Jeremiah's experience shows that even an apparent consensus of clerical opinion is not always to be trusted. The history of councils and synods is stained by many foul and shameful blots; it was the OEcumenical Council at Constance that burnt Huss, and most Churches have found themselves, at some time or other, engaged in building the tombs of the prophets whom their own officials had stoned in days gone by. We forget that Athanasius contra mundum implies also Athanasius contra ecclesiam.

Footnotes:

10. The expression is curious; it usually means all the cities of Judah, except Jerusalem; the LXX. reading varies between "all the Jews" and "all Judah."

11. See especially the exposition of chaps. vii.-x., which are often supposed to be a reproduction of Jeremiah's utterance on this occasion.

12. The Hebrew apparently implies that the discourse was a repetition of former prophecies.

13. vii. 12-14. Even if chaps. vii.-x. are not a report of Jeremiah's discourse on this occasion, the few lines in xxvi. are evidently a mere summary, and vii. will best indicate the substance of his utterance. The verses quoted occur towards the beginning of vii.-x., but from the emphatic reference to Shiloh in the brief abstract in xxvi., Jeremiah must have dwelt on this topic, and the fact that the outburst followed his conclusion suggests that he reserved this subject for his peroration.

14. v. 31.

15. Acts xxi. 27-30.

16. 2 Kings xv. 35.

17. Mark xiv. 58.

18. Acts vi. 13, 14, vii. 48.

19. 2 Kings xviii. 4, xxiii.; Isa. xxxvi. 7.

20. vii. 4.

21. Micah iii. 12. As the quotation exactly agrees with the verse in our extant Book of Micah, we may suppose that the elders were acquainted with his prophecies in writing.

22. Psalm xxxi. 13-15, 18, 19. The Psalm is sometimes ascribed to Jeremiah, because it can be so readily applied to this incident. The reader will recognise his characteristic phrase "Terror on every side" (Magor-missabib).

23. This incident cannot be part of the speech of the elders; it would only have told against the point they were trying to make. The various phases--prophesy, persecution, flight, capture, and execution--must have taken some time, and can scarcely have preceded Jeremiah's utterance "at the beginning of the reign of King Jehoiakim."

24. Assuming his sympathy with Deuteronomy.

25. 2 Tim. iv. 3.

CHAPTER III

THE ROLL

xxxvi.

"*Take thee a roll of a book, and write therein all the words that I have spoken unto thee.*"--Jer. xxxvi. 2.

The incidents which form so large a proportion of the contents of our book do not make up a connected narrative; they are merely a series of detached pictures: we can only conjecture the doings and experiences of Jeremiah during the intervals. Chapter xxvi. leaves him still exposed to the persistent hostility of the priests and prophets, who had apparently succeeded in once more directing popular feeling against their antagonist. At the same time, though the princes were not ill-disposed towards him, they were not inclined to resist the strong pressure brought to bear upon them. Probably the attitude of the populace varied from time to time, according to the presence among them of the friends or enemies of the prophet; and, in the same way, we cannot think of "the princes" as a united body, governed by a single impulse. The action of this group of notables might be determined by the accidental preponderance of one or other of two opposing parties. Jeremiah's only real assurance of safety lay in the personal protection extended to him by Ahikam ben Shaphan. Doubtless other princes associated themselves with Ahikam in his friendly action on behalf of the prophet.

Under these circumstances, Jeremiah would find it necessary to restrict his activity. Utter indifference to danger was one of the most ordinary characteristics of Hebrew prophets, and Jeremiah was certainly not wanting in the desperate courage which may be found in any Mohammedan dervish. At the same time he was far too practical, too free from morbid self-consciousness, to court martyrdom for its own sake. If he had presented himself again in the Temple when it was crowded with worshippers, his life might have been taken in a popular tumult, while his mission was still only half accomplished. Possibly his priestly enemies had found means to exclude him from the sacred precincts.

Man's extremity was God's opportunity; this temporary and partial silencing of Jeremiah led to a new departure, which made the influence of his teaching more extensive and permanent. He was commanded to commit his prophecies to writing. The restriction of his active ministry was to bear rich fruit, like Paul's imprisonment, and Athanasius' exile, and Luther's sojourn in the Wartburg. A short time since there was great danger that Jeremiah and the Divine message entrusted to him would perish together. He did not know how soon he might become once more the mark of popular fury, nor whether Ahikam would still be able to protect him. The roll of the book could speak even if he were put to death.

But Jeremiah was not thinking chiefly about what would become of his teaching if he himself perished. He had an immediate and particular end in view. His tenacious persistence was not to be baffled by the prospect of mob violence, or by exclusion from the most favourable vantage-ground. Renan is fond of comparing the prophets to modern journalists; and this incident is an early and striking instance of the substitution of pen, ink, and paper for the orator's tribune. Perhaps the closest modern parallel is that of the speaker who is howled down at a public meeting and hands his manuscript to the reporters.

In the record of the Divine command to Jeremiah, there is no express statement as to what was to be done with the roll; but as the object of writing it was that "perchance the house of Judah might hear and repent," it is evident that from the first it was intended to be read to the people.

There is considerable difference of opinion [26] as to the contents of the roll. They are described as: "All that I have spoken unto thee concerning [27] Jerusalem [28] and Judah, and all the nations, since I (first) spake unto thee, from the time of Josiah until now." At first sight this would seem to include all previous utterances, and therefore all the extant prophecies of a date earlier than b.c. 605, i.e. those contained in chapters i.-xii. and some portions of xiv.-xx. (we cannot determine which with any exactness), and probably most of those dated in the fourth year of Jehoiakim, i.e. xxv. and parts of xlv.-xlix. Cheyne, [29] however, holds that the roll simply contained the striking and comprehensive prophecy in chapter xxv. The whole series of chapters might very well be described as dealing with Jerusalem, Judah, and the nations; but at the same time xxv. might be considered equivalent, by way of summary, to all that had been spoken on these subjects. From various considerations which will appear as we proceed with the narrative, it seems probable that the larger estimate is the more correct, i.e. that the roll contained a large fraction of our Book of Jeremiah, and not merely one or two chapters. We need not, however, suppose that every previous utterance of the prophet, even though still extant, must have been included in the roll; the "all" would of course be understood to be conditioned by relevancy; and the narratives of various incidents are obviously not part of what Jehovah had spoken.

Jeremiah dictated his prophecies, as St. Paul did his epistles, to an amanuensis; he called his disciple Baruch [30] ben Neriah, and dictated to him "all that Jehovah had spoken, upon a book, in the form of a roll."

It seems clear that, as in xxvi., the narrative does not exactly follow the order of events, [31] and that verse 9, which records the proclamation of a fast in the ninth month of Jehoiakim's fifth year, should be read before verse 5, which begins the account of the circumstances leading up to the actual reading of the roll. We are not told in what month of Jehoiakim's fourth year Jeremiah received this command to write his prophecies in a roll, but as they were not read till the ninth month of the fifth year, there must have been an interval of at least ten months or a year between the Divine command and the reading by Baruch. We can scarcely suppose that all or nearly all this delay was caused by Jeremiah and Baruch's waiting for a suitable occasion. The long interval suggests that the dictation took some time, and that therefore the roll was somewhat voluminous in its contents, and that it was carefully compiled, not without a certain amount of revision.

When the manuscript was ready, its authors had to determine the right time at which to read it; they found their desired opportunity in the fast proclaimed in the ninth month. This was evidently an extraordinary fast, appointed in view of some pressing danger; and, in the year following the battle of Carchemish, this would naturally be the advance of Nebuchadnezzar. As our incident took place in the depth of winter, the months must be reckoned according to the Babylonian year, which began in April; and the ninth month, Kisleu, would roughly correspond to our December. The dreaded invasion would be looked for early in the following spring, "at the time when kings go out to battle." [32]

Jeremiah does not seem to have absolutely determined from the first that the reading of the roll by Baruch was to be a substitute for his own presence. He had probably hoped that some change for the better in the situation might justify his appearance before a great gathering in the Temple. But when the time came he was "hindered" [33] --we are not told how--and could not go into the Temple. He may have been restrained by his own prudence, or dissuaded by his friends, like Paul when he would have faced the mob in the theatre at Ephesus; the hindrance may have been some ban under which he had been placed by the priesthood, or it may have been some unexpected illness, or legal uncleanness, or some other passing accident, such as Providence often uses to protect its soldiers till their warfare is accomplished.

Accordingly it was Baruch who went up to the Temple. Though he is said to have read the book "in the ears of all the people," he does not seem to have challenged universal attention as openly as Jeremiah had done; he did not stand forth in the court of the Temple, [34] but betook himself to the "chamber" of the scribe, [35] or secretary of state, Gemariah ben Shaphan, the brother of Jeremiah's protector Ahikam. This chamber would be one of the cells built round the upper court, from which the "new gate" [36] led into an inner court of the Temple. Thus Baruch placed himself formally under the protection of the owner of the apartment, and any violence offered to him would have been resented and avenged by this powerful noble with his kinsmen and allies. Jeremiah's disciple and representative took his seat at the door of the chamber, and, in full view of the crowds who passed and repassed through the new gate, opened his roll and began to read aloud from its contents. His reading was yet another repetition of the exhortations, warnings, and threats which Jeremiah had rehearsed on the feast day when he spake to the people "all that Jehovah had commanded him"; and still both Jehovah and His prophet promised deliverance as the reward of repentance. Evidently the head and front of the nation's offence had been no open desertion of Jehovah for idols, else His servants would not have selected for their audience His enthusiastic worshippers as they thronged to His Temple. The fast itself might have seemed a token of penitence, but it was not accepted by Jeremiah, or put forward by the people, as a reason why the prophecies of ruin should not be fulfilled. No one offers the very natural plea: "In this fast we are humbling ourselves under the mighty hand of God, we are confessing our sins, and consecrating ourselves afresh to service of Jehovah. What more does He expect of us? Why does He still withhold His mercy and forgiveness? Wherefore have we fasted, and Thou seest not? Wherefore have we afflicted our soul, and Thou takest no knowledge?" Such a plea would probably have received an answer similar to that given by one of Jeremiah's successors: "Behold, in the day of your fast ye find your own pleasure, and oppress all your labourers. Behold, ye fast for strife and contention, and to smite with the fist of wickedness: ye fast not this day so as to make your voice to be heard on high. Is such the fast that I have chosen? the day for a man to afflict his soul? Is it to bow down his head as a rush, and to spread sackcloth and ashes under him? wilt thou call this a fast, and a day acceptable to Jehovah?"

"Is not this the fast that I have chosen? to loose the bonds of wickedness, to undo the bands of the yoke, and to let the oppressed go free, and that ye break every yoke? Is it not to deal thy bread to the hungry, and that thou bring the poor that are cast out to thy house? when thou seest the naked, that thou cover him; and that thou hide not thyself from thine own flesh? Then shall thy light break forth as the morning, and thy healing shall spring forth speedily: and thy righteousness shall go before thee; the glory of Jehovah shall be thy rearward." [37]

Jeremiah's opponents did not grudge Jehovah His burnt-offerings and calves of a year old; He was welcome to thousands of rams, and ten thousands of rivers of oil. They were even willing to give their firstborn for their transgression, the fruit of their body for the sin of their soul; but they were not prepared "to do justly, and to love mercy, and to walk humbly with their God." [38]

We are not told how Jeremiah and the priests and prophets formulated the points at issue between them, which were so thoroughly and universally understood that the record takes them for granted. Possibly Jeremiah contended for the recognition of Deuteronomy, with its lofty ideals of pure religion and a humanitarian order of society. But, in any case, these incidents were an early phase of the age-long struggle of the prophets of God against the popular attempt to make ritual and sensuous emotion into excuses for ignoring morality, and to offer the cheap sacrifice of a few unforbidden pleasures, rather than surrender the greed of grain, the lust of power, and the sweetness of revenge.

When the multitudes caught the sound of Baruch's voice and saw him sitting in the doorway of Gemariah's chamber, they knew exactly what they would hear. To them he was almost as antagonistic as a Protestant evangelist would be to the worshippers at some great Romanist feast; or perhaps we might find a closer parallel in a Low Church bishop addressing a ritualistic audience. For the hearts of these hearers were not steeled by the consciousness of any formal schism. Baruch and the great prophet whom he represented did not stand outside the recognised limits of Divine inspiration. While the priests and prophets and their adherents repudiated his teaching as heretical, they were still haunted by the fear that, at any rate, his threats might have some Divine authority. Apart from all theology, the prophet of evil always finds an ally in the nervous fears and guilty conscience of his hearer.

The feelings of the people would be similar to those with which they had heard the same threats against Judah, the city and the Temple, from Jeremiah himself. But the excitement aroused by the defeat of Pharaoh and the hasty return of Nebuchadnezzar to Babylon had died away. The imminence of a new invasion made it evident that this had not been the Divine deliverance of Judah. The people were cowed by what must have seemed to many the approaching fulfilments of former threatenings; the ritual of a fast was in itself depressing; so that they had little spirit to resent the message of doom. Perhaps too there was less to resent: the prophecies were the same, but Baruch may have been less unpopular than Jeremiah, and his reading would be tame and ineffective compared to the fiery eloquence of his master. Moreover the powerful protection which shielded him was indicated not only by the place he occupied, but also by the presence of Gemariah's son, Micaiah.

The reading passed off without any hostile demonstration on the part of the people, and Micaiah went in search of his father to describe to him the scene he had just witnessed. He found him in the palace, in the chamber of the secretary of state, Elishama, attending a council of the princes. There were present, amongst others, Elnathan ben Achbor, who brought Uriah back from Egypt, Delaiah ben Shemaiah, and Zedekiah ben Hananiah. Micaiah told them what he had heard. They at once sent for Baruch and the roll. Their messenger, Jehudi ben Nethaniah, seems to have been a kind of court-usher. His name signifies "the Jew," and as his great-grandfather was Cushi, "the Ethiopian," it has been suggested that he came of a family of Ethiopian descent, which had only attained in his generation to Jewish citizenship. [39]

When Baruch arrived, the princes greeted him with the courtesy and even deference due to the favourite disciple of a distinguished prophet. They invited him to sit down and read them the roll. Baruch obeyed; the method of reading suited the enclosed room and the quiet, interested audience of responsible men, better than the swaying crowd gathered round the door of Gemariah's chamber. Baruch now had before him ministers of state who knew from their official information and experience how extremely probable it was that the words to which they were listening would find a speedy and complete fulfilment. Baruch must almost have seemed to them like a doomster who announces to a condemned criminal the ghastly details of his coming execution. They exchanged looks of dismay and horror, and when the reading was over, they said to one another, [40] "We must tell the king of all these words." First, however, they inquired concerning the exact circumstances under which the roll had been written, that they might know how far responsibility in this matter was to be divided between the prophet and his disciple, and also whether all the contents rested upon the full authority of Jeremiah. Baruch assured them that it was simply a case of dictation: Jeremiah had uttered every word with his own mouth, and he had faithfully written it down; everything was Jeremiah's own. [41]

The princes were well aware that the prophet's action would probably be resented and punished by Jehoiakim. They said to Baruch: "Do you and Jeremiah go and hide yourselves, and let no one know where you are." They kept the roll and laid it up in Elishama's room; then they went to the king. They found him in his winter room, in the inner court of the palace, sitting in front of a brasier of burning charcoal. On this fast-day the king's mind might well be careful and troubled, as he meditated on the kind of treatment that he, the nominee of Pharaoh Necho, was likely to receive from Nebuchadnezzar. We cannot tell whether he contemplated resistance or had already resolved to submit to the conqueror.

In either case he would wish to act on his own initiative, and might be anxious lest a Chaldean party should get the upper hand in Jerusalem and surrender him and the city to the invader.

When the princes entered, their number and their manner would at once indicate to him that their errand was both serious and disagreeable. He seems to have listened in silence while they made their report of the incident at the door of Gemariah's chamber and their own interview with Baruch. [42] The king sent for the roll by Jehudi, who had accompanied the princes into the presence chamber; and on his return the same serviceable official read its contents before Jehoiakim and the princes, whose number was now augmented by the nobles in attendance upon the king. Jehudi had had the advantage of hearing Baruch read the roll, but ancient Hebrew manuscripts were not easy to decipher, and probably Jehudi stumbled somewhat; altogether the reading of prophecies by a court-usher would not be a very edifying performance, or very gratifying to Jeremiah's friends. Jehoiakim treated the matter with deliberate and ostentatious contempt. At the end of every three or four columns, [43] he put out his hand for the roll, cut away the portion that had been read, and threw it on the fire; then he handed the remainder back to Jehudi, and the reading was resumed till the king thought fit to repeat the process. It at once appeared that the audience was divided into two parties. When Gemariah's father, Shaphan, had read Deuteronomy to Josiah, the king rent his clothes; but now the writer tells us, half aghast, that neither Jehoiakim nor any of his servants were afraid or rent their clothes, but the audience, including doubtless both court officials and some of the princes, looked on with calm indifference. Not so the princes who had been present at Baruch's reading: they had probably induced him to leave the roll with them, by promising that it should be kept safely; they had tried to keep it out of the king's hands by leaving it in Elishama's room, and now they made another attempt to save it from destruction. They entreated Jehoiakim to refrain from open and insolent defiance of a prophet who might after all be speaking in the name of Jehovah. But the king persevered. The alternate reading and burning went on; the unfortunate usher's fluency and clearness would not be improved by the extraordinary conditions under which he had to read; and we may well suppose that the concluding columns were hurried over in a somewhat perfunctory fashion, if they were read at all. As soon as the last shred of parchment was shrivelling on the charcoal, Jehoiakim commanded three of his officers [44] to arrest Jeremiah and Baruch. But they had taken the advice of the princes and were not to be found: "Jehovah hid them."

Thus the career of Baruch's roll was summarily cut short. But it had done its work; it had been read on three separate occasions, first before the people, then before the princes, and last of all before the king and his court. If Jeremiah had appeared in person, he might have been at once arrested, and put to death like Uriah. No doubt this threefold recital was, on the whole, a failure; Jeremiah's party among the princes had listened with anxious deference, but the appeal had been received by the people with indifference and by the king with contempt. Nevertheless it must have strengthened individuals in the true faith, and it had proclaimed afresh that the religion of Jehovah gave no sanction to the policy of Jehoiakim: the ruin of Judah would be a proof of the sovereignty of Jehovah and not of His impotence. But probably this incident had more immediate influence over the king than we might at first sight suppose. When Nebuchadnezzar arrived in Palestine, Jehoiakim submitted to him, a policy entirely in accordance with the views of Jeremiah. We may well believe that the experiences of this fast-day had strengthened the hands of the prophet's friends, and cooled the enthusiasm of the court for more desperate and adventurous courses. Every year's respite for Judah fostered the growth of the true religion of Jehovah.

The sequel showed how much more prudent it was to risk the existence of a roll rather than the life of a prophet. Jeremiah was only encouraged to persevere. By the Divine command, he dictated his prophecies afresh to Baruch, adding besides unto them many like words. Possibly other copies were made of the whole or parts of this roll, and were secretly circulated, read, and talked about. We are not told whether Jehoiakim ever heard this new roll; but, as one of the many like things added to the older prophecies was a terrible personal condemnation of the king, [45] we may be sure that he was not allowed to remain in ignorance, at any rate, of this portion of it.

The second roll was, doubtless, one of the main sources of our present Book of Jeremiah, and the narrative of this chapter is of considerable importance for Old Testament criticism. It shows that a prophetic book may not go back to any prophetic autograph at all; its most original sources may be manuscripts written at the prophet's dictation, and liable to all the errors which are apt to creep into the most faithful work of an amanuensis. It shows further that, even when a prophet's utterances were written down during his lifetime, the manuscript may contain only his recollections [46] of what he said years before, and that these might be either expanded or abbreviated, sometimes even unconsciously modified, in the light of subsequent events. Verse 32 shows that Jeremiah did not hesitate to add to the record of his former prophecies "many like words": there is no reason to suppose that these were all contained in an appendix; they would often take the form of annotations.

The important part played by Baruch as Jeremiah's secretary and representative must have invested him with full authority to speak for his master and expound his views; such authority points to Baruch as the natural editor of our present book, which is virtually the "Life and Writings" of the prophet. The last words of our chapter are ambiguous, perhaps intentionally. They simply state that many like words were added, and do not say by whom; they might even include additions made later on by Baruch from his own reminiscences.

In conclusion, we may notice that both the first and second copies of the roll were written by the direct Divine command, just as in the Hexateuch and the Book of Samuel we read of Moses, Joshua, and Samuel committing certain matters to writing at the bidding of Jehovah. We have here the recognition of the inspiration of the scribe, as ancillary to that of the prophet. Jehovah not only gives His word to His servants, but watches over its preservation and transmission. [47] But there is no inspiration to write any new revelation: the spoken word, the consecrated life, are inspired; the book is only a record of inspired speech and action.

Footnotes:

26. See Cheyne, Giesebrecht, Orelli, etc.
27. R.V. "against." The Hebrew is ambiguous.
28. So Septuagint. The Hebrew text has Israel, which is a less accurate description of the prophecies, and is less relevant to this particular occasion.
29. Jeremiah (Men of the Bible), p. 132.
30. Cf. Chap. V. on "Baruch."
31. Verses 5-8 seem to be a brief alternative account to 9-26.
32. 1 Chron. xx. i.
33. 'ACÃ   ☐RarÃiV.,"rÌsÌVaiŕìsÌdúÎt ÎpÌ;tÌrÌM is used in xxxiii. 1, xxxix. 15, in the sense of "imprisoned," but here Jeremiah appears to be at liberty. The phrase 'AC?Ã   "ÌRuÌVuÌ^ZÃÎaÎBÎ¹ÌJDtuÌV_ xxxii. 36, etc.), has been understood, those under the restraints imposed upon ceremonial uncleanness and those free from these restraints, i.e. everybody; the same meaning has been given to 'AC?Ã   ☐R here.
34. xxvi. 2.
35. So Cheyne; the Hebrew does not make it clear whether the title "scribe" refers to the father or the son. Giesebrecht understands it of Shaphan, who appears as scribe in 2 Kings xxii. 8. He points out that in verse 20 Elishama is called the scribe, but we cannot assume that the title was limited to a single officer of state.
36. Cf. xxvi. 10.
37. Isa. lviii. 3-8.
38. Micah vi. 6-8.
39. So Orelli, in loco.
40. Hebrew text "to Baruch," which LXX. omits.
41. In verse 18 the word "with ink" is not in the LXX., and may be an accidental repetition of the similar word for "his mouth."
42. The A.V. and R.V. "all the words" is misleading: it should rather be "everything"; the princes did not recite all the contents of the roll.
43. The English tenses "cut," "cast," are ambiguous, but the Hebrew implies that the "cutting" and "casting on the fire" were repeated again and again.
44. One is called Jerahmeel the son of Hammelech (A.V.), or "the king's son" (R.V.); if the latter is correct we must understand merely a prince of the blood-royal and not a son of Jehoiakim, who was only thirty.
45. For verses 29-31 see Chap. [155]VI., where they are dealt with in connection with xxii. 13-19.
46. The supposition that Jeremiah had written notes of previous prophecies is not an impossible one, but it is a pure conjecture.
47. Cf. Orelli, in loco.

CHAPTER IV

THE RECHABITES

xxxv.

"Jonadab the son of Rechab shall not want a man to stand before Me for ever."--Jer. xxxv. 19.

This incident is dated "in the days of Jehoiakim." We learn from verse 11 that it happened at a time when the open country of Judah was threatened by the advance of Nebuchadnezzar with a Chaldean and Syrian army. If Nebuchadnezzar marched into the south of Palestine immediately after the battle of Carchemish, the incident may have happened, as some suggest, in the eventful fourth year of Jehoiakim; or if he did not appear in the neighbourhood of Jerusalem till after he had taken over the royal authority at Babylon, Jeremiah's interview with the Rechabites may have followed pretty closely upon the destruction of Baruch's roll. But we need not press the words "Nebuchadnezzar ... came up into the land"; they may only mean that Judah was invaded by an army acting under his orders. The mention of Chaldeans and Assyrians suggests that this invasion is the same as that mentioned in 2 Kings xxiv. 1, 2, where we are told that Jehoiakim served Nebuchadnezzar three years and then rebelled against him, whereupon Jehovah sent against him bands of Chaldeans, Syrians, Moabites, and Ammonites, and sent them against Judah to destroy it. If this is the invasion referred to in our chapter it falls towards the end of Jehoiakim's reign, and sufficient time had elapsed to allow the king's anger against Jeremiah to cool, so that the prophet could venture out of his hiding-place.

The marauding bands of Chaldeans and their allies had driven the country people in crowds into Jerusalem, and among them the nomad clan of the Rechabites. According to 1 Chron. ii. 55, the Rechabites traced their descent to a certain Hemath, and were a branch of the Kenites, an Edomite tribe dwelling for the most part in the south of Palestine. These Kenites had maintained an ancient and intimate alliance with Judah, and in time the allies virtually became a single people, so that after the Return from the Captivity all distinction of race between Kenites and Jews was forgotten, and the Kenites were reckoned among the families of Israel. In this fusion of their tribe with Judah, the Rechabite clan would be included. It is clear from all the references both to Kenites and to Rechabites that they had adopted the religion of Israel and worshipped Jehovah. We know nothing else of the early history of the Rechabites. The statement in Chronicles that the father of the house of Rechab was Hemath perhaps points to their having been at one time settled at some place called Hemath near Jabez in Judah. Possibly too Rechab, which means "rider," is not a personal name, but a designation of the clan as horsemen of the desert.

These Rechabites were conspicuous among the Jewish farmers and townsfolk by their rigid adherence to the habits of nomad life; and it was this peculiarity that attracted the notice of Jeremiah, and made them a suitable object-lesson to the recreant Jews. The traditional customs of the clan had been formulated into positive commands by Jonadab, the son of Rechab, i.e. the Rechabite. This must be the same Jonadab who co-operated with Jehu in overthrowing the house of Omri and suppressing the worship of Baal. Jehu's reforms concluded the long struggle of Elijah and Elisha against the house of Omri and its half-heathen religion. Hence we may infer that Jonadab and his Rechabites had come under the influence of these great prophets, and that their social and religious condition was one result of Elijah's work. Jeremiah stood in the true line of succession from the northern prophets in his attitude towards religion and politics; so that there would be bonds of sympathy between him and these nomad refugees.

The laws or customs of Jonadab, like the Ten Commandments, were chiefly negative: "Ye shall drink no wine, neither ye nor your sons for ever: neither shall ye build houses, nor sow seed, nor plant vineyards, nor have any: but all your days ye shall dwell in tents; that ye may live many days in the land wherein ye are strangers."

Various parallels have been found to the customs of the Rechabites. The Hebrew Nazarites abstained from wine and strong drink, from grapes and grape juice and everything made of the vine, "from the kernels even to the husk." [48] Mohammed forbade his followers to drink any sort of wine or strong drink. But the closest parallel is one often quoted from Diodorus Siculus, [49] who, writing about b.c. 8, tells us that the Nabatean Arabs were prohibited under the penalty of death from sowing corn or planting fruit trees, using wine or building houses. Such abstinence is not primarily ascetic; it expresses the universal contempt of the wandering hunter and herdsman for tillers of the ground, who are tied to one small spot of earth, and for burghers, who further imprison themselves in narrow houses and behind city walls. The nomad has a not altogether unfounded instinct that such acceptance of material restraints emasculates both soul and body. A remarkable parallel to the laws of Jonadab ben Rechab is found in the injunctions of the dying highlander, Ranald of the Mist, to his heir: "Son of the Mist! be free as thy forefathers. Own no lord--receive no law--take no hire--give no stipend--build no hut--enclose no pasture--sow no grain." [50] The Rechabite faith in the higher moral value of their primitive habits had survived their alliance with Israel, and Jonadab did his best to protect his clan from the taint of city life and settled civilisation. Abstinence from wine was not enjoined chiefly, if at all, to guard against intoxication, but because the fascinations of the grape might tempt the clan to plant vineyards, or, at any rate, would make them dangerously dependent upon vine-dressers and wine-merchants.

Till this recent invasion, the Rechabites had faithfully observed their ancestral laws, but the stress of circumstances had now driven them into a fortified city, possibly even into houses, though it is more probable that they were encamped in some open space within the walls. [51] Jeremiah was commanded to go and bring them into the Temple, that is, into one of the rooms in the Temple buildings, and offer them wine. The narrative proceeds in the first person, "I took Jaazaniah," so that the chapter will have been composed by the prophet himself. In somewhat legal fashion he tells us how he took "Jaazaniah ben Jeremiah, ben Habaziniah, and his brethren, and all his sons, and all the clan of the Rechabites." All three names are compounded of the Divine name Iah, Jehovah, and serve to emphasise the devotion of the clan to the God of Israel. It is a curious coincidence that the somewhat rare name Jeremiah [52] should occur twice in this connection. The room to which the prophet took his friends is described as the chamber of the disciples of the man of God [53] Hanan ben Igdaliah, which was by the chamber of the princes, which was above the chamber of the keeper of the threshold, Maaseiah ben Shallum. Such minute details probably indicate that this chapter was committed to writing while these buildings were still standing and still had the same occupants as at the time of this incident, but to us the topography is unintelligible. The "man of God" or prophet Hanan was evidently in sympathy with Jeremiah, and had a following of disciples who formed a sort of school of the prophets, and were a sufficiently permanent body to have a chamber assigned to them in the Temple buildings. The keepers of the threshold were Temple officials of high standing. The "princes" may have been the princes of Judah, who might very well have a chamber in the Temple courts; but the term is general, and may simply refer to other Temple officials. Hanan's disciples seem to have been in good company.

These exact specifications of person and place are probably designed to give a certain legal solemnity and importance to the incident, and seem to warrant us in rejecting Reuss' suggestion that our narrative is simply an elaborate prophetic figure. [54]

After these details Jeremiah next tells us how he set before his guests bowls of wine and cups, and invited them to drink. Probably Jaazaniah and his clansmen were aware that the scene was intended to have symbolic religious significance. They would not suppose that the prophet had invited them all, in this solemn fashion, merely to take a cup of wine; and they would welcome an opportunity of showing their loyalty to their own peculiar customs. They said: "We will drink no wine: for our father Jonadab the son of Rechab commanded us, saying, Ye shall drink no wine, neither ye nor your sons for ever." They further recounted Jonadab's other commands and their own scrupulous obedience in every point, except that now they had been compelled to seek refuge in a walled city.

Then the word of Jehovah came unto Jeremiah; he was commanded to make yet another appeal to the Jews, by contrasting their disobedience with the fidelity of the Rechabites. The Divine King and Father of Israel had been untiring in His instruction and admonitions: "I have spoken unto you, rising up early and speaking." He had addressed them in familiar fashion through their fellow-countrymen: "I have sent also unto you all My servants the prophets, rising up early and sending them." Yet they had not hearkened unto the God of Israel or His prophets. The Rechabites had received no special revelation; they had not been appealed to by numerous prophets. Their Torah had been simply given them by their father Jonadab; nevertheless the commands of Jonadab had been regarded and those of Jehovah had been treated with contempt.

Obedience and disobedience would bring forth their natural fruit. "I will bring upon Judah, and upon all the inhabitants of Jerusalem, all the evil that I have pronounced against them: because I have spoken unto them, but they have not heard; and I have called unto them, but they have not answered." But because the Rechabites obeyed the commandment of their father Jonadab, "Therefore thus saith Jehovah Sabaoth, Jonadab the son of Rechab shall not want a man to stand before Me for ever."

Jehovah's approval of the obedience of the Rechabites is quite independent of the specific commands which they obeyed. It does not bind us to abstain from wine any more than from building houses and sowing seed. Jeremiah himself, for instance, would have had no more hesitation in drinking wine than in sowing his field at Anathoth. The tribal customs of the Rechabites had no authority whatever over him. Nor is it exactly his object to set forth the merit of obedience and its certain and great reward. These truths are rather touched upon incidentally. What Jeremiah seeks to emphasise is the gross, extreme, unique wickedness of Israel's disobedience. Jehovah had not looked for any special virtue in His people. His Torah was not made up of counsels of perfection. He had only expected the loyalty that Moab paid to Chemosh, and Tyre and Sidon to Baal. He would have been satisfied if Israel had observed His laws as faithfully as the nomads of the desert kept up their ancestral habits. Jehovah had spoken through Jeremiah long ago and said: "Pass over the isles of Chittim, and see; and send unto Kedar, and consider diligently, and see if there be any such thing. Hath a nation changed their gods, which are yet no gods? but My people have changed their glory for that which doth not profit." [55] Centuries later Christ found Himself constrained to upbraid the cities of Israel, "wherein most of His mighty works were done": "Woe unto thee, Chorazin! woe unto thee, Bethsaida! for if the mighty works which were done in you had been done in Tyre and Sidon, they would have repented long ago in sackcloth and ashes.... It shall be more tolerable for Tyre and Sidon at the day of judgment than for you." [56] And again and again in the history of the Church the Holy Spirit has been grieved because those who profess and call themselves Christians, and claim to prophesy and do many mighty works in the name of Christ, are less loyal to the gospel than the heathen to their own superstitions.

Buddhists and Mohammedans have been held up as modern examples to rebuke the Church, though as a rule with scant justification. Perhaps material for a more relevant contrast may be found nearer home. Christian societies have been charged with conducting their affairs by methods to which a respectable business firm would not stoop; they are said to be less scrupulous in their dealings and less chivalrous in their honour than the devotees of pleasure; at their gatherings they are sometimes supposed to lack the mutual courtesy of members of a Legislature or a Chamber of Commerce. The history of councils and synods and Church meetings gives colour to such charges, which could never have been made if Christians had been as jealous for the Name of Christ as a merchant is for his credit or a soldier for his honour.

And yet these contrasts do not argue any real moral and religious superiority of the Rechabites over the Jews or of unbelievers over professing Christians. It was comparatively easy to abstain from wine and to wander over wide pasture lands instead of living cooped up in cities--far easier than to attain to the great ideals of Deuteronomy and the prophets. It is always easier to conform to the code of business and society than to live according to the Spirit of Christ. The fatal sin of Judah was not that it fell so far short of its ideals, but that it repudiated them. So long as we lament our own failures and still cling to the Name and Faith of Christ, we are not shut out from mercy; our supreme sin is to crucify Christ afresh, by denying the power of His gospel, while we retain its empty form.

The reward promised to the Rechabites for their obedience was that "Jonadab the son of Rechab shall not want a man to stand before Me for ever"; to stand before Jehovah is often used to describe the exercise of priestly or prophetic ministry. It has been suggested that the Rechabites were hereby promoted to the status of the true Israel, "a kingdom of priests"; but this phrase may merely mean that their clan should continue in existence. Loyal observance of national law, the subordination of individual caprice and selfishness to the interests of the community, make up a large part of that righteousness that establisheth a nation.

Here, as elsewhere, students of prophecy have been anxious to discover some literal fulfilment; and have searched curiously for any trace of the continued existence of the Rechabites. The notice in Chronicles implies that they formed part of the Jewish community of the Restoration. Apparently Alexandrian Jews were acquainted with Rechabites at a still later date. Psalm lxxi. is ascribed by the Septuagint to "the sons of Jonadab." Eusebius [57] mentions "priests of the sons of Rechab," and Benjamin of Tudela, a Jewish traveller of the twelfth century, states that he met with them in Arabia. More recent travellers have thought that they discovered the descendants of Rechab amongst the nomads in Arabia or the Peninsula of Sinai that still practised the old ancestral customs.

But the fidelity of Jehovah to His promises does not depend upon our unearthing obscure tribes in distant deserts. The gifts of God are without repentance, but they have their inexorable conditions; no nation can flourish for centuries on the virtues of its ancestors. The Rechabites may have vanished in the ordinary stream of history, and yet we can hold that Jeremiah's prediction has been fulfilled and is still being fulfilled. No scriptural prophecy is limited in its application to an individual or a race, and every nation possessed by the spirit of true patriotism shall "stand before Jehovah for ever."

Footnotes:

48. Num. vi. 2.
49. xix. 94.
50. Scott, Legend of Montrose, chap. xxii.
51. The term "house of the Rechabites" in verse 2 means "family" or "clan," and does not refer to a building.
52. Eight Jeremiahs occur in O.T.
53. Literally "sons of Hanan."
54. Jeremiah, according to this view, had no interview with the Rechabites, but made an imaginary

incident a text for his discourse.
    55. ii. 10, 11.
    56. Matt. xi. 21, 22.
    57. Ch. Hist., ii. 23.

CHAPTER V

BARUCH

xlv.

"Thy life will I give unto thee for a prey."--Jer. xlv. 5.

The editors of the versions and of the Hebrew text of the Old Testament have assigned a separate chapter to this short utterance concerning Baruch; thus paying an unconscious tribute to the worth and importance of Jeremiah's disciple and secretary, who was the first to bear the familiar Jewish name, which in its Latinised form of Benedict has been a favourite with saints and popes. Probably few who read of these great ascetics and ecclesiastics give a thought to the earliest recorded Baruch, nor can we suppose that Christian Benedicts have been named after him. One thing they may all have in common: either their own faith or that of their parents ventured to bestow upon a "man born unto trouble as the sparks fly upward" the epithet "Blessed." We can scarcely suppose that the life of any Baruch or Benedict has run so smoothly as to prevent him or his friends from feeling that such faith has not been outwardly justified and that the name suggested an unkind satire. Certainly Jeremiah's disciple, like his namesake Baruch Spinoza, had to recognise his blessings disguised as distress and persecution.

Baruch ben Neriah is said by Josephus [58] to have belonged to a most distinguished family, and to have been exceedingly well educated in his native language. These statements are perhaps legitimate deductions from the information supplied by our book. His title "scribe" [59] and his position as Jeremiah's secretary imply that he possessed the best culture of his time; and we are told in li. 59 that Seraiah ben Neriah, who must be Baruch's brother, was chief chamberlain (R.V.) to Zedekiah. According to the Old Latin Version of the Apocryphal Book of Baruch (i. 1) he was of the tribe of Simeon, a statement by no means improbable in view of the close connection between Judah and Simeon, but needing the support of some better authority.

Baruch's relation to Jeremiah is not expressly defined, but it is clearly indicated in the various narratives in which he is referred to. We find him in constant attendance upon the prophet, acting both as his "scribe," or secretary, and as his mouthpiece. The relation was that of Joshua to Moses, of Elisha to Elijah, of Gehazi to Elisha, of Mark to Paul and Barnabas, and of Timothy to Paul. It is described in the case of Joshua and Mark by the term "minister," while Elisha is characterised as having "poured water on the hands of Elijah." The "minister" was at once personal attendant, disciple, representative, and possible successor of the prophet. The position has its analogue in the service of the squire to the mediæval knight, and in that of an unpaid private secretary to a modern cabinet minister. Squires expected to become knights, and private secretaries hope for a seat in future cabinets. Another less perfect parallel is the relation of the members of a German theological "seminar" to their professor.

Baruch is first [60] introduced to us in the narrative concerning the roll. He appears as Jeremiah's amanuensis and representative, and is entrusted with the dangerous and honourable task of publishing his prophecies to the people in the Temple. Not long before, similar utterances had almost cost the master his life, so that the disciple showed high courage and devotion in undertaking such a commission. He was called to share with his master at once the same cup of persecution--and the same Divine protection.

We next hear of Baruch in connection with the symbolic purchase of the field at Anathoth. [61] He seems to have been attending on Jeremiah during his imprisonment in the court of the guard, and the documents containing the evidence of the purchase were entrusted to his care. Baruch's presence in the court of the guard does not necessarily imply that he was himself a prisoner. The whole incident shows that Jeremiah's friends had free access to him; and Baruch probably not only attended to his master's wants in prison, but also was his channel of communication with the outside world.

We are nowhere told that Baruch himself was either beaten or imprisoned, but it is not improbable that he shared Jeremiah's fortunes even to these extremities. We next hear of him as carried down to Egypt [62] with Jeremiah, when the Jewish refugees fled thither after the murder of Gedaliah. Apparently he had remained with Jeremiah throughout the whole interval, had continued to minister to him during his imprisonment, and had been among the crowd of Jewish captives whom Nebuchadnezzar found at Ramah. Josephus probably makes a similar conjecture [63] in telling us that, when Jeremiah was released and placed under the protection of Gedaliah at Mizpah, he asked and obtained from Nebuzaradan the liberty of his disciple Baruch. At any rate Baruch shared with his master the transient hope and bitter disappointment of this period; he supported him in dissuading the remnant of Jews from fleeing into Egypt, and was also compelled to share their flight. According to a tradition recorded by Jerome, Baruch and Jeremiah died in Egypt. But the Apocryphal Book of Baruch places him at Babylon, whither another tradition takes him after the death of Jeremiah in Egypt. [64] These legends are probably mere attempts of wistful imagination to supply unwelcome blanks in history.

It has often been supposed that our present Book of Jeremiah, in some stage of its formation, was edited or compiled by Baruch, and that this book may be ranked with biographies--like Stanley's Life of Arnold--of great teachers by their old disciples. He was certainly the amanuensis of the roll, which must have been the most valuable authority for any editor of Jeremiah's prophecies. And the amanuensis might very easily become the editor. If an edition of the book was compiled in Jeremiah's lifetime, we should naturally expect him to use Baruch's assistance; if it first took shape after the prophet's death, and if Baruch survived, no one would be better able to compile the "Life and Works of Jeremiah" than his favourite and faithful disciple. The personal prophecy about Baruch does not occur in its proper place in connection with the episode of the roll, but is appended at the end of the prophecies, [65] possibly as a kind of subscription on the part of the editor. These data do not constitute absolute proof, but they afford strong probability that Baruch compiled a book, which was substantially our Jeremiah. The evidence is similar in character to, but much more conclusive than, that adduced for the authorship of the Epistle to the Hebrews by Apollos.

Almost the final reference to Baruch suggests another aspect of his relation to Jeremiah. The Jewish captains accused him of unduly influencing his master against Egypt and in favour of Chaldea. Whatever truth there may have been in this particular charge, we gather that popular opinion credited Baruch with considerable influence over Jeremiah, and probably popular opinion was not far wrong. Nothing said about Baruch suggests any vein of weakness in his character, such as Paul evidently recognised in Timothy. His few appearances upon the scene rather leave the impression of strength and self-reliance, perhaps even self-assertion. If we knew more about him, possibly indeed if any one else had compiled these "Memorabilia," we might discover that much in Jeremiah's policy and teaching was due to Baruch, and that the master leaned somewhat heavily upon the sympathy of the disciple. The qualities that make a successful man of action do not always exempt their possessor from being directed or even controlled by his followers. It would be interesting to discover how much of Luther is Melanchthon. Of many a great minister, his secretaries and subordinates might say safely, in private, Cujus pars magna fuimus.

The short prophecy which has furnished a text for this chapter shows that Jeremiah was not unaware of Baruch's tendency to self-assertion, and even felt that sometimes it required a check. Apparently chapter xlv. once formed the immediate continuation of chapter xxxvi., the narrative of the incident of the roll. It was "the word spoken by Jeremiah the prophet to Baruch ben Neriah, when he wrote these words in a book at the dictation of Jeremiah in the fourth year of Jehoiakim." The reference evidently is to xxxvi. 32, where we are told that Baruch wrote, at Jeremiah's dictation, all the words of the book that had been burnt, and many like words.

Clearly Baruch had not received Jeremiah's message as to the sin and ruin of Judah without strong protest. It was as distasteful to him as to all patriotic Jews and even to Jeremiah himself. Baruch had not yet been able to accept this heavy burden or to look beyond to the brighter promise of the future. He broke out into bitter complaint: "Woe is me now! for Jehovah hath added sorrow to my pain; I am weary with my groaning, and find no rest." [66] Strong as these words are, they are surpassed by many of Jeremiah's complaints to Jehovah, and doubtless even now they found an echo in the prophet's heart. Human impatience of suffering revolts desperately against the conviction that calamity is inevitable; hope whispers that some unforeseen Providence will yet disperse the storm-clouds, and the portents of ruin will dissolve like some evil dream. Jeremiah had, now as always, the harsh, unwelcome task of compelling himself and his fellows to face the sad and appalling reality. "Thus saith Jehovah, Behold, I am breaking down that which I built, I am plucking up that which I planted." [67] This was his familiar message concerning Judah, but he had also a special word for Baruch: "And as for thee, dost thou seek great things for thyself?" What "great things" could a devout and patriotic Jew, a disciple of Jeremiah, seek for himself in those disastrous times? The answer is at once suggested by the renewed prediction of doom. Baruch, in spite of his master's teaching, had still ventured to look for better things, and had perhaps fancied that he might succeed where Jeremiah had failed and might become the mediator who should reconcile Israel to Jehovah. He may have thought that Jeremiah's threats and entreaties had prepared the way for some message of reconciliation. Gemariah ben Shaphan and other princes had been greatly moved when Baruch read the roll. Might not their emotion be an earnest of the repentance of the people? If he could carry on his master's work to a more blessed issue than the master himself had dared to hope, would not this be a "great thing" indeed? We gather from the tone of the chapter that Baruch's aspirations were unduly tinged with personal ambition. While kings, priests, and prophets were sinking into a common ruin from which even the most devoted servants of Jehovah would not escape, Baruch was indulging himself in visions of the honour to be obtained from a glorious mission, successfully accomplished. Jeremiah reminds him that he will have to take his share in the common misery. Instead of setting his heart upon "great things" which are not according to the Divine purpose, he must be prepared to endure with resignation the evil which Jehovah "is bringing upon all flesh." Yet there is a word of comfort and promise: "I will give thee thy life for a prey in all places whither thou goest." Baruch was to be protected from violent or premature death.

According to Renan, [68] this boon was flung to Baruch half-contemptuously, in order to silence his unworthy and unseasonable importunity:--

"Dans une catastrophe qui va englober l'humanité tout entière, il est beau de venir réclamer de petites faveurs d'exception! Baruch aura la vie sauve partout où il ira; qu'il s'en contente!"

We prefer a more generous interpretation. To a selfish man, unless indeed he clung to bare life in craven terror or mere animal tenacity, such an existence as Baruch was promised would have seemed no boon at all. Imprisonment in a besieged and starving city, captivity and exile, his fellow-countrymen's ill-will and resentment from first to last--these experiences would be hard to recognise as privileges bestowed by Jehovah. Had Baruch been wholly self-centred, he might well have craved death instead, like Job, nay, like Jeremiah himself. But life meant for him continued ministry to his master, the high privilege of supporting him in his witness to Jehovah. If, as seems almost certain, we owe to Baruch the preservation of Jeremiah's prophecies, then indeed the life that was given him for a prey must have been precious to him as the devoted servant of God. Humanly speaking, the future of revealed religion and of Christianity depended on the survival of Jeremiah's teaching, and this hung upon the frail thread of Baruch's life. After all, Baruch was destined to achieve "great things," even though not those which he sought after; and as no editor's name is prefixed to our book, he cannot be accused of self-seeking. So too for every faithful disciple, his life, even if given for a prey, even if spent in sorrow, poverty, and pain, is still a Divine gift, because nothing can spoil its opportunity of ministering to men and glorifying God, even if only by patient endurance of suffering.

We may venture on a wider application of the promise, "Thy life shall be given thee for a prey." Life is not merely continued existence in the body: life has come to mean spirit and character, so that Christ could say, "He that loseth his life for My sake shall find it." In this sense the loyal servant of God wins as his prey, out of all painful experiences, a fuller and nobler life. Other rewards may come in due season, but this is the most certain and the most sufficient. For Baruch, constant devotion to a hated and persecuted master, uncompromising utterance of unpopular truth, had their chief issue in the redemption of his own inward life.

Footnotes:

58. Antt., x. 9, 1.
59. xxxvi. 26, 32.
60. In order of time, ch. xxxvi.
61. xxxii.
62. xliii.
63. Antt., x. 9, 1.
64. Bissell's Introduction to Baruch in Lange's Commentary.
65. So LXX., which here probably gives the true order.
66. The clause "I am weary with my groaning" also occurs in Psalm vi. 6.
67. The concluding clause of the verse is omitted by LXX., and is probably a gloss added to indicate that the ruin would not be confined to Judah, but would extend "over the whole earth." Cf. Kautzsch.
68. Hist. of Israel, iii., 293.

CHAPTER VI

THE JUDGMENT ON JEHOIAKIM

xxii. 13-19, xxxvi. 30, 31.

"Jehoiakim ... slew him (Uriah) with the sword, and cast his dead body into the graves of the common people."--Jer. xxvi. 23.

"Therefore thus saith Jehovah concerning Jehoiakim, ... He shall be buried with the burial of an ass, drawn and cast forth beyond the gates of Jerusalem."--Jer. xxii. 18, 19.

"Jehoiakim ... did that which was evil in the sight of Jehovah, according to all that his fathers had done."--2 Kings xxiii. 36, 37.

Our last four chapters have been occupied with the history of Jeremiah during the reign of Jehoiakim, and therefore necessarily with the relations of the prophet to the king and his government. Before we pass on to the reigns of Jehoiachin and Zedekiah, we must consider certain utterances which deal with the personal character and career of Jehoiakim. We are helped to appreciate these passages by what we here read, and by the brief paragraph concerning this reign in the Second Book of Kings. In Jeremiah the king's policy and conduct are specially illustrated by two incidents, the murder of the prophet Uriah and the destruction of the roll. The historian states his judgment of the reign, but his brief record [69] adds little to our knowledge of the sovereign.

Jehoiakim was placed upon the throne as the nominee and tributary of Pharaoh Necho; but he had the address or good fortune to retain his authority under Nebuchadnezzar, by transferring his allegiance to the new suzerain of Western Asia. When a suitable opportunity offered, the unwilling and discontented vassal naturally "turned and rebelled against" his lord. Even then his good fortune did not forsake him; although in his latter days Judah was harried by predatory bands of Chaldeans, Syrians, Moabites, and Ammonites, yet Jehoiakim "slept with his fathers" before Nebuchadnezzar had set to work in earnest to chastise his refractory subject. He was not reserved, like Zedekiah, to endure agonies of mental and physical torture, and to rot in a Babylonian dungeon.

Jeremiah's judgment upon Jehoiakim and his doings is contained in the two passages which form the subject of this chapter. The utterance in xxxvi. 30, 31, was evoked by the destruction of the roll, and we may fairly assume that xxii. 13-19 was also delivered after that incident. The immediate context of the latter paragraph throws no light on the date of its origin. Chapter xxii. is a series of judgments on the successors of Josiah, and was certainly composed after the deposition of Jehoiachin, probably during the reign of Zedekiah; but the section on Jehoiakim must have been uttered at an earlier period. Renan indeed imagines [70] that Jeremiah delivered this discourse at the gate of the royal palace at the very beginning of the new reign. The nominee of Egypt was scarcely seated on the throne, his "new name" Jehoiakim--"He whom Jehovah establisheth"--still sounded strange in his ears, when the prophet of Jehovah publicly menaced the king with condign punishment. Renan is naturally surprised that Jehoiakim tolerated Jeremiah, even for a moment. But, here as often elsewhere, the French critic's dramatic instinct has warped his estimate of evidence. We need not accept the somewhat unkind saying that picturesque anecdotes are never true, but, at the same time, we have always to guard against the temptation to accept the most dramatic interpretation of history as the most accurate. The contents of this passage, the references to robbery, oppression, and violence, clearly imply that Jehoiakim had reigned long enough for his government to reveal itself as hopelessly corrupt. The final breach between the king and the prophet was marked by the destruction of the roll, and xxii. 13-19, like xxxvi. 30, 31, may be considered a consequence of this breach.

Let us now consider these utterances. In xxxvi. 30a we read, "Therefore thus saith Jehovah concerning Jehoiakim king of Judah, He shall have none to sit upon the throne of David." Later on, [71] a like judgment was pronounced upon Jehoiakim's son and successor Jehoiachin. The absence of this threat from xxii. 13-19 is doubtless due to the fact that the chapter was compiled when the letter of the prediction seemed to have been proved to be false by the accession of Jehoiachin. Its spirit and substance were amply satisfied by the latter's deposition and captivity after a brief reign of a hundred days.

The next clause in the sentence on Jehoiakim runs: "His dead body shall be cast out in the day to the heat, and in the night to the frost." The same doom is repeated in the later prophecy:--

"They shall not lament for him,
Alas my brother! Alas my brother!
They shall not lament for him,
Alas lord! Alas lord! [72]
He shall be buried with the burial of an ass,
Dragged forth and cast away without the gates of Jerusalem."

Jeremiah did not need to draw upon his imagination for this vision of judgment. When the words were uttered, his memory called up the murder of Uriah ben Shemaiah and the dishonour done to his corpse. Uriah's only guilt had been his zeal for the truth that Jeremiah had proclaimed. Though Jehoiakim and his party had not dared to touch Jeremiah or had not been able to reach him, they had struck his influence by killing Uriah. But for their hatred of the master, the disciple might have been spared. And Jeremiah had neither been able to protect him, nor allowed to share his fate. Any generous spirit will understand how Jeremiah's whole nature was possessed and agitated by a tempest of righteous indignation, how utterly humiliated he felt to be compelled to stand by in helpless impotence. And now, when the tyrant had filled up the measure of his iniquity, when the imperious impulse of the Divine Spirit bade the prophet speak the doom of his king, there breaks forth at last the long pent-up cry for vengeance: "Avenge, O Lord, Thy slaughtered saint"--let the persecutor suffer the agony and shame which he inflicted on God's martyr, fling out the murderer's corpse unburied, let it lie and rot upon the dishonoured grave of his victim.

Can we say, Amen? Not perhaps without some hesitation. Yet surely, if our veins run blood and not water, our feelings, had we been in Jeremiah's place, would have been as bitter and our words as fierce. Jehoiakim was more guilty than our Queen Mary, but the memory of the grimmest of the Tudors still stinks in English nostrils. In our own days, we have not had time to forget how men received the news of Hannington's murder at Uganda, and we can imagine what European Christians would say and feel if their missionaries were massacred in China.

And yet, when we read such a treatise as Lactantius wrote Concerning the Deaths of Persecutors, we cannot but recoil. We are shocked at the stern satisfaction he evinces in the miserable ends of Maximin and Galerius, and other enemies of the true faith. Discreet historians have made large use of this work, without thinking it desirable to give an explicit account of its character and spirit. Biographers of Lactantius feel constrained to offer a half-hearted apology for the De Morte Persecutorum. Similarly we find ourselves of one mind with Gibbon, [73] in refusing to derive edification from a sermon in which Constantine the Great, or the bishop who composed it for him, affected to relate the miserable end of all the persecutors of the Church. Nor can we share the exultation of the Covenanters in the Divine judgment which they saw in the death of Claverhouse; and we are not moved to any hearty sympathy with more recent writers, who have tried to illustrate from history the danger of touching the rights and privileges of the Church. Doubtless God will avenge His own elect; nevertheless Nemo me impune lacessit is no seemly motto for the Kingdom of God. Even Greek mythologists taught that it was perilous for men to wield the thunderbolts of Zeus. Still less is the Divine wrath a weapon for men to grasp in their differences and dissensions, even about the things of God. Michael the Archangel, even when contending with the devil he disputed about the body of Moses, durst not bring against him a railing judgment, but said, The Lord rebuke thee. [74]

How far Jeremiah would have shared such modern sentiment, it is hard to say. At any rate his personal feeling is kept in the background; it is postponed to the more patient and deliberate judgment of the Divine Spirit, and subordinated to broad considerations of public morality. We have no right to contrast Jeremiah with our Lord and His proto-martyr Stephen, because we have no prayer of the ancient prophet to rank with, "Father, forgive them; for they know not what they do," or again with, "Lord, lay not this sin to their charge." Christ and His disciple forgave wrongs done to themselves: they did not condone the murder of their brethren. In the Apocalypse, which concludes the English Bible, and was long regarded as God's final revelation, His last word to man, the souls of the martyrs cry out from beneath the altar: "How long, O Master, the holy and true, dost Thou not judge and avenge our blood on them that dwell on the earth?" [75]

Doubtless God will avenge His own elect, and the appeal for justice may be neither ignoble nor vindictive. But such prayers, beyond all others, must be offered in humble submission to the Judge of all. When our righteous indignation claims to pass its own sentence, we do well to remember that our halting intellect and our purblind conscience are ill qualified to sit as assessors of the Eternal Justice.

When Saul set out for Damascus, "breathing out threatening and slaughter against the disciples of the Lord," the survivors of his victims cried out for a swift punishment of the persecutor, and believed that their prayers were echoed by martyred souls in the heavenly Temple. If that ninth chapter of the Acts had recorded how Saul of Tarsus was struck dead by the lightnings of the wrath of God, preachers down all the Christian centuries would have moralised on the righteous Divine judgment. Saul would have found his place in the homiletic Chamber of Horrors with Ananias and Sapphira, Herod and Pilate, Nero and Diocletian. Yet the Captain of our salvation, choosing His lieutenants, passes over many a man with blameless record, and allots the highest post to this blood-stained persecutor. No wonder that Paul, if only in utter self-contempt, emphasised the doctrine of Divine election. Verily God's ways are not our ways and His thoughts are not our thoughts.

Still, however, we easily see that Paul and Jehoiakim belong to two different classes. The persecutor who attempts in honest but misguided zeal to make others endorse his own prejudices, and turn a deaf ear with him to the teaching of the Holy Spirit, must not be ranked with politicians who sacrifice to their own private interests the Revelation and the Prophets of God.

This prediction which we have been discussing of Jehoiakim's shameful end is followed in the passage in chapter xxxvi. by a general announcement of universal judgment, couched in Jeremiah's usual comprehensive style:--

"I will visit their sin upon him and upon his children and upon his servants, and I will bring upon them and the inhabitants of Jerusalem and the men of Judah all the evil which I spake unto them and they did not hearken."

In chapter xxii. the sentence upon Jehoiakim is prefaced by a statement of the crimes for which he was punished. His eyes and his heart were wholly possessed by avarice and cruelty; as an administrator he was active in oppression and violence. [76] But Jeremiah does not confine himself to these general charges; he specifies and emphasises one particular form of Jehoiakim's wrong-doing, the tyrannous exaction of forced labour for his buildings. To the sovereigns of petty Syrian states, old Memphis and Babylon were then what London and Paris are to modern Ameers, Khedives, and Sultans. Circumstances, indeed, did not permit a Syrian prince to visit the Egyptian or Chaldean capital with perfect comfort and unrestrained enjoyment. Ancient Eastern potentates, like mediæval suzerains, did not always distinguish between a guest and a hostage. But the Jewish kings would not be debarred from importing the luxuries and imitating the vices of their conquerors.

Renan says [77] of this period: "L'Egypte était, à cette époque, le pays où les industries de luxe étaient le plus développées. Tout le monde raffolaient, en particulier, de sa carrosserie et de ses meubles ouvragés. Joiaquin et la noblesse de Jérusalem ne songeaient qu'à se procurer ces beaux objets, qui réalisaient ce qu'on avait vu de plus exquis en fait de goût jusque-là."

The supreme luxury of vulgar minds is the use of wealth as a means of display, and monarchs have always delighted in the erection of vast and ostentatious buildings. At this time Egypt and Babylon vied with one another in pretentious architecture. In addition to much useful engineering work, Psammetichus I. made large additions to the temples and public edifices at Memphis, Thebes, Sais, and elsewhere, so that "the entire valley of the Nile became little more than one huge workshop, where stone-cutters and masons, bricklayers and carpenters, laboured incessantly." [78] This activity in building continued even after the disaster to the Egyptian arms at Carchemish.

Nebuchadnezzar had an absolute mania for architecture. His numerous inscriptions are mere catalogues of his achievements in building. His home administration and even his extensive conquests are scarcely noticed; he held them of little account compared with his temples and palaces--"this great Babylon, which I have built for the royal dwelling-place, by the might of my power and for the glory of my majesty." [79] Nebuchadnezzar created most of the magnificence that excited the wonder and admiration of Herodotus a century later.

Jehoiakim had been moved to follow the notable example of Chaldea and Egypt. By a strange irony of fortune, Egypt, once the cynosure of nations, has become in our own time the humble imitator of Western civilisation, and now boulevards have rendered the suburbs of Cairo "a shabby reproduction of modern Paris." Possibly in the eyes of Egyptians and Chaldeans Jehoiakim's efforts only resulted in a "shabby reproduction" of Memphis or Babylon. Nevertheless these foreign luxuries are always expensive; and minor states had not then learnt the art of trading on the resources of their powerful neighbours by means of foreign loans. Moreover Judah had to pay tribute first to Pharaoh Necho, and then to Nebuchadnezzar. The times were bad, and additional taxes for building purposes must have been felt as an intolerable oppression. Naturally the king did not pay for his labour; like Solomon and all other great Eastern despots, he had recourse to the corvee, and for this in particular Jeremiah denounced him.

"Woe unto him that buildeth his house by unrighteousness
And his chambers by injustice;
That maketh his neighbour toil without wages,
And giveth him no hire;
That saith, 'I will build me a wide house
And spacious chambers,'
And openeth out broad windows, with woodwork of cedar
And vermilion painting."
Then the denunciation passes into biting sarcasm:--
"Art thou indeed a king,
Because thou strivest to excel in cedar?" [80]

Poor imitations of Nebuchadnezzar's magnificent structures could not conceal the impotence and dependence of the Jewish king. The pretentiousness of Jehoiakim's buildings challenged a comparison which only reminded men that he was a mere puppet, with its strings pulled now by Egypt and now by Babylon. At best he was only reigning on sufferance.

Jeremiah contrasts Jehoiakim's government both as to justice and dignity with that of Josiah:--

"Did not thy father eat and drink?" [81]
(He was no ascetic, but, like the Son of Man, lived a full, natural, human life.)
"And do judgment and justice?
Then did he prosper.
He judged the cause of the poor and needy,
Then was there prosperity.
Is not this to know Me?
Jehovah hath spoken it."

Probably Jehoiakim claimed by some external observance, or through some subservient priest or prophet, to "know Jehovah"; and Jeremiah repudiates the claim.

Josiah had reigned in the period when the decay of Assyria left Judah dominant in Palestine, until Egypt or Chaldea could find time to gather up the outlying fragments of the shattered empire. The wisdom and justice of the Jewish king had used this breathing space for the advantage and happiness of his people; and during part of his reign Josiah's power seems to have been as extensive as that of any of his predecessors on the throne of Judah. And yet, according to current theology, Jeremiah's appeal to the prosperity of Josiah as a proof of God's approbation was a startling anomaly. Josiah had been defeated and slain at Megiddo in the prime of his manhood, at the age of thirty-nine. None but the most independent and enlightened spirits could believe that the Reformer's premature death, at the moment when his policy had resulted in national disaster, was not an emphatic declaration of Divine displeasure. Jeremiah's contrary belief might be explained and justified. Some such justification is suggested by the prophet's utterance concerning Jehoahaz: "Weep not for the dead, neither bemoan him: but weep sore for him that goeth away." Josiah had reigned with real authority, he died when independence was no longer possible; and therein he was happier and more honourable than his successors, who held a vassal throne by the uncertain tenure of time-serving duplicity, and were for the most part carried into captivity. "The righteous was taken away from the evil to come." [82]

The warlike spirit of classical antiquity and of Teutonic chivalry welcomed a glorious death upon the field of battle:--

"And how can man die better
Than facing fearful odds,
For the ashes of his fathers,
And the temples of his Gods?"

No one spoke of Leonidas as a victim of Divine wrath. Later Judaism caught something of the same temper. Judas MaccabÃ¦us, when in extreme danger, said, "It is better for us to die in battle, than to look upon the evils of our people and our sanctuary"; and later on, when he refused to flee from inevitable death, he claimed that he would leave behind him no stain upon his honour. [83] Islam also is prodigal in its promises of future bliss to those soldiers who fall fighting for its sake.

But the dim and dreary SheÃ´l of the ancient Hebrews was no glorious Valhalla or houri-peopled Paradise. The renown of the battle-field was poor compensation for the warm, full-blooded life of the upper air. When David sang his dirge for Saul and Jonathan, he found no comfort in the thought that they had died fighting for Israel. Moreover the warrior's self-sacrifice for his country seems futile and inglorious, when it neither secures victory nor postpones defeat. And at Megiddo Josiah and his army perished in a vain attempt to come

"Between the pass and fell incensed points
Of mighty opposites."

We can hardly justify to ourselves Jeremiah's use of Josiah's reign as an example of prosperity as the reward of righteousness; his contemporaries must have been still more difficult to convince. We cannot understand how the words of this prophecy were left without any attempt at justification, or why Jeremiah did not meet by anticipation the obvious and apparently crushing rejoinder that the reign terminated in disgrace and disaster.

Nevertheless these difficulties do not affect the terms of the sentence upon Jehoiakim, or the ground upon which he was condemned. We shall be better able to appreciate Jeremiah's attitude and to discover its lessons if we venture to reconsider his decisions. We cannot forget that there was, as Cheyne puts it, a duel between Jeremiah and Jehoiakim; and we should hesitate to accept the verdict of Hildebrand upon Henry IV. of Germany, or of Thomas Ã

Becket on Henry II. of England. Moreover the data upon which we have to base our judgment, including the unfavourable estimate in the Book of Kings, come to us from Jeremiah or his disciples. Our ideas about Queen Elizabeth would be more striking than accurate if our only authorities for her reign were Jesuit historians of England. But Jeremiah is absorbed in lofty moral and spiritual issues; his testimony is not tainted with that sectarian and sacerdotal casuistry which is always so ready to subordinate truth to the interests of "the Church." He speaks of facts with a simple directness which leaves us in no doubt as to their reality; his picture of Jehoiakim may be one-sided, but it owes nothing to an inventive imagination.

Even Renan, who, in Ophite fashion, holds a brief for the bad characters of the Old Testament, does not seriously challenge Jeremiah's statements of fact. But the judgment of the modern critic seems at first sight more lenient than that of the Hebrew prophet: the former sees in Jehoiakim "un prince libÃ§ral et modÃ§rÃ§," [84] but when this favourable estimate is coupled with an apparent comparison with Louis Philippe, we must leave students of modern history to decide whether Renan is really less severe than Jeremiah. Cheyne, on the other hand, holds [85] that "we have no reason to question Jeremiah's verdict upon Jehoiakim, who, alike from a religious and a political point of view, appears to have been unequal to the crisis in the fortunes of Israel." No doubt this is true; and yet perhaps Renan is so far right that Jehoiakim's failure was rather his misfortune than his fault. We may doubt whether any king of Israel or Judah would have been equal to the supreme crisis which Jehoiakim had to face. Our scanty information seems to indicate a man of strong will, determined character, and able statesmanship. Though the nominee of Pharaoh Necho, he retained his sceptre under Nebuchadnezzar, and held his own against Jeremiah and the powerful party by which the prophet was supported. Under more favourable conditions he might have rivalled Uzziah or Jeroboam II. In the time of Jehoiakim, a supreme political and military genius would have been as helpless on the throne of Judah as were the PalÃ¦ologi in the last days of the Empire at Constantinople. Something may be said to extenuate his religious attitude. In opposing Jeremiah he was not defying clear and acknowledged truth. Like the Pharisees in their conflict with Christ, the persecuting king had popular religious sentiment on his side. According to that current theology which had been endorsed in some measure even by Isaiah and Jeremiah, the defeat at Megiddo proved that Jehovah repudiated the religious policy of Josiah and his advisers. The inspiration of the Holy Spirit enabled Jeremiah to resist this shallow conclusion, and to maintain through every crisis his unshaken faith in the profounder truth. Jehoiakim was too conservative to surrender at the prophet's bidding the long-accepted and fundamental doctrine of retribution, and to follow the forward leading of Revelation. He "stood by the old truth" as did Charles V. at the Reformation. "Let him that is without sin" in this matter "first cast a stone at" him.

Though we extenuate Jehoiakim's conduct, we are still bound to condemn it; not however because he was exceptionally wicked, but because he failed to rise above a low spiritual average: yet in this judgment we also condemn ourselves for our own intolerance, and for the prejudice and self-will which have often blinded our eyes to the teachings of our Lord and Master.

But Jeremiah emphasises one special charge against the king--his exaction of forced and unpaid labour. This form of taxation was in itself so universal that the censure can scarcely be directed against its ordinary and moderate exercise. If Jeremiah had intended to inaugurate a new departure, he would have approached the subject in a more formal and less casual fashion. It was a time of national danger and distress, when all moral and material resources were needed to avert the ruin of the state, or at any rate to mitigate the sufferings of the people; and at such a time Jehoiakim exhausted and embittered his subjects--that he might dwell in spacious halls with woodwork of cedar. The Temple and palaces of Solomon had been built at the expense of a popular resentment, which survived for centuries, and with which, as their silence seems to show, the prophets fully sympathised. If even Solomon's exactions were culpable, Jehoiakim was altogether without excuse.

His sin was that common to all governments, the use of the authority of the state for private ends. This sin is possible not only to sovereigns and secretaries of state, but to every town councillor and every one who has a friend on a town council, nay, to every clerk in a public office and to every workman in a government dockyard. A king squandering public revenues on private pleasures, and an artisan pilfering nails and iron with an easy conscience because they only belong to the state, are guilty of crimes essentially the same. On the one hand, Jehoiakim as the head of the state was oppressing individuals; and although modern states have grown comparatively tender as to the rights of the individual, yet even now their action is often cruelly oppressive to insignificant minorities. But, on the other hand, the right of exacting labour was only vested in the king as a public trust; its abuse was as much an injury to the community as to individuals. If Jeremiah had to deal with modern civilisation, we might, perchance, be startled by his passing lightly over our religious and political controversies to denounce the squandering of public resources in the interests of individuals and classes, sects and

The Expositor's Bible: Jeremiah Volumes I & II
parties.

Footnotes:
    69. 2 Kings xxiii. 34-xxiv. 7.
    70. iii. 274.
    71. xxii. 30.
    72. R.V., "Ah my brother! or Ah sister!... Ah lord! or Ah his glory!" The text is based on an emendation of Graetz, following the Syriac. (Giesebrecht.)
    73. Chap. xiii.
    74. Jude 9.
    75. Apc. vi. 10.
    76. xxii. 17. The exact meaning of the word translated "violence" (so A.V., R.V.) is very doubtful.
    77. Hist., etc., iii. 266.
    78. Rawlinson, Ancient Egypt (Story of the Nations).
    79. Dan. iv. 30.
    80. I have followed R.V., but the text is probably corrupt. Cheyne follows LXX. (A) in reading "because thou viest with Ahab": LXX. (B) has "Ahaz" (so Ewald). Giesebrecht proposes to neglect the accents and translate, "viest in cedar buildings with thy father" (i.e. Solomon).
    81. According to Giesebrecht (cf. however the last note) this clause is an objection which the prophet puts into the mouth of the king. "My father enjoyed the good things of life--why should not I?" The prophet rejoins, "Nay, but he did judgment," etc.
    82. Isa. lvii. (English Versions).
    83. Macc. ii. 59, ix. 10.
    84. iii. 269.
    85. P. 142.

CHAPTER VII

JEHOIACHIN [86]

xxii. 20-30.

"*A despised broken vessel,*"--Jer. xxii. 28.
"*A young lion. And he went up and down among the lions, he became a young lion and he learned to catch the prey, he devoured men.*"--Ezek. xix. 5, 6.
"*Jehoiachin ... did evil in the sight of Jehovah, according to all that his father had done.*"--2 Kings xxiv. 8, 9.

We have seen that our book does not furnish a consecutive biography of Jeremiah; we are not even certain as to the chronological order of the incidents narrated. Yet these chapters are clear and full enough to give us an accurate idea of what Jeremiah did and suffered during the eleven years of Jehoiakim's reign. He was forced to stand by while the king lent the weight of his authority to the ancient corruptions of the national religion, and conducted his home and foreign policy without any regard to the will of Jehovah, as expressed by His prophet. His position was analogous to that of a Romanist priest under Elizabeth or a Protestant divine in the reign of James II. According to some critics, Nebuchadnezzar was to Jeremiah what Philip of Spain was to the priest and William of Orange to the Puritan.

During all these long and weary years, the prophet watched the ever multiplying tokens of approaching ruin. He was no passive spectator, but a faithful watchman to the house of Israel; again and again he risked his life in a vain attempt to make his fellow-countrymen aware of their danger. [87] The vision of the coming sword was ever before his eyes, and he blew the trumpet and warned the people; but they would not be warned, and the prophet knew that the sword would come and take them away in their iniquity. He paid the penalty of his faithfulness; at one time or another he was beaten, imprisoned, proscribed, and driven to hide himself; still he persevered in his mission, as time and occasion served. Yet he survived Jehoiakim, partly because he was more anxious to serve Jehovah than to gain the glorious deliverance of martyrdom; partly because his royal enemy feared to proceed to extremities against a prophet of Jehovah, who was befriended by powerful nobles, and might possibly have relations with Nebuchadnezzar himself. Jehoiakim's religion--for like the Athenians he was probably "very religious"--was saturated with superstition, and it was only when deeply moved that he lost the sense of an external sanctity attaching to Jeremiah's person. In Israel prophets were hedged by a more potent divinity than kings.

Meanwhile Jeremiah was growing old in years and older in experience. When Jehoiakim died, it was nearly forty years since the young priest had first been called "to pluck up and to break down, and to destroy and to overthrow; to build and to plant"; it was more than eleven since his brighter hopes were buried in Josiah's grave. Jehovah had promised that He would make His servant into "an iron pillar and brasen walls." [88] The iron was tempered and hammered into shape during these days of conflict and endurance, like--

> "... *iron dug from central gloom,*
> *And heated hot with burning fears*
> *And dipt in baths of hissing tears,*
> *And battered with the shocks of doom,*
> *To shape and use.*"

He had long lost all trace of that sanguine youthful enthusiasm which promises to carry all before it. His opening manhood had felt its happy illusions, but they did not dominate his soul and they soon passed away. At the Divine bidding, he had surrendered his most ingrained prejudices, his dearest desires. He had consented to be alienated from his brethren at Anathoth, and to live without home or family; although a patriot, he accepted the inevitable ruin of his nation as the just judgment of Jehovah; he was a priest, imbued by heredity and education with the religious traditions of Israel, yet he had yielded himself to Jehovah, to announce, as His herald, the destruction of the Temple, and the devastation of the Holy Land. He had submitted his shrinking flesh and reluctant spirit to God's most unsparing demands, and had dared the worst that man could inflict. Such surrender and such experiences wrought in him a certain stern and terrible strength, and made his life still more remote from the hopes and fears, the joys and sorrows of common men. In his isolation and his inspired self-sufficiency he had become an "iron pillar." Doubtless he seemed to many as hard and cold as iron; but this pillar of the faith could still glow with white heat of indignant passion, and within the shelter of the "brasen walls" there still beat a human heart, touched with tender sympathy for those less disciplined to endure.

We have thus tried to estimate the development of Jeremiah's character during the second period of his ministry, which began with the death of Josiah and terminated with the brief reign of Jehoiachin. Before considering Jeremiah's judgment upon this prince we will review the scanty data at our disposal to enable us to appreciate the prophet's verdict.

Jehoiakim died while Nebuchadnezzar was on the march to punish his rebellion. His son Jehoiachin, a youth of eighteen, [89] succeeded his father and continued his policy. Thus the accession of the new king was no new departure, but merely a continuance of the old order; the government was still in the hands of the party attached to Egypt, and opposed to Babylon and hostile to Jeremiah. Under these circumstances we are bound to accept the statement of Kings that Jehoiakim "slept with his fathers," i.e. was buried in the royal sepulchre. [90] There was no literal fulfilment of the prediction that he should "be buried with the burial of an ass." Jeremiah had also declared concerning Jehoiakim: "He shall have none to sit upon the throne of David." [91] According to popular superstition, the honourable burial of Jehoiakim and the succession of his son to the throne further discredited Jeremiah and his teaching. Men read happy omens in the mere observance of ordinary constitutional routine. The curse upon Jehoiakim seemed so much spent breath: why should not Jeremiah's other predictions of ruin and exile also prove a mere vox et prÃ¦terea nihil? In spite of a thousand disappointments, men's hopes still turned to Egypt; and if earthly resources failed they trusted to Jehovah Himself to intervene, and deliver Jerusalem from the advancing hosts of Nebuchadnezzar, as from the army of Sennacherib.

Ezekiel's elegy over Jehoiachin suggests that the young king displayed energy and courage worthy of a better fortune:--

"He walked up and down among the lions,
He became a young lion;
He learned to catch the prey,
He devoured men.
He broke down [92] *their palaces,*
He wasted their cities;
The land, was desolate, and the fulness thereof,
At the noise of his roaring." [93]

However figurative these lines may be, the hyperbole must have had some basis in fact. Probably before the regular Babylonian army entered Judah, Jehoiachin distinguished himself by brilliant but useless successes against the marauding bands of Chaldeans, Syrians, Moabites, and Ammonites, who had been sent to prepare the way for the main body. He may even have carried his victorious arms into the territory of Moab or Ammon. But his career was speedily cut short: "The servants of Nebuchadnezzar king of Babylon came up to Jerusalem and besieged the city." Pharaoh Necho made no sign, and Jehoiachin was forced to retire before the regular forces of Babylon, and soon found himself shut up in Jerusalem. Still for a time he held out, but when it was known in the beleaguered city that Nebuchadnezzar was present in person in the camp of the besiegers, the Jewish captains lost heart. Perhaps too they hoped for better treatment, if they appealed to the conqueror's vanity by offering him an immediate submission which they had refused to his lieutenants. The gates were thrown open; Jehoiachin and the Queen Mother, Nehushta, with his ministers and princes and the officers of his household, passed out in suppliant procession, and placed themselves and their city at the disposal of the conqueror. In pursuance of the policy which Nebuchadnezzar had inherited from the Assyrians, the king and his court and eight thousand picked men were carried away captive to Babylon. [94] For thirty-seven years Jehoiachin languished in a Chaldean prison, till at last his sufferings were mitigated by an act of grace, which signalised the accession of a new king of Babylon. Nebuchadnezzar's successor Evil Merodach, "in the year when he began to reign, lifted up the head of Jehoiachin king of Judah out of prison, and spake kindly to him, and set his throne above the throne of the kings that were with him in Babylon. And Jehoiachin changed his prison garments, and ate at the royal table continually all the days of his life, and had a regular allowance given him by the king, a daily portion, all the days of his life." [95] At the age of fifty-five, the last survivor of the reigning princes of the house of David emerges from his dungeon, broken in mind and body by his long captivity, to be a grateful dependent upon the charity of Evil Merodach, just as the survivor of the house of Saul had sat at David's table. The young lion that devoured the prey and caught men and wasted cities was thankful to be allowed to creep out of his cage and die in comfort--"a despised broken vessel."

We feel a shock of surprise and repulsion as we turn from this pathetic story to Jeremiah's fierce invectives against the unhappy king. But we wrong the prophet and misunderstand his utterance if we forget that it was delivered during that brief frenzy in which the young king and his advisers threw away the last chance of safety for Judah. Jehoiachin might have repudiated his father's rebellion against Babylon; Jehoiakim s death had removed the chief offender, no personal blame attached to his successor, and a prompt submission might have appeased Nebuchadnezzar's wrath against Judah and obtained his favour for the new king. If a hot-headed young rajah of some protected Indian state revolted against the English suzerainty and exposed his country to the misery of a hopeless war, we should sympathise with any of his counsellors who condemned such wilful folly; we have no right to find fault with Jeremiah for his severe censure of the reckless vanity which precipitated his country's fate.

Jeremiah's deep and absorbing interest in Judah and Jerusalem is indicated by the form of this utterance; it is addressed to the "Daughter of Zion" [96] :--

"Go up to Lebanon, and lament,
And lift up thy voice in Bashan,
And lament from Abarim, [97]
For thy lovers are all destroyed!"

Her "lovers," her heathen allies, whether gods or men, are impotent, and Judah is as forlorn and helpless as a lonely and unfriended woman; let her bewail her fate upon the mountains of Israel, like Jephthah's daughter in ancient days.

"I spake unto thee in thy prosperity;
Thou saidst, I will not hearken.
This hath been thy way from thy youth,
That thou hast not obeyed My voice.
The tempest shall be the shepherd to all thy shepherds."

Kings and nobles, priests and prophets, shall be carried off by the Chaldean invaders, as trees and houses are swept away by a hurricane. These shepherds who had spoiled and betrayed their flock would themselves be as silly sheep in the hands of robbers.

"Thy lovers shall go into captivity.
Then, verily, shalt thou be ashamed and confounded
Because of all thy wickedness.
O thou that dwellest in Lebanon!
O thou that hast made thy nest in the cedar!"

The former mention of Lebanon reminded Jeremiah of Jehoiakim's halls of cedar. With grim irony he links together the royal magnificence of the palace and the wild abandonment of the people's lamentation.

"How wilt thou groan [98] when pangs come upon thee,
Anguish as of a woman in travail!"

The nation is involved in the punishment inflicted upon her rulers. In such passages the prophets largely identify the nation with the governing classes--not without justification. No government, whatever the constitution may be, can ignore a strong popular demand for righteous policy, at home and abroad. A special responsibility of course rests on those who actually wield the authority of the state, but the policy of rulers seldom succeeds in effecting much either for good or evil without some sanction of public feeling. Our revolution which replaced the Puritan Protectorate by the restored Monarchy was rendered possible by the change of popular sentiment. Yet even under the purest democracy men imagine that they divest themselves of civic responsibility by neglecting their civic duties; they stand aloof, and blame officials and professional politicians for the injustice and crime wrought by the state. National guilt seems happily disposed of when laid on the shoulders of that convenient abstraction "the government"; but neither the prophets nor the Providence which they interpret recognise this convenient theory of vicarious atonement: the king sins, but the prophet's condemnation is uttered against and executed upon the nation.

Nevertheless a special responsibility rests upon the ruler, and now Jeremiah turns from the nation to its king.

"As I live--Jehovah hath spoken it--

Though Coniah ben Jehoiakim king of Judah were a signet ring upon My right hand----"

By a forcible Hebrew idiom Jehovah, as it were, turns and confronts the king and specially addresses him:--

"Yet would I pluck thee thence."

A signet ring was valuable in itself, and, as far as an inanimate object could be, was an "alter ego" of the sovereign; it scarcely ever left his finger, and when it did, it carried with it the authority of its owner. A signet ring could not be lost or even cast away without some reflection upon the majesty of the king. Jehoiachin's character was by no means worthless; he had courage, energy, and patriotism. The heir of David and Solomon, the patron and champion of the Temple, dwelt, as it were, under the very shadow of the Almighty. Men generally believed that Jehovah's honour was engaged to defend Jerusalem and the house of David. He Himself would be discredited by the fall of the elect dynasty and the captivity of the chosen people. Yet everything must be sacrificed--the career of a gallant young prince, the ancient association of the sacred Name with David and Zion, even the superstitious awe with which the heathen regarded the God of the Exodus and of the deliverance from Sennacherib. Nothing will be allowed to stand in the way of the Divine judgment. And yet we still sometimes dream that the working out of the Divine righteousness will be postponed in the interests of ecclesiastical traditions and in deference to the criticisms of ungodly men!

*"And I will give thee into the hand of them that seek thy life,
Into the hand of them of whom thou art afraid,
Into the hand of Nebuchadnezzar king of Babylon and the Chaldeans.
And I will hurl thee and the mother that bare thee into another land, where ye were not born:
There shall ye die.
And unto the land whereunto their soul longeth to return,
Thither they shall not return."*

Again the sudden change in the person addressed emphasises the scope of the Divine proclamation; the doom of the royal house is not only announced to them, but also to the world at large. The mention of the Queen Mother, Nehushta, reveals what we should in any case have conjectured, that the policy of the young prince was largely determined by his mother. Her importance is also indicated by xiii. 18, usually supposed to be addressed to Jehoiachin and Nehushta:---

*"Say unto the king and the queen mother,
Leave your thrones and sit in the dust,
For your glorious diadems are fallen."*

The Queen Mother is a characteristic figure of polygamous Eastern dynasties, but we may be helped to understand what Nehushta was to Jehoiachin if we remember the influence of Eleanor of Poitou over Richard I. and John, and the determined struggle which Margaret of Anjou made on behalf of her ill-starred son.

The next verse of our prophecy seems to be a protest against the severe sentence pronounced in the preceding clauses:--

*"Is then this man Coniah a despised vessel, only fit to be broken?
Is he a tool, that no one wants?"*

Thus Jeremiah imagines the citizens and warriors of Jerusalem crying out against him, for his sentence of doom against their darling prince and captain. The prophetic utterance seemed to them monstrous and incredible, only worthy to be met with impatient scorn. We may find a mediæval analogy to the situation at Jerusalem in the relations of Clement IV. to Conradin, the last heir of the house of Hohenstaufen. When this youth of sixteen was in the full career of victory, the Pope predicted that his army would be scattered like smoke, and pointed out the prince and his allies as victims for the sacrifice. When Conradin was executed after his defeat at Tagliacozzo, Christendom was filled with abhorrence at the suspicion that Clement had countenanced the doing to death of the hereditary enemy of the Papal See. Jehoiachin's friends felt towards Jeremiah somewhat as these thirteenth-century Ghibellines towards Clement.

Moreover the charge against Clement was probably unfounded; Milman [99] says of him, "He was doubtless moved with inner remorse at the cruelties of 'his champion' Charles of Anjou." Jeremiah too would lament the doom he was constrained to utter. Nevertheless he could not permit Judah to be deluded to its ruin by empty dreams of glory:--

> "O land, land, land,
> Hear the word of Jehovah."

Isaiah had called all Nature, heaven and earth to bear witness against Israel, but now Jeremiah is appealing with urgent importunity to Judah. "O Chosen Land of Jehovah, so richly blessed by His favour, so sternly chastised by His discipline, Land of prophetic Revelation, now at last, after so many warnings, believe the word of thy God and submit to His judgment. Hasten not thy unhappy fate by shallow confidence in the genius and daring of Jehoiachin: he is no true Messiah."

> "For saith Jehovah,
> Write this man childless,
> A man whose life shall not know prosperity:
> For none of his seed shall prosper;
> None shall sit upon the throne of David,
> Nor rule any more over Judah."

Thus, by Divine decree, the descendants of Jehoiakim were disinherited; Jehoiachin was to be recorded in the genealogies of Israel as having no heir. He might have offspring, [100] but the Messiah, the Son of David, would not come of his line.

Two points suggest themselves in connection with this utterance of Jeremiah; first as to the circumstances under which it was uttered, then as to its application to Jehoiachin.

A moment's reflection will show that this prophecy implied great courage and presence of mind on the part of Jeremiah--his enemies might even have spoken of his barefaced audacity. He had predicted that Jehoiakim's corpse should be cast forth without any rites of honourable sepulture; and that no son of his should sit upon the throne. Jehoiakim had been buried like other kings, he slept with his fathers, and Jehoiachin his son reigned in his stead. The prophet should have felt himself utterly discredited; and yet here was Jeremiah coming forward unabashed with new prophecies against the king, whose very existence was a glaring disproof of his prophetic inspiration. Thus the friends of Jehoiachin. They would affect towards Jeremiah's message the same indifference which the present generation feels for the expositors of Daniel and the Apocalypse, who confidently announce the end of the world for 1866, and in 1867 fix a new date with cheerful and undiminished assurance. But these students of sacred records can always save the authority of Scripture by acknowledging the fallibility of their calculations. When their predictions fail, they confess that they have done their sum wrong and start it afresh. But Jeremiah's utterances were not published as human deductions from inspired data; he himself claimed to be inspired. He did not ask his hearers to verify and acknowledge the accuracy of his arithmetic or his logic, but to submit to the Divine message from his lips. And yet it is clear that he did not stake the authority of Jehovah or even his own prophetic status upon the accurate and detailed fulfilment of his predictions. Nor does he suggest that, in announcing a doom which was not literally accomplished, he had misunderstood or misinterpreted his message. The details which both Jeremiah and those who edited and transmitted his words knew to be unfulfilled were allowed to remain in the record of Divine Revelation--not, surely, to illustrate the fallibility of prophets, but to show that an accurate forecast of details is not of the essence of prophecy; such details belong to its form and not to its substance. Ancient Hebrew prophecy clothed its ideas in concrete images; its messages of doom were made definite and intelligible in a glowing series of definite pictures. The prophets were realists and not impressionists. But they were also spiritual men, concerned with the great issues of history and religion. Their message had to do with these: they were little interested in minor matters; and they used detailed imagery as a mere instrument of exposition. Popular scepticism exulted when subsequent facts did not exactly correspond to Jeremiah's images, but the prophet himself was unconscious of either failure or mistake. Jehoiakim might be magnificently buried, but his name was branded with eternal dishonour; Jehoiachin might reign for a hundred days, but the doom of Judah was not averted, and the house of David ceased for ever to rule in Jerusalem.

Our second point is the application of this prophecy to Jehoiachin. How far did the king deserve his sentence? Jeremiah indeed does not explicitly blame Jehoiachin, does not specify his sins as he did those of his royal sire. The estimate recorded in the Book of Kings doubtless expresses the judgment of Jeremiah, but it may be directed not so much against the young king as against his ministers. Yet the king cannot have been entirely innocent of the guilt of his policy and government. In chapter xxiv., however, Jeremiah speaks of the captives at Babylon, those carried away with Jehoiachin, as "good figs"; but we scarcely suppose he meant to include the king himself in this favourable estimate, otherwise we should discern some note of sympathy in the personal sentence upon him. We are left, therefore, to conclude that Jeremiah's judgment was unfavourable; although, in view of the prince's youth and limited opportunities, his guilt must have been slight compared to that of his father.

And, on the other hand, we have the manifest sympathy and even admiration of Ezekiel. The two estimates stand side by side in the sacred record to remind us that God neither tolerates man's sins because there is a better side to his nature, nor yet ignores his virtues on account of his vices. For ourselves we may be content to leave the last word on this matter with Jeremiah. When he declares God's sentence on Jehoiachin, he does not suggest that it was undeserved, but he refrains from any explicit reproach. Probably if he had known how entirely his prediction would be fulfilled, if he had foreseen the seven-and-thirty weary years which the young lion was to spend in his Babylonian cage, Jeremiah would have spoken more tenderly and pitifully even of the son of Jehoiakim.

Footnotes:

86. Also called Coniah and Jeconiah.

87. Considerable portions of chaps. i.-xx. are referred to the reigns of Jehoiakim and Jehoiachin: see previous volume on Jeremiah.

88. i. 18.

89. The Chronicler's account of Jehoiakim's end (2 Chron. xxviii. 6-8) is due to a misunderstanding of the older records. According to Chronicles Jehoiachin was only eight, but all our data indicate that Kings is right.

90. In LXX. of 2 Chron. xxxvi. 8, Jehoiakim, like Manasseh and Amon, was "buried in the garden of Uzza": B, GanozÃ¦; A, Ganozan. Cheyne is inclined to accept this statement, which he regards as derived from tradition.

91. xxxvi. 30.

92. So A. B. Davidson in Cambridge Bible, etc., by a slight conjectural emendation; there have been many other suggested corrections of the text. The Hebrew text as it stands would mean literally "he knew their widows" (R.V. margin); A.V., R.V., by a slight change, "he knew their (A.V. desolate) palaces."

93. Ezek. xix. 5-7.

94. 2 Kings xxiv. 8-17.

95. 2 Kings xxv. 27-30; Jer. lii. 31-34.

96. The Hebrew verbs are in 2 s. fem.; the person addressed is not named, but from analogy she can only be the "Daughter of Zion," i.e. Jerusalem personified.

97. Identified with the mountains of Moab.

98. R.V. margin, with LXX., Vulg., and Syr.

99. Milman's Latin Christianity, vi. 392.

100. 1 Chron. iii. 17 mentions the "sons" of Jeconiah, and in Matt. i. 12 Shealtiel is called his "son," but in Luke iii. 27 Shealtiel is called the son of Neri.

Rev. C. J. Ball, M.A., & W. H. Bennett, M.A.

CHAPTER VIII

BAD SHEPHERDS AND FALSE PROPHETS

xxiii., xxiv.

"Woe unto the shepherds that destroy and scatter the sheep of My pasture!"--Jer. xxiii. 1.
"Of what avail is straw instead of grain?... Is not My word like fire, ... like a hammer that shattereth the rocks?"--Jer. xxiii. 28, 29.

    The captivity of Jehoiachin and the deportation of the flower of the people marked the opening of the last scene in the tragedy of Judah and of a new period in the ministry of Jeremiah. These events, together with the accession of Zedekiah as Nebuchadnezzar's nominee, very largely altered the state of affairs in Jerusalem. And yet the two main features of the situation were unchanged--the people and the government persistently disregarded Jeremiah's exhortations. "Neither Zedekiah, nor his servants, nor the people of the land, did hearken unto the words of Jehovah which He spake by the prophet Jeremiah." [101] They would not obey the will of Jehovah as to their life and worship, and they would not submit to Nebuchadnezzar. "Zedekiah ... did evil in the sight of Jehovah, according to all that Jehoiakim had done; ... and Zedekiah rebelled against the king of Babylon." [102]
    It is remarkable that though Jeremiah consistently urged submission to Babylon, the various arrangements made by Nebuchadnezzar did very little to improve the prophet's position or increase his influence. The Chaldean king may have seemed ungrateful only because he was ignorant of the services rendered to him--Jeremiah would not enter into direct and personal co-operation with the enemy of his country, even with him whom Jehovah had appointed to be the scourge of His disobedient people--but the Chaldean policy served Nebuchadnezzar as little as it profited Jeremiah. Jehoiakim, in spite of his forced submission, remained the able and determined foe of his suzerain, and Zedekiah, to the best of his very limited ability, followed his predecessor's example.
    Zedekiah was uncle of Jehoiachin, half-brother of Jehoiakim, and own brother to Jehoahaz. [103] Possibly the two brothers owed their bias against Jeremiah and his teaching to their mother, Josiah's wife Hamutal, the daughter of another Jeremiah, the Libnite. Ezekiel thus describes the appointment of the new king: "The king of Babylon ... took one of the seed royal, and made a covenant with him; he also put him under an oath, and took away the mighty of the land: that the kingdom might be base, that it might not lift itself up, but that by keeping of his covenant it might stand." [104] Apparently Nebuchadnezzar was careful to choose a feeble prince for his "base kingdom"; all that we read of Zedekiah suggests that he was weak and incapable. Henceforth the sovereign counted for little in the internal struggles of the tottering state. Josiah had firmly maintained the religious policy of Jeremiah, and Jehoiakim, as firmly, the opposite policy; but Zedekiah had neither the strength nor the firmness to enforce a consistent policy and to make one party permanently dominant. Jeremiah and his enemies were left to fight it out amongst themselves, so that now their antagonism grew more bitter and pronounced than during any other reign.
    But whatever advantage the prophet might derive from the weakness of the sovereign was more than counterbalanced by the recent deportation. In selecting the captives Nebuchadnezzar had sought merely to weaken Judah by carrying away every one who would have been an element of strength to the "base kingdom." Perhaps he rightly believed that neither the prudence of the wise nor the honour of the virtuous would overcome their patriotic hatred of subjection; weakness alone would guarantee the obedience of Judah. He forgot that even weakness is apt to be foolhardy--when there is no immediate prospect of penalty.
    One result of his policy was that the enemies and friends of Jeremiah were carried away indiscriminately; there was no attempt to leave behind those who might have counselled submission to Babylon as the acceptance of a Divine judgment, and thus have helped to keep Judah loyal to its foreign master. On the contrary Jeremiah's disciples were chiefly thoughtful and honourable men, and Nebuchadnezzar's policy in taking away "the mighty of the land" bereft the prophet of many friends and supporters, amongst them his disciple Ezekiel and doubtless a large class of whom Daniel and his three friends might be taken as types. When Jeremiah characterises the captives as "good figs" and those left behind as "bad figs," [105] and the judgment is confirmed and amplified by Ezekiel, [106] we may be sure that most of the prophet's adherents were in exile.
    We have already had occasion to compare the changes in the religious policy of the Jewish

government to the alternations of Protestant and Romanist sovereigns among the Tudors; but no Tudor was as feeble as Zedekiah. He may rather be compared to Charles IX. of France, helpless between the Huguenots and the League. Only the Jewish factions were less numerous, less evenly balanced; and by the speedy advance of Nebuchadnezzar civil dissensions were merged in national ruin.

The opening years of the new reign passed in nominal allegiance to Babylon. Jeremiah's influence would be used to induce the vassal king to observe the covenant he had entered into and to be faithful to his oath to Nebuchadnezzar. On the other hand a crowd of "patriotic" prophets urged Zedekiah to set up once more the standard of national independence, to "come to the help of the Lord against the mighty." Let us then briefly consider Jeremiah's polemic against the princes, prophets, and priests of his people. While Ezekiel in a celebrated chapter [107] denounces the idolatry of the princes, priests, and women of Judah, their worship of creeping things and abominable beasts, their weeping for Tammuz, their adoration of the sun, Jeremiah is chiefly concerned with the perverse policy of the government and the support it receives from priests and prophets, who profess to speak in the name of Jehovah. Jeremiah does not utter against Zedekiah any formal judgment like those on his three predecessors. Perhaps the prophet did not regard this impotent sovereign as the responsible representative of the state, and when the long-expected catastrophe at last befell the doomed people, neither Zedekiah nor his doings distracted men's attention from their own personal sufferings and patriotic regrets. At the point where a paragraph on Zedekiah would naturally have followed that on Jehoiachin, we have by way of summary and conclusion to the previous sections a brief denunciation of the shepherds of Israel.

"Woe unto the shepherds that destroy and scatter the sheep of My pasture!... Ye have scattered My flock, and driven them away, and have not cared for them; behold, I will visit upon you the evil of your doings."

These "shepherds" are primarily the kings, Jehoahaz, Jehoiakim, and Jehoiachin, who have been condemned by name in the previous chapter, together with the unhappy Zedekiah, who is too insignificant to be mentioned. But the term shepherds will also include the ruling and influential classes of which the king was the leading representative.

The image is a familiar one in the Old Testament and is found in the oldest literature of Israel, [108] but the denunciation of the rulers of Judah as unfaithful shepherds is characteristic of Jeremiah, Ezekiel, and one of the prophecies appended to the Book of Zechariah. [109] Ezekiel xxxiv. expands this figure and enforces its lessons:--

> *"Woe unto the shepherds of Israel that do feed themselves!*
> *Should not the shepherds feed the sheep? Ye eat the fat, and ye clothe you with the wool.*
> *Ye kill the fatlings; but ye feed not the sheep.*
> *The diseased have ye not strengthened,*
> *Neither have ye healed the sick,*
> *Neither have ye bound up the bruised,*
> *Neither have ye brought back again that which was driven away,*
> *Neither have ye sought for that which was lost,*
> *But your rule over them has been harsh and violent.*
> *And for want of a shepherd, they were scattered,*
> *And became food for every beast of the field."* [110]

So in Zechariah ix., etc., Jehovah's anger is kindled against the shepherds, because they do not pity His flock. [111] Elsewhere [112] Jeremiah speaks of the kings of all nations as shepherds, and pronounces against them also a like doom. All these passages illustrate the concern of the prophets for good government. They were neither Pharisees nor formalists; their religious ideals were broad and wholesome. Doubtless the elect remnant will endure through all conditions of society; but the Kingdom of God was not meant to be a pure Church in a rotten state. This present evil world is no manure heap to fatten the growth of holiness: it is rather a mass for the saints to leaven.

Both Jeremiah and Ezekiel turn from the unfaithful shepherds whose "hungry sheep look up and are not fed" to the true King of Israel, the "Shepherd of Israel that led Joseph like a flock, and dwelt between the Cherubim." In the days of the Restoration He will raise up faithful shepherds, and over them a righteous Branch, the real Jehovah Zidqenu, instead of the sapless twig who disgraced the name "Zedekiah." Similarly Ezekiel promises that God will set up one shepherd over His people, "even My servant David." The pastoral care of Jehovah for His people is most tenderly and beautifully set forth in the twenty-third Psalm. Our Lord, the root and the offspring of David, claims to be the fulfilment of ancient prophecy when He calls Himself "the Good Shepherd." The words of Christ and of the Psalmist receive new force and fuller meaning when we contrast their pictures of the true Shepherd with the portraits of the Jewish kings drawn by the prophets. Moreover the history of this metaphor warns us against ignoring the organic life of the Christian society, the Church, in our concern for the spiritual life of the individual. As Sir Thomas More said, in applying this figure to Henry VIII., "Of the multitude of sheep cometh the name of a shepherd." [113] A shepherd implies not merely a sheep, but a flock; His relation to each member is tender and personal, but He bestows blessings and requires service in fellowship with the Family of God.

By a natural sequence the denunciation of the unfaithful shepherds is followed by a similar utterance "concerning the prophets." It is true that the prophets are not spoken of as shepherds; and Milton's use of the figure in Lycidas suggests the New Testament rather than the Old. Yet the prophets had a large share in guiding the destinies of Israel in politics as well as in religion, and having passed sentence on the shepherds--the kings and princes--Jeremiah turns to the ecclesiastics, chiefly, as the heading implies, to the prophets. The priests indeed do not escape, but Jeremiah seems to feel that they are adequately dealt with in two or three casual references. We use the term "ecclesiastics" advisedly; the prophets were now a large professional class, more important and even more clerical than the priests. The prophets and priests together were the clergy of Israel. They claimed to be devoted servants of Jehovah, and for the most part the claim was made in all sincerity; but they misunderstood His character, and mistook for Divine inspiration the suggestions of their own prejudice and self-will.

Jeremiah's indictment against them has various counts. He accuses them of speaking without authority, and also of time-serving, plagiarism, and cant.

First, then, as to their unauthorised utterances: Jeremiah finds them guilty of an unholy licence in prophesying, a distorted caricature of that "liberty of prophesying" which is the prerogative of God's accredited ambassadors.

> "Hearken not unto the words of the prophets that prophesy unto you.
> They make fools of you:
> The visions which they declare are from their own hearts,
> And not from the mouth of Jehovah.

***

> Who hath stood in the council of Jehovah,
> To perceive and hear His word?
> Who hath marked His word and heard it?
> I sent not the prophets--yet they ran;
> I spake not unto them--yet they prophesied."

The evils which Jeremiah describes are such as will always be found in any large professional class. To use modern terms--in the Church, as in every profession, there will be men who are not qualified for the vocation which they follow. They are indeed not called to their vocation; they "follow," but do not overtake it. They are not sent of God, yet they run; they have no Divine message, yet they preach. They have never stood in the council of Jehovah; they might perhaps have gathered up scraps of the King's purposes from His true councillors; but when they had opportunity they neither "marked nor heard"; and yet they discourse concerning heavenly things with much importance and assurance. But their inspiration, at its best, has no deeper or richer source than their own shallow selves; their visions are the mere product of their own imaginations. Strangers to the true fellowship, their spirit is not "a well of water springing up unto eternal life," but a stagnant pool. And, unless the judgment and mercy of God intervene, that pool will in the end be fed from a fountain whose bitter waters are earthly, sensual, devilish.

We are always reluctant to speak of ancient prophecy or modern preaching as a "profession." We may gladly dispense with the word, if we do not thereby ignore the truth which it inaccurately expresses. Men lived by prophecy, as, with Apostolic sanction, men live by "the gospel." They were expected, as ministers are now, though in a less degree, to justify their claims to an income and an official status, by discharging religious functions so as to secure the approval of the people or the authorities. Then, as now, the prophet's reputation, influence, and social standing, probably even his income, depended upon the amount of visible success that he could achieve.

In view of such facts, it is futile to ask men of the world not to speak of the clerical life as a profession. They discern no ethical difference between a curate's dreams of a bishopric and the aspirations of a junior barrister to the woolsack. Probably a refusal to recognise the element common to the ministry with law, medicine, and other professions, injures both the Church and its servants. One peculiar difficulty and most insidious temptation of the Christian ministry consists in its mingled resemblances to and differences from the other professions. The minister has to work under similar worldly conditions, and yet to control those conditions by the indwelling power of the Spirit. He has to "run," it may be twice or even three times a week, whether he be sent or no: how can he always preach only that which God has taught him? He is consciously dependent upon the exercise of his memory, his intellect, his fancy: how can he avoid speaking "the visions of his own heart"? The Church can never allow its ministers to regard themselves as mere professional teachers and lecturers, and yet if they claim to be more, must they not often fall under Jeremiah's condemnation?

It is one of those practical dilemmas which delight casuists and distress honest and earnest servants of God. In the early Christian centuries similar difficulties peopled the Egyptian and Syrian deserts with ascetics, who had given up the world as a hopeless riddle. A full discussion of the problem would lead us too far away from the exposition of Jeremiah, and we will only venture to make two suggestions.

The necessity, which most ministers are under, of "living by the gospel," may promote their own spiritual life and add to their usefulness. It corrects and reduces spiritual pride, and helps them to understand and sympathise with their lay brethren, most of whom are subject to a similar trial.

Secondly, as a minister feels the ceaseless pressure of strong temptation to speak from and live for himself--his lower, egotistic self--he will be correspondingly driven to a more entire and persistent surrender to God. The infinite fulness and variety of Revelation is expressed by the manifold gifts and experience of the prophets. If only the prophet be surrendered to the Spirit, then what is most characteristic of himself may become the most forcible expression of his message. His constant prayer will be that he may have the child's heart and may never resist the Holy Ghost, that no personal interest or prejudice, no bias of training or tradition or current opinion, may dull his hearing when he stands in the council of the Lord, or betray him into uttering for Christ's gospel the suggestions of his own self-will or the mere watchwords of his ecclesiastical faction.

But to return to the ecclesiastics who had stirred Jeremiah's wrath. The professional prophets naturally adapted their words to the itching ears of their clients. They were not only officious, but also time-serving. Had they been true prophets, they would have dealt faithfully with Judah; they would have sought to convince the people of sin, and to lead them to repentance; they would thus have given them yet another opportunity of salvation.

"If they had stood in My council,
They would have caused My people to hear My words;
They would have turned them from their evil way,
And from the evil of their doings."

But now:--

"They walk in lies and strengthen the hands of evildoers,
That no one may turn away from his sin.

***

They say continually unto them that despise the word of Jehovah, [114]
Ye shall have peace;
And unto every one that walketh in the stubbornness of his heart they say,
No evil shall come upon you."

Unfortunately, when prophecy becomes professional in the lowest sense of the word, it is governed by commercial principles. A sufficiently imperious demand calls forth an abundant supply. A sovereign can "tune the pulpits"; and a ruling race can obtain from its clergy formal ecclesiastical sanction for such "domestic institutions" as slavery. When evildoers grow numerous and powerful, there will always be prophets to strengthen their hands and encourage them not to turn away from their sin. But to give the lie to these false prophets God sends Jeremiahs, who are often branded as heretics and schismatics, turbulent fellows who turn the world upside-down.

The self-important, self-seeking spirit leads further to the sin of plagiarism:--

"Therefore I am against the prophets, is the utterance of Jehovah,
Who steal My word from one another."

The sin of plagiarism is impossible to the true prophet, partly because there are no rights of private property in the word of Jehovah. The Old Testament writers make free use of the works of their predecessors. For instance, Isaiah ii. 2-4 is almost identical with Micah iv. 1-3; yet neither author acknowledges his indebtedness to the other or to any third prophet. [115] Uriah ben Shemaiah prophesied according to all the words of Jeremiah, [116] who himself owes much to Hosea, whom he never mentions. Yet he was not conscious of stealing from his predecessor, and he would have brought no such charge against Isaiah or Micah or Uriah. In the New Testament 2 Peter and Jude have so much in common that one must have used the other without acknowledgment. Yet the Church has not, on that ground, excluded either Epistle from the Canon. In the goodly fellowship of the prophets and the glorious company of the apostles no man says that the things which he utters are his own. But the mere hireling has no part in the spiritual communism wherein each may possess all things because he claims nothing. When a prophet ceases to be the messenger of God, and sinks into the mercenary purveyor of his own clever sayings and brilliant fancies, then he is tempted to become a clerical Autolycus, "a snapper-up of unconsidered trifles." Modern ideas furnish a curious parallel to Jeremiah's indifference to the borrowings of the true prophet, and his scorn of the literary pilferings of the false. We hear only too often of stolen sermons, but no one complains of plagiarism in prayers. Doubtless among these false prophets charges of plagiarism were bandied to and fro with much personal acrimony. But it is interesting to notice that Jeremiah is not denouncing an injury done to himself; he does not accuse them of thieving from him, but from one another. Probably assurance and lust of praise and power would have overcome any awe they felt for Jeremiah. He was only free from their depredations, because--from their point of view--his words were not worth stealing. There was nothing to be gained by repeating his stern denunciations, and even his promises were not exactly suited to the popular taste.

These prophets were prepared to cater for the average religious appetite in the most approved fashion--in other words, they were masters of cant. Their office had been consecrated by the work of true men of God like Elijah and Isaiah. They themselves claimed to stand in the genuine prophetic succession, and to inherit the reverence felt for their great predecessors, quoting their inspired utterances and adopting their weighty phrases. As Jeremiah's contemporaries listened to one of their favourite orators, they were soothed by his assurances of Divine favour and protection, and their confidence in the speaker was confirmed by the frequent sound of familiar formulÃ¦ in his unctuous sentences. These had the true ring; they were redolent of sound doctrine, of what popular tradition regarded as orthodox.

The solemn attestation NE'UM YAHWE, "It is the utterance of Jehovah," is continually appended to prophecies, almost as if it were the sign-manual of the Almighty. Isaiah and other prophets frequently use the term MASSA (A.V., R.V., "burden") as a title, especially for prophecies concerning neighbouring nations. The ancient records loved to tell how Jehovah revealed Himself to the patriarchs in dreams. Jeremiah's rivals included dreams in their clerical apparatus:--

> "Behold, I am against them that prophesy lying dreams--
> Ne'um Yahwe--
> And tell them, and lead astray My people
> By their lies and their rodomontade;
> It was not I who sent or commanded them,
> Neither shall they profit this people at all,
> Ne'um Yahwe"

These prophets "thought to cause the Lord's people to forget His name, as their fathers forgot His name for Baal, by their dreams which they told one another."
Moreover they could glibly repeat the sacred phrases as part of their professional jargon:--

> "Behold, I am against the prophets,
> It is the utterance of Jehovah (Ne'um Yahwe),
> That use their tongues
> To utter utterances (Wayyin'amu Ne'um)."

"To utter utterances"--the prophets uttered them, not Jehovah. These sham oracles were due to no Diviner source than the imagination of foolish hearts. But for Jeremiah's grim earnestness, the last clause would be almost blasphemous. It is virtually a caricature of the most solemn formula of ancient Hebrew religion. But this was really degraded when it was used to obtain credence for the lies which men prophesied out of the deceit of their own heart. Jeremiah's seeming irreverence was the most forcible way of bringing this home to his hearers. There are profanations of the most sacred things which can scarcely be spoken of without an apparent breach of the Third Commandment. The most awful taking in vain of the name of the Lord God is not heard among the publicans and sinners, but in pulpits and on the platforms of religious meetings.

But these prophets and their clients had a special fondness for the phrase "The burden of Jehovah," and their unctuous use of it most especially provoked Jeremiah's indignation:--

> "When this people, priest, or prophet shall ask thee,
> What is the burden of Jehovah?
> Then say unto them, Ye are the burden. [117]
> But I will cast you off, Ne'um Yahwe.
> If priest or prophet or people shall say, The burden of Jehovah,

> *I will punish that man and his house.*
> *And ye shall say to one another,*
> *What hath Jehovah answered? and, What hath Jehovah spoken?*
> *And ye shall no more make mention of the burden of Jehovah:*
> *For (if ye do) men's words shall become a burden to themselves.*

***

> *Thus shall ye inquire of a prophet,*
> *What hath Jehovah answered thee?*
> *What hath Jehovah spoken unto thee?*
> *But if ye say, The burden of Jehovah,*
> *Thus saith Jehovah: Because ye say this word, The burden of Jehovah,*
> *When I have sent unto you the command,*
> *Ye shall not say, The burden of Jehovah,*
> *Therefore I will assuredly take you up,*
> *And will cast away from before Me both you and the city which I gave to you and to your fathers.*
> *I will bring upon you everlasting reproach*
> *And everlasting shame, that shall not be forgotten."*

Jeremiah's insistence and vehemence speak for themselves. Their moral is obvious, though for the most part unheeded. The most solemn formulæ, hallowed by ancient and sacred associations, used by inspired teachers as the vehicle of revealed truths, may be debased till they become the very legend of Antichrist, blazoned on the Vexilla Regis Inferni. They are like a motto of one of Charles's Paladins flaunted by his unworthy descendants to give distinction to cruelty and vice. The Church's line of march is strewn with such dishonoured relics of her noblest champions. Even our Lord's own words have not escaped. There is a fashion of discoursing upon "the gospel" which almost tempts reverent Christians to wish they might never hear that word again. Neither is this debasing of the moral currency confined to religious phrases; almost every political and social watchword has been similarly abused. One of the vilest tyrannies the world has ever seen--the Reign of Terror--claimed to be an incarnation of "Liberty, Equality, and Fraternity."

Yet the Bible, with that marvellous catholicity which lifts it so high above the level of all other religious literature, not only records Jeremiah's prohibition to use the term "Burden," but also tells us that centuries later Malachi could still speak of "the burden of the word of Jehovah." A great phrase that has been discredited by misuse may yet recover itself; the tarnished and dishonoured sword of faith may be baptised and burnished anew, and flame in the forefront of the holy war.

Jeremiah does not stand alone in his unfavourable estimate of the professional prophets of Judah; a similar depreciation seems to be implied by the words of Amos: "I am neither a prophet nor of the sons of the prophets." [118] One of the unknown authors whose writings have been included in the Book of Zechariah takes up the teaching of Amos and Jeremiah and carries it a stage further:--

> *"In that day (it is the utterance of Jehovah Sabaoth) I will cut off the names of the idols from the land,*
> *They shall not be remembered any more;*
> *Also the prophets and the spirit of uncleanness*
> *Will I expel from the land.*
> *When any shall yet prophesy,*
> *His father and mother that begat him shall say unto him,*
> *Thou shalt not live, for thou speakest lies in the name of Jehovah:*
> *And his father and mother that begat him shall thrust him through when he prophesieth.*
> *In that day every prophet when he prophesieth shall be ashamed of his vision;*
> *Neither shall any wear a hairy mantle to deceive:*
> *He shall say, I am no prophet;*
> *I am a tiller of the ground,*
> *I was sold for a slave in my youth."* [119]

No man with any self-respect would allow his fellows to dub him prophet; slave was a less humiliating name. No family would endure the disgrace of having a member who belonged to this despised caste; parents would rather put their son to death than see him a prophet. To such extremities may the spirit of time-serving and cant reduce a national clergy. We are reminded of Latimer's words in his famous sermon to Convocation in 1536: "All good men in all places accuse your avarice, your exactions, your tyranny. I commanded you that ye should feed my sheep, and ye earnestly feed yourselves from day to day, wallowing in delights and idleness. I commanded you to teach my law; you teach your own traditions, and seek your own glory." [120]

Over against their fluent and unctuous cant Jeremiah sets the terrible reality of his Divine message. Compared to this, their sayings are like chaff to the wheat; nay, this is too tame a figure--Jehovah's word is like fire, like a hammer that shatters rocks. He says of himself:--

"My heart within me is broken; all my bones shake:
I am like a drunken man, like a man whom wine hath overcome,
Because of Jehovah and His holy words."

Thus we have in chapter xxiii. a full and formal statement of the controversy between Jeremiah and his brother-prophets. On the one hand, self-seeking and self-assurance winning popularity by orthodox phrases, traditional doctrine, and the prophesying of smooth things; on the other hand, a man to whom the word of the Lord was like a fire in his bones, who had surrendered prejudice and predilection that he might himself become a hammer to shatter the Lord's enemies, a man through whom God wrought so mightily that he himself reeled and staggered with the blows of which he was the instrument.

The relation of the two parties was not unlike that of St. Paul and his Corinthian adversaries: the prophet, like the Apostle, spoke "in demonstration of the Spirit and of power"; he considered "not the word of them which are puffed up, but the power. For the kingdom of God is not in word, but in power." In our next chapter we shall see the practical working of this antagonism which we have here set forth.

Footnotes:
101. xxxvii. 2.
102. 2 Kings xxiv. 18-20.
103. 2 Chron. xxxvi. 10 makes Zedekiah the brother of Jehoiachin, possibly using the word in the general sense of "relation." Zedekiah's age shows that he cannot have been the son of Jehoiakim.
104. Ezek. xvii. 13, 14.
105. xxiv.
106. vii.-xi.
107. viii.
108. Gen. xlix. 24, J. from older source. Micah v. 5.
109. ix.-xi., xiii. 7-9.
110. Ezek. xxxiv. 2-5.
111. Zech. x. 3, xi. 5.
112. xxv. 34-38.
113. Froude, i. 205.
114. LXX. See R.V. margin.
115. Possibly, however, the insertion of this passage in one of the books may have been the work of an editor, and we cannot be sure that, in Jeremiah's time, collections entitled Isaiah and Micah both included this section.
116. xxvi. 20.
117. So LXX. and modern editors: see Giesebrecht, in loco. R.V. "What burden!"
118. vii. 14; but cf. R.V.; "I was," etc.
119. Zech. xiii. 2-5. Post-exilic, according to most critics (Driver's Introduction, in loco).
120. Froude, ii. 474.

CHAPTER IX

HANANIAH

xxvii., xxviii.

"*Hear now, Hananiah; Jehovah hath not sent thee, but thou makest this people to trust in a lie.*"-- Jer. xxviii. 15.

The most conspicuous point at issue between Jeremiah and his opponents was political rather than ecclesiastical. Jeremiah was anxious that Zedekiah should keep faith with Nebuchadnezzar, and not involve Judah in useless misery by another hopeless revolt. The prophets preached the popular doctrine of an imminent Divine intervention to deliver Judah from her oppressors. They devoted themselves to the easy task of fanning patriotic enthusiasm, till the Jews were ready for any enterprise, however reckless.

During the opening years of the new reign, Nebuchadnezzar's recent capture of Jerusalem and the consequent wholesale deportation were fresh in men's minds; fear of the Chaldeans together with the influence of Jeremiah kept the government from any overt act of rebellion. According to li. 59, the king even paid a visit to Babylon, to do homage to his suzerain.

It was probably in the fourth year of his reign [121] that the tributary Syrian states began to prepare for a united revolt against Babylon. The Assyrian and Chaldean annals constantly mention such combinations, which were formed and broken up and reformed with as much ease and variety as patterns in a kaleidoscope. On the present occasion the kings of Edom, Moab, Ammon, Tyre, and Zidon sent their ambassadors to Jerusalem to arrange with Zedekiah for concerted action. But there were more important persons to deal with in that city than Zedekiah. Doubtless the princes of Judah welcomed the opportunity for a new revolt. But before the negotiations were very far advanced, Jeremiah heard what was going on. By Divine command, he made "bands and bars," i.e. yokes, for himself and for the ambassadors of the allies, or possibly for them to carry home to their masters. They received their answer, not from Zedekiah, but from the true King of Israel, Jehovah Himself. They had come to solicit armed assistance to deliver them from Babylon; they were sent back with yokes to wear as a symbol of their entire and helpless subjection to Nebuchadnezzar. This was the word of Jehovah:--

> "*The nation and the kingdom that will not put its neck beneath the yoke of the king of Babylon,
> That nation will I visit with sword and famine and pestilence until I consume them by his hand.*"

The allied kings had been encouraged to revolt by oracles similar to those uttered by the Jewish prophets in the name of Jehovah; but:--

> "*As for you, hearken not to your prophets, diviners, dreams, soothsayers and sorcerers,
> When they speak unto you, saying, Ye shall not serve the king of Babylon.
> They prophesy a lie unto you, to remove you far from your land;
> That I should drive you out, and that you should perish.
> But the nation that shall bring their neck under the yoke of the king of Babylon, and serve him,
> That nation will I maintain in their own land (it is the utterance of Jehovah), and they shall till it and dwell in it.*"

When he had sent his message to the foreign envoys, Jeremiah addressed an almost identical admonition to his own king. He bids him submit to the Chaldean yoke, under the same penalties for disobedience--sword, pestilence, and famine for himself and his people. He warns him also against delusive promises of the prophets, especially in the matter of the sacred vessels.

The popular doctrine of the inviolable sanctity of the Temple had sustained a severe shock when Nebuchadnezzar carried off the sacred vessels to Babylon. It was inconceivable that Jehovah would patiently submit to so gross an indignity. In ancient days the Ark had plagued its Philistine captors till they were only too thankful to be rid of it. Later on a graphic narrative in the Book of Daniel told with what swift vengeance God punished Belshazzar for his profane use of these very vessels. So now patriotic prophets were convinced that the golden candlestick, the bowls and chargers of gold and silver, would soon return in triumph, like the Ark of old; and their return would be the symbol of the final deliverance of Judah from Babylon. Naturally the priests above all others would welcome such a prophecy, and would industriously disseminate it. But Jeremiah "spake to the priests and all this people, saying, Thus saith Jehovah:--

> "Hearken not unto the words of your prophets, which prophesy unto you,
> Behold, the vessels of the house of Jehovah shall be brought back from Babylon now speedily:
> For they prophesy a lie unto you."

How could Jehovah grant triumphant deliverance to a carnally minded people who would not understand His Revelation, and did not discern any essential difference between Him and Moloch and Baal?

> "Hearken not unto them; serve the king of Babylon and live.
> Why should this city become a desolation?"

Possibly, however, even now, the Divine compassion might have spared Jerusalem the agony and shame of her final siege and captivity. God would not at once restore what was lost, but He might spare what was still left. Jeremiah could not endorse the glowing promises of the prophets, but he would unite with them to intercede for mercy upon the remnant of Israel.

> "If they are prophets and the word of Jehovah is with them,
> Let them intercede with Jehovah Sabaoth, that the rest of the vessels of the Temple, the Palace, and the City may not go to Babylon."

The God of Israel was yet ready to welcome any beginning of true repentance. Like the father of the Prodigal Son, He would meet His people when they were on the way back to Him. Any stirring of filial penitence would win an instant and gracious response.

We can scarcely suppose that this appeal by Jeremiah to his brother-prophets was merely sarcastic and denunciatory. Passing circumstances may have brought Jeremiah into friendly intercourse with some of his opponents; personal contact may have begotten something of mutual kindliness; and hence there arose a transient gleam of hope that reconciliation and co-operation might still be possible. But it was soon evident that the "patriotic" party would not renounce their vain dreams; Judah must drink the cup of wrath to the dregs: the pillars, the sea, the bases, the rest of the vessels left in Jerusalem must also be carried to Babylon, and remain there till Jehovah should visit the Jews and bring them back and restore them to their own land.

Thus did Jeremiah meet the attempt of the government to organise a Syrian revolt against Babylon, and thus did he give the lie to the promises of Divine blessing made by the prophets. In the face of his utterances, it was difficult to maintain the popular enthusiasm necessary to a successful revolt. In order to neutralise, if possible, the impression made by Jeremiah, the government put forward one of their prophetic supporters to deliver a counter-blast. The place and the occasion were similar to those chosen by Jeremiah for his own address to the people and for Baruch's reading of the roll--the court of the Temple where the priests and "all the people" were assembled. Jeremiah himself was there. Possibly it was a feast-day. The incident came to be regarded as of special importance, and a distinct heading is attached to it, specifying its exact date, "in the same year"--as the incidents of the previous chapter--"in the beginning of the reign of Zedekiah, in the fourth year, in the fifth month."

On such an occasion, Jeremiah's opponents would select as their representative some striking personality, a man of high reputation for ability and personal character. Such a man, apparently, they found in Hananiah ben Azzur of Gibeon. Let us consider for a moment this mouthpiece and champion of a great political and ecclesiastical party, we might almost say of a National Government and a National Church. He is never mentioned except in chapter xxviii., but what we read here is sufficiently characteristic, and receives much light from the other literature of the period. As Gibeon is assigned to the priests in Joshua xxi. 17, it has been conjectured that, like Jeremiah himself, Hananiah was a priest. The special stress laid on the sacred vessels would be in accordance with this theory.

In our last chapter we expounded Jeremiah's description of his prophetic contemporaries, as self-important and time-serving, guilty of plagiarism and cant. Now from this dim, inarticulate crowd of professional prophets, an individual steps for a moment into the light of history and speaks with clearness and emphasis. Let us gaze at him, and hear what he has to say.

If we could have been present at this scene immediately after a careful study of chapter xxvii. even the appearance of Hananiah would have caused us a shock of surprise--such as is sometimes experienced by a devout student of Protestant literature on being introduced to a live Jesuit, or by some budding secularist when he first makes the personal acquaintance of a curate. We might possibly have discerned something commonplace, some lack of depth and force in the man whose faith was merely conventional; but we should have expected to read "liar and hypocrite" in every line of his countenance, and we should have seen nothing of the sort. Conscious of the enthusiastic support of his fellow-countrymen and especially of his own order, charged--as he believed--with a message of promise for Jerusalem, Hananiah's face and bearing, as he came forward to address his sympathetic audience, betrayed nothing unworthy of the high calling of a prophet. His words had the true prophetic ring, he spoke with assured authority:--

> "Thus saith Jehovah Sabaoth, the God of Israel,
> I have broken the yoke of the king of Babylon."

His special object was to remove the unfavourable impression caused by Jeremiah's contradiction of the promise concerning the sacred vessels. Like Jeremiah, he meets this denial in the strongest and most convincing fashion. He does not argue--he reiterates the promise in a more definite form and with more emphatic asseveration. Like Jonah at Nineveh, he ventures to fix an exact date in the immediate future for the fulfilment of the prophecy. "Yet forty days," said Jonah, but the next day he had to swallow his own words; and Hananiah's prophetic chronology met with no better fate:--

> "Within two full years will I bring again to this place all the vessels of the Temple, that Nebuchadnezzar king of Babylon took away."

The full significance of this promise is shown by the further addition:--

> "And I will bring again to this place the king of Judah, Jeconiah ben Jehoiakim, and all the captives of Judah that went to Babylon (it is the utterance of Jehovah); for I will break the yoke of the king of Babylon."

This bold challenge was promptly met:--
"The prophet Jeremiah said unto the prophet Hananiah before the priests and all the people that stood in the Temple." Not "the true prophet" and "the false prophet," not "the man of God" and "the impostor," but simply "the prophet Jeremiah" and "the prophet Hananiah." The audience discerned no obvious difference of status or authority between the two--if anything the advantage lay with Hananiah; they watched the scene as a modern churchman might regard a discussion between ritualistic and evangelical bishops at a Church Congress, only Hananiah was their ideal of a "good churchman." The true parallel is not debates between atheists and the Christian Evidence Society, or between missionaries and Brahmins, but controversies like those between Arius and Athanasius, Jerome and Rufinus, Cyril and Chrysostom.

These prophets, however, display a courtesy and self-restraint that have, for the most part, been absent from Christian polemics.

> "Jeremiah the prophet said, Amen: may Jehovah bring it to pass; may He establish the words of thy prophecy, by bringing back again from Babylon unto this place both the vessels of the Temple and all the captives."

With that entire sincerity which is the most consummate tact, Jeremiah avows his sympathy with his opponents' patriotic aspirations, and recognises that they were worthy of Hebrew prophets. But patriotic aspirations were not a sufficient reason for claiming Divine authority for a cheap optimism. Jeremiah's reflection upon the past had led him to an entirely opposite philosophy of history. Behind Hananiah's words lay the claim that the religious traditions of Israel and the teaching of former prophets guaranteed the inviolability of the Temple and the Holy City. Jeremiah appealed to their authority for his message of doom:--

"The ancient prophets who were our predecessors prophesied war and calamity and pestilence against many countries and great kingdoms."

It was almost a mark of the true prophet that he should be the herald of disaster. The prophetical books of the Old Testament Canon fully confirm this startling and unwelcome statement. Their main burden is the ruin and misery that await Israel and its neighbours. The presumption therefore was in favour of the prophet of evil, and against the prophet of good. Jeremiah does not, of course, deny that there had been, and might yet be, prophets of good. Indeed every prophet, he himself included, announced some Divine promise, but:--

> "The prophet which prophesieth of peace shall be known as truly sent of Jehovah when his prophecy is fulfilled."

It seemed a fair reply to Hananiah's challenge. His prophecy of the return of the sacred vessels and the exiles within two years was intended to encourage Judah and its allies to persist in their revolt. They would be at once victorious, and recover all and more than all which they had lost. Under such circumstances Jeremiah's criterion of "prophecies of peace" was eminently practical. "You are promised these blessings within two years: very well, do not run the terrible risks of a rebellion; keep quiet and see if the two years bring the fulfilment of this prophecy--it is not long to wait." Hananiah might fairly have replied that this fulfilment depended on Judah's faith and loyalty to the Divine promise; and their faith and loyalty would be best shown by rebelling against their oppressors. Jehovah promised Canaan to the Hebrews of the Exodus, but their carcasses mouldered in the desert because they had not courage enough to attack formidable enemies. "Let us not," Hananiah might have said, "imitate their cowardice, and thus share alike their unbelief and its penalty."

Neither Jeremiah's premises nor his conclusions would commend his words to the audience, and he probably weakened his position by leaving the high ground of authority and descending to argument. Hananiah at any rate did not follow his example: he adheres to his former method, and reiterates with renewed emphasis the promise which his adversary had contradicted. Following Jeremiah in his use of the parable in action, so common with Hebrew prophets, he turned the symbol of the yoke against its author. As Zedekiah ben Chenaanah made him horns of iron and prophesied to Ahab and Jehoshaphat, "Thus saith Jehovah, With these shalt thou push the Syrians until thou have consumed them," [122] so now Hananiah took the yoke off Jeremiah's neck and broke it before the assembled people and said:--

"Thus saith Jehovah, Even so will I break the yoke of Nebuchadnezzar king of Babylon from the neck of all nations within two full years."

Naturally the promise is "for all nations"--not for Judah only, but for the other allies.

"And the prophet Jeremiah went his way." For the moment Hananiah had triumphed; he had had the last word, and Jeremiah was silenced. A public debate before a partisan audience was not likely to issue in victory for the truth. The situation may have even shaken his faith in himself and his message; he may have been staggered for a moment by Hananiah's apparent earnestness and conviction. He could not but remember that the gloomy predictions of Isaiah's earlier ministry had been followed by the glorious deliverance from Sennacherib. Possibly some similar sequel was to follow his own denunciations. He betook himself anew to fellowship with God, and awaited a fresh mandate from Jehovah.

"Then the word of Jehovah came unto Jeremiah, ... Go and tell Hananiah: Thou hast broken wooden yokes; thou shalt make iron yokes in their stead. For thus saith Jehovah Sabaoth, the God of Israel: I have put a yoke of iron upon the necks of all these nations, that they may serve Nebuchadnezzar king of Babylon." [123]

We are not told how long Jeremiah had to wait for this new message, or under what circumstances it was delivered to Hananiah. Its symbolism is obvious. When Jeremiah sent the yokes to the ambassadors of the allies and exhorted Zedekiah to bring his neck under the yoke of Nebuchadnezzar, they were required to accept the comparatively tolerable servitude of tributaries. Their impatience of this minor evil would expose them to the iron yoke of ruin and captivity.

Thus the prophet of evil received new Divine assurance of the abiding truth of his message and of the reality of his own inspiration. The same revelation convinced him that his opponent was either an impostor or woefully deluded:--

"Then said the prophet Jeremiah unto the prophet Hananiah, Hear now, Hananiah; Jehovah hath not sent thee, but thou makest this people to trust in a lie. Therefore thus saith Jehovah: I will cast thee away from on the face of the earth; this year thou shalt die, because thou hast preached rebellion against Jehovah."

By a judgment not unmixed with mercy, Hananiah was not left to be convicted of error or imposture, when the "two full years" should have elapsed, and his glowing promises be seen to utterly fail. He also was "taken away from the evil to come."

"So Hananiah the prophet died in the same year in the seventh month"--i.e. about two months after this incident. Such personal judgments were most frequent in the case of kings, but were not confined to them. Isaiah [124] left on record prophecies concerning the appointment to the treasurership of Shebna and Eliakim; and elsewhere Jeremiah himself pronounces the doom of Pashhur ben Immer, the governor of the Temple; but the conclusion of this incident reminds us most forcibly of the speedy execution of the apostolic sentence upon Ananias and Sapphira.

The subjects of this and the preceding chapter raise some of the most important questions as to authority in religion. On the one hand, on the subjective side, how may a man be assured of the truth of his own religious convictions; on the other hand, on the objective side, how is the hearer to decide between conflicting claims on his faith and obedience?

The former question is raised as to the personal convictions of the two prophets. We have ventured to assume that, however erring and culpable Hananiah may have been, he yet had an honest faith in his own inspiration and in the truth of his own prophecies. The conscious impostor, unhappily, is not unknown either in ancient or modern Churches; but we should not look for edification from the study of this branch of morbid spiritual pathology. There were doubtless Jewish counterparts to "Mr. Sludge the Medium" and to the more subtle and plausible "Bishop Blougram"; but Hananiah was of a different type. The evident respect felt for him by the people, Jeremiah's almost deferential courtesy and temporary hesitation as to his rival's Divine mission, do not suggest deliberate hypocrisy. Hananiah's "lie" was a falsehood in fact but not in intention. The Divine message "Jehovah hath not sent thee" was felt by Jeremiah to be no mere exposure of what Hananiah had known all along, but to be a revelation to his adversary as well as to himself.

The sweeping condemnation of the prophets in chapter xxiii. does not exclude the possibility of Hananiah's honesty, any more than our Lord's denunciation of the Pharisees as "devourers of widows' houses" necessarily includes Gamaliel. In critical times, upright, earnest men do not always espouse what subsequent ages hold to have been the cause of truth. Sir Thomas More and Erasmus remained in the communion which Luther renounced: Hampden and Falkland found themselves in opposite camps. If such men erred in their choice between right and wrong, we may often feel anxious as to our own decisions. When we find ourselves in opposition to earnest and devoted men, we may well pause to consider which is Jeremiah and which Hananiah.

The point at issue between these two prophets was exceedingly simple and practical--whether Jehovah approved of the proposed revolt and would reward it with success. Theological questions were only indirectly and remotely involved. Yet, in face of his opponent's persistent asseverations, Jeremiah-- perhaps the greatest of the prophets--went his way in silence to obtain fresh Divine confirmation of his message. And the man who hesitated was right.

Two lessons immediately follow, one as to practice, the other as to principle. It often happens that earnest servants of God find themselves at variance, not on simple practical questions, but on the history and criticism of the remote past, or on abstruse points of transcendental theology. Before any one ventures to denounce his adversary as a teacher of deadly error, let him, like Jeremiah, seek, in humble and prayerful submission to the Holy Spirit, a Divine mandate for such denunciation.

But again Jeremiah was willing to reconsider his position, not merely because he himself might have been mistaken, but because altered circumstances might have opened the way for a change in God's dealings. It was a bare possibility, but we have seen elsewhere that Jeremiah represents God as willing to make a gracious response to the first movement of compunction. Prophecy was the declaration of His will, and that will was not arbitrary, but at every moment and at every point exactly adapted to conditions with which it had to deal. Its principles were unchangeable and eternal; but prophecy was chiefly an application of these principles to existing circumstances. The true prophet always realised that his words were for men as they were when he addressed them. Any moment might bring a change which would abrogate or modify the old teaching, and require and receive a new message. Like Jonah, he might have to proclaim ruin one day and deliverance the next. A physician, even after the most careful diagnosis, may have to recognise unsuspected symptoms which lead him to cancel his prescription and write a new one. The sickening and healing of the soul involve changes equally unexpected. The Bible does not teach that inspiration, any more than science, has only one treatment for each and every spiritual condition and contingency. The true prophet's message is always a word in season.

We turn next to the objective question: How is the hearer to decide between conflicting claims on his faith and obedience? We say the right was with Jeremiah; but how were the Jews to know that? They were addressed by two prophets, or, as we might say, two accredited ecclesiastics of the national Church; each with apparent earnestness and sincerity claimed to speak in the name of Jehovah and of the ancient faith of Israel, and each flatly contradicted the other on an immediate practical question, on which hung their individual fortunes and the destinies of their country. What were the Jews to do? Which were they to believe? It is the standing difficulty of all appeals to external authority. You inquire of this supposed divine oracle and there issues from it a babel of discordant voices, and each demands that you shall unhesitatingly submit to its dictates on peril of eternal damnation; and some have the audacity to claim obedience, because their teaching is "quod semper, quod ubique, quod ab omnibus."

One simple and practical test is indeed suggested--the prophet of evil is more likely to be truly inspired than the prophet of good; but Jeremiah naturally does not claim that this is an invariable test. Nor can he have meant that you can always believe prophecies of evil without any hesitation, but that you are to put no faith in promises until they are fulfilled. Yet it is not difficult to discern the truth underlying Jeremiah's words. The prophet whose words are unpalatable to his hearers is more likely to have a true inspiration than the man who kindles their fancy with glowing pictures of an imminent millennium. The divine message to a congregation of country squires is more likely to be an exhortation to be just to their tenants than a sermon on the duty of the labourer to his betters. A true prophet addressing an audience of working men would perhaps deal with the abuses of trades unions rather than with the sins of capitalists.

But this principle, which is necessarily of limited application, does not go far to solve the great question of authority in religion, on which Jeremiah gives us no further help.

There is, however, one obvious moral. No system of external authority, whatever pains may be taken to secure authentic legitimacy, can altogether release the individual from the responsibility of private judgment. Unreserved faith in the idea of a Catholic Church is quite consistent with much hesitation between the Anglican, Roman, and Greek communions; and the most devoted Catholic may be called upon to choose between rival anti-popes.

Ultimately the inspired teacher is only discerned by the inspired hearer; it is the answer of the conscience that authenticates the divine message.

Footnotes:

121. The close connection between xxvii. and xxviii. shows that the date in xxviii. 1, "the fourth year of Zedekiah," covers both chapters. "Jehoiakim" in xxvii. 1 is a misreading for "Zedekiah": see R.V. margin.

122. 1 Kings xxii. 11.

123. The rest of this verse has apparently been inserted from xxvii. 6 by a scribe. It is omitted by the LXX.

124. xxii. 15-25.

CHAPTER X

CORRESPONDENCE WITH THE EXILES

xxix.
"*Jehovah make thee like Zedekiah and Ahab, whom the king of Babylon roasted in the fire.*"--Jer. xxix. 22.

Nothing further is said about the proposed revolt, so that Jeremiah's vigorous protest seems to have been successful. In any case, unless irrevocable steps had been taken, the enterprise could hardly have survived the death of its advocate, Hananiah. Accordingly Zedekiah sent an embassy to Babylon, charged doubtless with plausible explanations and profuse professions of loyalty and devotion. The envoys were Elasah ben Shaphan and Gemariah ben Hilkiah. Shaphan and Hilkiah were almost certainly the scribe and high priest who discovered Deuteronomy in the eighteenth year of Josiah, and Elasah was the brother of Ahikam ben Shaphan, who protected Jeremiah in the fourth year of Jehoiakim, and of Gemariah ben Shaphan, in whose chamber Baruch read the roll, and who protested against its destruction. Probably Elasah and Gemariah were adherents of Jeremiah, and the fact of the embassy, as well as the choice of ambassadors, suggests that, for the moment, Zedekiah was acting under the influence of the prophet. Jeremiah took the opportunity of sending a letter to the exiles at Babylon. Hananiah had his allies in Chaldea: Ahab ben Kolaiah, Zedekiah ben Maaseiah, and Shemaiah the Nehelamite, with other prophets, diviners, and dreamers, had imitated their brethren in Judah; they had prophesied without being sent and had caused the people to believe a lie. We are not expressly told what they prophesied, but the narrative takes for granted that they, like Hananiah, promised the exiles a speedy return to their native land. Such teaching naturally met with much acceptance, the people congratulating themselves because, as they supposed, "Jehovah hath raised us up prophets in Babylon." The presence of prophets among them was received as a welcome proof that Jehovah had not deserted His people in their house of bondage.

Thus when Jeremiah had confounded his opponents in Jerusalem he had still to deal with their friends in Babylon. Here again the issue was one of immediate practical importance. In Chaldea as at Jerusalem the prediction that the exiles would immediately return was intended to kindle the proposed revolt. The Jews at Babylon were virtually warned to hold themselves in readiness to take advantage of any success of the Syrian rebels, and, if opportunity offered, to render them assistance. In those days information travelled slowly, and there was some danger lest the captives should be betrayed into acts of disloyalty, even after the Jewish government had given up any present intention of revolting against Nebuchadnezzar. Such disloyalty might have involved their entire destruction. Both Zedekiah and Jeremiah would be anxious to inform them at once that they must refrain from any plots against their Chaldean masters. Moreover the prospect of an immediate return had very much the same effect upon these Jews as the expectation of Christ's Second Coming had upon the primitive Church at Thessalonica. It made them restless and disorderly. They could not settle to any regular work, but became busybodies--wasting their time over the glowing promises of their popular preachers, and whispering to one another wild rumours of successful revolts in Syria; or were even more dangerously occupied in planning conspiracies against their conquerors.

Jeremiah's letter sought to bring about a better state of mind. It is addressed to the elders, priests, prophets, and people of the Captivity. The enumeration reminds us how thoroughly the exiled community reproduced the society of the ancient Jewish state--there was already a miniature Judah in Chaldea, the first of those Israels of the Dispersion which have since covered the face of the earth.

This is Jehovah's message by His prophet:--

> "*Build houses and dwell in them;*
> *Plant gardens and eat the fruit thereof;*
> *Marry and beget sons and daughters;*
> *Marry your sons and daughters,*
> *That they may bear sons and daughters,*
> *That ye may multiply there and not grow few.*
> *Seek the peace of the city whither I have sent you into captivity:*
> *Pray for it unto Jehovah;*

For in its peace, ye shall have peace."

There was to be no immediate return; their captivity would last long enough to make it worth their while to build houses and plant gardens. For the present they were to regard Babylon as their home. The prospect of restoration to Judah was too distant to make any practical difference to their conduct of ordinary business. The concluding command to "seek the peace of Babylon" is a distinct warning against engaging in plots, which could only ruin the conspirators. There is an interesting difference between these exhortations and those addressed by Paul to his converts in the first century. He never counsels them to marry, but rather recommends celibacy as more expedient for the present necessity. Apparently life was more anxious and harassed for the early Christians than for the Jews in Babylon. The return to Canaan was to these exiles what the millennium and the Second Advent were to the primitive Church. Jeremiah having bidden his fellow-countrymen not to be agitated by supposing that this much-longed event might come at any moment, fortifies their faith and patience by a promise that it should not be delayed indefinitely.

"When ye have fulfilled seventy years in Babylon I will visit you,
And will perform for you My gracious promise to bring you back to this place." [125]

Seventy is obviously a round number. Moreover the constant use of seven and its multiples in sacred symbolism forbids us to understand the prophecy as an exact chronological statement.
We should adequately express the prophet's meaning by translating "in about two generations." We need not waste time and trouble in discovering or inventing two dates exactly separated by seventy years, one of which will serve for the beginning and the other for the end of the Captivity. The interval between the destruction of Jerusalem and the Return was fifty years (b.c. 586-536), but as our passage refers more immediately to the prospects of those already in exile, we should obtain an interval of sixty-five years from the deportation of Jehoiachin and his companions in b.c. 601. But there can be no question of approximation, however close. Either the "seventy years" merely stands for a comparatively long period, or it is exact. We do not save the inspiration of a date by showing that it is only five years wrong, and not twenty. For an inspired date must be absolutely accurate; a mistake of a second in such a case would be as fatal as a mistake of a century.
Israel's hope is guaranteed by God's self-knowledge of His gracious counsel:--

"I know the purposes which I purpose concerning you, is the utterance of Jehovah;
Purposes of peace and not of evil, to give you hope for the days to come."

In the former clause "I" is emphatic in both places, and the phrase is parallel to the familiar formula "by Myself have I sworn, saith Jehovah." The future of Israel was guaranteed by the divine consistency. Jehovah, to use a colloquial phrase, knew His own mind. His everlasting purpose for the Chosen People could not be set aside. "Did God cast off His people? God forbid."
Yet this persistent purpose is not fulfilled without reference to character and conduct:--

"Ye shall call upon Me, and come and pray unto Me,
And I will hearken unto you.
Ye shall seek Me, and find Me,
Because ye seek Me with all your heart.
I will be found of you--it is the utterance of Jehovah.
I will bring back your captivity, and will gather you from all nations and places whither I have scattered you--it is the utterance of Jehovah.
I will bring you back to this place whence I sent you away to captivity." [126]

As in the previous chapter, Jeremiah concludes with a personal judgment upon those prophets who had been so acceptable to the exiles. If verse 23 is to be understood literally, Ahab and Zedekiah had not only spoken without authority in the name of Jehovah, but had also been guilty of gross immorality. Their punishment was to be more terrible than that of Hananiah. They had incited the exiles to revolt by predicting the imminent ruin of Nebuchadnezzar. Possibly the Jewish king proposed to make his own peace by betraying his agents, after the manner of our own Elizabeth and other sovereigns.
They were to be given over to the terrible vengeance which a Chaldean king would naturally take on such offenders, and would be publicly roasted alive, so that the malice of him who desired to curse his enemy might find vent in such words as:--

"Jehovah make thee like Zedekiah and Ahab, whom the king of Babylon roasted alive."

We are not told whether this prophecy was fulfilled, but it is by no means unlikely. The Assyrian king Assurbanipal says, in one of his inscriptions concerning a viceroy of Babylon who had revolted, that Assur and the other gods "in the fierce burning fire they threw him and destroyed his life"--possibly through the agency of Assurbanipal's servants. [127] One of the seven brethren who were tortured to death in the persecutions of Antiochus Epiphanes is said to have been "fried in the pan." [128] Christian hagiology commemorates St. Lawrence and many other martyrs, who suffered similar torments. Such punishments remained part of criminal procedure until a comparatively recent date; they are still sometimes inflicted by lynch law in the United States, and have been defended even by Christian ministers.

Jeremiah's letter caused great excitement and indignation among the exiles. We have no rejoinder from Ahab and Zedekiah; probably they were not in a position to make any. But Shemaiah the Nehelamite tried to make trouble for Jeremiah at Jerusalem. He, in his turn, wrote letters to "all the people at Jerusalem and to the priest Zephaniah ben Maaseiah and to all the priests" to this effect:--

"Jehovah hath made thee priest in the room of Jehoiada the priest, to exercise supervision over the Temple, and to deal with any mad fanatic who puts himself forward to prophesy, by placing him in the stocks and the collar. Why then hast thou not rebuked Jeremiah of Anathoth, who puts himself forward to prophesy unto you? Consequently he has sent unto us at Babylon: It (your captivity) will be long; build houses and dwell in them, plant gardens and eat the fruit thereof."

Confidence in a speedy return had already been exalted into a cardinal article of the exiles' faith, and Shemaiah claims that any one who denied this comfortable doctrine must be ipso facto a dangerous and deluded fanatic, needing to be placed under strict restraint. This letter travelled to Jerusalem with the returning embassy, and was duly delivered to Zephaniah. Zephaniah is spoken of in the historical section common to Kings and Jeremiah as "the second priest," [129] Seraiah being the High Priest; like Pashhur ben Immer, he seems to have been the governor of the Temple. He was evidently well disposed to Jeremiah, to whom Zedekiah twice sent him on important missions. On the present occasion, instead of acting upon the suggestions made by Shemaiah, he read the letter to Jeremiah, in order that the latter might have an opportunity of dealing with it.

Jeremiah was divinely instructed to reply to Shemaiah, charging him, in his turn, with being a man who put himself forward to prophesy without any commission from Jehovah, and who thus deluded his hearers into belief in falsehoods. Personal sentence is passed upon him, as upon Hananiah, Ahab, and Zedekiah; no son of his shall be reckoned amongst God's people or see the prosperity which they shall hereafter enjoy. The words are obscure: it is said that Jehovah will "visit Shemaiah and his seed," so that it cannot mean that he will be childless; but it is further said that "he shall not have a man to abide amongst this people." It is apparently a sentence of excommunication against Shemaiah and his family.

Here the episode abruptly ends. We are not told whether the letter was sent, or how it was received, or whether it was answered. We gather that, here also, the last word rested with Jeremiah, and that at this point his influence became dominant both at Jerusalem and at Babylon, and that King Zedekiah himself submitted to his guidance.

Chapters xxviii., xxix., deepen the impression made by other sections of Jeremiah's intolerance and personal bitterness towards his opponents. He seems to speak of the roasting alive of the prophets at Babylon with something like grim satisfaction, and we are tempted to think of Torquemada and Bishop Bonner. But we must remember that the stake, as we have already said, has scarcely yet ceased to be an ordinary criminal punishment, and that, after centuries of Christianity, More and Cranmer, Luther and Calvin, had hardly any more tenderness for their ecclesiastical opponents than Jeremiah.

Indeed the Church is only beginning to be ashamed of the complacency with which she has contemplated the fiery torments of hell as the eternal destiny of unrepentant sinners. One of the most tolerant and catholic of our religious teachers has written: "If the unlucky malefactor, who in mere brutality of ignorance or narrowness of nature or of culture has wronged his neighbour, excite our anger, how much deeper should be our indignation when intellect and eloquence are abused to selfish purposes, when studious leisure and learning and thought turn traitors to the cause of human well-being and the wells of a nation's moral life are poisoned." [130] The deduction is obvious: society feels constrained to hang or burn "the unlucky malefactor"; consequently such punishments are, if anything, too merciful for the false prophet. Moreover the teaching which Jeremiah denounced was no mere dogmatism about abstruse philosophical and theological abstractions. Like the Jesuit propaganda under Elizabeth, it was more immediately concerned with politics than with religion. We are bound to be indignant with a man, gifted in exploiting the emotions of his docile audience, who wins the confidence and arouses the enthusiasm of his hearers, only to entice them into hopeless and foolhardy ventures.

And yet we are brought back to the old difficulty, how are we to know the false prophet? He has neither horns nor hoofs, his tie may be as white and his coat as long as those of the true messenger of God. Again, Jeremiah's method affords us some practical guidance. He does not himself order and superintend the punishment of false prophets; he merely announces a divine judgment, which Jehovah Himself is to execute. He does not condemn men by the code of any Church, but each sentence is a direct and special revelation from Jehovah. How many sentences would have been passed upon heretics, if their accusers and judges had waited for a similar sanction?

Footnotes:

125. Doubts have been expressed as to whether this verse originally formed part of Jeremiah's letter, or was ever written by him; but in view of his numerous references to a coming restoration those doubts are unnecessary.

126. The Hebrew Text inserts a paragraph (vv. 16-20) substantially identical with other portions of the book, especially xxiv. 8-10, announcing the approaching ruin and captivity of Zedekiah and the Jews still remaining in Judah. This section is omitted by the LXX., and breaks the obvious connection between verses 15 and 21.

127. Smith's Assurbanipal, p. 163.
128. 2 Macc. vii. 5.
129. lii. 24; 2 Kings xxv. 18.
130. Ecce Homo, xxi.

CHAPTER XI

A BROKEN COVENANT

xxi. 1-10, xxxiv., xxxvii. 1-10.
"*All the princes and people ... changed their minds and reduced to bondage again all the slaves whom they had set free.*"--Jer. xxxiv. 10, 11.

In our previous chapter we saw that, at the point where the fragmentary record of the abortive conspiracy in the fourth year of Zedekiah came to an abrupt conclusion, Jeremiah seemed to have regained the ascendency he enjoyed under Josiah. The Jewish government had relinquished their schemes of rebellion and acquiesced once more in the supremacy of Babylon. We may possibly gather from a later chapter [131] that Zedekiah himself paid a visit to Nebuchadnezzar to assure him of his loyalty. If so, the embassy of Elasah ben Shaphan and Gemariah ben Hilkiah was intended to assure a favourable reception for their master.

The history of the next few years is lost in obscurity, but when the curtain again rises everything is changed and Judah is once more in revolt against the Chaldeans. No doubt one cause of this fresh change of policy was the renewed activity of Egypt. In the account of the conspiracy in Zedekiah's fourth year, there is a significant absence of any reference to Egypt. Jeremiah succeeded in baffling his opponents partly because their fears of Babylon were not quieted by any assurance of Egyptian support. Now there seemed a better prospect of a successful insurrection.

About the seventh year of Zedekiah, Psammetichus II. of Egypt was succeeded by his brother Pharaoh Hophra, the son of Josiah's conqueror, Pharaoh Necho. When Hophra--the Apries of Herodotus--had completed the reconquest of Ethiopia, he made a fresh attempt to carry out his father's policy and to re-establish the ancient Egyptian supremacy in Western Asia; and, as of old, Egypt began by tampering with the allegiance of the Syrian vassals of Babylon. According to Ezekiel, [132] Zedekiah took the initiative: "he rebelled against him (Nebuchadnezzar) by sending his ambassadors into Egypt, that they might give him horses and much people."

The knowledge that an able and victorious general was seated on the Egyptian throne, along with the secret intrigues of his agents and partisans, was too much for Zedekiah's discretion. Jeremiah's advice was disregarded. The king surrendered himself to the guidance--we might almost say, the control--of the Egyptian party in Jerusalem; he violated his oath of allegiance to his suzerain, and the frail and battered ship of state was once more embarked on the stormy waters of rebellion. Nebuchadnezzar promptly prepared to grapple with the reviving strength of Egypt in a renewed contest for the lordship of Syria. Probably Egypt and Judah had other allies, but they are not expressly mentioned. A little later Tyre was besieged by Nebuchadnezzar; but as Ezekiel [133] represents Tyre as exulting over the fall of Jerusalem, she can hardly have been a benevolent neutral, much less a faithful ally. Moreover, when Nebuchadnezzar began his march into Syria, he hesitated whether he should first attack Jerusalem or Rabbath Ammon:--

"*The king of Babylon stood at the parting of the way, ... to use divination: he shook the arrows to and fro, he consulted the teraphim, he looked in the liver.*" [134]

Later on Baalis, king of Ammon, received the Jewish refugees and supported those who were most irreconcilable in their hostility to Nebuchadnezzar. Nevertheless the Ammonites were denounced by Jeremiah for occupying the territory of Gad, and by Ezekiel [135] for sharing the exultation of Tyre over the ruin of Judah. Probably Baalis played a double part. He may have promised support to Zedekiah, and then purchased his own pardon by betraying his ally.

Nevertheless the hearty support of Egypt was worth more than the alliance of any number of the petty neighbouring states, and Nebuchadnezzar levied a great army to meet this ancient and formidable enemy of Assyria and Babylon. He marched into Judah with "all his army, and all the kingdoms of the earth that were under his dominion, and all the peoples," and "fought against Jerusalem and all the cities thereof." [136]

At the beginning of the siege Zedekiah's heart began to fail him. The course of events seemed to confirm Jeremiah's threats, and the king, with pathetic inconsistency, sought to be reassured by the prophet himself. He sent Pashhur ben Malchiah and Zephaniah ben Maaseiah to Jeremiah with the message:--

"Inquire, I pray thee, of Jehovah for us, for Nebuchadnezzar king of Babylon maketh war against us: peradventure Jehovah will deal with us according to all His wondrous works, that he may go up from us."

The memories of the great deliverance from Sennacherib were fresh and vivid in men's minds. Isaiah's denunciations had been as uncompromising as Jeremiah's, and yet Hezekiah had been spared. "Peradventure," thought his anxious descendant, "the prophet may yet be charged with gracious messages that Jehovah repents Him of the evil and will even now rescue His Holy City." But the timid appeal only called forth a yet sterner sentence of doom. Formidable as were the enemies against whom Zedekiah craved protection, they were to be reinforced by more terrible allies; man and beast should die of a great pestilence, and Jehovah Himself should be their enemy:--

"I will turn back the weapons of war that are in your hands, wherewith ye fight against the king of Babylon and the Chaldeans.... I Myself will fight against you with an outstretched hand and a strong arm, in anger and fury and great wrath."

The city should be taken and burnt with fire, and the king and all others who survived should be carried away captive. Only on one condition might better terms be obtained:--

"Behold, I set before you the way of life and the way of death. He that abideth in this city shall die by the sword, the famine, and the pestilence; but he that goeth out, and falleth to the besieging Chaldeans, shall live, and his life shall be unto him for a prey." [137]

On another occasion Zephaniah ben Maaseiah with a certain Tehucal ben Shelemiah was sent by the king to the prophet with the entreaty, "Pray now unto Jehovah our God for us." We are not told the sequel to this mission, but it is probably represented by the opening verses of chapter xxxiv. This section has the direct and personal note which characterises the dealings of Hebrew prophets with their sovereigns. Doubtless the partisans of Egypt had had a severe struggle with Jeremiah before they captured the ear of the Jewish king, and Zedekiah was possessed to the very last with a half-superstitious anxiety to keep on good terms with the prophet. Jehovah's "iron pillar and brasen wall" would make no concession to these royal blandishments: his message had been rejected, his Master had been slighted and defied, the Chosen People and the Holy City were being betrayed to their ruin; Jeremiah would not refrain from denouncing this iniquity because the king who had sanctioned it tried to flatter his vanity by sending deferential deputations of important notables. This is the Divine sentence:--

"I will give this city into the hand of the king of Babylon,
And he shall burn it with fire.
Thou shalt not escape out of his hand;
Thou shalt assuredly be taken prisoner;
Thou shalt be delivered into his hand.
Thou shalt see the king of Babylon, face to face;
He shall speak to thee, mouth to mouth,
And thou shalt go to Babylon."
Yet there should be one doubtful mitigation of his punishment:--
"Thou shalt not die by the sword;
Thou shalt die in peace:
With the burnings of thy fathers, the former kings that were before thee,
So shall they make a burning for thee;
And they shall lament thee, saying, Alas lord!
For it is I that have spoken the word--it is the utterance of Jehovah."

King and people were not proof against the combined terrors of the prophetic rebukes and the besieging enemy. Jeremiah regained his influence, and Jerusalem gave an earnest of the sincerity of her repentance by entering into a covenant for the emancipation of all Hebrew slaves. Deuteronomy had re-enacted the ancient law that their bondage should terminate at the end of six years, [138] but this had not been observed: "Your fathers hearkened not unto Me, neither inclined their ear." [139] A large proportion of those then in slavery must have served more than six years; [140] and partly because of the difficulty of discrimination at such a crisis, partly by way of atonement, the Jews undertook to liberate all their slaves. This solemn reparation was made because the limitation of servitude was part of the national Torah, "the covenant that Jehovah made with their fathers in the day that He brought them forth out of the land of Egypt"--i.e. the Deuteronomic Code. Hence it implied the renewed recognition of Deuteronomy, and the restoration of the ecclesiastical order established by Josiah's reforms.

Even Josiah's methods were imitated. He had assembled the people at the Temple and made them enter into "a covenant before Jehovah, to walk after Jehovah, to keep His commandments and testimonies and statutes with all their heart and soul, to perform the words of this covenant that were written in this book. And all the people entered into the covenant." [141] So now Zedekiah in turn caused the people to make a covenant before Jehovah, "in the house which was called by His name," [142] "that every one should release his Hebrew slaves, male and female, and that no one should enslave a brother Jew." [143] A further sanction had been given to this vow by the observance of an ancient and significant rite. When Jehovah promised to Abraham a seed countless as the stars of heaven, He condescended to ratify His promise by causing the symbols of His presence--a smoking furnace and a burning lamp--to pass between the divided halves of a heifer, a she-goat, a ram, and between a turtle-dove and a young pigeon. [144] Now, in like manner, a calf was cut in twain, the two halves laid opposite each other, and "the princes of Judah and Jerusalem, the eunuchs, the priests, and all the people of the land, ... passed between the parts of the calf." [145] Similarly, after the death of Alexander the Great, the contending factions in the Macedonian army ratified a compromise by passing between the two halves of a dog. Such symbols spoke for themselves: those who used them laid themselves under a curse; they prayed that if they violated the covenant they might be slain and mutilated like the divided animals.

This covenant was forthwith carried into effect, the princes and people liberating their Hebrew slaves according to their vow. We cannot, however, compare this event with the abolition of slavery in British colonies or with Abraham Lincoln's Decree of Emancipation. The scale is altogether different: Hebrew bondage had no horrors to compare with those of the American plantations; and moreover, even at the moment, the practical results cannot have been great. Shut up in a beleaguered city, harassed by the miseries and terrors of a siege, the freedmen would see little to rejoice over in their new-found freedom. Unless their friends were in Jerusalem they could not rejoin them, and in most cases they could only obtain sustenance by remaining in the households of their former masters, or by serving in the defending army. Probably this special ordinance of Deuteronomy was selected as the subject of a solemn covenant, because it not only afforded an opportunity of atoning for past sin, but also provided the means of strengthening the national defence. Such expedients were common in ancient states in moments of extreme peril.

In view of Jeremiah's persistent efforts, both before and after this incident, to make his countrymen loyally accept the Chaldean supremacy, we cannot doubt that he hoped to make terms between Zedekiah and Nebuchadnezzar. Apparently no tidings of Pharaoh Hophra's advance had reached Jerusalem; and the non-appearance of his "horses and much people" had discredited the Egyptian party, and enabled Jeremiah to overthrow their influence with the king and people. Egypt, after all her promises, had once more proved herself a broken reed; there was nothing left but to throw themselves on Nebuchadnezzar's mercy.

But the situation was once more entirely changed by the news that Pharaoh Hophra had come forth out of Egypt "with a mighty army and a great company." [146] The sentinels on the walls of Jerusalem saw the besiegers break up their encampment, and march away to meet the relieving army. All thought of submitting to Babylon was given up. Indeed, if Pharaoh Hophra were to be victorious, the Jews must of necessity accept his supremacy. Meanwhile they revelled in their respite from present distress and imminent danger. Surely the new covenant was bearing fruit. Jehovah had been propitiated by their promise to observe the Torah; Pharaoh was the instrument by which God would deliver His people; or even if the Egyptians were defeated, the Divine resources were not exhausted. When Tirhakah advanced to the relief of Hezekiah, he was defeated at Eltekeh, yet Sennacherib had returned home baffled and disgraced. Naturally the partisans of Egypt, the opponents of Jeremiah, recovered their control of the king and the government. The king sent, perhaps at the first news of the Egyptian advance, to inquire of Jeremiah concerning their prospects of success. What seemed to every one else a Divine deliverance was to him a national misfortune; the hopes he had once more indulged of averting the ruin of Judah were again dashed to the ground. His answer is bitter and gloomy:--

> "Behold, Pharaoh's army, which is come forth to help you,
> Shall return to Egypt into their own land.
> The Chaldeans shall come again, and fight against this city;
> They shall take it, and burn it with fire.
> Thus saith Jehovah:
> Do not deceive yourselves, saying,
> The Chaldeans shall surely depart from us:
> They shall not depart.

> *Though ye had smitten the whole army of the Chaldeans that fight against you,*
> *And there remained none but wounded men among them,*
> *Yet should they rise up every man in his tent,*
> *And burn this city with fire."*

Jeremiah's protest was unavailing, and only confirmed the king and princes in their adherence to Egypt. Moreover Jeremiah had now formally disclaimed any sympathy with this great deliverance, which Pharaoh--and presumably Jehovah--had wrought for Judah. Hence it was clear that the people did not owe this blessing to the covenant to which they had submitted themselves by Jeremiah's guidance. As at Megiddo, Jehovah had shown once more that He was with Pharaoh and against Jeremiah. Probably they would best please God by renouncing Jeremiah and all his works--the covenant included. Moreover they could take back their slaves with a clear conscience, to their own great comfort and satisfaction. True, they had sworn in the Temple with solemn and striking ceremonies, but then Jehovah Himself had manifestly released them from their oath. "All the princes and people changed their mind, and reduced to bondage again all the slaves whom they had set free." The freedmen had been rejoicing with their former masters in the prospect of national deliverance; the date of their emancipation was to mark the beginning of a new era of Jewish happiness and prosperity. When the siege was raised and the Chaldeans driven away, they could use their freedom in rebuilding the ruined cities and cultivating the wasted lands. To all such dreams there came a sudden and rough awakening: they were dragged back to their former hopeless bondage--a happy augury for the new dispensation of Divine protection and blessing!

Jeremiah turned upon them in fierce wrath, like that of Elijah against Ahab when he met him taking possession of Naboth's vineyard. They had profaned the name of Jehovah, and--

> *"Therefore thus saith Jehovah:*
> *Ye have not hearkened unto Me to proclaim a release every one to his brother and his neighbour:*
> *Behold, I proclaim a release for you--it is the utterance of Jehovah--unto the sword, the pestilence, and the famine;*
> *And I will make you a terror among all the kingdoms of the earth."*

The prophet plays upon the word "release" with grim irony. The Jews had repudiated the "release" which they had promised under solemn oath to their brethren, but Jehovah would not allow them to be so easily quit of their covenant. There should be a "release" after all, and they themselves should have the benefit of it--a "release" from happiness and prosperity, from the sacred bounds of the Temple, the Holy City, and the Land of Promise--a "release" unto "the sword, the pestilence, and the famine."

> *"I will give the men that have transgressed My covenant into the hands of their enemies....*
> *Their dead bodies shall be meat for the fowls of heaven and for the beasts of the earth.*
> *Zedekiah king of Judah and his princes will I give into the hand of ... the host of the king of Babylon, which are gone up from you.*
> *Behold, I will command--it is the utterance of Jehovah--and will bring them back unto this city:*
> *They shall fight against it, and take it, and burn it with fire.*
> *I will lay the cities of Judah waste, without inhabitant."*

Another broken covenant was added to the list of Judah's sins, another promise of amendment speedily lost in disappointment and condemnation. Jeremiah might well say with his favourite Hosea:--

> *"O Judah, what shall I do unto thee?*
> *Your goodness is as a morning cloud,*
> *And as the dew that goeth early away."* [147]

This incident has many morals; one of the most obvious is the futility of the most stringent oaths and the most solemn symbolic ritual. Whatever influence oaths may have in causing a would-be liar to speak the truth, they are very poor guarantees for the performance of contracts. William the Conqueror profited little by Harold's oath to help him to the crown of England, though it was sworn over the relics of holy saints. Wulfnoth's whisper in Tennyson's drama--

> *"Swear thou to-day, to-morrow is thine own"--*

states the principle on which many oaths have been taken. The famous "blush of Sigismund" over the violation of his safe-conduct to Huss was rather a token of unusual sensitiveness than a confession of exceptional guilt. The Christian Church has exalted perfidy into a sacred obligation. As Milman says[148] :--

> *"The fatal doctrine, confirmed by long usage, by the decrees of Pontiffs, by the assent of all ecclesiastics, and the acquiescence of the Christian world, that no promise, no oath, was binding to a heretic, had hardly been questioned, never repudiated."*

At first sight an oath seems to give firm assurance to a promise; what was merely a promise to man is made into a promise to God. What can be more binding upon the conscience than a promise to God? True; but He to whom the promise is made may always release from its performance. To persist in what God neither requires nor desires because of a promise to God seems absurd and even wicked. It has been said that men "have a way of calling everything they want to do a dispensation of Providence." Similarly, there are many ways by which a man may persuade himself that God has cancelled his vows, especially if he belongs to an infallible Church with a Divine commission to grant dispensations. No doubt these Jewish slaveholders had full sacerdotal absolution from their pledge. The priests had slaves of their own. Failing ecclesiastical aid, Satan himself will play the casuist--it is one of his favourite parts--and will find the traitor full justification for breaking the most solemn contract with Heaven. If a man's whole soul and purpose go with his promise, oaths are superfluous; otherwise, they are useless.

However, the main lesson of the incident lies in its added testimony to the supreme importance which the prophets attached to social righteousness. When Jeremiah wished to knit together again the bonds of fellowship between Judah and its God, he did not make them enter into a covenant to observe ritual or to cultivate pious sentiments, but to release their slaves. It has been said that a gentleman may be known by the way in which he treats his servants; a man's religion is better tested by his behaviour to his helpless dependents than by his attendance on the means of grace or his predilection for pious conversation. If we were right in supposing that the government supported Jeremiah because the act of emancipation would furnish recruits to man the walls, this illustrates the ultimate dependence of society upon the working classes. In emergencies, desperate efforts are made to coerce or cajole them into supporting governments by which they have been neglected or oppressed. The sequel to this covenant shows how barren and transient are concessions begotten by the terror of imminent ruin. The social covenant between all classes of the community needs to be woven strand by strand through long years of mutual helpfulness and goodwill, of peace and prosperity, if it is to endure the strain of national peril and disaster.

Footnotes:

131. li. 59, Hebrew Text. According to the LXX., Zedekiah sent another embassy and did not go himself to Babylon. The section is apparently a late addition.
132. xvii. 15.
133. xxvi. 2.
134. Ezek. xxi. 21.
135. xxv. 1-7.
136. xxi. 1-10. The exact date of this section is not given, but it is closely parallel to xxxiv. 1-7, and seems to belong to the same period.
137. xxi. 1-10.
138. Deut. xv. 12. Cf. Exod. xxi. 2, xxiii. 10.
139. xxxiv. 14.
140. xxxiv. 13.
141. 2 Kings xxiii. 3.
142. xxxiv. 15.
143. xxxiv. 9.
144. Gen. xv.
145. xxxiv. 19.
146. Ezek. xvii. 17.
147. Hosea vi. 4.
148. Milman's Latin Christianity, viii. 255.

CHAPTER XII

JEREMIAH'S IMPRISONMENT

xxxvii. 11-21, xxxviii., xxxix. 15-18.
"Jeremiah abode in the court of the guard until the day that Jerusalem was taken."--Jer. xxxviii. 28.

"When the Chaldean army was broken up from Jerusalem for fear of Pharaoh's army, Jeremiah went forth out of Jerusalem to go into the land of Benjamin" to transact certain family business at Anathoth. [149]

He had announced that all who remained in the city should perish, and that only those who deserted to the Chaldeans should escape. In these troubled times all who sought to enter or leave Jerusalem were subjected to close scrutiny, and when Jeremiah wished to pass through the gate of Benjamin he was stopped by the officer in charge--Irijah ben Shelemiah ben Hananiah--and accused of being about to practise himself what he had preached to the people: "Thou fallest away to the Chaldeans." The suspicion was natural enough; for, although the Chaldeans had raised the siege and marched away to the south-west, while the gate of Benjamin was on the north of the city, Irijah might reasonably suppose that they had left detachments in the neighbourhood, and that this zealous advocate of submission to Babylon had special information on the subject. Jeremiah indeed had the strongest motives for seeking safety in flight. The party whom he had consistently denounced had full control of the government, and even if they spared him for the present any decisive victory over the enemy would be the signal for his execution. When once Pharaoh Hophra was in full march upon Jerusalem at the head of a victorious army, his friends would show no mercy to Jeremiah. Probably Irijah was eager to believe in the prophet's treachery, and ready to snatch at any pretext for arresting him. The name of the captain's grandfather--Hananiah--is too common to suggest any connection with the prophet who withstood Jeremiah; but we may be sure that at this crisis the gates were in charge of trusty adherents of the princes of the Egyptian party. Jeremiah would be suspected and detested by such men as these. His vehement denial of the charge was received with real or feigned incredulity; Irijah "hearkened not unto him."

The arrest took place "in the midst of the people." [150] The gate was crowded with other Jews hurrying out of Jerusalem: citizens eager to breathe more freely after being cooped up in the overcrowded city; countrymen anxious to find out what their farms and homesteads had suffered at the hands of the invaders; not a few, perhaps, bound on the very errand of which Jeremiah was accused, friends of Babylon, convinced that Nebuchadnezzar would ultimately triumph, and hoping to find favour and security in his camp. Critical events of Jeremiah's life had often been transacted before a great assembly; for instance, his own address and trial in the Temple, and the reading of the roll. He knew the practical value of a dramatic situation. This time he had sought the crowd, rather to avoid than attract attention; but when he was challenged by Irijah, the accusation and denial must have been heard by all around. The soldiers of the guard, necessarily hostile to the man who had counselled submission, gathered round to secure their prisoner; for a time the gate was blocked by the guards and spectators. The latter do not seem to have interfered. Formerly the priests and prophets and all the people had laid hold on Jeremiah, and afterwards all the people had acquitted him by acclamation. Now his enemies were content to leave him in the hands of the soldiers, and his friends, if he had any, were afraid to attempt a rescue. Moreover men's minds were not at leisure and craving for new excitement, as at Temple festivals; they were preoccupied, and eager to get out of the city. While the news quickly spread that Jeremiah had been arrested as he was trying to desert, his guards cleared a way through the crowd, and brought the prisoner before the princes. The latter seem to have acted as a Committee of National Defence; they may either have been sitting at the time, or a meeting, as on a previous occasion, [151] may have been called when it was known that Jeremiah had been arrested. Among them were probably those enumerated later on: [152] Shephatiah ben Mattan, Gedaliah ben Pashhur, Jucal ben Shelemiah, and Pashhur ben Malchiah. Shephatiah and Gedaliah are named only here; possibly Gedaliah's father was Pashhur ben Immer, who beat Jeremiah and put him in the stocks. Both Jucal and Pashhur ben Malchiah had been sent by the king to consult Jeremiah. Jucal may have been the son of the Shelemiah who was sent to arrest Jeremiah and Baruch after the reading of the roll. We note the absence of the princes who then formed Baruch's audience, some of whom tried to dissuade Jehoiakim from burning the roll; and we especially miss the prophet's former friend and protector, Ahikam ben Shaphan. Fifteen or sixteen years had elapsed since these earlier events; some of Jeremiah's adherents were dead, others in exile, others powerless to help him. We may safely conclude that his judges were his personal and political enemies. Jeremiah was now their discomfited rival: a few weeks before he had been master of the city and the court. Pharaoh Hophra's advance had enabled them to overthrow him. We can understand that they would at once take Irijah's view of the case. They treated their fallen antagonist as a criminal taken in the act: "they were wroth with him," i.e. they overwhelmed him with a torrent of abuse; "they beat him, and put him in prison in the house of Jonathan the secretary." But this imprisonment in a private house was not mild and honourable confinement under the care of a distinguished noble, who was rather courteous host than harsh gaoler. "They had made that the prison," duly provided with a dungeon and cells, to which Jeremiah was consigned and where he remained "many days." Prison accommodation at Jerusalem was limited; the Jewish government preferred more summary methods of dealing with malefactors. The revolution which had placed the present government in power had given them special occasion for a prison. They had defeated rivals whom they did not venture to execute publicly, but who might be more safely starved and tortured to death in secret. For such a fate they destined Jeremiah. We shall not do injustice to Jonathan the secretary if we compare the hospitality which he extended to his unwilling guests with the treatment of modern Armenians in Turkish prisons. Yet the prophet remained alive "for many days"; probably his enemies reflected that even if he did not succumb earlier to the hardships of his imprisonment, his execution would suitably adorn the looked-for triumph of Pharaoh Hophra.

Few however of the "many days" had passed, before men's exultant anticipations of victory and deliverance began to give place to anxious forebodings. They had hoped to hear that Nebuchadnezzar had been defeated and was in headlong retreat to Chaldea; they had been prepared to join in the pursuit of the routed army, to gratify their revenge by massacring the fugitives and to share the plunder with their Egyptian allies. The fortunes of war belied their hopes; Pharaoh retreated, either after a battle or perhaps even without fighting. The return of the enemy was announced by the renewed influx of the country people to seek the shelter of the fortifications, and soon the Jews crowded to the walls as Nebuchadnezzar's vanguard appeared in sight and the Chaldeans occupied their old lines and re-formed the siege of the doomed city.

There was no longer any doubt that prudence dictated immediate surrender. It was the only course by which the people might be spared some of the horrors of a prolonged siege, followed by the sack of the city. But the princes who controlled the government were too deeply compromised with Egypt to dare to hope for mercy. With Jeremiah out of the way, they were able to induce the king and the people to maintain their resistance, and the siege went on.

But though Zedekiah was, for the most part, powerless in the hands of the princes, he ventured now and then to assert himself in minor matters, and, like other feeble sovereigns, derived some consolation amidst his many troubles from intriguing with the opposition against his own ministers. His feeling and behaviour towards Jeremiah were similar to those of Charles IX. towards Coligny, only circumstances made the Jewish king a more efficient protector of Jeremiah.

At this new and disastrous turn of affairs, which was an exact fulfilment of Jeremiah's warnings, the king was naturally inclined to revert to his former faith in the prophet--if indeed he had ever really been able to shake himself free from his influence. Left to himself he would have done his best to make terms with Nebuchadnezzar, as Jehoiakim and Jehoiachin had done before him. The only trustworthy channel of help, human or divine, was Jeremiah. Accordingly he sent secretly to the prison and had the prophet brought into the palace. There in some inner chamber, carefully guarded from intrusion by the slaves of the palace, Zedekiah received the man who now for more than forty years had been the chief counsellor of the kings of Judah, often in spite of themselves. Like Saul on the eve of Gilboa, he was too impatient to let disaster be its own herald; the silence of Heaven seemed more terrible than any spoken doom, and again like Saul he turned in his perplexity and despair to the prophet who had rebuked and condemned him. "Is there any word from Jehovah? And Jeremiah said, There is: ... thou shalt be delivered into the hand of the king of Babylon."

The Church is rightly proud of Ambrose rebuking Theodosius at the height of his power and glory, and of Thomas Ã

Becket, unarmed and yet defiant before his murderers; but the Jewish prophet showed himself capable of a simpler and grander heroism. For "many days" he had endured squalor, confinement, and semi-starvation. His body must have been enfeebled and his spirit depressed. Weak and contemptible as Zedekiah was, yet he was the prophet's only earthly protector from the malice of his enemies. He intended to utilise this interview for an appeal for release from his present prison. Thus he had every motive for conciliating the man who asked him for a word from Jehovah. He was probably alone with Zedekiah, and was not nerved to self-sacrifice by any opportunity of making public testimony to the truth, and yet he was faithful alike to God and to the poor helpless king--"Thou shalt be delivered into the hand of the king of Babylon."

And then he proceeds, with what seems to us inconsequent audacity, to ask a favour. Did ever petitioner to a king preface his supplication with so strange a preamble? This was the request:--

"Now hear, I pray thee, O my lord the king: let my supplication, I pray thee, be accepted before thee; that thou do not cause me to return to the house of Jonathan the secretary, lest I die there.

"Then Zedekiah the king commanded, and they committed Jeremiah into the court of the guard, and they gave him daily a loaf of bread out of the bakers' street."

A loaf of bread is not sumptuous fare, but it is evidently mentioned as an improvement upon his prison diet: it is not difficult to understand why Jeremiah was afraid he would die in the house of Jonathan.

During this milder imprisonment in the court of the guard occurred the incident of the purchase of the field at Anathoth, which we have dealt with in another chapter. This low ebb of the prophet's fortunes was the occasion of Divine revelation of a glorious future in store for Judah. But this future was still remote, and does not seem to have been conspicuous in his public teaching. On the contrary Jeremiah availed himself of the comparative publicity of his new place of detention to reiterate in the ears of all the people the gloomy predictions with which they had so long been familiar: "This city shall assuredly be given into the hand of the army of the king of Babylon." He again urged his hearers to desert to the enemy: "He that abideth in this city shall die by the sword, the famine, and the pestilence; but he that goeth forth to the Chaldeans shall live." We cannot but admire the splendid courage of the solitary prisoner, helpless in the hands of his enemies and yet openly defying them. He left his opponents only two alternatives, either to give up the government into his hands or else to silence him. Jeremiah in the court of the guard was really carrying on a struggle in which neither side either would or could give quarter. He was trying to revive the energies of the partisans of Babylon, that they might overpower the government and surrender the city to Nebuchadnezzar. If he had succeeded, the princes would have had a short shrift. They struck back with the prompt energy of men fighting for their lives. No government conducting the defence of a besieged fortress could have tolerated Jeremiah for a moment. What would have been the fate of a French politician who should have urged Parisians to desert to the Germans during the siege of 1870? [153] The princes' former attempt to deal with Jeremiah had been thwarted by the king; this time they tried to provide beforehand against any officious intermeddling on the part of Zedekiah. They extorted from him a sanction of their proceedings.

"Then the princes said unto the king, Let this man, we pray thee, be put to death: for he weakeneth the hands of the soldiers that are left in this city, and of all the people, by speaking such words unto them: for this man seeketh not the welfare of this people, but the hurt." Certainly Jeremiah's word was enough to take the heart out of the bravest soldiers; his preaching would soon have rendered further resistance impossible. But the concluding sentence about the "welfare of the people" was merely cheap cant, not without parallel in the sayings of many "princes" in later times. "The welfare of the people" would have been best promoted by the surrender which Jeremiah advocated. The king does not pretend to sympathise with the princes; he acknowledges himself a mere tool in their hands. "Behold," he answers, "he is in your power, for the king can do nothing against you."

"Then they took Jeremiah, and cast him into the cistern of Malchiah ben Hammelech, that was in the court of the guard; and they let Jeremiah down with cords. And there was no water in the cistern, only mud, and Jeremiah sank in the mud."

The depth of this improvised oubliette is shown by the use of cords to let the prisoner down into it. How was it, however, that, after the release of Jeremiah from the cells in the house of Jonathan, the princes did not at once execute him? Probably, in spite of all that had happened, they still felt a superstitious dread of actually shedding the blood of a prophet. In some mysterious way they felt that they would be less guilty if they left him in the empty cistern to starve to death or be suffocated in the mud, than if they had his head cut off. They acted in the spirit of Reuben's advice concerning Joseph, who also was cast into an empty pit, with no water in it: "Shed no blood, but cast him into this pit in the wilderness, and lay no hand upon him." [154] By a similar blending of hypocrisy and superstition, the mediæval Church thought to keep herself unstained by the blood of heretics, by handing them over to the secular arm; and Macbeth having hired some one else to kill Banquo was emboldened to confront his ghost with the words:--

"Thou canst not say I did it. Never shake
Thy gory locks at me."

But the princes were again baffled; the prophet had friends in the royal household who were bolder than their master: Ebed-melech the Ethiopian, an eunuch, heard that they had put Jeremiah in the cistern. He went to the king, who was then sitting in the gate of Benjamin, where he would be accessible to any petitioner for favour or justice, and interceded for the prisoner:--

"My lord the king, these men have done evil in all that they have done to Jeremiah the prophet, whom they have cast into the cistern; and he is like to die in the place where he is because of the famine, for there is no more bread in the city."

Apparently the princes, busied with the defence of the city and in their pride "too much despising" their royal master, had left him for a while to himself. Emboldened by this public appeal to act according to the dictates of his own heart and conscience, and possibly by the presence of other friends of Jeremiah, the king acts with unwonted courage and decision.

"The king commanded Ebed-melech the Ethiopian, saying, Take with thee hence thirty men, and draw up Jeremiah the prophet out of the cistern, before he die. So Ebed-melech took the men with him, and went into the palace under the treasury, and took thence old cast clouts and rotten rags, and let them down by cords into the cistern to Jeremiah. And he said to Jeremiah, Put these old cast clouts and rotten rags under thine armholes under the cords. And Jeremiah did so. So they drew him up with the cords, and took him up out of the cistern: and he remained in the court of the guard."

Jeremiah's gratitude to his deliverer is recorded in a short paragraph in which Ebed-melech, like Baruch, is promised that "his life shall be given him for a prey." He should escape with his life from the sack of the city--"because he trusted" in Jehovah. As of the ten lepers whom Jesus cleansed only the Samaritan returned to give glory to God, so when none of God's people were found to rescue His prophet, the dangerous honour was accepted by an Ethiopian proselyte. [155]

Meanwhile the king was craving for yet another "word of Jehovah." True, the last "word" given him by the prophet had been, "Thou shalt be delivered into the hand of the king of Babylon." But now that he had just rescued Jehovah's prophet from a miserable death (he forgot that Jeremiah had been consigned to the cistern by his own authority), possibly there might be some more encouraging message from God. Accordingly he sent and took Jeremiah unto him for another secret interview, this time in the "corridor of the bodyguard," [156] a passage between the palace and the Temple.

Here he implored the prophet to give him a faithful answer to his questions concerning his own fate and that of the city: "Hide nothing from me." But Jeremiah did not respond with his former prompt frankness. He had had too recent a warning not to put his trust in princes. "If I declare it unto thee," said he, "wilt thou not surely put me to death? and if I give thee counsel, thou wilt not hearken unto me. So Zedekiah the king sware secretly to Jeremiah, As Jehovah liveth, who is the source and giver of our life, I will not put thee to death, neither will I give thee into the hand of these men that seek thy life.

"Then said Jeremiah unto Zedekiah, Thus saith Jehovah, the God of hosts, the God of Israel: If thou wilt go forth unto the king of Babylon's princes, thy life shall be spared, and this city shall not be burned, and thou and thine house shall live; but if thou wilt not go forth, then shall this city be given into the hand of the Chaldeans, and they shall burn it, and thou shalt not escape out of their hand.

"Zedekiah said unto Jeremiah, I am afraid of the Jews that have deserted to the Chaldeans, lest they deliver me into their hand, and they mock me."

He does not, however, urge that the princes will hinder any such surrender; he believed himself sufficiently master of his own actions to be able to escape to the Chaldeans if he chose.

But evidently, when he first revolted against Babylon, and more recently when the siege was raised, he had been induced to behave harshly towards her partisans: they had taken refuge in considerable numbers in the enemy's camp, and now he was afraid of their vengeance. Similarly, in Quentin Durward, Scott represents Louis XI. on his visit to Charles the Bold as startled by the sight of the banners of some of his own vassals, who had taken service with Burgundy, and as seeking protection from Charles against the rebel subjects of France.

Zedekiah is a perfect monument of the miseries that wait upon weakness: he was everybody's friend in turn--now a docile pupil of Jeremiah and gratifying the Chaldean party by his professions of loyalty to Nebuchadnezzar, and now a pliant tool in the hands of the Egyptian party persecuting his former friends. At the last he was afraid alike of the princes in the city, of the exiles in the enemy's camp, and of the Chaldeans. The mariner who had to pass between Scylla and Charybdis was fortunate compared to Zedekiah. To the end he clung with a pathetic blending of trust and fearfulness to Jeremiah. He believed him, and yet he seldom had courage to act according to his counsel.

Jeremiah made a final effort to induce this timid soul to act with firmness and decision. He tried to reassure him: "They shall not deliver thee into the hands of thy revolted subjects. Obey, I beseech thee, the voice of Jehovah, in that which I speak unto thee: so it shall be well with thee, and thy life shall be spared." He appealed to that very dread of ridicule which the king had just betrayed. If he refused to surrender, he would be taunted for his weakness and folly by the women of his own harem:--

"If thou refuse to go forth, this is the word that Jehovah hath showed me: Behold, all the women left in the palace shall be brought forth to the king of Babylon's princes, and those women shall say, Thy familiar friends have duped thee and got the better of thee; thy feet are sunk in the mire, and they have left thee in the lurch." He would be in worse plight than that from which Jeremiah had only just been rescued, and there would no Ebed-melech to draw him out. He would be humiliated by the suffering and shame of his own family: "They shall bring out all thy wives and children to the Chaldeans." He himself would share with them the last extremity of suffering: "Thou shalt not escape out of their hand, but shalt be taken by the hand of the king of Babylon."

And as Tennyson makes it the climax of Geraint's degeneracy that he was not only--

"Forgetful of his glory and his name,"

but also--

"Forgetful of his princedom and its cares,"

so Jeremiah appeals last of all to the king's sense of responsibility for his people: "Thou wilt be the cause of the burning of the city."

In spite of the dominance of the Egyptian party, and their desperate determination, not only to sell their own lives dearly, but also to involve king and people, city and temple, in their own ruin, the power of decisive action still rested with Zedekiah; if he failed to use it, he would be responsible for the consequences.

Thus Jeremiah strove to possess the king with some breath of his own dauntless spirit and iron will.

Zedekiah paused irresolute. A vision of possible deliverance passed through his mind. His guards and the domestics of the palace were within call. The princes were unprepared; they would never dream that he was capable of anything so bold. It would be easy to seize the nearest gate, and hold it long enough to admit the Chaldeans. But no! he had not nerve enough. Then his predecessors Joash, Amaziah, and Amon had been assassinated, and for the moment the daggers of the princes and their followers seemed more terrible than Chaldean instruments of torture. He lost all thought of his own honour and his duty to his people in his anxiety to provide against this more immediate danger. Never was the fate of a nation decided by a meaner utterance. "Then said Zedekiah to Jeremiah, No one must know about our meeting, and thou shalt not die. If the princes hear that I have talked with thee, and come and say unto thee, Declare unto us now what thou hast said unto the king; hide it not from us, and we will not put thee to death: declare unto us what the king said unto thee: then thou shalt say unto them, I presented my supplication unto the king, that he would not cause me to return to Jonathan's house, to die there.

"Then all the princes came to Jeremiah, and asked him; and he told them just what the king had commanded. So they let him alone, for no report of the matter had got abroad." We are a little surprised that the princes so easily abandoned their purpose of putting Jeremiah to death, and did not at once consign him afresh to the empty cistern. Probably they were too disheartened for vigorous action; the garrison were starving, and it was clear that the city could not hold out much longer. Moreover the superstition that had shrunk from using actual violence to the prophet would suspect a token of Divine displeasure in his release.

Another question raised by this incident is that of the prophet's veracity, which, at first sight, does not seem superior to that of the patriarchs. It is very probable that the prophet, as at the earlier interview, had entreated the king not to allow him to be confined in the cells in Jonathan's house, but the narrative rather suggests that the king constructed this pretext on the basis of the former interview. Moreover, if the princes let Jeremiah escape with nothing less innocent than a suppressio veri, if they were satisfied with anything less than an explicit statement that the place of the prophet's confinement was the sole topic of conversation, they must have been more guileless that we can easily imagine. But, at any rate, if Jeremiah did stoop to dissimulation, it was to protect Zedekiah, not to save himself.

Zedekiah is a conspicuous example of the strange irony with which Providence entrusts incapable persons with the decision of most momentous issues; It sets Laud and Charles I. to adjust the Tudor Monarchy to the sturdy self-assertion of Puritan England, and Louis XVI. to cope with the French Revolution. Such histories are after all calculated to increase the self-respect of those who are weak and timid. Moments come, even to the feeblest, when their action must have the most serious results for all connected with them. It is one of the crowning glories of Christianity that it preaches a strength that is made perfect in weakness.

Perhaps the most significant feature in this narrative is the conclusion of Jeremiah's first interview with the king. Almost in the same breath the prophet announces to Zedekiah his approaching ruin and begs from him a favour. He thus defines the true attitude of the believer towards the prophet.

Unwelcome teaching must not be allowed to interfere with wonted respect and deference, or to provoke resentment. Possibly if this truth were less obvious men would be more willing to give it a hearing and it might be less persistently ignored. But the prophet's behaviour is even more striking and interesting as a revelation of his own character and of the true prophetic spirit. His faithful answer to the king involved much courage, but that he should proceed from such an answer to such a petition shows a simple and sober dignity not always associated with courage. When men are wrought up to the pitch of uttering disagreeable truths at the risk of their lives, they often develop a spirit of defiance, which causes personal bitterness and animosity between themselves and their hearers, and renders impossible any asking or granting of favours. Many men would have felt that a petition compromised their own dignity and weakened the authority of the divine message. The exaltation of self-sacrifice which inspired them would have suggested that they ought not to risk the crown of martyrdom by any such appeal, but rather welcome torture and death. Thus some amongst the early Christians would present themselves before the Roman tribunals and try to provoke the magistrates into condemning them. But Jeremiah, like Polycarp and Cyprian, neither courted nor shunned martyrdom; he was as incapable of bravado as he was of fear. He was too intent upon serving his country and glorifying God, too possessed with his mission and his message, to fall a prey to the self-consciousness which betrays men, sometimes even martyrs, into theatrical ostentation.

Footnotes:

149. Cf. xxxii. 6-8.
150. xxxvii. 12; so R.V., Streane (Camb. Bible), Kautzsch, etc.
151. xxvi. 10.
152. xxxviii. 1.
153. Cf. Renan, iii. 333.
154. Gen. xxxvii. 22-24.
155. xxxix. 15-18.
156. So Giesebrecht, in loco; A.V., R.V., "third entry." In any case it will naturally be a passage from the palace to the Temple.

CHAPTER XIII

GEDALIAH

xxxix.-xli., lii. [157]

"Then arose Ishmael ben Nethaniah, and the ten men that were with him, and smote with the sword and slew Gedaliah ben Ahikam ben Shaphan, whom the king of Babylon had made king over the land."--Jer. xli. 2.

We now pass to the concluding period of Jeremiah's ministry. His last interview with Zedekiah was speedily followed by the capture of Jerusalem. With that catastrophe the curtain falls upon another act in the tragedy of the prophet's life. Most of the chief dramatis personæ make their final exit; only Jeremiah and Baruch remain. King and princes, priests and prophets, pass to death or captivity, and new characters appear to play their part for a while upon the vacant stage.

We would gladly know how Jeremiah fared on that night when the city was stormed, and Zedekiah and his army stole out in a vain attempt to escape beyond Jordan. Our book preserves two brief but inconsistent narratives of his fortunes.

One is contained in xxxix. 11-14. Nebuchadnezzar, we must remember, was not present in person with the besieging army. His headquarters were at Riblah, far away in the north. He had, however, given special instructions concerning Jeremiah to Nebuzaradan, the general commanding the forces before Jerusalem: "Take him, and look well to him, and do him no harm; but do with him even as he shall say unto thee."

Accordingly Nebuzaradan and all the king of Babylon's princes sent and took Jeremiah out of the court of the guard, and committed him to Gedaliah ben Ahikam ben Shaphan, to take him to his house.[158] And Jeremiah dwelt among the people.

This account is not only inconsistent with that given in the next chapter, but it also represents Nebuzaradan as present when the city was taken, whereas later on [159] we are told that he did not come upon the scene till a month later. For these and similar reasons, this version of the story is generally considered the less trustworthy. It apparently grew up at a time when the other characters and interests of the period had been thrown into the shade by the reverent recollection of Jeremiah and his ministry. It seemed natural to suppose that Nebuchadnezzar was equally preoccupied with the fortunes of the great prophet who had consistently preached obedience to his authority. The section records the intense reverence which the Jews of the Captivity felt for Jeremiah. We are more likely, however, to get a true idea of what happened by following the narrative in chapter xl.

According to this account, Jeremiah was not at once singled out for any exceptionally favourable treatment. When Zedekiah and the soldiers had left the city, there can have been no question of further resistance. The history does not mention any massacre by the conquerors, but we may probably accept Lamentations ii. 20, 21, as a description of the sack of Jerusalem:--

> "Shall the priest and the prophet be slain in the sanctuary of the Lord?
> The youth and the old man lie on the ground in the streets;
> My virgins and my young men are fallen by the sword:
> Thou hast slain them in the day of Thine anger;
> Thou hast slaughtered, and not pitied."

Yet the silence of Kings and Jeremiah as to all this, combined with their express statements as to captives, indicates that the Chaldean generals did not order a massacre, but rather sought to take prisoners. The soldiers would not be restrained from a certain slaughter in the heat of their first breaking into the city; but prisoners had a market value, and were provided for by the practice of deportation which Babylon had inherited from Nineveh. Accordingly the soldiers' lust for blood was satiated or bridled before they reached Jeremiah's prison. The court of the guard probably formed part of the precincts of the palace, and the Chaldean commanders would at once secure its occupants for Nebuchadnezzar. Jeremiah was taken with other captives and put in chains. If the dates in lii. 6, 12, be correct, he must have remained a prisoner till the arrival of Nebuzaradan, a month later on. He was then a witness of the burning of the city and the destruction of the fortifications, and was carried with the other captives to Ramah. Here the Chaldean general found leisure to inquire into the deserts of individual prisoners and to decide how they should be treated. He would be aided in this task by the Jewish refugees from whose ridicule Zedekiah had shrunk, and they would at once inform him of the distinguished sanctity of the prophet and of the conspicuous services he had rendered to the Chaldean cause.

Nebuzaradan at once acted upon their representations. He ordered Jeremiah's chains to be removed, gave him full liberty to go where he pleased, and assured him of the favour and protection of the Chaldean government:--

"If it seem good unto thee to come with me into Babylon, come, and I will look well unto thee; but if it seem ill unto thee to come with me into Babylon, forbear: behold, all the land is before thee; go whithersoever it seemeth to thee good and right."

These words are, however, preceded by two remarkable verses. For the nonce, the prophet's mantle seems to have fallen upon the Chaldean soldier. He speaks to his auditor just as Jeremiah himself had been wont to address his erring fellow-countrymen:--

"Thy God Jehovah pronounced this evil upon this place: and Jehovah hath brought it, and done according as He spake; because ye have sinned against Jehovah, and have not obeyed His voice, therefore this thing is come unto you."

Possibly Nebuzaradan did not include Jeremiah personally in the "ye" and "you"; and yet a prophet's message is often turned upon himself in this fashion. Even in our day outsiders will not be at the trouble to distinguish between one Christian and another, and will often denounce a man for his supposed share in Church abuses he has strenuously combated.

We need not be surprised that a heathen noble can talk like a pious Jew. The Chaldeans were eminently religious, and their worship of Bel and Merodach may often have been as spiritual and sincere as the homage paid by most Jews to Jehovah. The Babylonian creed could recognise that a foreign state might have its own legitimate deity and would suffer for disloyalty to him. Assyrian and Chaldean kings were quite willing to accept the prophetic doctrine that Jehovah had commissioned them to punish this disobedient people. Still Jeremiah must have been a little taken aback when one of the cardinal points of his own teaching was expounded to him by so strange a preacher; but he was too prudent to raise any discussion on the matter, and too chivalrous to wish to establish his own rectitude at the expense of his brethren. Moreover he had to decide between the two alternatives offered him by Nebuzaradan. Should he go to Babylon or remain in Judah?

According to a suggestion of Gratz, accepted by Cheyne, [160] xv. 10-21 is a record of the inner struggle through which Jeremiah came to a decision on this matter. The section is not very clear, but it suggests that at one time it seemed Jehovah's will that he should go to Babylon, and that it was only after much hesitation that he was convinced that God required him to remain in Judah. Powerful motives drew him in either direction. At Babylon he would reap the full advantage of Nebuchadnezzar's favour, and would enjoy the order and culture of a great capital. He would meet with old friends and disciples, amongst the rest Ezekiel. He would find an important sphere for ministry amongst the large Jewish community in Chaldea, where the flower of the whole nation was now in exile. In Judah he would have to share the fortunes of a feeble and suffering remnant, and would be exposed to all the dangers and disorder consequent on the break-up of the national government--brigandage on the part of native guerilla bands and raids by the neighbouring tribes. These guerilla bands were the final effort of Jewish resistance, and would seek to punish as traitors those who accepted the dominion of Babylon.

On the other hand, Jeremiah's surviving enemies, priests, prophets, and princes, had been taken en masse to Babylon. On his arrival he would find himself again plunged into the old controversies. Many if not the majority of his countrymen there would regard him as a traitor. The protégé of Nebuchadnezzar was sure to be disliked and distrusted by his less fortunate brethren. And Jeremiah was not a born courtier like Josephus. In Judah, moreover, he would be amongst friends of his own way of thinking; the remnant left behind had been placed under the authority of his friend Gedaliah, the son of his former protector Ahikam, the grandson of his ancient ally Shaphan. He would be free from the anathemas of corrupt priests and the contradiction of false prophets. The advocacy of true religion amongst the exiles might safely be left to Ezekiel and his school.

But probably the motives that decided Jeremiah's course of action were, firstly, that devoted attachment to the sacred soil which was a passion with every earnest Jew; and, secondly, the inspired conviction that Palestine was to be the scene of the future development of revealed religion. This conviction was coupled with the hope that the scattered refugees who were rapidly gathering at Mizpah under Gedaliah might lay the foundations of a new community, which should become the instrument of the divine purpose. Jeremiah was no deluded visionary, who would suppose that the destruction of Jerusalem had exhausted God's judgments, and that the millennium would forthwith begin for the special and exclusive benefit of his surviving companions in Judah. Nevertheless, while there was an organised Jewish community left on native soil, it would be regarded as the heir of the national religious hopes and aspirations, and a prophet, with liberty of choice, would feel it his duty to remain.

Accordingly Jeremiah decided to join Gedaliah. [161] Nebuzaradan gave him food and a present, and let him go.

Gedaliah's headquarters were at Mizpah, a town not certainly identified, but lying somewhere to the north-west of Jerusalem, and playing an important part in the history of Samuel and Saul. Men would remember the ancient record which told how the first Hebrew king had been divinely appointed at Mizpah, and might regard the coincidence as a happy omen that Gedaliah would found a kingdom more prosperous and permanent than that which traced its origin to Saul.

Nebuzaradan had left with the new governor "men, women, and children, ... of them that were not carried away captive to Babylon." These were chiefly of the poorer sort, but not altogether, for among them were "royal princesses" and doubtless others belonging to the ruling classes. Apparently after these arrangements had been made the Chaldean forces were almost entirely withdrawn, and Gedaliah was left to cope with the many difficulties of the situation by his own unaided resources. For a time all went well. It seemed at first as if the scattered bands of Jewish soldiers still in the field would submit to the Chaldean government and acknowledge Gedaliah's authority. Various captains with their bands came to him at Mizpah, amongst them Ishmael ben Nethaniah, Johanan ben Kareah and his brother Jonathan. Gedaliah swore to them that they should be pardoned and protected by the Chaldeans. He confirmed them in their possession of the towns and districts they had occupied after the departure of the enemy. They accepted his assurance, and their alliance with him seemed to guarantee the safety and prosperity of the settlement. Refugees from Moab, the Ammonites, Edom, and all the neighbouring countries flocked to Mizpah, and busied themselves in gathering in the produce of the oliveyards and vineyards which had been left ownerless when the nobles were slain or carried away captive. Many of the poorer Jews revelled in such unwonted plenty, and felt that even national ruin had its compensations.

Tradition has supplemented what the sacred record tells us of this period in Jeremiah's history. We are told [162] that "it is also found in the records that the prophet Jeremiah" commanded the exiles to take with them fire from the altar of the Temple, and further exhorted them to observe the law and to abstain from idolatry; and that "it was also contained in the same writing, that the prophet, being warned of God, commanded the tabernacle and the ark to go with him, as he went forth unto the mountain, where Moses climbed up, and saw the heritage of God. And when Jeremiah came thither, he found an hollow cave, wherein he laid the tabernacle and the ark and the altar of incense, and so stopped the door. And some of those that followed him came to mark the way, but they could not find it: which when Jeremiah perceived he blamed them, saying, As for that place, it shall be unknown until the time that God gather His people again together and receive them to His mercy."

A less improbable tradition is that which narrates that Jeremiah composed the Book of Lamentations shortly after the capture of the city. This is first stated by the Septuagint; it has been adopted by the Vulgate and various Rabbinical authorities, and has received considerable support from Christian scholars. [163] Moreover as the traveller leaves Jerusalem by the Damascus Gate, he passes great stone quarries, where Jeremiah's Grotto is still pointed out as the place where the prophet composed his elegy.

Without entering into the general question of the authorship of Lamentations, we may venture to doubt whether it can be referred to any period of Jeremiah's life which is dealt with in our book; and even whether it accurately represents his feelings at any such period. During the first month that followed the capture of Jerusalem the Chaldean generals held the city and its inhabitants at the disposal of their king. His decision was uncertain; it was by no means a matter of course that he would destroy the city. Jerusalem had been spared by Pharaoh Necho after the defeat of Josiah, and by Nebuchadnezzar after the revolt of Jehoiakim. Jeremiah and the other Jews must have been in a state of extreme suspense as to their own fate and that of their city, very different from the attitude of Lamentations. This suspense was ended when Nebuzaradan arrived and proceeded to burn the city. Jeremiah witnessed the fulfilment of his own prophecies when Jerusalem was thus overtaken by the ruin he had so often predicted. As he stood there chained amongst the other captives, many of his neighbours must have felt towards him as we should feel towards an anarchist gloating over the spectacle of a successful dynamite explosion; and Jeremiah could not be ignorant of their sentiments. His own emotions would be sufficiently vivid, but they would not be so simple as those of the great elegy. Probably they were too poignant to be capable of articulate expression; and the occasion was not likely to be fertile in acrostics.

Doubtless when the venerable priest and prophet looked from Ramah or Mizpah towards the blackened ruins of the Temple and the Holy City, he was possessed by something of the spirit of Lamentations. But from the moment when he went to Mizpah he would be busily occupied in assisting Gedaliah in his gallant effort to gather the nucleus of a new Israel out of the flotsam and jetsam of the shipwreck of Judah. Busy with this work of practical beneficence, his unconquerable spirit already possessed with visions of a brighter future, Jeremiah could not lose himself in mere regrets for the past.

He was doomed to experience yet another disappointment. Gedaliah had only held his office for about two months, [164] when he was warned by Johanan ben Kareah and the other captains that Ishmael ben Nethaniah had been sent by Baalis, king of the Ammonites, to assassinate him. Gedaliah refused to believe them. Johanan, perhaps surmising that the governor's incredulity was assumed, came to him privately and proposed to anticipate Ishmael: "Let me go, I pray thee, and slay Ishmael ben Nethaniah, and no one shall know it: wherefore should he slay thee, that all the Jews which are gathered unto thee should be scattered, and the remnant of Judah perish? But Gedaliah ben Ahikam said unto Johanan ben Kareah, Thou shalt not do this thing: for thou speakest falsely of Ishmael."

Gedaliah's misplaced confidence soon had fatal consequences. In the second month, about October, the Jews in the ordinary course of events would have celebrated the Feast of Tabernacles, to return thanks for their plentiful ingathering of grapes, olives, and summer fruit. Possibly this occasion gave Ishmael a pretext for visiting Mizpah. He came thither with ten nobles who, like himself, were connected with the royal family and probably were among the princes who persecuted Jeremiah. This small and distinguished company could not be suspected of intending to use violence. Ishmael seemed to be reciprocating Gedaliah's confidence by putting himself in the governor's power. Gedaliah feasted his guests. Johanan and the other captains were not present; they had done what they could to save him, but they did not wait to share the fate which he was bringing on himself.

"Then arose Ishmael ben Nethaniah and his ten companions and smote Gedaliah ben Ahikam ... and all the Jewish and Chaldean soldiers that were with him at Mizpah."

Probably the eleven assassins were supported by a larger body of followers, who waited outside the city and made their way in amidst the confusion consequent on the murder; doubtless, too, they had friends amongst Gedaliah's entourage. These accomplices had first lulled any suspicions that he might feel as to Ishmael, and had then helped to betray their master.

Not contented with the slaughter which he had already perpetrated, Ishmael took measures to prevent the news getting abroad, and lay in wait for any other adherents of Gedaliah who might come to visit him. He succeeded in entrapping a company of eighty men from Northern Israel: ten were allowed to purchase their lives by revealing hidden stores of wheat, barley, oil, and honey; the rest were slain and thrown into an ancient pit, "which King Asa had made for fear of Baasha king of Israel."

These men were pilgrims, who came with shaven chins and torn clothes, "and having cut themselves, bringing meal offerings and frankincense to the house of Jehovah." The pilgrims were doubtless on their way to celebrate the Feast of Tabernacles: with the destruction of Jerusalem and the Temple, all the joy of that festival would be changed to mourning and its songs to wailing. Possibly they were going to lament on the site of the ruined temple. But Mizpah itself had an ancient sanctuary. Hosea speaks of the priests, princes, and people of Israel as having been "a snare on Mizpah." Jeremiah may have sanctioned the use of this local temple thinking that Jehovah would "set His name there" till Jerusalem was restored, even as He had dwelt at Shiloh before He chose the City of David. But to whatever shrine these pilgrims were journeying, their errand should have made them sacrosanct to all Jews. Ishmael's hypocrisy, treachery, and cruelty in this matter go far to justify Jeremiah's bitterest invectives against the princes of Judah.

But after this bloody deed it was high time for Ishmael to be gone and betake himself back to his heathen patron, Baalis the Ammonite. These massacres could not long be kept a secret. And yet Ishmael seems to have made a final effort to suppress the evidence of his crimes. In his retreat he carried with him all the people left in Mizpah, "soldiers, women, children, and eunuchs," including the royal princesses, and apparently Jeremiah and Baruch. No doubt he hoped to make money out of his prisoners by selling them as slaves or holding them to ransom. He had not ventured to slay Jeremiah: the prophet had not been present at the banquet and had thus escaped the first fierce slaughter, and Ishmael shrank from killing in cold blood the man whose predictions of ruin had been so exactly and awfully fulfilled by the recent destruction of Jerusalem.

When Johanan ben Kareah and the other captains heard how entirely Ishmael had justified their warning, they assembled their forces and started in pursuit. Ishmael's band seems to have been comparatively small, and was moreover encumbered by the disproportionate number of captives with which they had burdened themselves. They were overtaken "by the great waters that are in Gibeon," only a very short distance from Mizpah.

However Ishmael's original following of ten may have been reinforced, his band cannot have been very numerous and was manifestly inferior to Johanan's forces. In face of an enemy of superior strength, Ishmael's only chance of escape was to leave his prisoners to their own devices--he had not even time for another massacre. The captives at once turned round and made their way to their deliverer. Ishmael's followers seem to have been scattered, taken captive, or slain, but he himself escaped with eight men--

possibly eight of the original ten--and found refuge with the Ammonites.

Johanan and his companions with the recovered captives made no attempt to return to Mizpah. The Chaldeans would exact a severe penalty for the murder of their governor Gedaliah, and their own fellow-countryman: their vengeance was not likely to be scrupulously discriminating. The massacre would be regarded as an act of rebellion on the part of the Jewish community in Judah, and the community would be punished accordingly. Johanan and his whole company determined that when the day of retribution came the Chaldeans should find no one to punish. They set out for Egypt, the natural asylum of the enemies of Babylon. On the way they halted in the neighbourhood of Bethlehem at a caravanserai [165] which bore the name of Chimham, [166] the son of David's generous friend Barzillai. So far the fugitives had acted on their first impulse of dismay; now they paused to take breath, to make a more deliberate survey of their situation, and to mature their plans for the future.

Footnotes:

157. Chapter lii. = 2 Kings xxiv. 18-xxv. 30, and xxxix. 1-10 = lii. 4-16, in each case with minor variations which do not specially bear upon our subject. Cf. Driver, Introduction, in loco. The detailed treatment of this section belongs to the exposition of the Book of Kings.

158. Literally "the house"--either Jeremiah's or Gedaliah's, or possibly the royal palace.

159. lii. 6, 12.

160. Pulpit Commentary, in loco. Cf. the previous volume on Jeremiah in this series.

161. The sequence of verses 4 and 5 has been spoilt by some corruption of the text. The versions diverge variously from the Hebrew. Possibly the original text told how Jeremiah found himself unable to give an immediate answer, and Nebuzaradan, observing his hesitation, bade him return to Gedaliah and decide at his leisure.

162. 2 Macc. ii. 1-8.

163. Cf. Professor Adeney's Canticles and Lamentations in this series.

164. Cf. lii. 12, "fifth month," and xli. 1, "seventh month." Cheyne however points out that no year is specified in xli. 1, and holds that Gedaliah's governorship lasted for over four years, and that the deportation four years (lii. 30) after the destruction of the city was the prompt punishment of his murder.

165. The reading is doubtful; possibly the word (geruth) translated "caravanserai," or some similar word to be read instead of it, merely forms a compound proper name with Chimham.

166. 2 Sam. xix. 31-40.

CHAPTER XIV

THE DESCENT INTO EGYPT

xlii., xliii.

"They came into the land of Egypt, for they obeyed not the voice of Jehovah."--Jer. xliii. 7.

Thus within a few days Jeremiah had experienced one of those sudden and extreme changes of fortune which are as common in his career as in a sensational novel. Yesterday the guide, philosopher, and friend of the governor of Judah, to-day sees him once more a helpless prisoner in the hands of his old enemies. To-morrow he is restored to liberty and authority, and appealed to by the remnant of Israel as the mouthpiece of Jehovah. Johanan ben Kareah and all the captains of the forces, "from the least even unto the greatest, came near" and besought Jeremiah to pray unto "Jehovah thy God," "that Jehovah thy God may show us the way wherein we may walk, and the thing we may do." Jeremiah promised to make intercession and to declare faithfully unto them whatsoever Jehovah should reveal unto him.

And they on their part said unto Jeremiah: "Jehovah be a true and faithful witness against us, if we do not according to every word that Jehovah thy God shall send unto us by thee. We will obey the voice of Jehovah our God, to whom we send thee, whether it be good or evil, that it may be well with us, when we obey the voice of Jehovah our God."

The prophet returned no hasty answer to this solemn appeal. As in his controversy with Hananiah, he refrained from at once announcing his own judgment as the Divine decision, but waited for the express confirmation of the Spirit. For ten days prophet and people were alike kept in suspense. The patience of Johanan and his followers is striking testimony to their sincere reverence for Jeremiah.

On the tenth day the message came, and Jeremiah called the people together to hear God's answer to their question, and to learn that Divine will to which they had promised unreserved obedience. It ran thus:--

> *"If you will still abide in this land,*
> *I will build you and not pull you down,*
> *I will plant you and not pluck you up."*
> The words of Jeremiah's original commission seem ever present to his mind:--
> *"For I repent Me of the evil I have done unto you."*

They need not flee from Judah as an accursed land; Jehovah had a new and gracious purpose concerning them, and therefore:--

> *"Be not afraid of the king of Babylon,*
> *Of whom ye are afraid;*
> *Be not afraid of him--it is the utterance of Jehovah--*
> *For I am with you,*
> *To save you and deliver you out of his hand.*
> *I will put kindness in his heart toward you,*
> *And he shall deal kindly with you,*
> *And restore you to your lands."*

It was premature to conclude that Ishmael's crime finally disposed of the attempt to shape the remnant into the nucleus of a new Israel. Hitherto Nebuchadnezzar had shown himself willing to discriminate; when he condemned the princes, he spared and honoured Jeremiah, and the Chaldeans might still be trusted to deal fairly and even generously with the prophet's friends and deliverers. Moreover the heart of Nebuchadnezzar, like that of all earthly potentates, was in the hands of the King of Kings.

But Jeremiah knew too well what mingled hopes and fears drew his hearers towards the fertile valley and rich cities of the Nile. He sets before them the reverse of the picture: they might refuse to obey God's command to remain in Judah; they might say, "No, we will go into the land of Egypt, where we shall see no war, nor hear the sound of the trumpet, nor hunger for bread, and there will we dwell."

As of old, they craved for the flesh-pots of Egypt; and with more excuse than their forefathers. They were worn out with suffering and toil, some of them had wives and children; the childless prophet was inviting them to make sacrifices and incur risks which he could neither share nor understand. Can we wonder if they fell short of his inspired heroism, and hesitated to forego the ease and plenty of Egypt in order to try social experiments in Judah?

"Let what is broken so remain.
The Gods are hard to reconcile:
'Tis hard to settle order once again.

***

Sore task to hearts worn out by many wars."

But Jeremiah had neither sympathy nor patience with such weakness. Moreover, now as often, valour was the better part of discretion, and the boldest course was the safest. The peace and security of Egypt had been broken in upon again and again by Asiatic invaders; only recently it had been tributary to Nineveh, till the failing strength of Assyria enabled the Pharaohs to recover their independence. Now that Palestine had ceased to be the seat of war the sound of Chaldean trumpets would soon be heard in the valley of the Nile. By going down into Egypt, they were leaving Judah where they might be safe under the broad shield of Babylonian power, for a country that would soon be afflicted by the very evils they sought to escape:--

"If ye finally determine to go to Egypt to sojourn there,
The sword, which ye fear, shall overtake you there in the land of Egypt,
The famine, whereof ye are afraid, shall follow hard after you there in Egypt,
And there shall ye die."

The old familiar curses, so often uttered against Jerusalem and its inhabitants, are pronounced against any of his hearers who should take refuge in Egypt:--

"As Mine anger and fury hath been poured forth upon the inhabitants of Jerusalem,
So shall My fury be poured forth upon you, when ye shall enter in Egypt."

They would die "by the sword, the famine, and the pestilence"; they would be "an execration and an astonishment, a curse and a reproach."

He had set before them two alternative courses, and the Divine judgment upon each: he had known beforehand that, contrary to his own choice and judgment, their hearts were set upon going down into Egypt; hence, as when confronted and contradicted by Hananiah, he had been careful to secure divine confirmation before he gave his decision. Already he could see the faces of his hearers hardening into obstinate resistance or kindling into hot defiance; probably they broke out into interruptions which left no doubt as to their purpose. With his usual promptness, he turned upon them with fierce reproof and denunciation:--

"Ye have been traitors to yourselves.
Ye sent me unto Jehovah your God, saying,
Pray for us unto Jehovah our God;
According unto all that Jehovah our God shall say,
Declare unto us, and we will do it.
I have this day declared it unto you,
But ye have in no wise obeyed the voice of Jehovah your God.

***

Ye shall die by the sword, the famine, and the pestilence,
In the place whither ye desire to go to sojourn."

His hearers were equally prompt with their rejoinder; Johanan ben Kareah and "all the proud men" answered him:--

The Expositor's Bible: Jeremiah Volumes I & II
"Thou liest! It is not Jehovah our God who hath sent thee to say, Ye shall not go into Egypt to sojourn there; but Baruch ben Neriah setteth thee on against us, to deliver us into the hand of the Chaldeans, that they may slay us or carry us away captive to Babylon."

Jeremiah had experienced many strange vicissitudes, but this was not the least striking. Ten days ago the people and their leaders had approached him in reverent submission, and had solemnly promised to accept and obey his decision as the word of God. Now they called him a liar; they asserted that he did not speak by any Divine inspiration, but was a feeble impostor, an oracular puppet, whose strings were pulled by his own disciple. [167]

Such scenes are, unfortunately, only too common in Church history. Religious professors are still ready to abuse and to impute unworthy motives to prophets whose messages they dislike, in a spirit not less secular than that which is shown when some modern football team tries to mob the referee who has given a decision against its hopes.

Moreover we must not unduly emphasise the solemn engagement given by the Jews to abide Jeremiah's decision. They were probably sincere, but not very much in earnest. The proceedings and the strong formulÃ¦ used were largely conventional. Ancient kings and generals regularly sought the approval of their prophets or augurs before taking any important step, but they did not always act upon their advice. The final breach between Saul and the prophet Samuel seems to have been due to the fact that the king did not wait for his presence and counsel before engaging the Philistines. [168] Before the disastrous expedition to Ramoth Gilead, Jehoshaphat insisted on consulting a prophet of Jehovah, and then acted in the teeth of his inspired warning. [169]

Johanan and his company felt it essential to consult some divine oracle; and Jeremiah was not only the greatest prophet of Jehovah, he was also the only prophet available. They must have known from his consistent denunciation of all alliance with Egypt that his views were likely to be at variance with their own. But they were consulting Jehovah--Jeremiah was only His mouthpiece; hitherto He had set His face against any dealings with Egypt, but circumstances were entirely changed, and Jehovah's purpose might change with them, He might "repent." They promised to obey, because there was at any rate a chance that God's commands would coincide with their own intentions. Butler's remark that men may be expected to act "not only upon an even chance, but upon much less," specially applies to such promises as the Jews made to Jeremiah. Certain tacit conditions may always be considered attached to a profession of willingness to be guided by a friend's advice. Our newspapers frequently record breaches of engagements that should be as binding as that entered into by Johanan and his friends, and they do so without any special comment. For instance, the verdicts of arbitrators in trade disputes have been too often ignored by the unsuccessful parties; and--to take a very different illustration--the most unlimited professions of faith in the infallibility of the Bible have sometimes gone along with a denial of its plain teaching and a disregard of its imperative commands. While Shylock expected a favourable decision, Portia was "a Daniel come to judgment": his subsequent opinion of her judicial qualities has not been recorded. Those who have never refused or evaded unwelcome demands made by an authority whom they have promised to obey may cast the first stone at Johanan.

After the scene we have been describing, the refugees set out for Egypt, carrying with them the princesses and Jeremiah and Baruch. They were following in the footsteps of Abraham, Isaac, and Jacob, of Jeroboam and many another Jew who had sought protection under the shadow of Pharaoh. They were the forerunners of that later Israel in Egypt which, through Philo and his disciples, exercised so powerful an influence on the doctrine, criticism, and exegesis of the early Christian Church.

Yet this exodus in the wrong direction was by no means complete. Four years later Nebuzaradan could still find seven hundred and forty-five Jews to carry away to Babylon. [170] Johanan's movements had been too hurried to admit of his gathering in the inhabitants of outlying districts.

When Johanan's company reached the frontier, they would find the Egyptian officials prepared to receive them. During the last few months there must have been constant arrivals of Jewish refugees, and rumour must have announced the approach of so large a company, consisting of almost all the Jews left in Palestine. The very circumstances that made them dread the vengeance of Nebuchadnezzar would ensure them a hearty welcome in Egypt. Their presence was an unmistakable proof of the entire failure of the attempt to create in Judah a docile and contented dependency and outpost of the Chaldean Empire. They were accordingly settled at Tahpanhes and in the surrounding district.

But no welcome could conciliate Jeremiah's implacable temper, nor could all the splendour of Egypt tame his indomitable spirit. Amongst his fellow-countrymen at Bethlehem, he had foretold the coming tribulations of Egypt. He now renewed his predictions within the very precincts of Pharaoh's palace, and enforced them by a striking symbol. At Tahpanhes--the modern Tell Defenneh--which was the ancient Egyptian frontier fortress and settlement on the more westerly route from Syria, "the word of Jehovah came to Jeremiah, saying, Take great stones in thine hand, and hide them in mortar in the brick pavement, at the entry of Pharaoh's palace in Tahpanhes, in the presence of the men of Judah; and say unto them, Thus saith Jehovah Sabaoth, the God of Israel:--

"Behold, I will send and take My servant Nebuchadnezzar king of Babylon:
I will set his throne upon these stones which I have hid,
And he shall spread his state pavilion over them."
He would set up his royal tribunal, and decide the fate of the conquered city and its inhabitants.
"He shall come and smite the land of Egypt;
Such as are for death shall be put to death,
Such as are for captivity shall be sent into captivity,
Such as are for the sword shall be slain by the sword.
I will kindle a fire in the temples of the gods of Egypt;
He shall burn their temples, and carry them away captive:
He shall array himself with the land of Egypt,
As a shepherd putteth on his garment."

The whole country would become a mere mantle for his dignity, a comparatively insignificant part of his vast possessions.

"He shall go forth from thence in peace."

A campaign that promised well at the beginning has often ended in despair, like Sennacherib's attack on Judah, and Pharaoh Necho's expedition to Carchemish. The invading army has been exhausted by its victories, or wasted by disease and compelled to beat an inglorious retreat. No such misfortunes should overtake the Chaldean king. He would depart with all his spoil, leaving Egypt behind him subdued into a loyal province of his empire.

Then the prophet adds, apparently as a kind of afterthought:--

"He also shall break the obelisks of Heliopolis, in the land of Egypt."
(so styled to distinguish this Beth-Shemesh from Beth-Shemesh in Palestine),
"And shall burn with fire the temples of the gods of Egypt."

The performance of this symbolic act and the delivery of its accompanying message are not recorded, but Jeremiah would not fail to make known the divine word to his fellow-countrymen. It is difficult to understand how the exiled prophet would be allowed to assemble the Jews in front of the main entrance of the palace, and hide "great stones" in the pavement. Possibly the palace was being repaired, [171] or the stones might be inserted under the front or side of a raised platform, or possibly the symbolic act was only to be described and not performed. Mr. Flinders Petrie recently discovered at Tell Defenneh a large brickwork pavement, with great stones buried underneath, which he supposed might be those mentioned in our narrative. He also found there another possible relic of these Jewish émigrés in the shape of the ruins of a large brick building of the twenty-sixth dynasty--to which Pharaoh Hophra belonged--still known as the "Palace of the Jew's Daughter." It is a natural and attractive conjecture that this was the residence assigned to the Jewish princesses whom Johanan carried with him into Egypt.

But while the ruined palace may testify to Pharaoh's generosity to the Royal House that had suffered through its alliance with him, the "great stones" remind us that, after a brief interval of sympathy and co-operation, Jeremiah again found himself in bitter antagonism to his fellow-countrymen. In our next chapter we shall describe one final scene of mutual recrimination. [172]

Footnotes:

167. Cf. chapter on "Baruch."
168. 1 Sam. xiii.
169. 1 Kings xxii.
170. lii. 30.
171. So Orelli, in loco.
172. For the prophecy against Egypt and its fulfilment see further chapter [156]XVII.

CHAPTER XV

THE QUEEN OF HEAVEN

xliv.

"*Since we left off burning incense and offering libations to the Queen of Heaven, we have been in want of everything, and have been consumed by the sword and the famine.*"--Jer. xliv. 18.

The Jewish exiles in Egypt still retained a semblance of national life, and were bound together by old religious ties. Accordingly we read that they came together from their different settlements--from Migdol and Tahpanhes on the north-eastern frontier, from Noph or Memphis on the Nile south of the site of Cairo, and from Pathros or Upper Egypt--to a "great assembly," no doubt a religious festival. The list of cities shows how widely the Jews were scattered throughout Egypt.

Nothing is said as to where and when this "great assembly" met; but for Jeremiah, such a gathering at all times and anywhere, in Egypt as at Jerusalem, became an opportunity for fulfilling his Divine commission. He once again confronted his fellow-countrymen with the familiar threats and exhortations. A new climate had not created in them either clean hearts or a right spirit.

Recent history had added force to his warnings. He begins therefore by appealing to the direful consequences which had come upon the Holy Land, through the sins of its inhabitants:--

> "*Ye have seen all the evil that I have brought upon Jerusalem, and upon all the cities of Judah.*
> *Behold, this day they are an uninhabited waste,*
> *Because of their wickedness which they wrought to provoke Me to anger,*
> *By going to burn incense and to serve other gods whom neither they nor their fathers knew.*"

The Israelites had enjoyed for centuries intimate personal relations with Jehovah, and knew Him by this ancient and close fellowship and by all His dealings with them. They had no such knowledge of the gods of surrounding nations. They were like foolish children who prefer the enticing blandishments of a stranger to the affection and discipline of their home. Such children do not intend to forsake their home or to break the bonds of filial affection, and yet the new friendship may wean their hearts from their father. So these exiles still considered themselves worshippers of Jehovah, and yet their superstition led them to disobey and dishonour Him.

Before its ruin, Judah had sinned against light and leading:--

> "*Howbeit I sent unto you all My servants the prophets,*
> *Rising up early and sending them, saying,*
> *Oh do not this abominable thing that I hate.*
> *But they hearkened not, nor inclined their ears, so as to turn from their evil,*
> *That they should not burn incense to other gods.*
> *Wherefore My fury and My anger was poured forth.*"

Political and social questions, the controversies with the prophets who contradicted Jeremiah in the name of Jehovah, have fallen into the background; the poor pretence of loyalty to Jehovah which permitted His worshippers to degrade Him to the level of Baal and Moloch is ignored as worthless: and Jeremiah, like Ezekiel, finds the root of the people's sin in their desertion of Jehovah. Their real religion was revealed by their heathenish superstitions. Every religious life is woven of many diverse strands; if the web as a whole is rotten, the Great Taskmaster can take no account of a few threads that have a form and profession of soundness. Our Lord declared that He would utterly ignore and repudiate men upon whose lips His name was a too familiar word, who had preached and cast out devils and done many mighty works in that Holy Name. These were men who had worked iniquity, who had combined promising externals with the worship of "other gods," Mammon or Belial or some other of those evil powers, who place

*"Within His sanctuary itself their shrines,
Abominations; and with cursed things
His holy rites and solemn feasts profane;
And with their darkness dare affront His light."*

This profane blending of idolatry with a profession of zeal for Jehovah had provoked the divine wrath against Judah: and yet the exiles had not profited by their terrible experience of the consequences of sin; they still burnt incense unto other gods. Therefore Jeremiah remonstrates with them afresh, and sets before their eyes the utter ruin which will punish persistent sin. This discourse repeats and enlarges the threats uttered at Bethlehem. The penalties then denounced on disobedience are now attributed to idolatry. We have here yet another example of the tacit understanding attaching to all the prophet's predictions. The most positive declarations of doom are often warnings and not final sentences. Jehovah does not turn a deaf ear to the penitent, and the doom is executed not because He exacts the uttermost farthing, but because the culprit perseveres in his uttermost wrong. Lack of faith and loyalty at Bethlehem and idolatry in Egypt were both symptoms of the same deep-rooted disease.

On this occasion there was no rival prophet to beard Jeremiah and relieve his hearers from their fears and scruples. Probably indeed no professed prophet of Jehovah would have cared to defend the worship of other gods. But, as at Bethlehem, the people themselves ventured to defy their aged mentor. They seem to have been provoked to such hardihood by a stimulus which often prompts timorous men to bold words. Their wives were specially devoted to the superstitious burning of incense, and these women were present in large numbers. Probably, like Lady Macbeth, they had already in private

*"Poured their spirits in their husbands' ears,
And chastised, with the valour of their tongues,
All that impeded"*

those husbands from speaking their minds to Jeremiah. In their presence, the men dared not shirk an obvious duty, for fear of more domestic chastisement. The prophet's reproaches would be less intolerable than such inflictions. Moreover the fair devotees did not hesitate to mingle their own shrill voices in the wordy strife.

These idolatrous Jews--male and female--carried things with a very high hand indeed:--

"We will not obey thee in that which thou hast spoken unto us in the name of Jehovah. We are determined to perform all the vows we have made to burn incense and other libations to the Queen of Heaven, exactly as we have said and as we and our fathers and kings and princes did in the cities of Judah and in the streets of Jerusalem." [173]

Moreover they were quite prepared to meet Jeremiah on his own ground and argue with him according to his own principles and methods. He had appealed to the ruin of Judah as a proof of Jehovah's condemnation of their idolatry and of His power to punish: they argued that these misfortunes were a divine spretā injuria formā, the vengeance of the Queen of Heaven, whose worship they had neglected. When they duly honoured her,--

"Then had we plenty of victuals, and were prosperous and saw no evil; but since we left off burning incense and offering libations to the Queen of Heaven, we have been in want of everything, and have been consumed by the sword and the famine."

Moreover the women had a special plea of their own:--

"When we burned incense and offered libations to the Queen of Heaven, did we not make cakes to symbolise her and offer libations to her with our husbands' permission?"

A wife's vows were not valid without her husband's sanction, and the women avail themselves of this principle to shift the responsibility for their superstition on the men's shoulders. Possibly too the unfortunate Benedicts were not displaying sufficient zeal in the good cause, and these words were intended to goad them into greater energy. Doubtless they cannot be entirely exonerated of blame for tolerating their wives' sins, probably they were guilty of participation as well as connivance. Nothing however but the utmost determination and moral courage would have curbed the exuberant religiosity of these devout ladies. The prompt suggestion that, if they have done wrong, their husbands are to blame for letting them have their own way, is an instance of the meanness which results from the worship of "other gods."

But these defiant speeches raise a more important question. There is an essential difference between regarding a national catastrophe as a divine judgment and the crude superstition to which an eclipse expresses the resentment of an angry god. But both involve the same practical uncertainty. The sufferers or the spectators ask what god wrought these marvels and what sins they are intended to punish, and to these questions neither catastrophe nor eclipse gives any certain answer.

Doubtless the altars of the Queen of Heaven had been destroyed by Josiah in his crusade against heathen cults; but her outraged majesty had been speedily avenged by the defeat and death of the iconoclast, and since then the history of Judah had been one long series of disasters. Jeremiah declared that these were the just retribution inflicted by Jehovah because Judah had been disloyal to Him; in the reign of Manasseh their sin had reached its climax:--

> "I will cause them to be tossed to and fro among all the nations of the earth, because of Manasseh ben Hezekiah, king of Judah, for that which he did in Jerusalem." [174]

His audience were equally positive that the national ruin was the vengeance of the Queen of Heaven. Josiah had destroyed her altars, and now the worshippers of Istar had retaliated by razing the Temple to the ground. A Jew, with the vague impression that Istar was as real as Jehovah, might find it difficult to decide between these conflicting theories.

To us, as to Jeremiah, it seems sheer nonsense to speak of the vengeance of the Queen of Heaven, not because of what we deduce from the circumstances of the fall of Jerusalem, but because we do not believe in any such deity. But the fallacy is repeated when, in somewhat similar fashion, Protestants find proof of the superiority of their faith in the contrast between England and Catholic Spain, while Romanists draw the opposite conclusion from a comparison of Holland and Belgium. In all such cases the assured truth of the disputant's doctrine, which is set forth as the result of his argument, is in reality the premise upon which his reasoning rests. Faith is not deduced from, but dictates an interpretation of history. In an individual the material penalties of sin may arouse a sleeping conscience, but they cannot create a moral sense: apart from a moral sense the discipline of rewards and punishments would be futile:--

> "Were no inner eye in us to tell,
> Instructed by no inner sense,
> The light of heaven from the dark of hell,
> That light would want its evidence."

Jeremiah, therefore, is quite consistent in refraining from argument and replying to his opponents by reiterating his former statements that sin against Jehovah had ruined Judah and would yet ruin the exiles. He spoke on the authority of the "inner sense," itself instructed by Revelation. But, after the manner of the prophets, he gave them a sign--Pharaoh Hophra should be delivered into the hand of his enemies as Zedekiah had been. Such an event would indeed be an unmistakable sign of imminent calamity to the fugitives who had sought the protection of the Egyptian king against Nebuchadnezzar.[175]

We have reserved for separate treatment the questions suggested by the references to the Queen of Heaven. [176] This divine name only occurs again in the Old Testament in vii. 18, and we are startled, at first sight, to discover that a cult about which all other historians and prophets have been entirely silent is described in these passages as an ancient and national worship. It is even possible that the "great assembly" was a festival in her honour. We have again to remind ourselves that the Old Testament is an account of the progress of Revelation and not a History of Israel. Probably the true explanation is that given by Kuenen. The prophets do not, as a rule, speak of the details of false worship; they use the generic "Baal" and the collective "other gods." Even in this chapter Jeremiah begins by speaking of "other gods," and only uses the term "Queen of Heaven" when he quotes the reply made to him by the Jews. Similarly when Ezekiel goes into detail concerning idolatry [177] he mentions cults and ritual [178] which do not occur elsewhere in the Old Testament. The prophets were little inclined to discriminate between different forms of idolatry, just as the average churchman is quite indifferent to the distinctions of the various Nonconformist bodies, which are to him simply "dissenters." One might read many volumes of Anglican sermons and even some English Church History without meeting with the term Unitarian.

It is easy to find modern parallels--Christian and heathen--to the name of this goddess. The Virgin Mary is honoured with the title Regina Coeli, and at Mukden, the Sacred City of China, there is a temple to the Queen of Heaven. But it is not easy to identify the ancient deity who bore this name. The Jews are accused elsewhere of worshipping "the sun and the moon and all the host of heaven," and one or other of these heavenly bodies--mostly either the moon or the planet Venus--has been supposed to have been the Queen of Heaven.

Neither do the symbolic cakes help us. Such emblems are found in the ritual of many ancient cults: at Athens cakes called Ἶ and shaped like a full-moon were offered to the moon-goddess Artemis; a similar usage seems to have prevailed in the worship of the Arabian goddess Al-Uzza, whose star was Venus, and also of connection with the worship of the sun. [179]

Moreover we do not find the title "Queen of Heaven" as an ordinary and well-established name of any neighbouring divinity. "Queen" is a natural title for any goddess, and was actually given to many ancient deities. Schrader [180] finds our goddess in the Atar-samain (Athar-Astarte) who is mentioned in the Assyrian ascriptions as worshipped by a North Arabian tribe of Kedarenes. Possibly too the Assyrian Istar is called Queen of Heaven. [181]

Istar, however, is connected with the moon as well as with the planet Venus. [182] For the present therefore we must be content to leave the matter an open question, [183] but any day some new discovery may solve the problem. Meanwhile it is interesting to notice how little religious ideas and practices are affected by differences in profession. St. Isaac the Great, of Antioch, who died about a.d. 460, tells us that the Christian ladies of Syria--whom he speaks of very ungallantly as "fools"--used to worship the planet Venus from the roofs of their houses, in the hope that she would bestow upon them some portion of her own brightness and beauty. His experience naturally led St. Isaac to interpret the Queen of Heaven as the luminary which his countrywomen venerated. [184]

The episode of the "great assembly" closes the history of Jeremiah's life. We leave him (as we so often met with him before) hurling ineffective denunciations at a recalcitrant audience. Vagrant fancy, holding this to be a lame and impotent conclusion, has woven romantic stories to continue and complete the narrative. There are traditions that he was stoned to death at Tahpanhes, and that his bones were removed to Alexandria by Alexander the Great; that he and Baruch returned to Judea or went to Babylon and died in peace; that he returned to Jerusalem and lived there three hundred years,--and other such legends. As has been said concerning the Apocryphal Gospels, these narratives serve as a foil to the history they are meant to supplement: they remind us of the sequels of great novels written by inferior pens, or of attempts made by clumsy mechanics to convert a bust by some inspired sculptor into a full-length statue.

For this story of Jeremiah's life is not a torso. Sacred biography constantly disappoints our curiosity as to the last days of holy men. We are scarcely ever told how prophets and apostles died. It is curious too that the great exceptions--Elijah in his chariot of fire and Elisha dying quietly in his bed--occur before the period of written prophecy. The deaths of Isaiah, Jeremiah, and Ezekiel, Peter, Paul, and John, are passed over in the Sacred Record, and when we seek to follow them beyond its pages, we are taught afresh the unique wisdom of inspiration. If we may understand Deuteronomy xxxiv. to imply that no eye was permitted to behold Moses in the hour of death, we have in this incident a type of the reticence of Scripture on such matters. Moreover a moment's reflection reminds us that the inspired method is in accordance with the better instincts of our nature. A death in opening manhood, or the death of a soldier in battle or of a martyr at the stake, rivets our attention; but when men die in a good old age, we dwell less on their declining years than on the achievements of their prime. We all remember the martyrdoms of Huss and Latimer, but how many of those in whose mouths Calvin and Luther are familiar as household words know how those great Reformers died?

There comes a time when we may apply to the aged saint the words of Browning's Death in the Desert:--

> "So is myself withdrawn into my depths,
> The soul retreated from the perished brain
> Whence it was wont to feel and use the world
> Through these dull members, done with long ago."

And the poet's comparison of this soul to

> "A stick once fire from end to end;
> Now, ashes save the tip that holds a spark."

Love craves to watch to the last, because the spark may

> "Run back, spread itself
> A little where the fire was....
> And we would not lose
> The last of what might happen on his face."

Such privileges may be granted to a few chosen disciples, probably they were in this case granted to Baruch; but they are mostly withheld from the world, lest blind irreverence should see in the aged saint nothing but

The Expositor's Bible: Jeremiah Volumes I & II
"Second childishness, and mere oblivion;
Sans teeth, sans eyes, sans taste, sans everything."

Footnotes:

173. Combined from verses 16, 17, and 25.
174. xv. 4.
175. As to the fulfilment of this prophecy see Chap. [157]XVII.
176. MELEKHETH HASHSHAMAYIM. The Masoretic pointing seems to indicate a rendering "service" or work of heaven, probably in the sense of "host of heaven," i.e. the stars,
177. Ezek. viii.
178. The worship of Tammuz and of "creeping things and abominable beasts" etc.
179. Kuenen, 208.
180. Schrader (Whitehouse's translation), ii. 207.
181. Kuenen, 206.
182. Sayce, Higher Criticism, etc., 80.
183. So Giesebrecht on vii. 18. Kuenen argues for the identification of the Queen of Heaven with the planet Venus.
184. Kuenen, 211.

Rev. C. J. Ball, M.A., & W. H. Bennett, M.A.

BOOK II

PROPHECIES CONCERNING FOREIGN NATIONS

CHAPTER XVI

JEHOVAH AND THE NATIONS

xxv. 15-38.
"*Jehovah hath a controversy with the nations.*"--Jer. xxv. 31.

    As the son of a king only learns very gradually that his father's authority and activity extend beyond the family and the household, so Israel in its childhood thought of Jehovah as exclusively concerned with itself.
    Such ideas as omnipotence and universal Providence did not exist; therefore they could not be denied; and the limitations of the national faith were not essentially inconsistent with later Revelation. But when we reach the period of recorded prophecy we find that, under the guidance of the Holy Spirit, the prophets had begun to recognise Jehovah's dominion over surrounding peoples. There was, as yet, no deliberate and formal doctrine of omnipotence, but, as Israel became involved in the fortunes first of one foreign power and then of another, the prophets asserted that the doings of these heathen states were overruled by the God of Israel. The idea of Jehovah's Lordship of the Nations enlarged with the extension of international relations, as our conception of the God of Nature has expanded with the successive discoveries of science. Hence, for the most part, the prophets devote special attention to the concerns of Gentile peoples. Hosea, Micah, Haggai, Zechariah, and Malachi are partial exceptions. Some of the minor prophets have for their main subject the doom of a heathen empire. Jonah and Nahum deal with Nineveh, Habbakuk with Chaldea, and Edom is specially honoured by being almost the sole object of the denunciations of Obadiah. Daniel also deals with the fate of the kingdoms of the world, but in the Apocalyptic fashion of the Pseudepigrapha. Jewish criticism rightly declined to recognise this book as prophetic, and relegated it to the latest collection of canonical scriptures.
    Each of the other prophetical books contains a longer or shorter series of utterances concerning the neighbours of Israel, its friends and foes, its enemies and allies. The fashion was apparently set by Amos, who shows God's judgment upon Damascus, the Philistines, Tyre, Edom, Ammon, and Moab. This list suggests the range of the prophet's religious interest in the Gentiles. Assyria and Egypt were, for the present, beyond the sphere of Revelation, just as China and India were to the average Protestant of the seventeenth century. When we come to the Book of Isaiah, the horizon widens in every direction. Jehovah is concerned with Egypt and Ethiopia, Assyria and Babylon. [185] In very short books like Joel and Zephaniah we could not expect exhaustive treatment of this subject. Yet even these prophets deal with the fortunes of the Gentiles: Joel, variously held one of the latest or one of the earliest of the canonical books, pronounces a divine judgment on Tyre and Sidon and the Philistines, on Egypt and Edom; and Zephaniah, an elder contemporary of Jeremiah, devotes sections to the Philistines, Moab and Ammon, Ethiopia and Assyria.
    The fall of Nineveh revolutionised the international system of the East. The judgment on Asshur was accomplished, and her name disappears from these catalogues of doom. In other particulars Jeremiah, as well as Ezekiel, follows closely in the footsteps of his predecessors. He deals, like them, with the group of Syrian and Palestinian states--Philistines, Moab, Ammon, Edom, and Damascus. [186] He dwells with repeated emphasis on Egypt, and Arabia is represented by Kedar and Hazor. In one section the prophet travels into what must have seemed to his contemporaries the very far East, as far as Elam. On the other hand, he is comparatively silent about Tyre, in which Joel, Amos, the Book of Isaiah, [187] and above all Ezekiel display a lively interest. Nebuchadnezzar's campaigns were directed against Tyre as much as against Jerusalem; and Ezekiel, living in Chaldea, would have attention forcibly directed to the Phoenician capital, at a time when Jeremiah was absorbed in the fortunes of Zion.
    But in the passage which we have chosen as the subject for this introduction to the prophecies of the nations, Jeremiah takes a somewhat wider range:--

The Expositor's Bible: Jeremiah Volumes I & II
> "Thus saith unto me Jehovah, the God of Israel:
> Take at My hand this cup of the wine of fury,
> And make all the nations, to whom I send thee, drink it.
> They shall drink, and reel to and fro, and be mad,
> Because of the sword that I will send among them."

First and foremost of these nations, pre-eminent in punishment as in privilege, stand "Jerusalem and the cities of Judah, with its kings and princes."

This bad eminence is a necessary application of the principle laid down by Amos [188] :--

> "You only have I known of all the families of the earth:
> Therefore I will visit upon you all your iniquities."

But as Jeremiah says later on, addressing the Gentile nations,--

> "I begin to work evil at the city which is called by My name.
> Should ye go scot-free? Ye shall not go scot-free."

And the prophet puts the cup of God's fury to their lips also, and amongst them, Egypt, the bête noir of Hebrew seers, is most conspicuously marked out for destruction: "Pharaoh king of Egypt, and his servants and princes and all his people, and all the mixed population of Egypt." [189] Then follows, in epic fashion, a catalogue of "all the nations" as Jeremiah knew them: "All the kings of the land of Uz, all the kings of the land of the Philistines; Ashkelon, Gaza, Ekron, and the remnant of Ashdod; [190] Edom, Moab, and the Ammonites; all the kings [191] of Tyre, all the kings of Zidon, and the kings of their colonies [192] beyond the sea; Dedan and Tema and Buz, and all that have the corners of their hair polled; [193] and all the kings of Arabia, and all the kings of the mixed populations that dwell in the desert; all the kings of Zimri, all the kings of Elam, and all the kings of the Medes." Jeremiah's definite geographical information is apparently exhausted, but he adds by way of summary and conclusion: "And all the kings of the north, far and near, one after the other; and all the kingdoms of the world, which are on the face of the earth."

There is one notable omission in the list. Nebuchadnezzar, the servant of Jehovah, [194] was the divinely appointed scourge of Judah and its neighbours and allies. Elsewhere [195] the nations are exhorted to submit to him, and here apparently Chaldea is exempted from the general doom, just as Ezekiel passes no formal sentence on Babylon. It is true that "all the kingdoms of the earth" would naturally include Babylon, possibly were even intended to do so. But the Jews were not long content with so veiled a reference to their conquerors and oppressors. Some patriotic scribe added the explanatory note, "And the king of Sheshach (i.e. Babylon) shall drink after them." [196] Sheshach is obtained from Babel by the cypher 'Athbash, according to which an alphabet is written out and a reversed alphabet written out underneath it, and the letters of the lower row used for those of the upper and vice versâ. Thus

    Aleph B
    K L T
    SH L K

The use of cypher seems to indicate that the note was added in Chaldea during the Exile, when it was not safe to circulate documents which openly denounced Babylon. Jeremiah's enumeration of the peoples and rulers of his world is naturally more detailed and more exhaustive than the list of the nations against which he prophesied. It includes the Phoenician states, details the Philistine cities, associates with Elam the neighbouring nations of Zimri and the Medes, and substitutes for Kedar and Hazor Arabia and a number of semi-Arab states, Uz, Dedan, Tema, and Buz. [197] Thus Jeremiah's world is the district constantly shown in Scripture atlases in a map comprising the scenes of Old Testament history, Egypt, Arabia, and Western Asia, south of a line from the north-east corner of the Mediterranean to the southern end of the Caspian Sea, and west of a line from the latter point to the northern end of the Persian Gulf. How much of history has been crowded into this narrow area! Here science, art, and literature won those primitive triumphs which no subsequent achievements could surpass or even equal. Here, perhaps for the first time, men tasted the Dead Sea apples of civilisation, and learnt how little accumulated wealth and national splendour can do for the welfare of the masses. Here was Eden, where God walked in the cool of the day to commune with man; and here also were many Mount Moriahs, where man gave his firstborn for his transgression, the fruit of his body for the sin of his soul, and no angel voice stayed his hand.

And now glance at any modern map and see for how little Jeremiah's world counts among the great Powers of the nineteenth century. Egypt indeed is a bone of contention between European states, but how often does a daily paper remind its readers of the existence of Syria or Mesopotamia? We may apply to this ancient world the title that Byron gave to Rome, "Lone mother of dead empires," and call it:--

"The desert, where we steer
Stumbling o'er recollections."

It is said that Scipio's exultation over the fall of Carthage was marred by forebodings that Time had a like destiny in store for Rome. Where Cromwell might have quoted a text from the Bible, the Roman soldier applied to his native city the Homeric lines:--

"Troy shall sink in fire,
And Priam's city with himself expire."

The epitaphs of ancient civilisations are no mere matters of archÃ¦ology; like the inscriptions on common graves, they carry a Memento mori for their successors.

But to return from epitaphs to prophecy: in the list which we have just given, the kings of many of the nations are required to drink the cup of wrath, and the section concludes with a universal judgment upon the princes and rulers of this ancient world under the familiar figure of shepherds, supplemented here by another, that of the "principal of the flock," or, as we should say, "bell-wethers." Jehovah would break out upon them to rend and scatter like a lion from his covert. Therefore:--

"Howl, ye shepherds, and cry!
Roll yourselves in the dust, ye bell-wethers!
The time has fully come for you to be slaughtered.
I will cast you down with a crash, like a vase of porcelain. [198]
Ruin hath overtaken the refuge of the shepherds,
And the way of escape of the bell-wethers."

Thus Jeremiah announces the coming ruin of an ancient world, with all its states and sovereigns, and we have seen that the prediction has been amply fulfilled. We can only notice two other points with regard to this section.

First, then, we have no right to accuse the prophet of speaking from a narrow national standpoint. His words are not the expression of the Jewish adversus omnes alios hostile odium; [199] if they were, we should not hear so much of Judah's sin and Judah's punishment. He applied to heathen states as he did to his own the divine standard of national righteousness, and they too were found wanting. All history confirms Jeremiah's judgment. This brings us to our second point. Christian thinkers have been engrossed in the evidential aspect of these national catastrophes. They served to fulfil prophecy, and therefore the squalor of Egypt and the ruins of Assyria to-day have seemed to make our way of salvation more safe and certain. But God did not merely sacrifice these holocausts of men and nations to the perennial craving of feeble faith for signs. Their fate must of necessity illustrate His justice and wisdom and love. Jeremiah tells us plainly that Judah and its neighbours had filled up the measure of their iniquity before they were called upon to drink the cup of wrath; national sin justifies God's judgments. Yet these very facts of the moral failure and decadence of human societies perplex and startle us. Individuals grow old and feeble and die, but saints and heroes do not become slaves of vice and sin in their last days. The glory of their prime is not buried in a dishonoured grave. Nay rather, when all else fails, the beauty of holiness grows more pure and radiant. But of what nation could we say:--

"Let me die the death of the righteous,
Let my last end be like his"?

Apparently the collective conscience is a plant of very slow growth; and hitherto no society has been worthy to endure honourably or even to perish nobly. In Christendom itself the ideals of common action are still avowedly meaner than those of individual conduct. International and collective morality is still in its infancy, and as a matter of habit and system modern states are often wantonly cruel and unjust towards obscure individuals and helpless minorities. Yet surely it shall not always be so; the daily prayer of countless millions for the coming of the Kingdom of God cannot remain unanswered.

Footnotes:

185. Doubts however have been raised as to whether any of the sections about Babylon are by Isaiah himself.
186. Doubts have been expressed as to the genuineness of the Damascus prophecy.
187. The Isaianic authorship of this prophecy (Isa. xxiii.) is rejected by very many critics.
188. Amos iii. 2.
189. So Giesebrecht, Orelli, etc.
190. Psammetichus had recently taken Ashdod, after a continuous siege of twenty-nine years.
191. The plural may refer to dependent chiefs or may be used for the sake of symmetry.
192. Lit. "the coasts" (i.e. islands and coastland) where the Phoenicians had planted their colonies.
193. See on xlix. 28-32.
194. xxv. 9.
195. xxvii. 8.
196. Sheshach (Sheshakh) for Babel also occurs in li. 41. This explanatory note is omitted by LXX.
197. As to Damascus cf. note on p. 213.
198. This line is somewhat paraphrased. Lit. "I will shatter you, and ye shall fall like an ornamental vessel" (KELI HEMDA).
199. Tacitus, History, v. 5.

Rev. C. J. Ball, M.A., & W. H. Bennett, M.A.

CHAPTER XVII

EGYPT

xliii. 8-13, xliv. 30, xlvi.

"*I will visit Amon of No, and Pharaoh, and Egypt, with their gods and their kings; even Pharaoh, and all them that trust in him.*"--Jer. xlvi. 25.

The kings of Egypt with whom Jeremiah was contemporary--Psammetichus II., Pharaoh Necho, and Pharaoh Hophra--belonged to the twenty-sixth dynasty. When growing distress at home compelled Assyria to loose her hold on her distant dependencies, Egypt still retained something of her former vigorous elasticity. In the rebound from subjection under the heavy hand of Sennacherib, she resumed her ancient forms of life and government. She regained her unity and independence, and posed afresh as an equal rival with Chaldea for the supremacy of Western Asia. At home there was a renascence of art and literature, and, as of old, the wealth and devotion of powerful monarchs restored the ancient temples and erected new shrines of their own.

But this revival was no new growth springing up with a fresh and original life from the seeds of the past; it cannot rank with the European Renascence of the fifteenth century. It is rather to be compared with the reorganisations by which Diocletian and Constantine prolonged the decline of the Roman Empire, the rally of a strong constitution in the grip of mortal disease. These latter-day Pharaohs failed ignominiously in their attempts to recover the Syrian dominion of the Thothmes and Rameses; and, like the Roman Empire in its last centuries, the Egypt of the twenty-sixth dynasty surrendered itself to Greek influence and hired foreign mercenaries to fight its battles. The new art and literature were tainted by pedantic archaism. According to Brugsch, [200] "Even to the newly created dignities and titles, the return to ancient times had become the general watchword.... The stone door-posts of this age reveal the old Memphian style of art, mirrored in its modern reflection after the lapse of four thousand years." Similarly Meyer [201] tells us that apparently the Egyptian state was reconstituted on the basis of a religious revival, somewhat in the fashion of the establishment of Deuteronomy by Josiah.

Inscriptions after the time of Psammetichus are written in archaic Egyptian of a very ancient past; it is often difficult to determine at first sight whether inscriptions belong to the earliest or latest period of Egyptian history.

The superstition that sought safety in an exact reproduction of a remote antiquity could not, however, resist the fascination of Eastern demonology. According to Brugsch, [202] in the age called the Egyptian Renascence the old Egyptian theology was adulterated with GrÃ¦co-Asiatic elements--demons and genii of whom the older faith and its purer doctrine had scarcely an idea; exorcisms became a special science, and are favourite themes for the inscriptions of this period. Thus, amid many differences, there are also to be found striking resemblances between the religious movements of the period in Egypt and amongst the Jews, and corresponding difficulties in determining the dates of Egyptian inscriptions and of sections of the Old Testament.

This enthusiasm for ancient custom and tradition was not likely to commend the Egypt of Jeremiah's age to any student of Hebrew history. He would be reminded that the dealings of the Pharaohs with Israel had almost always been to its hurt; he would remember the Oppression and the Exodus--how, in the time of Solomon, friendly intercourse with Egypt taught that monarch lessons in magnificent tyranny, how Shishak plundered the Temple, how Isaiah had denounced the Egyptian alliance as a continual snare to Judah. A Jewish prophet would be prompt to discern the omens of coming ruin in the midst of renewed prosperity on the Nile.

Accordingly at the first great crisis of the new international system, in the fourth year of Jehoiakim, either just before or just after the battle of Carchemish--it matters little which--Jeremiah takes up his prophecy against Egypt. First of all, with an ostensible friendliness which only masks his bitter sarcasm, he invites the Egyptians to take the field:--

"*Prepare buckler and shield, and draw near to battle.*
Harness the horses to the chariots, mount the chargers, stand forth armed cap-Ã -pie for battle;
Furbish the spears, put on the coats of mail."

This great host with its splendid equipment must surely conquer. The prophet professes to await its triumphant return; but he sees instead a breathless mob of panic-stricken fugitives, and pours upon them the torrent of his irony:--

"How is it that I behold this? These heroes are dismayed and have turned their backs;
Their warriors have been beaten down;
They flee apace, and do not look behind them:
Terror on every side--is the utterance of Jehovah."

Then irony passes into explicit malediction:--

"Let not the swift flee away, nor the warrior escape;
Away northward, they stumble and fall by the river Euphrates."

Then, in a new strophe, Jeremiah again recurs in imagination to the proud march of the countless hosts of Egypt:--

"Who is this that riseth up like the Nile,
Whose waters toss themselves like the rivers?
Egypt riseth up like the Nile,
His waters toss themselves like the rivers.
And he saith, I will go up and cover the land"
(like the Nile in flood);
"I will destroy the cities and their inhabitants"
(and, above all other cities, Babylon).

Again the prophet urges them on with ironical encouragement:--

"Go up, ye horses; rage, ye chariots;
Ethiopians and Libyans that handle the shield,
Lydians that handle and bend the bow"
(the tributaries and mercenaries of Egypt).

Then, as before, he speaks plainly of coming disaster:

"That day is a day of vengeance for the Lord Jehovah Sabaoth, whereon He will avenge Him of His adversaries"
(a day of vengeance upon Pharaoh Necho for Megiddo and Josiah).
"The sword shall devour and be sated, and drink its fill of their blood:
For the Lord Jehovah Sabaoth hath a sacrifice in the northern land, by the river Euphrates."

In a final strophe, the prophet turns to the land left bereaved and defenceless by the defeat at Carchemish:--

"Go up to Gilead and get thee balm, O virgin daughter of Egypt:
In vain dost thou multiply medicines; thou canst not be healed.
The nations have heard of thy shame, the earth is full of thy cry:
For warrior stumbles against warrior; they fall both together."

Nevertheless the end was not yet. Egypt was wounded to death, but she was to linger on for many a long year to be a snare to Judah and to vex the righteous soul of Jeremiah. The reed was broken, but it still retained an appearance of soundness, which more than once tempted the Jewish princes to lean upon it and find their hands pierced for their pains. Hence, as we have seen already, Jeremiah repeatedly found occasion to reiterate the doom of Egypt, of Necho's successor, Pharaoh Hophra, and of the Jewish refugees who had sought safety under his protection. In the concluding part of chapter xlvi., a prophecy of uncertain date sets forth the ruin of Egypt with rather more literary finish than in the parallel passages.

This word of Jehovah was to be proclaimed in Egypt, and especially in the frontier cities, which would have to bear the first brunt of invasion:--

Rev. C. J. Ball, M.A., & W. H. Bennett, M.A.

"Declare in Egypt, proclaim in Migdol, proclaim in Noph and Tahpanhes:
Say ye, Take thy stand and be ready, for the sword hath devoured round about thee.
Why hath Apis [203] fled and thy calf not stood? Because Jehovah overthrew it."

Memphis was devoted to the worship of Apis, incarnate in the sacred bull; but now Apis must succumb to the mightier divinity of Jehovah, and his sacred city become a prey to the invaders.

"He maketh many to stumble; they fall one against another.
Then they say, Arise, and let us return to our own people and to our native land, before the oppressing sword."

We must remember that the Egyptian armies were largely composed of foreign mercenaries. In the hour of disaster and defeat these hirelings would desert their employers and go home.

"Give unto Pharaoh king of Egypt the name [204] Crash; he hath let the appointed time pass by."

The form of this enigmatic sentence is probably due to a play upon Egyptian names and titles. When the allusions are forgotten, such paronomasia naturally results in hopeless obscurity. The "appointed time" has been explained as the period during which Jehovah gave Pharaoh the opportunity of repentance, or as that within which he might have submitted to Nebuchadnezzar on favourable terms.

"As I live, is the utterance of the King, whose name is Jehovah Sabaoth,
One shall come like Tabor among the mountains and like Carmel by the sea."

It was not necessary to name this terrible invader; it could be no other than Nebuchadnezzar.

"Get thee gear for captivity, O daughter of Egypt, that dwellest in thine own land:
For Noph shall become a desolation, and shall be burnt up and left without inhabitants.
Egypt is a very fair heifer, but destruction is come upon her from the north."

This tempest shattered the Greek phalanx in which Pharaoh trusted:--

"Even her mercenaries in the midst of her are like calves of the stall;
Even they have turned and fled together, they have not stood:
For their day of calamity hath come upon them, their day of reckoning."

We do not look for chronological sequence in such a poem, so that this picture of the flight and destruction of the mercenaries is not necessarily later in time than their overthrow and contemplated desertion in verse 15. The prophet is depicting a scene of bewildered confusion; the disasters that fell thick upon Egypt crowd into his vision without order or even coherence. Now he turns again to Egypt herself:--

"Her voice goeth forth like the (low hissing of) the serpent;
For they come upon her with a mighty army, and with axes like woodcutters."

A like fate is predicted in Isaiah xxix. 4 for "Ariel, the city where David dwelt":--

"Thou shalt be brought low and speak from the ground;
Thou shalt speak with a low voice out of the dust;
Thy voice shall come from the ground, like that of a familiar spirit,
And thou shalt speak in a whisper from the dust."

Thus too Egypt would seek to writhe herself from under the heel of the invader; hissing out the while her impotent fury, she would seek to glide away into some safe refuge amongst the underwood. Her dominions, stretching far up the Nile, were surely vast enough to afford her shelter somewhere; but no! the "woodcutters" are too many and too mighty for her:--

"They cut down her forest--it is the utterance of Jehovah--for it is impenetrable;
For they are more than the locusts, and are innumerable."

The whole of Egypt is overrun and subjugated; no district holds out against the invader, and remains unsubjugated to form the nucleus of a new and independent empire.

"The daughter of Egypt is put to shame; she is delivered into the hand of the northern people."

Her gods share her fate; Apis had succumbed at Memphis, but Egypt had countless other stately shrines whose denizens must own the overmastering might of Jehovah:--

"Thus saith Jehovah Sabaoth, the God of Israel:
Behold, I will visit Amon of No,
And Pharaoh, and Egypt, and all her gods and kings,
Even Pharaoh and all who trust in him."

Amon of No, or Thebes, known to the Greeks as Ammon and called by his own worshippers Amen, or "the hidden one," is apparently mentioned with Apis as sharing the primacy of the Egyptian divine hierarchy. On the fall of the twentieth dynasty, the high priest of the Theban Amen became king of Egypt, and centuries afterwards Alexander the Great made a special pilgrimage to the temple in the oasis of Ammon and was much gratified at being there hailed son of the deity.

Probably the prophecy originally ended with this general threat of "visitation" of Egypt and its human and divine rulers. An editor, however, has added, [205] from parallel passages, the more definite but sufficiently obvious statement that Nebuchadnezzar and his servants were to be the instruments of the Divine visitation.

A further addition is in striking contrast to the sweeping statements of Jeremiah:--

"Afterward it shall be inhabited, as in the days of old."

Similarly, Ezekiel foretold a restoration for Egypt:--

"At the end of forty years, I will gather the Egyptians, and will cause them to return ... to their native land; and they shall be there a base kingdom: it shall be the basest of the kingdoms." [206]

And elsewhere we read yet more gracious promises to Egypt:--

"Israel shall be a third with Egypt and Assyria, a blessing in the midst of the land: whom Jehovah Sabaoth shall bless, saying, Blessed be Egypt My people, and Assyria the work of My hands, and Israel Mine inheritance." [207]

Probably few would claim to discover in history any literal fulfilment of this last prophecy. Perhaps it might have been appropriated for the Christian Church in the days of Clement and Origen. We may take Egypt and Assyria as types of heathendom, which shall one day receive the blessings of the Lord's people and of the work of His hands. Of political revivals and restorations Egypt has had her share. But less interest attaches to these general prophecies than to more definite and detailed predictions; and there is much curiosity as to any evidence which monuments and other profane witnesses may furnish as to a conquest of Egypt and capture of Pharaoh Hophra by Nebuchadnezzar.

According to Herodotus, [208] Apries (Hophra) was defeated and imprisoned by his successor Amasis, afterwards delivered up by him to the people of Egypt, who forthwith strangled their former king. This event would be an exact fulfilment of the words, "I will give Pharaoh Hophra king of Egypt into the hand of his enemies, and into the hand of them that seek his life," [209] if it were not evident from parallel passages [210] that the Book of Jeremiah intends Nebuchadnezzar to be the enemy into whose hands Pharaoh is to be delivered. But Herodotus is entirely silent as to the relations of Egypt and Babylon during this period; for instance, he mentions the victory of Pharaoh Necho at Megiddo--which he miscalls Magdolium--but not his defeat at Carchemish. Hence his silence as to Chaldean conquests in Egypt has little weight. Even the historian's explicit statement as to the death of Apries might be reconciled with his defeat and capture by Nebuchadnezzar, if we knew all the facts. At present, however, the inscriptions do little to fill the gap left by the Greek historian; there are, however, references which seem to establish two invasions of Egypt by the Chaldean king, one of which fell in the reign of Pharaoh Hophra. But the spiritual lessons of this and the following prophecies concerning the nations are not dependent on the spade of the excavator or the skill of the decipherers of hieroglyphics and cuneiform script; whatever their relation may be to the details of subsequent historical events, they remain as monuments of the inspired insight of the prophet into the character and destiny alike of great empires and petty states. They assert the Divine government of the nations, and the subordination of all history to the coming of the Kingdom of God.

Footnotes:

200. Second edition, ii. 291, 292.
201. Meyer, Geschichte des alten Ägypten, 371, 373.
202. ii. 293.
203. Giesebrecht, with LXX.
204. Giesebrecht, Orelli, Kautzsch, with LXX., Syr., and Vulg., by an alteration of the pointing.
205. LXX. omits verse 26. Verses 27, 28 = xxx. 10, 11, and probably are an insertion here.
206. Ezek. xxix. 13-15.
207. Isa. xix. 25.
208. Herodotus, II. clxix.
209. xliv. 30.
210. xlvi. 25.

CHAPTER XVIII

THE PHILISTINES

xlvii.

"O sword of Jehovah, how long will it be ere thou be quiet? put up thyself into thy scabbard; rest, and be still."--Jer. xlvii. 6.

According to the title placed at the head of this prophecy, it was uttered "before Pharaoh smote Gaza." The Pharaoh is evidently Pharaoh Necho, and this capture of Gaza was one of the incidents of the campaign which opened with the victory at Megiddo and concluded so disastrously at Carchemish. Our first impulse is to look for some connection between this incident and the contents of the prophecy: possibly the editor who prefixed the heading may have understood by the northern enemy Pharaoh Necho on his return from Carchemish; but would Jeremiah have described a defeated army thus?

> "Behold, waters rise out of the north, and become an overflowing torrent;
> They overflow the land, and all that is therein, the city and its inhabitants.
> Men cry out, and all the inhabitants of the land howl,
> At the sound of the stamping of the hoofs of his stallions,
> At the rattling of his chariots and the rumbling of his wheels."

Here as elsewhere the enemy from the north is Nebuchadnezzar. Pharaohs might come and go, winning victories and taking cities, but these broken reeds count for little; not they, but the king of Babylon is the instrument of Jehovah's supreme purpose. The utter terror caused by the Chaldean advance is expressed by a striking figure:--

> "The fathers look not back to their children for slackness of hands."

Their very bodies are possessed and crippled with fear, their palsied muscles cannot respond to the impulses of natural affection; they can do nothing but hurry on in headlong flight, unable to look round or stretch out a helping hand to their children:--

> "Because of the day that cometh for the spoiling of all the Philistines,
> For cutting off every ally that remaineth unto Tyre and Zidon:
> For Jehovah spoileth the Philistines, the remnant of the coast of Caphtor. [211]
> Baldness cometh upon Gaza; Ashkelon is destroyed:
> O remnant of the Anakim, [212] how long wilt thou cut thyself?"

This list is remarkable both for what it includes and what it omits. In order to understand the reference to Tyre and Zidon, we must remember that Nebuchadnezzar's expedition was partly directed against these cities, with which the Philistines had evidently been allied. The Chaldean king would hasten the submission of the Phoenicians, by cutting off all hope of succour from without. There are various possible reasons why out of the five Philistine cities only two--Ashkelon and Gaza--are mentioned; Ekron, Gath, and Ashdod may have been reduced to comparative insignificance. Ashdod had recently been taken by Psammetichus after a twenty-nine years' siege. Or the names of two of these cities may be given by way of paronomasia in the text: Ashdod may be suggested by the double reference to the spoiling and the spoiler, Shdod and Shoded; Gath may be hinted at by the word used for the mutilation practised by mourners, Tithgoddadi, and by the mention of the Anakim, who are connected with Gath, Ashdod, and Gaza in Joshua xi. 22.

As Jeremiah contemplates this fresh array of victims of Chaldean cruelty, he is moved to protest against the weary monotony of ruin:--

"O sword of Jehovah, how long will it be ere thou be quiet?
Put up thyself into thy scabbard; rest, and be still."

The prophet ceases to be the mouthpiece of God, and breaks out into the cry of human anguish. How often since, amid the barbarian inroads that overwhelmed the Roman Empire, amid the prolonged horrors of the Thirty Years' War, amid the carnage of the French Revolution, men have uttered a like

Rev. C. J. Ball, M.A., & W. H. Bennett, M.A.

appeal to an unanswering and relentless Providence! Indeed, not in war only, but even in peace, the tide of human misery and sin often seems to flow, century after century, with undiminished volume, and ever and again a vain "How long" is wrung from pallid and despairing lips. For the Divine purpose may not be hindered, and the sword of Jehovah must still strike home.

> "How can it be quiet, seeing that Jehovah hath given it a charge?
> Against Ashkelon and against the sea-shore, there hath He appointed it."

Yet Ashkelon survived to be a stronghold of the Crusaders, and Gaza to be captured by Alexander and even by Napoleon. Jehovah has other instruments besides His devastating sword; the victorious endurance and recuperative vitality of men and nations also come from Him.

> "Come, and let us return unto Jehovah:
> For He hath torn, and He will heal us;
> He hath smitten, and He will bind us up." [213]

Footnotes:

211. Referring to their ancient immigration from Caphtor, probably Crete.
212. Kautzsch, Giesebrecht, with LXX., reading 'Nqm for the Masoretic 'Mqm; Eng. Vers., "their valley."
213. Hosea vi. 1.

CHAPTER XIX

MOAB

xlviii.

"Moab shall be destroyed from being a people, because he hath magnified himself against Jehovah."--Jer. xlviii. 42.

"Chemosh said to me, Go, take Nebo against Israel ... and I took it ... and I took from it the vessels of Jehovah, and offered them before Chemosh."--Moabite Stone.

"Yet will I bring again the captivity of Moab in the latter days."--Jer. xlviii. 47.

The prophets show a very keen interest in Moab. With the exception of the very short Book of Joel, all the prophets who deal in detail with foreign nations devote sections to Moab. The unusual length of such sections in Isaiah and Jeremiah is not the only resemblance between the utterances of these two prophets concerning Moab. There are many parallels [214] of idea and expression, which probably indicate the influence of the elder prophet upon his successor; unless indeed both of them adapted some popular poem which was early current in Judah. [215]

It is easy to understand why the Jewish Scriptures should have much to say about Moab, just as the sole surviving fragment of Moabite literature is chiefly occupied with Israel. These two Terahite tribes--the children of Jacob and the children of Lot--had dwelt side by side for centuries, like the Scotch and English borderers before the accession of James I. They had experienced many alternations of enmity and friendship, and had shared complex interests, common and conflicting, after the manner of neighbours who are also kinsmen. Each in its turn had oppressed the other; and Moab had been the tributary of the Israelite monarchy till the victorious arms of Mesha had achieved independence for his people and firmly established their dominion over the debatable frontier lands. There are traces, too, of more kindly relations: the House of David reckoned Ruth the Moabitess amongst its ancestors, and Jesse, like Elimelech and Naomi, had taken refuge in Moab.

Accordingly this prophecy concerning Moab, in both its editions, frequently strikes a note of sympathetic lamentation and almost becomes a dirge.

> *"Therefore will I howl for Moab;*
> *Yea, for all Moab will I cry out.*
> *For the men of Kir-heres shall they mourn.*
> *With more than the weeping of Jazer*
> *Will I weep for thee, O vine of Sibmah.*

***

> *Therefore mine heart soundeth like pipes for Moab,*
> *Mine heart soundeth like pipes for the men of Kir-heres."*

But this pity could not avail to avert the doom of Moab; it only enabled the Jewish prophet to fully appreciate its terrors. The picture of coming ruin is drawn with the colouring and outlines familiar to us in the utterances of Jeremiah--spoiling and destruction, fire and sword and captivity, dismay and wild abandonment of wailing.

> *"Chemosh shall go forth into captivity, his priests and his princes together.*
> *Every head is bald, and every beard clipped;*
> *Upon all the hands are cuttings, and upon the loins sackcloth.*
> *On all the housetops and in all the streets of Moab there is everywhere lamentation;*
> *For I have broken Moab like a useless vessel--it is the utterance of Jehovah.*
> *How is it broken down! Howl ye! Be thou ashamed!*
> *How hath Moab turned the back!*
> *All the neighbours shall laugh and shudder at Moab.*

***

The heart of the mighty men of Moab at that day
Shall be like the heart of a woman in her pangs."

This section of Jeremiah illustrates the dramatic versatility of the prophet's method. He identifies himself now with the blood-thirsty invader, now with his wretched victims, and now with the terror-stricken spectators; and sets forth the emotions of each in turn with vivid realism. Hence at one moment we have the pathos and pity of such verses as we have just quoted, and at another such stern and savage words as these:--

"Cursed be he that doeth the work of Jehovah negligently,
Cursed be he that stinteth his sword of blood."

These lines might have served as a motto for Cromwell at the massacre of Drogheda, for Tilly's army at the sack of Magdeburg, or for Danton and Robespierre during the Reign of Terror. Jeremiah's words were the more terrible because they were uttered with the full consciousness that in the dread Chaldean king [216] a servant of Jehovah was at hand who would be careful not to incur any curse for stinting his sword of blood. We shrink from what seems to us the prophet's brutal assertion that relentless and indiscriminate slaughter is sometimes the service which man is called upon to render to God. Such sentiment is for the most part worthless and unreal; it does not save us from epidemics of war fever, and is at once ignored under the stress of horrors like the Indian Mutiny. There is no true comfort in trying to persuade ourselves that the most awful events of history lie outside of the Divine purpose, or in forgetting that the human scourges of their kind do the work that God has assigned to them.

In this inventory, as it were, of the ruin of Moab our attention is arrested by the constant and detailed references to the cities. This feature is partly borrowed from Isaiah. Ezekiel too speaks of the Moabite cities which are the glory of the country; [217] but Jeremiah's prophecy is a veritable Domesday Book of Moab. With his epic fondness for lists of sonorous names--after the manner of Homer's catalogue of the ships--he enumerates Nebo, Kiriathaim, Heshbon, and Horonaim, city after city, till he completes a tale of no fewer than twenty-six, [218] and then summarises the rest as "all the cities of the land of Moab, far and near." Eight of these cities are mentioned in Joshua [219] as part of the inheritance of Reuben and Gad. Another, Bozrah, is usually spoken of as a city of Edom. [220]

The Moabite Stone explains the occurrence of Reubenite cities in these lists. It tells us how Mesha took Nebo, Jahaz, and Horonaim from Israel. Possibly in this period of conquest Bozrah became tributary to Moab, without ceasing to be an Edomite city. This extension of territory and multiplication of towns points to an era of power and prosperity, of which there are other indications in this chapter. "We are mighty and valiant for war," said the Moabites. When Moab fell "there was broken a mighty sceptre and a glorious staff." Other verses imply the fertility of the land and the abundance of its vintage.

Moab in fact had profited by the misfortunes of its more powerful and ambitious neighbours. The pressure of Damascus, Assyria, and Chaldea prevented Israel and Judah from maintaining their dominion over their ancient tributary. Moab lay less directly in the track of the invaders; it was too insignificant to attract their special attention, perhaps too prudent to provoke a contest with the lords of the East. Hence, while Judah was declining, Moab had enlarged her borders and grown in wealth and power.

And even as Jeshurun kicked, when he was waxen fat, [221] so Moab in its prosperity was puffed up with unholy pride. Even in Isaiah's time this was the besetting sin of Moab; he says in an indictment which Jeremiah repeats almost word for word:--

"We have heard of the pride of Moab, that he is very proud,
Even of his arrogancy and his pride and his wrath." [222]

This verse is a striking example of the Hebrew method of gaining emphasis by accumulating derivatives of the same and similar roots. The verse in Jeremiah runs thus: "We have heard of the pride (Ge'ON) of Moab, that he is very proud (GE'EH); his loftiness (GABHeHO), and his pride (Ge'ONO), and his proudfulness (GA'aWATHO)."
Jeremiah dwells upon this theme:--

"Moab shall be destroyed from being a people,
Because he hath magnified himself against Jehovah."

Zephaniah bears like testimony [223] :--

> "This shall they have for their pride,
> Because they have been insolent, and have magnified themselves
> Against the people of Jehovah Sabaoth."

Here again the Moabite Stone bears abundant testimony to the justice of the prophet's accusations; for there Mesha tells how in the name and by the grace of Chemosh he conquered the cities of Israel; and how, anticipating Belshazzar's sacrilege, he took the sacred vessels of Jehovah from His temple at Nebo and consecrated them to Chemosh. Truly Moab had "magnified himself against Jehovah."

Prosperity had produced other baleful effects beside a haughty spirit, and pride was not the only cause of the ruin of Moab. Jeremiah applies to nations the dictum of Polonius--

> "Home-keeping youths have ever homely wits,"

and apparently suggests that ruin and captivity were necessary elements in the national discipline of Moab:--

> "Moab hath been undisturbed from his youth;
> He hath settled on his lees;
> He hath not been emptied from vessel to vessel;
> He hath not gone into captivity:
> Therefore his taste remaineth in him,
> His scent is not changed.
> Wherefore, behold, the days come--it is the utterance of Jehovah--
> That I will send men unto him that shall tilt him up;
> They shall empty his vessels and break his [224] bottles."

As the chapter, in its present form, concludes with a note--

> "I will bring again the captivity of Moab in the latter days--it is the utterance of Jehovah"--

we gather that even this rough handling was disciplinary; at any rate, the former lack of such vicissitudes had been to the serious detriment of Moab. It is strange that Jeremiah did not apply this principle to Judah. For, indeed, the religion of Israel and of mankind owes an incalculable debt to the captivity of Judah, a debt which later writers are not slow to recognise. "Behold," says the prophet of the Exile,--

> "I have refined thee, but not as silver;
> I have chosen thee in the furnace of affliction." [225]

History constantly illustrates how when Christians were undisturbed and prosperous the wine of truth settled on the lees and came to taste of the cask; and--to change the figure--how affliction and persecution proved most effectual tonics for a debilitated Church. Continental critics of modern England speak severely of the ill-effects which our prolonged freedom from invasion and civil war, and the unbroken continuity of our social life have had on our national character and manners. In their eyes England is a perfect Moab, concerning which they are ever ready to prophesy after the manner of Jeremiah. The Hebrew Chronicler blamed Josiah because he would not listen to the advice and criticism of Pharaoh Necho. There may be warnings which we should do well to heed, even in the acrimony of foreign journalists.

But any such suggestion raises wider and more difficult issues; for ordinary individuals and nations the discipline of calamity seems necessary. What degree of moral development exempts from such discipline, and how may it be attained? Christians cannot seek to compound for such discipline by self-inflicted loss or pain, like Polycrates casting away his ring or Browning's Caliban, who in his hour of terror,--

> "Lo! 'Lieth flat and loveth Setebos!
> 'Maketh his teeth meet through his upper lip,
> Will let those quails fly, will not eat this month
> One little mess of whelks, so he may 'scape."

But though it is easy to counsel resignation and the recognition of a wise loving Providence in national as in personal suffering, yet mankind longs for an end to the period of pupilage and chastisement and would fain know how it may be hastened.

Footnotes:

214. E.g. xlviii. 5, "For by the ascent of Luhith with continual weeping shall they go up; for in going down of Horonaim they have heard the distress of the cry of destruction," is almost identical with Isa. xv. 5. Cf. also xlviii. 29-34 with Isa. xv. 4, xvi. 6-11.
215. Verse 47 with the subscription, "Thus far is the judgment of Moab," is wanting in the LXX.
216. The exact date of the prophecy is uncertain, but it must have been written during the reign of Nebuchadnezzar.
217. Ezek. xxv. 9.
218. Some of the names, however, may be variants.
219. Josh. xiii. 15-28 (possibly on JE. basis).
220. xlix. 13, possibly this is not the Edomite Bozrah.
221. Deut. xxxii. 15.
222. Isa. xvi. 6.
223. ii. 10.
224. Kautzsch, Giesebrecht, with LXX.; A.V., R.V., with Hebrew Text, "their bottles."
225. Isa. xlviii. 10.

CHAPTER XX

AMMON

xlix. 1-6.

"Hath Israel no sons? hath he no heir? why then doth Moloch possess Gad, and his people dwell in the cities thereof?"--Jer. xlix. 1

The relations of Israel with Ammon were similar but less intimate than they were with his twin-brother Moab. Hence this prophecy is, mutatis mutandis, an abridgment of that concerning Moab. As Moab was charged with magnifying himself against Jehovah, and was found to be occupying cities which Reuben claimed as its inheritance, so Ammon had presumed to take possession of the Gadite cities, whose inhabitants had been carried away captive by the Assyrians. Here again the prophet enumerates Heshbon, Ai, Rabbah, and the dependent towns, "the daughters of Rabbah." Only in the territory of this half-nomadic people the cities are naturally not so numerous as in Moab; and Jeremiah mentions also the fertile valleys wherein the Ammonites gloried. The familiar doom of ruin and captivity is pronounced against city and country and all the treasures of Ammon; Moloch, [226] like Chemosh, must go into captivity with his priests and princes. This prophecy also concludes with a promise of restoration:--

"*Afterward I will bring again the captivity of the children of Ammon--it is the utterance of Jehovah.*"

Footnotes:

226. xlix. 3: A.V., "their king"; R.V., "Malcam," which here and in verse 1 is a form of Moloch.

Rev. C. J. Ball, M.A., & W. H. Bennett, M.A.

CHAPTER XXI

EDOM

xlix. 7-22.

"*Bozrah shall become an astonishment, a reproach, a waste, and a curse.*"--Jer. xlix. 13.

The prophecy concerning Edom is not formulated along the same line as those which deal with the twin children of Lot, Moab and Ammon. Edom was not merely the cousin, but the brother of Israel. His history, his character and conduct, had marked peculiarities, which received special treatment. Edom had not only intimate relations with Israel as a whole, but was also bound by exceptionally close ties to the Southern Kingdom. The Edomite clan Kenaz had been incorporated in the tribe of Judah; [227] and when Israel broke up into two states, Edom was the one tributary which was retained or reconquered by the House of David, and continued subject to Judah till the reign of Jehoram ben Jehoshaphat. [228]

Much virtuous indignation is often expressed at the wickedness of Irishmen in contemplating rebellion against the dominion of England: we cannot therefore be surprised that the Jews resented the successful revolt of Edom, and regarded the hostility of Mount Seir to its former masters as ingratitude and treachery. In moments of hot indignation against the manifold sins of Judah Jeremiah might have announced with great vehemence that Judah should be made a "reproach and a proverb"; but when, as Obadiah tells us, the Edomites stood gazing with eager curiosity on the destruction of Jerusalem, and rejoiced and exulted in the distress of the Jews, and even laid hands on their substance in the day of their calamity, and occupied the roads to catch fugitives and deliver them up to the Chaldeans, [229] then the patriotic fervour of the prophet broke out against Edom. Like Moab and Ammon, he was puffed up with pride, and deluded by baseless confidence into a false security. These hardy mountaineers trusted in their reckless courage and in the strength of their inaccessible mountain fastnesses.

> "*Men shall shudder at thy fate,* [230] *the pride of thy heart hath deceived thee,*
> *O thou that dwellest in the clefts of the rock, that holdest the height of the hill:*
> *Though thou shouldest make thy nest as high as the eagle,* [231]
> *I will bring thee down from thence--it is the utterance of Jehovah.*"

Pliny speaks of the Edomite capital as "*oppidum circumdatum montibus inaccessis,*" [232] and doubtless the children of Esau had often watched from their eyrie Assyrian and Chaldean armies on the march to plunder more defenceless victims, and trusted that their strength, their good fortune, and their ancient and proverbial wisdom would still hold them scatheless. Their neighbours--the Jews amongst the rest--might be plundered, massacred, and carried away captive, but Edom could look on in careless security, and find its account in the calamities of kindred tribes. If Jerusalem was shattered by the Chaldean tempest, the Edomites would play the part of wreckers. But all this shrewdness was mere folly: how could these Solons of Mount Seir prove so unworthy of their reputation?

> "*Is wisdom no more in Teman?*
> *Has counsel perished from the prudent?*
> *Has their wisdom vanished?*"

They thought that Jehovah would punish Jacob whom He loved, and yet spare Esau whom He hated. But:--

> "*Thus saith Jehovah:*
> *Behold, they to whom it pertained not to drink of the cup shall assuredly drink.*
> *Art thou he that shall go altogether unpunished?*
> *Thou shalt not go unpunished, but thou shalt assuredly drink*" (12).

Ay, and drink to the dregs:--

> "If grape-gatherers come to thee, would they not leave gleanings?
> If thieves came by night, they would only destroy till they had enough.
> But I have made Esau bare, I have stripped him stark naked; he shall not be able to hide himself.
> His children, and his brethren, and his neighbours are given up to plunder, and there is an end of him" (9, 10).
> "I have sworn by Myself--is the utterance of Jehovah--
> That Bozrah shall become an astonishment, a reproach, a desolation, and a curse;
> All her cities shall become perpetual wastes.
> I have heard tidings from Jehovah, and an ambassador is sent among the nations, saying,
> Gather yourselves together and come against her, arise to battle" (13, 14).

There was obviously but one leader who could lead the nations to achieve the overthrow of Edom and lead her little ones away captive, who could come up like a lion from the thickets of Jordan, or "flying like an eagle and spreading his wings against Bozrah" (22)--Nebuchadnezzar, king of Babylon, who had come up against Judah with all the kingdoms and peoples of his dominions. [233]

In this picture of chastisement and calamity, there is one apparent touch of pitifulness:--

> "Leave thine orphans, I will preserve their lives;
> Let thy widows put their trust in Me" (11).

At first sight, at any rate, these seem to be the words of Jehovah. All the adult males of Edom would perish, yet the helpless widows and orphans would not be without a protector. The God of Israel would watch over the lambs of Edom, [234] when they were dragged away into captivity. We are reluctant to surrender this beautiful and touching description of a God, who, though He may visit the iniquity of the fathers upon the children unto the third and fourth generation, yet even in such judgment ever remembers mercy. It is impossible, however, to ignore the fact that such ideas are widely different from the tone and sentiment of the rest of the section. These words may be an immediate sequel to the previous verse, "No Edomite survives to say to his dying brethren, Leave thine orphans to me," or possibly they may be quoted, in bitter irony, from some message from Edom to Jerusalem, inviting the Jews to send their wives and children for safety to Mount Seir. Edom, ungrateful and treacherous Edom, shall utterly perish--Edom that offered an asylum to Jewish refugees, and yet shared the plunder of Jerusalem and betrayed her fugitives to the Chaldeans.

There is no word of restoration. Moab and Ammon and Elam might revive and flourish again, but for Esau, as of old, there should be no place of repentance. For Edom, in the days of the Captivity, trespassed upon the inheritance of Israel more grievously than Ammon and Moab upon Reuben and Gad. The Edomites possessed themselves of the rich pastures of the south of Judah, and the land was thenceforth called Idumea. Thus they earned the undying hatred of the Jews, in whose mouths Edom became a curse and a reproach, a term of opprobrium. Like Babylon, Edom was used as a secret name for Rome, and later on for the Christian Church.

Nevertheless, even in this prophecy, there is a hint that these predictions of utter ruin must not be taken too literally:--

> "For, behold, I will make thee small among the nations,
> Despised among men" (15).

These words are scarcely consistent with the other verses, which imply that, as a people, Edom would utterly perish from off the face of the earth. As a matter of fact, Edom flourished in her new territory till the time of the Maccabees, and when the Messiah came to establish the Kingdom of God, instead of "saviours standing on Mount Zion to judge the Mount of Esau," [235] an Edomite dynasty was reigning in Jerusalem.

Footnotes:

227. Cf. the designation of Caleb "ben Jephunneh the Kenizzite," Num. xxxii. 12, etc., with the genealogies which trace the descent of Kenaz to Esau, Gen. xxxvi. 11, etc. Cf. also Expositor's Bible, Chronicles.

228. Cf. 1 Kings xxii. 47 with 2 Kings viii. 20.

229. Obadiah 11-15. The difference between A.V. and R.V. is more apparent than real. The prohibition which R.V. gives must have been based on experience. The short prophecy of Obadiah has very much in common with this section of Jeremiah: Obad. 1-6, 8, are almost identical with Jer. xlix.

14-16, 9, 10a, 7. The relation of the two passages is a matter of controversy, but probably both use a common original. Cf. Driver's Introduction on Obadiah.

230. Lit. "thy terror," i.e. the terror inspired by thy fate. A.V., R.V., "thy terribleness," suggests that Edom trusted in the terror felt for him by his enemies, but we can scarcely suppose that even the fiercest highlanders expected Nebuchadnezzar to be terrified at them.

231. Obad. 4: "Though thou set thy nest among the stars."
232. Hist. Nat., vi. 28. Orelli.
233. xxxiv. 1.
234. Verse 20.
235. Obadiah 21.

CHAPTER XXII

DAMASCUS

xlix. 23-27.
"*I will kindle a fire in the wall of Damascus, and it shall devour the palaces of Benhadad.*"--Jer. xlix. 27.

We are a little surprised to meet with a prophecy of Jeremiah concerning Damascus and the palaces of Benhadad. The names carry our minds back for more than a couple of centuries. During Elisha's ministry, Damascus and Samaria were engaged in their long, fierce duel for the supremacy over Syria and Palestine. In the reign of Ahaz these ancient rivals combined to attack Judah, so that Isaiah is keenly interested in Damascus and its fortunes. But about b.c. 745, about a hundred and fifty years before Jeremiah's time, the Assyrian king Tiglath-Pileser [236] overthrew the Syrian kingdom and carried its people into captivity. We know from Ezekiel, [237] what we might have surmised from the position and later history of Damascus, that this ancient city continued a wealthy commercial centre; but Ezekiel has no oracle concerning Damascus, and the other documents of the period and of later times do not mention the capital of Benhadad. Its name does not even occur in Jeremiah's exhaustive list of the countries of his world in xxv. 15-26. Religious interest in alien races depended on their political relations with Israel; when the latter ceased, the prophets had no word from Jehovah concerning foreign nations. Such considerations have suggested doubts as to the authenticity of this section, and it has been supposed that it may be a late echo of Isaiah's utterances concerning Damascus.

We know, however, too little of the history of the period to warrant such a conclusion. Damascus would continue to exist as a tributary state, and might furnish auxiliary forces to the enemies of Judah or join with her to conspire against Babylon, and would in either case attract Jeremiah's attention. Moreover, in ancient as in modern times, commerce played its part in international politics. Doubtless slaves were part of the merchandise of Damascus, just as they were among the wares of the Apocalyptic Babylon. Joel [238] denounces Tyre and Zidon for selling Jews to the Greeks, and the Damascenes may have served as slave-agents to Nebuchadnezzar and his captains, and thus provoked the resentment of patriot Jews. So many picturesque and romantic associations cluster around Damascus, that this section of Jeremiah almost strikes a jarring note. We love to think of this fairest of Oriental cities, "half as old as time," as the "Eye of the East" which Mohammed refused to enter--because "Man," he said, "can have but one paradise, and my paradise is fixed above"--and as the capital of Noureddin and his still more famous successor Saladin. And so we regret that, when it emerges from the obscurity of centuries into the light of Biblical narrative, the brief reference should suggest a disaster such as it endured in later days at the hands of the treacherous and ruthless Tamerlane.

"*Damascus hath grown feeble:*
She turneth herself to flee;
Trembling hath seized on her.

***

How is the city of praise forsaken, [239]
The city of joy!
Her young men shall fall in the streets,
All the warriors shall be put to silence in that day."

We are moved to sympathy with the feelings of Hamath and Arpad, when they heard the evil tidings, and were filled with sorrow, "like the sea that cannot rest."

Yet even here this most uncompromising of prophets may teach us, after his fashion, wholesome though perhaps unwelcome truths. We are reminded how often the mystic glamour of romance has served to veil cruelty and corruption, and how little picturesque scenery and interesting associations can do of themselves to promote a noble life. Feudal castles, with their massive grandeur, were the strongholds of avarice and cruelty; and ancient abbeys which, even in decay, are like a dream of fairyland, were sometimes the home of abominable corruption.

Footnotes:

236. 2 Kings xvi. 9.
237. Ezek. xxvii. 18.
238. Joel iii. 4.
239. So Giesebrecht, with most of the ancient versions. A.V., R.V., with Masoretic Text, "not forsaken ... my joy," possibly meaning, "Why did not the inhabitants forsake the doomed city?"

CHAPTER XXIII

KEDAR AND HAZOR

xlix. 28-33.

"Concerning Kedar, and the kingdoms of Hazor which Nebuchadnezzar king of Babylon smote."--Jer. xlix. 28.

From an immemorial seat of human culture, an "eternal city" which antedates Rome by centuries, if not millenniums, we turn to those Arab tribes whose national life and habits were as ancient and have been as persistent as the streets of Damascus. While Damascus has almost always been in the forefront of history, the Arab tribes--except in the time of Mohammed and the early Caliphs--have seldom played a more important part than that of frontier marauders. Hence, apart from a few casual references, the only other passage in the Old Testament which deals, at any length, with Kedar is the parallel prophecy of Isaiah. And yet Kedar was the great northern tribe, which ranged the deserts between Palestine and the Euphrates, and which must have had closer relations with Judah than most Arab peoples.

"The kingdoms of Hazor" are still more unknown to history. There were several "Hazors" in Palestine, besides sundry towns whose names are also derived from HaÃ§er, a village; and some of these are on or beyond the southern frontier of Judah, in the wilderness of the Exodus, where we might expect to find nomad Arabs. But even these latter cities can scarcely be the "Hazor" of Jeremiah, and the more northern are quite out of the question. It is generally supposed that Hazor here is either some Arabian town, or, more probably, a collective term for the district inhabited by Arabs, who lived not in tents, but in HaÃ§erÃ®m, or villages. This district would be in Arabia itself, and more distant from Palestine than the deserts over which Kedar roamed. Possibly Isaiah's "villages (HaÃ§erÃ®m) that Kedar doth inhabit" were to be found in the Hazor of Jeremiah, and the same people were called Kedar and Hazor respectively according as they lived a nomad life or settled in more permanent dwellings.

The great warlike enterprises of Egypt, Assyria, and Chaldea during the last centuries of the Jewish monarchy would bring these desert horsemen into special prominence. They could either further or hinder the advance of armies marching westward from Mesopotamia, and could command their lines of communication. Kedar, and possibly Hazor too, would not be slack to use the opportunities of plunder presented by the calamities of the Palestinian states. Hence their conspicuous position in the pages of Isaiah and Jeremiah.

As the Assyrians, when their power was at its height, had chastised the aggressions of the Arabs, so now Nebuchadnezzar "smote Kedar and the kingdoms of Hazor." Even the wandering nomads and dwellers by distant oases in trackless deserts could not escape the sweeping activity of this scourge of God. Doubtless the ravages of Chaldean armies might serve to punish many sins besides the wrongs they were sent to revenge. The Bedouin always had their virtues, but the wild liberty of the desert easily degenerated into unbridled licence. Judah and every state bordering on the wilderness knew by painful experience how large a measure of rapine and cruelty might coexist with primitive customs, and the Jewish prophet gives Nebuchadnezzar a Divine commission as for a holy war:--

> "Arise, go up to Kedar;
> Spoil the men of the east.
> They (the Chaldeans) shall take away their tents and flocks;
> They shall take for themselves their tent-coverings,
> And all their gear and their camels:
> Men shall cry concerning them,
> Terror on every side." [240]

Then the prophet turns to the more distant Hazor with words of warning:--

> "Flee, get you far off, dwell in hidden recesses of the land, O inhabitants of Hazor--
> It is the utterance of Jehovah--
> For Nebuchadnezzar king of Babylon hath counselled a counsel and purposed a purpose against you."

But then, as if this warning were a mere taunt, he renews his address to the Chaldeans and directs their attack against Hazor:--

"*Arise, go up against a nation that is at ease, that dwelleth without fear--it is the utterance of Jehovah--*
Which abide alone, without gates or bars"--

like the people of Laish before the Danites came, and like Sparta before the days of Epaminondas.

Possibly we are to combine these successive "utterances," and to understand that it was alike Jehovah's will that the Chaldeans should invade and lay waste Hazor, and that the unfortunate inhabitants should escape--but escape plundered and impoverished: for

"Their camels shall become a spoil,
The multitude of their cattle a prey:
I will scatter to every wind them that have the corners of their hair polled; [241]
I will bring their calamity upon them from all sides.
Hazor shall be a haunt of jackals, a desolation for ever:
No one shall dwell there,
No soul shall sojourn therein."

Footnotes:

240. Magor-missabib: cf. xlvi. 5.
241. I.e. cut off.

CHAPTER XXIV

ELAM

xlix. 34-39
"I will break the bow of Elam, the chief of their might."--Jer. xlix. 35.

We do not know what principle or absence of principle determined the arrangement of these prophecies; but, in any case, these studies in ancient geography and politics present a series of dramatic contrasts. From two ancient and enduring types of Eastern life, the city of Damascus and the Bedouin of the desert, we pass to a state of an entirely different order, only slightly connected with the international system of Western Asia. Elam contended for the palm of supremacy with Assyria and Babylon in the farther east, as Egypt did to the south-west. Before the time of Abraham Elamite kings ruled over Chaldea, and Genesis xiv. tells us how Chedorlaomer with his subject-allies collected his tribute in Palestine. Many centuries later, the Assyrian king Ashur-bani-pal (b.c. 668-626) conquered Elam, sacked the capital Shushan, and carried away many of the inhabitants into captivity. According to Ezra iv. 9, 10, Elamites were among the mingled population whom "the great and noble Asnapper" (probably Ashur-bani-pal) settled in Samaria.

When we begin to recall even a few of the striking facts concerning Elam discovered in the last fifty years, and remember that for millenniums Elam had played the part of a first-class Asiatic power, we are tempted to wonder that Jeremiah only devotes a few conventional sentences to this great nation. But the prophet's interest was simply determined by the relations of Elam with Judah; and, from this point of view, an opposite difficulty arises. How came the Jews in Palestine in the time of Jeremiah to have any concern with a people dwelling beyond the Euphrates and Tigris, on the farther side of the Chaldean dominions? One answer to this question has already been suggested: the Jews may have learnt from the Elamite colonists in Samaria something concerning their native country; it is also probable that Elamite auxiliaries served in the Chaldean armies that invaded Judah.

Accordingly the prophet sets forth, in terms already familiar to us, how Elamite fugitives should be scattered to the four quarters of the earth and be found in every nation under heaven, how the sword should follow them into their distant places of refuge and utterly consume them.

"I will set My throne in Elam;
I will destroy out of it both king and princes--
It is the utterance of Jehovah."

In the prophecy concerning Egypt, Nebuchadnezzar was to set his throne at Tahpanhes to decide the fate of the captives; but here Jehovah Himself is pictured as the triumphant and inexorable conqueror, holding His court as the arbiter of life and death. The vision of the "great white throne" was not first accorded to John in his Apocalypse. Jeremiah's eyes were opened to see beside the tribunals of heathen conquerors the judgment-seat of a mightier Potentate; and his inspired utterances remind the believer that every battle may be an Armageddon, and that at every congress there is set a mystic throne from which the Eternal King overrules the decisions of plenipotentiaries.

But this sentence of condemnation was not to be the final "utterance of Jehovah" with regard to Elam. A day of renewed prosperity was to dawn for Elam, as well as for Moab, Ammon, Egypt, and Judah:--

"In the latter days I will bring again the captivity of Elam--
It is the utterance of Jehovah."

The Apostle Peter [242] tells us that the prophets "sought and searched diligently" concerning the application of their words, "searching what time and what manner of time the Spirit of Christ which was in them did point unto." We gather from these verses that, as Newton could not have foreseen all that was contained in the law of gravitation, so the prophets often understood little of what was involved in their own inspiration. We could scarcely have a better example than this prophecy affords of the knowledge of the principles of God's future action combined with ignorance of its circumstances and details. If we may credit the current theory, Cyrus, the servant of Jehovah, the deliverer of Judah, was a

Rev. C. J. Ball, M.A., & W. H. Bennett, M.A.

king of Elam. If Jeremiah had foreseen how his prophecies of the restoration of Elam and of Judah would be fulfilled, we may be sure that this utterance would not have been so brief, its hostile tone would have been mitigated, and the concluding sentence would not have been so cold and conventional.

Footnotes:

242. 1 Peter i. 10, 11.

CHAPTER XXV

BABYLON

l., li.

"*Babylon is taken, Bel is confounded, Merodach is broken in pieces.*"--Jer. l., 2.

These chapters present phenomena analogous to those of Isaiah xl.-lxvi., and have been very commonly ascribed to an author writing at Babylon towards the close of the Exile, or even at some later date. The conclusion has been arrived at in both cases by the application of the same critical principles to similar data. In the present case the argument is complicated by the concluding paragraph of chapter li., which states that "Jeremiah wrote in a book all the evil that should come upon Babylon, even all these words that are written against Babylon," in the fourth year of Zedekiah, and gave the book to Seraiah ben Neriah to take to Babylon and tie a stone to it and throw it into the Euphrates.

Such a statement, however, cuts both ways. On the one hand, we seem to have--what is wanting in the case of Isaiah xl.-lxvi.--a definite and circumstantial testimony as to authorship. But, on the other hand, this very testimony raises new difficulties. If l. and li. had been simply assigned to Jeremiah, without any specification of date, we might possibly have accepted the tradition according to which he spent his last years at Babylon, and have supposed that altered, circumstances and novel experiences account for the differences between these chapters and the rest of the book. But Zedekiah's fourth year is a point in the prophet's ministry at which it is extremely difficult to account for his having composed such a prophecy. If, however, li. 59-64 is mistaken in its exact and circumstantial account of the origin of the preceding section, we must hesitate to recognise its authority as to that section's authorship.

A detailed discussion of the question would be out of place here, [243] but we may notice a few passages which illustrate the arguments for an exilic date. We learn from Jeremiah xxvii.-xxix. that, in the fourth year of Zedekiah, [244] the prophet was denouncing as false teachers those who predicted that the Jewish captives in Babylon would speedily return to their native land. He himself asserted that judgment would not be inflicted upon Babylon for seventy years, and exhorted the exiles to build houses and marry, and plant gardens, and to pray for the peace of Babylon. [245] We can hardly imagine that, in the same breath almost, he called upon these exiles to flee from the city of their captivity, and summoned the neighbouring nations to execute Jehovah's judgment against the oppressors of His people. And yet we read:--

> "*There shall come the Israelites, they and the Jews together:*
> *They shall weep continually, as they go to seek Jehovah their God;*
> *They shall ask their way to Zion, with their faces hitherward*" [246] *(l. 4, 5).*

***

> "*Remove from the midst of Babylon, and be ye as he-goats before the flock*" *(l. 8).*

These verses imply that the Jews were already in Babylon, and throughout the author assumes the circumstances of the Exile. "The vengeance of the Temple," i.e. vengeance for the destruction of the Temple at the final capture of Jerusalem, is twice threatened. [247] The ruin of Babylon is described as imminent:--

> "*Set up a standard on the earth,*
> *Blow the trumpet among the nations,*
> *Prepare the nations against her.*"

If these words were written by Jeremiah in the fourth year of Zedekiah, he certainly was not practising his own precept to pray for the peace of Babylon.

Various theories have been advanced to meet the difficulties which are raised by the ascription of this prophecy to Jeremiah. It may have been expanded from an authentic original. Or again, li. 59-64 may not really refer to l. 1-li. 58; the two sections may once have existed separately, and may owe their connection to an editor, who met with l. 1-li. 58 as an anonymous document, and thought he recognised in it the "book" referred to in li. 59-64. Or again, l. 1-li. 58 may be a hypothetical reconstruction of a lost prophecy of Jeremiah; li. 59-64 mentioned such a prophecy and none was extant, and some student and disciple of Jeremiah's school utilised the material and ideas of extant writings to supply the gap. In any case, it must have been edited more than once, and each time with modifications. Some support might be obtained for any one of these theories from the fact that l. 1-li. 58 is primÃ¢ facie partly a cento of passages from the rest of the book and from the Book of Isaiah. [248]

In view of the great uncertainty as to the origin and history of this prophecy, we do not intend to attempt any detailed exposition. Elsewhere whatever non-Jeremianic matter occurs in the book is mostly by way of expansion and interpretation, and thus lies in the direct line of the prophet's teaching. But the section on Babylon attaches itself to the new departure in religious thought that is more fully expressed in Isaiah xl.-lxvi. Chapters l., li., may possibly be Jeremiah's swan-song, called forth by one of those Pisgah visions of a new dispensation sometimes granted to aged seers; but such visions of a new era and a new order can scarcely be combined with earlier teaching. We will therefore only briefly indicate the character and contents of this section.

It is apparently a mosaic, complied from lost as well as extant sources; and dwells upon a few themes with a persistent iteration of ideas and phrases hardly to be paralleled elsewhere, even in the Book of Jeremiah. It has been reckoned [249] that the imminence of the attack on Babylon is introduced afresh eleven times, and its conquest and destruction nine times. The advent of an enemy from the north is announced four times. [250]

The main theme is naturally that dwelt upon most frequently, the imminent invasion of Chaldea by victorious enemies who shall capture and destroy Babylon. Hereafter the great city and its territory will be a waste, howling wilderness:--

"Your mother shall be sore ashamed,
She that bare you shall be confounded;
Behold, she shall be the hindmost of the nations,
A wilderness, a parched land, and a desert.
Because of the wrath of Jehovah, it shall be uninhabited;
The whole land shall be a desolation.
Every one that goeth by Babylon
Shall hiss with astonishment because of all her plagues." [251]

The gods of Babylon, Bel and Merodach, and all her idols, are involved in her ruin, and reference is made to the vanity and folly of idolatry. [252] But the wrath of Jehovah has been chiefly excited, not by false religion, but by the wrongs inflicted by the Chaldeans on His Chosen People. He is moved to avenge His Temple [253] :--

"I will recompense unto Babylon
And all the inhabitants of Chaldea
All the evil which they wrought in Zion,
And ye shall see it--it is the utterance of Jehovah" (li. 24).

Though He thus avenge Judah, yet its former sins are not yet blotted out of the book of His remembrance:--

"Their adversaries said, We incur no guilt,
Because they have sinned against Jehovah, the Pasture of Justice,
Against the Hope of their fathers, even Jehovah" (l. 7).

Yet now there is forgiveness:--

"The iniquity of Israel shall be sought for, and there shall be none;
And the sins of Judah, and they shall not be found:
For I will pardon the remnant that I preserve" (l. 20).

The Jews are urged to flee from Babylon, lest they should be involved in its punishment, and are encouraged to return to Jerusalem and enter afresh into an everlasting covenant with Jehovah. As in Jeremiah xxxi., Israel is to be restored as well as Judah:--

"I will bring Israel again to his Pasture:
He shall feed on Carmel and Bashan;
His desires shall be satisfied on the hills of Ephraim and in Gilead" (l. 19).

Footnotes:

243. See against the authenticity Driver's Introduction, in loco; and in support of it Speaker's Commentary, Streane (C.B.S.). Cf. also Sayce, Higher Criticism, etc., pp. 484-486.

244. In xxvii. 1 we must read, "In the beginning of the reign of Zedekiah," not Jehoiakim.

245. xxix. 4-14.

246. "Hitherward" seems to indicate that the writers local standpoint is that of Palestine.

247. l. 28, li. 11.

248. Cf. l. 8, li. 6, with Isa. xlviii. 20; l. 13 with xlix. 17; l. 41-43 with vi. 22-24; l. 44-46 with xlix. 19-21; li. 15-19 with x. 12-16.

249. Budde ap. Giesebrecht, in loco.

250. l. 3, 9, li. 41, 48.

251. l. 12, 13: cf. l. 39, 40, li. 26, 29, 37, 41-43.

252. li. 17, 18.

253. l. 28.

Rev. C. J. Ball, M.A., & W. H. Bennett, M.A.

BOOK III

JEREMIAH'S TEACHING CONCERNING ISRAEL AND JUDAH

CHAPTER XXVI

INTRODUCTORY

"I will be the God of all the families of Israel, and they shall be My people."--Jer. xxxi. 1.

In this third book an attempt is made to present a general view of Jeremiah's teaching on the subject with which he was most preoccupied--the political and religious fortunes of Judah. Certain [254] chapters detach themselves from the rest, and stand in no obvious connection with any special incident of the prophet's life. These are the main theme of this book, and have been dealt with in the ordinary method of detailed exposition. They have been treated separately, and not woven into the continuous narrative, partly because we thus obtain a more adequate emphasis upon important aspects of their teaching, but chiefly because their date and occasion cannot be certainly determined. With them other sections have been associated, on account of the connection of subject. Further material for a synopsis of Jeremiah's teaching has been collected from chapters xxi.-xlix. generally, supplemented by brief [255] references to the previous chapters. Inasmuch as the prophecies of our book do not form an ordered treatise on dogmatic theology, but were uttered with regard to individual conduct and critical events, topics are not exclusively dealt with in a single section, but are referred to at intervals throughout. Moreover, as both the individuals and the crises were very much alike, ideas and phrases are constantly reappearing, so that there is an exceptionally large amount of repetition in the Book of Jeremiah. The method we have adopted avoids some of the difficulties which would arise if we attempted to deal with these doctrines in our continuous exposition.

Our general sketch of the prophet's teaching is naturally arranged under categories suggested by the book itself, and not according to the sections of a modern treatise on Systematic Theology. No doubt much may legitimately be extracted or deduced concerning Anthropology, Soteriology, and the like; but true proportion is as important in exposition as accurate interpretation. If we wish to understand Jeremiah, we must be content to dwell longest upon what he emphasised most, and to adopt the standpoint of time and race which was his own. Accordingly in our treatment we have followed the cycle of sin, punishment, and restoration, so familiar to students of Hebrew prophecy.

NOTE: SOME CHARACTERISTIC EXPRESSIONS OF JEREMIAH

This note is added partly for convenience of reference, and partly to illustrate the repetition just mentioned as characteristic of Jeremiah. The instances are chosen from expressions occurring in chapters xxi.-lii. The reader will find fuller lists dealing with the whole book in the Speaker's Commentary and the Cambridge Bible for Schools and Colleges. The Hebrew student is referred to the list in Driver's Introduction, upon which the following is partly based.

1. Rising up early: vii. 13, 25; xi. 7; xxv. 3, 4; xxvi. 5; xxix. 19; xxxii. 33; xxxv. 14, 15; xliv. 4. This phrase, familiar to us in the narratives of Genesis and in the historical books, is used here, as in 2 Chron. xxxvi. 15, of God addressing His people on sending the prophets.

2. Stubbornness of heart (A.V. imagination of heart): iii. 17; vii. 24; ix. 14; xi. 8; xiii. 10; xvi. 12; xviii. 12; xxiii. 17; also found Deut. xxix. 19 and Ps. lxxxi. 15.

3. The evil of your doings: iv. 4; xxi. 12; xxiii. 2, 22; xxv. 5; xxvi. 3; xliv. 22; also Deut. xxviii. 20; 1 Sam. xxv. 3; Isa. i. 16; Hos. ix. 15; Ps. xxviii. 4; and in slightly different form in xi. 18 and Zech. i. 4.

The fruit of your doings: xvii. 10; xxi. 14; xxxii. 19; also found in Micah vii. 13.

Doings, your doings, etc., are also found in Jeremiah and elsewhere.

4. The sword, the pestilence, and the famine, in various orders, and either as a phrase or each word occurring in one of three successive clauses: xiv. 12; xv. 2; xxi. 7, 9; xxiv. 10; xxvii. 8, 13; xxix. 17, 18; xxxii. 24, 36; xxxiv. 17; xxxviii. 2; xlii. 17, 22; xliv. 13.

The sword and the famine, with similar variations: v. 12; xi. 22; xiv. 13, 15, 16, 18; xvi. 4; xviii.

21; xlii. 16; xliv. 12, 18, 27.

Cf. similar lists, etc., "death ... sword ... captivity" in xliii. 11; "war ... evil ... pestilence," xxviii. 8.

5. Kings ... princes ... priests ... prophets, in various orders and combinations: ii. 26; iv. 9; viii. 1; xiii. 13; xxiv. 8; xxxii. 32.

Cf. Prophet ... priest ... people, xxiii. 33, 34. Prophets ... divines ... dreamers ... enchanters ... sorcerers, xxvii. 9.

Footnotes:

254. xxx., xxxi., and, in part, xxxiii.

255. Brief, in order not to trespass more than is absolutely necessary upon the ground covered by the previous Expositor's Bible volume on Jeremiah.

Rev. C. J. Ball, M.A., & W. H. Bennett, M.A.

CHAPTER XXVII

SOCIAL AND RELIGIOUS CORRUPTION

"*Very bad figs, ... too bad to be eaten.*"--Jer. xxiv. 2, 8, xxix. 17.

Prophets and preachers have taken the Israelites for God's helots, as if the Chosen People had been made drunk with the cup of the Lord's indignation, in order that they might be held up as a warning to His more favoured children throughout after ages. They seem depicted as "sinners above all men," that by this supreme warning the heirs of a better covenant may be kept in the path of righteousness. Their sin is no mere inference from the long tragedy of their national history, "because they have suffered such things"; their own prophets and their own Messiah testify continually against them. Religious thought has always singled out Jeremiah as the most conspicuous and uncompromising witness to the sins of his people. One chief feature of his mission was to declare God's condemnation of ancient Judah. Jeremiah watched and shared the prolonged agony and overwhelming catastrophes of the last days of the Jewish monarchy, and ever and anon raised his voice to declare that his fellow-countrymen suffered, not as martyrs, but as criminals. He was like the herald who accompanies a condemned man on the way to execution, and proclaims his crime to the spectators.

What were these crimes? How was Jerusalem a sink of iniquity, an Augean stable, only to be cleansed by turning through it the floods of Divine chastisement? The annalists of Egypt and Chaldea show no interest in the morality of Judah; but there is no reason to believe that they regarded Jerusalem as more depraved than Tyre, or Babylon, or Memphis. If a citizen of one of these capitals of the East visited the city of David he might miss something of accustomed culture, and might have occasion to complain of the inferiority of local police arrangements, but he would be as little conscious of any extraordinary wickedness in the city as a Parisian would in London. Indeed, if an English Christian familiar with the East of the nineteenth century could be transported to Jerusalem under King Zedekiah, in all probability its moral condition would not affect him very differently from that of Cabul or Ispahan.

When we seek to learn from Jeremiah wherein the guilt of Judah lay, his answer is neither clear nor full: he does not gather up her sins into any complete and detailed indictment; we are obliged to avail ourselves of casual references scattered through his prophecies. For the most part Jeremiah speaks in general terms; a precise and exhaustive catalogue of current vices would have seemed too familiar and commonplace for the written record.

The corruption of Judah is summed up by Jeremiah in the phrase "the evil of your doings," [256] and her punishment is described in a corresponding phrase as "the fruit of your doings," or as coming upon her "because of the evil of your doings." The original of "doings" is a peculiar word [257] occurring most frequently in Jeremiah, and the phrases are very common in Jeremiah, and hardly occur at all elsewhere. The constant reiteration of this melancholy refrain is an eloquent symbol of Jehovah's sweeping condemnation. In the total depravity of Judah, no special sin, no one group of sins, stood out from the rest. Their "doings" were evil altogether.

The picture suggested by the scattered hints as to the character of these evil doings is such as might be drawn of almost any Eastern state in its darker days. The arbitrary hand of the government is illustrated by Jeremiah's own experience of the bastinado [258] and the dungeon, [259] and by the execution of Uriah ben Shemaiah. [260] The rights of less important personages were not likely to be more scrupulously respected. The reproach of shedding innocent blood is more than once made against the people and their rulers; [261] and the more general charge of oppression occurs still more frequently. [262]

The motive for both these crimes was naturally covetousness; [263] as usual, they were specially directed against the helpless, "the poor," [264] "the stranger, the fatherless, and the widow"; and the machinery of oppression was ready to hand in venal judges and rulers. Upon occasion, however, recourse was had to open violence--men could "steal and murder," as well as "swear falsely"; [265] they lived in an atmosphere of falsehood, they "walked in a lie." [266] Indeed the word "lie" is one of the keynotes of these prophecies. [267] The last days of the monarchy offered special temptations to such vices. Social wreckers reaped an unhallowed harvest in these stormy times. Revolutions were frequent, and each in its turn meant fresh plunder for unscrupulous partisans. Flattery and treachery could always find a market in the court of the suzerain or the camp of the invader. Naturally, amidst this general demoralisation, the life of the family did not remain untouched: "the land was full of adulterers." [268] Zedekiah and Ahab, the false prophets at Babylon, are accused of having committed adultery with their neighbours' wives. [269] In these passages "adultery" can scarcely be a figure for idolatry; and even if it is, idolatry always involved immoral ritual.

In accordance with the general teaching of the Old Testament, Jeremiah traces the roots of the people's depravity to a certain moral stupidity; they are "a foolish people, without understanding," who, like the idols in Psalm cxv. 5, 6, "have eyes and see not" and "have ears and hear not." [270] In keeping with their stupidity was an unconsciousness of guilt which even rose into proud self-righteousness. They could still come with pious fervour to worship in the temple of Jehovah and to claim the protection of its inviolable sanctity. They could still assail Jeremiah with righteous indignation because he announced the coming destruction of the place where Jehovah had chosen to set His name. [271] They said that they had no sin, and met the prophet's rebukes with protests of conscious innocence: "Wherefore hath Jehovah pronounced all this great evil against us? or what is our iniquity? or what is our sin that we have committed against Jehovah our God?" [272]

When the public conscience condoned alike the abuse of the forms of law and its direct violation, actual legal rights would be strained to the utmost against debtors, hired labourers, and slaves. In their extremity, the princes and people of Judah sought to propitiate the anger of Jehovah by emancipating their Hebrew slaves; when the immediate danger had passed away for a time, they revoked the emancipation. [273] The form of their submission to Jehovah reveals their consciousness that their deepest sin lay in their behaviour to their helpless dependents. This prompt repudiation of a most solemn covenant illustrated afresh their callous indifference to the well-being of their inferiors.

The depravity of Judah was not only total, it was also universal. In the older histories we read how Achan's single act of covetousness involved the whole people in misfortune, and how the treachery of the bloody house of Saul brought three years' famine upon the land; but now the sins of individuals and classes were merged in the general corruption. Jeremiah dwells with characteristic reiteration of idea and phrase upon this melancholy truth. Again and again he enumerates the different classes of the community: "kings, princes, priests, prophets, men of Judah and inhabitants of Jerusalem." They had all done evil and provoked Jehovah to anger; they were all to share the same punishment. [274] They were all arch-rebels, given to slander; nothing but base metal; [275] corrupters, every one of them. [276] The universal extent of total depravity is most forcibly expressed when Zedekiah with his court and people are summarily described as a basket of "very bad figs, too bad to be eaten."

The dark picture of Israel's corruption is not yet complete--Israel's corruption, for now the prophet is no longer exclusively concerned with Judah. The sin of these last days is no new thing; it is as old as the Israelite occupation of Jerusalem. "This city hath been to Me a provocation of My anger and of My fury from the day that they built it even unto this day"; from the earliest days of Israel's national existence, from the time of Moses and the Exodus, the people have been given over to iniquity. "The children of Israel and the children of Judah have done nothing but evil before Me from their youth up."[277] Thus we see at last that Jeremiah's teaching concerning the sin of Judah can be summed up in one brief and comprehensive proposition. Throughout their whole history all classes of the community have been wholly given over to every kind of wickedness.

This gloomy estimate of God's Chosen People is substantially confirmed by the prophets of the later monarchy, from Amos and Hosea onwards. Hosea speaks of Israel in terms as sweeping as those of Jeremiah. "Hear the word of Jehovah, ye children of Israel; for Jehovah hath a controversy with the inhabitants of the land, because there is no truth, nor mercy, nor knowledge of God in the land. Swearing and lying and killing and stealing and committing adultery, they cast off all restraint, and blood toucheth blood." [278] As a prophet of the Northern Kingdom, Hosea is mainly concerned with his own country, but his casual references to Judah include her in the same condemnation. [279] Amos again condemns both Israel and Judah: Judah, "because they have despised the law of Jehovah, and have not kept His commandments, and their lies caused them to err, after the which their fathers walked"; Israel, "because they sold the righteous for silver and the poor for a pair of shoes, and pant after the dust of the earth on the head of the poor and turn aside the way of the meek." [280] The first chapter of Isaiah is in a similar strain: Israel is "a sinful nation, a people laden with iniquity, a seed of evil-doers"; "the whole head is sick, the whole heart faint. From the sole of the foot even unto the head there is no soundness in it, but wounds and bruises and putrefying sores." According to Micah, "Zion is built up with blood and Jerusalem with iniquity. The heads thereof judge for reward, and the priests thereof teach for hire, and the prophets thereof divine for money." [281]

Jeremiah's older and younger contemporaries, Zephaniah and Ezekiel, alike confirm his testimony. In the spirit and even the style afterwards used by Jeremiah, Zephaniah enumerates the sins of the nobles and teachers of Jerusalem. "Her princes within her are roaring lions; her judges are evening wolves.... Her prophets are light and treacherous persons: her priests have polluted the sanctuary, they have done violence to the law." [282] Ezekiel xx. traces the defections of Israel from the sojourn in Egypt to the Captivity. Elsewhere Ezekiel says that "the land is full of bloody crimes, and the city is full of violence"; [283] and in xxii. 23-31 he catalogues the sins of priests, princes, prophets, and people, and proclaims that Jehovah "sought for a man among them that should make up the hedge, and stand in the gap before Me for the land, that I should not destroy it: but I found none."

We have now fairly before us the teaching of Jeremiah and the other prophets as to the condition of Judah: the passages quoted or referred to represent its general tone and attitude; it remains to estimate its significance. We should naturally suppose that such sweeping statements as to the total depravity of the whole people throughout all their history were not intended to be interpreted as exact mathematical formulÃ¦. And the prophets themselves state or imply qualifications. Isaiah insists upon the existence of a righteous remnant. When Jeremiah speaks of Zedekiah and his subjects as a basket of very bad figs, he also speaks of the Jews who had already gone into captivity as a basket of very good figs. The mere fact of going into captivity can hardly have accomplished an immediate and wholesale conversion. The "good figs" among the captives were presumably good before they went into exile. Jeremiah's general statements that "they were all arch-rebels" do not therefore preclude the existence of righteous men in the community. Similarly, when he tells us that the city and people have always been given over to iniquity, Jeremiah is not ignorant of Moses and Joshua, David and Solomon, and the kings "who did right in the eyes of Jehovah"; nor does he intend to contradict the familiar accounts of ancient history. On the other hand, the universality which the prophets ascribe to the corruption of their people is no mere figure of rhetoric, and yet it is by no means incompatible with the view that Jerusalem, in its worst days, was not more conspicuously wicked than Babylon or Tyre; or even, allowing for the altered circumstances of the times, than London or Paris. It would never have occurred to Jeremiah to apply the average morality of Gentile cities as a standard by which to judge Jerusalem; and Christian readers of the Old Testament have caught something of the old prophetic spirit. The very introduction into the present context of any comparison between Jerusalem and Babylon may seem to have a certain flavour of irreverence. We perceive with the prophets that the City of Jehovah and the cities of the Gentiles must be placed in different categories. The popular modern explanation is that heathenism was so utterly abominable that Jerusalem at its worst was still vastly superior to Nineveh or Tyre. However exaggerated such views may be, they still contain an element of truth; but Jeremiah's estimate of the moral condition of Judah was based on entirely different ideas. His standards were not relative but absolute, not practical but ideal. His principles were the very antithesis of the tacit ignoring of difficult and unusual duties, the convenient and somewhat shabby compromise represented by the modern word "respectable." Israel was to be judged by its relation to Jehovah's purpose for His people. Jehovah had called them out of Egypt, and delivered them from a thousand dangers. He had raised up for them judges and kings, Moses, David, and Isaiah. He had spoken to them by Torah and by prophecy. This peculiar munificence of Providence and Revelation was not meant to produce a people only better by some small percentage than their heathen neighbours.

The comparison between Israel and its neighbours would no doubt be much more favourable under David than under Zedekiah, but even then the outcome of Mosaic religion as practically embodied in the national life was utterly unworthy of the Divine ideal; to have described the Israel of David or the Judah of Hezekiah as Jehovah's specially cherished possession, a kingdom of priests and a holy nation, [284] would have seemed a ghastly irony even to the sons of Zeruiah, far more to Nathan, Gad, or Isaiah. Nor had any class, as a class, been wholly true to Jehovah at any period of the history. If for any considerable time the numerous order of professional prophets had had a single eye to the glory of Jehovah, the fortunes of Israel would have been altogether different, and where prophets failed, priests and princes and common people were not likely to succeed.

Hence, judged as citizens of God's Kingdom on earth, the Israelites were corrupt in every faculty of their nature: as masters and servants, as rulers and subjects, as priests, prophets, and worshippers of Jehovah, they succumbed to selfishness and cowardice, and perpetrated the ordinary crimes and vices of ancient Eastern life.

The reader is perhaps tempted to ask: Is this all that is meant by the fierce and impassioned denunciations of Jeremiah? Not quite all. Jeremiah had had the mortification of seeing the great religious revival under Josiah spend itself, apparently in vain, against the ingrained corruption of the people. The reaction, as under Manasseh, had accentuated the worst features of the national life. At the same time the constant distress and dismay caused by disastrous invasions tended to general licence and anarchy. A long period of decadence reached its nadir.

But these are mere matters of degree and detail; the main thing for Jeremiah was not that Judah had become worse, but that it had failed to become better. One great period of Israel's probation was finally closed. The kingdom had served its purpose in the Divine Providence; but it was impossible to hope any longer that the Jewish monarchy was to prove the earthly embodiment of the Kingdom of God. There was no prospect of Judah attaining a social order appreciably better than that of the surrounding nations. Jehovah and His Revelation would be disgraced by any further association with the Jewish state.

Certain schools of socialists bring a similar charge against the modern social order; that it is not a

Kingdom of God upon earth is sufficiently obvious; and they assert that our social system has become stereotyped on lines that exclude and resist progress towards any higher ideal. Now it is certainly true that every great civilisation hitherto has grown old and obsolete; if Christian society is to establish its right to abide permanently, it must show itself something more than an improved edition of the Athens of Pericles or the Empire of the Antonines.

All will agree that Christendom falls sadly short of its ideal, and therefore we may seek to gather instruction from Jeremiah's judgment on the shortcomings of Judah. Jeremiah specially emphasises the universality of corruption in individual character, in all classes of society and throughout the whole duration of history. Similarly we have to recognise that prevalent social and moral evils lower the general tone of individual character. Moral faculties are not set apart in watertight compartments. "Whosoever shall keep the whole law, and yet offend in one point, is guilty of all," is no mere forensic principle. The one offence impairs the earnestness and sincerity with which a man keeps the rest of the law, even though there may be no obvious lapse. There are moral surrenders made to the practical exigencies of commercial, social, political, and ecclesiastical life. Probably we should be startled and dismayed if we understood the consequent sacrifice of individual character.

We might also learn from the prophet that the responsibility for our social evils rests with all classes. Time was when the lower classes were plentifully lectured as the chief authors of public troubles; now it is the turn of the capitalist, the parson, and the landlord. The former policy had no very marked success, possibly the new method may not fare better.

Wealth and influence imply opportunity and responsibility which do not belong to the poor and feeble; but power is by no means confined to the privileged classes; and the energy, ability, and self-denial embodied in the great Trades Unions have sometimes shown themselves as cruel and selfish towards the weak and destitute as any association of capitalists. A necessary preliminary to social amendment is a General Confession by each class of its own sins.

Finally, the Divine Spirit had taught Jeremiah that Israel had always been sadly imperfect. He did not deny Divine Providence and human hope by teaching that the Golden Age lay in the past, that the Kingdom of God had been realised and allowed to perish. He was under no foolish delusion as to "the good old times"; in his most despondent moods he was not given over to wistful reminiscence. His example may help us not to become discouraged through exaggerated ideas about the attainments of past generations.

In considering modern life it may seem that we pass to an altogether different quality of evil to that denounced by Jeremiah, that we have lost sight of anything that could justify his fierce indignation, and thus that we fail in appreciating his character and message. Any such illusion may be corrected by a glance at the statistics of congested town districts, sweated industries, and prostitution. A social reformer, living in contact with these evils, may be apt to think Jeremiah's denunciations specially adapted to the society which tolerates them with almost unruffled complacency.

Footnotes:

256. Characteristic Expressions (1), p. 269.
257. ×   □×¦×□×□.
258. xx. 2, xxxvii. 15.
259. xxxvii., xxxviii.
260. xxvi. 20-24.
261. ii. 34, xix. 4, xxii. 17.
262. v. 25, vi. 6, vii. 5.
263. vi. 13.
264. ii. 34.
265. vii. 5-9.
266. xxiii. 14.
267. Characteristic Expressions (2), p. 269.
268. xxiii. 10, 14.
269. xxix. 23.
270. v. 21, quoted by Ezekiel, xii. 2. The verse is also the foundation of the description of Israel as "the blind people that have eyes, and the deaf that have ears," in Isa. xlii. 18 ff., xliii. 8. Cf. Giesebrecht on Jer. v. 21.
271. vii., xxvi.
272. xvi. 10.
273. xxxiv.
274. xxxii. 26-35: cf. p. 269, Characteristic Expressions (3).
275. Literally "copper and iron."
276. vi. 28.

277. xxxii. 26-35.
278. Hosea iv. 1, 2; also Hosea's general picture of the kingdom of Samaria.
279. The A.V. translation of xi. 12 ("Judah yet ruleth with God, and is faithful with the saints") must be set aside. The sense is obscure and the text doubtful.
280. Amos ii. 4-8.
281. Micah iii. 10, 11.
282. Zeph. iii. 3, 4.
283. Ezek. vii. 23: cf. vii. 9, xxii. 1-12.
284. Exod. xix. 6.

CHAPTER XXVIII

PERSISTENT APOSTASY

"They have forsaken the covenant of Jehovah their God, and worshipped other gods, and served them."--Jer. xxii. 9.

"Every one that walketh in the stubbornness of his heart."--Jer. xxiii. 17.

The previous chapter has been intentionally confined, as far as possible, to Jeremiah's teaching upon the moral condition of Judah. Religion, in the narrower sense, was kept in the background, and mainly referred to as a social and political influence. In the same way the priests and prophets were mentioned chiefly as classes of notables--estates of the realm. This method corresponds with a stage in the process of Revelation; it is that of the older prophets. Hosea, as a native of the Northern Kingdom, may have had a fuller experience and clearer understanding of religious corruption than his contemporaries in Judah. But, in spite of the stress that he lays upon idolatry and the various corruptions of worship, many sections of his book simply deal with social evils. We are not explicitly told why the prophet was "a fool" and "a snare of a fowler," but the immediate context refers to the abominable immorality of Gibeah. [285] The priests are not reproached with incorrect ritual, but with conspiracy to murder. [286] In Amos, the land is not so much punished on account of corrupt worship, as the sanctuaries are destroyed because the people are given over to murder, oppression, and every form of vice. In Isaiah again the main stress is constantly upon international politics and public and private morality. [287] For instance, none of the woes in v. 8-24 are directed against idolatry or corrupt worship, and in xxviii. 7 the charge brought against Ephraim does not refer to ecclesiastical matters; they have erred through strong drink.

In Jeremiah's treatment of the ruin of Judah, he insists, as Hosea had done as regards Israel, on the fatal consequences of apostasy from Jehovah to other gods. This very phrase "other gods" is one of Jeremiah's favourite expressions, and in the writings of the other prophets only occurs in Hosea iii. 1. On the other hand, references to idols are extremely rare in Jeremiah. These facts suggest a special difficulty in discussing the apostasy of Judah. The Jews often combined the worship of other gods with that of Jehovah. According to the analogy of other nations, it was quite possible to worship Baal and Ashtaroth, and the whole heathen Pantheon, without intending to show any special disrespect to the national Deity. Even devout worshippers, who confined their adorations to the one true God, sometimes thought they did honour to Him by introducing into His services the images and all the paraphernalia of the splendid cults of the great heathen empires. It is not always easy to determine whether statements about idolatry imply formal apostasy from Jehovah, or merely a debased worship. When the early Mohammedans spoke with lofty contempt of image-worshippers, they were referring to the Eastern Christians; the iconoclast heretics denounced the idolatry of the Orthodox Church, and the Covenanters used similar terms as to prelacy. Ignorant modern Jews are sometimes taught that Christians worship idols.

Hence when we read of the Jews, "They set their abominations in the house which is called by My name, to defile it," we are not to understand that the Temple was transferred from Jehovah to some other deities, but that the corrupt practices and symbols of heathen worship were combined with the Mosaic ritual. Even the high places of Baal, in the Valley of Ben-Hinnom, where children were passed through the fire unto Moloch, professed to offer an opportunity of supreme devotion to the God of Israel. Baal and Melech, Lord and King, had in ancient times been amongst His titles; and when they became associated with the more heathenish modes of worship, their misguided devotees still claimed that they were doing homage to the national Deity. The inhuman sacrifices to Moloch were offered in obedience to sacred tradition and Divine oracles, which were supposed to emanate from Jehovah. In three different places, Jeremiah explicitly and emphatically denies that Jehovah had required or sanctioned these sacrifices: "I commanded them not, neither came it into My mind, that they should do this abomination, to cause Judah to sin." [288] The Pentateuch preserves an ancient ordinance which the Moloch-worshippers probably interpreted in support of their unholy rites, and Jeremiah's protests are partly directed against the misinterpretation of the command "the first-born of thy sons shalt thou give Me." The immediate context also commanded that the firstlings of sheep and oxen should be given to Jehovah. The beasts were killed; must it not be intended that the children should be killed too? [289] A similar blind literalism has been responsible for many of the follies and crimes perpetrated in the name of Christ. The Church is apt to justify its most flagrant enormities by appealing to a misused and misinterpreted Old Testament. "Thou shalt not suffer a witch to live" and "Cursed be Canaan" have been proof-texts for witch-hunting and negro-slavery; and the book of Joshua has been regarded as a Divine charter, authorising the unrestrained indulgence of the passion for revenge and blood.

When it was thus necessary to put on record reiterated denials that inhuman rites of Baal and Moloch were a divinely sanctioned adoration of Jehovah, we can understand that the Baal-worship constantly referred to by Hosea, Jeremiah, and Zephaniah [290] was not generally understood to be apostasy. The worship of "other gods," "the sun, the moon, and all the host of heaven," [291] and of the "Queen of Heaven," would be more difficult to explain as mere syncretism, but the assimilation of Jewish worship to heathen ritual and the confusion of the Divine Name with the titles of heathen deities masked the transition from the religion of Moses and Isaiah to utter apostasy.

Such assimilation and confusion perplexed and baffled the prophets. [292] Social and moral wrongdoing were easily exposed and denounced; and the evils thus brought to light were obvious symptoms of serious spiritual disease. The Divine Spirit taught the prophets that sin was often most rampant in those who professed the greatest devotion to Jehovah and were most punctual and munificent in the discharge of external religious duties. When the prophecy in Isaiah i. was uttered it almost seemed as if the whole system of Mosaic ritual would have to be sacrificed, in order to preserve the religion of Jehovah. But the further development of the disease suggested a less heroic remedy. The passion for external rites did not confine itself to the traditional forms of ancient Israelite worship. The practices of unspiritual and immoral ritualism were associated specially with the names of Baal and Moloch and with the adoration of the host of heaven; and the departure from the true worship became obvious when the deities of foreign nations were openly worshipped.

Jeremiah clearly and constantly insisted on the distinction between the true and the corrupt worship. The worship paid to Baal and Moloch was altogether unacceptable to Jehovah. These and other objects of adoration were not to be regarded as forms, titles, or manifestations of the one God, but were "other gods," distinct and opposed in nature and attributes; in serving them the Jews were forsaking Him. So far from recognising such rites as homage paid to Jehovah, Jeremiah follows Hosea in calling them "backsliding," [293] a falling away from true loyalty. When they addressed themselves to their idols, even if they consecrated them in the Temple and to the glory of the Most High, they were not really looking to Him in reverent supplication, but with impious profanity were turning their backs upon Him: "They have turned unto Me the back, and not the face." [294] These proceedings were a violation of the covenant between Jehovah and Israel. [295]

The same anxiety to discriminate the true religion from spurious imitations and adulterations underlies the stress which Jeremiah lays upon the Divine Name. His favourite formula, "Jehovah Sabaoth is His name," [296] may be borrowed from Amos, or may be an ancient liturgical sentence; in any case, its use would be a convenient protest against the doctrine that Jehovah could be worshipped under the names of and after the manner of Baal and Moloch. When Jehovah speaks of the people forgetting "My name," He does not mean either that the people would forget all about Him, or would cease to use the name Jehovah; but that they would forget the character and attributes, the purposes and ordinances, which were properly expressed by His Name. The prophets who "prophesy lies in My name" "cause My people to forget My name." [297] Baal and Moloch had sunk into fit titles for a god who could be worshipped with cruel, obscene, and idolatrous rites, but the religion of Revelation had been for ever associated with the one sacred Name, when "Elohim said unto Moses, Thou shalt say unto the Israelites: Jehovah, the God of your fathers, the God of Abraham, the God of Isaac, and the God of Jacob, hath sent me unto you: this is My name for ever, and this is My memorial unto all generations." All religious life and practice inconsistent with this Revelation given through Moses and the prophets—all such worship, even if offered to beings which, as Jehovah, sat in the Temple of Jehovah, professing to be Jehovah—were nevertheless service and obedience paid to other and false gods. Jeremiah's mission was to hammer these truths into dull and unwilling minds.

His work seems to have been successful. Ezekiel, who is in a measure his disciple, [298] drops the phrase "other gods," and mentions "idols" very frequently. [299] Argument and explanation were no longer necessary to show that idolatry was sin against Jehovah; the word "idol" could be freely used and universally understood as indicating what was wholly alien to the religion of Israel. [300] Jeremiah was too anxious to convince the Jews that all syncretism was apostasy to distinguish it carefully from the avowed neglect of Jehovah for other gods. It is not even clear that such neglect existed in his day. In chap. xliv. we have one detailed account of false worship to the Queen of Heaven. It was offered by the Jewish refugees in Egypt; shortly before, these refugees had unanimously entreated Jeremiah to pray for them to Jehovah, and had promised to obey His commands. The punishment of their false worship was that they should no longer be permitted to name the Holy Name. Clearly, therefore, they had supposed that offering incense to the Queen of Heaven was not inconsistent with worshipping Jehovah. We need not dwell on a distinction which is largely ignored by Jeremiah; the apostasy of Judah was real and widespread, it matters little how far the delinquents ventured to throw off the cloak of orthodox profession. [301] The most lapsed masses in a Christian country do not utterly break their connection with the Church; they consider themselves legitimate recipients of its alms, and dimly contemplate as a vague and distant possibility the reformation of their life and character through Christianity. So the blindest worshippers of stocks and stones claimed a vested interest in the national Deity, and in the time of their trouble they turned to Jehovah with the appeal "Arise and save us." [302]

Jeremiah also dwells on the deliberate and persistent character of the apostasy of Judah. Nations have often experienced a sort of satanic revival when the fountains of the nether deep seemed broken up, and flood-tides of evil influence swept all before them. Such, in a measure, was the reaction from the Puritan Commonwealth, when so much of English society lapsed into reckless dissipation. Such too was the carnival of wickedness into which the First French Republic was plunged in the Reign of Terror. But these periods were transient, and the domination of lust and cruelty soon broke down before the reassertion of an outraged national conscience. But we noticed, in the previous chapter, that Israel and Judah alike steadily failed to attain the high social ideal of the Mosaic dispensation. Naturally, this continuous failure is associated with persistent apostasy from true religious teaching of the Mosaic and prophetic Revelation. Exodus, Deuteronomy and the Chronicler agree with Jeremiah that the Israelites were a stiff-necked people; [303] and, in the Chronicler's time at any rate, Israel had played a part in the world long enough for its character to be accurately ascertained; and subsequent history has shown that, for good or for evil, the Jews have never lacked tenacity. Syncretism, the tendency to adulterate true teaching and worship with elements from heathen sources, had been all along a morbid affection of Israelite religion. The Pentateuch and the historical books are full of rebukes of the Israelite passion for idolatry, which must for the most part be understood as introduced into or associated with the worship of Jehovah. Jeremiah constantly refers to "the stubbornness of their evil heart": [304] "they ... have walked after the stubbornness of their own heart and after the Baalim." This stubbornness was shown in their resistance to all the means which Jehovah employed to wean them from their sin. Again and again, in our book, Jehovah speaks of Himself as "rising up early" [305] to speak to the Jews, to teach them, to send prophets to them, to solemnly adjure them to submit themselves to Him; but they would not hearken either to Jehovah or to His prophets, they would not accept His teaching or obey His commands, they made themselves stiff-necked and would not bow to His will. He had subjected them to the discipline of affliction, instruction had become correction; Jehovah had wounded them "with the wound of an enemy, with the chastisement of a cruel one"; but as they had been deaf to exhortation, so they were proof against chastisement--"they refused to receive correction." Only the ruin of the state and the captivity of the people could purge out this evil leaven.

Apostasy from the Mosaic and prophetic religion was naturally accompanied by social corruption. It has recently been maintained that the universal instinct which inclines man to be religious is not necessarily moral, and that it is the distinguishing note of the true faith, or of religion proper, that it enlists this somewhat neutral instinct in the cause of a pure morality. The Phoenician and Syrian cults, with which Israel was most closely in contact, sufficiently illustrated the combination of fanatical religious feeling with gross impurity. On the other hand, the teaching of Revelation to Israel consistently inculcated a high morality and an unselfish benevolence. The prophets vehemently affirmed the worthlessness of religious observances by men who oppressed the poor and helpless. Apostasy from Jehovah to Baal and Moloch involved the same moral lapse as a change from loyal service of Christ to a pietistic antinomianism. Widespread apostasy meant general social corruption. The most insidious form of apostasy was that specially denounced by Jeremiah, in which the authority of Jehovah was more or less explicitly claimed for practices and principles which defied His law. The Reformer loves a clear issue, and it was more difficult to come to close quarters with the enemy when both sides professed to be fighting in the King's name. Moreover the syncretism which still recognised Jehovah was able without any violent revolution to control the established institutions and orders of the state--palace and temple, king and princes, priests and prophets. For a moment the Reformation of Josiah, and the covenant entered into by king and people to observe the law as laid down in the newly discovered Book of Deuteronomy, seemed to have raised Judah from its low estate. But the defeat and death of Josiah and the deposition of Jehoahaz followed to discredit Jeremiah and his friends. In the consequent reaction it seemed as if the religion of Jehovah and the life of His people had become hopelessly corrupt.

We are too much accustomed to think of the idolatry of Israel as something openly and avowedly distinct from and opposed to the worship of Jehovah. Modern Christians often suppose that the true worshipper and the ancient idolater were as contrasted as a pious Englishman and a devotee of one of the hideous images seen on missionary platforms; or, at any rate, that they were as easily distinguishable as a native Indian evangelist from his unconverted fellow-countrymen.

This mistake deprives us of the most instructive lessons to be derived from the record. The sin which Jeremiah denounced is by no means outside Christian experience; it is much nearer to us than conversion to Buddhism--it is possible to the Church in every stage of its history. The missionary finds that the lives of his converts continually threaten to revert to a nominal profession which cloaks the immorality and superstition of their old heathenism. The Church of the Roman Empire gave the sanction of Christ's name and authority to many of the most unchristian features of Judaism and Paganism; once more the rites of strange gods were associated with the worship of Jehovah, and a new Queen of Heaven was honoured with unlimited incense. The Reformed Churches in their turn, after the first "kindness of their youth," the first "love of their espousals," have often fallen into the very abuses against which their great leaders protested; they have given way to the ritualistic spirit, have put the Church in the place of Christ, and have claimed for human formulÃ¦ the authority that can only belong to the inspired Word of God. They have immolated their victims to the Baals and Molochs of creeds and confessions, and thought that they were doing honour to Jehovah thereby.

Moreover we have still to contend like Jeremiah with the continual struggle of corrupt human nature to indulge in the luxury of religious sentiment and emotion without submitting to the moral demands of Christ. The Church suffers far less by losing the allegiance of the lapsed masses than it does by those who associate with the service of Christ those malignant and selfish vices which are often canonised as Respectability and Convention.

Footnotes:

285. Hosea ix. 7-9: cf. Judges xix. 22.
286. Hosea vi. 9.
287. Isaiah xl.-lxvi. is excluded from this statement.
288. xxxii. 34, 35, repeating vii. 30, 31, with slight variations. A similar statement occurs in xix. 4, 5. Cf. 2 Kings xvi. 3, xxi. 6, xxiii. 10; also Giesebrecht and Orelli in loco.
289. Exod. xxii. 29 (JE.). Exod. xxxiv. 20 is probably a later interpretation intended to guard against misunderstandings.
290. Baal is not mentioned in the other prophetical books.
291. vii. 2.
292. Here and elsewhere, "prophet," unless specially qualified by the context, is used of the true prophet, the messenger of Divine Revelation, and does not include the mere professional prophets. Cf. Chap. VIII.
293. ii. 19, etc.
294. xxxii. 33, etc.
295. xxii. 9: cf. xi. 10, xxxi. 32, and Hosea vi. 7, viii. 1.
296. x. 16: cf. Amos iv. 13.
297. xxiii. 25-27: cf. Giesebrecht, in loco.
298. Cheyne, Jeremiah: Life and Times, p. 150.
299. Jeremiah hardly mentions idols.
300. Cf. on this whole subject, Cheyne, Jeremiah: Life and Times, p. 319.
301. The strongest expressions are in chap. ii., for which see previous volume on Jeremiah.
302. ii. 27.
303. xvii. 23: cf. Exod. xxxii. 9, etc. (JE.); Deut. ix. 6; 2 Chron. xxx. 8.
304. Characteristic Expressions, p. 269.
305. Ibid., p. 269.

CHAPTER XXIX

RUIN

xxii. 1-9, xxvi. 14.
"The sword, the pestilence, and the famine."--Jer. xxi. 9 and passim. [306]
"Terror on every side."--Jer. vi. 25, xx. 10, xlvi. 5, xlix. 29; also as proper name, MAGOR-MISSABIB, xx. 3.

We have seen, in the two previous chapters, that the moral and religious state of Judah not only excluded any hope of further progress towards the realisation of the Kingdom of God, but also threatened to involve Revelation itself in the corruption of His people. The Spirit that opened Jeremiah's eyes to the fatal degradation of his country showed him that ruin must follow as its swift result. He was elect from the first to be a herald of doom, to be set "over the nations and over the kingdoms, to pluck up and to break down, and to destroy and to overthrow." [307] In his earliest vision he saw the thrones of the northern conquerors set over against the walls of Jerusalem and the cities of Judah. [308]

But Jeremiah was called in the full vigour of early manhood; [309] he combined with the uncompromising severity of youth its ardent affection and irrepressible hope. The most unqualified threats of Divine wrath always carried the implied condition that repentance might avert the coming judgment; [310] and Jeremiah recurred again and again to the possibility that, even in these last days, amendment might win pardon. Like Moses at Sinai and Samuel at Ebenezer, he poured out his whole soul in intercession for Judah, only to receive the answer, "Though Moses and Samuel stood before Me, yet My mind could not be toward this people: cast them out of My sight and let them go forth." [311] The record of these early hopes and prayers is chiefly found in chapters i.-xx., and is dealt with in the previous volume on Jeremiah. The prophecies in xiv. 1-xvii. 18 seem to recognise the destiny of Judah as finally decided, and to belong to the latter part of the reign of Jehoiakim, [312] and there is little in the later chapters of an earlier date. In xxii. 1-5 the king of Judah is promised that if he and his ministers and officers will refrain from oppression, faithfully administer justice, and protect the helpless, kings of the elect dynasty shall still pass with magnificent retinues in chariots and on horses through the palace gates to sit upon the throne of David. Possibly this section belongs to the earlier part of Jeremiah's career. But there were pauses and recoils in the advancing tide of ruin, alternations of hope and despair; and these varying experiences were reflected in the changing moods of the court, the people, and the prophet himself. We may well believe that Jeremiah hastened to greet any apparent zeal for reformation with a renewed declaration that sincere and radical amendment would be accepted by Jehovah. The proffer of mercy did not avert the ruin of the state, but it compelled the people to recognise that Jehovah was neither harsh nor vindictive. His sentence was only irrevocable because the obduracy of Israel left no other way open for the progress of Revelation, except that which led through fire and blood. The Holy Spirit has taught mankind in many ways that when any government or church, any school of thought or doctrine, ossifies so as to limit the expansion of the soul, that society or system must be shattered by the forces it seeks to restrain. The decadence of Spain and the distractions of France sufficiently illustrate the fruits of persistent refusal to abide in the liberty of the Spirit.

But, until the catastrophe is clearly inevitable, the Christian, both as patriot and as churchman,[313] will be quick to cherish all those symptoms of higher life which indicate that society is still a living organism. He will zealously believe and teach that even a small leaven may leaven the whole mass. He will remember that ten righteous men might have saved Sodom; that, so long as it is possible, God will work by encouraging and rewarding willing obedience rather than by chastising and coercing sin.

Thus Jeremiah, even when he teaches that the day of grace is over, recurs wistfully to the possibilities of salvation once offered to repentance. [314] Was not this the message of all the prophets: "Return ye now every one from his evil way, and from the evil of your doings, and dwell in the land that Jehovah hath given unto your fathers"? [315] Even at the beginning of Jehoiakim's reign Jehovah entrusted Jeremiah with a message of mercy, saying: "It may be they will hearken, and turn every man from his evil way; that I may repent Me of the evil, which I purpose to do unto them because of the evil of their doings." [316] When the prophet multiplied the dark and lurid features of his picture, he was not gloating with morbid enjoyment over the national misery, but rather hoped that the awful vision of judgment might lead them to pause, and reflect and repent. In his age history had not accumulated her now abundant proofs that the guilty conscience is panoplied in triple brass against most visions of judgment. The sequel of Jeremiah's own mission was added evidence for this truth.

Yet it dawned but slowly on the prophet's mind. The covenant of emancipation [317] in the last days of Zedekiah was doubtless proposed by Jeremiah as a possible beginning of better things, an omen of salvation, even at the eleventh hour. To the very last the prophet offered the king his life and promised that Jerusalem should not be burnt, if only he would submit to the Chaldeans, and thus accept the Divine judgment and acknowledge its justice.

Faithful friends have sometimes stood by the drunkard or the gambler, and striven for his deliverance through all the vicissitudes of his downward career; to the very last they have hoped against hope, have welcomed and encouraged every feeble stand against evil habit, every transient flash of high resolve. But, long before the end, they have owned, with sinking heart, that the only way to salvation lay through the ruin of health, fortune, and reputation. So, when the edge of youthful hopefulness had quickly worn itself away, Jeremiah knew in his inmost heart that, in spite of prayers and promises and exhortations, the fate of Judah was sealed. Let us therefore try to reproduce the picture of coming ruin which Jeremiah kept persistently before the eyes of his fellow-countrymen. The pith and power of his prophecies lay in the prospect of their speedy fulfilment. With him, as with Savonarola, a cardinal doctrine was that "before the regeneration must come the scourge," and that "these things will come quickly." Here again, Jeremiah took up the burden of Hosea's utterances. The elder prophet said of Israel, "The days of visitation are come"; [318] and his successor announced to Judah the coming of "the year of visitation." [319] The long-deferred assize was at hand, when the Judge would reckon with Judah for her manifold infidelities, would pronounce sentence and execute judgment.

If the hour of doom had struck, it was not difficult to surmise whence destruction would come or the man who would prove its instrument. The North (named in Hebrew the hidden quarter) was to the Jews the mother of things unforeseen and terrible. Isaiah menaced the Philistines with "a smoke out of the north," [320] i.e. the Assyrians. Jeremiah and Ezekiel both speak very frequently of the destroyers of Judah as coming from the north. Probably the early references in our book to northern enemies denote the Scythians, who invaded Syria towards the beginning of Josiah's reign; but later on the danger from the north is the restored Chaldean Empire, under its king Nebuchadnezzar. "North" is even less accurate geographically for Chaldea than for Assyria. Probably it was accepted in a somewhat symbolic sense for Assyria, and then transferred to Chaldea as her successor in the hegemony of Western Asia.

Nebuchadnezzar is first [321] introduced in the fourth year of Jehoiakim; after the decisive defeat of Pharaoh Necho by Nebuchadnezzar at Carchemish, Jeremiah prophesied the devastation of Judah by the victor; it is also prophesied that he is to carry Jehoiachin away captive, [322] and similar prophecies were repeated during the reign of Zedekiah. [323] Nebuchadnezzar and his Chaldeans very closely resembled the Assyrians, with whose invasions the Jews had long been only too familiar; indeed, as Chaldea had long been tributary to Assyria, it is morally certain that Chaldean princes must have been present with auxiliary forces at more than one of the many Assyrian invasions of Palestine. Under Hezekiah, on the other hand, Judah had been allied with Merodach-baladan of Babylon against his Assyrian suzerain. So that the circumstances of Chaldean invasions and conquests were familiar to the Jews before the forces of the restored empire first attacked them; their imagination could readily picture the horrors of such experiences.

But Jeremiah does not leave them to their unaided imagination, which they might preferably have employed upon more agreeable subjects. He makes them see the future reign of terror, as Jehovah had revealed it to his shuddering and reluctant vision. With his usual frequency of iteration, he keeps the phrase "the sword, the famine, and the pestilence" ringing in their ears. The sword was the symbol of the invading hosts, "the splendid and awful military parade" of the "bitter and hasty nation" that were "dreadful and terrible." [324] "The famine" inevitably followed from the ravages of the invaders, and the impossibility of ploughing, sowing, and reaping. It became most gruesome in the last desperate agonies of besieged garrisons, when, as in Elisha's time and the last siege of Jerusalem, "men ate the flesh of their sons and the flesh of their daughters, and ate every one the flesh of his friend." [325] Among such miseries and horrors, the stench of unburied corpses naturally bred a pestilence, which raged amongst the multitudes of refugees huddled together in Jerusalem and the fortified towns. We are reminded how the great plague of Athens struck down its victims from among the crowds driven within its walls during the long siege of the Peloponnesian war.

An ordinary Englishman can scarcely do justice to such prophecies; his comprehension is limited by a happy inexperience. The constant repetition of general phrases seems meagre and cold, because they carry few associations and awaken no memories. Those who have studied French and Russian realistic art, and have read Erckmann-Chatrain, Zola, and Tolstoï, may be stirred somewhat more by Jeremiah's grim rhetoric. It will not be wanting in suggestiveness to those who have known battles and sieges. For students of missionary literature we may roughly compare the Jews, when exposed to the full fury of a Chaldean attack, to the inhabitants of African villages raided by slave-hunters.

The Jews, therefore, with their extensive, first-hand knowledge of the miseries denounced against them, could not help filling in for themselves the rough outline drawn by Jeremiah. Very probably, too, his speeches were more detailed and realistic than the written reports. As time went on, the inroads of the Chaldeans and their allies provided graphic and ghastly illustrations of the prophecies that Jeremiah still reiterated. In a prophecy, possibly originally referring to the Scythian inroads and afterwards adapted to the Chaldean invasions, Jeremiah speaks of himself: "I am pained at my very heart; my heart is disquieted in me; I cannot hold my peace; for my soul heareth [326] the sound of the trumpet, the alarm of war.... How long shall I see the standard, and hear the sound of the trumpet?" [327] Here, for once, Jeremiah expressed emotions that throbbed in every heart. There was "terror on every hand"; men seemed to be walking "through slippery places in darkness," [328] or to stumble along rough paths in a dreary twilight. Wormwood was their daily food, and their drink maddening draughts of poison. [329]

Jeremiah and his prophecies were no mean part of the terror. To the devotees of Baal and Moloch Jeremiah must have appeared in much the same light as the fanatic whose ravings added to the horrors of the Plague of London, while the very sanity and sobriety of his utterances carried a conviction of their fatal truth.

When the people and their leaders succeeded in collecting any force of soldiers or store of military equipment, and ventured on a sally, Jeremiah was at once at hand to quench any reviving hope of effective resistance. How could soldiers and weapons preserve the city which Jehovah had abandoned to its fate? "Thus saith Jehovah, the God of Israel: Behold, I will turn back the weapons in your hands, with which ye fight without the walls against your besiegers, the king of Babylon and the Chaldeans, and will gather them into the midst of this city. I Myself will fight against you in furious anger and in great wrath, with outstretched hand and strong arm. I will smite the inhabitants of this city, both man and beast: they shall die of a great pestilence." [330]

When Jerusalem was relieved for a time by the advance of an Egyptian army, and the people allowed themselves to dream of another deliverance like that from Sennacherib, the relentless prophet only turned upon them with renewed scorn: "Though ye had smitten the whole hostile army of the Chaldeans, and all that were left of them were desperately wounded, yet should they rise up every man in his tent and burn this city." [331] Not even the most complete victory could avail to save the city.

The final result of invasions and sieges was to be the overthrow of the Jewish state, the capture and destruction of Jerusalem, and the captivity of the people. This unhappy generation were to reap the harvest of centuries of sin and failure. As in the last siege of Jerusalem there came upon the Jews "all the righteous blood shed on the earth, from the blood of righteous Abel unto the blood of Zachariah son of Barachiah," [332] so now Jehovah was about to bring upon His Chosen People all the evil that He had spoken against them [333] --all that had been threatened by Isaiah and his brother-prophets, all the curses written in Deuteronomy. But these threats were to be fully carried out, not because predictions must be fulfilled, nor even merely because Jehovah had spoken and His word must not return to Him void, but because the people had not hearkened and obeyed. His threats were never meant to exclude the penitent from the possibility of pardon.

As Jeremiah had insisted upon the guilt of every class of the community, so he is also careful to enumerate all the classes as about to suffer from the coming judgment: "Zedekiah king of Judah and his princes"; [334] "the people, the prophet, and the priest." [335] This Last Judgment of Judah, as it took the form of the complete overthrow of the State, necessarily included all under its sentence of doom. One of the mysteries of Providence is that those who are most responsible for national sins seem to suffer least by public misfortunes. Ambitious statesmen and bellicose journalists do not generally fall in battle and leave destitute widows and children. When the captains of commerce and manufacture err in their industrial policy, one great result is the pauperism of hundreds of families who had no voice in the matter. A spendthrift landlord may cripple the agriculture of half a county. And yet, when factories are closed and farmers ruined, the manufacturer and the landlord are the last to see want. In former invasions of Judah, the princes and priests had some share of suffering; but wealthy nobles might incur losses and yet weather the storm by which poorer men were overwhelmed. Fines and tribute levied by the invaders would, after the manner of the East, be wrung from the weak and helpless. But now ruin was to fall on all alike. The nobles had been flagrant in sin, they were now to be marked out for most condign punishment--"To whomsoever much is given, of him shall much be required."

Part of the burden of Jeremiah's prophecy, one of the sayings constantly on his lips, was that the city would be taken and destroyed by fire. [336] The Temple would be laid in ruins like the ancient sanctuary of Israel at Shiloh. [337] The palaces [338] of the king and princes would be special marks for the destructive fury of the enemy, and their treasures and all the wealth of the city would be for a spoil; those who survived the sack of the city would be carried captive to Babylon. [339]

In this general ruin the miseries of the people would not end with death. All nations have attached much importance to the burial of the dead and the due performance of funeral rites. In the touching Greek story Antigone sacrificed her life in order to bury the remains of her brother. Later Judaism attached exceptional importance to the burial of the dead, and the Book of Tobit lays great stress on this sacred duty. The angel Raphael declares that one special reason why the Lord had been merciful to

Tobias was that he had buried dead bodies, and had not delayed to rise up and leave his meal to go and bury the corpse of a murdered Jew, at the risk of his own life. [340]

Jeremiah prophesied of the slain in this last overthrow: "They shall not be lamented, neither shall they be buried; they shall be as dung on the face of the ground; ... their carcases shall be meat for the fowls of the heaven, and for the beasts of the earth."

When these last had done their ghastly work, the site of the Temple, the city, the whole land would be left silent and desolate. The stranger, wandering amidst the ruins, would hear no cheerful domestic sounds; when night fell, no light gleaming through chink or lattice would give the sense of human neighbourhood. Jehovah "would take away the sound of the millstones and the light of the candle."[341] The only sign of life amidst the desolate ruins of Jerusalem and the cities of Judah would be the melancholy cry of the jackals round the traveller's tent. [342]

The Hebrew prophets and our Lord Himself often borrowed their symbols from the scenes of common life, as they passed before their eyes. As in the days of Noah, as in the days of Lot, as in the days of the Son of Man, so in the last agony of Judah there was marrying and giving in marriage. Some such festive occasion suggested to Jeremiah one of his favourite formulÃ¦; it occurs four times in the Book of Jeremiah, and was probably uttered much oftener. Again and again it may have happened that, as a marriage procession passed through the streets, the gay company were startled by the grim presence of the prophet, and shrank back in dismay as they found themselves made the text for a stern homily of ruin: "Thus saith Jehovah Sabaoth, I will take away from them the voice of mirth and the voice of gladness, the voice of the bridegroom and the voice of the bride." At any rate, however, and whenever used, the figure could not fail to arrest attention, and to serve as an emphatic declaration that the ordinary social routine would be broken up and lost in the coming calamity.

Henceforth the land would be as some guilty habitation of sinners, devoted to eternal destruction, an astonishment and a hissing and a perpetual desolation. [343] When the heathen sought some curse to express the extreme of malignant hatred, they would use the formula, "God make thee like Jerusalem." [344] Jehovah's Chosen People would become an everlasting reproach, a perpetual shame, which should not be forgotten. [345] The wrath of Jehovah pursued even captives and fugitives. In chapter xxix. Jeremiah predicts the punishment of the Jewish prophets at Babylon. When we last hear of him, in Egypt, he is denouncing ruin against "the remnant of Judah that have set their faces to go into the land of Egypt to sojourn there." He still reiterates the same familiar phrases: "Ye shall die by the sword, by the famine, and by the pestilence"; they shall be "an execration, and an astonishment, and a curse, and a reproach."

We have now traced the details of the prophet's message of doom. Fulfilment followed fast upon the heels of prediction, till Jeremiah rather interpreted than foretold the thick-coming disasters. When his book was compiled, the prophecies were already, as they are now, part of the history of the last days of Judah. The book became the record of this great tragedy, in which these prophecies take the place of the choric odes in a Greek drama.

Footnotes:

306. Characteristic Expressions, p. 269.
307. i. 10.
308. i. 15.
309. i. 7. The word for "child" (na'ar) is an elastic term, equalling "boy" or "young man," with all the range of meaning possible in English to the latter phrase.
310. Cf. the Book of Jonah.
311. xv. 1.
312. Driver, Introduction, p. 242.
313. "Church" is used, in the true Catholic sense, to embrace all Christians.
314. xxvii. 18.
315. xxv. 5, xxxv. 15.
316. xxvi. 3, xxxvi. 2.
317. Chap. XI.
318. Hosea ix. 7.
319. xxiii. 12.
320. Isa. xiv. 31.
321. xxv. 1-14: "first," i.e., in time, not in the order of chapters in our Book of Jeremiah.
322. xxii. 25. Jehoiachin (Kings, Chronicles, and Jer. lii. 31) is also called Coniah (Jer. xxii. 24, 28, xxxvii. 1) and Jeconiah (Chronicles, Esther, Jer. xxiv. 1, xxvii. 20, xxviii. 4, xxix. 2). They are virtually forms of the same name, the "Yah" of the Divine Name being prefixed in the first and affixed in the last two.
323. xxi. 7, xxviii. 14.

324. Habakkuk i. 6, 7.
325. xix. 9.
326. R.V. margin.
327. iv. 21.
328. xxiii. 12.
329. xxiii. 15.
330. xxi. 3-6.
331. xxxvii. 10.
332. Matt. xxiii. 35.
333. xxxv. 17: cf. xix. 15, xxxvi. 31.
334. xxxiv. 21.
335. xxiii. 33, 34.
336. xxxiv. 2, 22, xxxvii. 8.
337. vii. and xxvi.
338. vi. 5.
339. xx. 5.
340. Tobit xii. 13: cf. ii.
341. xxv. 10.
342. ix. 11, x. 22.
343. xxv. 9, 10.
344. xxvi. 6.
345. xxiii. 40.

CHAPTER XXX

RESTORATION--I. THE SYMBOL

xxxii

"And I bought the field of Hanameel."--Jer. xxxii. 9.

When Jeremiah was first called to his prophetic mission, after the charge "to pluck up and to break down, and to destroy and to overthrow," there were added--almost as if they were an afterthought--the words "to build and to plant." [346] Throughout a large part of the book little or nothing is said about building and planting; but, at last, four consecutive chapters, xxx.-xxxiii., are almost entirely devoted to this subject. Jeremiah's characteristic phrases are not all denunciatory; we owe to him the description of Jehovah as "the Hope of Israel." [347] Sin and ruin, guilt and punishment, could not quench the hope that centred in Him. Though the day of Jehovah might be darkness and not light, [348] yet, through the blackness of this day turned into night, the prophets beheld a radiant dawn. When all other building and planting were over for Jeremiah, when it might seem that much that he had planted was being rooted up again in the overthrow of Judah, he was yet permitted to plant shoots in the garden of the Lord, which have since become trees whose leaves are for the healing of the nations.

The symbolic act dealt with in this chapter is a convenient introduction to the prophecies of restoration, especially as chapters xxx., xxxi., have no title and are of uncertain date.

The incident of the purchase of Hanameel's field is referred by the title to the year 587 b.c., when Jeremiah was in prison and the capture of the city was imminent. Verses 2-6 are an introduction by some editor, who was anxious that his readers should fully understand the narrative that follows. They are compiled from the rest of the book, and contain nothing that need detain us.

When Jeremiah was arrested and thrown into prison, he was on his way to Anathoth "to receive his portion there," [349] i.e., as we gather from this chapter, to take possession of an inheritance that devolved upon him. As he was now unable to attend to this business at Anathoth, his cousin Hanameel came to him in the prison, to give him the opportunity of observing the necessary formalities. In his enforced leisure Jeremiah would often recur to the matter on which he had been engaged when he was arrested. An interrupted piece of work is apt to intrude itself upon the mind with tiresome importunity; moreover his dismal surroundings would remind him of his business--it had been the cause of his imprisonment. The bond between an Israelite and the family inheritance was almost as close and sacred as that between Jehovah and the Land of Promise. Naboth had died a martyr to the duty he owed to the land. "Jehovah forbid that I should give thee the inheritance of my fathers," [350] said he to Ahab. And now, in the final crisis of the fortunes of Judah, the prophet whose heart was crushed by the awful task laid upon him had done what he could to secure the rights of his family in the "field" at Anathoth.

Apparently he had failed. The oppression of his spirits would suggest that Jehovah had disapproved and frustrated his purpose. His failure was another sign of the utter ruin of the nation. The solemn grant of the Land of Promise to the Chosen People was finally revoked; and Jehovah no longer sanctioned the ancient ceremonies which bound the households and clans of Israel to the soil of their inheritance.

In some such mood, Jeremiah received the intimation that his cousin Hanameel was on his way to see him about this very business. "The word of Jehovah came unto him: Behold, thine uncle Shallum's son Hanameel is coming to thee, to say unto thee, Buy my field in Anathoth, for it is thy duty to buy it by way of redemption." The prophet was roused to fresh perplexity. The opportunity might be a Divine command to proceed with the redemption. And yet he was a childless man doomed to die in exile. What had he to do with a field at Anathoth in that great and terrible day of the Lord? Death or captivity was staring every one in the face; land was worthless. The transaction would put money into Hanameel's pocket. The eagerness of a Jew to make sure of a good bargain seemed no very safe indication of the will of Jehovah.

In this uncertain frame of mind Hanameel found his cousin, when he came to demand that Jeremiah should buy his field. Perhaps the prisoner found his kinsman's presence a temporary mitigation of his gloomy surroundings, and was inspired with more cheerful and kindly feelings. The solemn and formal appeal to fulfil a kinsman's duty towards the family inheritance came to him as a Divine command: "I knew that this was the word of Jehovah."

The cousins proceeded with their business, which was in no way hindered by the arrangements of the prison. We must be careful to dismiss from our minds all the associations of the routine and discipline of a modern English gaol. The "court of the guard" in which they were was not properly a prison; it was a place of detention, not of punishment. The prisoners may have been fettered, but they were together and could communicate with each other and with their friends. The conditions were not unlike those of a debtors' prison such as the old Marshalsea, as described in Little Dorrit.

Our information as to this right or duty of the next-of-kin to buy or buy back land is of the scantiest. [351] The leading case is that in the Book of Ruth, where, however, the purchase of land is altogether secondary to the levirate marriage. The land custom assumes that an Israelite will only part with his land in case of absolute necessity, and it was evidently supposed that some member of the clan would feel bound to purchase. On the other hand, in Ruth, the next-of-kin is readily allowed to transfer the obligation to Boaz. Why Hanameel sold his field we cannot tell; in these days of constant invasion, most of the small landowners must have been reduced to great distress, and would gladly have found purchasers for their property. The kinsman to whom land was offered would pretty generally refuse to pay anything but a nominal price. Formerly the demand that the next-of-kin should buy an inheritance was seldom made, but the exceptional feature in this case was Jeremiah's willingness to conform to ancient custom.

The price paid for the field was seventeen shekels of silver, but, however precise this information may seem, it really tells us very little. A curious illustration is furnished by modern currency difficulties. The shekel, in the time of the Maccabees, when we are first able to determine its value with some certainty, contained about half an ounce of silver, i.e. about the amount of metal in an English half-crown. The commentaries accordingly continue to reckon the shekel as worth half-a-crown, whereas its value by weight according to the present price of silver would be about fourteenpence. Probably the purchasing power of silver was not more stable in ancient Palestine than it is now. Fifty shekels seemed to David and Araunah a liberal price for a threshing-floor and its oxen, but the Chronicler thought it quite inadequate. [352] We know neither the size of Hanameel's field nor the quality of the land, nor yet the value of the shekels; [353] but the symbolic use made of the incident implies that Jeremiah paid a fair and not a panic price.

The silver was duly weighed in the presence of witnesses and of all the Jews that were in the court of the guard, apparently including the prisoners; their position as respectable members of society was not affected by their imprisonment. A deed or deeds were drawn up, signed by Jeremiah and the witnesses, and publicly delivered to Baruch to be kept safely in an earthen vessel. The legal formalities are described with some detail; possibly they were observed with exceptional punctiliousness; at any rate, great stress is laid upon the exact fulfilment of all that law and custom demanded. Unfortunately, in the course of so many centuries, much of the detail has become unintelligible. For instance, Jeremiah the purchaser signs the record of the purchase, but nothing is said about Hanameel signing. When Abraham bought the field of Machpelah of Ephron the Hittite there was no written deed, the land was simply transferred in public at the gate of the city. [354] Here the written record becomes valid by being publicly delivered to Baruch in the presence of Hanameel and the witnesses. The details with regard to the deeds are very obscure, and the text is doubtful. The Hebrew apparently refers to two deeds, but the Septuagint for the most part to one only. The R.V. of verse 11 runs: "So I took the deed of the purchase, both that which was sealed, according to the law and the custom, and that which was open." The Septuagint omits everything after "that which was sealed"; and, in any case, the words "the law and the custom"--better, as R.V. margin, "containing the terms and the conditions"--are a gloss. In verse 14 the R.V. has: "Take these deeds, this deed of the purchase, both that which is sealed, and this deed which is open, and put them in an earthen vessel." The Septuagint reads: "Take this book of the purchase and this book that has been read, [355] and thou shalt put it in an earthen vessel." [356] It is possible that, as has been suggested, the reference to two deeds has arisen out of a misunderstanding of the description of a single deed. Scribes may have altered or added to the text in order to make it state explicitly what they supposed to be implied. No reason is given for having two deeds. We could have understood the double record if each party had retained one of the documents, or if one had been buried in the earthen vessel and the other kept for reference, but both are put into the earthen vessel. The terms "that which is sealed" and "that which is open" may, however, be explained of either of one or two documents [357] somewhat as follows: the record was written, signed, and witnessed; it was then folded up and sealed; part or the whole of the contents of this sealed-up record was then written again on the outside or on a separate parchment, so that the purport of the deed could easily be ascertained without exposing the original record. The Assyrian and Chaldean contract-tablets were constructed on this principle; the contract was first written on a clay tablet, which was further enclosed in an envelope of clay, and on the outside was engraved an exact copy of the writing within. If the outer writing became indistinct or was tampered with, the envelope could be broken and the exact terms of the contract ascertained from the first tablet. Numerous examples of this method can be seen in the British Museum. The Jews had been vassals of Assyria and Babylon for about a century, and thus must have had ample opportunity to become acquainted with their legal procedure; and, in this instance, Jeremiah and his friends may have imitated the Chaldeans. Such an imitation would be specially significant in what was intended to symbolise the transitoriness of the Chaldean conquest.

The earthen vessel would preserve the record from being spoilt by the damp; similarly bottles are used nowadays to preserve the documents that are built up into the memorial stones of public buildings. In both cases the object is that "they may continue many days."

So far the prophet had proceeded in simple obedience to a Divine command to fulfil an obligation which otherwise might excusably have been neglected. He felt that his action was a parable which suggested that Judah might retain its ancient inheritance, [358] but Jeremiah hesitated to accept an interpretation seemingly at variance with the judgments he had pronounced upon the guilty people. When he had handed over the deed to Baruch, and his mind was no longer occupied with legal minutiæ, he could ponder at leisure on the significance of his purchase. The prophet's meditations naturally shaped themselves into a prayer; he laid his perplexity before Jehovah. [359] Possibly, even from the court of the guard, he could see something of the works of the besiegers; and certainly men would talk constantly of the progress of the siege. Outside the Chaldeans were pushing their mounds and engines nearer and nearer to the walls, within famine and pestilence decimated and enfeebled the defenders; the city was virtually in the enemy's hands. All this was in accordance with the will of Jehovah and the mission entrusted to His prophet. "What thou hast spoken of is come to pass, and, behold, thou seest it." And yet, in spite of all this, "Thou hast said unto me, O Lord Jehovah, Buy the field for money and take witnesses--and the city is in the hands of the Chaldeans!"

Jeremiah had already predicted the ruin of Babylon and the return of the captives at the end of seventy years. [360] It is clear, therefore, that he did not at first understand the sign of the purchase as referring to restoration from the Captivity. His mind, at the moment, was preoccupied with the approaching capture of Jerusalem; apparently his first thought was that his prophecies of doom were to be set aside, and at the last moment some wonderful deliverance might be wrought out for Zion. In the Book of Jonah, Nineveh is spared in spite of the prophet's unconditional and vehement declaration: "Yet forty days and Nineveh shall be overthrown." Was it possible, thought Jeremiah, that after all that had been said and done, buying and selling, building and planting, marrying and giving in marriage, were to go on as if nothing had happened? He was bewildered and confounded by the idea of such a revolution in the Divine purposes.

Jehovah in His answer at once repudiates this idea. He asserts His universal sovereignty and omnipotence; these are to be manifested, first in judgment and then in mercy. He declares afresh that all the judgments predicted by Jeremiah shall speedily come to pass. Then He unfolds His gracious purpose of redemption and deliverance. He will gather the exiles from all lands and bring them back to Judah, and they shall dwell there securely. They shall be His people and He will be their God. Henceforth He will make an everlasting covenant with them, that He will never again abandon them to misery and destruction, but will always do them good. By Divine grace they shall be united in purpose and action to serve Jehovah; He Himself will put His fear in their hearts.

And then returning to the symbol of the purchased field, Jehovah declares that fields shall be bought, with all the legal formalities usual in settled and orderly societies, deeds shall be signed, sealed, and delivered in the presence of witnesses. This restored social order shall extend throughout the territory of the Southern Kingdom, Benjamin, the environs of Jerusalem, the cities of Judah, of the hill country, of the Shephelah and the Negeb. The exhaustive enumeration partakes of the legal character of the purchase of Hanameel's field.

Thus the symbol is expounded: Israel's tenure of the Promised Land will survive the Captivity; the Jews will return to resume their inheritance, and will again deal with the old fields and vineyards and oliveyards, according to the solemn forms of ancient custom.

The familiar classical parallel to this incident is found in Livy, xxvi. 11, where we are told that when Hannibal was encamped three miles from Rome, the ground he occupied was sold in the Forum by public auction, and fetched a good price.

Both at Rome and at Jerusalem the sale of land was a symbol that the control of the land would remain with or return to its original inhabitants. The symbol recognised that access to land is essential to all industry, and that whoever controls this access can determine the conditions of national life. This obvious and often forgotten truth was constantly present to the minds of the inspired writers: to them the Holy Land was almost as sacred as the Chosen People; its right use was a matter of religious obligation, and the prophets and legislators always sought to secure for every Israelite family some rights in their native soil.

The selection of a legal ceremony and the stress laid upon its forms emphasise the truth that social order is the necessary basis of morality and religion. The opportunity to live healthily, honestly, and purely is an antecedent condition of the spiritual life. This opportunity was denied to slaves in the great heathen empires, just as it is denied to the children in our slums. Both here and more fully in the sections we shall deal with in the following chapters, Jeremiah shows that he was chiefly interested in the restoration of the Jews because they could only fulfil the Divine purpose as a separate community in

Judah.

Moreover, to use a modern term, he was no anarchist; spiritual regeneration might come through material ruin, but the prophet did not look for salvation either in anarchy or through anarchy. While any fragment of the State held together, its laws were to be observed; as soon as the exiles were re-established in Judah, they would resume the forms and habits of an organised community. The discipline of society, like that of an army, is most necessary in times of difficulty and danger, and, above all, in the crisis of defeat.

Footnotes:

346. i. 10.
347. xiv. 8, xvii. 13.
348. Amos v. 18, 20.
349. xxxvii. 12 (R.V.).
350. 1 Kings xxi. 3.
351. Lev. xxv. 25, Law of Holiness; Ruth iv.
352. 2 Sam. xxiv. 24: cf. 1 Chron. xxi. 25, where the price is six hundred shekels of gold. It is scarcely necessary to point out that "threshing-floor" (Sam.) and "place of the threshing-floor" (Chron.) are synonymous.
353. By value here is meant purchasing power, to which the weight denoted by the term shekel is now no clue.
354. Gen. xxiii. (P.).
355. á¼   a½Îµ Î³Î½Ï Î Î¼á½³Î½Î¿Î¹ Î½á½¶ probably it
356. The text varies in different MSS. of the LXX.
357. Cf. Cheyne, etc., in loco.
358. Verse 15 anticipates by way of summary verses 42-44, and is apparently ignored in verse 25. It probably represents Jeremiah's interpretation of God's command at the time when he wrote the chapter. In the actual development of the incident, the conviction of the Divine promise of restoration came to him somewhat later.
359. What was said of verse 15 partly applies to verses 17-23 (with the exception of the introductory words: "Ah, Lord Jehovah!"). These verses are not dealt with in the text, because they largely anticipate the ideas and language of the following Divine utterance. Kautzsch and Cornill, following Stade, mark these verses as a later addition; Giesebrecht is doubtful. Cf. v. 20 ff. and xxvii. 5 f.
360. xxv. 12, xxix. 10.

CHAPTER XXXI

RESTORATION--II. THE NEW ISRAEL

xxiii. 3-8, xxiv. 6, 7, xxx., xxxi., xxxiii. [361]

"In those days shall Judah be saved, and Jerusalem shall dwell safely: and this is the name whereby she shall be called."--Jer. xxxiii. 16.

The Divine utterances in chapter xxxiii. were given to Jeremiah when he was shut up in the "court of the guard" during the last days of the siege. It may, however, have been committed to writing at a later date, possibly in connection with chapters xxx. and xxxi., when the destruction of Jerusalem was already past. It is in accordance with all analogy that the final record of a "word of Jehovah" should include any further light which had come to the prophet through his inspired meditations on the original message. Chapters xxx., xxxi., and xxxiii. mostly expound and enforce leading ideas contained in xxxii. 37-44 and in earlier utterances of Jeremiah. They have much in common with II. Isaiah. The ruin of Judah and the captivity of the people were accomplished facts to both writers, and they were both looking forward to the return of the exiles and the restoration of the kingdom of Jehovah. We shall have occasion to notice individual points of resemblance later on.

In xxx. 2 Jeremiah is commanded to write in a book all that Jehovah has spoken to him; and according to the present context the "all," in this case, refers merely to the following four chapters. These prophecies of restoration would be specially precious to the exiles; and now that the Jews were scattered through many distant lands, they could only be transmitted and preserved in writing. After the command "to write in a book" there follows, by way of title, a repetition of the statement that Jehovah would bring back His people to their fatherland. Here, in the very forefront of the Book of Promise, Israel and Judah are named as being recalled together from exile. As we read twice [362] elsewhere in Jeremiah, the promised deliverance from Assyria and Babylon was to surpass all earlier manifestations of the Divine power and mercy. The Exodus would not be named in the same breath with it: "Behold, the days come, saith Jehovah, that it shall no more be said, As Jehovah liveth, that brought up the Israelites out of the land of Egypt; but, As Jehovah liveth, that brought up the Israelites from the land of the north, and from all the countries whither He had driven them." This prediction has waited for fulfilment to our own times: hitherto the Exodus has occupied men's minds much more than the Return; we are now coming to estimate the supreme religious importance of the latter event.

Elsewhere again Jeremiah connects his promise with the clause in his original commission "to build and to plant": [363] "I will set My eyes upon them (the captives) for good, and I will bring them again to this land; and I will build them, and not pull them down; and I will plant them, and not pluck them up." [364] As in xxxii. 28-35, the picture of restoration is rendered more vivid by contrast with Judah's present state of wretchedness; the marvellousness of Jehovah's mercy is made apparent by reminding Israel of the multitude of its iniquities. The agony of Jacob is like that of a woman in travail. But travail shall be followed by deliverance and triumph. In the second Psalm the subject nations took counsel against Jehovah and against His Anointed:--

"Let us break their bands asunder,
And cast away their cords from us";

but now this is the counsel of Jehovah concerning His people and their Babylonian conqueror:--

"I will break his yoke from off thy neck,
And break thy bands asunder." [365]

Judah's lovers, her foreign allies, Assyria, Babylon, Egypt, and all the other states with whom she had intrigued, had betrayed her; they had cruelly chastised her, so that her wounds were grievous and her bruises incurable. She was left without a champion to plead her cause, without a friend to bind up her wounds, without balm to allay the pain of her bruises. "Because thy sins were increased, I have done these things unto thee, saith Jehovah." Jerusalem was an outcast, of whom men said contemptuously: "This is Zion, whom no man seeketh after." [366] But man's extremity was God's opportunity; because Judah was helpless and despised, therefore Jehovah said, "I will restore health unto thee, and I will heal thee of thy wounds." [367]

While Jeremiah was still watching from his prison the progress of the siege, he had seen the houses and palaces beyond the walls destroyed by the Chaldeans to be used for their mounds; and had known that every sally of the besieged was but another opportunity for the enemy to satiate themselves with slaughter, as they executed Jehovah's judgments upon the guilty city. Even at this extremity He announced solemnly and emphatically the restoration and pardon of His people. "Thus saith Jehovah, who established the earth, when He made and fashioned it--Jehovah is His name: Call upon Me, and I will answer thee, and will show thee great mysteries, which thou knowest not." [368]

"I will bring to this city healing and cure, and will cause them to know all the fulness of steadfast peace.... I will cleanse them from all their iniquities, and will pardon all their iniquities, whereby they have sinned and transgressed against Me." [369]

The healing of Zion naturally involved the punishment of her cruel and treacherous lovers. [370] The Return, like other revolutions, was not wrought by rose-water; the yokes were broken and the bands rent asunder by main force. Jehovah would make a full end of all the nations whither He had scattered them. Their devourers should be devoured, all their adversaries should go into captivity, those who had spoiled and preyed upon them should become a spoil and a prey. Jeremiah had been commissioned from the beginning to pull down foreign nations and kingdoms as well as his native Judah. [371] Judah was only one of Israel's evil neighbours who were to be plucked up out of their land. [372] And at the Return, as at the Exodus, the waves at one and the same time opened a path of safety for Israel and overwhelmed her oppressors.

Israel, pardoned and restored, would again be governed by legitimate kings of the House of David. In the dying days of the monarchy Israel and Judah had received their rulers from the hands of foreigners. Menahem and Hoshea bought the confirmation of their usurped authority from Assyria. Jehoiakim was appointed by Pharaoh Necho, and Zedekiah by Nebuchadnezzar. We cannot doubt that the kings of Egypt and Babylon were also careful to surround their nominees with ministers who were devoted to the interests of their suzerains. But now "their nobles were to be of themselves, and their ruler was to proceed out of their midst," [373] i.e. nobles and rulers were to hold their offices according to national custom and tradition.

Jeremiah was fond of speaking of the leaders of Judah as shepherds. We have had occasion already [374] to consider his controversy with the "shepherds" of his own time. In his picture of the New Israel he uses the same figure. In denouncing the evil shepherds, he predicts that, when the remnant of Jehovah's flock is brought again to their folds, He will set up shepherds over them which shall feed them, [375] shepherds according to Jehovah's own heart, who should feed them with knowledge and understanding. [376]

Over them Jehovah would establish as Chief Shepherd a Prince of the House of David. Isaiah had already included in his picture of Messianic times the fertility of Palestine; its vegetation, [377] by the blessing of Jehovah, should be beautiful and glorious: he had also described the Messianic King as a fruitful Branch [378] out of the root of Jesse. Jeremiah takes the idea of the latter passage, but uses the language of the former. For him the King of the New Israel is, as it were, a Growth (Ã§ema?) out of the sacred soil, or perhaps more definitely from the roots of the House of David, that ancient tree whose trunk had been hewn down and burnt. Both the Growth (Ã§ema?) and the Branch (neÃ§er) had the same vital connection with the soil of Palestine and the root of David. Our English versions exercised a wise discretion when they sacrificed literal accuracy and indicated the identity of idea by translating both "Ã§ema?" and "neÃ§er" by "Branch."

"Behold, the days come, saith Jehovah, that I will raise up unto David a righteous Branch; and He shall be a wise and prudent King, and He shall execute justice and maintain the right. In His days Judah shall be saved and Israel shall dwell securely, and His name shall be Jehovah 'Ã idqenu,' our righteousness." [379] Jehovah Ã idqenu might be the personal name of a Jewish king, though the form would be unusual; but what is chiefly intended is that His character shall be such as the "name" describes. The "name" is a brief and pointed censure upon a king whose character was the opposite of that described in these verses, yet who bore a name of almost identical meaning--Zedekiah, Jehovah is my righteousness. The name of the last reigning Prince of the House of David had been a standing condemnation of his unworthy life, but the King of the New Israel, Jehovah's true Messiah, would realise in His administration all that such a name promised. Sovereigns delight to accumulate sonorous epithets in their official designations--Highness, High and Mighty, Majesty, Serene, Gracious. The glaring contrast between character and titles often only serves to advertise the worthlessness of those who are labelled with such epithets: the Majesty of James I., the Graciousness of Richard III. Yet these titles point to a standard of true royalty, whether the sovereign be an individual or a class or the people; they describe that Divine Sovereignty which will be realised in the Kingdom of God. [380]

The material prosperity of the restored community is set forth with wealth of glowing imagery.

Cities and palaces are to be rebuilt on their former sites with more than their ancient splendour. "Out of them shall proceed thanksgiving, and the voice of them that make merry: and I will multiply them, and they shall not be few; I will also glorify them, and they shall not be small. And the children of Jacob shall be as of old, and their assembly shall be established before Me." [381] The figure often used of the utter desolation of the deserted country is now used to illustrate its complete restoration: "Yet again there shall be heard in this place ... the voice of joy and the voice of gladness, the voice of the bridegroom and the voice of the bride." Throughout all the land "which is waste, without man and without beast, and in all the cities thereof," shepherds shall dwell and pasture and fold their flocks; and in the cities of all the districts of the Southern Kingdom (enumerated as exhaustively as in xxxii. 44) shall the flocks again pass under the shepherd's hands to be told. [382]

Jehovah's own peculiar flock, His Chosen People, shall be fruitful and multiply according to the primÃ¦val blessing; under their new shepherds they shall no more fear nor be dismayed, neither shall any be lacking. [383] Jeremiah recurs again and again to the quiet, the restfulness, the freedom from fear and dismay of the restored Israel. In this, as in all else, the New Dispensation was to be an entire contrast to those long weary years of alternate suspense and panic, when men's hearts were shaken by the sound of the trumpet and the alarm of war. [384] Israel is to dwell securely at rest from fear of harm. [385] When Jacob returns, he "shall be quiet and at ease, and none shall make him afraid." [386] Egyptian, Assyrian, and Chaldean shall all cease from troubling; the memory of past misery shall become dim and shadowy.

The finest expansion of this idea is a passage which always fills the soul with a sense of utter rest. "He shall dwell on high: his refuge shall be the inaccessible rocks: his bread shall be given him; his waters shall be sure. Thine eyes shall see the king in his beauty: they shall behold a far-stretching land. Thine heart shall muse on the terror: where is he that counted, where is he that weighed the tribute? where is he that counted the towers? Thou shalt not see the fierce people, a people of a deep speech that thou canst not perceive; of a strange tongue that thou canst not understand. Look upon Zion, the city of our solemnities: thine eyes shall see Jerusalem a quiet habitation, a tent that shall not be removed, the stakes whereof shall never be plucked up, neither shall any of the cords thereof be broken. There Jehovah will be with us in majesty, a place of broad rivers and streams; wherein shall go no galley with oars, neither shall gallant ship pass thereby." [387]

For Jeremiah too the presence of Jehovah in majesty was the only possible guarantee of the peace and prosperity of Israel. The voices of joy and gladness in the New Jerusalem were not only those of bride and bridegroom, but also of those that said, "Give thanks to Jehovah Sabaoth, for Jehovah is good, for His mercy endureth for ever," and of those that "came to offer sacrifices of thanksgiving in the house of Jehovah." [388] This new David, as the Messianic King is called, [389] is to have the priestly right of immediate access to God: "I will cause Him to draw near, and He shall approach unto Me: for else who would risk his life by daring to approach Me?" [390] Israel is liberated from foreign conquerors to serve Jehovah their God and David their King; and the Lord Himself rejoices in His restored and ransomed people.

The city that was once a desolation, an astonishment, a hissing, and a curse among all nations shall now be to Jehovah "a name of joy, a praise and a glory, before all the nations of the earth, which shall hear all the good that I do unto them, and shall tremble with fear for all the good and all the peace that I procure unto it." [391]

Footnotes:

361. Vatke and Stade reject chapters xxx., xxxi., xxxiii., but they are accepted by Driver, Cornill, Kautzsch (for the most part). Giesebrecht assigns them partly to Baruch and partly to a later editor. It is on this account that the full exposition of certain points in xxxii. and elsewhere has been reserved for the present chapter. Moreover, if the cardinal ideas come from Jeremiah, we need not be over-anxious to decide whether the expansion, illustration, and enforcing of them is due to the prophet himself, or to his disciple Baruch, or to some other editor. The question is somewhat parallel to that relating to the discourses of our Lord in the Fourth Gospel.

362. xvi. 14, 15, xxiii. 7, 8.
363. i. 10.
364. xxiv. 6.
365. xxx. 5-8.
366. xxx. 12-17.
367. The two verses xxx. 10, 11, present some difficulty here. According to Kautzsch, and of course Giesebrecht, they are a later addition. The ideas can mostly be paralleled elsewhere in Jeremiah. Verse 11 b, "I will correct thee with judgment, and will in no wise leave thee unpunished," seems inconsistent with the context, which represents the punishment as actually inflicted. Still, the verses might be a genuine fragment misplaced. Driver (Introduction, 246) says: "The title of honour 'My

servant'... appears to have formed the basis upon which II. Isaiah constructs his great conception of Jehovah's ideal servant."

368. xxxiii. 2, 3; "earth" is inserted with the LXX. Many regard these verses as a later addition, based on II. Isaiah: cf. Isa. xlviii. 6. The phrase "Jehovah is His name" and the terms "make" and "fashion" are specially common in II. Isaiah. xxxiii. so largely repeats the ideas of xxx. that it is most convenient to deal with them together.

369. xxxiii. 6-8, slightly paraphrased and condensed.

370. xxx. 8, 11, 16, 20. Cf. also the chapters on the prophecies concerning foreign nations.

371. i. 10.

372. xii. 14. xxx. 23, 24, is apparently a gloss, added as a suitable illustration of this chapter, from xxiii. 19, 20, which are almost identical with these two verses.

373. xxx. 21.

374. Cf. Chap. VIII.

375. xxiii. 3, 4.

376. iii. 15.

377. Isa. iv. 2, Ã§ema?; A.V. and R.V. Branch, R.V. margin Shoot or Bud.

378. Isa. xi. 1.

379. xxv. 5, 6; repeated in xxxiii. 15, 16, with slight variations.

380. In xxxiii. 14-26 the permanence of the Davidic dynasty, the Levitical priests, and the people of Israel is solemnly assured by a Divine promise. These verses are not found in the LXX., and are considered by many to be a later addition; see Kautzsch, Giesebrecht, Cheyne, etc. They are mostly of a secondary character--15, 16, = xxiii. 5, 6; here Jerusalem and not its king is called Jehovah C?idqenu, possibly because the addition was made when there was no visible prospect of the restoration of the Davidic dynasty. Verse 17 is based on the original promise in 2 Sam. vii. 14-16, and is equivalent to Jer. xxii. 4, 30. The form and substance of the Divine promise imitate xxxi. 35-37.

381. xxx. 18-20.

382. xxxiii. 10-13.

383. xxiii. 3, 4.

384. iv. 19.

385. xxiii. 6.

386. xxx. 10.

387. Isa. xxxiii. 16-21: cf. xxxii. 15-18.

388. xxxiii. 11.

389. xxx. 9.

390. xxx. 21, as Kautzsch.

391. xxxiii. 9.

Rev. C. J. Ball, M.A., & W. H. Bennett, M.A.

CHAPTER XXXII

RESTORATION--III. REUNION

xxxi.

"I will sow the house of Israel and the house of Judah with the seed of man, and with the seed of beast."--Jer. xxxi. 27.

In his prophecies of restoration, Jeremiah continually couples together Judah and Israel. [392] Israel, it is true, often stands for the whole elect nation, and is so used by Jeremiah. After the disappearance of the Ten Tribes, the Jewish community is spoken of as Israel. But Israel, in contrast to Judah, will naturally mean the Northern Kingdom or its exiled inhabitants. In this chapter Jeremiah clearly refers to this Israel; he speaks of it under its distinctive title of Ephraim, and promises that vineyards shall again be planted on the mountains of Samaria. Jehovah had declared that He would cast Judah out of His sight, as He had cast out the whole seed of Ephraim. [393] In the days to come Jehovah would make His new covenant with the House of Israel, as well as with the House of Judah. Amos, [394] who was sent to declare the captivity of Israel, also prophesied its return; and similar promises are found in Micah and Isaiah. [395] But, in his attitude towards Ephraim, Jeremiah, as in so much else, is a disciple of Hosea. Both prophets have the same tender, affectionate interest in this wayward child of God. Hosea mourns over Ephraim's sin and punishment: "How shall I give thee up, Ephraim? how shall I deliver thee to thine enemies, O Israel? how shall I make thee as Admah? how shall I set thee as Zeboim?" [396] Jeremiah exults in the glory of Ephraim's restoration. Hosea barely attains to the hope that Israel will return from captivity, or possibly that its doom may yet be averted. "Mine heart is turned within Me, My compassions are kindled together. I will not execute the fierceness of Mine anger, I will not again any more destroy Ephraim: for I am God, and not man; the Holy One of Israel in the midst of thee." [397] But Jehovah rather longs to pardon than finds any sign of the repentance that makes pardon possible; and similarly the promise--"I will be as the dew unto Israel: he shall blossom as the lily, and cast forth his roots as Lebanon. His branches shall spread, and his beauty shall be as the olive tree, and his smell as Lebanon"--is conditioned upon the very doubtful response to the appeal "O Israel, return unto Jehovah thy God." [398] But Jeremiah's confidence in the glorious future of Ephraim is dimmed by no shade of misgiving. "They shall be My people, and I will be their God," is the refrain of Jeremiah's prophecies of restoration; this chapter opens with a special modification of the formula, which emphatically and expressly includes both Ephraim and Judah--"I will be the God of all the clans of Israel, and they shall be My people."

The Assyrian and Chaldean captivities carried men's thoughts back to the bondage in Egypt; and the experiences of the Exodus provided phrases and figures to describe the expected Return. The judges had delivered individual tribes or groups of tribes. Jeroboam II. had been the saviour of Samaria; and the overthrow of Sennacherib had rescued Jerusalem. But the Exodus stood out from all later deliverances as the birth of the whole people. Hence the prophets often speak of the Return as a New Exodus.

This prophecy takes the form of a dialogue between Jehovah and the Virgin of Israel, i.e. the nation personified. Jehovah announces that the Israelite exiles, the remnant left by the sword of Shalmaneser and Sargon, were to be more highly favoured than the fugitives from the sword of Pharaoh, of whom Jehovah sware in His wrath "that they should not enter into My rest; whose carcases fell in the wilderness." "A people that hath survived the sword hath found favour in the wilderness; Israel hath entered into his rest," [399] --hath found favour--hath entered--because Jehovah regards His purpose as already accomplished.

Jehovah speaks from his ancient dwelling-place in Jerusalem, and, when the Virgin of Israel hears Him in her distant exile, she answers:--

"From afar hath Jehovah appeared unto me (saying),
With My ancient love do I love thee;
Therefore My lovingkindness is enduring toward thee." [400]

His love is as old as the Exodus, His mercy has endured all through the long, weary ages of Israel's sin and suffering.

Then Jehovah replies:--

"Again will I build thee, and thou shalt be built, O Virgin of Israel;
Again shalt thou take thy tabrets, and go forth in the dances of them that make merry;
Again shalt thou plant vineyards on the mountains of Samaria, while they that plant shall enjoy the fruit."

This contrasts with the times of invasion when the vintage was destroyed or carried off by the enemy. Then follows the Divine purpose, the crowning mercy of Israel's renewed prosperity:--

"For the day cometh when the vintagers [401] shall cry in the hill-country of Ephraim,
Arise, let us go up to Zion, to Jehovah our God."

Israel will no longer keep her vintage feasts in schism at Samaria and Bethel and her countless high places, but will join with Judah in the worship of the Temple, which Josiah's covenant had accepted as the one sanctuary of Jehovah.

The exultant strain continues stanza after stanza:--

"Thus saith Jehovah:
Exult joyously for Jacob, and shout for the chief of the nations;
Make your praises heard, and say, Jehovah hath saved His people, [402] even the remnant of Israel.
Behold, I bring them from the land of the north, and gather them from the uttermost ends of the earth;
Among them blind and lame, pregnant women and women in travail together."

None are left behind, not even those least fit for the journey.

"A great company shall return hither.
They shall come with weeping, and with supplications will I lead them."

Of old, weeping and supplication had been heard upon the heights of Israel because of her waywardness and apostasy; [403] but now the returning exiles offer prayers and thanksgiving mingled with tears, weeping partly for joy, partly for pathetic memories.

"I will bring them to streams of water, by a plain path, wherein they cannot stumble:
For I am become once more a father to Israel, and Ephraim is My first-born son."

Of the two Israelite states, Ephraim, the Northern Kingdom, had long been superior in power, wealth, and religion. Judah was often little more than a vassal of Samaria, and owed her prosperity and even her existence to the barrier which Samaria interposed between Jerusalem and invaders from Assyria or Damascus. Until the latter days of Samaria, Judah had no prophets that could compare with Elijah and Elisha. The Jewish prophet is tenacious of the rights of Zion, but he does not base any claim for the ascendency of Judah on the geographical position of the Temple; he does not even mention the sacerdotal tribe of Levi. Jew and priest as he was, he acknowledges the political and religious hegemony of Ephraim. The fact is a striking illustration of the stress laid by the prophets on the unity of Israel, to which all sectional interests were to be sacrificed. If Ephraim was required to forsake his ancient shrines, Jeremiah was equally ready to forego any pride of tribe or caste. Did we, in all our different Churches, possess the same generous spirit, Christian reunion would no longer be a vain and distant dream. But, passing on to the next stanza,--

"Hear the word of Jehovah, O ye nations, and make it known in the distant islands.
Say, He that scattered Israel doth gather him, and watcheth over him as a shepherd over his flock.
For Jehovah hath ransomed Jacob and redeemed him from the hand of him that was too strong for him.
They shall come and sing for joy in the height of Zion;
They shall come in streams to the bounty of Jehovah, for corn and new wine and oil and lambs and calves."

Jeremiah does not dwell, in any grasping sacerdotal spirit, on the contributions which these reconciled schismatics would pay to the Temple revenues, but rather delights to make mention of their share in the common blessings of God's obedient children.

"They shall be like a well-watered garden; they shall no more be faint and weary:
Then shall they rejoice--the damsels in the dance--the young men and the old together.
I will turn their mourning into gladness, and will comfort them, and will bring joy out of their wretchedness.
I will fill the priests with plenty, and My people shall be satisfied with My bounty--
It is the utterance of Jehovah."

It is not quite clear how far, in this chapter, Israel is to be understood exclusively of Ephraim. If the foregoing stanza is, as it seems, perfectly general, the priests are simply those of the restored community, ministering at the Temple; but if the reference is specially to Ephraim, the priests belong to families involved in the captivity of the ten tribes, and we have further evidence of the catholic spirit of the Jewish prophet.

Another stanza:--

"Thus saith Jehovah:
A voice is heard in Ramah, lamentation and bitter weeping, Rachel weeping for her children.
She refuseth to be comforted for her children, for they are not."

Rachel, as the mother of Benjamin and Joseph, claimed an interest in both the Israelite kingdoms. Jeremiah shows special concern for Benjamin, in whose territory his native Anathoth was situated.[404]

"Her children" would be chiefly the Ephraimites and Manassites, who formed the bulk of the Northern Kingdom; but the phrase was doubtless intended to include other Jews, that Rachel might be a symbol of national unity.

The connection of Rachel with Ramah is not obvious; there is no precedent for it. Possibly Ramah is not intended for a proper name, and we might translate "A voice is heard upon the heights." In Gen. xxxv. 19, Rachel's grave is placed between Bethel and Ephrath, [405] and in 1 Sam. x. 2, in the border of Benjamin at Zelzah; only here has Rachel anything to do with Ramah. The name, however, in its various forms, was not uncommon. Ramah, to the north of Jerusalem, seems to have been a frontier town, and debatable territory [406] between the two kingdoms; and Rachel's appearance there might symbolise her relation to both. This Ramah was also a slave depot for the Chaldeans [407] after the fall of Jerusalem, and Rachel might well revisit the glimpses of the moon at a spot where her descendants had drunk the first bitter draught of the cup of exile. In any case, the lines are a fresh appeal to the spirit of national unity. The prophet seems to say: "Children of the same mother, sharers in the same fate, whether of ruin or restoration, remember the ties that bind you and forget your ancient feuds." Rachel, wailing in ghostly fashion, was yet a name to conjure with, and the prophet hoped that her symbolic tears could water the renewed growth of Israel's national life. Christ, present in His living Spirit, lacerated at heart by the bitter feuds of those who call Him Lord, should temper the harsh judgments that Christians pass on servants of their One Master. The Jewish prophet lamenting the miseries of schismatic Israel contrasts with the Pope singing Te Deums over the massacre of St. Bartholomew.

Then comes the answer:--

"Thus saith Jehovah:
Refrain thy voice from weeping, and thine eyes from tears.
Thou shalt have wages for thy labour--it is the utterance of Jehovah--they shall return from the enemy's land.
There is hope for thee in the days to come--it is the utterance of Jehovah--thy children shall return to their own border." [408]

The Niobe of the nation is comforted, but now is heard another voice:--

"Surely I hear Ephraim bemoaning himself: Thou hast chastised me; I am chastised like a calf not yet broken to the yoke.
Restore me to Thy favour, that I may return unto Thee, for Thou art Jehovah my God.
In returning unto Thee, I repent; when I come to myself, I smite upon my thigh in penitence."[409]

The image of the calf is another reminiscence of Hosea, with whom Israel figures as a "backsliding heifer" and Ephraim as a "heifer that has been broken in and loveth to tread out the corn"; though apparently in Hosea Ephraim is broken in to wickedness. Possibly this figure was suggested by the calves at Bethel and Dan.

The moaning of Ephraim, like the wailing of Rachel, is met and answered by the Divine compassion. By a bold and touching figure, Jehovah is represented as surprised at the depth of His passionate affection for His prodigal son:--

> "Can it be that Ephraim is indeed a son that is precious to Me? is he indeed a darling child?
> As often as I speak against him, I cannot cease to remember him, [410]
> Wherefore My tender compassion is moved towards him: verily I will have mercy on him--
> It is the utterance of Jehovah."

As with Hosea, Israel is still the child whom Jehovah loved, the son whom He called out of Egypt. But now Israel is called with a more effectual calling:--

> "Set thee up pillars of stone, [411] to mark the way; make thee guide-posts: set thy heart toward the highway whereby thou wentest.
> Return, O Virgin of Israel, return unto these thy cities."

The following verse strikes a note of discord, that suggests the revulsion of feeling, the sudden access of doubt, that sometimes follows the most ecstatic moods:--

> "How long wilt thou wander to and fro, O backsliding daughter?
> Jehovah hath created a new thing in the earth--a woman shall compass a man."

It is just possible that this verse is not intended to express doubt of Israel's cordial response, but is merely an affectionate urgency that presses the immediate appropriation of the promised blessings. But such an exegesis seems forced, and the verse is a strange termination to the glowing stanzas that precede. It may have been added when all hope of the return of the ten tribes was over. [412]

The meaning of the concluding enigma is as profound a mystery as the fate of the lost tribes, and the solutions rather more unsatisfactory. The words apparently denote that the male and the female shall interchange functions, and an explanation often given is that, in the profound peace of the New Dispensation, the women will protect the men. This portent seems to be the sign which is to win the Virgin of Israel from her vacillation and induce her to return at once to Palestine.

In Isaiah xliii. 19 the "new thing" which Jehovah does is to make a way in the untrodden desert and rivers in the parched wilderness. A parallel interpretation, suggested for our passage, is that women should develop manly strength and courage, as abnormal to them as roads and rivers to a wilderness. When women were thus endowed, men could not for shame shrink from the perils of the Return.

In Isaiah iv. 1 seven women court one man, and it has been suggested [413] that the sense here is "women shall court men," but it is difficult to see how this would be relevant. Another parallel has been sought for in the Immanuel and other prophecies of Isaiah, in which the birth of a child is set forth as a sign. Our passage would then assume a Messianic character; the return of the Virgin of Israel would be postponed till her doubts and difficulties should be solved by the appearance of a new Moses. [414] This view has much to commend it, but does not very readily follow from the usage of the word translated "compass." Still less can we regard these words as a prediction of the miraculous conception of our Lord.

The next stanza connects the restoration of Judah with that of Ephraim, and, for the most part, goes over ground already traversed in our previous chapters; one or two points only need be noticed here. It is in accordance with the catholic and gracious spirit which characterises this chapter that the restoration of Judah is expressly connected with that of Ephraim. The combination of the future fortunes of both in a single prophecy emphasises their reunion. The heading of this stanza, "Thus saith Jehovah Sabaoth, the God of Israel," is different from that hitherto used, and has a special significance in its present context. It is "the God of Israel" to whom Ephraim is a darling child and a first-born son, the God of that Israel which for centuries stood before the world as Ephraim; it is this God who blesses and redeems Judah. Her faint and weary soul is also to be satisfied with His plenty; Zion is to be honoured as the habitation of justice and the mountain of holiness.

"Hereupon," saith the prophet, "I awaked and looked about me, and felt that my sleep had been pleasant to me." The vision had come to him, in some sense, as a dream. Zechariah [415] had to be aroused, like a man wakened out of his sleep, in order to receive the Divine message; and possibly Zechariah's sleep was the ecstatic trance in which he had beheld previous visions. Jeremiah, however, shows scant confidence [416] in the inspiration of those who dream dreams, and it does not seem likely that this is a unique exception to his ordinary experience. Perhaps we may say with Orelli that the prophet had become lost in the vision of future blessedness as in some sweet dream.

In the following stanza Jehovah promises to recruit the dwindled numbers of Israel and Judah;

with a sowing more gracious and fortunate than that of Cadmus, He will scatter [417] over the land, not dragons' teeth, but the seed of man and beast. Recurring [418] to Jeremiah's original commission, He promises that as He watched over Judah to pluck up and to break down, to overthrow and to destroy and to afflict, so now He will watch over them to build and to plant.

The next verse is directed against a lingering dread, by which men's minds were still possessed. More than half a century elapsed between the death of Manasseh and the fall of Jerusalem. He was succeeded by Josiah, who "turned to Jehovah with all his heart, and with all his soul, and with all his might." [419] Yet Jehovah declared to Jeremiah that Manasseh's sins had irrevocably fixed the doom of Judah, so that not even the intercession of Moses and Samuel could procure her pardon. [420] Men might well doubt whether the guilt of that wicked reign was even yet fully expiated, whether their teeth might not still be set on edge because of the sour grapes which Manasseh had eaten. Therefore the prophet continues: "In those days men shall no longer say, The fathers have eaten sour grapes, and the children's teeth are set on edge; but every man shall die for his own transgression, all who eat sour grapes shall have their own teeth set on edge." Or to use the explicit words of Ezekiel, in the great chapter in which he discusses this permanent theological difficulty: "The soul that sinneth, it shall die. The son shall not bear the iniquity of the father, neither shall the father bear the iniquity of the son; the righteousness of the righteous shall be upon him, and the wickedness of the wicked shall be upon him." [421] With the fall of Jerusalem, a chapter in the history of Israel was concluded for ever; Jehovah blotted out the damning record of the past, and turned over a new leaf in the annals of His people. The account between Jehovah and the Israel of the monarchy was finally closed, and no penal balance was carried over to stand against the restored community.

The last portion of this chapter is so important that we must reserve it for separate treatment, but we may pause for a moment to consider the prophecy of the restoration of Ephraim from two points of view--the unity of Israel and the return of the ten tribes.

In the first place, this chapter is an eirenicon, intended to consign to oblivion the divisions and feuds of the Chosen People. After the fall of Samaria, the remnant of Israel had naturally looked to Judah for support and protection, and the growing weakness of Assyria had allowed the Jewish kings to exercise a certain authority over the territory of northern tribes. The same fate--the sack of the capital and the deportation of most of the inhabitants--had successively befallen Ephraim and Judah. His sense of the unity of the race was too strong to allow the prophet to be satisfied with the return of Judah and Benjamin, apart from the other tribes. Yet it would have been monstrous to suppose that Jehovah would bring back Ephraim from Assyria, and Judah from Babylon, only that they might resume their mutual hatred and suspicion. Even wild beasts are said not to rend one another when they are driven by floods to the same hill-top.

Thus various causes contributed to produce a kindlier feeling between the survivors of the catastrophes of Samaria and Jerusalem; and from henceforth those of the ten tribes who found their way back to Palestine lived in brotherly union with the other Jews. And, on the whole, the Jews have since remained united both as a race and a religious community. It is true that the relations of the later Jews to Samaria were somewhat at variance both with the letter and spirit of this prophecy, but that Samaria had only the slightest claim to be included in Israel. Otherwise the divisions between Hillel and Shammai, Sadducees and Pharisees, Karaites, Sephardim and Ashkenazim, Reformed and Unreformed Jews, have rather been legitimate varieties of opinion and practice within Judaism than a rending asunder of the Israel of God.

Matters stand very differently with regard to the restoration of Ephraim. We know that individual members and families of the ten tribes were included in the new Jewish community, and that the Jews reoccupied Galilee and portions of Eastern Palestine. But the husbandmen who had planted vineyards on the hills of Samaria were violently repulsed by Ezra and Nehemiah, and were denied any part or lot in the restored Israel. The tribal inheritance of Ephraim and Manasseh was never reoccupied by Ephraimites and Manassites who came to worship Jehovah in His Temple at Jerusalem. There was no return of the ten tribes that in any way corresponded to the terms of this prophecy or that could rank with the return of their brethren. Our growing acquaintance with the races of the world seems likely to exclude even the possibility of any such restoration of Ephraim. Of the two divisions of Israel, so long united in common experiences of grace and chastisement, the one has been taken and the other left.

Christendom is the true heir of the ideals of Israel, but she is mostly content to inherit them as counsels of perfection. Isaiah [422] struck the keynote of this chapter when he prophesied that Ephraim should not envy Judah, nor Judah vex Ephraim. Our prophet, in the same generous spirit, propounds a programme of reconciliation. It might serve for a model to those who construct schemes for Christian Reunion. When two denominations are able to unite on such terms that the one admits the other to be the first-born of God, His darling child and precious in His sight, and the latter is willing to accept the former's central sanctuary as the headquarters of the united body, we shall have come some way towards realising this ancient Jewish ideal. Meanwhile Ephraim remains consumed with envy of Judah; and Judah apparently considers it her most sacred duty to vex Ephraim.

Moreover the disappearance of what was at one time the most flourishing branch of the Hebrew Church has many parallels in Church History. Again and again religious dissension has been one of the causes of political ruin, and the overthrow of a Christian state has sometimes involved the extinction of its religion. Christian thought and doctrine owe an immense debt to the great Churches of Northern Africa and Egypt. But these provinces were torn by the dissensions of ecclesiastical parties; and the quarrels of Donatists, Arians, and Catholics in North Africa, the endless controversies over the Person of Christ in Egypt, left them helpless before the Saracen invader. To-day the Church of Tertullian and Augustine is blotted out, and the Church of Origen and Clement is a miserable remnant. Similarly the ecclesiastical strife between Rome and Constantinople lost to Christendom some of the fairest provinces of Europe and Asia, and placed Christian races under the rule of the Turk.

Even now the cause of Christians in heathen and Mohammedan countries suffers from the jealousy of Christian states, and modern Churches sometimes avail themselves of this jealousy to try and oust their rivals from promising fields for mission work.

It is a melancholy reflection that Jeremiah's effort at reconciliation came too late, when the tribes whom it sought to reunite were hopelessly set asunder. Reconciliation, which involves a kind of mutual repentance, can ill afford to be deferred to the eleventh hour. In the last agonies of the Greek Empire, there was more than one formal reconciliation between the Eastern and Western Churches; but they also came too late, and could not survive the Empire which they failed to preserve.

Footnotes:

392. xxxiii., 7, etc.
393. vii. 15.
394. Amos ix. 14.
395. Micah ii. 12; Isa. xi. 10-16.
396. Hosea xi. 8.
397. Hosea xi. 9.
398. Hosea xiv.
399. So Giesebrecht, reading with Jerome and Targum l'margÃ'Ã´ for the obscure and obviously corrupt l'hargÃ®'Ã´. The other versions vary widely in their readings.
400. R.V. "with lovingkindness have I drawn thee," R.V. margin "have I continued lovingkindness unto thee"; the word for "drawn" occurs also in Hosea xi. 4, "I drew them ... with bands of love."
401. So Giesebrecht's conjecture of bocerim (vintages), for the nocerim (watchmen, R.V.). The latter is usually explained of the watcher who looked for the appearance of the new moon, in order to determine the time of the feasts. The practice is stated on negative grounds to be post-exilic, but seems likely to be ancient. On the other hand "vintagers" seems a natural sequel to the preceding clauses.
402. According to the reading of the LXX. and the Targum, the Hebrew Text has (as R.V.) "O Jehovah, save Thy people."
403. iii. 21.
404. Isaiah does not mention Benjamin.
405. "Which is Bethlehem," in Genesis, is probably a later explanatory addition; and the explanation is not necessarily a mistake. Cf. Matt. ii. 18.
406. 1 Kings xv. 17.
407. xl. 1.
408. LXX. omits verse 17 b, i.e. from "Jehovah" to "border."
409. Slightly paraphrased.
410. More literally as R.V., "I do earnestly remember him still."
411. The Hebrew Text has the same word, "tamrurim," here that is used in verse 15 in the phrase "bekhi tamrurim," "weeping of bitternesses" or "bitter weeping." It is difficult to believe that the coincidence is accidental, and Hebrew literature is given to paronomasia; at the same time the distance of the words and the complete absence of point in this particular instance are remarkable. The LXX., not understanding the word, represented it more suo by the similar Greek word Ĭ may indicate that the original reading was "timorim," and the assimilation to "tamrurim" may be a scribe's caprice. In any case, the word here connects with "tamar," a palm, the post being made of or like a palm tree. Cf. Giesebrecht, Orelli, Cheyne, etc.
412. Giesebrecht treats verses 21-26 as a later addition, but this seems unnecessary.
413. So Kautzsch.
414. Cf. Streane, Cambridge Bible.
415. Zech. iv. 1.
416. xxiii, 25-32, xxvii. 9, xxix. 8: cf. Deut. xiii. 1-5.
417. Cf. Hosea ii. 23, "I will sow her unto Me in the earth" (or land), in reference to Jezreel, understood as "Whom God soweth" (R.V. margin).

418. i. 10-12.
419. 2 Kings xxiii. 25.
420. xv. 1-4.
421. Ezek. xviii. 20: cf. Cheyne, Jeremiah (Men of the Bible), p. 150.
422. Isa. xi. 13.

CHAPTER XXXIII

RESTORATION--IV. THE NEW COVENANT

xxxi. 31-38: cf. Hebrews viii.
"I will make a new covenant with the house of Israel and the house of Judah."--Jer. xxxi. 31.

The religious history of Israel in the Old Testament has for its epochs a series of covenants: Jehovah declared His gracious purposes towards His people, and made known the conditions upon which they were to enjoy His promised blessings; they, on their part, undertook to observe faithfully all that Jehovah commanded. We are told that covenants were made with Noah, after the Flood; with Abraham, when he was assured that his descendants should inherit the land of Canaan; at Sinai, when Israel first became a nation; with Joshua, after the Promised Land was conquered; and, at the close of Old Testament history, when Ezra and Nehemiah established the Pentateuch as the Code and Canon of Judaism.

One of the oldest sections of the Pentateuch, Exodus xx. 20-xxiii. 33, is called the "Book of the Covenant," [423] and Ewald named the Priestly Code the "Book of the Four Covenants." Judges and Samuel record no covenants between Jehovah and Israel; but the promise of permanence to the Davidic dynasty is spoken of as an everlasting covenant. Isaiah, [424] Amos, and Micah make no mention of the Divine covenants. Jeremiah, however, imitates Hosea [425] in emphasising this aspect of Jehovah's relation to Israel, and is followed in his turn by Ezekiel and II. Isaiah.

Jeremiah had played his part in establishing covenants between Israel and its God. He is not, indeed, even so much as mentioned in the account of Josiah's reformation; and it is not clear that he himself makes any express reference to it; so that some doubt must still be felt as to his share in that great movement. At the same time indirect evidence seems to afford proof of the common opinion that Jeremiah was active in the proceedings which resulted in the solemn engagement to observe the code of Deuteronomy. But yet another covenant occupies a chapter [426] in the Book of Jeremiah, and in this case there is no doubt that the prophet was the prime mover in inducing the Jews to release their Hebrew slaves. This act of emancipation was adopted in obedience to an ordinance of Deuteronomy, [427] so that Jeremiah's experience of former covenants was chiefly connected with the code of Deuteronomy and the older Book of the Covenant upon which it was based.

The Restoration to which Jeremiah looked forward was to throw the Exodus into the shade, and to constitute a new epoch in the history of Israel more remarkable than the first settlement in Canaan. The nation was to be founded anew, and its regeneration would necessarily rest upon a New Covenant, which would supersede the Covenant of Sinai.

"Behold, the days come--it is the utterance of Jehovah--when I will enter into a new covenant with the House of Israel and the House of Judah: not according to the covenant into which I entered with your fathers, when I took them by the hand to bring them out of the land of Egypt."

The Book of the Covenant and Deuteronomy had both been editions of the Mosaic Covenant, and had neither been intended nor regarded as anything new. Whatever was fresh in them, either in form or substance, was merely the adaptation of existing ordinances to altered circumstances. But now the Mosaic Covenant was declared obsolete, the New Covenant was not to be, like Deuteronomy, merely a fresh edition of the earliest code. The Return from Babylon, like the primitive Migration from Ur and like the Exodus from Egypt, was to be the occasion of a new Revelation, placing the relations of Jehovah and His people on a new footing.

When Ezra and Nehemiah established, as the Covenant of the Restoration, yet another edition of the Mosaic ordinances, they were acting in the teeth of this prophecy--not because Jehovah had changed His purpose, but because the time of fulfilment had not yet come. [428]

The rendering of the next clause is uncertain, and, in any case, the reason given for setting aside the old covenant is not quite what might have been expected. The Authorised and Revised Versions translate: "Which My covenant they brake, although I was an husband unto them"; [429] thus introducing that Old Testament figure of marriage between Jehovah and Israel which is transferred in Ephesians and the Apocalypse to Christ and the Church. The margin of the Revised Version has: "Forasmuch as they brake My covenant, although I was lord over them." There is little difference between these two translations, both of which imply that in breaking the covenant Israel was setting aside Jehovah's legitimate claim to obedience. A third translation, on much the same lines, would be "although I was Baal unto or over them"; [430] Baal or ba'al being found for lord, husband, in ancient times as a name of Jehovah, and in Jeremiah's time as a name of heathen gods. Jeremiah is fond of paronomasia, and frequently refers to Baal, so that he may have been here deliberately ambiguous. The phrase might suggest to the Hebrew reader that Jehovah was the true lord or husband of Israel, and the true Baal or God, but that Israel had come to regard Him as a mere Baal, like one of the Baals of the heathen. "Forasmuch as they, on their part, set at nought My covenant; so that I, their true Lord, became to them as a mere heathen Baal." The covenant and the God who gave it were alike treated with contempt.

The Septuagint, which is quoted in Hebrews viii. 9, has another translation: "And I regarded them not." [431] Unless this represents a different reading, [432] it is probably due to a feeling that the form of the Hebrew sentence required a close parallelism. Israel neglected to observe the covenant, and Jehovah ceased to feel any interest in Israel. But the idea of the latter clause seems alien to the context.

In any case, the new and better covenant is offered to Israel, after it has failed to observe the first covenant. This Divine procedure is not quite according to many of our theories. The law of ordinances is often spoken of as adapted to the childhood of the race. We set children easy tasks, and when these are successfully performed we require of them something more difficult. We grant them limited privileges, and if they make a good use of them the children are promoted to higher opportunities. We might perhaps have expected that when the Israelites failed to observe the Mosaic ordinances, they would have been placed under a narrower and harsher dispensation; yet their very failure leads to the promise of a better covenant still. Subsequent history, indeed, qualifies the strangeness of the Divine dealing. Only a remnant of Israel survived as the people of God. The Covenant of Ezra was very different from the New Covenant of Jeremiah; and the later Jews, as a community, [433] did not accept that dispensation of grace which ultimately realised Jeremiah's prophecy. In a narrow and unspiritual fashion the Jews of the Restoration observed the covenant of external ordinances; so that, in a certain sense, the Law was fulfilled before the new Kingdom of God was inaugurated. But if Isaiah and Jeremiah had reviewed the history of the restored community, they would have declined to receive it as, in any sense, the fulfilling of a Divine covenant. The Law of Moses was not fulfilled, but made void, by the traditions of the Pharisees. The fact therefore remains, that failure in the lower forms, so to speak, of God's school is still followed by promotion to higher privileges. However little we may be able to reconcile this truth with a priori views of Providence, it has analogies in nature, and reveals new depths of Divine love and greater resourcefulness of Divine grace. Boys whose early life is unsatisfactory nevertheless grow up into the responsibilities and privileges of manhood; and the wilful, disobedient child does not always make a bad man. We are apt to think that the highest form of development is steady, continuous, and serene, from good to better, from better to best. The real order is more awful and stupendous, combining good and evil, success and failure, victory and defeat, in its continuous advance through the ages. The wrath of man is not the only evil passion that praises God by its ultimate subservience to His purpose. We need not fear lest such Divine overruling of sin should prove any temptation to wrongdoing, seeing that it works, as in the exile of Israel, through the anguish and humiliation of the sinner.

The next verse explains the character of the New Covenant; once Jehovah wrote His law on tables of stone, but now:--

"This is the covenant which I will conclude with the House of Israel after those days--it is the utterance of Jehovah--
I will put My law within them, and will write it upon their heart;
And I will be their God, and they shall be My people."

These last words were an ancient formula for the immemorial relation of Jehovah and Israel, but they were to receive new fulness of meaning. The inner law, written on the heart, is in contrast to Mosaic ordinances. It has, therefore, two essential characteristics: first, it governs life, not by fixed external regulations, but by the continual control of heart and conscience by the Divine Spirit; secondly, obedience is rendered to the Divine Will, not from external compulsion, but because man's inmost nature is possessed by entire loyalty to God. The new law involves no alteration of the standards of morality or of theological doctrine, but it lays stress on the spiritual character of man's relation to God, and therefore on the fact that God is a spiritual and moral being. When man's obedience is claimed on the ground of God's irresistible power, and appeal is made to material rewards and punishments, God's personality is obscured and the way is opened for the deification of political or material Force. This doctrine of setting aside of ancient codes by the authority of the Inner Law is implied in many passages of our book. The superseding of the Mosaic Law is set forth by a most expressive symbol, [434] "When ye are multiplied and increased in the land, 'The Ark of the Covenant of Jehovah' shall no longer be the watchword of Israel: men shall neither think of the ark nor remember it; they shall neither miss the ark nor make another in its place." The Ark and the Mosaic Torah were inseparably connected; if the Ark was to perish and be forgotten, the Law must also be annulled.

Jeremiah moreover discerned with Paul that there was a law in the members warring against the Law of Jehovah: "The sin of Judah is written with a pen of iron, and with the point of a diamond: it is graven upon the table of their heart, and upon the horns of their altars." [435]

Hence the heart of the people had to be changed before they could enter into the blessings of the Restoration: "I will give them an heart to know Me, that I am Jehovah: and they shall be My people, and I will be their God: for they shall return unto Me with their whole heart." [436] In the exposition of the symbolic purchase of Hanameel's field, Jehovah promises to make an everlasting covenant with His people, that He will always do them good and never forsake them. Such continual blessings imply that Israel will always be faithful. Jehovah no longer seeks to ensure their fidelity by an external law, with its alternate threats and promises: He will rather control the inner life by His grace. "I will give them one heart and one way, that they may fear Me for ever; ... I will put My fear in their hearts, that they may not depart from Me." [437]

We must not, of course, suppose that these principles--of obedience from loyal enthusiasm, and of the guidance of heart and conscience by the Spirit of Jehovah--were new to the religion of Israel. They are implied in the idea of prophetic inspiration. When Saul went home to Gibeah, "there went with him a band of men, whose hearts God had touched." [438] In Deuteronomy, Israel is commanded to "love Jehovah thy God with all thine heart, and with all thy soul, and with all thy might. And these words, which I command thee this day, shall be in thine heart." [439]

The novelty of Jeremiah's teaching is that these principles are made central in the New Covenant. Even Deuteronomy, which approaches so closely to the teaching of Jeremiah, was a new edition of the Covenant of the Exodus, an attempt to secure a righteous life by exhaustive rules and by external sanctions. Jeremiah had witnessed and probably assisted the effort to reform Judah by the enforcement of the Deuteronomic Code. But when Josiah's religious policy collapsed after his defeat and death at Megiddo, Jeremiah lost faith in elaborate codes, and turned from the letter to the spirit.

The next feature of the New Covenant naturally follows from its being written upon men's hearts by the finger of Jehovah:--

> "Men shall no longer teach one another and teach each other, saying, Know ye Jehovah!
> For all shall know Me, from the least to the greatest--it is the utterance of Jehovah."

In ancient times men could only "know Jehovah" and ascertain His will by resorting to some sanctuary, where the priests preserved and transmitted the sacred tradition and delivered the Divine oracles. Written codes scarcely altered the situation; copies would be few and far between, and still mostly in the custody of the priests. Whatever drawbacks arise from attaching supreme religious authority to a printed book were multiplied a thousandfold when codes could only be copied. But, in the New Israel, men's spiritual life would not be at the mercy of pen, ink, and paper, of scribe and priest. The man who had a book and could read would no longer be able, with the self-importance of exclusive knowledge, to bid his less fortunate brethren to know Jehovah. He Himself would be the one teacher, and His instruction would fall, like the sunshine and the rain, upon all hearts alike.

And yet again Israel is assured that past sin shall not hinder the fulfilment of this glorious vision:--

> "For I will forgive their iniquity, and their sin will I remember no more."

Recurring to the general topic of the Restoration of Israel, the prophet affixes the double seal of two solemn Divine asseverations. Of old, Jehovah had promised Noah: "While the earth remaineth, seedtime and harvest, cold and heat, summer and winter, day and night, shall not cease." [440] Now He promises that while sun and moon and stars and sea continue in their appointed order, Israel shall not cease from being a nation. And, again, Jehovah will not cast off Israel on account of its sin till the height of heaven can be measured and the foundations of the earth searched out. [441]

Footnotes:

423. Exod. xxiv. 7.
424. I.e. in the sections generally acknowledged.
425. Hosea ii. 18, vi. 7, viii. 1.
426. xxxiv.
427. Cf. xxxiv. 14 with Deut. xv. 12 and Exod. xxi. 2.
428. Cf. Prof. Adeney's Ezra, Nehemiah, etc., in this series.
429. So also Kautzsch, Reuss, Sugfried, and Stade. The same phrase is thus translated in iii. 14.

430. "I was Baal" = "ba'alti."
431. á¼ Î¼á½³Î»Î·Ï   Î±.
432. × ×|×   and R. ᵛ "loatheth occurs in xiv. 19, and is tran
433. We usually underrate the proportion of Jews who embraced Christianity. Hellenistic Judaism disappeared as Christianity became widely diffused, and was probably for the most part absorbed into the new faith.
434. iii. 16, slightly paraphrased.
435. xvii. 1.
436. xxiv. 7.
437. xxxii. 39, 40.
438. 1 Sam. x. 26.
439. Deut. vi. 5, 6.
440. Gen. viii. 22 (J.).
441. Verses 35-37 occur in the LXX. in the order 37, 35, 36. They are considered by many critics to be a later addition. The most remarkable feature of the paragraph is the clause translated by the Authorised Version "which divideth [Revised Version, text "stirreth up," margin "stilleth"] the sea when the waves thereof roar; The Lord of Hosts is His name." This whole clause is taken word for word from Isa. li. 15, "I am Jehovah thy God, which stirreth up," etc. It seems clear that either this clause or 35-37 as a whole were added by an editor acquainted with II. Isaiah. The prophecy, as it stands in the Masoretic text, is concluded by a detailed description of the site of the restored Jerusalem. The contrast between the glorious vision of the New Israel and these architectural specifications is almost grotesque. Verses 38-40 are regarded by many as a later addition; and even if they are by Jeremiah, they form an independent prophecy and have no connection with the rest of the chapter. Our knowledge of the geographical points mentioned is not sufficient to enable us to define the site assigned to the restored city. The point of verse 40 is that the most unclean districts of the ancient city shall partake of the sanctity of the New Jerusalem.

CHAPTER XXXIV

RESTORATION--V. REVIEW

xxx.-xxxiii.

In reviewing these chapters we must be careful not to suppose that Jeremiah knew all that would ultimately result from his teaching. When he declared that the conditions of the New Covenant would be written, not in a few parchments, but on every heart, he laid down a principle which involved the most characteristic teaching of the New Testament and the Reformers, and which might seem to justify extreme mysticism. When we read these prophecies in the light of history, they seem to lead by a short and direct path to the Pauline doctrines of Faith and Grace. Constraining grace is described in the words: "I will put My fear in their hearts, that they shall not depart from Me." [442] Justification by faith instead of works substitutes the response of the soul to the Spirit of God for conformity to a set of external regulations--the writing on the heart for the carving of ordinances on stone. Yet, as Newton's discovery of the law of gravitation did not make him aware of all that later astronomers have discovered, so Jeremiah did not anticipate Paul and Augustine, Luther and Calvin: he was only their forerunner. Still less did he intend to affirm all that has been taught by the Brothers of the Common Life or the Society of Friends. We have followed the Epistle to the Hebrews in interpreting his prophecy of the New Covenant as abrogating the Mosaic code and inaugurating a new departure upon entirely different lines. This view is supported by his attitude towards the Temple, and especially the Ark. At the same time we must not suppose that Jeremiah contemplated the summary and entire abolition of the previous dispensation. He simply delivers his latest message from Jehovah, without bringing its contents into relation with earlier truth, without indeed waiting to ascertain for himself how the old and the new were to be combined. But we may be sure that the Divine writing on the heart would have included much that was already written in Deuteronomy, and that both books and teachers would have had their place in helping men to recognise and interpret the inner leadings of the Spirit.

In rising from the perusal of these chapters the reader is tempted to use the prophet's words with a somewhat different meaning: "I awaked and looked about me, and felt that I had had a pleasant dream." [443] Renan, with cynical frankness, heads a chapter on such prophecies with the title "Pious Dreams." While Jeremiah's glowing utterances rivet our attention, the gracious words fall like balm upon our aching hearts, and we seem, like the Apostle, caught up into Paradise. But as soon as we try to connect our visions with any realities, past, present, or in prospect, there comes a rude awakening. The restored community attained to no New Covenant, but was only found worthy of a fresh edition of the written code. Instead of being committed to the guidance of the ever-present Spirit of Jehovah, they were placed under a rigid and elaborate system of externals--"carnal ordinances, concerned with meats and drinks and divers washings, imposed until a time of reformation." [444] They still remained under the covenant "from Mount Sinai, bearing children unto bondage, which is Hagar. Now this Hagar is Mount Sinai in Arabia, and answereth to the Jerusalem that now is: for she is in bondage with her children." [445]

For these bondservants of the letter, there arose no David, no glorious Scion of the ancient stock. For a moment the hopes of Zechariah rested on Zerubbabel, but this Branch quickly withered away and was forgotten. We need not underrate the merits and services of Ezra and Nehemiah, of Simon the Just and Judas Maccabæus; and yet we cannot find any one of them who answers to the Priestly King of Jeremiah's visions. The new Growth of Jewish royalty came to an ignominious end in Aristobulus, Hyrcanus, and the Herods, Antichrists rather than Messiahs.

The Reunion of long-divided Israel is for the most part a misnomer; there was no healing of the wound, and the offending member was cut off.

Even now, when the leaven of the Kingdom has been working in the lump of humanity for nearly two thousand years, any suggestion that these chapters are realised in Modern Christianity would seem cruel irony. Renan accuses Christianity of having quickly forgotten the programme which its Founder borrowed from the prophets, and of having become a religion like other religions, a religion of priests and sacrifices, of external observances and superstitions. [446] It is sometimes asserted that Protestants lack faith and courage to trust to any law written on the heart, and cling to a printed book, as if there were no Holy Spirit--as if the Branch of David had borne fruit once for all, and Christ were dead. The movement for Christian Reunion seems thus far chiefly to emphasise the feuds that make the Church a kingdom divided against itself.

Rev. C. J. Ball, M.A., & W. H. Bennett, M.A.

But we must not allow the obvious shortcomings of Christendom to blind us to brighter aspects of truth. Both in the Jews of the Restoration and in the Church of Christ we have a real fulfilment of Jeremiah's prophecies. The fulfilment is no less real because it is utterly inadequate. Prophecy is a guide-post and not a mile-stone; it shows the way to be trodden, not the duration of the journey. Jews and Christians have fulfilled Jeremiah's prophecies because they have advanced by the road along which he pointed towards the spiritual city of his vision. The "pious dreams" of a little group of enthusiasts have become the ideals and hopes of humanity. Even Renan ranks himself among the disciples of Jeremiah: "The seed sown in religious tradition by inspired Israelites will not perish; all of us who seek a God without priests, a revelation without prophets, a covenant written in the heart, are in many respects the disciples of these ancient fanatics (ces vieux égarés)." [447]

The Judaism of the Return, with all its faults and shortcomings, was still an advance in the direction Jeremiah had indicated. However ritualistic the Pentateuch may seem to us, it was far removed from exclusive trust in ritual. Where the ancient Israelite had relied upon correct observance of the forms of his sanctuary, the Torah of Ezra introduced a large moral and spiritual element, which served to bring the soul into direct fellowship with Jehovah. "Pity and humanity are pushed to their utmost limits, always of course in the bosom of the family of Israel." [448] The Torah moreover included the great commands to love God and man, which once for all placed the religion of Israel on a spiritual basis. If the Jews often attached more importance to the letter and form of Revelation than to its substance, and were more careful for ritual and external observances than for inner righteousness, we have no right to cast a stone at them.

It is a curious phenomenon that after the time of Ezra the further developments of the Torah were written no longer on parchment, but, in a certain sense, on the heart. The decisions of the rabbis interpreting the Pentateuch, "the fence which they made round the law," were not committed to writing, but learnt by heart and handed down by oral tradition. Possibly this custom was partly due to Jeremiah's prophecy. It is a strange illustration of the way in which theology sometimes wrests the Scriptures to its own destruction, that the very prophecy of the triumph of the spirit over the letter was made of none effect by a literal interpretation.

Nevertheless, though Judaism moved only a very little way towards Jeremiah's ideal, yet it did move, its religion was distinctly more spiritual than that of ancient Israel. Although Judaism claimed finality and did its best to secure that no future generation should make further progress, yet in spite of, nay, even by means of, Pharisee and Sadducee, the Jews were prepared to receive and transmit that great resurrection of prophetic teaching which came through Christ.

If even Judaism did not altogether fail to conform itself to Jeremiah's picture of the New Israel, clearly Christianity must have shaped itself still more fully according to his pattern. In the Old Testament both the idea and the name of a "New Covenant," [449] superseding that of Moses, are peculiar to Jeremiah, and the New Testament consistently represents the Christian dispensation as a fulfilment of Jeremiah's prophecy. Besides the express and detailed application in the Epistle to the Hebrews, Christ instituted the Lord's Supper as the Sacrament of His New Covenant—"This cup is the New Covenant in My blood"; [450] and St. Paul speaks of himself as "a minister of the New Covenant." [451] Christianity has not been unworthy of the claim made on its behalf by its Founder, but has realised, at any rate in some measure, the visible peace, prosperity, and unity of Jeremiah's New Israel, as well as the spirituality of his New Covenant. Christendom has its hideous blots of misery and sin, but, on the whole, the standard of material comfort and intellectual culture has been raised to a high average throughout the bulk of a vast population. Internal order and international concord have made enormous strides since the time of Jeremiah. If an ancient Israelite could witness the happy security of a large proportion of English workmen and French peasants, he would think that many of the predictions of his prophets had been fulfilled. But the advance of large classes to a prosperity once beyond the dreams of the most sanguine only brings out in darker relief the wretchedness of their less fortunate brethren. In view of the growing knowledge and enormous resources of modern society, any toleration of its cruel wrongs is an unpardonable sin. Social problems are doubtless urgent because a large minority are miserable, but they are rendered still more urgent by the luxury of many and the comfort of most. The high average of prosperity shows that we fail to right our social evils, not for want of power, but for want of devotion. Our civilisation is a Dives, at whose gate Lazarus often finds no crumbs.

Again Christ's Kingdom of the New Covenant has brought about a larger unity. We have said enough elsewhere on the divisions of the Church. Doubtless we are still far from realising the ideals of chapter xxxi., but, at any rate, they have been recognised as supreme, and have worked for harmony and fellowship in the world. Ephraim and Judah are forgotten, but the New Covenant has united into brotherhood a worldwide array of races and nations. There are still divisions in the Church, and a common religion will not always do away with national enmities; but in spite of all, the influence of our common Christianity has done much to knit the nations together and promote mutual amity and goodwill. The vanguard of the modern world has accepted Christ as its standard and ideal, and has thus attained an essential unity, which is not destroyed by minor differences and external divisions.

And, finally, the promise that the New Covenant should be written on the heart is far on the way towards fulfilment. If Roman and Greek orthodoxy interposes the Church between the soul and Christ, yet the inspiration claimed for the Church to-day is, at any rate in some measure, that of the living Spirit of Christ speaking to the souls of living men. On the other hand, a predilection for Rabbinical methods of exegesis sometimes interferes with the influence and authority of the Bible. Yet in reality there is no serious attempt to take away the key of knowledge or to forbid the individual soul to receive the direct teaching of the Holy Ghost. The Reformers established the right of private judgment in the interpretation of the Scriptures; and the interpretation of the Library of Sacred Literature, the spiritual harvest of a thousand years, affords ample scope for reverent development of our knowledge of God.

One group of Jeremiah's prophecies has indeed been entirely fulfilled. [452] In Christ, God has raised up a Branch of Righteousness unto David, and through Him judgment and righteousness are wrought in the earth.

Footnotes:

442. xxxii. 40.
443. xxxi. 26.
444. Heb. ix. 10.
445. Gal. iv. 24, 25.
446. Histoire du Peuple d'Israel, iii., 340.
447. Renan, iii., 340.
448. Renan, iii., 425.
449. We have the idea of a spiritual covenant in Isa. lix. 21, "This is My covenant with them: ... My spirit that is upon thee, and My words which I have put in thy mouth, shall not depart out of thy mouth, nor out of the mouth of thy seed, nor out of the mouth of thy seed's seed, ... from henceforth and for ever"; but nothing is said as to a new covenant.
450. Luke xxii. 20; 1 Cor. xi. 25. The word "new" is omitted by Codd. Sin. and Vat. and the R.V. in Matt. xxvi. 28 and Mark xiv. 24.
451. 2 Cor. iii. 6.
452. xxxiii. 15.

EPILOGUE

CHAPTER XXXV

JEREMIAH AND CHRIST

"Jehovah thy God will raise up unto thee a prophet from amongst thee, of thy brethren, like unto me; unto him shall ye hearken."--Deut. xviii. 15.

"Jesus ... asked His disciples, saying, Who do men say that the Son of Man is? And they said, Some say John the Baptist; some, Elijah: and others, Jeremiah, or one of the prophets."--Matt. xvi. 13, 14.

English feeling about Jeremiah has long ago been summed up and stereotyped in the single word "jeremiad." The contempt and dislike which this word implies are partly due to his supposed authorship of Lamentations; but, to say the least, the Book of Jeremiah is not sufficiently cheerful to remove the impression created by the linked wailing, long drawn out, which has been commonly regarded as an appendix to its prophecies. We can easily understand the unpopularity of the prophet of doom in modern Christendom. Such prophets are seldom acceptable, except to the enemies of the people whom they denounce; and even ardent modern advocates of Jew-baiting would not be entirely satisfied with Jeremiah--they would resent his patriotic sympathy with sinful and suffering Judah. Most modern Christians have ceased to regard the Jews as monsters of iniquity, whose chastisement should give profound satisfaction to every sincere believer. History has recorded but few of the crimes which provoked and justified our prophet's fierce indignation, and those of which we do read repel our interest by a certain lack of the picturesque, so that we do not take the trouble to realise their actual and intense wickedness. Ahab is a by-word, but how many people know anything about Ishmael ben Nethaniah? The cruelty of the nobles and the unctuous cant of their prophetic allies are forgotten in--nay, they seem almost atoned for by--the awful calamities that befell Judah and Jerusalem. Jeremiah's memory may even be said to have suffered from the speedy and complete fulfilment of his prophecies. The national ruin was a triumphant vindication of his teaching, and his disciples were eager to record every utterance in which he had foretold the coming doom. Probably the book, in its present form, gives an exaggerated impression of the stress which Jeremiah laid upon this topic.

Moreover, while the prophet's life is essentially tragic, its drama lacks an artistic close and climax. Again and again Jeremiah took his life in his hand, but the good confession which he witnessed for so long does not culminate in the crown of martyrdom. A final scene like the death of John the Baptist would have won our sympathy and conciliated our criticism.

We thus gather that the popular attitude towards Jeremiah rests on a superficial appreciation of his character and work; it is not difficult to discern that a careful examination of his history establishes important claims on the veneration and gratitude of the Christian Church.

For Judaism was not slow to pay her tribute of admiration and reverence to Jeremiah as to a Patron Saint and Confessor. His prophecy of the Restoration of Israel is appealed to in Ezra and Daniel; and the Hebrew Chronicler, who says as little as he can of Isaiah, adds to the references made by the Book of Kings to Jeremiah. We have already seen that apocryphal legends clustered round his honoured name. He was credited with having concealed the Tabernacle and the Ark in the caves of Sinai. [453] On the eve of a great victory, he appeared to Judas Maccabæus, in a vision, as "a man distinguished by grey hairs, and a majestic appearance; but something wonderful and exceedingly magnificent was the grandeur about him," and was made known to Judas as a "lover of the brethren, who prayeth much for the people and for the holy city, to wit, Jeremiah the prophet of God. And Jeremiah stretching forth his right hand delivered over to Judas a sword of gold." [454] The Son of Sirach does not fail to include Jeremiah in his praise of famous men; [455] and there is an apocryphal epistle purporting to be written by our prophet. [456] It is noteworthy that in the New Testament Jeremiah is only mentioned by name in the Judaistic Gospel of St. Matthew.

In the Christian Church, notwithstanding the lack of popular sympathy, earnest students of the prophet's life and words have ranked him with some of the noblest characters of history. A modern writer enumerates as amongst those with whom he has been compared Cassandra, Phocion,

Demosthenes, Dante, Milton, and Savonarola. [457] The list might easily be enlarged, but another parallel has been drawn which has supreme claims on our consideration. The Jews in New Testament times looked for the return of Elijah or Jeremiah to usher in Messiah's reign; and it seemed to some among them that the character and teaching of Jesus of Nazareth identified him with the ancient prophet who had been commissioned "to root out, pull down, destroy and throw down, to build and to plant." The suggested comparison has often been developed, but undue stress has been laid on such accidental and external circumstances as the prophet's celibacy and the statement that he was "sanctified from the womb." The discussion of such details does not greatly lend itself to edification. But it has also been pointed out that there is an essential resemblance between the circumstances and mission of Jeremiah and his Divine Successor, and to this some little space may be devoted.

Jeremiah and our Lord appeared at similar crises in the history of Israel and of revealed religion. The prophet foretold the end of the Jewish monarchy, the destruction of the First Temple and of ancient Jerusalem; Christ, in like manner, announced the end of the restored Israel, the destruction of the Second Temple and of the newer Jerusalem. In both cases the doom of the city was followed by the dispersion and captivity of the people. At both eras the religion of Jehovah was supposed to be indissolubly bound up with the Temple and its ritual; and, as we have seen, Jeremiah, like Stephen and Paul and our Lord Himself, was charged with blasphemy because he predicted its coming ruin. The prophet, like Christ, was at variance with the prevalent religious sentiment of his time and with what claimed to be orthodoxy. Both were regarded and treated by the great body of contemporary religious teachers as dangerous and intolerable heretics; and their heresy, as we have said, was practically one and the same. To the champions of the Temple, their teaching seemed purely destructive, an irreverent attack upon fundamental doctrines and indispensable institutions. But the very opposite was the truth; they destroyed nothing but what deserved to perish. Both in Jeremiah's time and in our Lord's, men tried to assure themselves of the permanence of erroneous dogmas and obsolete rites by proclaiming that these were of the essence of Divine Revelation. In either age to succeed in this effort would have been to plunge the world into spiritual darkness: the light of Hebrew prophecy would have been extinguished by the Captivity, or, again, the hope of the Messiah would have melted away like a mirage, when the legions of Titus and Hadrian dispelled so many Jewish dreams. But before the catastrophe came, Jeremiah had taught men that Jehovah's Temple and city were destroyed of His own set purpose, because of the sins of His people; there was no excuse for supposing that He was discredited by the ruin of the place where He had once chosen to set His Name. Thus the Captivity was not the final page in the history of Hebrew religion, but the opening of a new chapter. In like manner Christ and His Apostles, more especially Paul, finally dissociated Revelation from the Temple and its ritual, so that the light of Divine truth was not hidden under the bushel of Judaism, but shone forth upon the whole world from the many-branched candlestick of the Universal Church.

Again, in both cases, not only was ancient faith rescued from the ruin of human corruption and commentary, but the purging away of the old leaven made room for a positive statement of new teaching. Jeremiah announced a new covenant--that is, a formal and complete change in the conditions and method of man's service to God and God's beneficence to men. The ancient Church, with its sanctuary, its clergy, and its ritual, was to be superseded by a new order, without sanctuary, clergy, or ritual, wherein every man would enjoy immediate fellowship with his God. This great ideal was virtually ignored by the Jews of the Restoration, but it was set forth afresh by Christ and His Apostles. The "New Covenant" was declared to be ratified by His sacrifice, and was confirmed anew at every commemoration of His death. We read in John iv. 21-23: "The hour cometh, when neither in this mountain, nor in Jerusalem, shall ye worship the Father.... The hour cometh, and now is, when the true worshippers shall worship the Father in spirit and truth."

Thus when we confess that the Church is built upon the foundation of the Prophets and Apostles, we have to recognise that to this foundation Jeremiah's ministry supplied indispensable elements, alike by its positive and in its negative parts. This fact was manifest even to Renan, who fully shared the popular prejudices against Jeremiah. Nothing short of Christianity, according to him, is the realisation of the prophet's dream: "Il ajoute un facteur essentiel à

l'oeuvre humaine; Jérémie est, avant Jean-Baptiste, l'homme qui a le plus contribué à la fondation du Christianisme; il doit compter, malgré la distance des siècles, entre les précurseurs immédiats de Jésus." [458]

Rev. C. J. Ball, M.A., & W. H. Bennett, M.A.

Footnotes:

453. 2 Macc. ii. 1-8.
454. 2 Macc. xv. 12-16.
455. Ecclus. xlix. 6, 7.
456. Sometimes appended to the Book of Baruch as a sixth chapter.
457. Smith's Dictionary of the Bible, art. "Jeremiah."
458. Hist., iii., 251, 305.

www.ingramcontent.com/pod-product-compliance
Lightning Source LLC
Chambersburg PA
CBHW022107150426
43195CB00008B/309